Grade 6

Teacher Edition

Spelling

Colorado Springs, CO

Development Team

First Edition

Editorial Team

Dr. Sharon Berry — *Managing Editor*
Dr. Barry Morris — *Content Manager*
Dr. Ollie Gibbs — *Project Manager*

Author Team

Sharon Bird
Cathy Guy
Eunice Harris
Linda Miller
Nancy Wetsel
Connie Williams

Project Consultants

Dr. Barbara Bode
Dr. Richard Edlin
Dr. Omer Bonenberger
Dr. Linda Goodson
Dr. Alex Lackey
Ruth McBride
Dr. Connie Pearson
Patti Rhan
Dr. Milton Uecker
Dr. Ray White

Second Edition

Editorial Team

JoAnn Keenan — *Managing Editor*
Maria Linn Deckard — *Editor*
Cynthia C. Shipman — *Editor*
Lorraine Wadman — *Editor*
Dr. June Hetzel — *Senior Content Editor*
Dr. Claire Sibold — *Content Editor*

Design Team

Monica Starr Brown — *Graphic Designer, Photographer*
Susanna Garmany — *Graphic Designer*
Daron Short — *Graphic Designer, Photographer*

Project Consultants

Dr. Derek Keenan — *ACSI Vice President for Academic Affairs*
Steven Babbitt — *Director, Purposeful Design Publications*
Don Hulin — *Assistant Director, Textbook Development*

Purposeful Design

Grade 6
Teacher Edition

Spelling

Managing Editor
JoAnn Keenan

Editors
Maria Linn Deckard
Cynthia C. Shipman
Lorraine Wadman

Designers
Monica Starr Brown
Susanna Garmany
Daron Short

Senior Content Editor
Dr. June Hetzel

Content Editor
Dr. Claire Sibold

First edition 1991
Second edition 2009

Purposeful Design Publications is the publishing division of the Association of Christian Schools International (ACSI) and is committed to the ministry of Christian school education, to enable Christian educators and schools worldwide to effectively prepare students for life. As the publisher of textbooks, trade books, and other educational resources within ACSI, Purposeful Design Publications strives to produce biblically sound materials that reflect Christian scholarship and stewardship and that address the identified needs of Christian schools around the world.

References to books, computer software, and other ancillary resources in this series are not endorsements by ACSI. These materials were selected to provide teachers with additional resources appropriate to the concepts being taught and to promote student understanding and enjoyment.

Photograph of Eric Liddell on Student Edition page 100 courtesy of the Liddell family.

Printed in the United States of America
18 17 16 15 14 13 12 11 10 09 1 2 3 4 5 6 7

Spelling, grade six
Purposeful Design Spelling series
Second edition
ISBN 978-1-58331-247-6 Teacher edition Catalog #7418S

Purposeful Design Publications
A Division of ACSI
PO Box 65130 • Colorado Springs, CO 80962-5130
Customer Service: 800-367-0798 • www.acsi.org

Table of Contents

Lesson		Page

Teacher Resources

Blackline Master List

Parent Letter

Lesson 1

SP6-01A	A Spelling Study Strategy
SP6-01B	Flash Cards Template
SP6-01C	Lesson 1 Homework

Lesson 2

SP6-02A	Lesson 2 Homework

Lesson 3

SP6-03A	Lesson 3 Homework

Lesson 4

SP6-04A	Lesson 4 Homework

Lesson 5

SP6-05A	T-3 Answer Key
SP6-05B	Lesson 5 Homework

Lesson 6

SP6-06A	Lessons 1–5 Study Sheet
SP6-06B	Lesson 6 Homework I
SP6-06C	Lesson 6 Homework II
SP6-06D	Lessons 1–5 Test Prep
SP6-06E	Lessons 1–5 Test I
SP6-06F	Lessons 1–5 Test II
SP6-06G	Student Answer Form
SP6-06H	Lessons 1–5 Answer Key

Lesson 7

SP6-07A	Lesson 7 Homework

Lesson 8

SP6-08A	T-6 Answer Key
SP6-08B	Venn Diagram
SP6-08C	Lesson 8 Homework

Lesson 9

SP6-09A	T-7 Answer Key
SP6-09B	Lesson 9 Homework

Lesson 10

SP6-10A	Lesson 10 Homework

Lesson 11

SP6-11A	Lesson 11 Homework

Lesson 12

SP6-12A	Lessons 7–11 Study Sheet
SP6-12B	Lesson 12 Homework I
SP6-12C	Lesson 12 Homework II
SP6-12D	Lessons 7–11 Test Prep
SP6-12E	Lessons 7–11 Test I
SP6-12F	Lessons 7–11 Test II
SP6-12G	Lessons 7–11 Answer Key

Lesson 13

SP6-13A	Lesson 13 Homework

Lesson 14

SP6-14A	Lesson 14 Homework

Lesson 15

SP6-15A T-11 Answer Key
SP6-15B Lesson 15 Homework

Lesson 16

SP6-16A Lesson 16 Homework

Lesson 17

SP6-17A Graphic Organizer for a Narrative
SP6-17B Lesson 17 Homework

Lesson 18

SP6-18A Lessons 13–17 Study Sheet
SP6-18B Lesson 18 Homework I
SP6-18C Lesson 18 Homework II
SP6-18D Lessons 13–17 Test Prep
SP6-18E Lessons 13–17 Test I
SP6-18F Lessons 13–17 Test II
SP6-18G Lessons 13–17 Answer Key

Lesson 19

SP6-19A Lesson 19 Homework

Lesson 20

SP6-20A T-14 Answer Key
SP6-20B Lesson 20 Homework

Lesson 21

SP6-21A Lesson 21 Homework

Lesson 22

SP6-22A Lesson 22 Homework

Lesson 23

SP6-23A Lesson 23 Homework

Lesson 24

SP6-24A Lessons 19–23 Study Sheet
SP6-24B Lesson 24 Homework I
SP6-24C Lesson 24 Homework II
SP6-24D Lessons 19–23 Test Prep
SP6-24E Lessons 19–23 Test I
SP6-24F Lessons 19–23 Test II
SP6-24G Lessons 19–23 Answer Key

Lesson 25

SP6-25A Lesson 25 Homework

Lesson 26

SP6-26A T-16 Answer Key
SP6-26B Lesson 26 Homework

Lesson 27

SP6-27A Flow Chart
SP6-27B Lesson 27 Homework

Lesson 28

SP6-28A T-18 Answer Key
SP6-28B Lesson 28 Homework

Lesson 29

SP6-29A Lesson 29 Homework

Lesson 30

SP6-30A Lessons 25–29 Study Sheet
SP6-30B Lesson 30 Homework I
SP6-30C Lesson 30 Homework II
SP6-30D Lessons 25–29 Test Prep
SP6-30E Lessons 25–29 Test I
SP6-30F Lessons 25–29 Test II
SP6-30G Lessons 25–29 Answer Key

Transparency List

T-1 A Spelling Study Strategy
T-2 Word Origins Practice
T-3 Proofreading an Informative Essay
T-4 Lessons 1–5 Study Sheet
T-5 Word Search Grid
T-6 Venn Diagram
T-7 Proofreading an Action Story
T-8 Basketball Dialogue
T-9 Lessons 7–11 Study Sheet
T-10 Homophones and Homographs
T-11 Proofreading a Narrative
T-12 Graphic Organizer for a Narrative
T-13 Lessons 13–17 Study Sheet
T-14 Proofreading an Advertisement
T-15 Lessons 19–23 Study Sheet
T-16 Proofreading an Informative Article
T-17 Flow Chart Graphic Organizer
T-18 Shot Put and Javelin
T-19 Lessons 25–29 Study Sheet
T-20 Proofreading a Blog
T-21 Words from French and Italian
T-22 Words from Spanish
T-23 Words from German
T-24 A Friendly Letter About Archery
T-25 Words from Asian Languages
T-26 Lessons 31–35 Study Sheet

Poster List

P-1 A Spelling Study Strategy
P-2 Latin Roots
P-3 Latin Roots
P-4 Greek Roots

Foreword

The fourfold educational mission of Christian schools is to prepare young people as disciples of Christ who are spiritually-formed thinkers. Education implies the development of the mind by the acquisition of knowledge and the ability to think and understand. Schools also equip students with a set of skills that are essential for life and vocation. In addition, the training process seeks to ground pupils with a worldview that is biblical and that shapes their lives into a God-pleasing spiritual pattern. In order to fulfill this Kingdom mandate, schools need to do their educational work carefully and responsibly. Purposeful Design Publications exists to assist educators in the fulfillment of that mission.

Over the past decades there continues to be a plethora of approaches to many aspects of the language arts. The research literature is somewhat conflicted about what is most effective in preparing students to be good readers, but it is quite clear about developing strong spellers. We have been through an era where spelling did not need to be taught explicitly but as an outgrowth of reading (Smith 1971). Several things from the research about spelling instruction are quite clear:

- Effective spelling instruction strengthens reading
- There are multiple benefits to explicit spelling instruction
- Strategies must be matched according to the age and level of spelling ability
- Well-developed and current spelling resources incorporate comprehensive tested strategies that match a variety of learners

(Gentry 2004)

The revised Purposeful Design Spelling series approaches spelling as a critical literacy skill that strengthens reading and writing ability. Spelling strategies such as word sorting by phonetic pattern, developing vocabulary through word study, and using the writing process to compose original stories pervade the books. Each of these strategies has a direct correlation to more effective and efficient reading and writing. Just as manipulatives are critical to mathematics understanding, spelling activities are crucial to the long-term acquisition by students of a significant bank of words they can spell correctly.

Each grade level and each lesson in the series has been thoroughly revised with updated strategies and research-based activities. Every page has been redesigned for readability, instructional flow and sequence, and attractive pictures and illustrations that draw students into and through each lesson.

Purposeful Design Publications, the publishing division of the Association of Christian Schools International, is indebted to a fine team of consultants, editors, and contributors who have invested themselves in this revision project. It was clear from the outset that some of the core concepts of the original spelling series were sound, but this team, backed by extensive research findings, has thoroughly revised these books into an outstanding series.

Your students will be well served by utilizing Purposeful Design Spelling in your classroom. We are certain that it will assist you to produce students who know how to spell, enjoy the activities of learning to spell, and embed in their minds a growing bank of words that support and strengthen vocabulary acquisition and reading skills.

Derek J. Keenan, Ed.D.
Vice President, Academic Affairs

Gentry, J. Richard. 2004 *The Science of Spelling.* Portsmouth, New Hampshire: Heinemann.

Smith, F. 1971 *Understanding Reading: A Psycholinguistic Analysis of Reading and Learning to Read.* New York: Holt, Rinehart and Winston.

"Glorify God in your body
and in your spirit."
1 Corinthians 6:20

Preface

The Purposeful Design Publications Team carefully crafted this revised spelling series with you and your Christian School students in mind. The philosophical underpinnings of this grades 1–6 series are as follows:

The ultimate aim of Christian education is to bring students to a saving knowledge of Jesus Christ, to know His Word, and to live Christianly in right relationship with God and others. Therefore, literacy contributes to a child's spiritual maturity as he or she develops as a reader and a writer, processing the truths of Scripture. Mastery of conventional spelling and word study become critical subsets of the writing branch of literacy, sharpening the student's literacy tools and his/her ability to accurately convey love and truth to others through the written word.

Conventional spelling contributes to the accuracy with which a writer can convey his message. Therefore, this series provides delightfully interesting and varied word study activities for both phonetically-consistent pattern words as well as high-frequency words. Study of phonetically-consistent pattern words supports students' acquisition of spelling generalizations, and study of high-frequency words promotes writing fluency with high-utility words. Writing assignments provide opportunities for learners to apply spelling in context, accurately conveying messages to readers through the encoding process.

Children are unique image bearers of God. Therefore, the learning process must take into account child development, academic strengths and weaknesses, learning styles, learning modalities, and learning rates. The Purposeful Design editorial team has ensured that you have straightforward methods to differentiate the learning process for high achievers, average performers, and struggling learners. Each lesson provides opportunities for high achievers to study challenge words and for struggling learners to receive additional spelling support. Additionally, a website has been developed to provide a plethora of resources to assist you in strategically planning for all learners.

Parents and teachers jointly share the responsibility of the child's education. Therefore, this series provides spelling study activities for both school and home, conceptualizing the training of the child as a partnership between parents and teachers.

Learning should satisfy the God-given curiosity of a child and inspire increased desire for learning. Therefore, the creative design team of Purposeful Design Publications has provided inviting images of God's creation and attractive layouts of student workbook pages and blackline masters. Additionally, the editorial team has carefully crafted lessons to include games, puzzles, stories, poems, and other inspiring, fun activities.

The Purposeful Design Publications Team desires that this series ministers to the educational needs of your students and that spelling becomes a favorite part of their day and your day as students study spelling "their way"—actively and joyfully! May the Lord bless you as you continue to press on in the name of the Lord Jesus Christ, training the next generation of Kingdom writers.

June Hetzel, Ph.D.
Professor of Education
Biola University

Acknowledgments

The Peer Review process is an important step in the development of this textbook series. ACSI and the Purposeful Design staff greatly appreciate the feedback we receive from the schools and teachers who participate. We highly value the efforts and input of these faculty members; their recommendations and suggestions are extremely helpful. The institutions listed below have assisted us in this way.

American Christian Academy, Tuscaloosa, AL
Asheville Christian Academy, Swannanoa, NC
Calvary Christian Academy, Philadelphia, PA
Cedar Park Christian School, Bothell, WA
Cincinnati Hills Christian Academy, Cincinnati, OH
Colorado Springs Christian Schools, Colorado Springs, CO
Cypress Christian School, Houston, TX
Dayton Christian School, Miamisburg, OH
Evangelical Christian Academy, Colorado Springs, CO
Faith Christian Academy, Arvada, CO
Faith Christian School, Rocky Mount, NC
Forest Lake Christian School, Auburn, CA
Fresno Christian Schools, Fresno, CA
Grace Community School, Tyler, TX
Greenbrier Christian Academy, Chesapeake, VA
Harvest Christian Academy, Elgin, IL
Heritage Christian School, Brookfield, WI
Jupiter Christian School, Jupiter, FL
Kodiak Christian School, Kodiak, AK
Lee's Summit Community Christian School, Lee's Summit, MO
Light and Life Christian School, Escondido, CA
Mount Hope School, Burlington, MA
North Cobb Christian School, Kennesaw, GA
North County Christian School, Florissant, MO
North Heights Christian Academy, Roseville, MN
Northwest Christian School, Phoenix, AZ
Oak Park Christian Academy, Oak Park, IL
Oakland Christian School, Auburn Hills, MI
Peoria Christian School, Peoria, IL
Pine Castle Christian Academy, Orlando, FL
Rocky Bayou Christian School, Niceville, FL
Salisbury Christian School, Salisbury, MD
Santiam Christian School, Corvallis, OR
Schenectady Christian School, Schenectady, NY
Smithtown Christian School, Smithtown, NY
Southwest Christian School, Fort Worth, TX
The Pilgrim Academy, Egg Harbor City, NJ
Timothy Christian School, Piscataway, NJ
Traders Point Christian Academy, Indianapolis, IN
Tri-City Christian Schools, Vista, CA
Trinity Christian Academy, Jackson, TN
Trinity Christian School of Fairfax, Fairfax, VA
Trinity Christian School, Addison, TX
Wesleyan School, Norcross, GA
West Bay Christian Academy, North Kingston, RI
West-Mont Christian Academy, Pottstown, PA

Spelling Series Task Force

June Hetzel, Ph.D.
Biola University

Pam Levicki
St. Stephen's Episcopal Day School

Anne Lichlyter
Evangelical Christian Academy

Victoria Lierheimer
Evergreen Academy

Keith McAdams
Cornerstone University

Rebecca Pennington
Covenant College

Julia Taves
Colorado Springs Christian School

Carolyn Ware
North Cobb Christian School

Amy Young
Rocky Mountain Christian Academy

Using the Teacher and Student Editions

Welcome to Purposeful Design Grade Six Spelling!

We believe that you will enjoy the new format, including beautiful, full-color photographs; well-researched word lists that include pattern words, content area words, and vocabulary words with Greek and Latin roots; and teacher-friendly lesson instructions. This instructional program, comprised of a Teacher Edition, Student Edition, Blackline Masters CD, Color Transparencies, and Posters, are all designed to assist you in engaging and challenging your students to become excellent spellers.

Visit www.acsi.org/kwspelling *for a listing of a wide variety of resources specifically selected to provide you with classroom tools in support of spelling and language arts instruction. Resources listed, although not endorsed by Purposeful Design Publications, are recommended by local educators for supporting grade six spelling.*

Grade six of the revised spelling series consists of 36 lessons, primarily using whole-group activities; however, guidance for supporting students who struggle as well as students who are advanced is also included. Each weekly word list lesson is designed for five days, 30–40 minutes of instruction per day. After each five-week set of word list lessons, a review lesson is provided.

Teacher Edition

Each Teacher Edition lesson includes an instructional "Objective," lesson "Introduction," and "Directed Instruction" in a step-by-step format. All the materials needed to teach each lesson are listed in the Lesson Materials. Instructional objectives and lesson content meet criteria set by state and national language arts standards.

The five-day instructional format of the word list lessons begins with the "Pretest" on Day 1 and concludes with the "Posttest" on Day 5. On Day 1, students use their auditory skills to encode and write the words. On Day 2, students see the words and sort the words by spelling patterns. They write the definition for each word and complete the "Word Analysis and Vocabulary" pages. Day 3 is reserved for "Word Study Strategies" and Day 4 promotes "Writing" skills. Lesson activities strengthen the students' skills in decoding, encoding, vocabulary, word building, proofreading, and creative word application in daily writing.

The "Pretest" is written on the students' own paper. It is self-corrected for immediate feedback without formal grades recorded. Each "Pretest" assesses current skill levels of individual students, as well as the skills of the entire class, in the context of the list words provided. If your students miss several words on the "Pretest," more practice will be needed throughout the week. It is important to teach your students to check the accuracy of their own "Pretest" so that they strengthen proofreading skills and understand their own error patterns. An extremely helpful tool for spelling practice is "A Spelling Study Strategy" found on a poster (P-1), color transparency (T-1), and blackline master (BLM SP6-01A). "A Spelling Study Strategy" is also found on the inside cover of the Student Edition. Demonstrate the use of "A Spelling Study Strategy" before beginning Lesson 1.

On weekly "Posttests," students write their spelling words and six dictated sentences on lined paper. Your students may write the dictation sentences as a paragraph. Dictation is an excellent way to integrate auditory and visual memory skills, as well as writing skills and conventions, such as capitalization and punctuation, in context. Dictation also provides a model of a complete sentence or paragraph. Many dictation sentences include words on previous spelling lists for review. We suggest that you read each sentence slowly, have the students repeat the sentence, and then read it once again before the students begin to write the sentence. Score the dictation sentences as a part of the overall grade on the "Posttest"; however, the scoring procedure is up to you.

Every sixth lesson is a review lesson and the "Assessment" for each review lesson is given on Day 5. The "Assessment" is cumulative, covering words from the five previous lessons. Due to the cumulative nature of the test, it is suggested that students retain the weekly flash cards, suggested for homework, as a study aid. Each "Assessment" is helpful in preparation for achievement testing since it is in standardized test format; words are presented in the context of a sentence that contains three underlined words, one of which may be misspelled, and a fourth choice of *All correct*. Students use a Student Answer Form to indicate the misspelled word or choose *All correct* if there are no misspellings. To extend each "Assessment," you may choose to have the students rewrite each misspelled word correctly.

The "Student Spelling Support" appears as a sidebar. The "Student Spelling Support" is a selection of optional activities that extends the spelling lessons, provides additional ideas for different learning styles, and incorporates spelling with other curriculum areas. The "Student Spelling Support" also gives ideas for discussion of the Scripture verses on the Student Edition pages, lists additional Scripture references, and promotes biblical integration. There are suggested writing challenge activities. You will not be able to use every suggestion listed for each lesson; however, a rich selection of spelling support strategies enables you to pick and choose as you carefully craft activities tailored to student needs. All materials needed for the "Student Spelling Support" are listed in "Student Spelling Support Materials."

One of the "Student Spelling Support" suggestions calls for starting and adding words to a classroom "Word Wall." Develop student-generated "Word Walls," using each week's spelling words. Write the words, categorize the Pattern, Content, and Vocabulary Words, and attach to the wall. The example given in Lesson one and the example shown below contain only a few of the list words, but teachers should add all of the words to their Word Wall. Allow students to spontaneously add new words to the list during the week. Categorizing words by patterns helps students internalize generalizations.

Word Wall

Short Vowel Sounds		Motocross	Vocabulary Words
a	attitude	circuit	fin + al = final
e	method	terrain	fin + al + ist = finalist
i	insist	engine	re + vers + ed = reversed
o	contact	physical	tra + vers + ed = traversed
u	subtotal	equipment	

Blackline Masters and Other Resources

Each lesson includes one or more blackline masters on CD. The CD is found on the inside back cover of the Teacher Edition. You will find the title and other useful information in the upper right-hand corner. The title is in the uppermost box. The second box contains the abbreviation, BLM SP6, followed by the lesson number and a letter. For example, BLM SP6-07C indicates that this blackline master is found in grade six (SP6), lesson seven (07), and is the third (C) blackline master in that lesson. Additionally, each blackline master has a circled letter code that indicates the primary use for the blackline.

- The blackline masters labeled **A for Assessment** are needed for the Review Assessment. Day 5 of each review lesson indicates the blackline masters needed. (A)
- The blackline masters labeled **H for Homework** provide practice with the skills taught in class. Answers are provided on the blackline master CD. Homework suggestions are given for three nights per week to accommodate evening worship schedules. Some of the activities call for students to choose a correctly spelled word from a group of misspelled words. This can be extremely challenging for students with visual processing disorders. You may choose to reduce the number of exercises, or choose to assign a different activity to these students. (H)
- The blackline masters labeled **P for Practice** mirror the concepts and skills taught in the Student Edition. 
- The blackline masters labeled **T for Teacher Tools** are the answer keys for transparencies and review "Assessments." 

Note to Macintosh Users: Double-click the disc icon on the desktop, go to the folder named "PDF," open the file containing the blackline masters, and access the list.

Color transparencies are coded with *T* plus a number and posters are coded with *P* plus a number for identification. Transparencies and Posters are used in different lessons, and instructions for their use are included in the Teacher Edition.

Student Edition

The theme of grade six is Sports. Students will be introduced to various team sports and individual sports with an emphasis on sportsmanlike conduct and godly attitudes toward competition. The weekly theme provides an opportunity for students to spell words from a variety of content areas related to the theme sport.

The handwriting styles presented as penmanship models in the lessons include both standard manuscript and cursive forms commonly used in Christian schools. Word lists are presented in a manuscript form on odd-numbered pages; word lists are presented in a standard cursive form on even-numbered pages. Either handwriting form can be viewed by flipping the page or looking at the adjacent page. Please note that most visual memory and recall of spelling words is in manuscript. Students struggling with spelling should study their words exclusively in manuscript.

Most word list lessons are organized around phonetic generalizations, content themes, and morphemic patterns. We use the term generalizations as opposed to rules because we realize that most, but not all, words follow these principles. Understanding these generalizations will give your students knowledge of the spelling patterns that are required to spell phonetically-consistent Pattern Words and morphemically-consistent Vocabulary Words. Vocabulary Words contain roots or affixes originating from Greek or Latin. Etymology, or the study of word orgins, is important in helping students develop strong spelling and vocabulary skills. Word lists also incorporate content area words. Content Words do not always follow a phonetic pattern, but they provide additional vocabulary to enhance students' ability to write proficiently within a subject area. Lists also include space on the student pages for the assignment of Challenge Words. You may choose Challenge Words based on the phonetic pattern targeted in the lesson, words previously misspelled, or content area words from other subjects you are studying, including social studies, science, and Bible. Students are often motivated to spell content area words by their interest in those subjects. You may also want to have your students self-select their own Challenge Words.

Some instructions on the Student Edition pages specify using only Pattern, Content, and/or Vocabulary Words. Other instructions specify using list words—a combination of all three categories.

A "Word Bank" is found in the back of the Student and Teacher Editions. In this section, students add Challenge Words that serve as a reference for their writing. Following this section is a Pronunciation Key, showing the diacritical marks used in the pronunciation of each list word. Review the symbols for each sound with your students. The "Spelling Dictionary," which is needed for the completion of several student pages, follows. The syllabication, pronunciation, part(s) of speech, definition(s), and sample sentence(s) are provided for each sixth grade spelling word. Elements of the Student Edition include the following:

- Pages are perforated and each lesson may be removed without losing a page from the next lesson.
- Colored boxes at the top of the page highlight the skill(s) practiced on each page.
- Exercises are numbered from left to right on pages with columns. Otherwise, the numbers are read vertically.
- Terminology that may be new to students is highlighted in yellow the first time it appears.
- The first letter of each Content Word is provided as a clue for students to complete sentences on the Word Analysis page of each lesson.

Differentiated Instruction

We have included options for differentiating instruction because no textbook series is "one size fits all." These suggestions for "Differentiated Instruction" include changing the number of spelling words for learners who are either behind or ahead of their peers in spelling so as to secure an appropriate level of difficulty for each student.

There are important considerations when spelling is differentiated. The first is clear communication with parents, and the second is evaluation and grading. Parents need to be partners in the differentiation process. Parents need to know which words their child will be responsible for learning and how he or she will be evaluated. We suggest that you hold a meeting early in the school year with parents of students whose skills were below grade level expectations, or who missed more than half of the words on the first two or three spelling list lessons. Assign more words as each student's progress dictates. Develop a method of communicating with parents, such as a weekly e-mail, which words students need to study.

It is suggested that, if possible, the students attempt to spell every word on the "Pretest" and "Posttest," even though they will be graded only on words that they were assigned. This is not only good practice for the students, but it reduces the chance of students being questioned or ridiculed for having fewer words on their tests. All students should complete every page in the Student Edition in preparation for the weekly "Posttest." The "Assessment" for the review lessons is cumulative and has been organized so that the first twelve sentences contain the spelling words that have been assigned to students who have reduced word lists.

For students who are ahead of their peers, we suggest that Extra Challenge Words be assigned. The words suggested are taken from lists of words that are ranked by usage and grade level. You may use the words suggested, develop your own list from content area study, or invite advanced students to suggest their own Extra Challenge Words. Extra Challenge Words may be sent home via e-mail. Decide with parents whether or not to include these words in each student's overall spelling grade.

Discuss the evaluation and grading of students who have differentiated lists with your administrator and teammates to provide grade level and/or schoolwide consistency.

Finally, enjoy using Purposeful Design Spelling, Grade Six. It has been our pleasure to receive teacher input and revise this series to better meet your students' needs. Enjoy the journey.

Preparing a Lesson

Read through the lesson and make notes regarding preparation.

Read the lesson objective so that it is clear in your mind.

Note the materials needed to teach the lesson as well as where and how each item is used.

Read the Sports theme presented on the sidebar.

Lesson 10

Words with ci, si, ti, and xi

Student Pages

Pages 37–40

Lesson Materials

BLM SP6-01B
Card stock
Index cards
T-8
BLM SP6-10A

Sports

The theme of this lesson is basketball. One of the most popular games in the world, the sport of basketball has a long history, dating back to its invention in 1891 by James Naismith. Although it was originally played by men, basketball quickly gained popularity with women. Disabled athletes began to play basketball using wheelchairs at the end of World War II. Today, wheelchair basketball is a recognized Paralympic sport.

Day 1 Pretest

Objective

The students will accurately spell and write **words with ci, si, ti, and xi.** They will spell and write content, vocabulary, and challenge words.

Introduction

Before class, select Challenge Words for numbers 24 and 25 from a cross-curricular subject, words misspelled on previous assignments, or words that interest your students. The word *crucifixion* has **xi** and is suggested for number 24. Explain that they are to attempt to write all the spelling words.

Directed Instruction

1 Say each word, use it in a sentence, and then repeat the word.

Pattern Words

1. The teammates were anxious when one of the players was injured.
2. Basketball and other aerobic sports are beneficial to one's health.
3. Was there a discussion held about wheelchair basketball?
4. Kareema had the distinction of being the tallest player on the team.
5. It is especially important to practice free throws.
6. It is essential to warm up before practice.
7. A basket was accompanied by an explosion of applause.
8. The crowd's behavior during the game was obnoxious.
9. God is omniscient, omnipotent, and omnipresent.
10. Did the coach feel the team had a lot of potential ability?
11. Players who do not drink sufficient water risk dehydration.
12. Is this a transitional period for the Paralympics?

Content Words

13. Basketball is played in arenas throughout the world.
14. Because of her height, Nicole played center.
15. The official began the game with a jump ball.
16. The athletes were opponents on the court, but friends elsewhere.
17. The rebound changed the possession of the basketball.
18. Strategy and skill are vital to playing basketball.
19. A technical foul was called for poor sportsmanship.

Vocabulary Words

20. Todd did not want to appear disrespectful and interrupt a game.
21. Natasha was an immigrant from Russia.
22. The Petrov family wanted to migrate to North America.
23. It is important to demonstrate respectable conduct at all times.

Challenge Words

24. ______
25. ______

2 Allow students to self-correct their Pretest. Write each word on the board. Point out the *ci, si, ti,* or *xi* spelling in each Pattern Word. The spellings are variant spellings for the sounds /sh/ or /zh/. The *si* in *explosion* is pronounced /zh/. Note the roots *migr* and *spect* in the Vocabulary Words. The Vocabulary Word *disrespectful* has two prefixes, *dis-* and *re-*.

3 As a class, read, spell, and read each word. Direct students to highlight misspelled words and rewrite them correctly.

4 Proof each student's Pretest. This becomes an individualized study sheet that can be used at school or at home.

38

© Spelling Grade 6

5 Homework suggestion: Duplicate **BLM SP6-01B Flash Cards Template** on CARD STOCK for students to write the list words, using the flash cards as a study aid. Another option is to use INDEX CARDS.

Day 2 Word Analysis and Vocabulary

Objective

The students will sort and write **words with ci, si, ti, and xi** and complete sentences with content words. They will use a table to write vocabulary words, select words to match definitions, and complete sentences in context. They will choose the best meaning for given words.

Introduction

Invite students to turn to page 37 and refer to the list words. Write the following headings on the board and select students to state examples of words containing each spelling:

ci	si	ti	xi
sufficient	explosion	potential	anxious
beneficial	discussion	essential	obnoxious
especially		distinction	
omniscient		transitional	

Because each spelling has the /sh/ or the /zh/ sound, the spellings must be memorized. Encourage students to highlight or underline each spelling in a different color on the Pattern Words in their set of flash cards that were suggested for homework on Day 1.

Directed Instruction

1 Proceed to page 37. Say, spell, and say each Pattern, Content, and Vocabulary Word. Provide this week's Challenge Words and have students write them in the spaces provided before completing the page.

2 Proceed to page 38. Remind students to use the table to assist in building each Vocabulary Word. For example, the prefix *im-* goes with the root *migr* and the suffix *-ant* to build the word *immigrant*. Allow students to complete the page independently.

Differentiated Instruction

- For students who spelled all the words correctly on the Pretest, select and assign Extra Challenge Words from the following list: cylindrical, chromosomes, onomatopoeia, ideological, immunization, dramatization.
- For students who spelled less than half correctly, assign the following Pattern, Content, and Vocabulary Words: anxious, potential, essential, sufficient, discussion, obnoxious, official, arenas, technical, opponents, immigrant, disrespectful. On the Posttest, evaluate these students on the twelve words assigned; however, encourage them to attempt to spell all the list words to the best of their ability. They are also responsible for writing the dictated sentences.

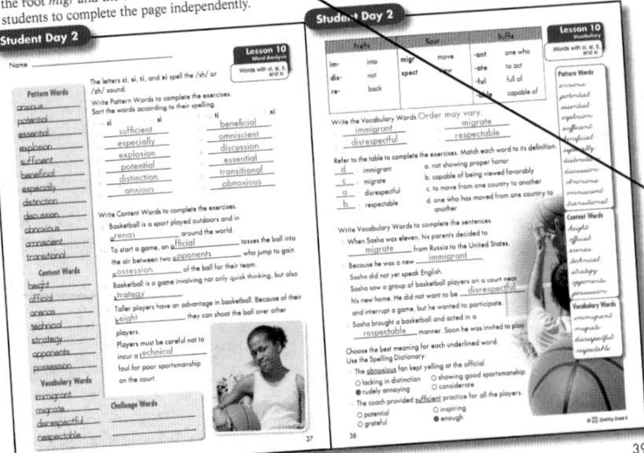

© Spelling Grade 6

Take note of the suggestions given in the Differentiated Instruction section if you plan to differentiate instruction.

Look at the lesson Introduction for ways to engage the students' interest in the lesson.

Review the Directed Instruction section to become familiar with the sequence of procedures to follow.

Look at the Student Spelling Support section of suggested activities to extend the spelling lessons, provide additional ideas for different learning styles, and incorporate spelling with other curriculum areas, including biblical integration.

Note the blackline masters, posters, and color transparencies provided.

Prepare the classroom for the activity noted in the lesson Introduction.

Student Spelling Support Materials

BLM SP6-01A

Student Spelling Support

1. Use **BLM SP6-01A A Spelling Study Strategy** in instructional groups to provide assistance with some or all of the words.
2. Invite students to write the Challenge Words, numbers 24 and 25, in the Word Bank, in the back of their textbook.
3. Challenge students to research the Paralympic games, using the Internet. Students choose a sport of interest and describe the sport in the progressive, sport journal that was started in Lesson 1.
4. Write this week's words, categorize the Pattern, Content, and Vocabulary Words, and attach them to the Word Wall.
5. Read Galatians 6:9: "And let us not grow weary while doing good, for in due season we shall reap if we do not lose heart." Just as athletes must not get discouraged through many practice sessions and drills, we as Christians need to persevere in doing good for others. Challenge students to write a paragraph describing how a good deed made a difference in the life of another person, or how a good deed done on another student's behalf helped him or her.
6. Expand students' study skills by providing a method for memorizing the *ci, si, ti,* and *xi* spellings in each Pattern Word. Instruct students to sort words according to their spellings and then to write a sentence using each spelling pattern; for example, The explo*si*on was the subject of discus*si*on, or The obno*xi*ous fan made the

Cont. on page 41

40

3 Homework suggestion: Students use their Spelling Dictionary to write the definition of each word on the back of the corresponding flash card that was suggested for homework on Day 1.

Day 3 Word Study Strategies

Objective

The students will complete riddles with Pattern Words. Students will write words that are related forms of given words. Students will use the meaning of related word forms to define list words.

Introduction

Invite students to turn to page 39 and refer to the Pattern Words. Ask the following riddles:

- Which word with *ti* is absolutely necessary? **(essential)**
- Which word with *si* is an oral consideration of a question or idea? **(discussion)**
- Which word with *ci* is that which improves one's well-being? **(beneficial)**

Select volunteers to provide the answer to each riddle.

Directed Instruction

1 Write the following sentences on the board, underlining words and leaving a blank space as shown:
- Something transitory tends to move away.
- A transient is a person who moves from place to place.
- Something _______ moves from one stage to another. **(transitional)**

Explain that the underlined words are related forms of the Pattern Word needed to complete the final sentence. Chorally read each sentence and choose a volunteer to write the word on the blank. Note that the meaning of each related form provides a clue to the meaning of the Pattern Word. Assist students to conclude that the prefix *trans-* implies movement. Knowing the meaning of a related form helps students in understanding new vocabulary.

2 Proceed to page 39. Students complete the page independently.

Day 4 Writing

Objective

The students will complete sentences in a descriptive dialogue with list words that match pronunciations.

Introduction

Display **T-8 Basketball Dialogue**, keeping the bottom portion covered. Define *dialogue* as a conversation between two or more people. The dialogue on the transparency gives the pronunciation for several list words followed by a blank. Students can refer to the list words found on page 40. Solicit volunteers to write the list word that matches each pronunciation by sounding out each word. Check the bottom of the transparency for accuracy. When complete, choose two volunteers to read the parts of CHRIS and PAT in the dialogue, substituting the pronunciation in the text for the list words.

Directed Instruction

1 Inform students that they will be reading a dialogue about a Paralympic sport, wheelchair basketball. The International Paralympics are a series of contests for athletes with disabilities held at the conclusion of the summer and winter Olympic Games.

2 Proceed to page 40. Encourage students to use the Spelling Dictionary to check the pronunciations of the list words as they complete the page independently.

3 Homework suggestion: Distribute a copy of **BLM SP6-10A Lesson 10 Homework** to each student.

© Spelling Grade 6

Locate definitions of new terms printed in blue italics.

Day 5 Posttest

Objective

The students will correctly write dictated spelling words and sentences.

Introduction

Review by using flash cards noted in Day 1 and Day 2 Homework suggestion.

Directed Assessment

1 Dictate the list words by using the Pretest sentences or developing original ones. Reserve *anxious, potential, sufficient, official, opponents,* and *disrespectful* for the dictation sentences.

2 Read each sentence. Repeat as needed.
- Timothy was anxious before the basketball tournament.
- He was concerned about a potential loss.
- Timothy knew the team had sufficient practice to play their best.
- The official on the court was ready for a jump ball.
- The opponents faced each other.
- None of the fans were disrespectful, and the tournament went well.

3 If assigned, dictate Extra Challenge Words.

4 Score the test, counting each misspelled word as an error. Correct the dictation sentences by grading only the spelling words or grading the complete sentences.

Student Spelling Support

Cont. from page 40

official feel anxious.

7. Invite students to write and perform their own sports dialogue centered around one of the following topics:
   - A young athlete argues with the referee's call and receives the consequences of his actions.
   - A young athlete gets in a fight on court and has to face a difficult conversation with his coach after the game.
   - A player is excited because his team is going to the finals, however, his parents have asked him to skip the game and attend his uncle's funeral.

Encourage students to incorporate spelling words into their dialogue, utilize Scriptures to back up their dialogue content, and to frame each athlete's appropriate or inappropriate response to authority.

Student Day 3

Student Day 4

Dialogue About Wheelchair Basketball

41

© Spelling Grade 6

Use the suggestions listed for assessment to monitor student progress.

Use the answers provided on the reduced student pages for correction and evaluation of student work.

A Spelling Study Strategy

Teacher Note: Instruct students in the use of **A Spelling Study Strategy** prior to Lesson 1.

Display P-1 A Spelling Study Strategy.

A Spelling Study Strategy
1
• Look at the word.
• Say the word and listen to the sounds.
• Think about how each sound is spelled.
2
• Picture the word in your mind.
• Are there any spelling patterns?
3
• Write the word.
• Check your spelling.
• Does your spelling match the correct spelling?
A Spelling Study Strategy P-1

Duplicate one copy of **BLM SP6-01A A Spelling Study Strategy** for each student. Write *insist, hiccup, difficult, contact,* and *subtotal* in the left-hand column.

Model each step.

- Look at the first spelling word, say it, and listen to the sounds. Think about the sounds.
- Fold the paper.
- Picture the word in your mind, identify spelling patterns, and write the word.
- Unfold the paper.
- Use a colored pencil for checking and making corrections. If a word is misspelled, direct students to circle it, go back to the first column, and write the word in the faded column.

Lesson 1

Short Vowels

Student Pages

Pages 1–4

Lesson Materials

BLM SP6-01B
Card stock
Index cards
T-2
P-2
P-3
P-4
BLM SP6-01C

Sports

Sportsmanship is the desired conduct at sporting events. Our loving God exemplifies the behavior that He desires to see in each of us as we go about our daily activities, including sports. 1 John 4:7 reads, "Beloved, let us love one another, for love is of God; and everyone who loves is born of God and knows God."

Lessons 1–5 utilize the theme of extreme sports. Lesson 1 begins with motocross. Motocross is a popular motorcycle sport that occurs over natural terrain—dirt. Events may encompass freestyle acrobatic tricks and racing. Motocross events can take place in a natural setting, an open-air arena, or an enclosed arena. The word *motocross* is a portmanteau /pôrt 'man tō/, a combination of the words *motorcycle* and *cross-country.*

Day 1 Pretest

Objective

The students will accurately spell and write words with **short vowels**, content, vocabulary, and challenge words.

Introduction

The Pretest is an ungraded assessment to assist students in studying the list words—Pattern, Content, Vocabulary, and Challenge. To meet your students' needs, select Challenge Words from a cross-curricular subject, common misspellings for sixth graders, or words that interest your students. The word *reminisce* has **short e** in the first syllable and is suggested for number 24. Explain that they are to attempt to write all the spelling words.

Directed Instruction

1 Use the sentences that follow or develop original ones.

2 Say each word, use it in a sentence, and then repeat the word.

Pattern Words

1. A motocross racer should anticipate racing in all types of weather.
2. Simon heard Matt hiccup after the championship Grand Prix.
3. Ryan's attitude improved when he took time to pray.
4. The motorcycling federation does insist on strict safety measures.
5. Tarah benefitted from hours of practice on the racecourse.
6. Sherri followed a specific training method when preparing to race.
7. Alisa came into contact with many professional racers at Supercross.
8. Modern engineering technology enables motorcycles to run faster.
9. Carrie maneuvered through the difficult course on her motorcycle.
10. The subtotal came to fifty-five dollars, before tax.
11. What is the function of large wheels on a race motorcycle?
12. Kirsten made significant progress in the latest motocross race.

Content Words

13. Chad maintained good form as he followed the challenging circuit.
14. The computerized game effectively simulated motocross events.
15. The sport of motocross racing is very dangerous.
16. Jerome felt confident as he raced along the bumpy terrain.
17. Jake's motorcycle has a modified and powerful engine.
18. Motocross racing involves intense, physical demands.
19. Motocross racers wear safety equipment such as body armor and boots.

Vocabulary Words

20. Meika successfully traversed the course during the women's event.
21. Lauren qualified for the final Pro Motocross event.
22. Due to the weather, the judges reversed the order of race events.
23. Curtis was a finalist in the Motocross World Championship.

Challenge Words

24. ______________________ **(Insert your choice.)**
25. ______________________ **(Insert your choice.)**

3 Allow students to self-correct their Pretest. Write each word on the board. Point out the **short vowels** in the first syllable of each Pattern Word. The Pattern Word *progress* is a noun and is pronounced /'pro grəs/. Note the roots *fin* and *vers* in the Vocabulary Words. The Vocabulary Word *finalist* contains two suffixes, *-al* and *-ist*.

4 As a class, read, spell, and read each word. Direct students to highlight misspelled words and rewrite them correctly.

5 Proof each student's Pretest. This becomes an individualized study sheet that can be used at school or at home.

6 Homework suggestion: Duplicate **BLM SP6-01B Flash Cards Template** on CARD STOCK for students to write the list words, using the flash cards as a study aid. Another option is to use INDEX CARDS. The pursuance of good study skills is a critical learning tool that will allow students to succeed as they move on to secondary school. One effective note-taking skill is using flash cards. Flash cards can be secured by a ring fastener or rubber band and reviewed each week. Students should retain the flash cards from the first five lessons for the review lesson.

Day 2 Word Analysis and Vocabulary

Objective

The students will sort words with **short vowels** according to the first syllable sound and complete sentences with content words. They will use a table to write vocabulary words, match vocabulary words to their definitions, and complete a sentence.

Introduction

Proceed to page 1. Define the following categories of words: Pattern Words—words with similar spellings or sounds; Content Words—words related to a specific content area indicated by the lesson theme; Vocabulary Words—words with prefixes, suffixes, and Greek and Latin Roots; and Challenge Words—words that may be harder to spell. Provide this week's Challenge Words and have students write the words on their page.

Directed Instruction

1 Invite students to refer to the list words, found on page 1, for this activity. Chorally read each Pattern Word. Point out that the Pattern Words in this lesson all contain a short vowel sound in the first syllable. Have students identify each beginning short vowel sound. Categorize the words on the board. (**short a—attitude, anticipate; short e—method, benefitted, technology; short i—insist, hiccup, difficult; short o—contact, progress; short u—subtotal, function**)

Differentiated Instruction

Differentiating spelling instruction is an option to consider. Additional information can be found on page xvii in the front of this book.

- For students who spelled all the words correctly on the Pretest, select and assign Extra Challenge Words from the following list: algebraic, abiotic, demonstrative, bureaucracy, apparatus, accelerando.
- For students who spelled less than half correctly, assign the following Pattern, Content, and Vocabulary Words: difficult, contact, method, attitude, function, anticipate, circuit, terrain, equipment, dangerous, finalist, reversed. On the Posttest, evaluate these students on the twelve words assigned; however, encourage them to attempt to spell all the list words to the best of their ability. They are also responsible for writing the dictated sentences.

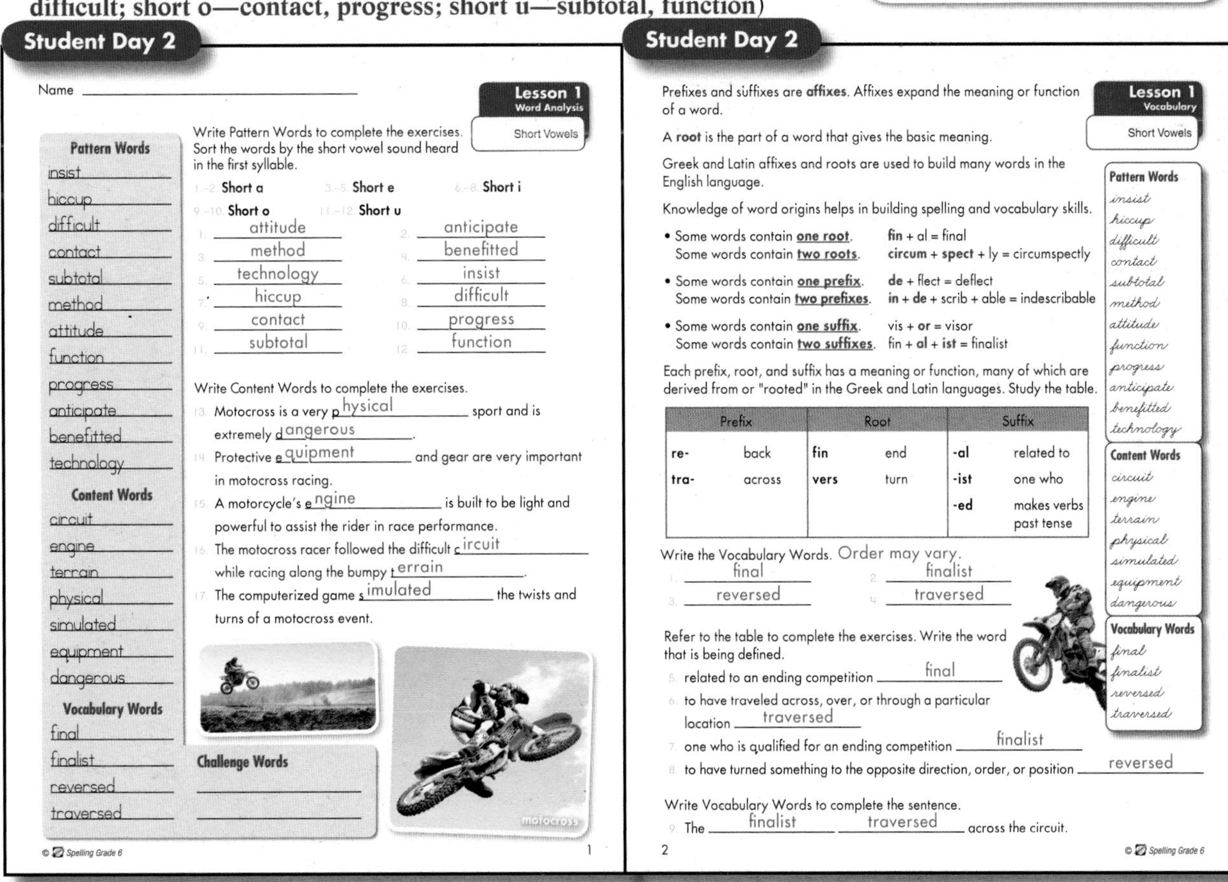

Student Day 2

Name ______________________

Lesson 1 Word Analysis — Short Vowels

Pattern Words: insist, hiccup, difficult, contact, subtotal, method, attitude, function, progress, anticipate, benefitted, technology

Content Words: circuit, engine, terrain, physical, simulated, equipment, dangerous

Vocabulary Words: final, finalist, reversed, traversed

Write Pattern Words to complete the exercises. Sort the words by the short vowel sound heard in the first syllable.

1–2 Short a; 3–5 Short e; 6–8 Short i; 9–10 Short o; 11–12 Short u

1. attitude 2. anticipate
3. method 4. benefitted
5. technology 6. insist
7. hiccup 8. difficult
9. contact 10. progress
11. subtotal 12. function

Write Content Words to complete the exercises.

13. Motocross is a very physical sport and is extremely dangerous.
14. Protective equipment and gear are very important in motocross racing.
15. A motorcycle's engine is built to be light and powerful to assist the rider in race performance.
16. The motocross racer followed the difficult circuit while racing along the bumpy terrain.
17. The computerized game simulated the twists and turns of a motocross event.

Challenge Words

motocross

© Spelling Grade 6 1

Student Day 2

Lesson 1 Vocabulary — Short Vowels

Prefixes and suffixes are **affixes**. Affixes expand the meaning or function of a word.

A **root** is the part of a word that gives the basic meaning.

Greek and Latin affixes and roots are used to build many words in the English language.

Knowledge of word origins helps in building spelling and vocabulary skills.

- Some words contain one root. — fin + al = final
  Some words contain two roots. — circum + spect + ly = circumspectly
- Some words contain one prefix. — de + flect = deflect
  Some words contain two prefixes. — in + de + scrib + able = indescribable
- Some words contain one suffix. — vis + or = visor
  Some words contain two suffixes. — fin + al + ist = finalist

Each prefix, root, and suffix has a meaning or function, many of which are derived from or "rooted" in the Greek and Latin languages. Study the table.

Prefix		Root		Suffix	
re-	back	fin	end	-al	related to
tra-	across	vers	turn	-ist	one who
				-ed	makes verbs past tense

Write the Vocabulary Words. Order may vary.

1. final 2. finalist
3. reversed 4. traversed

Refer to the table to complete the exercises. Write the word that is being defined.

5. related to an ending competition final
6. to have traveled across, over, or through a particular location traversed
7. one who is qualified for an ending competition finalist
8. to have turned something to the opposite direction, order, or position reversed

Write Vocabulary Words to complete the sentence.

9. The finalist traversed across the circuit.

Pattern Words: insist, hiccup, difficult, contact, subtotal, method, attitude, function, progress, anticipate, benefitted, technology

Content Words: circuit, engine, terrain, physical, simulated, equipment, dangerous

Vocabulary Words: final, finalist, reversed, traversed

2 © Spelling Grade 6

Student Spelling Support Materials

T-1
BLM SP6-01A
BLM Parent Letter

Student Spelling Support

1. Use **T-1 A Spelling Study Strategy** and **BLM SP6-01A A Spelling Study Strategy** for students who demonstrate the need for additional practice with some or all of the words.
2. Invite students to write the Challenge Words, numbers 24 and 25, in the Word Bank, in the back of their textbook.
3. Challenge students to research and write a few interesting facts of the lesson theme—motocross. Compile facts and draw pictures in a journal or notebook to build an informative resource. Do this with each lesson theme, in the textbook, as the year progresses. At the end of the year, invite students to share their progressive journals on sports.
4. Make a Word Wall using this week's spelling words. Write the words, categorize the Pattern, Content, and Vocabulary Words, and attach to the wall. Allow students to spontaneously add new words to the list during the week. Categorizing by patterns helps students internalize generalizations.

Short vowel in the first syllable

attitude method insist
contact subtotal

Content: Motocross

circuit engine

Vocabulary

final reversed

Cont. on page 5

Students independently complete the page.

2 Proceed to page 2. Display **T-2 Word Origins Practice** on the overhead and invite students to follow along as you build the foundation of studying word origins. The transparency is an exact replica of student page 2. Use the transparency to instruct students on how to build each Vocabulary Word. For example, the root *fin* goes with the suffix *-al* to build the word *final.* Read each sentence and complete the page as a class.

3 Display **P-2** and **P-3 Latin Roots** and **P-4 Greek Roots** for students to reference roots and meanings. Leave posters up throughout the year.

4 Homework suggestion: Students use their Spelling Dictionary to write the definition of each word on the back of the corresponding flash card that was suggested for homework on Day 1.

Day 3 Word Study Strategies

Objective

The students will utilize dictionary skills by answering questions about the different components of a dictionary entry. They will underline and write list words that are used as nouns in paragraphs.

Introduction

Direct students to turn to page 155 in the back of their textbook. Review the basic components of a dictionary entry.

Directed Instruction

1 Invite students to refer to the list words on page 3. Brainstorm ideas about how to approach looking up list words in the dictionary. Explain that there are many approaches to developing study skills and encourage students to figure out which approach(es) is suitable to them.

2 Ask a volunteer to state the definition of a noun. A *noun* is a person, place, thing, or idea. Review that a noun can be in singular or plural form. Parts of speech vary, depending upon how a word is used in context, so a word may be used as a noun in one sentence and a different part of speech in another sentence.

3 Proceed to page 3. Students independently complete the page. Select a volunteer to read Psalm 139:14. Discuss how we should praise God for how He made our bodies. Our brain, skeleton, and muscles are just a few examples of God's intricate design in us. Through this design, He has enabled us to actively participate in daily activities, such as sports.

Day 4 Writing

Objective

The students will complete an informative e-mail in the context of a cloze activity using pattern, content, and vocabulary words.

Introduction

Teacher Note: The informative domain is the focus for the writing pages in Lessons 1–5.

Remind students that a *cloze activity* consists of a sentence or passage with blanks. Students complete the blanks with appropriate list words. Inform students that you will be reading aloud a short cloze activity in the form of an e-mail. Read the following:

> Dear Natasha,
> Today, I attended a local motocross event and watched in amazement as the motocross riders raced through the _1_. They _2_ the course and sped around the dirt _3_. I didn't _4_ that I would have that much fun! I will let you know when I go again and would love it if you joined me!
> Sincerely,
> Julia

Directed Instruction

1 Invite students to refer to the list words on page 4. Reread the e-mail and challenge students to locate the appropriate list word that will fit into sentence context when you pause at the end of each sentence requiring a missing word or words. (**1—circuit or terrain; 2—traversed; 3—circuit or terrain; 4—anticipate**)

2 Proceed to page 4 and select a volunteer to read the sentences at the top of the page. Students independently complete the cloze activity. When complete, select a student to read the e-mail aloud.

3 Homework suggestion: Distribute a copy of **BLM SP6-01C Lesson 1 Homework** to each student.

Day 5 Posttest

Objective

The students will correctly write dictated spelling words and sentences.

Introduction

Review by using flash cards noted in Day 1 and Day 2 Homework suggestion.

Directed Assessment

1 Dictate the list words by using the Pretest sentences or developing original ones. Reserve *attitude, circuit, anticipate, difficult, terrain,* and *finalist* for the dictation sentences.

2 Read each sentence. Repeat as needed.

- Ben asked the Lord to help him have a good <u>attitude</u> before the race.
- He was excited to race on the new <u>circuit</u>.
- Ben did <u>anticipate</u> the race to be very intense.
- He knew it was a <u>difficult</u> course.
- Ben carefully studied the design of the <u>terrain</u>.
- Ben did his best and was a <u>finalist</u> in the race.

3 If assigned, dictate Extra Challenge Words.

4 Score the test, counting each misspelled word as an error. Correct the dictation sentences by grading only the spelling words or grading the complete sentences.

Student Spelling Support

Cont. from page 4

5. Read 1 John 4:7: "Beloved, let us love one another, for love is of God; and everyone who loves is born of God and knows God." Encourage students to share ideas as to why it is important for us to love one another. Discuss the consequences of not loving one another. How does this positive or negative behavior and attitude affect the way we participate in sports? Most importantly, how do these behaviors affect others for Christ?
6. Provide a copy of the **BLM Parent Letter** for each student to take home. This will inform parents about their child's spelling class.

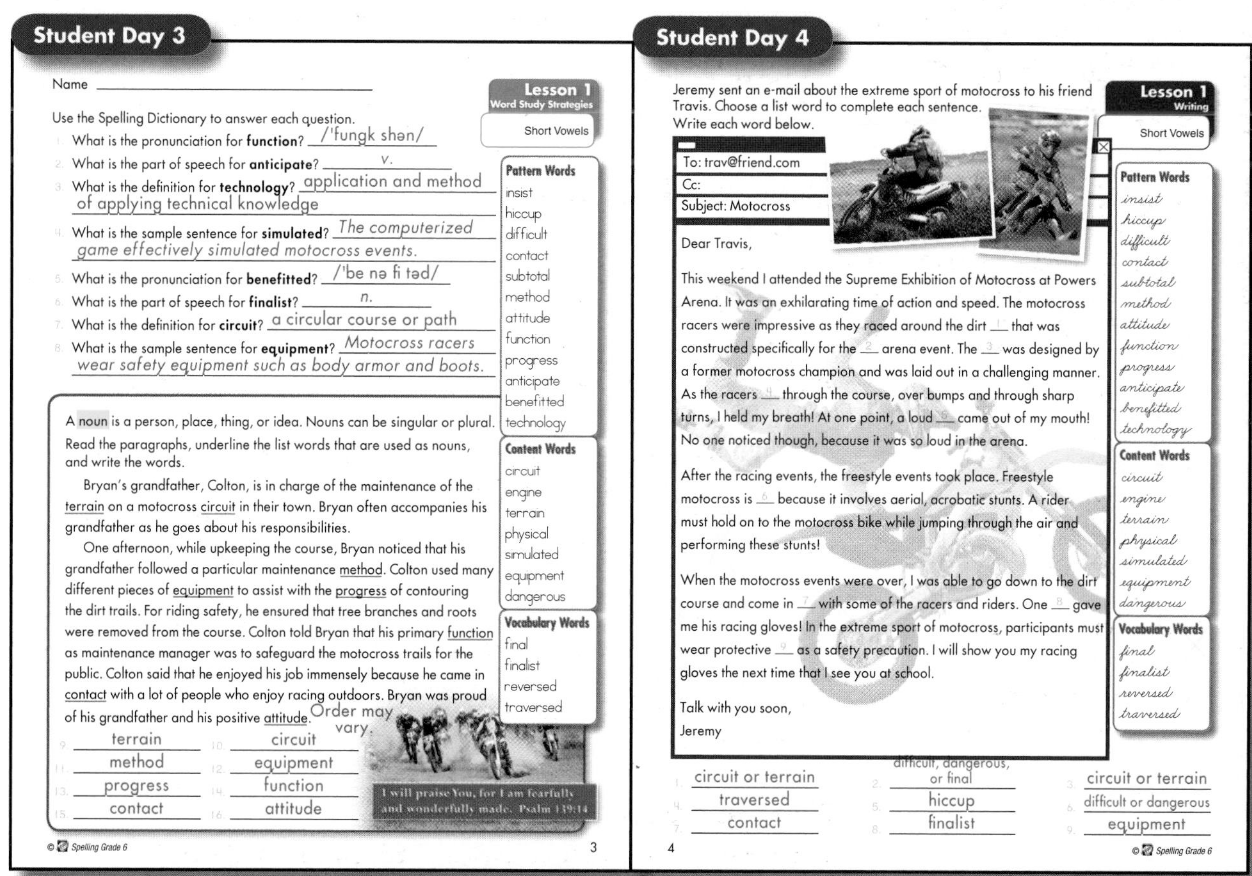

Student Day 3

Name ______________________

Lesson 1 Word Study Strategies — Short Vowels

Use the Spelling Dictionary to answer each question.

1. What is the pronunciation for **function**? /ˈfungk shən/
2. What is the part of speech for **anticipate**? v.
3. What is the definition for **technology**? application and method of applying technical knowledge
4. What is the sample sentence for **simulated**? The computerized game effectively simulated motocross events.
5. What is the pronunciation for **benefitted**? /ˈbe nə fi təd/
6. What is the part of speech for **finalist**? n.
7. What is the definition for **circuit**? a circular course or path
8. What is the sample sentence for **equipment**? Motocross racers wear safety equipment such as body armor and boots.

A noun is a person, place, thing, or idea. Nouns can be singular or plural. Read the paragraphs, underline the list words that are used as nouns, and write the words.

Bryan's grandfather, Colton, is in charge of the maintenance of the <u>terrain</u> on a motocross <u>circuit</u> in their town. Bryan often accompanies his grandfather as he goes about his responsibilities.

One afternoon, while upkeeping the course, Bryan noticed that his grandfather followed a particular maintenance <u>method</u>. Colton used many different pieces of <u>equipment</u> to assist with the <u>progress</u> of contouring the dirt trails. For riding safety, he ensured that tree branches and roots were removed from the course. Colton told Bryan that his primary <u>function</u> as maintenance manager was to safeguard the motocross trails for the public. Colton said that he enjoyed his job immensely because he came in <u>contact</u> with a lot of people who enjoy racing outdoors. Bryan was proud of his grandfather and his positive <u>attitude</u>.

Order may vary.

9. terrain 10. circuit
11. method 12. equipment
13. progress 14. function
15. contact 16. attitude

I will praise You, for I am fearfully and wonderfully made. Psalm 139:14

Pattern Words: insist, hiccup, difficult, contact, subtotal, method, attitude, function, progress, anticipate, benefitted, technology

Content Words: circuit, engine, terrain, physical, simulated, equipment, dangerous

Vocabulary Words: final, finalist, reversed, traversed

© Spelling Grade 6 3

Student Day 4

Lesson 1 Writing — Short Vowels

Jeremy sent an e-mail about the extreme sport of motocross to his friend Travis. Choose a list word to complete each sentence. Write each word below.

To: trav@friend.com
Cc:
Subject: Motocross

Dear Travis,

This weekend I attended the Supreme Exhibition of Motocross at Powers Arena. It was an exhilarating time of action and speed. The motocross racers were impressive as they raced around the dirt __1__ that was constructed specifically for the __2__ arena event. The __3__ was designed by a former motocross champion and was laid out in a challenging manner. As the racers __4__ through the course, over bumps and through sharp turns, I held my breath! At one point, a loud __5__ came out of my mouth! No one noticed though, because it was so loud in the arena.

After the racing events, the freestyle events took place. Freestyle motocross is __6__ because it involves aerial, acrobatic stunts. A rider must hold on to the motocross bike while jumping through the air and performing these stunts!

When the motocross events were over, I was able to go down to the dirt course and come in __7__ with some of the racers and riders. One __8__ gave me his racing gloves! In the extreme sport of motocross, participants must wear protective __9__ as a safety precaution. I will show you my racing gloves the next time that I see you at school.

Talk with you soon,
Jeremy

1. circuit or terrain 2. difficult, dangerous, or final 3. circuit or terrain
4. traversed 5. hiccup 6. difficult or dangerous
7. contact 8. finalist 9. equipment

Pattern Words: insist, hiccup, difficult, contact, subtotal, method, attitude, function, progress, anticipate, benefitted, technology

Content Words: circuit, engine, terrain, physical, simulated, equipment, dangerous

Vocabulary Words: final, finalist, reversed, traversed

4 © Spelling Grade 6

Lesson 2

Long Vowels

Student Pages

Pages 5–8

Lesson Materials

BLM SP6-01B
Card stock
Index cards
BLM SP6-02A

Sports

The theme of this lesson is bicycle motocross cycling, known by the acronym BMX. BMX cycling is an offshoot of motocross racing. Riders race or perform stunts on small, specially designed bikes. Courses for BMX bikes feature a variety of surfaces that challenge riders. Enthusiasts of BMX cycling are taught to follow safety rules and wear protective gear when riding.

Day 1 Pretest

Objective

The students will accurately spell and write words with **long vowels**, content, vocabulary, and challenge words.

Introduction

The Pretest is an ungraded assessment to assist students in studying the Pattern, Content, Vocabulary, and Challenge Words. To meet your students' needs, select Challenge Words from a cross-curricular subject or words misspelled on previous assignments. The word *globalization* has **long o** in the first syllable and is suggested for number 24. Explain that they are to attempt to write all the spelling words.

Directed Instruction

1 Use the sentences that follow or develop original ones.

2 Say each word, use it in a sentence, and then repeat the word.

Pattern Words

1. Working together will unify the team.
2. Motorcycle cross-country riding became the basis for BMX.
3. Each of the BMX riders followed closely behind the other.
4. BMX riders need to cooperate with each other.
5. Alana was lost in a daydream about a bike race.
6. Renee's visor shields her eyes from the sun.
7. One of the race highlights was a spectacular jump.
8. Ideally, one should remove the kickstand on a BMX bike.
9. Cindi chose a track of medium length.
10. Racers do not always line up in numerical order.
11. There are good reasons for every rule in BMX racing.
12. I could tell that the wheel was bent from its wobbly rotation.

Content Words

13. Is BMX cycling an Olympic sport?
14. A circle's diameter passes through its midpoint.
15. It is important to wear a sturdy helmet when riding a bike.
16. Hybrid bikes are a cross between motorcycles and mountain bikes.
17. The sport of motocross was the inspiration for BMX.
18. The agile rider could maneuver her bike around sharp corners.
19. The BMX bike was designed with smaller wheels than other bikes.

Vocabulary Words

20. Sunglasses deflect light rays from a rider's eyes.
21. The heat of the race caused many riders to perspire.
22. Owen wore a jacket with a reflective stripe down each sleeve.
23. My aspiration is to become like Jesus.

Challenge Words

24. ______________________ **(Insert your choice.)**
25. ______________________ **(Insert your choice.)**

3 Allow students to self-correct their Pretest. Write each word on the board. Point out the long vowel spellings in each Pattern Word. Note the roots *flect* and *spir* in the Vocabulary Words. The silent *e* in the word *perspire* is not included in the original root spelling *spir.*

4 As a class, read, spell, and read each word. Direct students to highlight misspelled words and rewrite them correctly.

5 Proof each student's Pretest. This becomes an individualized study sheet that can be used at school or at home.

6 Homework suggestion: Duplicate **BLM SP6-01B Flash Cards Template** on CARD STOCK for students to write the list words, using the flash cards as a study aid. Another option is to use INDEX CARDS.

Day 2 Word Analysis and Vocabulary

Objective

The students will sort and write words with **long vowels** and complete sentences with content words. They will use a table to write vocabulary words, select words to match definitions, and complete sentences in context. They will choose the best meaning for given words.

Introduction

Before class, write the following long vowel spelling generalizations on the board:

- Vowels at the end of an open syllable are usually long. (**u|nify, vi|sor, ba|sis, i|deally, ro|tation, me|dium, nu|merical, co|operate**)
- Vowels followed by a silent vowel are usually long. (**reasons, daydream**)
- Vowels followed by a consonant and silent *e* are usually long. (**closely**)
- The *long i* sound is heard in the phoneme *igh*. (**highlights**)

Challenge students to turn to the list words found on page 5 and to state which long vowel spelling pattern is demonstrated in the first syllable of each Pattern Word.

Directed Instruction

1 Inform students that the theme for this lesson is BMX cycling. Define *BMX cycling* as *bicycle motocross cycling,* an offshoot of motorcycle motocross. Point out the following to clarify Content Words:

- The word *motocross* is a portmanteau, a combination of the words *motorcycle* and *cross-country.*
- *Hybrid* means *something formed by merging two original designs.*

Differentiated Instruction

Differentiating spelling instruction is an option to consider.

- For students who spelled all the words correctly on the Pretest, select and assign Extra Challenge Words from the following list: algorithm, accelerator, documentary, cartography, autonomous, acoustic.
- For students who spelled less than half correctly, assign the following Pattern, Content, and Vocabulary Words: basis, ideally, closely, medium, numerical, cooperate, cycling, designed, diameter, motocross, deflect, aspiration. On the Posttest, evaluate these students on the twelve words assigned; however, encourage them to attempt to spell all the list words to the best of their ability. They are also responsible for writing the dictated sentences.

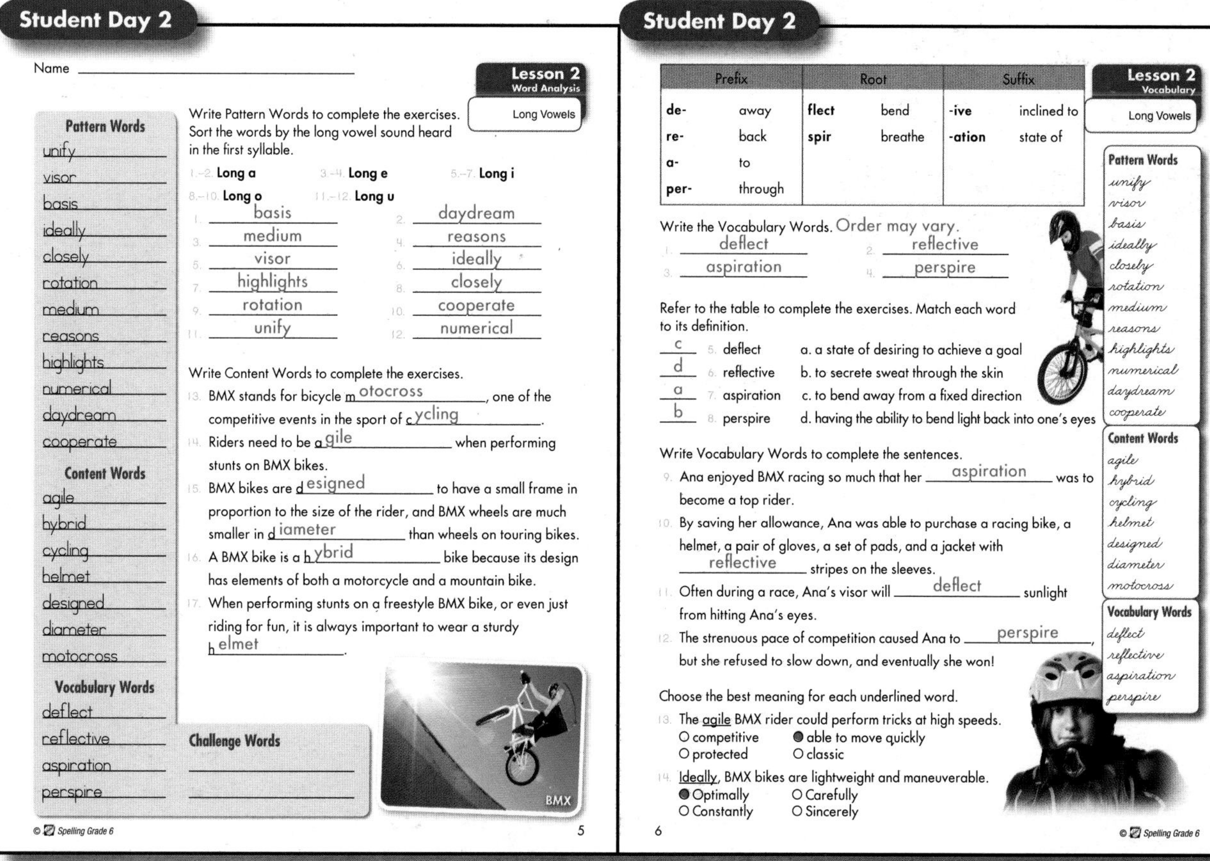

Student Day 2

Name ______

Lesson 2 Word Analysis — Long Vowels

Pattern Words: unify, visor, basis, ideally, closely, rotation, medium, reasons, highlights, numerical, daydream, cooperate

Content Words: agile, hybrid, cycling, helmet, designed, diameter, motocross

Vocabulary Words: deflect, reflective, aspiration, perspire

Challenge Words

Write Pattern Words to complete the exercises. Sort the words by the long vowel sound heard in the first syllable.

1.–2. Long a 3.–4. Long e 5.–7. Long i 8.–10. Long o 11.–12. Long u

1. basis 2. daydream
3. medium 4. reasons
5. visor 6. ideally
7. highlights 8. closely
9. rotation 10. cooperate
11. unify 12. numerical

Write Content Words to complete the exercises.

13. BMX stands for bicycle m otocross, one of the competitive events in the sport of c ycling.
14. Riders need to be a gile when performing stunts on BMX bikes.
15. BMX bikes are d esigned to have a small frame in proportion to the size of the rider, and BMX wheels are much smaller in d iameter than wheels on touring bikes.
16. A BMX bike is a h ybrid bike because its design has elements of both a motorcycle and a mountain bike.
17. When performing stunts on a freestyle BMX bike, or even just riding for fun, it is always important to wear a sturdy h elmet.

© Spelling Grade 6 5

Student Day 2

Lesson 2 Vocabulary — Long Vowels

Prefix		Root		Suffix	
de-	away	flect	bend	-ive	inclined to
re-	back	spir	breathe	-ation	state of
a-	to				
per-	through				

Write the Vocabulary Words. Order may vary.

1. deflect 2. reflective
3. aspiration 4. perspire

Refer to the table to complete the exercises. Match each word to its definition.

c 5. deflect — a. a state of desiring to achieve a goal
d 6. reflective — b. to secrete sweat through the skin
a 7. aspiration — c. to bend away from a fixed direction
b 8. perspire — d. having the ability to bend light back into one's eyes

Write Vocabulary Words to complete the sentences.

9. Ana enjoyed BMX racing so much that her aspiration was to become a top rider.
10. By saving her allowance, Ana was able to purchase a racing bike, a helmet, a pair of gloves, a set of pads, and a jacket with reflective stripes on the sleeves.
11. Often during a race, Ana's visor will deflect sunlight from hitting Ana's eyes.
12. The strenuous pace of competition caused Ana to perspire, but she refused to slow down, and eventually she won!

Choose the best meaning for each underlined word.

13. The agile BMX rider could perform tricks at high speeds.
○ competitive ● able to move quickly
○ protected ○ classic

14. Ideally, BMX bikes are lightweight and maneuverable.
● Optimally ○ Carefully
○ Constantly ○ Sincerely

Pattern Words: unify, visor, basis, ideally, closely, rotation, medium, reasons, highlights, numerical, daydream, cooperate

Content Words: agile, hybrid, cycling, helmet, designed, diameter, motocross

Vocabulary Words: deflect, reflective, aspiration, perspire

6 © Spelling Grade 6

Student Spelling Support Materials

BLM SP6-01A

Student Spelling Support

1. Use **BLM SP6-01A A Spelling Study Strategy** in instructional groups to provide assistance with some or all of the words.
2. Invite students to write the Challenge Words, numbers 24 and 25, in the Word Bank, in the back of their textbook.
3. Challenge students to work in small, collaborative groups to produce a poster, listing rules for a particular playground game. Encourage students to be as specific as possible when writing the rules. Students will need to compromise and cooperate as they draft their lists of rules.
4. Write this week's words, categorize the Pattern, Content, and Vocabulary Words, and attach them to the Word Wall.
5. Choose a student to read 1 Peter 2:13–15: "Therefore submit yourselves to every ordinance of man for the Lord's sake, whether to the king as supreme, or to governors, as to those who are sent by him for the punishment of evildoers and for the praise of those who do good. For this is the will of God, that by doing good you may put to silence the ignorance of foolish men." Define *ordinance* as *a rule*. Emphasize that our submission to rules is part of God's will for our lives. Challenge students to write a journal entry on the topic of obedience.
6. To further develop students' study skills, instruct students to fold a piece of notebook paper lengthwise into four columns. Demonstrate how

Cont. on page 9

BMX bikes are hybrid bikes because they have design elements of both a motorcycle and a mountain bike.

2 Proceed to page 5. Say, spell, and say each Pattern, Content, and Vocabulary Word. Provide this week's Challenge Words and have students write them in the spaces provided before completing the page.

3 Proceed to page 6. Encourage students to use the table as an aid in building each Vocabulary Word. For example, the prefix *de-* goes with the root *flect* to build the word *deflect*. Remind students that the silent *e* in the word *perspire* is not in the original root spelling *spir.* Allow students to complete the page independently.

4 Homework suggestion: Students use their Spelling Dictionary to write the definition of each word on the back of the corresponding flash card that was suggested for homework on Day 1.

Day 3 Word Study Strategies

Objective

The students will write list words to complete analogies. Students will identify and write the complete and simple subject of given sentences.

Introduction

Invite students to turn to the list words on page 7. Write the following incomplete statements on the board:

- Draw is to drawn as design is to ______. (**designed**)
- Shirt is to collar as helmet is to ______. (**visor**)

Identify these statements as analogies. An *analogy* is made up of two word pairs. Both pairs of words have the same kind of relationship. Read the first analogy and ask a volunteer to state how the words *draw* and *drawn* are related. (**Possible answer: *Drawn* is the past tense form of *draw.***) Apply the same relationship to the second part of the analogy by asking students which list word is the past tense form of *design*. (**designed**) In the next analogy, assist students in understanding the relationship between *shirt* and *collar.* (**A *collar* is an extension of the body of a *shirt.***) Challenge students to select a list word with the same type of relationship to *helmet.* (**visor**) Select a volunteer to complete the analogies.

Directed Instruction

1 Write the following sentences on the board:

- The agile (rider) had to cooperate with other members of his team.
- The entire BMX (team) followed closely behind the leader.

Remind students that every sentence in English is composed of a subject and a predicate. In English sentence structure, the subject usually precedes the predicate. The *complete subject* includes all the words that tell **whom** or **what** the sentence is about. The *simple subject* is the main word within the complete subject. The simple subject is a noun or pronoun. Choose volunteers to read each sentence, underline the complete subject and circle the simple subject.

2 Proceed to page 7. Allow students to work independently.

Day 4 Writing

Objective

The students will complete a list of safety rules in the context of a cloze activity using pattern, content, and vocabulary words. They will select a sport of their choice, write a list of safety rules pertaining to that sport, and list the reasons for the importance of each rule.

Introduction

Invite students to name a familiar sport. Brainstorm a list of four safety rules that pertain to the sport and write these in the form of a numbered list on the board. Discuss each rule in turn, selecting volunteers to explain why each rule is important to the safety of the players.

Directed Instruction

1 Encourage students to review the definition for each list word written on the back of their flash cards as suggested for homework on Day 2.

2 Proceed to page 8. Allow students to use the flash cards to complete the cloze activity independently. Invite students to write a rough draft of the writing assignment on a separate piece of paper and to edit their work before copying it onto the bottom of page 8.

3 Homework suggestion: Distribute a copy of **BLM SP6-02A Lesson 2 Homework** to each student.

Day 5 Posttest

Objective

The students will correctly write dictated spelling words and sentences.

Introduction

Review by using flash cards noted in Day 1 and Day 2 Homework suggestion.

Directed Assessment

1 Dictate the list words by using the Pretest sentences or developing original ones. Reserve *ideally, medium, cooperate, cycling, designed,* and *aspiration* for the dictation sentences

2 Read each sentence. Repeat as needed.

- Ideally, BMX riders should remove the kickstand for safety.
- Riders with a medium level of skill should not ride with advanced riders.
- It is very important that all riders cooperate fully with the track rules.
- BMX cycling can be dangerous if the rules are not followed.
- BMX bikes are designed to take jumps and make sharp turns.
- Your attitude will help you achieve your aspiration to become a top rider.

3 If assigned, dictate Extra Challenge Words.

4 Score the test, counting each misspelled word as an error. Correct the dictation sentences by grading only the spelling words or grading the complete sentences.

Student Spelling Support

Cont. from page 8

to syllabicate each Pattern Word by writing each syllable in its own column. The Spelling Dictionary shows the syllabication of each entry word, and it may be used if the students are unfamiliar with syllabication. Syllabication is a valuable tool for students to learn and retain the spelling of each word.

u	ni	fy	
vi	sor		
ba	sis		
i	de	al	ly

folds

7. To **cooperate** is to demonstrate love and respect for others. Invite students to read 1 Corinthians 13 and think about how love informs their role as a respectful, cooperative racer. Challenge students to write rules of cooperation and courtesy required for bicycle **motocross**.

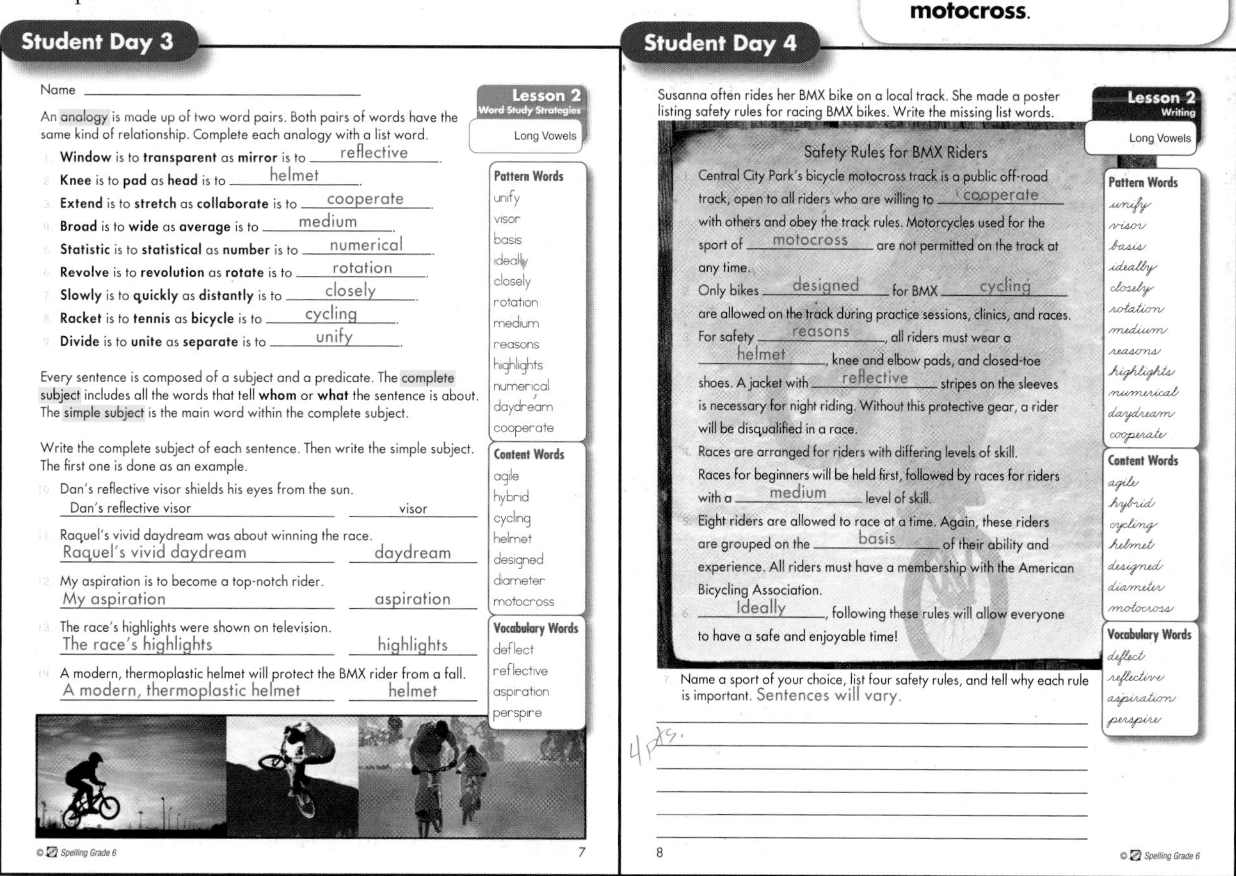

Student Day 3

Name

Lesson 2 Word Study Strategies — Long Vowels

An analogy is made up of two word pairs. Both pairs of words have the same kind of relationship. Complete each analogy with a list word.

1. **Window** is to **transparent** as **mirror** is to reflective.
2. **Knee** is to **pad** as **head** is to helmet.
3. **Extend** is to **stretch** as **collaborate** is to cooperate.
4. **Broad** is to **wide** as **average** is to medium.
5. **Statistic** is to **statistical** as **number** is to numerical.
6. **Revolve** is to **revolution** as **rotate** is to rotation.
7. **Slowly** is to **quickly** as **distantly** is to closely.
8. **Racket** is to **tennis** as **bicycle** is to cycling.
9. **Divide** is to **unite** as **separate** is to unify.

Every sentence is composed of a subject and a predicate. The complete subject includes all the words that tell **whom** or **what** the sentence is about. The simple subject is the main word within the complete subject.

Write the complete subject of each sentence. Then write the simple subject. The first one is done as an example.

10. Dan's reflective visor shields his eyes from the sun. Dan's reflective visor — visor
11. Raquel's vivid daydream was about winning the race. Raquel's vivid daydream — daydream
12. My aspiration is to become a top-notch rider. My aspiration — aspiration
13. The race's highlights were shown on television. The race's highlights — highlights
14. A modern, thermoplastic helmet will protect the BMX rider from a fall. A modern, thermoplastic helmet — helmet

Pattern Words: unify, visor, basis, ideally, closely, rotation, medium, reasons, highlights, numerical, daydream, cooperate

Content Words: agile, hybrid, cycling, helmet, designed, diameter, motocross

Vocabulary Words: deflect, reflective, aspiration, perspire

© Spelling Grade 6 — 7

Student Day 4

Lesson 2 Writing — Long Vowels

Susanna often rides her BMX bike on a local track. She made a poster listing safety rules for racing BMX bikes. Write the missing list words.

Safety Rules for BMX Riders

1. Central City Park's bicycle motocross track is a public off-road track, open to all riders who are willing to cooperate with others and obey the track rules. Motorcycles used for the sport of motocross are not permitted on the track at any time.
2. Only bikes designed for BMX cycling are allowed on the track during practice sessions, clinics, and races.
3. For safety reasons, all riders must wear a helmet, knee and elbow pads, and closed-toe shoes. A jacket with reflective stripes on the sleeves is necessary for night riding. Without this protective gear, a rider will be disqualified in a race.
4. Races are arranged for riders with differing levels of skill. Races for beginners will be held first, followed by races for riders with a medium level of skill.
5. Eight riders are allowed to race at a time. Again, these riders are grouped on the basis of their ability and experience. All riders must have a membership with the American Bicycling Association.
6. Ideally, following these rules will allow everyone to have a safe and enjoyable time!

7. Name a sport of your choice, list four safety rules, and tell why each rule is important. Sentences will vary.

4 pts.

Pattern Words: unify, visor, basis, ideally, closely, rotation, medium, reasons, highlights, numerical, daydream, cooperate

Content Words: agile, hybrid, cycling, helmet, designed, diameter, motocross

Vocabulary Words: deflect, reflective, aspiration, perspire

8 — © Spelling Grade 6

Lesson 3

Words with ei and ie

Student Pages

Pages 9–12

Lesson Materials

BLM SP6-01B
Card stock
Index cards
Newspaper
BLM SP6-03A

Sports

The theme of this lesson is skateboarding and in-line skating. Skateboarding emerged as an offshoot of surfing in the 1950s and was originally known as sidewalk surfing. The first skateboards were made either from scooters with their handlebars removed or roller skates nailed to a piece of wood. In-line skating originated in the 1700s in the Netherlands. However, it never gained popularity and succumbed to the design of the traditional roller skates. In the 1980s, in-line skating emerged once again and has remained a popular sport.

Day 1 Pretest

Objective

The students will accurately spell and write **words with ei and ie**, content, vocabulary, and challenge words.

Introduction

The Pretest is an ungraded assessment to assist students in studying the Pattern, Content, Vocabulary, and Challenge Words. To meet your students' needs, select Challenge Words from a cross-curricular subject or words misspelled on previous assignments. The word *deceivable* has **ei** and is suggested for number 24. Explain that they are to attempt to write all the spelling words.

Directed Instruction

1 Use the sentences that follow or develop original ones.

2 Say each word, use it in a sentence, and then repeat the word.

Pattern Words

1. Bragging about one's own abilities shows conceit.
2. The young lieutenant enjoys in-line skating during his free time.
3. A foreigner was a spectator at an international skating competition.
4. Kyle took the receipt from the clerk when he paid for the skateboard.
5. At his leisure, Grandpa watches professional skaters on television.
6. The team is working diligently to seize the championship this year.
7. The team experienced grief when it was disqualified last year.
8. Many skateboards have weird designs on their decks.
9. Joe was in disbelief when he qualified for the competition.
10. Have you received Jesus Christ as your Savior?
11. Believers in Christ have the promise of eternal salvation.
12. Our God is loving, just, and sovereign.

Content Words

13. The axles help hold the wheels on skateboards and in-line skates.
14. Competitive athletes enjoy the thrill of a competition.
15. It is difficult for wheels to have traction on wet surfaces.
16. Experienced skaters have flexibility to perform stunts.
17. Skateboard decks made of wood are preferred over composite ones.
18. In-line skaters and skateboarders develop their own technique.
19. Can you perform any maneuvers on in-line skates?

Vocabulary Words

20. Hank began to inquire about the new skate park hours.
21. Ethan's inquiry helped him plan his weekend schedule.
22. Cole rejoined his friends after attending his sister's soccer game.
23. The soccer field and the skate park are adjoining.

Challenge Words

24. ______________________ **(Insert your choice.)**
25. ______________________ **(Insert your choice.)**

3 Allow students to self-correct their Pretest. Write each word on the board. Point out the *ei* and *ie* spellings in each Pattern Word. Note the roots *join* and *quir* in the Vocabulary Words. The silent *e* in the word *inquire* is not included in the original root spelling *quir.*

4 As a class, read, spell, and read each word. Direct students to highlight misspelled words and rewrite them correctly.

5 Proof each student's Pretest. This becomes an individualized study sheet that can be used at school or at home.

6 Homework suggestion: Duplicate **BLM SP6-01B Flash Cards Template** on CARD STOCK for students to write the list words, using the flash cards as a study aid. Another option is to use INDEX CARDS.

Day 2 Word Analysis and Vocabulary

Objective

The students will accurately sort and write **words with ei and ie**, write content words to complete sentences, and use a table to correctly write vocabulary words. They will select list words to match definitions.

Introduction

Invite students to turn to page 9 for the list words. Have volunteers state the Pattern Words that follow the given generalizations. Write the
board:

lieutenant

Would I lie to u about the ten ant?

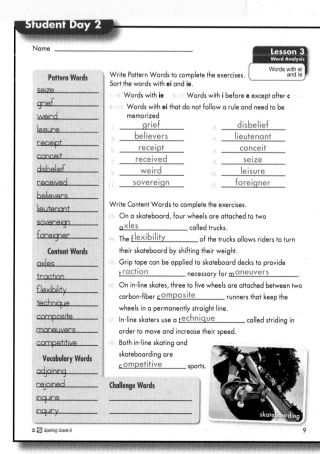

g *i* (**grief, disbelief, believers**)
u to make the /o͞o/ sound.

conceit, received)
e and have to be memorized.
ier) In these words, the *ei*
ure) In these words, the *ei* is

to assist them in learning to
out ten ants." Show the students
u and follows the letters *lie*
ining part of the word (tenants).
e the saying ends in *ants*.
s relate to the theme of

Differentiated Instruction

Differentiating spelling instruction is an option to consider.

- For students who spelled all the words correctly on the Pretest, select and assign Extra Challenge Words from the following list: analysis, advection, figurative, compensation, calisthenics, allegro.
- For students who spelled less than half correctly, assign the following Pattern, Content, and Vocabulary Words: weird, receipt, disbelief, received, lieutenant, foreigner, axles, traction, technique, competitive, rejoined, inquire. On the Posttest, evaluate these students on the twelve words assigned; however, encourage them to attempt to spell all the list words to the best of their ability. They are also responsible for writing the dictated sentences.

63 pts.

Student Day 2

Name ______________________

Lesson 3
Word Analysis
Words with ei and ie

Pattern Words
seize
grief
weird
leisure
receipt
conceit
disbelief
received
believers
lieutenant
sovereign
foreigner

Content Words
axles
traction
flexibility
technique
composite
maneuvers
competitive

Vocabulary Words
adjoining
rejoined
inquire
inquiry

Challenge Words

Write Pattern Words to complete the exercises. Sort the words with **ei** and **ie**.

1.–4. Words with **ie** 5.–7. Words with **i** before **e** except after **c**
8.–12. Words with **ei** that do not follow a rule and need to be memorized

1. grief 2. disbelief
3. believers 4. lieutenant
5. receipt 6. conceit
7. received 8. seize
9. weird 10. leisure
11. sovereign 12. foreigner

Write Content Words to complete the exercises.

13. On a skateboard, four wheels are attached to two axles called trucks.
14. The flexibility of the trucks allows riders to turn their skateboard by shifting their weight.
15. Grip tape can be applied to skateboard decks to provide traction necessary for maneuvers.
16. On in-line skates, three to five wheels are attached between two carbon-fiber composite runners that keep the wheels in a permanently straight line.
17. In-line skaters use a technique called striding in order to move and increase their speed.
18. Both in-line skating and skateboarding are competitive sports.

skateboarding

© Spelling Grade 6 9

Student Day 2

Lesson 3
Vocabulary
Words with ei and ie

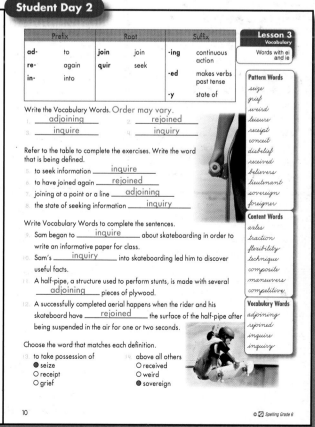

Prefix		Root		Suffix	
ad-	to	**join**	join	**-ing**	continuous action
re-	again	**quir**	seek	**-ed**	makes verbs past tense
in-	into			**-y**	state of

Write the Vocabulary Words. Order may vary.

1. adjoining 2. rejoined
3. inquire 4. inquiry

Refer to the table to complete the exercises. Write the word that is being defined.

5. to seek information inquire
6. to have joined again rejoined
7. joining at a point or a line adjoining
8. the state of seeking information inquiry

Write Vocabulary Words to complete the sentences.

9. Sam began to inquire about skateboarding in order to write an informative paper for class.
10. Sam's inquiry into skateboarding led him to discover useful facts.
11. A half-pipe, a structure used to perform stunts, is made with several adjoining pieces of plywood.
12. A successfully completed aerial happens when the rider and his skateboard have rejoined the surface of the half-pipe after being suspended in the air for one or two seconds.

Choose the word that matches each definition.

13. to take possession of
● seize
○ receipt
○ grief

14. above all others
○ received
○ weird
● sovereign

Pattern Words
seize
grief
weird
leisure
receipt
conceit
disbelief
received
believers
lieutenant
sovereign
foreigner

Content Words
axles
traction
flexibility
technique
composite
maneuvers
competitive

Vocabulary Words
adjoining
rejoined
inquire
inquiry

10 © Spelling Grade 6

Student Spelling Support Materials

BLM SP6-01A

Student Spelling Support

1. Use **BLM SP6-01A A Spelling Study Strategy** in instructional groups to provide assistance with some or all of the words.
2. Invite students to write the Challenge Words, numbers 24 and 25, in the Word Bank, in the back of their textbook.
3. Challenge students to write informational paragraphs describing the various parts of a skateboard or in-line skates. Have students include why each part is essential in the overall function of the skateboard or in-line skates.
4. Write this week's words, categorize the Pattern, Content, and Vocabulary Words, and attach them to the Word Wall.
5. Read Philippians 2:3: "Let nothing be done through selfish ambition or **conceit**, but in lowliness of mind let each esteem others better than himself." Discuss how students can esteem one another when playing a sport—as a casual activity on the playground or as part of an organized team. Help students understand how **conceit** can affect the way others are treated. God has given each person talents and abilities, and people should not look down on others who do not excel in the same activities, nor should they be jealous of those who are more skillful.

Cont. on page 13

skateboarding and in-line skating. Take a quick survey of the class by having students raise their hand if they enjoy either of these sports activities. Have students involved in these two sports share about their favorite maneuvers.

3 Proceed to page 9. Say, spell, and say each Pattern, Content, and Vocabulary Word. Provide this week's Challenge Words and have students write them in the spaces provided. Instruct students to look up the Content Words in the Spelling Dictionary. Select volunteers to read the definition of each word. Students complete the page.

4 Proceed to page 10. Encourage students to use the table as an aid in building each Vocabulary Word. For example, the prefix *ad-* goes with the root *join* and the suffix *-ing* to get the word *adjoining*. Allow students to complete the page independently.

5 Homework suggestion: Students use their Spelling Dictionary to write the definition of each word on the back of the corresponding flash card that was suggested for homework on Day 1.

Day 3 Word Study Strategies

Objective

The students will write list words that are synonyms for given words. They will identify and write verbs, helping verbs, and verb phrases in sentences.

Introduction

Remind students that a *synonym* is a word that means the same or almost the same as another word. Select a volunteer to state a synonym for *foreigner*. (**Possible answers: stranger, outsider, alien**) As a challenge, select volunteers to name several synonyms and write them on the board.

Directed Instruction

1 Write the following bulleted sentences on the board:

- The lieutenant received his new orders. (**received**)

Teach that the main word in a predicate is the *verb*. The verb may be an action verb. Select a student to identify the action verb in the sentence above.

- The lieutenant has received his new orders. (**has received**)

Continue by stating that the predicate may also contain a helping verb. Select a volunteer to identify the helping verb and the main verb in the sample sentence. Teach that a verb phrase contains both a helping verb (**has**) and an action verb (**received**). Write the verb phrase *has received* on the board.

2 Proceed to page 11. Allow students to read the directions and complete the page independently. Assist as needed.

Day 4 Writing

Objective

The students will complete a graphic organizer using information from a news article. They will find, underline, and write list words used in the article.

Introduction

Read a short news article from a NEWSPAPER. Select volunteers to state the who, what, where, and when facts contained in the article.

Directed Instruction

1 Explain that today's assignment has to do with a news article about a skate park. The students will find the four w's—who, what, where, and when, then write the facts in the appropriate areas on the graphic organizer. A *graphic organizer* is a drawing that shows how words or ideas fit together. Students will also find, underline, and write list words used in the story.

2 Proceed to page 12. Allow students to work independently. When complete, select volunteers to read the who, what, where, and when facts found in the article.

3 Homework suggestion: Distribute a copy of **BLM SP6-03A Lesson 3 Homework** to each student.

Day 5 Posttest

Objective

The students will correctly write dictated spelling words and sentences.

Introduction

Review by using flash cards noted in Day 1 and Day 2 Homework suggestion.

Directed Assessment

1 Dictate the list words by using the Pretest sentences or developing original ones. Reserve *weird, disbelief, received, axles, traction,* and *rejoined* for the dictation sentences.

2 Read each sentence. Repeat as needed.

- Charlie performed a weird stunt on his skateboard.
- At first the crowd stared in disbelief.
- Later Charlie received applause.
- Charlie ran both axles of his skateboard along a bar.
- The wheels provided the traction for the trick.
- When he rejoined his class, they congratulated him.

3 If assigned, dictate Extra Challenge Words.

4 Score the test, counting each misspelled word as an error. Correct the dictation sentences by grading only the spelling words or grading the complete sentences.

Student Spelling Support

Cont. from page 12

6. **Conceit** often leads individuals into sin. Invite students to read the book of *Esther* and write a news article with the four w's—who, what, where, and when, describing how Haman's **conceit** led to his downfall. Discuss how, had he chosen to be a team player, his life would have been blessed.
7. Discuss that the opposite of **conceit** is humility. I Peter 5:5 reads, "Likewise you younger people, submit yourselves to your elders. Yes, all of you be submissive to one another, and be clothed with humility, for 'God resists the proud, but gives grace to the humble.'"

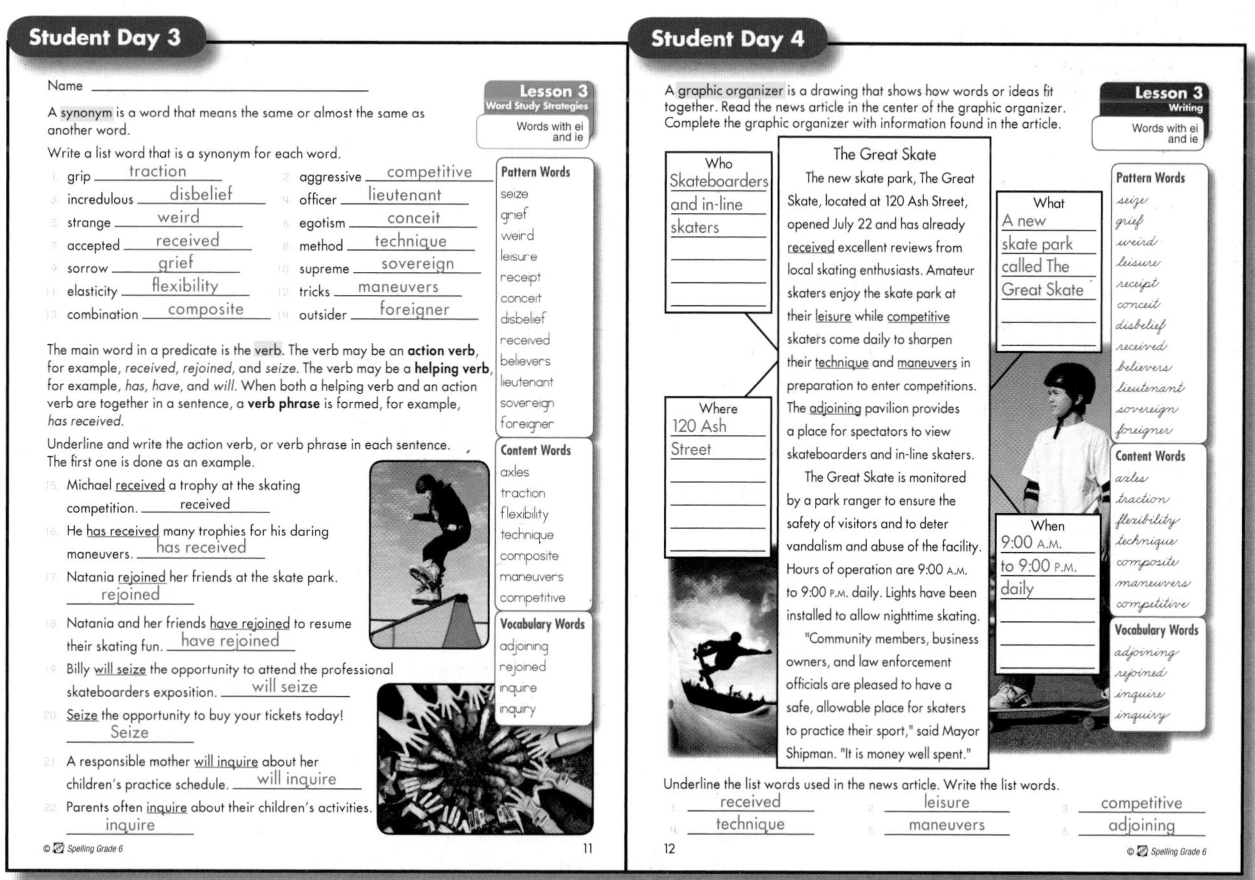

Student Day 3

Name ____________

Lesson 3 — Word Study Strategies — Words with ei and ie

A synonym is a word that means the same or almost the same as another word.

Write a list word that is a synonym for each word.

1. grip traction
2. aggressive competitive
3. incredulous disbelief
4. officer lieutenant
5. strange weird
6. egotism conceit
7. accepted received
8. method technique
9. sorrow grief
10. supreme sovereign
11. elasticity flexibility
12. tricks maneuvers
13. combination composite
14. outsider foreigner

The main word in a predicate is the verb. The verb may be an **action verb**, for example, *received, rejoined,* and *seize*. The verb may be a **helping verb**, for example, *has, have,* and *will*. When both a helping verb and an action verb are together in a sentence, a **verb phrase** is formed, for example, *has received*.

Underline and write the action verb, or verb phrase in each sentence. The first one is done as an example.

15. Michael received a trophy at the skating competition. received
16. He has received many trophies for his daring maneuvers. has received
17. Natania rejoined her friends at the skate park. rejoined
18. Natania and her friends have rejoined to resume their skating fun. have rejoined
19. Billy will seize the opportunity to attend the professional skateboarders exposition. will seize
20. Seize the opportunity to buy your tickets today! Seize
21. A responsible mother will inquire about her children's practice schedule. will inquire
22. Parents often inquire about their children's activities. inquire

Pattern Words: seize, grief, weird, leisure, receipt, conceit, disbelief, received, believers, lieutenant, sovereign, foreigner

Content Words: axles, traction, flexibility, technique, composite, maneuvers, competitive

Vocabulary Words: adjoining, rejoined, inquire, inquiry

© Spelling Grade 6 — 11

Student Day 4

Lesson 3 — Writing — Words with ei and ie

A graphic organizer is a drawing that shows how words or ideas fit together. Read the news article in the center of the graphic organizer. Complete the graphic organizer with information found in the article.

Who: Skateboarders and in-line skaters

What: A new skate park called The Great Skate

Where: 120 Ash Street

When: 9:00 A.M. to 9:00 P.M. daily

The Great Skate

The new skate park, The Great Skate, located at 120 Ash Street, opened July 22 and has already received excellent reviews from local skating enthusiasts. Amateur skaters enjoy the skate park at their leisure while competitive skaters come daily to sharpen their technique and maneuvers in preparation to enter competitions. The adjoining pavilion provides a place for spectators to view skateboarders and in-line skaters.

The Great Skate is monitored by a park ranger to ensure the safety of visitors and to deter vandalism and abuse of the facility. Hours of operation are 9:00 A.M. to 9:00 P.M. daily. Lights have been installed to allow nighttime skating.

"Community members, business owners, and law enforcement officials are pleased to have a safe, allowable place for skaters to practice their sport," said Mayor Shipman. "It is money well spent."

Underline the list words used in the news article. Write the list words.

1. received
2. leisure
3. competitive
4. technique
5. maneuvers
6. adjoining

Pattern Words: seize, grief, weird, leisure, receipt, conceit, disbelief, received, believers, lieutenant, sovereign, foreigner

Content Words: axles, traction, flexibility, technique, composite, maneuvers, competitive

Vocabulary Words: adjoining, rejoined, inquire, inquiry

12 — © Spelling Grade 6

Lesson 4

Words with ou

Student Pages

Pages 13–16

Lesson Materials

BLM SP6-01B
Card stock
Index cards
BLM SP6-04A

Sports

The theme of this lesson is snowboarding and skiing. Snowboarding originated in the late 1960s in the United States and has quickly gained popularity. The development of snowboarding is owed much to the sports of skateboarding and surfing. Skiing became popular, worldwide, in the twentieth century. The two basic types of recreational winter skiing are Alpine and Nordic. A fundamental, technical difference between snowboarders and skiers is that skiers shift their weight from ski to ski, while snowboarders shift their weight from heels to toes.

Day 1 Pretest

Objective

The students will accurately spell and write **words with ou**, content, vocabulary, and challenge words.

Introduction

The Pretest is an ungraded assessment to assist students in studying the Pattern, Content, Vocabulary, and Challenge Words. To meet your students' needs, select Challenge Words from a cross-curricular subject or words misspelled on previous assignments. The word *countenance* has **ou** and is suggested for number 24. Explain that they are to attempt to write all the spelling words.

Directed Instruction

1 Use the sentences that follow or develop original ones.

2 Say each word, use it in a sentence, and then repeat the word.

Pattern Words

1. Al heard the announcements about the Nordic skiing event.
2. The ski jumper thoughtlessly broke form and landed awkwardly.
3. Selena will couple her boots to her skis before riding the ski lift.
4. Nick eagerly sought the results of the men's big air competition.
5. Falling snow was a welcome sight after the period of drought.
6. Dimitri had a positive attitude throughout the competition.
7. A snowboarder should be ready to encounter numerous hazards.
8. Justin thoroughly practiced before the finals competition.
9. After the competition, contestants were served poultry for dinner.
10. Though it was snowing, the Alpine events continued.
11. Martin carved a route in the fresh snow as he descended the mountain.
12. With resounding joy, Eloise sang a worship song of praise.

Content Words

13. Regan submitted her snowboard designs into the competition.
14. Britt competed in the freestyle, half-pipe event.
15. Erich completed an extraordinary feat when he ski jumped 400 feet!
16. The popularity of winter sports has risen in the last few years.
17. Mel will facilitate the freestyle skiing competition as a judge.
18. Hannah entered the competition for the women's giant slalom.
19. Felix secured the fasteners on his boot before riding the half-pipe.

Vocabulary Words

20. There was an eclectic selection of ski equipment at the store.
21. A detailed inspection of ski equipment should be performed regularly.
22. Professional athletes are respected when they make wise choices.
23. There was a large selection of ski apparel to purchase.

Challenge Words

24. ______________________ **(Insert your choice.)**
25. ______________________ **(Insert your choice.)**

3 Allow students to self-correct their Pretest. Write each word on the board. Point out the *ou* or *ough* spelling pattern in each Pattern Word. The Pattern Word *throughout* contains both *ou* and *ough*. Note the roots *lect* and *spect* in the Vocabulary Words.

4 As a class, read, spell, and read each word. Direct students to highlight misspelled words and rewrite them correctly.

5 Proof each student's Pretest. This becomes an individualized study sheet that can be used at school or at home.

6 Homework suggestion: Duplicate **BLM SP6-01B Flash Cards Template** on CARD STOCK for students to write the list words, using the flash cards as a study aid. Another option is to use INDEX CARDS.

Day 2 Word Analysis and Vocabulary

Objective

The students will sort and write **words with ou** and complete sentences with content words. They will use a table to write vocabulary words, match given definitions in context, and choose list words that match definitions.

Introduction

Remind students that the target of this lesson's Pattern Words is **words with ou**, and the spelling patterns are *ou* and *ough*. Dictate each Pattern Word and instruct students to listen carefully and to visualize the word. Students raise the correct number of fingers—two for *ou* and four for *ough*—that represents the correct spelling pattern in each word. Remind students that *throughout* contains both *ou* and *ough*.

Directed Instruction

1 Invite students to refer to the list words, found on page 13, for this activity. Challenge students to quickly locate the definition of each Content Word from this lesson in their Spelling Dictionary. Students read the definitions aloud.

2 Proceed to page 13. Say, spell, and say each Pattern, Content, and Vocabulary Word. Provide this week's Challenge Words and have students write them in the spaces provided before completing the page.

3 Proceed to page 14. Encourage students to use the table as an aid in building each Vocabulary Word. For example, the prefix *ec-* goes with

Differentiated Instruction

Differentiating spelling instruction is an option to consider.

- For students who spelled all the words correctly on the Pretest, select and assign Extra Challenge Words from the following list: approximations, amplitude, generalization, constitutionalism, cardiorespiratory, articulation.
- For students who spelled less than half correctly, assign the following Pattern, Content, and Vocabulary Words: couple, sought, poultry, encounter, thoroughly, throughout, designs, freestyle, popularity, extraordinary, selection, respected. On the Posttest, evaluate these students on the twelve words assigned; however, encourage them to attempt to spell all the list words to the best of their ability. They are also responsible for writing the dictated sentences.

Student Day 2

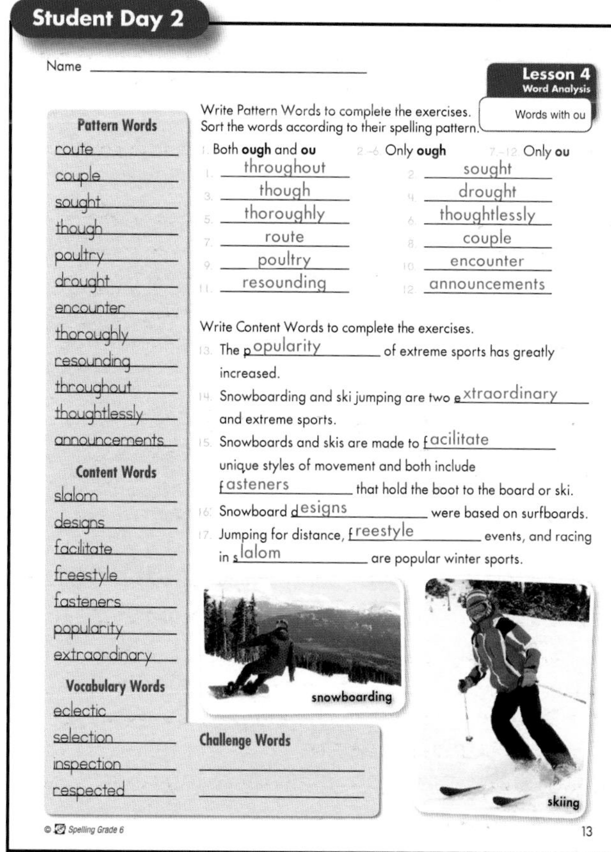

Name
Lesson 4
Word Analysis
Words with ou
Pattern Words
route
couple
sought
though
poultry
drought
encounter
thoroughly
resounding
throughout
thoughtlessly
announcements
Content Words
slalom
designs
facilitate
freestyle
fasteners
popularity
extraordinary
Vocabulary Words
eclectic
selection
inspection
respected
Write Pattern Words to complete the exercises. Sort the words according to their spelling pattern.
1 Both ough and ou
1. throughout
3. though
5. thoroughly
7. route
9. poultry
11. resounding
2–6 Only ough
2. sought
4. drought
6. thoughtlessly
7–12 Only ou
8. couple
10. encounter
12. announcements
Write Content Words to complete the exercises.
13. The popularity of extreme sports has greatly increased.
14. Snowboarding and ski jumping are two extraordinary and extreme sports.
15. Snowboards and skis are made to facilitate unique styles of movement and both include fasteners that hold the boot to the board or ski.
16. Snowboard designs were based on surfboards.
17. Jumping for distance, freestyle events, and racing in slalom are popular winter sports.
snowboarding
skiing
Challenge Words
© Spelling Grade 6
13

Student Day 2

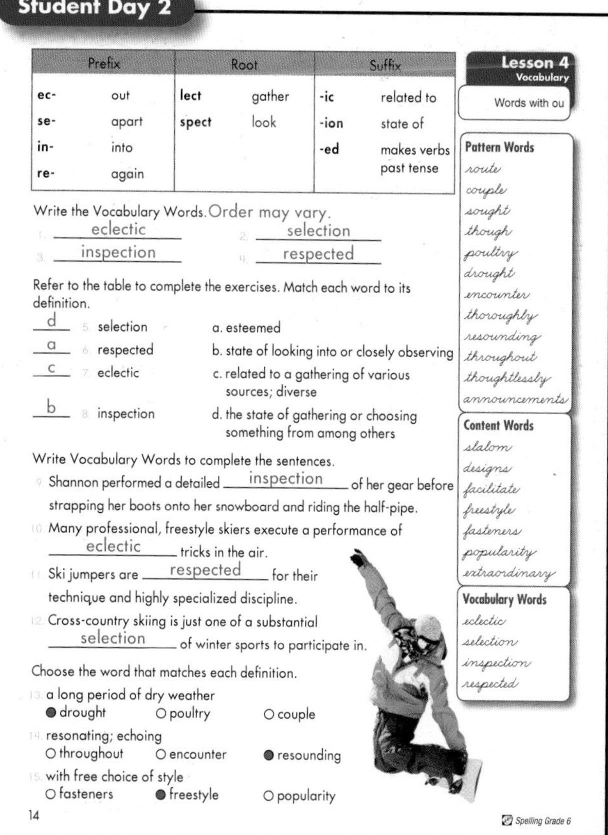

Lesson 4
Vocabulary
Words with ou
Prefix
ec- out
se- apart
in- into
re- again
Root
lect gather
spect look
Suffix
-ic related to
-ion state of
-ed makes verbs past tense
Write the Vocabulary Words. Order may vary.
1. eclectic
2. selection
3. inspection
4. respected
Refer to the table to complete the exercises. Match each word to its definition.
d 5. selection
a 6. respected
c 7. eclectic
b 8. inspection
a. esteemed
b. state of looking into or closely observing
c. related to a gathering of various sources; diverse
d. the state of gathering or choosing something from among others
Write Vocabulary Words to complete the sentences.
9. Shannon performed a detailed inspection of her gear before strapping her boots onto her snowboard and riding the half-pipe.
10. Many professional, freestyle skiers execute a performance of eclectic tricks in the air.
11. Ski jumpers are respected for their technique and highly specialized discipline.
12. Cross-country skiing is just one of a substantial selection of winter sports to participate in.
Choose the word that matches each definition.
13. a long period of dry weather
drought poultry couple
14. resonating; echoing
throughout encounter resounding
15. with free choice of style
fasteners freestyle popularity
Pattern Words
route
couple
sought
though
poultry
drought
encounter
thoroughly
resounding
throughout
thoughtlessly
announcements
Content Words
slalom
designs
facilitate
freestyle
fasteners
popularity
extraordinary
Vocabulary Words
eclectic
selection
inspection
respected
14
Spelling Grade 6

Student Spelling Support Materials

BLM SP6-01A

Student Spelling Support

1. Use **BLM SP6-01A A Spelling Study Strategy** in instructional groups to provide assistance with some or all of the words.
2. Invite students to write the Challenge Words, numbers 24 and 25, in the Word Bank, in the back of their textbook.
3. Challenge students to research and write a brief biography of a professional snowboarder or skier. Compile information in the progressive, sport journal that was started in Lesson 1.
4. Write this week's words, categorize the Pattern, Content, and Vocabulary Words, and attach them to the Word Wall.
5. Read Philippians 4:13: "I can do all things through Christ who strengthens me." Encourage students to share about an experience that the Lord helped them get through. Lead a discussion by asking the following questions: How did God help you? What were the circumstances? What did you learn from this experience? How did your faith strengthen you in this situation?

the root *lect* and the suffix *-ic* to build the word *eclectic.* Allow students to complete the page independently. When complete, select a volunteer to read exercises 9–12 aloud.

4 Homework suggestion: Students use their Spelling Dictionary to write the definition of each word on the back of the corresponding flash card that was suggested for homework on Day 1.

Day 3 Word Study Strategies

Objective

The students will alphabetize list words. They will identify and write the complete and simple predicate of given sentences.

Introduction

Dictate the following words aloud: couple, sought, slalom, facilitate, extraordinary, eclectic, selection, respected. Inform students that you will repeat the series of words, and they are to use their listening skills to alphabetize the words. Students raise their hand when they hear the first word in the dictated series. When a word is correctly identified, write the word on the board. Continue dictating the remaining words until the written alphabetized list is complete. (**couple, eclectic, extraordinary, facilitate, respected, selection, slalom, sought**)

Directed Instruction

1 Remind students that every sentence is composed of a subject and a predicate. Write the following definitions on the board: A *complete predicate* includes all the words that tell **what** the subject **does** or **is**. The *simple predicate* is the main verb or verb phrase within the complete predicate.

2 Write the following sentences on the board:

- Val sought a weather report on a news channel. (**sought—verb**)
- Val will encounter bad weather in the mountains. (**will encounter—verb phrase**)

Have students read each sentence and underline the complete predicate in each sentence. Students then write the simple predicate.

3 Proceed to page 15. Students complete the page independently.

Day 4 Writing

Objective

The students will complete sentences in an informative biographical sketch with list words that match pronunciations.

Introduction

Review the following definition: A *biography* is a written account of someone's life. Inform students that most biographies start off as written work but can be adapted into movies, plays, or television shows. Select a student to narrate a brief biography about an athlete that he or she respects.

Directed Instruction

1 Inform students that they will be reading a biography about a professional, Christian snowboarder named Dave Downing in today's lesson. Dave is a strong believer in Christ and leads a lifestyle that is to be admired. He has used his position in the sports world to be a godly influence on the next generation of snowboarders. God has called each of us to follow His example.

2 Write the following pronunciations on the board:

- /e 'klek tik/ (**eclectic**)
- /ə 'nount smənts/ (**announcements**)
- /ik 'strôr də nâr ē/ (**extraordinary**)

Invite students to refer to the list words, found on page 16, for this activity. Select volunteers to choose a list word that fits each pronunciation and write each word.

3 Proceed to page 16 and select a volunteer to read the sentences at the top of the page. Instruct students to … to complete the activity independent… biography. Select a volunteer to read … discuss how the Lord strengthens us…

4 Homework suggestion: Distribute a … **Homework** to each student.

The coach had an amplitude of money.

Her careful articulation of words made it easy to understand.

Day 5 Posttest

Objective

The students will correctly write dictat…

Introduction

Review by using flash cards noted in Da…

Directed Assessment

1 Dictate the list words by using the F… original ones. Reserve *selection, de…* and *thoroughly* for the dictation sen…

2 Read each sentence. Repeat as needed.

- Leah saw a wide selection of snowboards at the store.
- She looked at many different designs before purchasing one.
- Leah sought a friend to go snowboarding with.
- She decided to practice her freestyle tricks.
- The weather was great throughout the day.
- Leah and her friend thoroughly enjoyed themselves.

3 If assigned, dictate Extra Challenge Words.

4 Score the test, counting each misspelled word as an error. Correct the dictation sentences by grading only the spelling words or grading the complete sentences.

Notes

Student Day 3

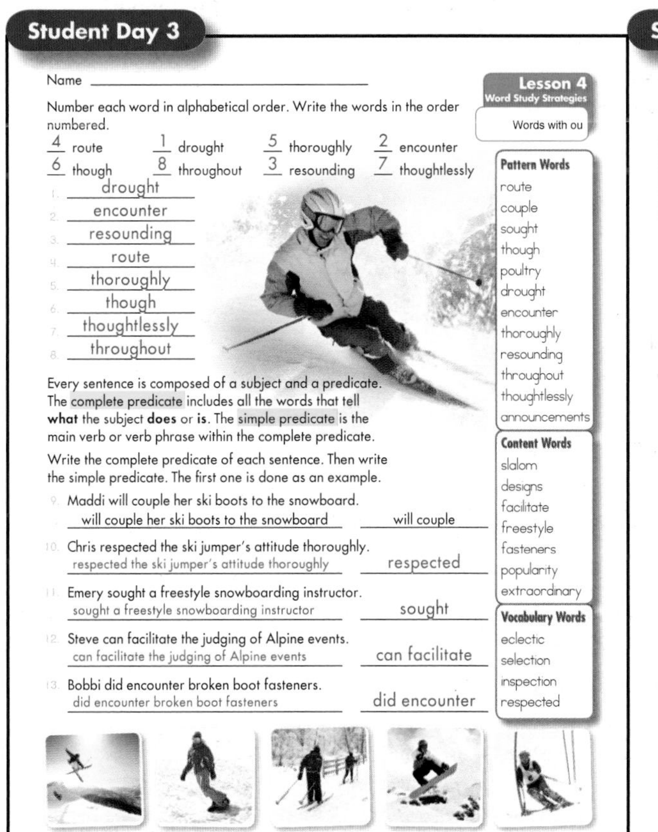
Name ______

Lesson 4 Word Study Strategies — Words with ou

Number each word in alphabetical order. Write the words in the order numbered.

4 route, 1 drought, 5 thoroughly, 2 encounter, 6 though, 8 throughout, 3 resounding, 7 thoughtlessly

1. drought
2. encounter
3. resounding
4. route
5. thoroughly
6. though
7. thoughtlessly
8. throughout

Every sentence is composed of a subject and a predicate. The complete predicate includes all the words that tell **what** the subject **does** or **is**. The simple predicate is the main verb or verb phrase within the complete predicate.

Write the complete predicate of each sentence. Then write the simple predicate. The first one is done as an example.

9. Maddi will couple her ski boots to the snowboard. — will couple her ski boots to the snowboard — will couple
10. Chris respected the ski jumper's attitude thoroughly. — respected the ski jumper's attitude thoroughly — respected
11. Emery sought a freestyle snowboarding instructor. — sought a freestyle snowboarding instructor — sought
12. Steve can facilitate the judging of Alpine events. — can facilitate the judging of Alpine events — can facilitate
13. Bobbi did encounter broken boot fasteners. — did encounter broken boot fasteners — did encounter

Pattern Words: route, couple, sought, though, poultry, drought, encounter, thoroughly, resounding, throughout, thoughtlessly, announcements

Content Words: slalom, designs, facilitate, freestyle, fasteners, popularity, extraordinary

Vocabulary Words: eclectic, selection, inspection, respected

© Spelling Grade 6 — 15

Student Day 4

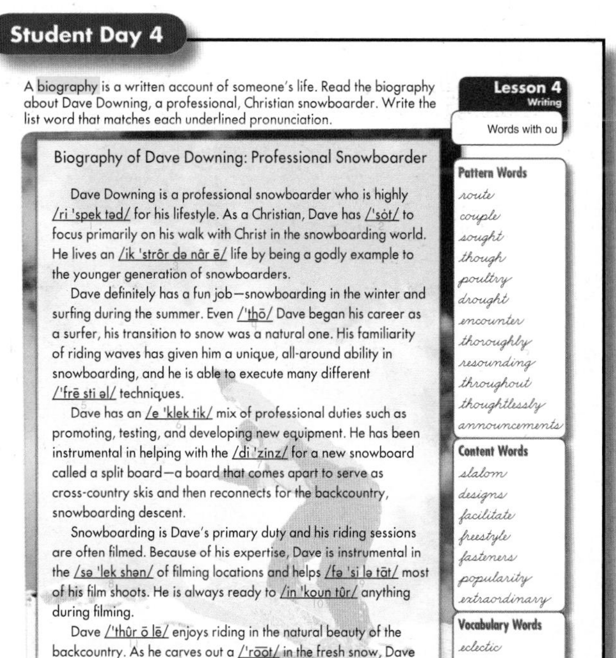
A biography is a written account of someone's life. Read the biography about Dave Downing, a professional, Christian snowboarder. Write the list word that matches each underlined pronunciation.

Lesson 4 Writing — Words with ou

Biography of Dave Downing: Professional Snowboarder

Dave Downing is a professional snowboarder who is highly /ri 'spek təd/ for his lifestyle. As a Christian, Dave has /'sȯt/ to focus primarily on his walk with Christ in the snowboarding world. He lives an /ik 'strôr də nâr ē/ life by being a godly example to the younger generation of snowboarders.

Dave definitely has a fun job—snowboarding in the winter and surfing during the summer. Even /'thō/ Dave began his career as a surfer, his transition to snow was a natural one. His familiarity of riding waves has given him a unique, all-around ability in snowboarding, and he is able to execute many different /'frē sti əl/ techniques.

Dave has an /e 'klek tik/ mix of professional duties such as promoting, testing, and developing new equipment. He has been instrumental in helping with the /di 'zinz/ for a new snowboard called a split board—a board that comes apart to serve as cross-country skis and then reconnects for the backcountry, snowboarding descent.

Snowboarding is Dave's primary duty and his riding sessions are often filmed. Because of his expertise, Dave is instrumental in the /sə 'lek shən/ of filming locations and helps /fə 'si lə tāt/ most of his film shoots. He is always ready to /in 'koun tər/ anything during filming.

Dave /'thûr ō lē/ enjoys riding in the natural beauty of the backcountry. As he carves out a /'rüt/ in the fresh snow, Dave marvels at God's creation and feels His presence. Dave believes that being a witness for God is what he is called to do, and he looks to the Lord for the strength to be an effective witness.

1. respected
2. sought
3. extraordinary
4. though
5. freestyle
6. eclectic
7. designs
8. selection
9. facilitate
10. encounter
11. thoroughly
12. route

I can do all things through Christ who strengthens me. Philippians 4:13

Pattern Words: route, couple, sought, though, poultry, drought, encounter, thoroughly, resounding, throughout, thoughtlessly, announcements

Content Words: slalom, designs, facilitate, freestyle, fasteners, popularity, extraordinary

Vocabulary Words: eclectic, selection, inspection, respected

16 — © Spelling Grade 6

Lesson 5

Vowel Combinations

Student Pages

Pages 17–20

Lesson Materials

BLM SP6-01B
Card stock
Index cards
T-3
BLM SP6-05A
BLM SP6-05B

Sports

The theme of this lesson is rock climbing. Rock climbing began as a form of training for mountain climbing but developed into its own sport. It requires as much mental strength as it does physical strength. A grading system is used to determine the level of difficulty for rock-climbing routes. Climbers who enjoy multiday ascents sleep in a portaledge, a tent anchored to the side of a rock wall.

Day 1 Pretest

Objective

The students will accurately spell and write words with **vowel combinations**, content, vocabulary, and challenge words.

Introduction

The Pretest is an ungraded assessment to assist students in studying the Pattern, Content, Vocabulary, and Challenge Words. To meet your students' needs, select Challenge Words from a cross-curricular subject or words misspelled on previous assignments. The word *nonpoisonous* has **oi** and is suggested for number 24. Explain that they are to attempt to write all the spelling words.

Directed Instruction

1 Use the sentences that follow or develop original ones.

2 Say each word, use it in a sentence, and then repeat the word.

Pattern Words

1. Climbers should always avoid wandering into unauthorized areas.
2. The decoy was used to help the climber to not be fearful.
3. Crash pads are used as a precaution to avoid injuries.
4. Permits to rock climb are renewable every year.
5. Sometimes rock climbers have awkward maneuvers.
6. The blind man's ascent up the granite rock was a newsworthy event.
7. Our wonderful world was beautifully designed by our loving God.
8. Our God is absolutely awesome!
9. The team was euphoric after reaching the summit of the rock.
10. The colorful flowers surrounded the neutral hue of the rocks.
11. Moisture on rocks can cause a climber to slip.
12. Our Lord is always ready to help us and is never exhausted.

Content Words

13. Yosemite National Park is known for its beautiful rock formations.
14. The climbers will be ascending the mountain for two days.
15. A portaledge is a tent that is anchored to the side of a rock.
16. Climbers often put their hands into fissures when climbing.
17. Thea began to slowly rappel to the ground.
18. Sloan rested on one of the outcroppings along the trail.
19. Lani and her family enjoy bouldering on weekends.

Vocabulary Words

20. Matthias wrote a story describing his rock-climbing adventure.
21. Drew was very careful and did not make an error.
22. The feeling of success in reaching the top was indescribable.
23. An errant climber greeted Ty when he reached the summit.

Challenge Words

24. ______________________ **(Insert your choice.)**
25. ______________________ **(Insert your choice.)**

3 Allow students to self-correct their Pretest. Write each word on the board. Point out the following vowel combinations in the Pattern Words: au, aw, eau, eu, ew, oi, oy. Note the roots *err* and *scrib* in the Vocabulary Words. Note that *indescribable* contains two prefixes, *in-* and *de-*.

4 As a class, read, spell, and read each word. Direct students to highlight misspelled words and rewrite them correctly.

5 Proof each student's Pretest. This becomes an individualized study sheet that can be used at school or at home.

6 Homework suggestion: Duplicate **BLM SP6-01B Flash Cards Template** on CARD STOCK for students to write the list words, using the flash cards as a study aid. Another option is to use INDEX CARDS.

Day 2 Word Analysis and Vocabulary

Objective

The students will sort and write pattern words by **vowel combinations**. They will write content words to complete sentences. They will use a table to write vocabulary words and choose the best meaning for given words.

Introduction

Write the following **vowel combinations** on the board: au, aw, eau, eu, ew, oi, oy. Pronounce the sound of a vowel pattern and have students refer to their flash cards to identify words containing the specified pattern. Instruct students to highlight or underline the vowel combination in each word on the flash cards. Brainstorm other words with the **vowel combinations** that are on the board.

Directed Instruction

1 Explain that this week's Content Words relate to the theme of rock climbing. Select a volunteer to read the Content Words found on page 17. Refer to the Spelling Dictionary to discuss the meaning of any unfamiliar words.

2 Proceed to page 17. Say, spell, and say each Pattern, Content, and Vocabulary Word. Provide this week's Challenge Words and have students write them in the spaces provided before completing the page.

3 Proceed to page 18. Encourage students to use the table as an aid in building each Vocabulary Word. For example, the root *err* goes with the suffix *-ant* to get the word *errant*. Allow students to complete the page independently.

Differentiated Instruction

Differentiating spelling instruction is an option to consider.

- For students who spelled all the words correctly on the Pretest, select and assign Extra Challenge Words from the following list: asymptote, anatomical, intonation, deregulation, cardiovascular, complementary.
- For students who spelled less than half correctly, assign the following Pattern, Content, and Vocabulary Words: euphoric, moisture, awesome, beautifully, exhausted, newsworthy, rappel, ascending, bouldering, formations, error, describing. On the Posttest, evaluate these students on the twelve words assigned; however, encourage them to attempt to spell all the list words to the best of their ability. They are also responsible for writing the dictated sentences.

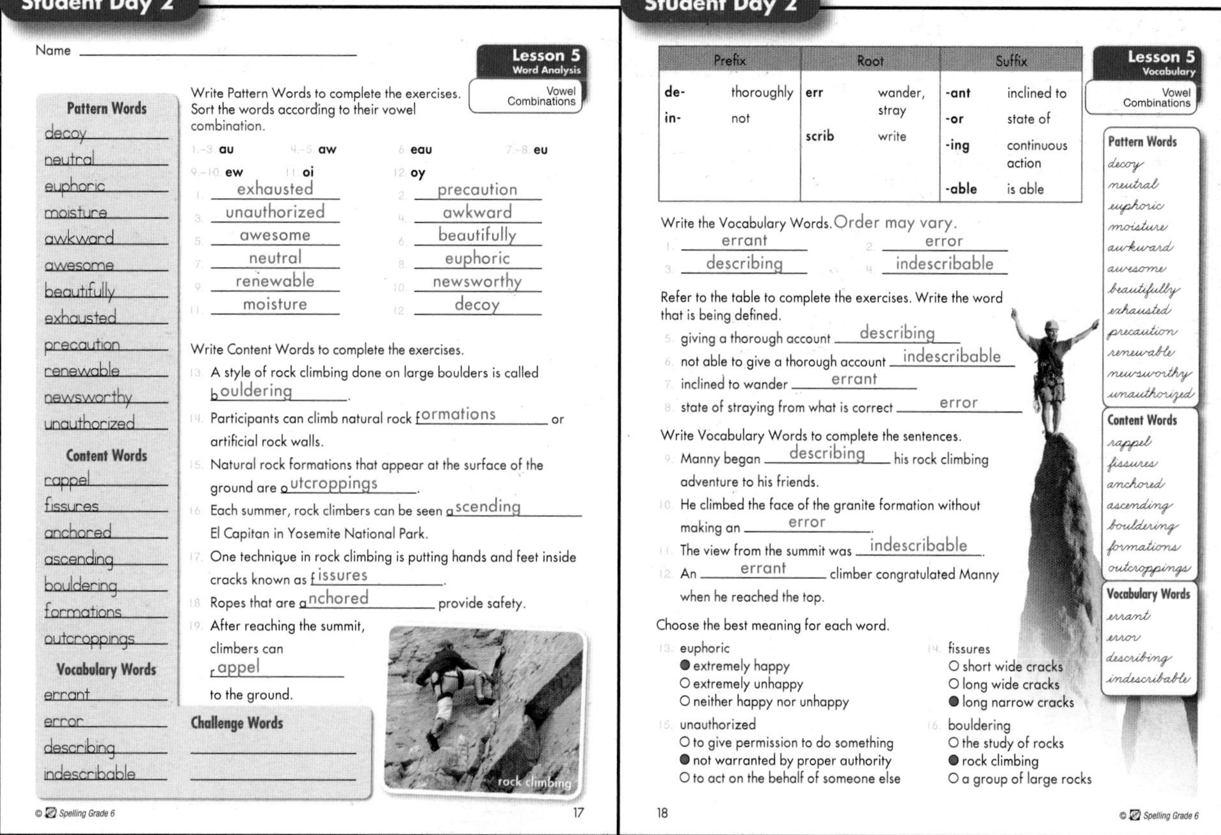

Student Day 2

Name

Lesson 5 Word Analysis — Vowel Combinations

Pattern Words: decoy, neutral, euphoric, moisture, awkward, awesome, beautifully, exhausted, precaution, renewable, newsworthy, unauthorized

Content Words: rappel, fissures, anchored, ascending, bouldering, formations, outcroppings

Vocabulary Words: errant, error, describing, indescribable

Challenge Words

Write Pattern Words to complete the exercises. Sort the words according to their vowel combination.

1–3 au 4–5 aw 6 eau 7–8 eu 9–10 ew 11 oi 12 oy

1. exhausted 2. precaution
3. unauthorized 4. awkward
5. awesome 6. beautifully
7. neutral 8. euphoric
9. renewable 10. newsworthy
11. moisture 12. decoy

Write Content Words to complete the exercises.

13. A style of rock climbing done on large boulders is called bouldering.
14. Participants can climb natural rock formations or artificial rock walls.
15. Natural rock formations that appear at the surface of the ground are outcroppings.
16. Each summer, rock climbers can be seen ascending El Capitan in Yosemite National Park.
17. One technique in rock climbing is putting hands and feet inside cracks known as fissures.
18. Ropes that are anchored provide safety.
19. After reaching the summit, climbers can rappel to the ground.

rock climbing

© Spelling Grade 6 17

Student Day 2

Lesson 5 Vocabulary — Vowel Combinations

Prefix		Root		Suffix	
de-	thoroughly	err	wander, stray	-ant	inclined to
in-	not			-or	state of
		scrib	write	-ing	continuous action
				-able	is able

Write the Vocabulary Words. Order may vary.

1. errant 2. error
3. describing 4. indescribable

Refer to the table to complete the exercises. Write the word that is being defined.

5. giving a thorough account describing
6. not able to give a thorough account indescribable
7. inclined to wander errant
8. state of straying from what is correct error

Write Vocabulary Words to complete the sentences.

9. Manny began describing his rock climbing adventure to his friends.
10. He climbed the face of the granite formation without making an error.
11. The view from the summit was indescribable.
12. An errant climber congratulated Manny when he reached the top.

Choose the best meaning for each word.

13. euphoric
- ● extremely happy
- ○ extremely unhappy
- ○ neither happy nor unhappy

14. fissures
- ○ short wide cracks
- ○ long wide cracks
- ● long narrow cracks

15. unauthorized
- ○ to give permission to do something
- ● not warranted by proper authority
- ○ to act on the behalf of someone else

16. bouldering
- ○ the study of rocks
- ● rock climbing
- ○ a group of large rocks

Pattern Words: decoy, neutral, euphoric, moisture, awkward, awesome, beautifully, exhausted, precaution, renewable, newsworthy, unauthorized

Content Words: rappel, fissures, anchored, ascending, bouldering, formations, outcroppings

Vocabulary Words: errant, error, describing, indescribable

18 © Spelling Grade 6

4 Homework suggestion: Students use their Spelling Dictionary to write the definition of each word on the back of the corresponding flash card that was suggested for homework on Day 1.

Day 3 Word Study Strategies

Objective

The students will write list words that are related forms of given words. They will write list words to complete similes.

Introduction

Write *anchored* and *moisture* on the board and challenge students to identify any related words. (**Possible answers: anchors, anchorman, anchor; moisturizes, moisturizing, moisturizer**)

Directed Instruction

1 Write the following similes on the board:
- The toddler in the nursery was as busy as a bee.
- The outcroppings in the field looked like sleeping elephants.
- The algebra problem was as clear as mud.
- We did not go bouldering today, since the weather was as hot as an oven.

Explain that these sentences are examples of a simile. Define a *simile* as a figure of speech that compares two different things using the word *like* or *as*. Solicit volunteers to identify the two things in each sentence that are being compared. (**outcroppings and elephants; weather and oven**)

2 Write the following similes on the board and invite students to complete them:
- … as cool as a cucumber.
- … like a rock.
- The fuzzy sweater felt like …

(**Possible answers: The confident student was** as cool as a cucumber. **The exhausted climber slept** like a rock. The fuzzy sweater felt like **scratchy sandpaper.**)

3 Proceed to page 19. Allow students to read the directions and complete the page independently. Assist as needed. Select a student to read Psalm 61:2 and discuss how the Lord is our rock and our stronghold when we encounter difficult times in our lives.

Day 4 Writing

Objective

The students will use proofreading marks to identify mistakes in an informative essay. They will correctly write misspelled words.

Introduction

Display **T-3 Proofreading an Informative Essay** on the overhead, keeping the bottom portion covered. Tell students that the errors will be corrected using proofreading marks located in the Proofreading Marks box. Review each proofreading mark. Orally read the text and challenge students to locate the mistakes. Correct the mistakes on the transparency using the appropriate proofreading mark. Use **BLM SP6-05A T-3 Answer Key** as a guide. Uncover the bottom portion of the transparency so students can see a corrected version.

Directed Instruction

1 Proceed to page 20. Select a student to read the sentences at the top of the page. Allow students to work independently, assisting as needed to ensure each error is corrected. (**9 misspellings; 4 capital letters needed; 2 periods needed; 3 deletes; 2 add something—*of*, *is*; 3 small letters needed; 1 new paragraph**) When finished, select a volunteer to read the essay.

2 Homework suggestion: Distribute a copy of **BLM SP6-05B Lesson 5**

Student Spelling Support Materials

BLM SP6-01A

Student Spelling Support

1. Use **BLM SP6-01A A Spelling Study Strategy** in instructional groups to provide assistance with some or all of the words.
2. Invite students to write the Challenge Words, numbers 24 and 25, in the Word Bank, in the back of their textbook.
3. Have students research and write an informational essay on a style of rock climbing other than bouldering. Styles of rock climbing include free climbing; traditional climbing, also called trad climbing; aid climbing; solo climbing; and ice climbing.
4. Write this week's words, categorize the Pattern, Content, and Vocabulary Words, and attach them to the Word Wall.
5. Read Psalm 61:2: "From the end of the earth I will cry to You, when my heart is overwhelmed; lead me to the rock that is higher than I." Explain that when we encounter situations that are overwhelming, our Lord is ready and willing to help. God is our rock and our strength. He is able to give us the strength we need to overcome trials. There are several verses in Psalms that refer to God as a rock. Have students look up the word *rock* in a paper or electronic concordance and read a few verses. Instruct students to write their own psalm referring to God as a rock. Encourage students to use list words.

Cont. on page 21

Homework to each student.

Day 5 Posttest

Objective

The students will correctly write dictated spelling words and sentences.

Introduction

Review by using flash cards noted in Day 1 and Day 2 Homework suggestion.

Directed Assessment

1 Dictate the list words by using the Pretest sentences or developing original ones. Reserve *bouldering, formations, error, moisture, euphoric,* and *exhausted* for the dictation sentences.

2 Read each sentence. Repeat as needed.
- Tim and Sue went bouldering on Saturday.
- They climbed several formations.
- Tim made an error and skinned his knee.
- Sue used chalk to absorb the moisture from her hands.
- They were both euphoric when they reached the top.
- Sue was exhausted and slept while Tim drove home.

3 If assigned, dictate Extra Challenge Words.

4 Score the test, counting each misspelled word as an error. Correct the dictation sentences by grading only the spelling words or grading the complete sentences.

Student Spelling Support

Cont. from page 20

6. Invite students to investigate Yosemite National Park or another national park of interest. Challenge students to write their own informative essay about the park, using as many spelling words as possible. Share the essays with the class.

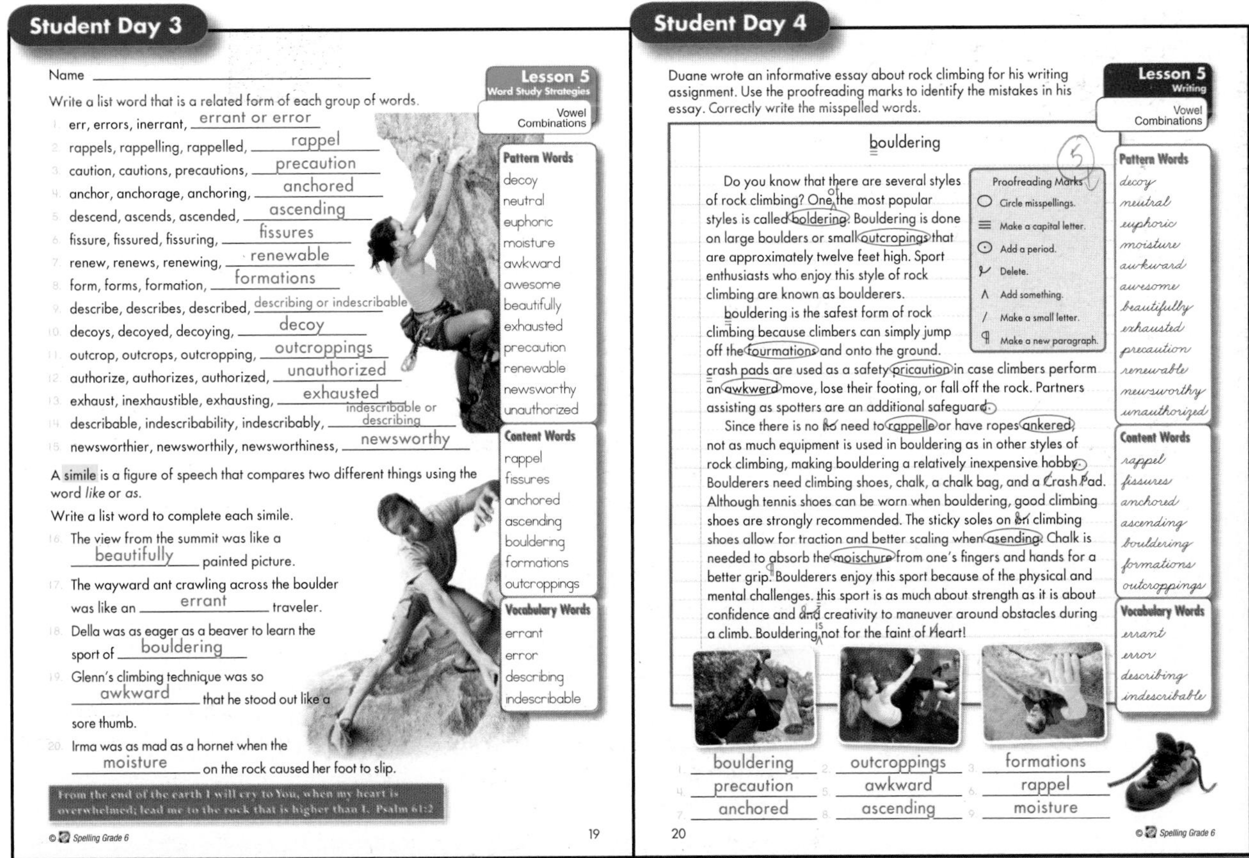

Lesson 6

Review Lessons 1–5

Student Pages

Pages 21–24

Lesson Materials

T-4
BLM SP6-06A
BLM SP6-06B
BLM SP6-06C
T-5
P-2
P-3
BLM SP6-06D
BLMs SP6-06E–F
BLM SP6-06G
BLM SP6-06H

Day 1 Short Vowels

Objective

The students will spell, identify, and sort words with **short vowels** in the first syllable.

Introduction

Teacher Note: This week's lesson incorporates the Pattern, Content, and Vocabulary Words taught in Lessons 1–5 using a variety of activities such as sorting, a crossword puzzle, filling in the correct answer circle, a word search, unscrambling words, shape boxes in sentence context, and using a coordinate grid to write words.

Display **T-4 Lessons 1–5 Study Sheet** on the overhead to review Lesson 1 words in unison, following this technique: say the word, spell the word, say the word. Challenge students to identify the short vowel sounds found in Lesson 1 Pattern Words. Use a different color transparency pen to circle each of the letters that represent the short vowel sounds in the first syllable of each Pattern Word. (**short a—attitude, anticipate; short e—method, benefitted, technology; short i—insist, hiccup, difficult; short o—contact, progress; short u—subtotal, function**)

Directed Instruction

1 Proceed to page 21. Explain that the box contains all the Pattern, Content, and Vocabulary Words in Lessons 1–5. These lists are a review tool and contain the same words that were previously reviewed on the overhead transparency. Allow students to complete the page independently.

2 Distribute a copy of **BLM SP6-06A Lessons 1–5 Study Sheet** to each student to take home for study. Each review lesson includes a study sheet for student use.

3 Homework suggestion: Distribute a copy of **BLM SP6-06B Lesson 6 Homework I** to each student to practice with **short vowels**, **long vowels**, **words with ei and ie**, and **words with ou**. Remind students to review their weekly sets of flash cards.

Day 2 Long Vowels and Words with ei and ie

Objective

The students will complete a crossword puzzle with words containing **long vowels**. They will select the appropriate answer circle to indicate if **words with ei and ie** are spelled correctly or incorrectly, and correctly write each word.

Introduction

Divide the class into two teams and instruct each of the teams to form a line. Write a Pattern Word from Lesson 2 on the board twice, allowing room to write the definition below each word. At your signal, the first player from each team comes to the board and writes the definition for the word below the Pattern Word. Players use either the definitions from their flash cards, suggested as weekly homework, or look up each word in the Spelling Dictionary. The first team to write the definition accurately scores one point. Players return to the end of their line and the game continues with a second Pattern Word until all the words have been defined. If you have a large class, you will need to repeat some Pattern Words.

Directed Instruction

1 Display **T-4 Lessons 1–5 Study Sheet** to review Lessons 2–3 words in unison, using the say-spell-say technique.

2 Write the following activity on the board to provide practice for the exercises on the student page:

	Correct	Incorrect	
reciept	○	○	**(incorrect; receipt)**
disbeleif	○	○	**(incorrect; disbelief)**
lieutenant	○	○	**(correct; lieutenant)**

Read each word and select volunteers to identify if each word is spelled correctly or incorrectly. Fill in each appropriate answer circle. Write each word correctly.

3 Proceed to page 22. Instruct students to read the directions silently and to complete the page independently. Encourage students to use their Spelling Dictionary to assist in completing the crossword puzzle.

4 Homework suggestion: Distribute a copy of **BLM SP6-06C Lesson 6 Homework II** to each student to practice with **vowel combinations**, Content Words, and Vocabulary Words.

Day 3 Words with ou and Vowel Combinations

Objective

The students will find and circle **words with ou** in a word search. They will unscramble words containing **vowel combinations.**

Introduction

Before class, make a word search, using **T-5 Word Search Grid**. Select a volunteer to write the following Pattern Words from Lesson 4 in the squares of the grid: route, sought, though, throughout. Assist the volunteer in positioning the words across, down, diagonally, and backwards. Fill in the surrounding squares with letters to conceal the words. When complete, display the transparency on the overhead and challenge students to find the Pattern Words, referring to the list words on the top of page 23. Circle each word as it is found. An example word search is shown.

c	k	c	r	s	e	l	y	a	e
u	w	k	b	o	a	w	r	x	a
v	n	r	e	u	u	r	u	t	s
m	l	t	r	g	i	t	i	u	i
p	y	e	y	h	r	m	e	l	l
t	x	s	g	t	h	o	u	g	h
t	u	o	h	g	u	o	r	h	t

Directed Instruction

1 Display **T-4 Lessons 1–5 Study Sheet** to review Lessons 4–5 words in unison, using the say-spell-say technique.

2 Direct students' attention to the words in Lesson 5 as you write the following scrambled words on the board:

- k a r d a w w (**awkward**)
- t h o r z e d i u n a u (**unauthorized**)
- w y n e r t h w s o (**newsworthy**)

Challenge students to unscramble the words by

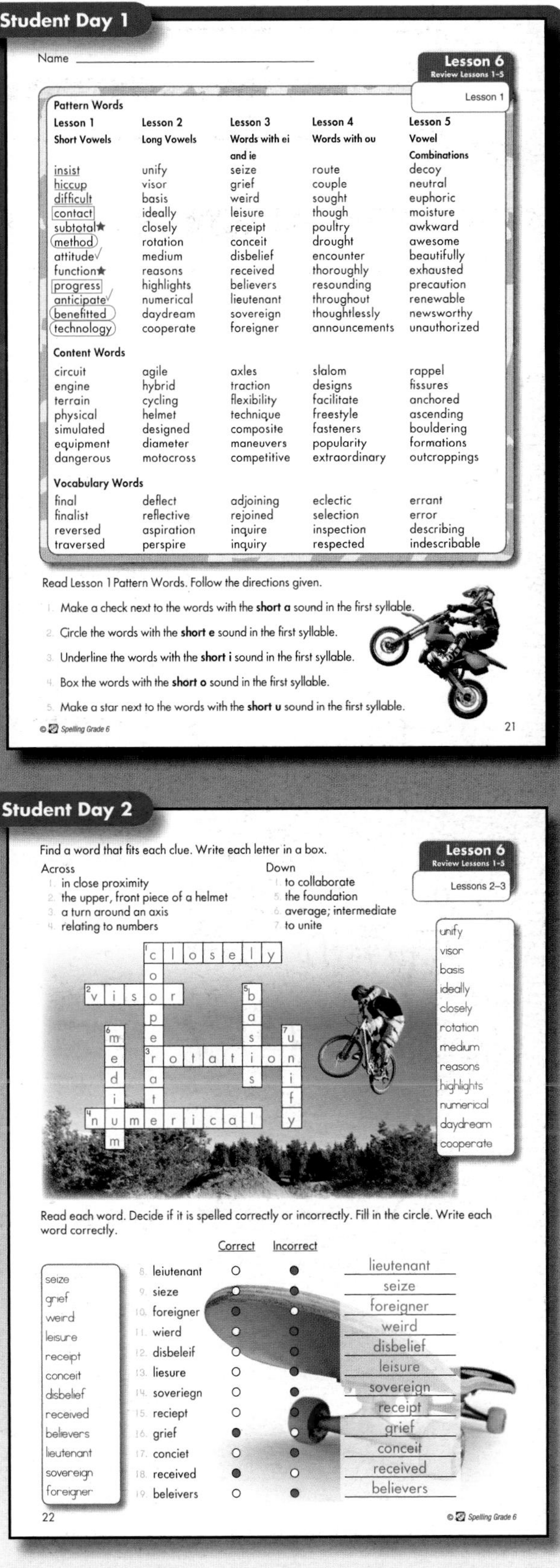
Student Day 1

Name ______________________

Lesson 6 Review Lessons 1–5

Lesson 1

Pattern Words

Lesson 1 Short Vowels	Lesson 2 Long Vowels	Lesson 3 Words with ei and ie	Lesson 4 Words with ou	Lesson 5 Vowel Combinations
insist	unify	seize	route	decoy
hiccup	visor	grief	couple	neutral
difficult	basis	weird	sought	euphoric
contact	ideally	leisure	though	moisture
subtotal★	closely	receipt	poultry	awkward
method	rotation	conceit	drought	awesome
attitude√	medium	disbelief	encounter	beautifully
function★	reasons	received	thoroughly	exhausted
progress	highlights	believers	resounding	precaution
anticipate√	numerical	lieutenant	throughout	renewable
benefitted	daydream	sovereign	thoughtlessly	newsworthy
technology	cooperate	foreigner	announcements	unauthorized

Content Words

circuit	agile	axles	slalom	rappel
engine	hybrid	traction	designs	fissures
terrain	cycling	flexibility	facilitate	anchored
physical	helmet	technique	freestyle	ascending
simulated	designed	composite	fasteners	bouldering
equipment	diameter	maneuvers	popularity	formations
dangerous	motocross	competitive	extraordinary	outcroppings

Vocabulary Words

final	deflect	adjoining	eclectic	errant
finalist	reflective	rejoined	selection	error
reversed	aspiration	inquire	inspection	describing
traversed	perspire	inquiry	respected	indescribable

Read Lesson 1 Pattern Words. Follow the directions given.

1. Make a check next to the words with the **short a** sound in the first syllable.
2. Circle the words with the **short e** sound in the first syllable.
3. Underline the words with the **short i** sound in the first syllable.
4. Box the words with the **short o** sound in the first syllable.
5. Make a star next to the words with the **short u** sound in the first syllable.

© Spelling Grade 6 21

Student Day 2

Lesson 6 Review Lessons 1–5

Lessons 2–3

Find a word that fits each clue. Write each letter in a box.

Across
1. in close proximity
2. the upper, front piece of a helmet
3. a turn around an axis
4. relating to numbers

Down
1. to collaborate
5. the foundation
6. average; intermediate
7. to unite

unify, visor, basis, ideally, closely, rotation, medium, reasons, highlights, numerical, daydream, cooperate

Read each word. Decide if it is spelled correctly or incorrectly. Fill in the circle. Write each word correctly.

	Correct	Incorrect	
8. leiutenant	○	●	lieutenant
9. sieze	○	●	seize
10. foreigner	●	○	foreigner
11. wierd	○	●	weird
12. disbeleif	○	●	disbelief
13. liesure	○	●	leisure
14. sovereign	●	○	sovereign
15. reciept	○	●	receipt
16. grief	●	○	grief
17. conciet	○	●	conceit
18. received	●	○	received
19. beleivers	○	●	believers

seize, grief, weird, leisure, receipt, conceit, disbelief, received, believers, lieutenant, sovereign, foreigner

22 © Spelling Grade 6

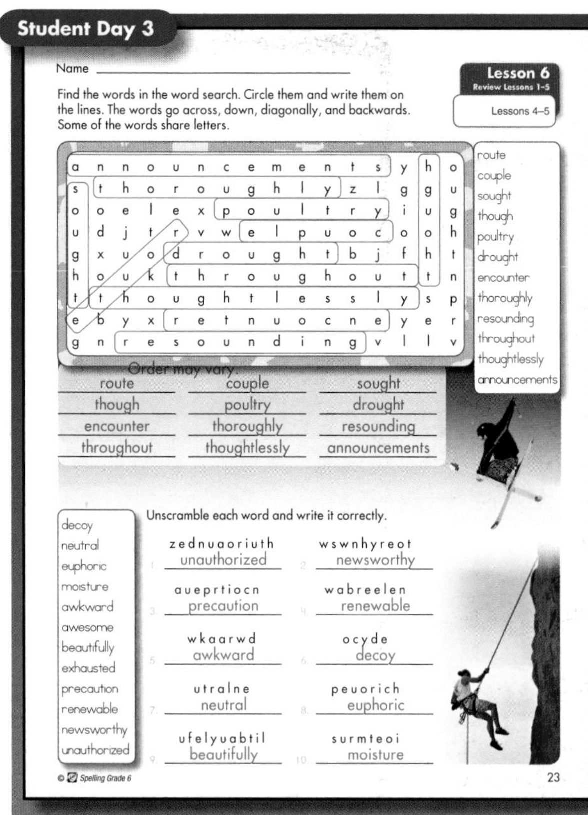
Student Day 3

Name ____________

Lesson 6 Review Lessons 1–5

Lessons 4–5

Find the words in the word search. Circle them and write them on the lines. The words go across, down, diagonally, and backwards. Some of the words share letters.

```
a n n o u n c e m e n t s y h o
s t h o r o u g h l y z l g g u
o o e l e x p o u l t r y i u g
u d j t r v w e l p u o c o o h
g x u o d r o u g h t b j f h t
h o u k t h r o u g h o u t t n
t t h o u g h t l e s s l y s p
e b y x r e t n u o c n e y e r
g n r e s o u n d i n g v l l v
```

route, couple, sought, though, poultry, drought, encounter, thoroughly, resounding, throughout, thoughtlessly, announcements

Order may vary.

route	couple	sought
though	poultry	drought
encounter	thoroughly	resounding
throughout	thoughtlessly	announcements

decoy, neutral, euphoric, moisture, awkward, awesome, beautifully, exhausted, precaution, renewable, newsworthy, unauthorized

Unscramble each word and write it correctly.

1. zednuaoriuth — unauthorized
2. wswnhyreot — newsworthy
3. aueprtiocn — precaution
4. wabreelen — renewable
5. wkaarwd — awkward
6. ocyde — decoy
7. utralne — neutral
8. peuorich — euphoric
9. ufelyuabtil — beautifully
10. surmteoi — moisture

© Spelling Grade 6 23

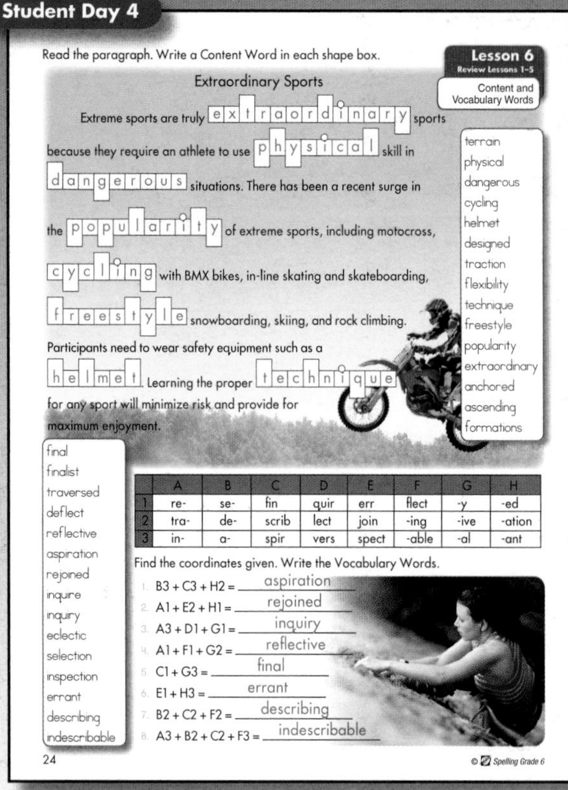
Student Day 4

Read the paragraph. Write a Content Word in each shape box.

Lesson 6 Review Lessons 1–5

Content and Vocabulary Words

Extraordinary Sports

Extreme sports are truly extraordinary sports because they require an athlete to use physical skill in dangerous situations. There has been a recent surge in the popularity of extreme sports, including motocross, cycling with BMX bikes, in-line skating and skateboarding, freestyle snowboarding, skiing, and rock climbing. Participants need to wear safety equipment such as a helmet. Learning the proper technique for any sport will minimize risk and provide for maximum enjoyment.

terrain, physical, dangerous, cycling, helmet, designed, traction, flexibility, technique, freestyle, popularity, extraordinary, anchored, ascending, formations

final, finalist, traversed, deflect, reflective, aspiration, rejoined, inquire, inquiry, eclectic, selection, inspection, errant, describing, indescribable

	A	B	C	D	E	F	G	H
1	re-	se-	fin	quir	err	flect	-y	-ed
2	tra-	de-	scrib	lect	join	-ing	-ive	-ation
3	in-	a-	spir	vers	spect	-able	-al	-ant

Find the coordinates given. Write the Vocabulary Words.

1. B3 + C3 + H2 = aspiration
2. A1 + E2 + H1 = rejoined
3. A3 + D1 + G1 = inquiry
4. A1 + F1 + G2 = reflective
5. C1 + G3 = final
6. E1 + H3 = errant
7. B2 + C2 + F2 = describing
8. A3 + B2 + C2 + F3 = indescribable

24 © Spelling Grade 6

looking for the following vowel combinations: au, aw, eau, eu, ew, oi, oy. Select three volunteers to write the correct spellings on the board.

3 Proceed to page 23. Instruct students to complete the page independently.

Day 4 Content Words and Vocabulary Words

Objective

The students will write content words in shape boxes to complete sentences. Students will use a coordinate grid to spell and write vocabulary words.

Introduction

Invite students to refer to the list of Content Words, found on the top of page 24, for this activity. Write the following sentences on the board:

- Miguel had to modify his technique to ride on rough terrain. (technique, terrain)
- The popularity of freestyle snowboarding intrigued Paula. (popularity, freestyle)

Choose a student to come to the board, locate the Content Words in each sentence, and to trace around the words, outlining their configuration. Studying the configuration of words promotes visual memory.

Directed Instruction

	A	B	C
1	re-	flect	-ion
2	in-	spect	-ive

1 To reinforce the Vocabulary Words, draw the grid shown on the board. Demonstrate how to go across to read the letter and down to read the number. Invite volunteers to write the Vocabulary Word formed by combining the roots and affixes found on the grid:

- A1 + B1 + C2 **(re-) (flect) (-ive) (reflective)**
- A2 + B2 + C1 **(in-) (spect) (-ion) (inspection)**

2 Display **T-4 Lessons 1–5 Study Sheet** to review Content and Vocabulary Words in unison, using the say-spell-say technique.

3 Reinforce the meaning of each root in the Vocabulary Words on **T-4 Lessons 1–5 Study Sheet** by displaying **P-2** and **P-3 Latin Roots**. Read each Vocabulary Word and select a student to tell the root and its meaning.

- *fin* means *end*
- *flect* means *bend*
- *join* means *join*
- *lect* means *gather*
- *err* means *wander, stray*
- *vers* means *turn*
- *spir* means *breathe*
- *quir* means *seek*
- *spect* means *look*
- *scrib* means *write*

4 Proceed to page 24. Allow students to complete the page independently.

5 Homework suggestion: Distribute a copy of **BLM SP6-06D Lessons 1–5 Test Prep** to each student to practice with many of the words that may appear on the Assessment. Students prepare for the Assessment by studying the words on **BLM SP6-06A Lessons 1–5 Study Sheet** that was sent home on Day 1 or by using their flash card sets.

Day 5 Assessment

Objective

The students will accurately select the appropriate answer within the context of a sentence. They will fill in the corresponding answer circle.

Introduction

Teacher Note: The Test makes provision for Differentiated Instruction. The first twelve sentences include the words assigned to students with shortened lists. Encourage these students to try all the sentences, but only grade the first twelve sentences. The Test is found on two blackline masters.

Distribute a copy of **BLMs SP6-06E–F Lessons 1–5 Test I** and **II** to each student. Duplicate **BLM SP6-06G Student Answer Form** and cut apart. Distribute one answer form to each student. Remind students to fill in each answer circle completely and to erase completely to change an answer.

Directed Assessment

1 Instruct students to listen as you dictate the following Sample:

Sample

It is often difficult (A) to anticipate (B) problems with equipement (C). All correct (D)

Say, "Are any of the first three underlined words misspelled?" Pause for replies. Inform students that the letter *C* is below the underlined word that is misspelled. (**equipment**) Guide students to the answer form that was previously distributed. Lead students to find the Sample box and fill in the appropriate answer circle containing the same letter. Say, "You will continue in the same way. You will read each sentence, choose the word that you think is misspelled, and fill in the corresponding circle on the answer form. If all the words are spelled correctly, fill in the fourth circle, labeled *D*, for *All correct*."

2 Assist students as needed while they read the sentences and complete the Test on their own.

1. Bikes designed for BMX cycling have wheels with a small diameter.
2. Contact with moisture may cause a climber to make an error.
3. Ideally, competitive ski jumpers demonstrate great technique.
4. Everyone stared in disbelief as the finalist did a weird stunt.
5. The dangerous terrain was imperfect for motocross.
6. An exhausted climber was euphoric as he viewed the awesome sight.
7. Climbing shoes provide traction while ascending when bouldering.
8. A good attitude is the basis for achieving your aspiration.
9. Is the popularity of extreme sports extraordinary or newsworthy?
10. Jan was thoroughly prepared to rappel beautifully down the cliff.
11. Tina was describing several designs for freestyle BMX bikes.
12. Teammates sought to cooperate and rejoined the race.
13. The progress of extreme sports has benefitted from technology.
14. Grant received a receipt for the purchase of his new helmet.
15. Announcements for the upcoming slalom were seen along the route.
16. Even though it felt awkward, Li continued to climb the rock formations.
17. Physical strength and flexibility are traits of agile BMX riders.
18. We insist that skaters do not thoughtlessly skate in unauthorized areas.
19. One of the reasons for a visor is to deflect sunlight away from one's eyes.
20. Throughout the race, the lieutenant was respected by the fans.
21. Bill made an inquiry into buying a reflective composite skateboard.
22. New fasteners will facilitate Jack's maneuvers with his snowboard.
23. Climbers, once firmly anchored, use fissures to seize a handhold.
24. As he traversed the final lap, Mario began to perspire.
25. At her leisure, Lily assembled an eclectic selection of skis.

3 Refer to **BLM SP6-06H Lessons 1–5 Answer Key** when correcting the Test.

Notes

Lesson 7

Schwa o

Student Pages

Pages 25–28

Lesson Materials

BLM SP6-01B
Card stock
Index cards
BLM SP6-07A

Sports

Lessons 7–11 utilize the theme of team sports. The theme of this lesson is football. Football is one of the most popular sports in the United States. It is played by professionals and amateurs alike, including students from elementary school through college and beyond. The game involves two opposing teams, with each team trying to score points by throwing or carrying an oval ball across their opponent's goal line or by kicking the ball through the opponent's goalposts.

Day 1 Pretest

Objective

The students will accurately spell and write words with **schwa o**. They will spell and write content, vocabulary, and challenge words.

Introduction

Before class, select Challenge Words for numbers 24 and 25 from a cross-curricular subject, words misspelled on previous assignments, or words that interest your students. The word *governmental* has **schwa o** in the first syllable and is suggested for number 24. Explain that they are to attempt to write all the spelling words.

Directed Instruction

1 Say each word, use it in a sentence, and then repeat the word.

Pattern Words

1. Could you hear the announcer over the accolades of the fans?
2. Players in the collegiate conference are university students.
3. Offensive and defensive players often collide.
4. The committee will seek land to build a new stadium.
5. Our community has an indoor football stadium.
6. When the game concludes, we will celebrate.
7. The coach configured the plays on a chalkboard.
8. We were unconvinced that the scoreboard was accurate.
9. Coach's halftime speech was not eloquent, but it was effective.
10. An improvement to the equipment was a positive development.
11. I recollect the score from last year's final game.
12. Experts recommend that you warm up before playing football.

Content Words

13. The best football team won the championship.
14. A defender caught a pass for an interception.
15. A penalty was called for offensive interference.
16. Numerous penalties caused the home team to lose.
17. Michelle plays quarterback for her flag football team.
18. Our offensive and defensive teams practice during a scrimmage.
19. The Mountain Goats scored a touchdown!

Vocabulary Words

20. The Eagles sought to dominate the competition.
21. Did the placekicker need to reposition the ball?
22. Jesus has dominion over all the earth.
23. The teams lined up on opposite sides of the field.

Challenge Words

24. ________________
25. ________________

The apparatus for making cider made a lot of noise.

The entrepreneur helped raise money for the company.

2 Allow students to self-corre
board. Inform students tha
The symbol ə indicates th
Spelling Dictionary. Point
letter *o* in each Pattern W
Vocabulary Words. The si
the original root spelling *p*

3 As a class, read, spell, and
misspelled words and rew

4 Proof each student's Pretest. This becomes an individualized study sheet that can be used at school or at home.

5 Homework suggestion: Duplicate **BLM SP6-01B Flash Cards Template** on CARD STOCK for students to write the list words, using the flash cards as a study aid. Another option is to use INDEX CARDS.

Day 2 Word Analysis and Vocabulary

Objective

The students will sort and write words with **schwa o** and complete sentences with content words. Students will use a table to write vocabulary words, match vocabulary words to their definitions, complete sentences, and choose list words that match definitions.

Introduction

Chorally read each Pattern Word. Remind students that the Pattern Words in this lesson all contain a schwa sound spelled with an *o*. The schwa sound is identical to the sound of *short u*. Have students identify each **schwa o** and state which syllable contains the schwa. (**first syllable—collide, collegiate, concludes, configured, committee, community; second syllable—eloquent, recollect, accolades, unconvinced, recommend; third syllable—development**)

Directed Instruction

1 Invite students to refer to the list words, found on page 25, for this activity. Challenge students to quickly locate the definition of *eloquent, accolades, scrimmage, interception*, and *interference* in their Spelling Dictionary. Students read the definitions aloud.

2 Proceed to page 25. Say, spell, and say each Pattern, Content, and Vocabulary Word. Provide this week's Challenge Words and have students write them in the spaces provided. Students complete the page.

3 Proceed to page 26. Remind students to use the table to assist in building each Vocabulary Word. For example, the root *domin* goes

Differentiated Instruction

- For students who spelled all the words correctly on the Pretest, select and assign Extra Challenge Words from the following list: bivariate, apparatus, rhetoric, entrepreneur, exclusionary, compositional.
- For students who spelled less than half correctly, assign the following Pattern, Content, and Vocabulary Words: collide, recollect, concludes, configured, recommend, development, touchdown, scrimmage, quarterback, championship, dominate, opposite. On the Posttest, evaluate these students on the twelve words assigned; however, encourage them to attempt to spell all the list words to the best of their ability. They are also responsible for writing the dictated sentences.

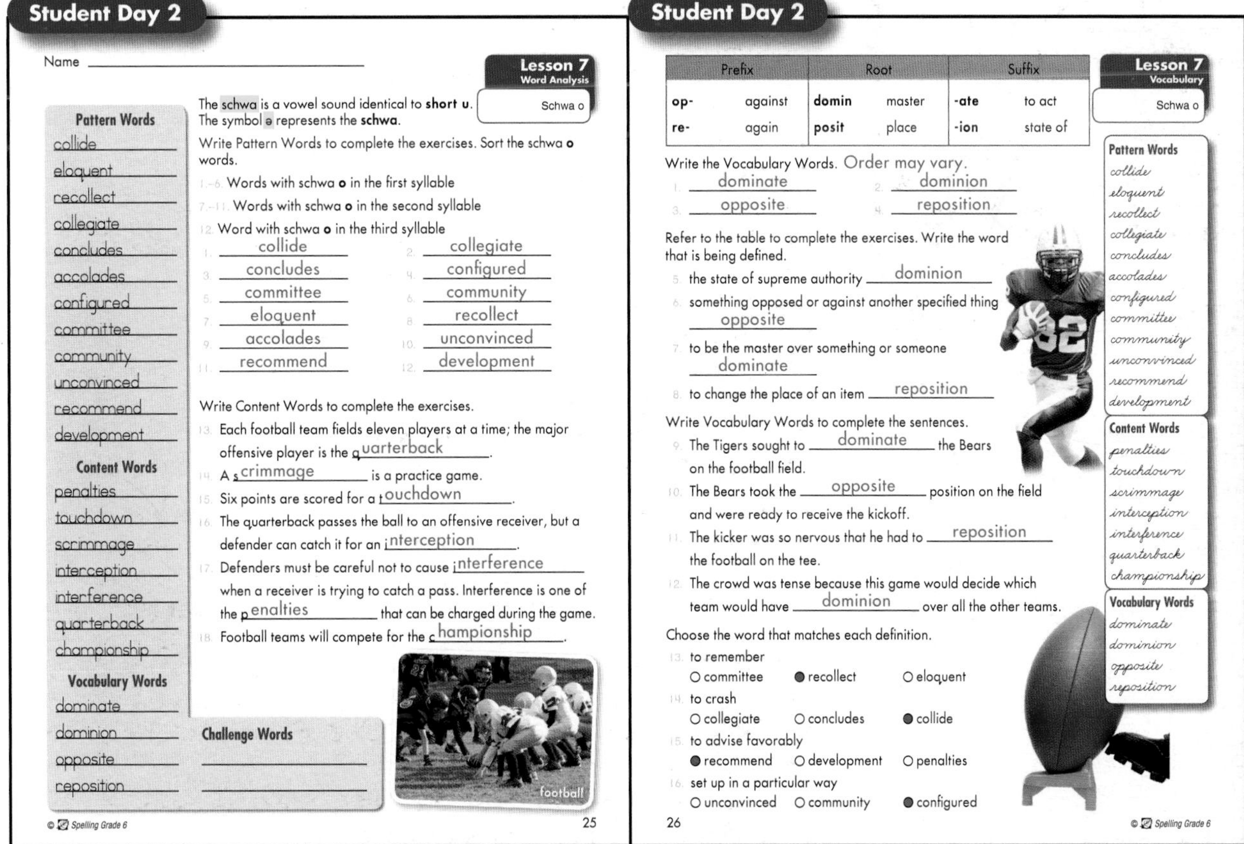

Student Day 2

Name

Lesson 7 Word Analysis — Schwa o

Pattern Words: collide, eloquent, recollect, collegiate, concludes, accolades, configured, committee, community, unconvinced, recommend, development

Content Words: penalties, touchdown, scrimmage, interception, interference, quarterback, championship

Vocabulary Words: dominate, dominion, opposite, reposition

The schwa is a vowel sound identical to **short u**. The symbol ə represents the **schwa**.

Write Pattern Words to complete the exercises. Sort the schwa **o** words.

1–6 Words with schwa **o** in the first syllable
7–11 Words with schwa **o** in the second syllable
12 Word with schwa **o** in the third syllable

1. collide 2. collegiate
3. concludes 4. configured
5. committee 6. community
7. eloquent 8. recollect
9. accolades 10. unconvinced
11. recommend 12. development

Write Content Words to complete the exercises.

13. Each football team fields eleven players at a time; the major offensive player is the quarterback.
14. A scrimmage is a practice game.
15. Six points are scored for a touchdown.
16. The quarterback passes the ball to an offensive receiver, but a defender can catch it for an interception.
17. Defenders must be careful not to cause interference when a receiver is trying to catch a pass. Interference is one of the penalties that can be charged during the game.
18. Football teams will compete for the championship.

Challenge Words

football

© Spelling Grade 6 25

Student Day 2

Prefix		Root		Suffix	
op-	against	**domin**	master	**-ate**	to act
re-	again	**posit**	place	**-ion**	state of

Lesson 7 Vocabulary — Schwa o

Write the Vocabulary Words. Order may vary.

1. dominate 2. dominion
3. opposite 4. reposition

Refer to the table to complete the exercises. Write the word that is being defined.

5. the state of supreme authority dominion
6. something opposed or against another specified thing opposite
7. to be the master over something or someone dominate
8. to change the place of an item reposition

Write Vocabulary Words to complete the sentences.

9. The Tigers sought to dominate the Bears on the football field.
10. The Bears took the opposite position on the field and were ready to receive the kickoff.
11. The kicker was so nervous that he had to reposition the football on the tee.
12. The crowd was tense because this game would decide which team would have dominion over all the other teams.

Choose the word that matches each definition.

13. to remember — ○ committee ● recollect ○ eloquent
14. to crash — ○ collegiate ○ concludes ● collide
15. to advise favorably — ● recommend ○ development ○ penalties
16. set up in a particular way — ○ unconvinced ○ community ● configured

Pattern Words: collide, eloquent, recollect, collegiate, concludes, accolades, configured, committee, community, unconvinced, recommend, development

Content Words: penalties, touchdown, scrimmage, interception, interference, quarterback, championship

Vocabulary Words: dominate, dominion, opposite, reposition

26 © Spelling Grade 6

Student Spelling Support Materials

BLM SP6-01A

Student Spelling Support

1. Use **BLM SP6-01A A Spelling Study Strategy** in instructional groups to provide assistance with some or all of the words.
2. Invite students to write the Challenge Words, numbers 24 and 25, in the Word Bank, in the back of their textbook.
3. Challenge students to write a fictional, descriptive article of a football game in their progressive journals on sports. Students should use a variety of precise verbs and nouns and descriptive adjectives, including as many spelling words as possible.
4. Write this week's words, categorize the Pattern, Content, and Vocabulary Words, and attach them to the Word Wall.
5. Read Philippians 3:14: "I press toward the goal for the prize of the upward call of God in Christ Jesus." Explain that the goal of every Christian should be to become like Jesus. We press toward this goal as we trust, obey, fellowship with other believers, and seek a deeper relationship with Him through the power of the Holy Spirit.
6. Enhance study skills by providing a list of this week's spelling words for each student. Students pronounce each word on the list and use a highlighter to highlight tricky or difficult spellings within each word. Encourage students to notice spelling patterns, such as double consonants, silent letters, or schwa spellings that must be memorized. Focusing on the visual

Cont. on page 29

with the suffix *-ate* to build the word *dominate.* Allow students to complete the page independently.

4 Homework suggestion: Students use their Spelling Dictionary to write the definition of each word on the back of the corresponding flash card that was suggested for homework on Day 1.

Day 3 Word Study Strategies

Objective

The students will write words from the given pronunciations. Students will identify and write compound subjects and simple subjects.

Introduction

Write the following pronunciations on the board:

- /kə 'lē jət/ (**collegiate**)
- /re kə 'mend/ (**recommend**)
- /kən 'fi gyûrd/ (**configured**)

Challenge students to sound out the pronunciations and identify the words.

Directed Instruction

1 Write the following sentences on the board:
- Power and dominion belong to the Lord.
- Stricter rules and sturdier equipment have made football safer.

Remind students that every sentence in English is composed of a subject and a predicate. Explain that some sentences may have a compound subject. A *compound subject* is made up of two or more subjects that share the same predicate. Choose volunteers to read each sentence, identify the subjects that share the same predicate, underline the compound subject, and circle each simple subject.

2 Proceed to page 27. Assist students as needed in completing the page. Select a volunteer to read Philippians 3:14. Discuss how football can deepen our understanding of Philippians 3:14 and how students may persevere in their spiritual growth.

Day 4 Writing

Objective

The students will complete a descriptive news article in the context of a cloze activity using pattern, content, and vocabulary words.

Introduction

Teacher Note: The descriptive domain is the focus for the writing pages in Lessons 7–11.

Remind students that a cloze activity consists of a sentence or passage with blanks. Direct students to the list words, found on page 28, and challenge students to locate the appropriate Pattern Word that will fit into the context of each sentence. (**collegiate or community; development**) Dictate the following brief paragraph, saying, "blank" where blank spaces are indicated:

> College football teams participate in ____ football events. Players on these teams are students as well as athletes. Together, they learn to work as a team. These student athletes see football as a positive ____ in their college careers. The skills gained through participation in football will have a lasting impact.

Directed Instruction

1 Explain that the activity in today's lesson involves a news article about a football game. Although the article on the page is fiction, the type and format of the article is similar to what students would read in an actual newspaper. It is an example of descriptive writing because it describes an event using vivid adjectives and adverbs that help the reader to be able to imagine being present at the football game.

2 Proceed to page 28. Instruct students to silently read the news article and to complete the cloze activity independently. Chorally read the completed article. Focus the students' attention on the effective use of description in the article. Some of the effective narrative and descriptive techniques that the writer uses include the following: sequence of events as in the beginning, middle, and end; rising action/suspense; precise verbs such as *configured* and *dominate*; precise nouns such as *accolades* and *interference*; sensory detail used in *cheering, yelling,* and *deafening.*

3 Homework suggestion: Distribute a copy of **BLM SP6-07A Lesson 7 Homework** to each student.

Day 5 Posttest

Objective

The students will correctly write dictated spelling words and sentences.

Introduction

Review by using flash cards noted in Day 1 and Day 2 Homework suggestion.

Directed Assessment

1 Dictate the list words by using the Pretest sentences or developing original ones. Reserve *recollect, quarterback, touchdown, opposite, recommend,* and *concludes* for the dictation sentences.

2 Read each sentence. Repeat as needed.

- I recollect an exciting football game that I saw on television.
- The quarterback was under pressure.
- He threw a pass for a touchdown.
- Later, a running back carried the ball to the opposite end of the field.
- I would recommend that you watch each football play.
- This concludes my memories of the game that I watched on television.

3 If assigned, dictate Extra Challenge Words.

4 Score the test, counting each misspelled word as an error. Correct the dictation sentences by grading only the spelling words or grading the complete sentences.

Student Spelling Support

Cont. from page 28

image of these spellings will assist in memorization.

7. Invite students to read 1 Corinthians 12. Discuss how the body of Christ, the human body, and a football team are all alike. Then, ask the students to read 1 Corinthians 13. Ask, "How does each member of a team display love when playing out his or her part on a team?" Challenge each student to pray to God about the following:
   - What is my role on the team?
   - How am I fulfilling that role?
   - How do I demonstrate responsibility in this role?
   - How do I show love in this role?

   Ask students to write a prayer, describing what they are doing well and how the Lord may have prompted them to improve.

Student Day 3

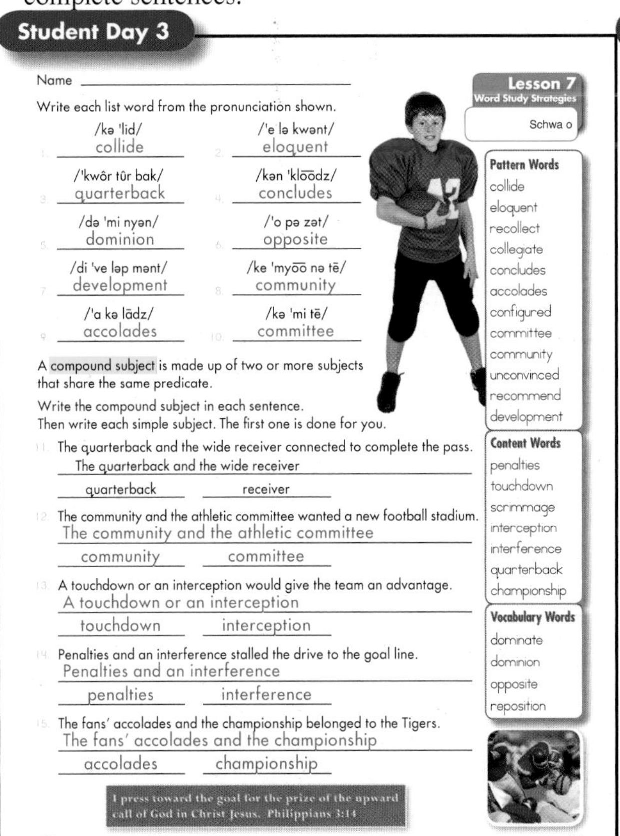

Lesson 7 Word Study Strategies

Schwa o

Name

Write each list word from the pronunciation shown.

1. /kə 'lid/ collide
2. /'e lə kwənt/ eloquent
3. /'kwôr tûr bak/ quarterback
4. /kən 'klo͞odz/ concludes
5. /də 'mi nyən/ dominion
6. /'o pə zət/ opposite
7. /di 've ləp mənt/ development
8. /kə 'myo͞o nə tē/ community
9. /'a kə lädz/ accolades
10. /kə 'mi tē/ committee

A compound subject is made up of two or more subjects that share the same predicate.

Write the compound subject in each sentence. Then write each simple subject. The first one is done for you.

11. The quarterback and the wide receiver connected to complete the pass.
    The quarterback and the wide receiver — quarterback — receiver
12. The community and the athletic committee wanted a new football stadium.
    The community and the athletic committee — community — committee
13. A touchdown or an interception would give the team an advantage.
    A touchdown or an interception — touchdown — interception
14. Penalties and an interference stalled the drive to the goal line.
    Penalties and an interference — penalties — interference
15. The fans' accolades and the championship belonged to the Tigers.
    The fans' accolades and the championship — accolades — championship

Pattern Words: collide, eloquent, recollect, collegiate, concludes, accolades, configured, committee, community, unconvinced, recommend, development

Content Words: penalties, touchdown, scrimmage, interception, interference, quarterback, championship

Vocabulary Words: dominate, dominion, opposite, reposition

I press toward the goal for the prize of the upward call of God in Christ Jesus. Philippians 3:14

© Spelling Grade 6 — 27

Student Day 4

Lesson 7 Writing

Schwa o

Scott wrote an article describing an exciting football game for the school newspaper. Read the article. Write the missing words.

EAGLES WIN!

It is almost impossible to describe the excitement at yesterday's play-off football game! The undefeated Eagles took on last year's bowl winners, the Rams. This game was for the _1_. It would prove which team had _2_ over all the other teams in the football conference.

The Rams' _3_ called several exciting plays that he and the coach had _4_ on a chalkboard and practiced during a _5_ before the game. An injury occurred when an offensive player happened to _6_ with a defender. Then the quarterback threw a long pass that was intended for a receiver downfield. A defender got in the way, and a penalty was called for _7_. The quarterback threw another long pass on the next play, but it was caught by the defending team for an _8_! The Rams' offense looked very disappointed as the defense took the field. The Eagles' offense began to _9_ the Rams' defense and soon the Eagles had scored the first _10_. The cheering, yelling, and other _11_ of the fans were deafening! It appeared that the Eagles would have an easy win, but in the next quarter they had a number of costly _12_ that kept them from scoring.

The game was tied at the beginning of the fourth quarter. The fans were _13_ that the undefeated Eagles would win to continue their record. The Rams' offense looked very good. They ran the first play from the five-yard line all the way to the five-yard line on the _14_ end of the field and scored on the next play. Yet, it was the Eagles who proved that they could fight back by scoring the next two touchdowns to win the game. It seemed as if the entire _15_ ran down onto the field to congratulate the coach and players. What a thrilling event!

1. championship 2. dominion 3. quarterback
4. configured 5. scrimmage 6. collide
7. interference 8. interception 9. dominate
10. touchdown 11. accolades 12. penalties
13. unconvinced 14. opposite 15. community

Pattern Words: collide, eloquent, recollect, collegiate, concludes, accolades, configured, committee, community, unconvinced, recommend, development

Content Words: penalties, touchdown, scrimmage, interception, interference, quarterback, championship

Vocabulary Words: dominate, dominion, opposite, reposition

28 — © Spelling Grade 6

Lesson **8**

Schwa in Final Syllables

Student Pages

Pages 29–32

Lesson Materials

BLM SP6-01B
Card stock
Index cards
T-6
BLM SP6-08A
BLM SP6-08B
BLM SP6-08C

Sports

The theme of this lesson is baseball and softball. Both baseball and softball originated in the 1800s in the United States. While baseball has always been an outdoor sport, softball emerged as an indoor sport. Softball was originally known as Kitten Ball, then Diamond Ball, and finally, softball.

Day 1 Pretest

Objective

The students will accurately spell and write words with **schwa in final syllables.** They will spell and write content, vocabulary, and challenge words.

Introduction

Before class, select Challenge Words for numbers 24 and 25 from a cross-curricular subject, words misspelled on previous assignments, or words that interest your students. The word *heightened* has a **schwa in the final syllable** and is suggested for number 24. Explain that they are to attempt to write all the spelling words.

Directed Instruction

1 Say each word, use it in a sentence, and then repeat the word.

Pattern Words

1. The team is accustomed to playing on their home field.
2. A softball player's status depends on his or her performance.
3. Do you know any trivia about baseball?
4. The news bulletin informed the viewers of the winning team.
5. It was a momentous occasion when the Vipers defeated the Lions.
6. The obstinate player would not quit despite being injured.
7. Callie is the pitcher on her intramural softball team.
8. In a random sequence of errors, the home team scored three runs.
9. A versatile player is very good at batting and also at fielding.
10. The game was so close that the coach wanted to broaden the score.
11. Uncle Ted and I watched the World Series on the sports channel.
12. In a raucous voice, the coach objected to the umpire's call.

Content Words

13. Keith's baseball team is in the south central league.
14. Two outfielders collided when they tried to catch the fly ball.
15. Being a spectator is not as much fun as playing in a baseball game.
16. Kim's statistics are so impressive that scouts are watching her.
17. Hal visited the concessions to get some snacks during the game.
18. Ivan is an amateur player who is dreaming of becoming a professional.
19. An athlete trains hard to improve his or her skills.

Vocabulary Words

20. I am grateful that God forgives me of my sins.
21. Does it gratify you that the Lord provides for our needs?
22. Does the life of the apostle Paul inspire you?
23. The faith of our forefathers is inspiring.

Challenge Words

24. ____________________
25. ____________________

2 Allow students to self-correct their Pretest. Write each word on the board. Remind students that a schwa is a vowel sound identical to *short u*. The symbol ə indicates the schwa in the pronunciation shown in the Spelling Dictionary. Point out that the schwa sound is spelled with the letters *a*, *e*, *i*, *ou*, *o*, and *u* and is in the final syllable of each Pattern Word. Note the roots *grat* and *spir* in the Vocabulary Words. The silent *e* in the words *grateful* and *inspire* is not included in the original root spellings *grat* and *spir*.

3 As a class, read, spell, and read each word. Direct students to highlight misspelled words and rewrite them correctly.

4 Proof each student's Pretest. This becomes an individualized study sheet that can be used at school or at home.

5 Homework suggestion: Distribute **BLM SP6-01B Flash Cards Template** on CARD STOCK for students to write the list words, using the flash cards as a study aid. Another option is to use INDEX CARDS.

Day 2 Word Analysis and Vocabulary

Objective

The students will sort and write pattern words containing a **schwa in final syllables**. They will write content words to complete sentences. Students will use a table to write vocabulary words, select words to match definitions, and complete sentences in context. They will choose words to match given definitions.

Introduction

Write the Pattern Words on the board, categorizing them by the vowel(s) that represent the schwa sound in the final syllable. Solicit volunteers to divide the words into syllables. Read each word.

- a—tri|vi|a, ob|sti|nate, in|tra|mu|ral
- i—bul|le|tin, ver|sa|tile
- o—ran|dom, ac|cus|tomed
- e—chan|nel, broad|en
- ou—rau|cous, mo|men|tous
- u—sta|tus

Teach that the schwa sound can be spelled with any of the vowels or a combination of vowels, and therefore the schwa spelling in each word must be memorized. Instruct students to highlight the vowel(s) that represent the schwa in the final syllable of each Pattern Word on the flash cards that were suggested for homework on Day 1.

Directed Instruction

1 Select volunteers to read the words in each category, while emphasizing the schwa sound in the final syllable.

2 Explain that this week's Content Words relate to the theme of baseball and softball. Select a volunteer to read the Content Words found on

Differentiated Instruction

- For students who spelled all the words correctly on the Pretest, select and assign Extra Challenge Words from the following list: categorical, biological, logographic, externalities, psychological, consonance.
- For students who spelled less than half correctly, assign the following Pattern, Content, and Vocabulary Words: trivia, status, bulletin, channel, random, momentous, league, athlete, spectator, outfielders, grateful, inspiring. On the Posttest, evaluate these students on the twelve words assigned; however, encourage them to attempt to spell all the list words to the best of their ability. They are also responsible for writing the dictated sentences.

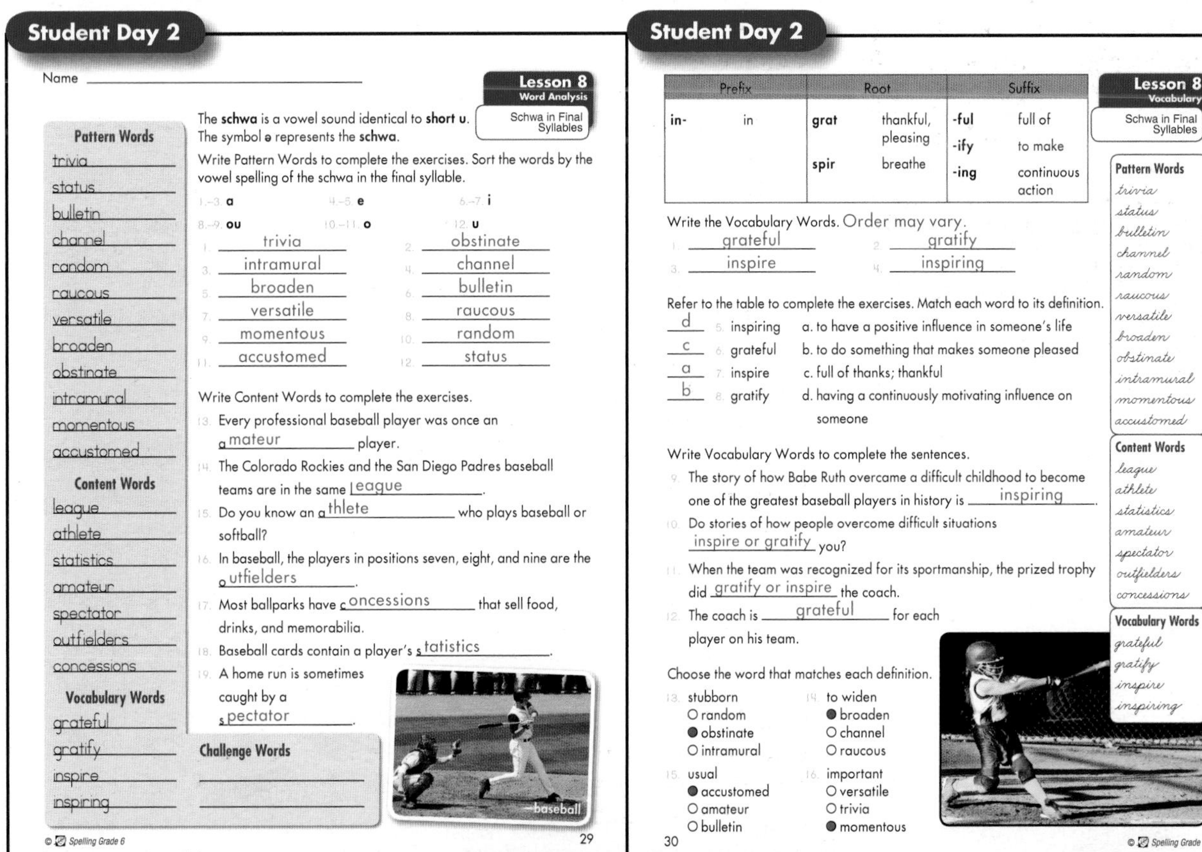

Student Day 2

Name ____________

Lesson 8 Word Analysis — Schwa in Final Syllables

Pattern Words: trivia, status, bulletin, channel, random, raucous, versatile, broaden, obstinate, intramural, momentous, accustomed

Content Words: league, athlete, statistics, amateur, spectator, outfielders, concessions

Vocabulary Words: grateful, gratify, inspire, inspiring

The **schwa** is a vowel sound identical to **short u**. The symbol ə represents the **schwa**.

Write Pattern Words to complete the exercises. Sort the words by the vowel spelling of the schwa in the final syllable.

1.–3. **a** 4.–5. **e** 6.–7. **i** 8.–9. **ou** 10.–11. **o** 12. **u**

1. trivia
2. obstinate
3. intramural
4. channel
5. broaden
6. bulletin
7. versatile
8. raucous
9. momentous
10. random
11. accustomed
12. status

Write Content Words to complete the exercises.

13. Every professional baseball player was once an amateur player.
14. The Colorado Rockies and the San Diego Padres baseball teams are in the same league.
15. Do you know an athlete who plays baseball or softball?
16. In baseball, the players in positions seven, eight, and nine are the outfielders.
17. Most ballparks have concessions that sell food, drinks, and memorabilia.
18. Baseball cards contain a player's statistics.
19. A home run is sometimes caught by a spectator.

Challenge Words

—baseball

© Spelling Grade 6 29

Student Day 2

Lesson 8 Vocabulary — Schwa in Final Syllables

Prefix		Root		Suffix	
in-	in	**grat**	thankful, pleasing	**-ful**	full of
				-ify	to make
		spir	breathe	**-ing**	continuous action

Write the Vocabulary Words. Order may vary.

1. grateful
2. gratify
3. inspire
4. inspiring

Refer to the table to complete the exercises. Match each word to its definition.

d 5. inspiring — a. to have a positive influence in someone's life
c 6. grateful — b. to do something that makes someone pleased
a 7. inspire — c. full of thanks; thankful
b 8. gratify — d. having a continuously motivating influence on someone

Write Vocabulary Words to complete the sentences.

9. The story of how Babe Ruth overcame a difficult childhood to become one of the greatest baseball players in history is inspiring.
10. Do stories of how people overcome difficult situations inspire or gratify you?
11. When the team was recognized for its sportmanship, the prized trophy did gratify or inspire the coach.
12. The coach is grateful for each player on his team.

Choose the word that matches each definition.

13. stubborn: ○ random ● obstinate ○ intramural
14. to widen: ● broaden ○ channel ○ raucous
15. usual: ● accustomed ○ amateur ○ bulletin
16. important: ○ versatile ○ trivia ● momentous

Pattern Words: trivia, status, bulletin, channel, random, raucous, versatile, broaden, obstinate, intramural, momentous, accustomed

Content Words: league, athlete, statistics, amateur, spectator, outfielders, concessions

Vocabulary Words: grateful, gratify, inspire, inspiring

30 © Spelling Grade 6

Student Spelling Support Materials

BLM SP6-01A

Student Spelling Support

1. Use **BLM SP6-01A A Spelling Study Strategy** in instructional groups to provide assistance with some or all of the words.
2. Invite students to write the Challenge Words, numbers 24 and 25, in the Word Bank, in the back of their textbook.
3. Challenge students to research and write about Billy Sunday. He was a baseball player for the Chicago White Stockings (currently known as the Chicago White Sox) in the late 1800s. After becoming a Christian, Sunday gave up a lucrative baseball career to be an evangelist.
4. Write this week's words, categorize the Pattern, Content, and Vocabulary Words, and attach them to the Word Wall.
5. Read I Corinthians 10:31: "Therefore, whether you eat or drink, or whatever you do, do all to the glory of God." Discuss with the students how attitudes, behavior, and words should be a reflection of Christ in our lives. Sometimes players and spectators become unruly at a sports event. As Christians, our lives are a testimony to others. Our actions and words do not go unnoticed. Invite students to write a descriptive paragraph or essay, describing the challenges to Christian living that they experience when participating in sports events. Challenge students to propose a biblically based behavioral intervention and then write an essay comparing and contrasting how this intervention could help them, as well as others.

Cont. on page 33

page 29. Refer to the Spelling Dictionary for unfamiliar words.

3 Proceed to page 29. Say, spell, and say each Pattern, Content, and Vocabulary Word. Provide this week's Challenge Words and have students write them in the spaces provided before completing the page.

4 Proceed to page 30. Encourage students to use the table as an aid in building each Vocabulary Word. For example, the root *grat* goes with the suffix *-ful* to get the word *grateful.* Remind students that silent *e* is not included in the original root spellings of *grat* and *spir.* Allow students to complete the page independently.

5 Homework suggestion: Students use their Spelling Dictionary to write the definition of each word on the back of the corresponding flash card that was suggested for homework on Day 1.

Day 3 Word Study Strategies

Objective

The students will write list words to complete sentences with inferences and alliterations.

Introduction

Write the following definition on the board: An *inference* is a conclusion reached by looking at facts. Have students refer to page 31 for the list words. Read the following sentences, and then ask students to use the facts to infer the missing word:

- Ten softball teams play against one another during the season. They are all in the same ______. (**league**)

Discuss the facts in the sentences that led to the inference.
(**ten teams, play against one another, are all in the same**)

Directed Instruction

1 Write the following alliterative sentences on the board:
- Betty bought a bat and a baseball for the birthday boy.
- Leah lost her left-handed mitt in the locker room.

Select a volunteer to read each sentence and underline the repeated initial consonant. Explain that these are examples of alliteration. *Alliteration* is a repetition of initial consonant sounds of several consecutive words in a phrase and is used by authors to add auditory interest to their writing.

2 Proceed to page 31. Allow students to complete the page. Conclude the lesson by asking volunteers to suggest inferences or alliterative sentences using list words that were not used.

Day 4 Writing

Objective

The students will read paragraphs about baseball and softball, and underline list words. They will write complete sentences comparing and contrasting baseball and softball. Students will complete a Venn diagram.

Introduction

Display **T-6 Venn Diagram**. Explain that a Venn diagram is a graphic organizer that is used to compare and contrast two topics. Hold a discussion about the similarities and differences of ice-skating and roller-skating. Title the left circle *Ice-skating* and write the unique features of that sport inside the circle. Above the right circle, write the title *Roller-skating* and list its unique aspects. Use the area of the overlapping circles to write the similarities of the two sports. On the board, write two sentences stating the similarities and two sentences stating the differences. Refer to **BLM SP6-08A T-6 Answer Key**.

Directed Instruction

1 Explain that the previous activity is an example of comparing and contrasting. To *compare* and *contrast* means to look and see how two or more things are alike or different. Tell students that comparing and contrasting while reading is a useful skill in comprehension.

2 Proceed to page 32. Select a volunteer to read the directions. Remind students to write the answers at the bottom of the page in complete sentences. Distribute a copy of **BLM SP6-08B Venn Diagram** to each student. Instruct them to write the similarities and differences of baseball and softball on the Venn diagram.

3 Homework suggestion: Distribute a copy of **BLM SP6-08C Lesson 8 Homework** to each student.

Day 5 Posttest

Objective

The students will correctly write dictated spelling words and sentences.

Introduction

Review by using flash cards noted in Day 1 and Day 2 Homework suggestion.

Directed Assessment

1 Dictate the list words by using the Pretest sentences or developing original ones. Reserve *trivia, athlete, channel, outfielders, status,* and *inspiring* for the dictation sentences.

2 Read each sentence. Repeat as needed.

- Sam knows a lot of baseball trivia.
- He reads a book about an athlete each week.
- He also watches baseball games on the sports channel.
- His favorite players are the outfielders.
- They each have a different status.
- Many players have stories about their life that are inspiring.

3 If assigned, dictate Extra Challenge Words.

4 Score the test, counting each misspelled word as an error. Correct the dictation sentences by grading only the spelling words or grading the complete sentences.

Student Spelling Support

Cont. from page 32

6. Young players are often inspired by the life of athletes who have been outstanding pitchers, catchers, and hitters. Some players acknowledge that they could not succeed without God and give the glory to Him. Invite students to research and describe the lives of Dave Dravecky, Cal Ripken, and Albert Pujols.

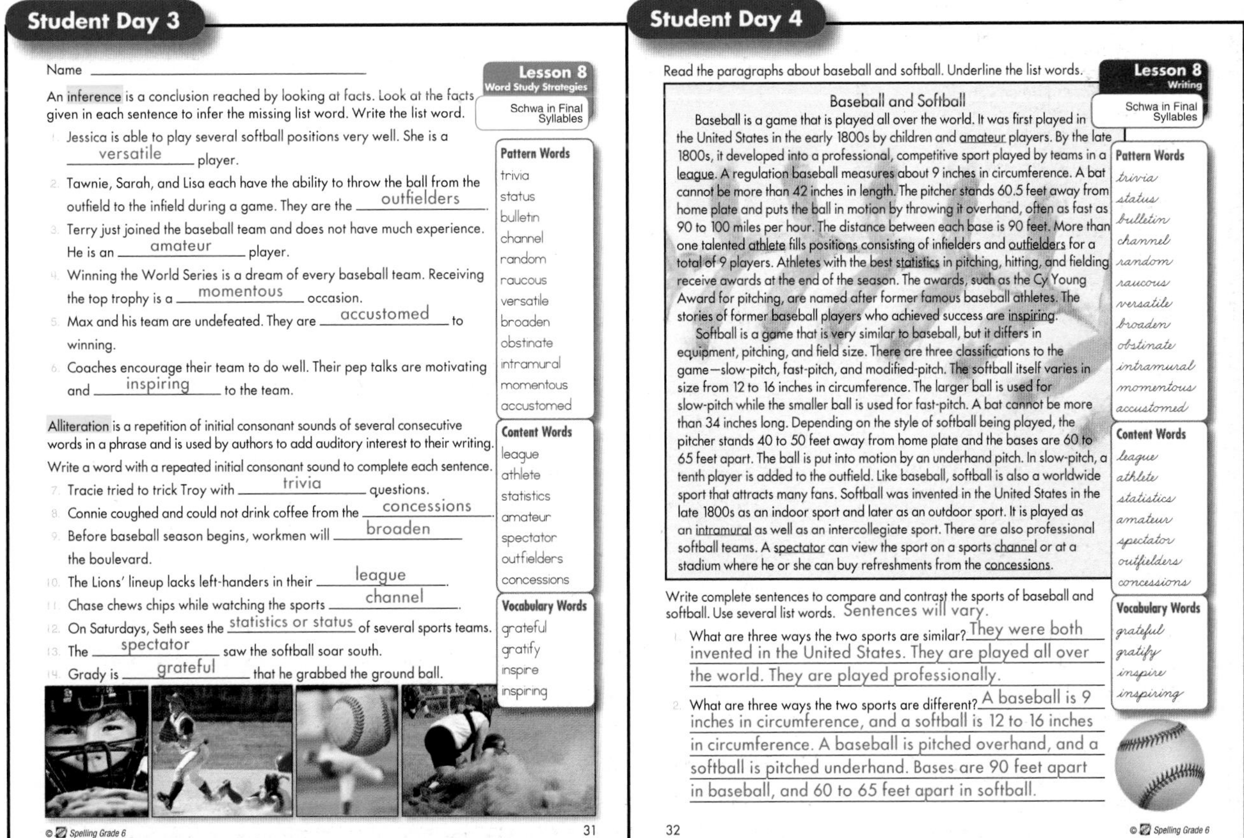

Student Day 3

Name ______

Lesson 8 Word Study Strategies — Schwa in Final Syllables

An inference is a conclusion reached by looking at facts. Look at the facts given in each sentence to infer the missing list word. Write the list word.

1. Jessica is able to play several softball positions very well. She is a versatile player.
2. Tawnie, Sarah, and Lisa each have the ability to throw the ball from the outfield to the infield during a game. They are the outfielders.
3. Terry just joined the baseball team and does not have much experience. He is an amateur player.
4. Winning the World Series is a dream of every baseball team. Receiving the top trophy is a momentous occasion.
5. Max and his team are undefeated. They are accustomed to winning.
6. Coaches encourage their team to do well. Their pep talks are motivating and inspiring to the team.

Alliteration is a repetition of initial consonant sounds of several consecutive words in a phrase and is used by authors to add auditory interest to their writing. Write a word with a repeated initial consonant sound to complete each sentence.

7. Tracie tried to trick Troy with trivia questions.
8. Connie coughed and could not drink coffee from the concessions.
9. Before baseball season begins, workmen will broaden the boulevard.
10. The Lions' lineup lacks left-handers in their league.
11. Chase chews chips while watching the sports channel.
12. On Saturdays, Seth sees the statistics or status of several sports teams.
13. The spectator saw the softball soar south.
14. Grady is grateful that he grabbed the ground ball.

Pattern Words: trivia, status, bulletin, channel, random, raucous, versatile, broaden, obstinate, intramural, momentous, accustomed

Content Words: league, athlete, statistics, amateur, spectator, outfielders, concessions

Vocabulary Words: grateful, gratify, inspire, inspiring

© Spelling Grade 6 — 31

Student Day 4

Lesson 8 Writing — Schwa in Final Syllables

Read the paragraphs about baseball and softball. Underline the list words.

Baseball and Softball

Baseball is a game that is played all over the world. It was first played in the United States in the early 1800s by children and amateur players. By the late 1800s, it developed into a professional, competitive sport played by teams in a league. A regulation baseball measures about 9 inches in circumference. A bat cannot be more than 42 inches in length. The pitcher stands 60.5 feet away from home plate and puts the ball in motion by throwing it overhand, often as fast as 90 to 100 miles per hour. The distance between each base is 90 feet. More than one talented athlete fills positions consisting of infielders and outfielders for a total of 9 players. Athletes with the best statistics in pitching, hitting, and fielding receive awards at the end of the season. The awards, such as the Cy Young Award for pitching, are named after former famous baseball athletes. The stories of former baseball players who achieved success are inspiring.

Softball is a game that is very similar to baseball, but it differs in equipment, pitching, and field size. There are three classifications to the game—slow-pitch, fast-pitch, and modified-pitch. The softball itself varies in size from 12 to 16 inches in circumference. The larger ball is used for slow-pitch while the smaller ball is used for fast-pitch. A bat cannot be more than 34 inches long. Depending on the style of softball being played, the pitcher stands 40 to 50 feet away from home plate and the bases are 60 to 65 feet apart. The ball is put into motion by an underhand pitch. In slow-pitch, a tenth player is added to the outfield. Like baseball, softball is also a worldwide sport that attracts many fans. Softball was invented in the United States in the late 1800s as an indoor sport and later as an outdoor sport. It is played as an intramural as well as an intercollegiate sport. There are also professional softball teams. A spectator can view the sport on a sports channel or at a stadium where he or she can buy refreshments from the concessions.

Write complete sentences to compare and contrast the sports of baseball and softball. Use several list words. Sentences will vary.

1. What are three ways the two sports are similar? They were both invented in the United States. They are played all over the world. They are played professionally.
2. What are three ways the two sports are different? A baseball is 9 inches in circumference, and a softball is 12 to 16 inches in circumference. A baseball is pitched overhand, and a softball is pitched underhand. Bases are 90 feet apart in baseball, and 60 to 65 feet apart in softball.

Pattern Words: trivia, status, bulletin, channel, random, raucous, versatile, broaden, obstinate, intramural, momentous, accustomed

Content Words: league, athlete, statistics, amateur, spectator, outfielders, concessions

Vocabulary Words: grateful, gratify, inspire, inspiring

32 — © Spelling Grade 6

Lesson 9

Schwa in Unstressed Syllables

Student Pages

Pages 33–36

Lesson Materials

BLM SP6-01B
Card stock
Index cards
Cash register paper tape
Sentence strips
T-7
BLM SP6-09A
BLM SP6-09B

Sports

The theme of this lesson is soccer. Soccer is the world's most popular sport and consists of eleven players on a regulation team. Players use any part of the body, except hands and arms, and attempt to bump or strike a ball into the opponent's goal. The sport's official name is *association football* and is more commonly known today as *football* or *soccer*. The word *soccer* is an altered term from the abbreviation of *association*.

Day 1 Pretest

Objective

The students will accurately spell and write words with **schwa in unstressed syllables**. They will spell and write content, vocabulary, and challenge words.

Introduction

Before class, select Challenge Words for numbers 24 and 25 from a cross-curricular subject, words misspelled on previous assignments, or words that interest your students. The word *metallic* has a **schwa in the unstressed syllable**, spelled *e*, and is suggested for number 24. Explain that they are to attempt to write all the spelling words.

Directed Instruction

1 Say each word, use it in a sentence, and then repeat the word.

Pattern Words

1. The crowd was aghast when the soccer player broke her ankle.
2. Tavonia did her algebra homework before soccer practice.
3. The new soccer stadium's layout antiquated the older stadium's design.
4. An apology was due after unsportsmanlike conduct was exhibited.
5. Donavan will celebrate the victory with his teammates.
6. The Lord wants us to have fervent charity toward each other.
7. Coach Sid drew a diagram of the new play strategy.
8. Many children try to imitate the athletic style of their favorite athlete.
9. Each individual on a soccer team is responsible for his or her actions.
10. The team manager placed the trophy on the pedestal.
11. The best teams qualified for the World Cup competition.
12. Billions of people received the World Cup broadcast via satellite.

Content Words

13. The amateur soccer association voted on the yearly budget.
14. Celeste played on defense during the last four games.
15. The goalkeeper dove and successfully blocked the kick.
16. Jerry led the offense to a victory in the final game.
17. Did you know that there is only one referee in a soccer game?
18. Tammy warmed up by stretching with other strikers on the team.
19. The soccer tournament began with a parade of athletes.

Vocabulary Words

20. The new coach was bilingual and was able to communicate effectively.
21. Soccer players receive a lot of exposure due to the sport's popularity.
22. Reina did impose her rules about penalties during the game.
23. Lester is proficient in the area of linguistics.

Challenge Words

24. ______________________________
25. ______________________________

2 Allow students to self-correct their Pretest. Write each word on the board. Point out that the Pattern Words contain at least one schwa in an unstressed syllable. Remind students that a schwa is a vowel sound identical to *short u*. The symbol ə indicates the schwa in the pronunciation shown in the Spelling Dictionary. An *unstressed syllable* is a syllable that is pronounced with less emphasis than the stressed syllable in the word. There is no accent mark on an unstressed syllable. Note the roots *lingu* and *pos* in the Vocabulary Words. Point out the following in the Vocabulary Words: *linguistics* contains two suffixes, *-ist* and *-ics*, silent *e* in *impose* is not included in the original root spelling *pos*.

3 As a class, read, spell, and read each word. Direct students to highlight misspelled words and rewrite them correctly.

4 Proof each student's Pretest. This becomes an individualized study sheet that can be used at school or at home.

5 Homework suggestion: Duplicate **BLM SP6-01B Flash Cards Template** on CARD STOCK for students to write the list words, using the flash cards as a study aid. Another option is to use INDEX CARDS.

Day 2 Word Analysis and Vocabulary

Objective

The students will read pronunciations and circle letters that make the schwa sound in unstressed syllables. They will complete sentences with content words. Students will use a table to write vocabulary words, complete sentences, and choose list words that match definitions.

Introduction

Invite students to refer to the list words, found on page 33, for this activity. Students locate the pronunciation for each Pattern Word, write each word on the board, and circle the letter(s) in the unaccented syllable(s) that make the schwa sound. Select seven volunteers to look up Content Words and read the definitions aloud.

Directed Instruction

1 Proceed to page 33. Say, spell, and say each Pattern, Content, and Vocabulary Word. Provide this week's Challenge Words and have students write them in the spaces provided. Students complete the page.

2 Proceed to page 34. Encourage students to use the table as an aid in building each Vocabulary Word. For example, the prefix *bi-* goes with the root *lingu* and the suffix *-al* to build the word *bilingual*. Allow students to complete the page independently. When complete, select a volunteer to read exercises 9–12 aloud.

Differentiated Instruction

- For students who spelled all the words correctly on the Pretest, select and assign Extra Challenge Words from the following list: congruence, characteristics, incongruity, feudalism, inheritability, crescendo.
- For students who spelled less than half correctly, assign the following Pattern, Content, and Vocabulary Words: charity, apology, qualified, pedestal, individual, celebrate, offense, defense, association, tournament, bilingual, exposure. On the Posttest, evaluate these students on the twelve words assigned; however, encourage them to attempt to spell all the list words to the best of their ability. They are also responsible for writing the dictated sentences.

Student Day 2

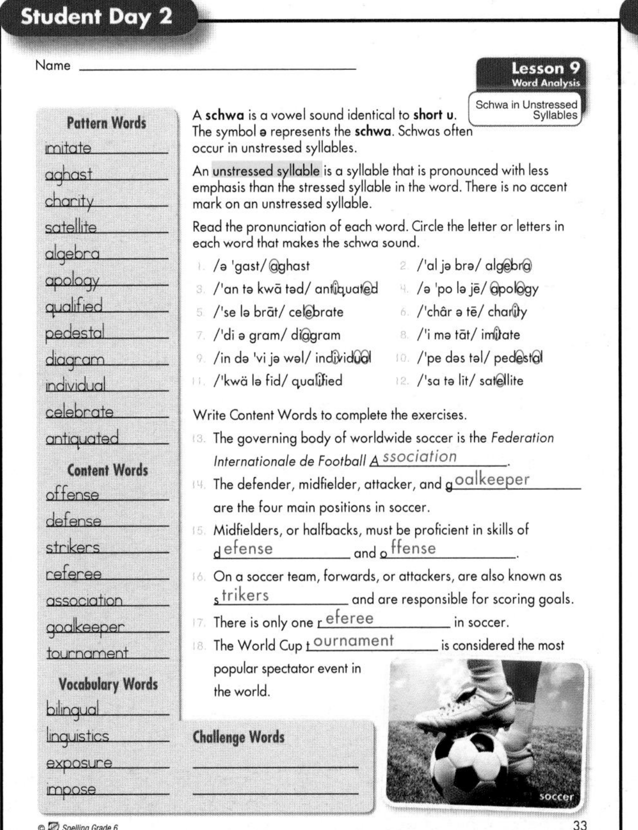

Student Day 2

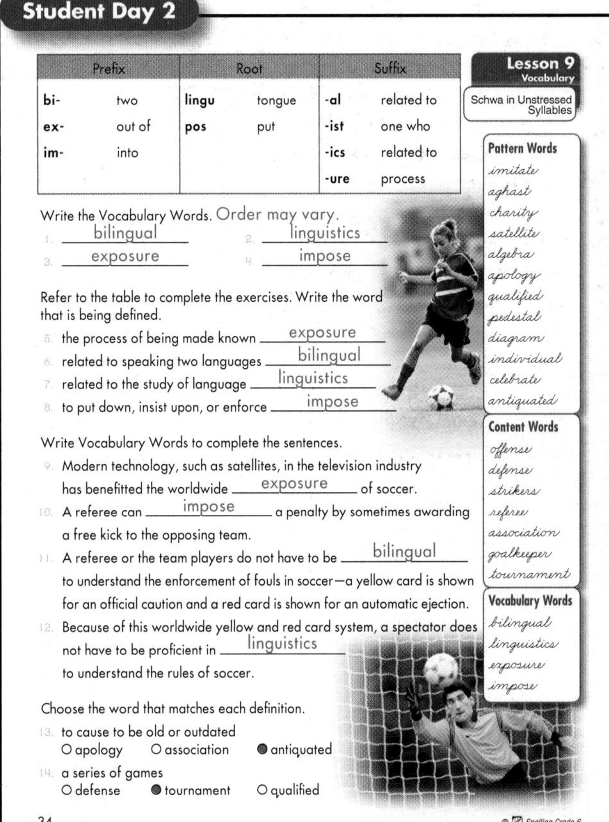

Student Spelling Support Materials

BLM SP6-01A
Soccer ball

Student Spelling Support

1. Use **BLM SP6-01A A Spelling Study Strategy** in instructional groups to provide assistance with some or all of the words.
2. Invite students to write the Challenge Words, numbers 24 and 25, in the Word Bank, in the back of their textbook.
3. Challenge students to research and write a brief report on the World Cup international tournament. Compile information in the progressive, sport journal that was started in Lesson 1.
4. Write this week's words, categorize the Pattern, Content, and Vocabulary Words, and attach them to the Word Wall.
5. Read 3 John 11: "Beloved, do not imitate what is evil, but what is good." Share about the dangers of imitating bad behaviors and the benefits of imitating good behaviors. Encourage students to share about personal experiences that others can learn from. Ask students to discuss how they can be imitators of Christ in their behavior.
6. To assist kinesthetic and visual learners, write the list words on small pieces of paper and tape to a SOCCER BALL. Have a student toss the ball to another student who selects a word and spells it.

3 Homework suggestion: Students use their Spelling Dictionary to write the definition of each word on the back of the corresponding flash card that was suggested for homework on Day 1.

Day 3 Word Study Strategies

Objective

The students will utilize dictionary skills by answering questions about the different components of dictionary entries. They will identify and write the compound predicate and simple predicate of given sentences.

Introduction

Select a few Pattern, Content, and Vocabulary Words. Write them on the board and instruct students to turn to their Spelling Dictionary. Challenge students to locate and verbalize the following components for each word: entry word, pronunciation, part of speech, definition, sample sentence.

Directed Instruction

1 Remind students that most every sentence in English is composed of a subject and predicate. Explain that some sentences may have a compound predicate. A *compound predicate* is made up of two or more predicates that share the same subject. Write the following sentence on the board:

- The soccer tournament finalists will celebrate their victory and run across the field. (**compound predicate: will celebrate their victory and run across the field; simple predicates: will celebrate, run**)

Invite a volunteer to come to the board, write the compound predicate, and then write each simple predicate. Note that simple predicates can be verbs or verb phrases.

2 Proceed to page 35. Allow students to work in collaborative groups to complete the page. When complete, review the page as a class.

Day 4 Writing

Objective

The students will use proofreading marks to identify mistakes in an action story. They will correctly write misspelled words and rewrite a run-on sentence as three complete sentences.

Introduction

Write the following run-on sentence on CASH REGISTER PAPER TAPE or on SENTENCE STRIPS that are taped together and display:

- The World Cup soccer tournament was being broadcast via satellite to millions of viewers a soccer tournament is very intense the soccer association does not tolerate rude conduct from its players.

Read the run-on sentence aloud without pausing. Ask students to state what is incorrect grammar. (**The ideas in the sentence are all jumbled together, and there are no punctuation marks.**) Define the following: A *run-on sentence* is an incorrect combination of two or more complete sentences. Select a volunteer to reread the sentence, stopping where a complete sentence ends. Cut the paper tape or sentence strip apart and insert a period at the end of the sentence. Capitalize the first letter of the next word. Select another volunteer to continue until the run-on sentence is broken into three complete sentences. (**The World Cup soccer tournament was being broadcast via satellite to millions of viewers. A soccer tournament is very intense. The soccer association does not tolerate rude conduct from its players.**)

Directed Instruction

1 Display **T-7 Proofreading an Action Story** on the overhead, keeping the bottom portion of the transparency covered. Read the text aloud. Correct the identified mistakes using the appropriate proofreading marks. Challenge students to identify the run-on sentence. Use **BLM SP6-09A T-7 Answer Key** as a guide. Uncover the bottom of the transparency and read the corrected version of the text.

2 Proceed to page 36. Students independently proofread the descriptive action story. Review all the necessary proofreading marks and corrections. (**6 misspellings; 2 capital letters needed; 2 periods needed; 3 deletes; 1 add something—*the*; 3 small letters needed; 1 new paragraph**) Select a volunteer to read 3 John 11. Compare and contrast the consequences of imitating good or bad behaviors.

3 Homework suggestion: Distribute a copy of **BLM SP6-09B Lesson 9 Homework** to each student.

Day 5 Posttest

Objective

The students will correctly write dictated spelling words and sentences.

Introduction

Review by using flash cards noted in Day 1 and Day 2 Homework suggestion.

Directed Assessment

1 Dictate the list words by using the Pretest sentences or developing original ones. Reserve *qualified, association, exposure, tournament, pedestal,* and *celebrate* for the dictation sentences.

2 Read each sentence. Repeat as needed.

- Our team qualified for the soccer finals.
- We were representing our local soccer association.
- The game was televised and provided a lot of exposure.
- We were successful in winning the tournament.
- Our coach placed our victory trophy on a pedestal.
- We decided to celebrate our victory with a pizza party.

3 If assigned, dictate Extra Challenge Words.

4 Score the test, counting each misspelled word as an error. Correct the dictation sentences by grading only the spelling words or grading the complete sentences.

Notes

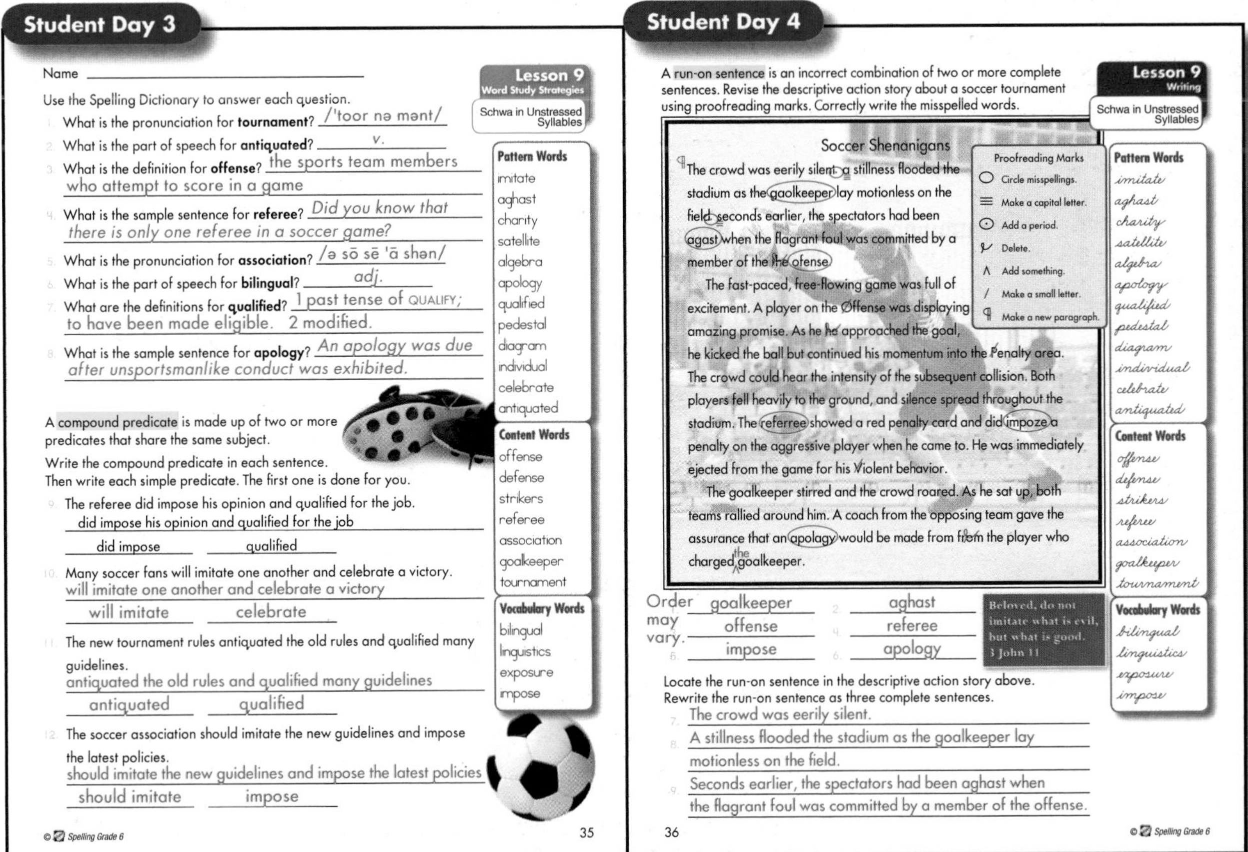

Lesson 10

Words with ci, si, ti, and xi

Student Pages

Pages 37–40

Lesson Materials

BLM SP6-01B
Card stock
Index cards
T-8
BLM SP6-10A

Sports

The theme of this lesson is basketball. One of the most popular games in the world, the sport of basketball has a long history, dating back to its invention in 1891 by James Naismith. Although it was originally played by men, basketball quickly gained popularity with women. Disabled athletes began to play basketball using wheelchairs at the end of World War II. Today, wheelchair basketball is a recognized Paralympic sport.

Day 1 Pretest

Objective

The students will accurately spell and write **words with ci, si, ti, and xi.** They will spell and write content, vocabulary, and challenge words.

Introduction

Before class, select Challenge Words for numbers 24 and 25 from a cross-curricular subject, words misspelled on previous assignments, or words that interest your students. The word *crucifixion* has **xi** and is suggested for number 24. Explain that they are to attempt to write all the spelling words.

Directed Instruction

1 Say each word, use it in a sentence, and then repeat the word.

Pattern Words

1. The teammates were anxious when one of the players was injured.
2. Basketball and other aerobic sports are beneficial to one's health.
3. Was there a discussion held about wheelchair basketball?
4. Kareema had the distinction of being the tallest player on the team.
5. It is especially important to practice free throws.
6. It is essential to warm up before practice.
7. A basket was accompanied by an explosion of applause.
8. The crowd's behavior during the game was obnoxious.
9. God is omniscient, omnipotent, and omnipresent.
10. Did the coach feel the team had a lot of potential ability?
11. Players who do not drink sufficient water risk dehydration.
12. Is this a transitional period for the Paralympics?

Content Words

13. Basketball is played in arenas throughout the world.
14. Because of her height, Nicole played center.
15. The official began the game with a jump ball.
16. The athletes were opponents on the court, but friends elsewhere.
17. The rebound changed the possession of the basketball.
18. Strategy and skill are vital to playing basketball.
19. A technical foul was called for poor sportsmanship.

Vocabulary Words

20. Todd did not want to appear disrespectful and interrupt a game.
21. Natasha was an immigrant from Russia.
22. The Petrov family wanted to migrate to North America.
23. It is important to demonstrate respectable conduct at all times.

Challenge Words

24. ______________________________
25. ______________________________

2 Allow students to self-correct their Pretest. Write each word on the board. Point out the *ci, si, ti,* or *xi* spelling in each Pattern Word. The spellings are variant spellings for the sounds /sh/ or /zh/. The *si* in *explosion* is pronounced /zh/. Note the roots *migr* and *spect* in the Vocabulary Words. The Vocabulary Word *disrespectful* has two prefixes, *dis-* and *re-*.

3 As a class, read, spell, and read each word. Direct students to highlight misspelled words and rewrite them correctly.

4 Proof each student's Pretest. This becomes an individualized study sheet that can be used at school or at home.

5 Homework suggestion: Duplicate **BLM SP6-01B Flash Cards Template** on CARD STOCK for students to write the list words, using the flash cards as a study aid. Another option is to use INDEX CARDS.

Day 2 Word Analysis and Vocabulary

Objective

The students will sort and write **words with ci, si, ti, and xi** and complete sentences with content words. They will use a table to write vocabulary words, select words to match definitions, and complete sentences in context. They will choose the best meaning for given words.

Introduction

Invite students to turn to page 37 and refer to the list words. Write the following headings on the board and select students to state examples of words containing each spelling:

ci	si	ti	xi
sufficient	explosion	potential	anxious
beneficial	discussion	essential	obnoxious
especially		distinction	
omniscient		transitional	

Because each spelling has the /sh/ or the /zh/ sound, the spellings must be memorized. Encourage students to highlight or underline each spelling in a different color on the Pattern Words in their set of flash cards that were suggested for homework on Day 1.

Directed Instruction

1 Proceed to page 37. Say, spell, and say each Pattern, Content, and Vocabulary Word. Provide this week's Challenge Words and have students write them in the spaces provided before completing the page.

2 Proceed to page 38. Remind students to use the table to assist in building each Vocabulary Word. For example, the prefix *im-* goes with the root *migr* and the suffix *-ant* to build the word *immigrant*. Allow students to complete the page independently.

Differentiated Instruction

- For students who spelled all the words correctly on the Pretest, select and assign Extra Challenge Words from the following list: cylindrical, chromosomes, onomatopoeia, ideological, immunization, dramatization.
- For students who spelled less than half correctly, assign the following Pattern, Content, and Vocabulary Words: anxious, potential, essential, sufficient, discussion, obnoxious, official, arenas, technical, opponents, immigrant, disrespectful.

On the Posttest, evaluate these students on the twelve words assigned; however, encourage them to attempt to spell all the list words to the best of their ability. They are also responsible for writing the dictated sentences.

Student Day 2

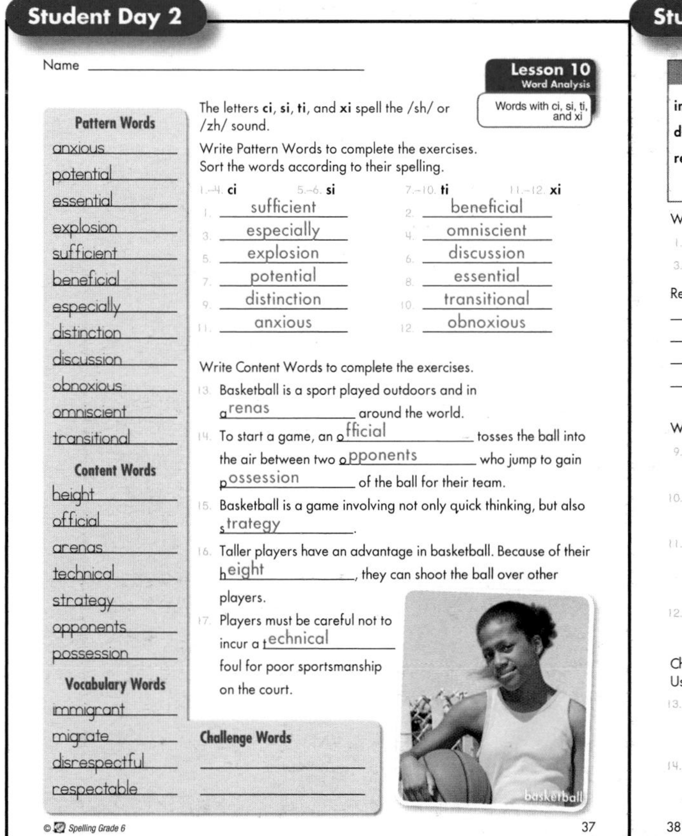

Name

Lesson 10 Word Analysis — Words with ci, si, ti, and xi

Pattern Words: anxious, potential, essential, explosion, sufficient, beneficial, especially, distinction, discussion, obnoxious, omniscient, transitional

Content Words: height, official, arenas, technical, strategy, opponents, possession

Vocabulary Words: immigrant, migrate, disrespectful, respectable

The letters **ci**, **si**, **ti**, and **xi** spell the /sh/ or /zh/ sound.

Write Pattern Words to complete the exercises. Sort the words according to their spelling.

1.–4. **ci** 5.–6. **si** 7.–10. **ti** 11.–12. **xi**

1. sufficient 2. beneficial
3. especially 4. omniscient
5. explosion 6. discussion
7. potential 8. essential
9. distinction 10. transitional
11. anxious 12. obnoxious

Write Content Words to complete the exercises.

13. Basketball is a sport played outdoors and in arenas around the world.
14. To start a game, an official tosses the ball into the air between two opponents who jump to gain possession of the ball for their team.
15. Basketball is a game involving not only quick thinking, but also strategy.
16. Taller players have an advantage in basketball. Because of their height, they can shoot the ball over other players.
17. Players must be careful not to incur a technical foul for poor sportsmanship on the court.

Challenge Words

© Spelling Grade 6 37

Student Day 2

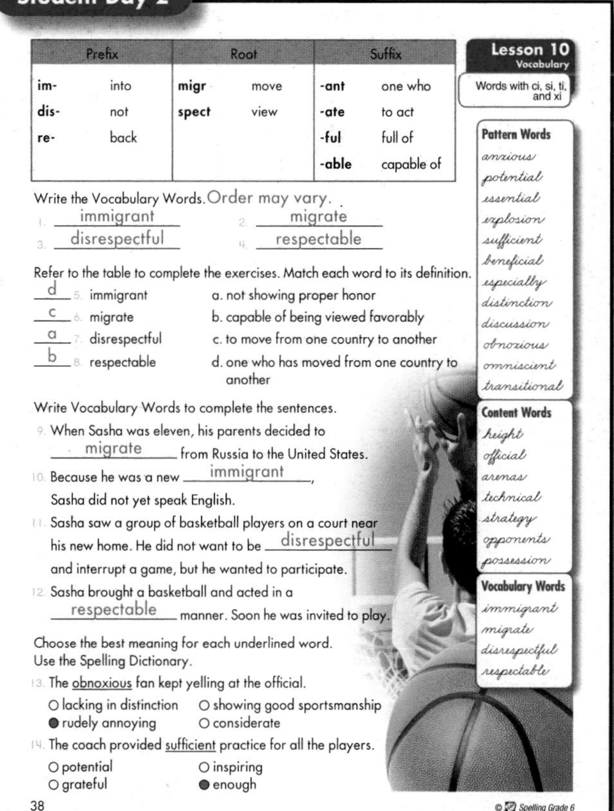

Prefix		Root		Suffix	
im-	into	**migr**	move	**-ant**	one who
dis-	not	**spect**	view	**-ate**	to act
re-	back			**-ful**	full of
				-able	capable of

Lesson 10 Vocabulary — Words with ci, si, ti, and xi

Write the Vocabulary Words. Order may vary.

1. immigrant 2. migrate
3. disrespectful 4. respectable

Refer to the table to complete the exercises. Match each word to its definition.

d 5. immigrant — a. not showing proper honor
c 6. migrate — b. capable of being viewed favorably
a 7. disrespectful — c. to move from one country to another
b 8. respectable — d. one who has moved from one country to another

Write Vocabulary Words to complete the sentences.

9. When Sasha was eleven, his parents decided to migrate from Russia to the United States.
10. Because he was a new immigrant, Sasha did not yet speak English.
11. Sasha saw a group of basketball players on a court near his new home. He did not want to be disrespectful and interrupt a game, but he wanted to participate.
12. Sasha brought a basketball and acted in a respectable manner. Soon he was invited to play.

Choose the best meaning for each underlined word. Use the Spelling Dictionary.

13. The obnoxious fan kept yelling at the official.
○ lacking in distinction ○ showing good sportsmanship
● rudely annoying ○ considerate

14. The coach provided sufficient practice for all the players.
○ potential ○ inspiring
○ grateful ● enough

Pattern Words: anxious, potential, essential, explosion, sufficient, beneficial, especially, distinction, discussion, obnoxious, omniscient, transitional

Content Words: height, official, arenas, technical, strategy, opponents, possession

Vocabulary Words: immigrant, migrate, disrespectful, respectable

38 © Spelling Grade 6

Student Spelling Support Materials

BLM SP6-01A

Student Spelling Support

1. Use **BLM SP6-01A A Spelling Study Strategy** in instructional groups to provide assistance with some or all of the words.
2. Invite students to write the Challenge Words, numbers 24 and 25, in the Word Bank, in the back of their textbook.
3. Challenge students to research the Paralympic games, using the Internet. Students choose a sport of interest and describe the sport in the progressive, sport journal that was started in Lesson 1.
4. Write this week's words, categorize the Pattern, Content, and Vocabulary Words, and attach them to the Word Wall.
5. Read Galatians 6:9: "And let us not grow weary while doing good, for in due season we shall reap if we do not lose heart." Just as athletes must not get discouraged through many practice sessions and drills, we as Christians need to persevere in doing good for others. Challenge students to write a paragraph describing how a good deed made a difference in the life of another person, or how a good deed done on another student's behalf helped him or her.
6. Expand students' study skills by providing a method for memorizing the *ci*, *si*, *ti*, and *xi* spellings in each Pattern Word. Instruct students to sort words according to their spellings and then to write a sentence using each spelling pattern; for example, The explo<u>si</u>on was the subject of discus<u>si</u>on, or The obno<u>xi</u>ous fan made the

Cont. on page 41

3 Homework suggestion: Students use their Spelling Dictionary to write the definition of each word on the back of the corresponding flash card that was suggested for homework on Day 1.

Day 3 Word Study Strategies

Objective

The students will complete riddles with Pattern Words. Students will write words that are related forms of given words. Students will use the meaning of related word forms to define list words.

Introduction

Invite students to turn to page 39 and refer to the Pattern Words. Ask the following riddles:

- Which word with *ti* is absolutely necessary? (**essential**)
- Which word with *si* is an oral consideration of a question or idea? (**discussion**)
- Which word with *ci* is that which improves one's well-being? (**beneficial**)

Select volunteers to provide the answer to each riddle.

Directed Instruction

1 Write the following sentences on the board, underlining words and leaving a blank space as shown:

- Something <u>transitory</u> tends to move away.
- A <u>transient</u> is a person who moves from place to place.
- Something _______ moves from one stage to another. (**transitional**)

Explain that the underlined words are related forms of the Pattern Word needed to complete the final sentence. Chorally read each sentence and choose a volunteer to write the word on the blank. Note that the meaning of each related form provides a clue to the meaning of the Pattern Word. Assist students to conclude that the prefix *trans-* implies movement. Knowing the meaning of a related form helps students in understanding new vocabulary.

2 Proceed to page 39. Students complete the page independently.

Day 4 Writing

Objective

The students will complete sentences in a descriptive dialogue with list words that match pronunciations.

Introduction

Display **T-8 Basketball Dialogue**, keeping the bottom portion covered. Define *dialogue* as <u>a conversation between two or more people</u>. The dialogue on the transparency gives the pronunciation for several list words followed by a blank. Students can refer to the list words found on page 40. Solicit volunteers to write the list word that matches each pronunciation by sounding out each word. Check the bottom of the transparency for accuracy. When complete, choose two volunteers to read the parts of CHRIS and PAT in the dialogue, substituting the pronunciation in the text for the list words.

Directed Instruction

1 Inform students that they will be reading a dialogue about a Paralympic sport, wheelchair basketball. The International Paralympics are a series of contests for athletes with disabilities held at the conclusion of the summer and winter Olympic Games.

2 Proceed to page 40. Encourage students to use the Spelling Dictionary to check the pronunciations of the list words as they complete the page independently.

3 Homework suggestion: Distribute a copy of **BLM SP6-10A Lesson 10 Homework** to each student.

Day 5 Posttest

Objective

The students will correctly write dictated spelling words and sentences.

Introduction

Review by using flash cards noted in Day 1 and Day 2 Homework suggestion.

Directed Assessment

1 Dictate the list words by using the Pretest sentences or developing original ones. Reserve *anxious, potential, sufficient, official, opponents*, and *disrespectful* for the dictation sentences.

2 Read each sentence. Repeat as needed.
- Timothy was anxious before the basketball tournament.
- He was concerned about a potential loss.
- Timothy knew the team had sufficient practice to play their best.
- The official on the court was ready for a jump ball.
- The opponents faced each other.
- None of the fans were disrespectful, and the tournament went well.

3 If assigned, dictate Extra Challenge Words.

4 Score the test, counting each misspelled word as an error. Correct the dictation sentences by grading only the spelling words or grading the complete sentences.

Student Spelling Support

Cont. from page 40

official feel anxious.

7. Invite students to write and perform their own sports dialogue centered around one of the following topics:
   - A young athlete argues with the referee's call and receives the consequences of his actions.
   - A young athlete gets in a fight on court and has to face a difficult conversation with his coach after the game.
   - A player is excited because his team is going to the finals, however, his parents have asked him to skip the game and attend his uncle's funeral.

   Encourage students to incorporate spelling words into their dialogue, utilize Scriptures to back up their dialogue content, and to frame each athlete's appropriate or inappropriate response to authority.

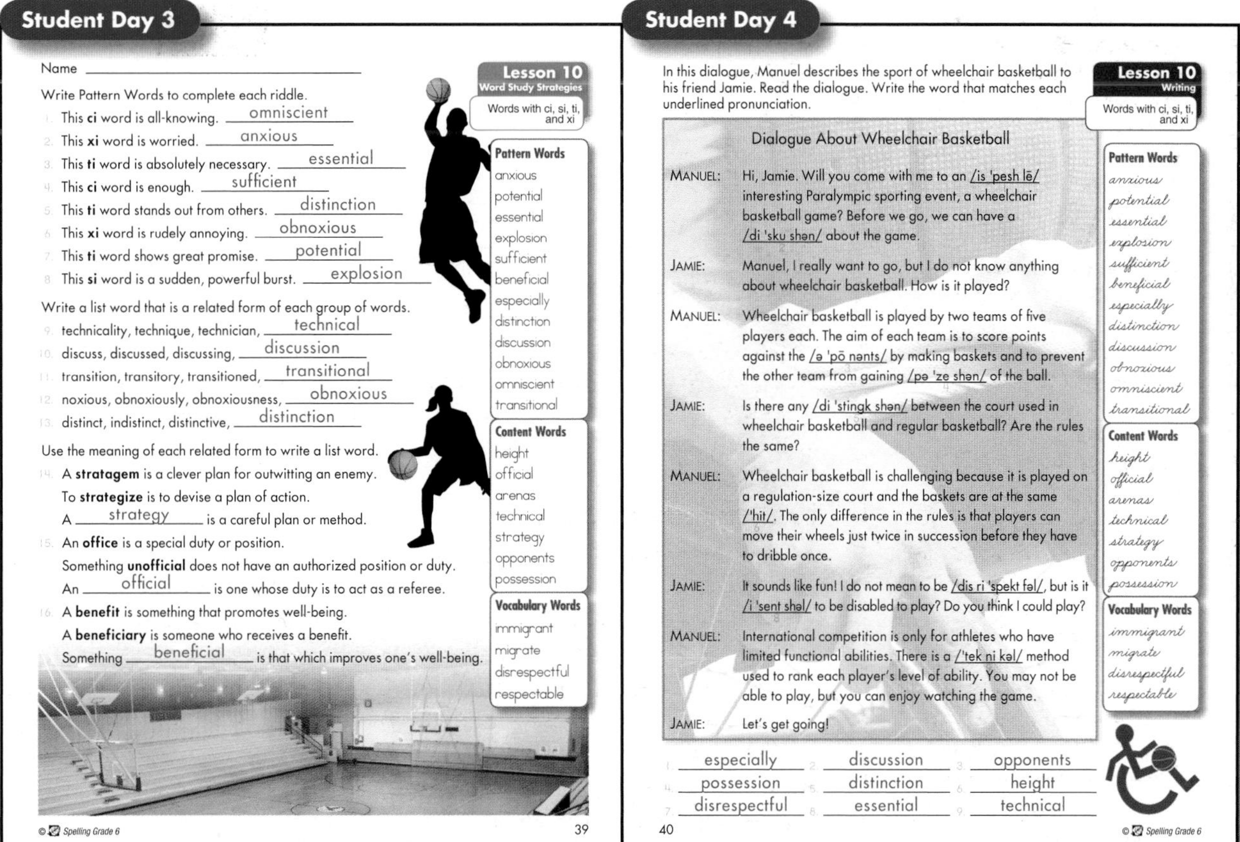

Student Day 3

Lesson 10 — Word Study Strategies — Words with ci, si, ti, and xi

Name ____________

Write Pattern Words to complete each riddle.
1. This **ci** word is all-knowing. omniscient
2. This **xi** word is worried. anxious
3. This **ti** word is absolutely necessary. essential
4. This **ci** word is enough. sufficient
5. This **ti** word stands out from others. distinction
6. This **xi** word is rudely annoying. obnoxious
7. This **ti** word shows great promise. potential
8. This **si** word is a sudden, powerful burst. explosion

Write a list word that is a related form of each group of words.
9. technicality, technique, technician, technical
10. discuss, discussed, discussing, discussion
11. transition, transitory, transitioned, transitional
12. noxious, obnoxiously, obnoxiousness, obnoxious
13. distinct, indistinct, distinctive, distinction

Use the meaning of each related form to write a list word.
14. A **stratagem** is a clever plan for outwitting an enemy. To **strategize** is to devise a plan of action. A strategy is a careful plan or method.
15. An **office** is a special duty or position. Something **unofficial** does not have an authorized position or duty. An official is one whose duty is to act as a referee.
16. A **benefit** is something that promotes well-being. A **beneficiary** is someone who receives a benefit. Something beneficial is that which improves one's well-being.

Pattern Words: anxious, potential, essential, explosion, sufficient, beneficial, especially, distinction, discussion, obnoxious, omniscient, transitional

Content Words: height, official, arenas, technical, strategy, opponents, possession

Vocabulary Words: immigrant, migrate, disrespectful, respectable

© Spelling Grade 6 — 39

Student Day 4

Lesson 10 — Writing — Words with ci, si, ti, and xi

In this dialogue, Manuel describes the sport of wheelchair basketball to his friend Jamie. Read the dialogue. Write the word that matches each underlined pronunciation.

Dialogue About Wheelchair Basketball

MANUEL: Hi, Jamie. Will you come with me to an /is 'pesh lē/ interesting Paralympic sporting event, a wheelchair basketball game? Before we go, we can have a /di 'sku shən/ about the game.

JAMIE: Manuel, I really want to go, but I do not know anything about wheelchair basketball. How is it played?

MANUEL: Wheelchair basketball is played by two teams of five players each. The aim of each team is to score points against the /ə 'pō nənts/ by making baskets and to prevent the other team from gaining /pə 'ze shən/ of the ball.

JAMIE: Is there any /di 'stingk shən/ between the court used in wheelchair basketball and regular basketball? Are the rules the same?

MANUEL: Wheelchair basketball is challenging because it is played on a regulation-size court and the baskets are at the same /'hīt/. The only difference in the rules is that players can move their wheels just twice in succession before they have to dribble once.

JAMIE: It sounds like fun! I do not mean to be /dis ri 'spekt fəl/, but is it /i 'sent shəl/ to be disabled to play? Do you think I could play?

MANUEL: International competition is only for athletes who have limited functional abilities. There is a /'tek ni kəl/ method used to rank each player's level of ability. You may not be able to play, but you can enjoy watching the game.

JAMIE: Let's get going!

1. especially 2. discussion 3. opponents
4. possession 5. distinction 6. height
7. disrespectful 8. essential 9. technical

Pattern Words: anxious, potential, essential, explosion, sufficient, beneficial, especially, distinction, discussion, obnoxious, omniscient, transitional

Content Words: height, official, arenas, technical, strategy, opponents, possession

Vocabulary Words: immigrant, migrate, disrespectful, respectable

40 — © Spelling Grade 6

Lesson 11 Consonants Before i and u

Student Pages

Pages 41–44

Lesson Materials

BLM SP6-01B
Card stock
Index cards
BLM SP6-11A

Sports

The theme of this lesson is volleyball. Volleyball is a popular team sport that can be played indoors or outdoors. The goal of volleyball is to hit an inflated, spherical ball back and forth over a high net that divides a rectangular court. Volleyball was invented in 1895 by an American named William Morgan. At the time, Morgan was the director of physical education at the YMCA in Holyoke, Massachusetts.

Day 1 Pretest

Objective

The students will accurately spell and write words with **consonants before i and u**. They will spell and write content, vocabulary, and challenge words.

Introduction

Before class, select Challenge Words for numbers 24 and 25 from a cross-curricular subject, words misspelled on previous assignments, or words that interest your students. The word *opinionated* has **consonant n before i, pronounced /y/**, and is suggested for number 24. Explain that they are to attempt to write all the spelling words.

Directed Instruction

1 Say each word, use it in a sentence, and then repeat the word.

Pattern Words

1. The volleyball player's behavior was exemplary.
2. Misty exhibited brilliant technique on the court.
3. Kevin played a casual game of beach volleyball yesterday.
4. Jesus is our ever faithful and loyal companion.
5. Gabe gave a cordial smile to his new teammate.
6. A spike is a familiar offensive technique in volleyball.
7. Kari noticed that the day was gradually getting warmer.
8. An athlete can become a millionaire through product endorsements.
9. Trisha tried to persuade the referee to change his decision.
10. The team doctor followed the proper procedure to treat the injury.
11. The coach checked all of the time schedules before the big meet.
12. Franklin is a senior member of the volleyball team.

Content Words

13. Team cooperation is necessary for a successful outcome.
14. Volleyball players need to have a lot of endurance.
15. The college volleyball match was held in the gymnasium.
16. The sand court was rectangular and bordered by bleachers.
17. A tall net separated the two volleyball teams.
18. The inflated, spherical volleyball was white and black.
19. A volleyball player is not allowed to hit the ball twice in succession.

Vocabulary Words

20. The announcer gave a detailed description of the game's highlights.
21. Jesse renewed his sport's magazine subscription last week.
22. Capitalism is characterized as a free, competitive market.
23. An athlete may capitalize on an opponent's mistake during a game.

Challenge Words

24. ______________________
25. ______________________

2 Allow students to self-correct their Pretest. Write each word on the board. Point out the following in the Pattern Words: words with *li*, *ni*, or *vi* that make the /y/ sound, words with *di* or *du* that make the /j/ sound, words with *su* that make the /sw/ or /zh/ sound. Note the roots *capit* and *script* in the Vocabulary Words. Point out the following in the Vocabulary Words: *capitalism* contains two suffixes, *-al* and *-ism*, *capitalize* contains two suffixes, *-al* and *-ize*.

3 As a class, read, spell, and read each word. Direct students to highlight misspelled words and rewrite them correctly.

4 Proof each student's Pretest. This becomes an individualized study sheet that can be used at school or at home.

5 Homework suggestion: Distribute **BLM SP6-01B Flash Cards Template** on CARD STOCK for students to write the list words, using the flash cards as a study aid. Another option is to use INDEX CARDS.

Day 2 Word Analysis and Vocabulary

Objective

The students will sort and write words with **consonants before i and u**. They will complete sentences with content words. Students will use a table to write vocabulary words, complete sentences, and choose list words that match definitions.

Introduction

Write the following categories on the board: *li, ni,* or *vi* pronounced /y/, *di* or *du* pronounced /j/, *su* pronunced /sw/, *su* pronounced /zh/. Invite students to refer to the list words, found on page 41, for this activity. Challenge students to locate Pattern Words that fall under the categories written on the board. **(*li, ni,* or *vi* pronounced /y/: senior, brilliant, familiar, behavior, millionaire, companion; *di* or *du* pronounced /j/: cordial, gradually, schedules, procedure; *su* pronounced /sw/: persuade; *su* pronounced /zh/: casual)**

Directed Instruction

1 Select a few Content Words from the lesson and challenge students to a race to look up each correlating definition in their Spelling Dictionary. Students raise their hand and read each definition aloud.

2 Proceed to page 41. Say, spell, and say each Pattern, Content, and Vocabulary Word. Provide this week's Challenge Words and have students write them in the spaces provided. Students complete the page.

3 Proceed to page 42. Encourage students to use the table as an aid in building each Vocabulary Word. For example, the root *capit* goes with the suffixes *-al* and *-ism* to build the word *capitalism*. Allow students

Differentiated Instruction

- For students who spelled all the words correctly on the Pretest, select and assign Extra Challenge Words from the following list: variance, criteria, neoclassical, immobility, osteoporosis, orchestral.
- For students who spelled less than half correctly, assign the following Pattern, Content, and Vocabulary Words: senior, casual, brilliant, behavior, schedules, persuade, separated, endurance, gymnasium, cooperation, capitalize, description. On the Posttest, evaluate these students on the twelve words assigned; however, encourage them to attempt to spell all the list words to the best of their ability. They are also responsible for writing the dictated sentences.

61 pts.

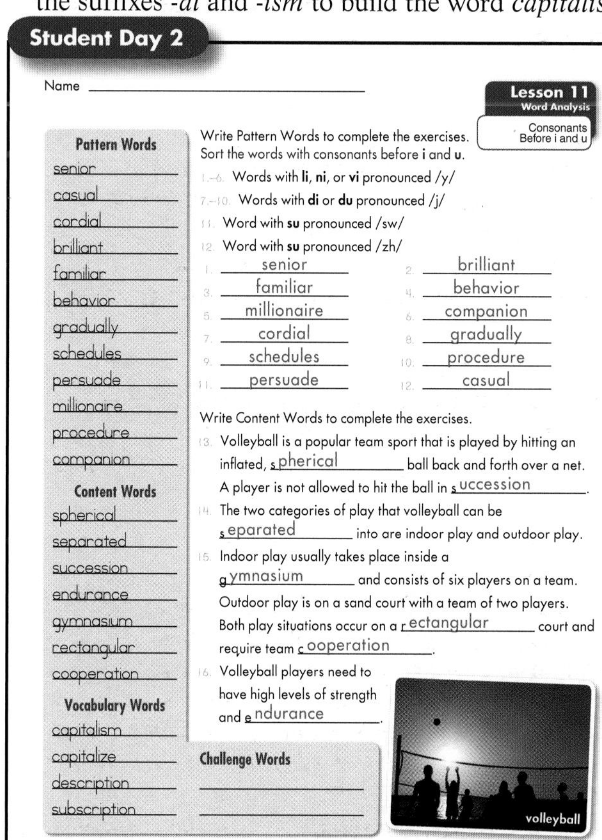

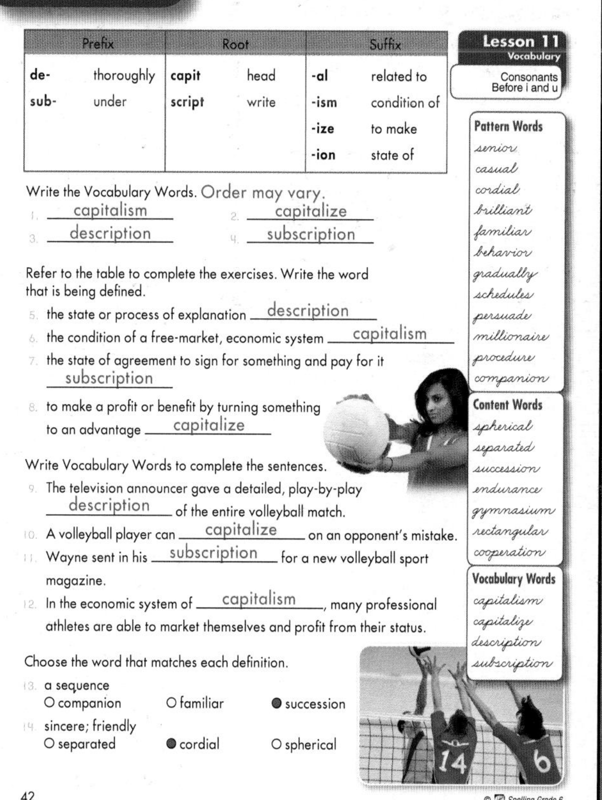

Student Spelling Support Materials

BLM SP6-01A

Student Spelling Support

1. Use **BLM SP6-01A A Spelling Study Strategy** in instructional groups to provide assistance with some or all of the words.
2. Invite students to write the Challenge Words, numbers 24 and 25, in the Word Bank, in the back of their textbook.
3. Challenge students to research and write a brief report on the origins of the team sport of volleyball. Compile information in the progressive, sport journal that was started in Lesson 1.
4. Write this week's words, categorize the Pattern, Content, and Vocabulary Words, and attach them to the Word Wall.
5. Read Romans 12:10, 16: "Be kindly affectionate to one another with brotherly love, in honor giving preference to one another.... Be of the same mind toward one another." Discuss how the Lord wants us to exemplify a loving behavior and attitude in all that we do, including sports. Encourage students to share about a time that they displayed proper, sportsmanlike conduct and the results that ensued. Students may also wish to share about an experience when a bad attitude was displayed and how that behavior choice affected them and others.
6. Invite students to meet in small groups and design a poster of biblically based sportsmanship rules for classroom games or sports of choice.

Cont. on page 45

to complete the page independently. When complete, select a volunteer to read exercises 9–12 aloud.

4 Homework suggestion: Students use their Spelling Dictionary to write the definition of each word on the back of the corresponding flash card that was suggested for homework on Day 1.

Day 3 Word Study Strategies

Objective

The students will categorize list words. They will identify and write compound subjects and compound predicates.

Introduction

Before class, write the following incomplete word lists on the board:

- talented, skillful, gifted, ______ (**brilliant**)
- sequence, series, progression, ______ (**succession**)
- payment, contribution, donation, ______ (**subscription**)

Review the following: A *category* is a group or set of things that are classified together. Point out that the words in each list have common characteristics, forming a category. Invite students to refer to the list words, found on page 43, as you choose volunteers to select a list word that belongs in each category. Have volunteers state the category and why they chose each word before filling in the blank.

Directed Instruction

1 Review the following definitions: A compound subject is made up of two or more subjects that share the same predicate. A compound predicate is made up of two or more predicates that share the same subject. Inform students that a sentence can contain both a compound subject and a compound predicate.

2 Write the following on the board:

- The coach and the team did persuade the officials and convinced the federation to review the rules.

Challenge students to locate the compound subject and compound predicate in the sentence. (**compound subject: The coach and the team; compound predicate: did persuade the officials and convinced the federation to review the rules**)

3 Proceed to page 43. Allow students to work in collaborative groups to complete exercises 1–15. When complete, review the page as a class.

Day 4 Writing

Objective

The students will read stanzas in a poem and replace synonyms with list words.

Introduction

Write the following short poem, with underlines, on the board:

A divided team will not perform at its best;
All should cooperate and certainly invest.
Collaboration and teamwork are key,
To assist the team in a victory!

Select a volunteer to read the poem aloud. Note that the first and second lines rhyme, and the third and fourth lines of the poem rhyme. This is an example of an AABB rhyme scheme.

Directed Instruction

1 Invite students to refer to the list words, found on page 44, for this activity. Students may also use their Spelling Dictionary. Challenge students to locate list words that are synonyms for the underlined words in the poem. (**separated; cooperation**) For each list word identified, erase the synonym on the board and write the list word in its place. Chorally read the rewritten poem.

2 Proceed to page 44. Students complete the page. When complete, select volunteers to read the stanzas of the poem. Challenge students to identify the rhyming words and the rhyme scheme in the poem.

3 Select a volunteer to read Romans 12:10,16. Use the verses and the last stanza of the poem as a discussion starter on what it means and what one should do to exemplify successful sportsmanship.

4 Homework suggestion: Distribute a copy of **BLM SP6-11A Lesson 11 Homework** to each student.

Day 5 Posttest

Objective

The students will correctly write dictated spelling words and sentences.

Introduction

Review by using flash cards noted in Day 1 and Day 2 Homework suggestion.

Directed Assessment

1 Dictate the list words by using the Pretest sentences or developing original ones. Reserve *senior, description, behavior, endurance, schedules,* and *cooperation* for the dictation sentences.

2 Read each sentence. Repeat as needed.

- Ron is a senior staff reporter for the local newspaper.
- He wrote a detailed description of a volleyball tournament.
- Ron noted the behavior of each athlete in the tournament.
- The players were very competitive and had a lot of endurance.
- The rotation of play schedules was very demanding.
- Every player contributed, and team cooperation was noticeable.

3 If assigned, dictate Extra Challenge Words.

4 Score the test, counting each misspelled word as an error. Correct the dictation sentences by grading only the spelling words or grading the complete sentences.

Student Spelling Support

Cont. from page 44

7. Challenge students to use selected list words to write AABB rhyme scheme poems that teach biblically based sportsmanship principles. The poems can be four lines, eight lines, twelve lines, or sixteen lines. Invite students to read their poems aloud and post them on the bulletin board.

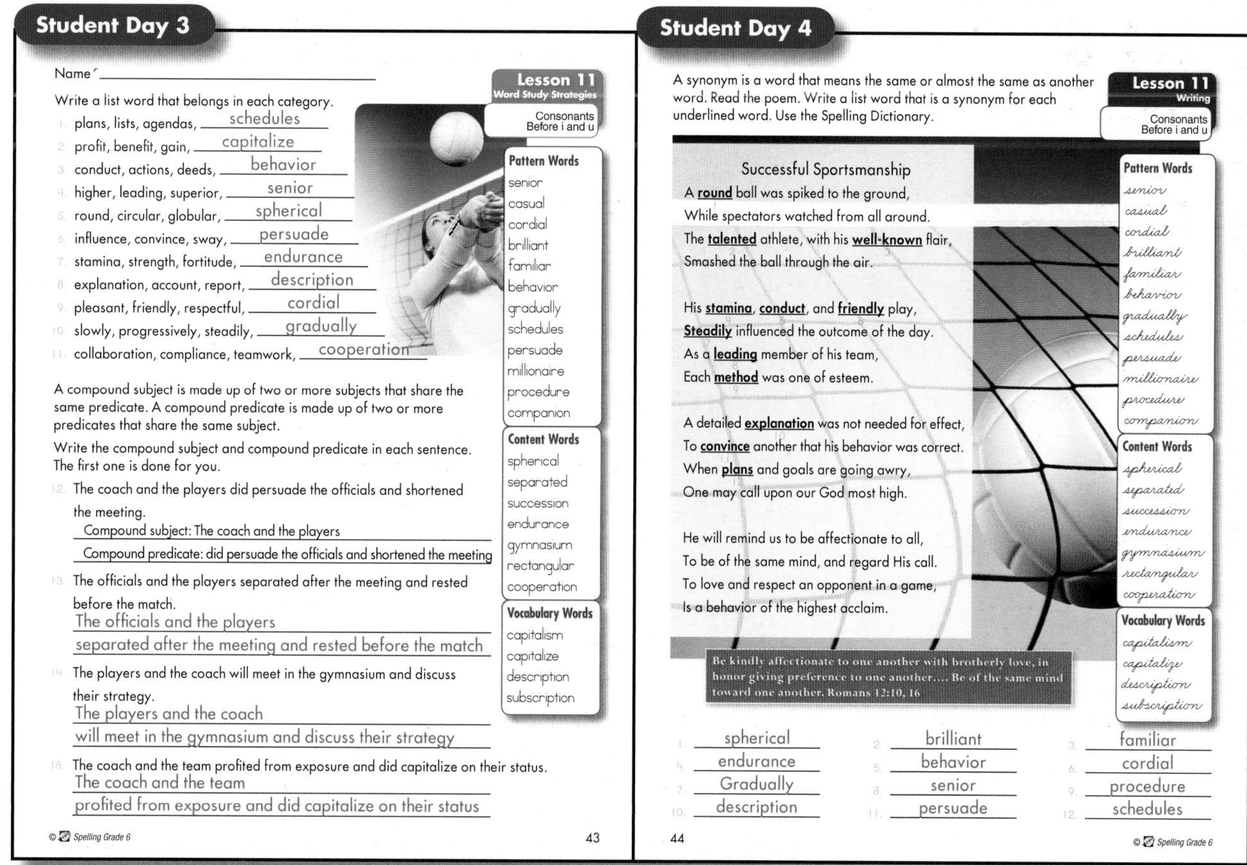

Lesson 12

Review Lessons 7–11

Student Pages

Pages 45–48

Lesson Materials

T-9
BLM SP6-12A
BLM SP6-12B
T-5
BLM SP6-12C
BLM SP6-12D
BLMs SP6-12E–F
BLM SP6-06G
BLM SP6-12G

Day 1 Schwa o

Objective

The students will identify and sort words that have a **schwa o** in the first, second, or third syllable.

Introduction

Teacher Note: This week's lesson incorporates the Pattern, Content, and Vocabulary Words taught in Lessons 7–11 using a variety of activities such as sorting, filling in the correct answer circle, a word search, a coordinate grid, a crossword puzzle, shape boxes in a story format, and writing words from given roots.

Display **T-9 Lessons 7–11 Study Sheet** on the overhead to review Lesson 7 words in unison, using the say-spell-say technique. Remind students that a schwa is a vowel sound identical to *short u*.

Directed Instruction

1 Pronounce each word and challenge students to raise one, two, or three fingers to indicate the syllable that contains the **schwa o**.
- first syllable—**collide, collegiate, concludes, configured, committee, community**
- second syllable—**eloquent, recollect, accolades, unconvinced, recommend**
- third syllable—**development**

2 Proceed to page 45. Explain that the box contains all the Pattern, Content, and Vocabulary Words in Lessons 7–11. This list is the same list of words that was previously displayed on the overhead. Encourage students to use this list as a review tool. Instruct students to read the directions and independently complete the page.

3 Distribute a copy of **BLM SP6-12A Lessons 7–11 Study Sheet** to each student to take home for study.

4 Homework suggestion: Distribute a copy of **BLM SP6-12B Lesson 12 Homework I** to each student to practice words with **schwa o, schwa in final syllables**, **schwa in unstressed syllables**, and **words with ci, si, ti, and xi**. Remind students to review their weekly sets of flash cards from Lessons 7–11.

Day 2 Schwa in Final Syllables and Schwa in Unstressed Syllables

Objective

The students will select an appropriate answer circle to indicate if words with **schwa in final syllables** are spelled correctly or incorrectly, and correctly write the word. They will find and write words with **schwa in unstressed syllables** in a word search.

Introduction

Display **T-9 Lessons 7–11 Study Sheet** to review Lessons 8–9 words in unison, using the say-spell-say technique. Remind students that although schwa has the *short u* sound, it can be spelled with the letters *a, e, i, ou, o,* or *u*. Challenge students to identify the vowel that makes the schwa sound in Lessons 8–9 words.

Directed Instruction

1 Write the following activity on the board to provide practice for the exercises on the student page:

	Correct	Incorrect	
trivia	O	O	**(correct; trivia)**
bulleten	O	O	**(incorrect; bulletin)**
momentus	O	O	**(incorrect; momentous)**

Read each word and select volunteers to identify if each word is spelled correctly or incorrectly. Fill in each appropriate answer circle. Correctly write each word.

2 Before class, prepare **T-5 Word Search Grid** by writing the following Pattern Words from Lesson 9: imitate, aghast, charity, diagram. Position the words across, down, backwards, and diagonally. Fill in the remaining boxes with various letters to hide the words. Write the words hidden in the word search on the board. Place the transparency on the overhead, and challenge students to find and circle the words. An example word search is shown.

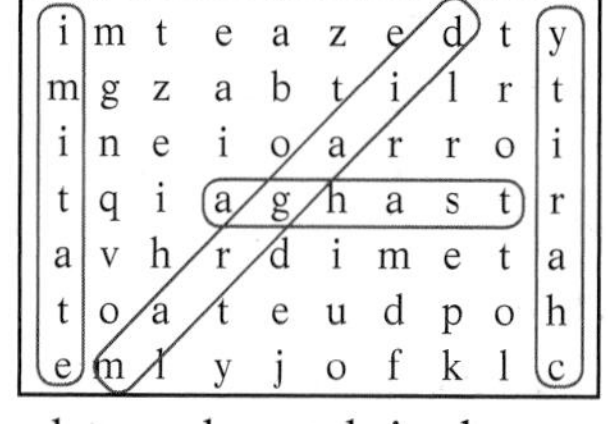

3 Proceed to page 46. Students complete the page.

4 Homework suggestion: Distribute a copy of **BLM SP6-12C Lesson 12 Homework II** to each student to practice **consonants before i and u**, Content Words, and Vocabulary Words.

Day 3 Words with ci, si, ti, and xi and Consonants Before i and u

Objective

The students will use a grid to spell **words with ci, si, ti, and xi**. They will complete a crossword puzzle with words containing **consonants before i and u**.

Introduction

Display **T-9 Lessons 7–11 Study Sheet** to review Lessons 10–11 words in unison, using the say-spell-say technique.

Directed Instruction

1 Draw the following grid on the board:

	A	B	C
1	si	ni	al
2	in	tion	scient
3	tran	ly	om

Demonstrate how to go across the top to find the letter and then down the correct number of boxes to find the syllables to build a word. Invite volunteers to find the Pattern Word from Lesson 10, using the following coordinates:

- C3 + B1 + C2 = _______ **(omniscient)**
- A3 + A1 + B2 + C1 = _______ **(transitional)**

2 Pronounce a Pattern Word from Lesson 11, found on page 47, and have students locate the word in their Spelling Dictionary. The first student to find the definition stands and reads the word and

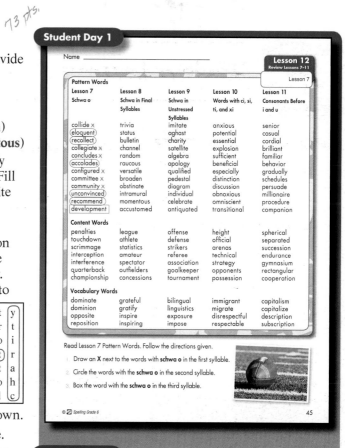

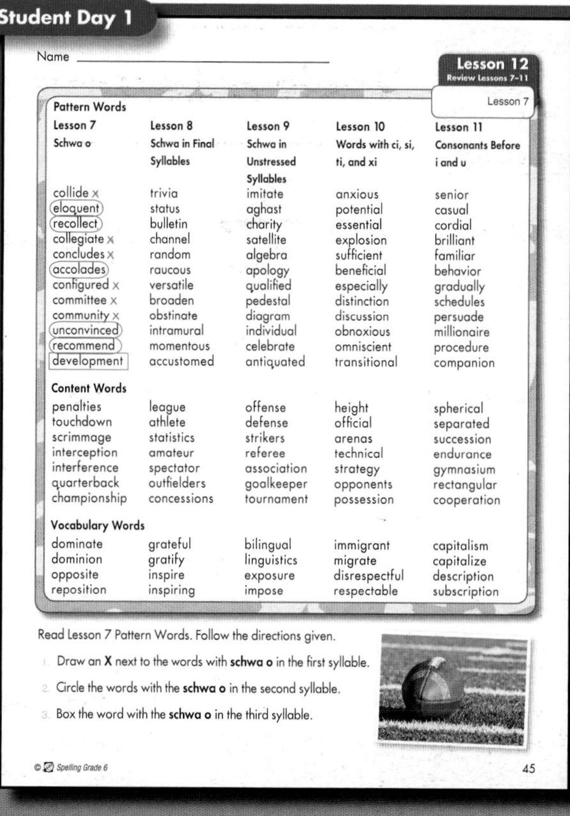

Student Day 1

Name ______________________

Lesson 12 Review Lessons 7–11

Lesson 7

Pattern Words

Lesson 7 Schwa o	**Lesson 8** Schwa in Final Syllables	**Lesson 9** Schwa in Unstressed Syllables	**Lesson 10** Words with ci, si, ti, and xi	**Lesson 11** Consonants Before i and u
collide x	trivia	imitate	anxious	senior
(eloquent)	status	aghast	potential	casual
(recollect)	bulletin	charity	essential	cordial
collegiate x	channel	satellite	explosion	brilliant
concludes x	random	algebra	sufficient	familiar
(accolades)	raucous	apology	beneficial	behavior
configured x	versatile	qualified	especially	gradually
committee x	broaden	pedestal	distinction	schedules
community x	obstinate	diagram	discussion	persuade
(unconvinced)	intramural	individual	obnoxious	millionaire
(recommend)	momentous	celebrate	omniscient	procedure
[development]	accustomed	antiquated	transitional	companion

Content Words

penalties	league	offense	height	spherical
touchdown	athlete	defense	official	separated
scrimmage	statistics	strikers	arenas	succession
interception	amateur	referee	technical	endurance
interference	spectator	association	strategy	gymnasium
quarterback	outfielders	goalkeeper	opponents	rectangular
championship	concessions	tournament	possession	cooperation

Vocabulary Words

dominate	grateful	bilingual	immigrant	capitalism
dominion	gratify	linguistics	migrate	capitalize
opposite	inspire	exposure	disrespectful	description
reposition	inspiring	impose	respectable	subscription

Read Lesson 7 Pattern Words. Follow the directions given.

1. Draw an **X** next to the words with **schwa o** in the first syllable.
2. Circle the words with the **schwa o** in the second syllable.
3. Box the word with the **schwa o** in the third syllable.

© Spelling Grade 6 45

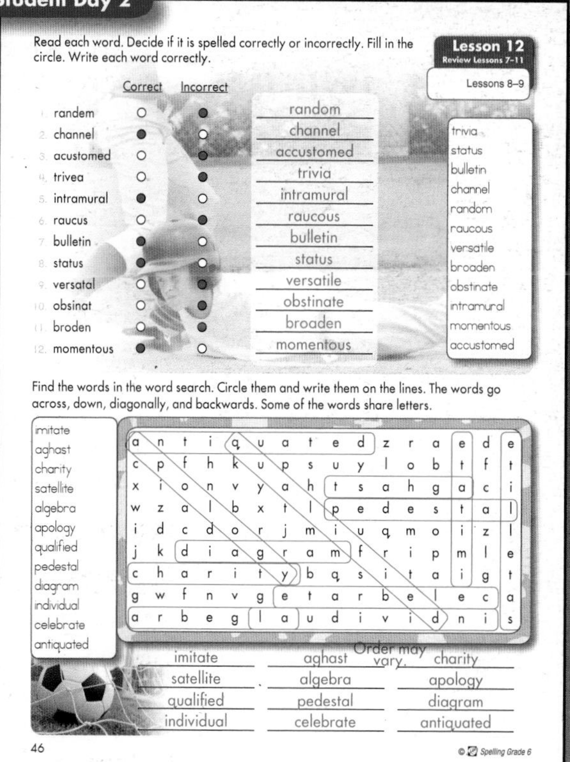

Student Day 2

Read each word. Decide if it is spelled correctly or incorrectly. Fill in the circle. Write each word correctly.

Lesson 12 Review Lessons 7–11

Lessons 8–9

		Correct	Incorrect	
1.	randem	O	●	random
2.	channel	●	O	channel
3.	acustomed	O	●	accustomed
4.	trivea	O	●	trivia
5.	intramural	●	O	intramural
6.	raucus	O	●	raucous
7.	bulletin	●	O	bulletin
8.	status	●	O	status
9.	versatal	O	●	versatile
10.	obsinat	O	●	obstinate
11.	broden	O	●	broaden
12.	momentous	●	O	momentous

trivia, status, bulletin, channel, random, raucous, versatile, broaden, obstinate, intramural, momentous, accustomed

Find the words in the word search. Circle them and write them on the lines. The words go across, down, diagonally, and backwards. Some of the words share letters.

imitate, aghast, charity, satellite, algebra, apology, qualified, pedestal, diagram, individual, celebrate, antiquated

a	n	t	i	q	u	a	t	e	d	z	r	a	e	d	e
c	p	f	h	k	u	p	s	u	y	l	o	b	t	f	t
x	i	o	n	v	y	a	h	t	s	a	h	g	a	c	i
w	z	a	l	b	x	t	l	p	e	d	e	s	t	a	l
i	d	c	d	o	r	j	m	i	u	q	m	o	i	z	l
j	k	d	i	a	g	r	a	m	f	r	i	p	m	l	e
c	h	a	r	i	t	y	b	q	s	i	t	a	i	g	t
g	w	f	n	v	g	e	t	a	r	b	e	l	e	c	a
a	r	b	e	g	l	a	u	d	i	v	i	d	n	i	s

Order may vary.

imitate	aghast	charity
satellite	algebra	apology
qualified	pedestal	diagram
individual	celebrate	antiquated

46 © Spelling Grade 6

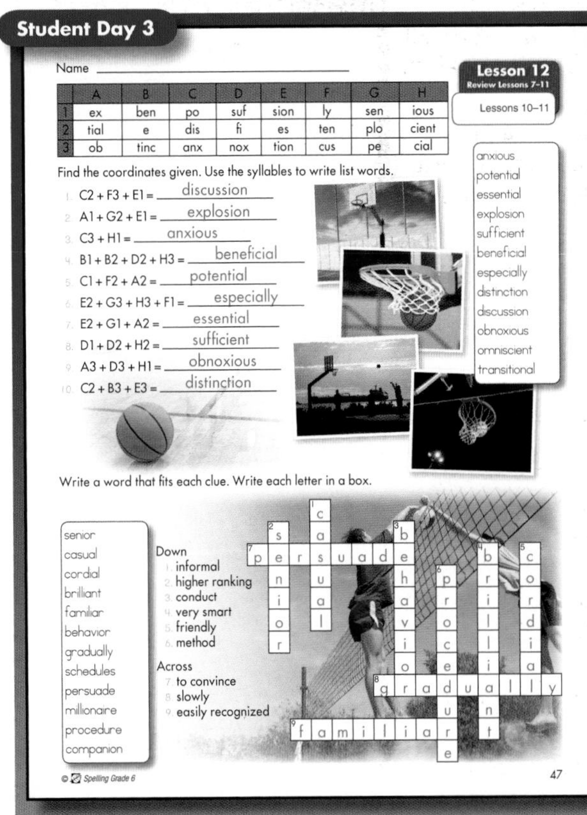
Student Day 3

Name ______________________

Lesson 12
Review Lessons 7–11
Lessons 10–11

	A	B	C	D	E	F	G	H
1	ex	ben	po	suf	sion	ly	sen	ious
2	tial	e	dis	fi	es	ten	plo	cient
3	ob	tinc	anx	nox	tion	cus	pe	cial

Find the coordinates given. Use the syllables to write list words.

1. C2 + F3 + E1 = discussion
2. A1 + G2 + E1 = explosion
3. C3 + H1 = anxious
4. B1 + B2 + D2 + H3 = beneficial
5. C1 + F2 + A2 = potential
6. E2 + G3 + H3 + F1 = especially
7. E2 + G1 + A2 = essential
8. D1 + D2 + H2 = sufficient
9. A3 + D3 + H1 = obnoxious
10. C2 + B3 + E3 = distinction

anxious, potential, essential, explosion, sufficient, beneficial, especially, distinction, discussion, obnoxious, omniscient, transitional

Write a word that fits each clue. Write each letter in a box.

senior, casual, cordial, brilliant, familiar, behavior, gradually, schedules, persuade, millionaire, procedure, companion

Down
1. informal
2. higher ranking
3. conduct
4. very smart
5. friendly
6. method

Across
7. to convince
8. slowly
9. easily recognized

© Spelling Grade 6 47

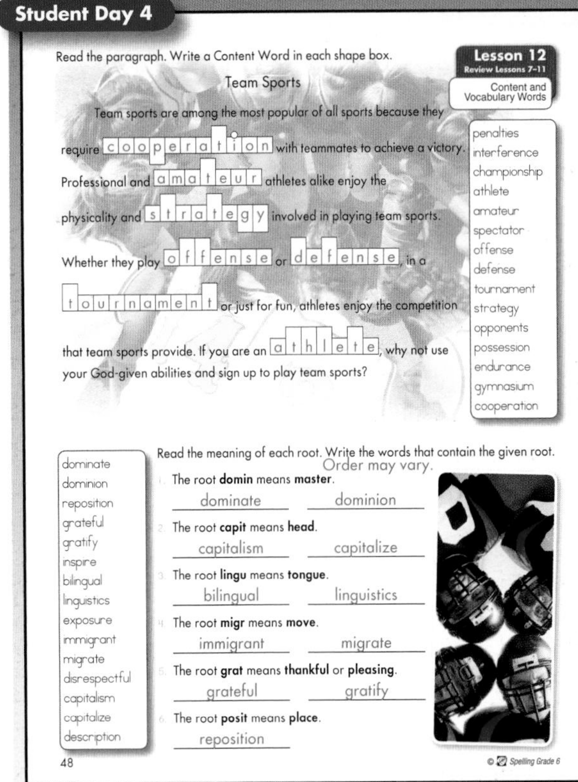
Student Day 4

Read the paragraph. Write a Content Word in each shape box.

Lesson 12
Review Lessons 7–11
Content and Vocabulary Words

Team Sports

Team sports are among the most popular of all sports because they require cooperation with teammates to achieve a victory. Professional and amateur athletes alike enjoy the physicality and strategy involved in playing team sports. Whether they play offense or defense in a tournament or just for fun, athletes enjoy the competition that team sports provide. If you are an athlete, why not use your God-given abilities and sign up to play team sports?

penalties, interference, championship, athlete, amateur, spectator, offense, defense, tournament, strategy, opponents, possession, endurance, gymnasium, cooperation

dominate, dominion, reposition, grateful, gratify, inspire, bilingual, linguistics, exposure, immigrant, migrate, disrespectful, capitalism, capitalize, description

Read the meaning of each root. Write the words that contain the given root.
Order may vary.

1. The root **domin** means **master**. dominate dominion
2. The root **capit** means **head**. capitalism capitalize
3. The root **lingu** means **tongue**. bilingual linguistics
4. The root **migr** means **move**. immigrant migrate
5. The root **grat** means **thankful** or **pleasing**. grateful gratify
6. The root **posit** means **place**. reposition

48 © Spelling Grade 6

its definition. As a challenge, read the Spelling Dictionary definition of a Pattern Word from Lesson 11. Have students determine which Pattern Word is being defined. Students verify the accuracy of the Pattern Word and its definition by looking it up in their Spelling Dictionary. Students volunteer to name the Pattern Word.

3 Proceed to page 47. Allow students to complete the page independently.

Day 4 Content Words and Vocabulary Words

Objective

The students will write content words in shape boxes to complete sentences. They will write vocabulary words from a given root and its meaning.

Introduction

Display **T-9 Lessons 7–11 Study Sheet** to review Content and Vocabulary Words in unison, using the say-spell-say technique.

Directed Instruction

1 Invite five volunteers to select a Content Word and draw its corresponding shape box on the board. Each volunteer should select a Content Word from a different column in order to prevent any duplicates. Select additional volunteers to write the correct Content Word in the shape boxes. Students may refer to the list of Content Words displayed on **T-9 Lessons 7–11 Study Sheet**.

2 Write the following meaning of each root on the board:
- The root *spir* means *breathe.* **(inspire, inspiring)**
- The root *script* means *write.* **(description, subscription)**

Select volunteers to read the root, its meaning, and state two Vocabulary Words containing that root. Students may refer to **T-9 Lessons 7–11 Study Sheet** on the overhead for the Vocabulary Words.

3 Proceed to page 48. Students complete the page independently. When completed, select a student to read the paragraph titled "Team Sports" at the top of the page.

4 Homework suggestion: Distribute a copy of **BLM SP6-12D Lessons 7–11 Test Prep** to each student to practice with many of the words that may appear on the Assessment. Prepare for the Assessment by studying the words on **BLM SP6-12A Lessons 7–11 Study Sheet** that was sent home on Day 1 or by using their flash card sets.

Day 5 Assessment

Objective

The students will accurately select the appropriate answer within the context of a sentence. They will fill in the corresponding answer circle.

Introduction

Teacher Note: The Test makes provision for

Differentiated Instruction. The first twelve sentences include the words assigned to students with shortened lists. Encourage these students to try all the sentences, but only grade the first twelve sentences. The Test is found on two blackline masters.

Duplicate a copy of **BLMs SP6-12E–F Lessons 7–11 Test I** and **II** and distribute to each student. Duplicate **BLM SP6-06G Student Answer Form** and cut apart. Distribute one answer form to each student. Remind students to fill in each answer circle completely and to erase completely if they wish to change an answer.

Directed Assessment

1 Instruct students to listen as you dictate the following Sample:

Sample

Outfelders will sometimes collide when playing defense. All correct
A B C D

Say, "Are any of the first three underlined words misspelled?" Pause for replies. Inform students that the letter *A* is below the underlined word that is misspelled. (**Outfielders**) Guide students to the answer form that was previously distributed. Lead students to find the Sample box and fill in the appropriate answer circle containing the same letter. Say, "You will continue in the same way. You will read each sentence, choose the word that you think is misspelled, and fill in the corresponding circle on the answer form. If all the words are spelled correctly, fill in the fourth circle, labeled *D*, for *All correct*."

2 Assist students as needed while they read the sentences and complete the Test on their own.

1. The offense scored a touchdown during the scrimmage.
2. The obnoxious spectator gave an apology before he left.
3. Raul, a bilingual immigrant, is inspiring to his soccer team.
4. A potential championship gave the team good reason to celebrate.
5. A quarterback from a major league shows charity at an orphanage.
6. The official separated the aggressive opponents.
7. The anchors on the sports channel recollect the momentous play.
8. The endurance of an individual is essential to the success of a team.
9. Tom configured the schedule of the tournament and did a brilliant job.
10. We would be grateful if you would recommend our gymnasium.
11. The athlete is anxious that the trophy will fall off the pedestal.
12. The bulletin contained a description of the new arenas.
13. The millionaire received accolades from the community for his gift.
14. The subscription to the magazine will gratify the amateur player.
15. Our spiritual development will broaden with exposure to the Word.
16. It is the job of the strikers to impose goal attempts upon the goalkeeper.
17. The obstinate player gradually collected too many penalties.
18. Paul concludes our Lord is omniscient and His grace is sufficient.
19. The senior player qualified for a collegiate scholarship.
20. The raucous crowd burst into an explosion after the interception.
21. The diagram included spherical and rectangular shapes.
22. Before the game, the coaches' discussion was casual and cordial.
23. The pastor is not accustomed to less than respectable behavior.
24. The referee had to reposition the ball according to the procedure.
25. Height is a physical distinction that is beneficial in basketball.

3 Refer to **BLM SP6-12G Lessons 7–11 Answer Key** when correcting the Test.

Notes

Lesson 13

Homophones and Homographs

Student Pages

Pages 49–52

Lesson Materials

BLM SP6-01B
Card stock
Index cards
T-10
BLM SP6-13A

Sports

Lessons 13–17 utilize the theme of water sports. The theme of this lesson is swimming and diving. Swimming is a major aspect of most water sports as well as its own individual sport. Swimming is considered one of the most complete forms of exercise because it works the majority of the muscles and provides resistance and aerobic benefits. Divers perform basic dives, somersaults, and twists from a platform or springboard. Divers have about two seconds to perform acrobatics before straightening their body and entering the water headfirst.

Day 1 Pretest

Objective

The students will accurately spell and write words that are **homophones** and **homographs**. They will spell and write content, vocabulary, and challenge words.

Introduction

Before class, select Challenge Words for numbers 24 and 25 from a cross-curricular subject, words misspelled on previous assignments, or words that interest your students. The word *discussed* is a **homophone** for *disgust* and is suggested for number 24. Administer the Pretest.

Directed Instruction

1 Say each word, use it in a sentence, and then repeat the word.

Pattern Words

1. The captain used stationery to write thank-you notes to the team.
2. A diving board is stationary since it is bolted to the concrete.
3. Rae received a compliment from Bonnie for her improved time.
4. Judd's skills complement the swim team.
5. A good coach will counsel athletes to help improve their skills.
6. The swim council meets every Tuesday.
7. The principal congratulated the team for its winning performance.
8. Judges at a swim and diving meet must be people of principle.
9. Michaella began to compact the swim gear into her bag.
10. The community pool director does not permit swimming alone.
11. Wade did his best at the meet, so he is content with his diving score.
12. The contrast of colors on the swimsuits was striking.

Content Words

13. Aquatics include swimming and diving.
14. A diver implements acrobatics into his or her routine.
15. Each dive is assigned a level of difficulty.
16. Do you wear goggles when you swim?
17. A medley relay consists of swimmers doing different strokes.
18. Can you smell the chlorine in a swimming pool?
19. A diver can dive off of a springboard or platform.

Vocabulary Words

20. The transparency of the water allowed Seth to see the sunken rings.
21. It is apparent that Marcus has a God-given talent for swimming.
22. The boys slept in a dormitory during sports camp.
23. The flowers that had been dormant began to bloom.

Challenge Words

24. ______________________
25. ______________________

2 Allow students to self-correct their Pretest. Write each word on the board. Point out that this week's list contains Pattern Words that are **homophones** and **homographs**. Teach that *homophones* are words that sound the same but have different meanings and spellings. *Homographs* are words that are spelled alike but have different meanings. They may also be pronounced differently. The pronunciation of the homograph depends upon the way the word is used in context. Note the roots *dorm*, *it*, and *par* in the Vocabulary Words. Words may have more than one root. The word *dormitory* has two roots, *dorm* and *it*.

3 As a class, read, spell, and read each word. Direct students to highlight misspelled words and rewrite them correctly.

4 Proof each student's Pretest. This becomes an individualized study sheet that can be used at school or at home.

5 Homework suggestion: Duplicate **BLM SP6-01B Flash Cards Template** on CARD STOCK for students to write the list words, using the flash cards as a study aid. Another option is to use INDEX CARDS.

Day 2 Word Analysis and Vocabulary

Objective

The students will sort and write pattern words that are **homophones** and **homographs**. They will write content words to complete sentences. Students will use a table to write vocabulary words and complete sentences in context. They will choose words to match given definitions.

Introduction

Teacher Note: The Pretest sentences include each of the **homophones** but only one of each homograph. A homograph for each Pattern Word is shown on **T-10 Homophones and Homographs**. The Spelling Dictionary lists each homograph as a separate entry word.

Select volunteers to find the definition(s) in the Spelling Dictionary of each homophone pair—council/counsel, principal/principle, stationary/stationery, compliment/complement—and both the first and second entry word of each homograph—permit, content, contrast, compact. Recite each word and invite the volunteer to read the definition.

Directed Instruction

1 Display **T-10 Homophones and Homographs**, covering the bottom portion on **Homographs** and the answers, to teach the following:

- The men of the *council* sat at a table to conduct their meetings. The homophone *counsel* can be a noun meaning *advice*—Jennifer went to her mother for counsel. *Counsel* can also be a verb meaning *to advise*—Mother is always willing to counsel her.

Differentiated Instruction

- For students who spelled all the words correctly on the Pretest, select and assign Extra Challenge Words from the following list: tangency, crystalline, acronym, instinctive, antioxidant, pentatonic.
- For students who spelled less than half correctly, assign the following Pattern, Content, and Vocabulary Words: counsel, principal, stationery, permit, content, contrast, goggles, aquatics, difficulty, springboard, dormant, apparent. On the Posttest, evaluate these students on the twelve words assigned; however, encourage them to attempt to spell all the list words to the best of their ability. They are also responsible for writing the dictated sentences.

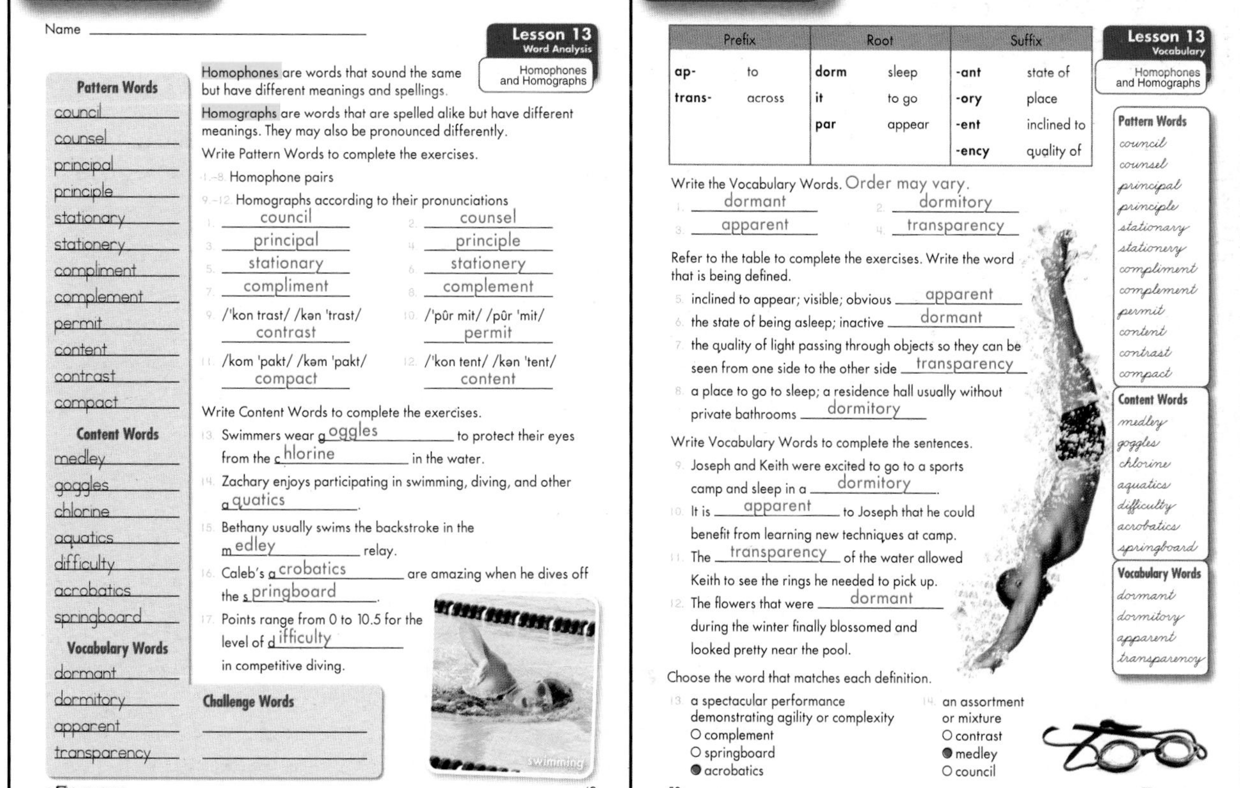

Student Day 2

Name ______________

Lesson 13 Word Analysis — Homophones and Homographs

Pattern Words: council, counsel, principal, principle, stationary, stationery, compliment, complement, permit, content, contrast, compact

Content Words: medley, goggles, chlorine, aquatics, difficulty, acrobatics, springboard

Vocabulary Words: dormant, dormitory, apparent, transparency

Homophones are words that sound the same but have different meanings and spellings.

Homographs are words that are spelled alike but have different meanings. They may also be pronounced differently.

Write Pattern Words to complete the exercises.

1.–8. Homophone pairs

9.–12. Homographs according to their pronunciations

1. council 2. counsel
3. principal 4. principle
5. stationary 6. stationery
7. compliment 8. complement
9. /'kon trast/ /kən 'trast/ contrast 10. /'pûr mit/ /pûr 'mit/ permit
11. /kom 'pakt/ /kəm 'pakt/ compact 12. /'kon tent/ /kən 'tent/ content

Write Content Words to complete the exercises.

13. Swimmers wear goggles to protect their eyes from the chlorine in the water.
14. Zachary enjoys participating in swimming, diving, and other aquatics.
15. Bethany usually swims the backstroke in the medley relay.
16. Caleb's acrobatics are amazing when he dives off the springboard.
17. Points range from 0 to 10.5 for the level of difficulty in competitive diving.

Challenge Words

swimming

© Spelling Grade 6 49

Student Day 2

Prefix		Root		Suffix	
ap-	to	dorm	sleep	-ant	state of
trans-	across	it	to go	-ory	place
		par	appear	-ent	inclined to
				-ency	quality of

Lesson 13 Vocabulary — Homophones and Homographs

Write the Vocabulary Words. Order may vary.

1. dormant 2. dormitory
3. apparent 4. transparency

Refer to the table to complete the exercises. Write the word that is being defined.

5. inclined to appear; visible; obvious apparent
6. the state of being asleep; inactive dormant
7. the quality of light passing through objects so they can be seen from one side to the other side transparency
8. a place to go to sleep; a residence hall usually without private bathrooms dormitory

Write Vocabulary Words to complete the sentences.

9. Joseph and Keith were excited to go to a sports camp and sleep in a dormitory.
10. It is apparent to Joseph that he could benefit from learning new techniques at camp.
11. The transparency of the water allowed Keith to see the rings he needed to pick up.
12. The flowers that were dormant during the winter finally blossomed and looked pretty near the pool.

Choose the word that matches each definition.

13. a spectacular performance demonstrating agility or complexity
   - O complement
   - O springboard
   - ● acrobatics

14. an assortment or mixture
   - O contrast
   - ● medley
   - O council

Pattern Words: council, counsel, principal, principle, stationary, stationery, compliment, complement, permit, content, contrast, compact

Content Words: medley, goggles, chlorine, aquatics, difficulty, acrobatics, springboard

Vocabulary Words: dormant, dormitory, apparent, transparency

50 © Spelling Grade 6

Student Spelling Support Materials

BLM SP6-01A

Student Spelling Support

1. Use **BLM SP6-01A A Spelling Study Strategy** in instructional groups to provide assistance with some or all of the words.
2. Invite students to write the Challenge Words, numbers 24 and 25, in the Word Bank, in the back of their textbook.
3. Have students write a narrative about a time they went swimming either in a pool or at the beach. Have them include several list words.
4. Write this week's words, categorize the Pattern, Content, and Vocabulary Words, and attach them to the Word Wall.
5. Read Job 12:13: "With Him are wisdom and strength, He has **counsel** and understanding." Explain that the wisest **counsel** a person could ever receive is from our Lord God. His wisdom and understanding far exceed our own. He is ready and willing to help us and He completely understands our needs.
6. Challenge students to conduct key word searches by using the Internet to locate a Bible concordance. Ask students to identify three biblically based principles as they relate to **counsel** from God, parents, teachers, peers, or pastors.
7. Invite students to write a narration of a story, factual or fiction, that teaches a **principle**.

- *Principal* can be remembered as the principal is your pal. *Principle* can be remembered as a principle is a rule.
- *Stationary* can be remembered by the a in, "Stay stationary!" *Stationery* can be remembered by the e in a pen, used with stationery.
- *Compliment* can be remembered by the letter *i* in, "I can give someone a compliment." *Complement* can be remembered by the e in complete, as in Sean's skills complement the swim team.

2 Uncover the bottom portion but keep the answers covered. Read each sentence and the pronunciations. Circle the correct pronunciation. Read the uncircled pronunciations and ask students to generate sentences.

3 Proceed to page 49. Say, spell, and say each Pattern, Content, and Vocabulary Word. Provide this week's Challenge Words and have students write them in the spaces provided before completing the page.

4 Proceed to page 50. Encourage students to use the table as an aid in building each Vocabulary Word. For example, the root *dorm* goes with the suffix *-ant* to get the word *dormant*. Refer to *apparent* and point out that the letter *p* is attached to the prefix *a-* because *a-* takes on the first letter of the root it is attached to—*par*. This forms a double consonant pattern that only occurs when the prefix *a-* means *to* or *toward*. Students complete the page.

5 Homework suggestion: Students use their Spelling Dictionary to write the definition of each word on the back of the corresponding flash card that was suggested for homework on Day 1.

Day 3 Word Study Strategies

Objective

The students will write parts of speech and definitions and circle the correct pronunciations for **homographs**. They will write the correct **homophones** in sentences.

Introduction

Write the pronunciations for the following **homographs**: /'pûr mit/, /pûr 'mit/; /'kon tent/, /kən 'tent/; /'kon trast/, /kən 'trast/; /kom 'pakt/, /kəm 'pakt/. Pronounce each word, pointing out the stressed syllable. Use each word in a sentence and identify the part of speech.

Directed Instruction

1 Say each bulleted pronunciation and the two definitions. Have volunteers name the definition that matches the pronunciation.

- /pûr 'mit/—to allow; give consent; authorize, or a license (**to allow; give consent; authorize**)
- /kən 'tent/—satisfied, or something contained (**satisfied**)
- /kən 'trast/—a sharp or striking difference, or to compare the differences of (**to compare the differences of**)
- /kəm 'pakt/—combine; to press together, or occupying a small space (**combine; to press together**)

2 Have students refer to page 51 for the list words. Say the following riddles and have volunteers spell the correct homophone:

- I stay in one place. (**stationary**)
- I am your pal. (**principal**)
- I am an expression of praise. (**compliment**)
- I am a club. (**council**)

3 Proceed to page 51. Allow students to complete the page independently.

Day 4 Writing

Objective

The students will read a friendly note in the form of a narrative. They will circle the correct **homophones** and **homographs**.

Introduction

Teacher Note: The narrative domain is the focus for the writing pages in Lessons 13–17. Explain that today's activity is a narrative, a story told from

th… ive
fo…

Di…

1 … oys.

2 … ts … les,

3 … 13

A Beka Book abeka.com 1-877-A BEKA BOOK (223-5226) toll free

Use an acronym to remember the sentences.

His instictive reaction saved the little dog's life.

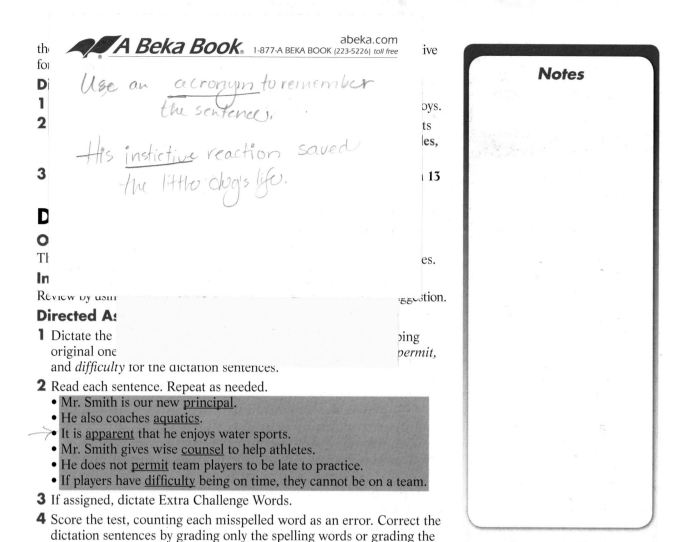

D…

O…

Th… es.

In…

Review by usi… ggestion.

Directed As…

1 Dictate the … ping original one… *permit,* and *difficulty* for the dictation sentences.

2 Read each sentence. Repeat as needed.
- Mr. Smith is our new principal.
- He also coaches aquatics.
- It is apparent that he enjoys water sports.
- Mr. Smith gives wise counsel to help athletes.
- He does not permit team players to be late to practice.
- If players have difficulty being on time, they cannot be on a team.

3 If assigned, dictate Extra Challenge Words.

4 Score the test, counting each misspelled word as an error. Correct the dictation sentences by grading only the spelling words or grading the complete sentences.

Notes

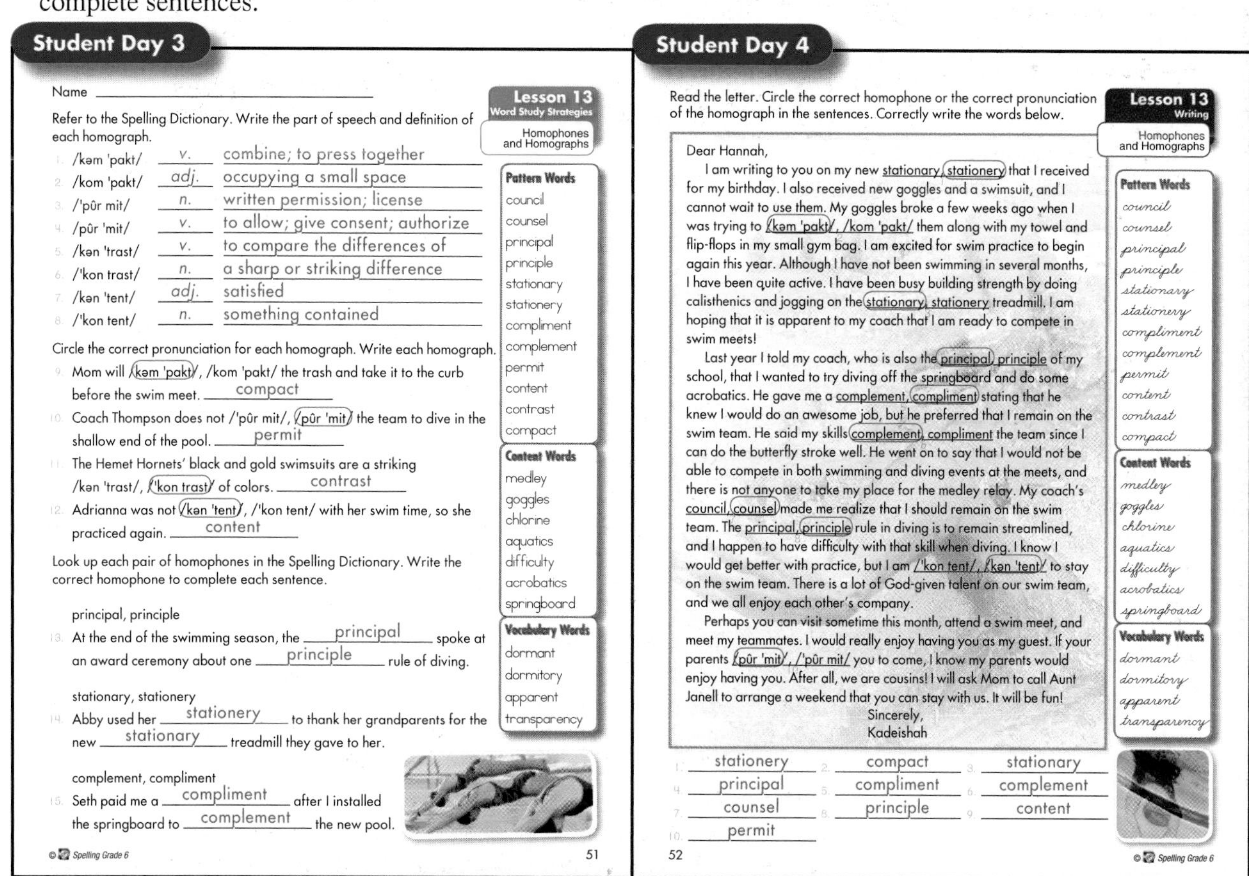

Student Day 3

Name ____

Lesson 13 Word Study Strategies — Homophones and Homographs

Refer to the Spelling Dictionary. Write the part of speech and definition of each homograph.

1. /kəm 'pakt/ v. combine; to press together
2. /kom 'pakt/ adj. occupying a small space
3. /'pûr mit/ n. written permission; license
4. /pûr 'mit/ v. to allow; give consent; authorize
5. /kən 'trast/ v. to compare the differences of
6. /'kon trast/ n. a sharp or striking difference
7. /kən 'tent/ adj. satisfied
8. /'kon tent/ n. something contained

Circle the correct pronunciation for each homograph. Write each homograph.

9. Mom will /kəm 'pakt/, /kom 'pakt/ the trash and take it to the curb before the swim meet. compact
10. Coach Thompson does not /'pûr mit/, /pûr 'mit/ the team to dive in the shallow end of the pool. permit
11. The Hemet Hornets' black and gold swimsuits are a striking /kən 'trast/, /'kon trast/ of colors. contrast
12. Adrianna was not /kən 'tent/, /'kon tent/ with her swim time, so she practiced again. content

Look up each pair of homophones in the Spelling Dictionary. Write the correct homophone to complete each sentence.

principal, principle
13. At the end of the swimming season, the principal spoke at an award ceremony about one principle rule of diving.

stationary, stationery
14. Abby used her stationery to thank her grandparents for the new stationary treadmill they gave to her.

complement, compliment
15. Seth paid me a compliment after I installed the springboard to complement the new pool.

Pattern Words: council, counsel, principal, principle, stationary, stationery, compliment, complement, permit, content, contrast, compact

Content Words: medley, goggles, chlorine, aquatics, difficulty, acrobatics, springboard

Vocabulary Words: dormant, dormitory, apparent, transparency

© Spelling Grade 6 51

Student Day 4

Read the letter. Circle the correct homophone or the correct pronunciation of the homograph in the sentences. Correctly write the words below.

Lesson 13 Writing — Homophones and Homographs

Dear Hannah,

I am writing to you on my new stationary, stationery that I received for my birthday. I also received new goggles and a swimsuit, and I cannot wait to use them. My goggles broke a few weeks ago when I was trying to /kəm 'pakt/, /kom 'pakt/ them along with my towel and flip-flops in my small gym bag. I am excited for swim practice to begin again this year. Although I have not been swimming in several months, I have been quite active. I have been busy building strength by doing calisthenics and jogging on the stationary, stationery treadmill. I am hoping that it is apparent to my coach that I am ready to compete in swim meets!

Last year I told my coach, who is also the principal, principle of my school, that I wanted to try diving off the springboard and do some acrobatics. He gave me a complement, compliment stating that he knew I would do an awesome job, but he preferred that I remain on the swim team. He said my skills complement, compliment the team since I can do the butterfly stroke well. He went on to say that I would not be able to compete in both swimming and diving events at the meets, and there is not anyone to take my place for the medley relay. My coach's council, counsel made me realize that I should remain on the swim team. The principal, principle rule in diving is to remain streamlined, and I happen to have difficulty with that skill when diving. I know I would get better with practice, but I am /'kon tent/, /kən 'tent/ to stay on the swim team. There is a lot of God-given talent on our swim team, and we all enjoy each other's company.

Perhaps you can visit sometime this month, attend a swim meet, and meet my teammates. I would really enjoy having you as my guest. If your parents /pûr 'mit/, /'pûr mit/ you to come, I know my parents would enjoy having you. After all, we are cousins! I will ask Mom to call Aunt Janell to arrange a weekend that you can stay with us. It will be fun!

Sincerely,
Kadeishah

1. stationery 2. compact 3. stationary
4. principal 5. compliment 6. complement
7. counsel 8. principle 9. content
10. permit

52 © Spelling Grade 6

Lesson **14** Compound Words

Student Pages

Pages 53–56

Lesson Materials

BLM SP6-01B
Card stock
Index cards
Photographs
BLM SP6-14A

Sports

The theme of this lesson is water polo. Water Polo is the oldest continuous Olympic team sport. A water-polo team consists of seven players—one goalkeeper and six players. Six substitutes are also allowed on a team. The game involves swimming, ball-handling skills, reflexes and awareness, and treading water. The *egg-beater* technique is the most common form of treading water. The circular movement of the athlete's legs during treading resembles the motion of the hand-operated kitchen device.

Day 1 Pretest

Objective

The students will accurately spell and write **compound words**. They will spell and write content, vocabulary, and challenge words.

Introduction

Before class, select Challenge Words for numbers 24 and 25 from a cross-curricular subject, words misspelled on previous assignments, or words that interest your students. The word *well-informed* is a **hyphenated compound word** and is suggested for number 24. Administer the Pretest.

Directed Instruction

1 Say each word, use it in a sentence, and then repeat the word.

Pattern Words

1. Marlene was an able-bodied athlete and played in the entire game.
2. Becka had a backache after being kicked by another player.
3. Reno and Austin are beachcombing in Laguna Niguel.
4. One should use common sense when playing in or around water.
5. During renovations, the team used the pool at the community center.
6. Jeb is unique because he is the only left-handed player on the team.
7. The water-polo team prayed in the locker room before the big meet.
8. Kaitlin's sportsmanlike and respectful behavior was praiseworthy.
9. Jennifer jumped into the swimming pool and began to warm up.
10. The floating water-polo nets touched the waterline in the pool.
11. The well-conditioned athlete effortlessly swam laps.
12. After a major win, the news of the team's success was widespread.

Content Words

13. Matthew threw the buoyant water-polo ball into the opponent's net.
14. Goalkeepers may use two hands when handling the ball in water polo.
15. Different colored caps provide identification in water polo.
16. An infraction was called when Allison took the ball underwater.
17. Jocelyn rested during the interval and encouraged her teammates.
18. Was Theo the only substitute player for the team in last week's game?
19. Different versions of water polo can involve variations in play area.

Vocabulary Words

20. The added pool chemicals should dissolve after a few minutes.
21. After an extensive delay, the water-polo meet finally began.
22. Coach David asked the team to refine their throwing techniques.
23. The arguing teammates resolved to put aside their differences.

Challenge Words

24. ____________________
25. ____________________

2 Allow students to self-correct their Pretest. Write each word on the board. Point out that the Pattern Words in this lesson are **compound words**. Define the following: A *compound word* is made of two or more smaller words. Compound words can be closed, open, or hyphenated. Point out the roots *fin* and *solv* in the Vocabulary Words. Note that *finally* contains two suffixes and that both *refine* and *dissolve* end in silent *e*. The silent *e* does not appear in the original root spellings of *fin* and *solv*.

3 As a class, read, spell, and read each word. Direct students to highlight misspelled words and rewrite them correctly.

4 Proof each student's Pretest. This becomes an individualized study sheet that can be used at school or at home.

5 Homework suggestion: Duplicate **BLM SP6-01B Flash Cards Template** on CARD STOCK for students to write the list words, using the flash cards as a study aid. Another option is to use INDEX CARDS.

Day 2 Word Analysis and Vocabulary

Objective

The students will sort and write **compound words** and complete sentences with content words. They will use a table to write vocabulary words, match given definitions in context, and complete sentences.

Introduction

Remind students that a compound word is made of two or more smaller words. **Compound words** can be closed, open, or hyphenated. Review the following:

- A closed compound word is a single closed word.
- An open compound word is two separate words. Open compound words are usually nouns.
- A hyphenated compound word can contain two or more words joined by hyphens. Hyphenated compound words are usually adjectives.

Instruct students to have their flash card pile from this lesson on hand for this activity. Call out a Pattern Word from this week's lesson. Students look through their flash card pile, locate the dictated words, and arrange them into three piles according to the compound word categories listed above. Upon dictation completion, check for accuracy by asking students to read the words in each pile and state the name of the category.

Directed Instruction

1 Write the following on the board:
• Lori played water polo. • Lori played in the water-polo meet.
Underline the compound word in each sentence. Ask students to point out a distinguishing feature of both underlined words. **(The word**

Differentiated Instruction

- For students who spelled all the words correctly on the Pretest, select and assign Extra Challenge Words from the following list: dispersion, cytoplasm, palindrome, microeconomics, benign, chiaroscuro.
- For students who spelled less than half correctly, assign the following Pattern, Content, and Vocabulary Words: backache, praiseworthy, locker room, swimming pool, left-handed, well-conditioned, buoyant, handling, versions, substitute, refine, resolved. On the Posttest, evaluate these students on the twelve words assigned; however, encourage them to attempt to spell all the list words to the best of their ability. They are also responsible for writing the dictated sentences.

Student Day 2

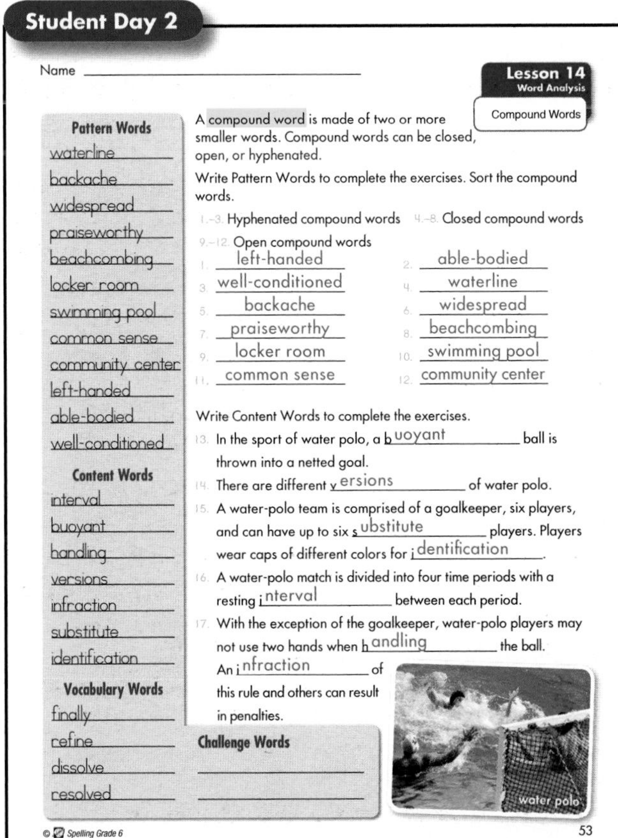
Name ______

Lesson 14 Word Analysis

Compound Words

Pattern Words: waterline, backache, widespread, praiseworthy, beachcombing, locker room, swimming pool, common sense, community center, left-handed, able-bodied, well-conditioned

Content Words: interval, buoyant, handling, versions, infraction, substitute, identification

Vocabulary Words: finally, refine, dissolve, resolved

Challenge Words

A compound word is made of two or more smaller words. Compound words can be closed, open, or hyphenated.

Write Pattern Words to complete the exercises. Sort the compound words.

1.–3. Hyphenated compound words 4.–8. Closed compound words 9.–12. Open compound words

1. left-handed 2. able-bodied
3. well-conditioned 4. waterline
5. backache 6. widespread
7. praiseworthy 8. beachcombing
9. locker room 10. swimming pool
11. common sense 12. community center

Write Content Words to complete the exercises.

13. In the sport of water polo, a buoyant ball is thrown into a netted goal.
14. There are different versions of water polo.
15. A water-polo team is comprised of a goalkeeper, six players, and can have up to six substitute players. Players wear caps of different colors for identification.
16. A water-polo match is divided into four time periods with a resting interval between each period.
17. With the exception of the goalkeeper, water-polo players may not use two hands when handling the ball. An infraction of this rule and others can result in penalties.

water polo

© Spelling Grade 6 53

Student Day 2

Lesson 14 Vocabulary

Compound Words

Prefix		Root		Suffix	
re-	again	fin	end	-al	related to
dis-	apart	solv	loosen, solve	-ly	forms an adverb from an adjective
				-ed	makes verbs past tense

Write the Vocabulary Words. Order may vary.

1. finally 2. refine
3. dissolve 4. resolved

Refer to the table to complete the exercises. Match each word to its definition.

c 5. dissolve — a. to improve or perfect again
a 6. refine — b. related to the end of a series or process; at last
d 7. resolved — c. to loosen or melt apart
b 8. finally — d. to have determined, solved, or settled

Write Vocabulary Words to complete the sentences.

9. The maintenance technician pours chemicals into the pool so they can dissolve before water-polo practice.
10. The team resolved to train hard so that they could do well in the national meet for water polo.
11. To prepare for the national meet, the coach wanted the team to refine their swimming, treading, passing, and throwing techniques.
12. Finally, after three weeks, practice came to an end, and the team felt confident and prepared for the national meet.
13. The coaching staff and the entire team resolved to do their best to refine as many technical aspects of water polo as possible before the important championship match.

Pattern Words: waterline, backache, widespread, praiseworthy, beachcombing, locker room, swimming pool, common sense, community center, left-handed, able-bodied, well-conditioned

Content Words: interval, buoyant, handling, versions, infraction, substitute, identification

Vocabulary Words: finally, refine, dissolve, resolved

54 © Spelling Grade 6

Student Spelling Support Materials

BLM SP6-01A

Student Spelling Support

1. Use **BLM SP6-01A A Spelling Study Strategy** in instructional groups to provide assistance with some or all of the words.
2. Invite students to write the Challenge Words, numbers 24 and 25, in the Word Bank, in the back of their textbook.
3. Challenge students to research and write a brief report on the differences between water polo in the levels of high school, college, and the Olympics. Compile information in the progressive, sport journal that was started in Lesson 1.
4. Write this week's words, categorize the Pattern, Content, and Vocabulary Words, and attach them to the Word Wall.
5. Read Philippians 4:8: "Finally, brethren, whatever things are true, whatever things are noble, whatever things are just, whatever things are pure, whatever things are lovely, whatever things are of good report, if there is any virtue and if there is anything **praiseworthy**—meditate on these things." Ask students to share about a **praiseworthy** event. Discuss how thinking on **praiseworthy** things reminds us to focus on the Lord and His goodness. Invite students to write a list of things that are **praiseworthy** and tell which of those things they would like to focus on this week.

***water polo* is an open compound word in the first sentence and a hyphenated compound word in the second sentence.**)
Challenge students to identify why *water polo* is an open compound word in the first sentence and a hyphenated compound word in the second sentence. (***Water polo* is a noun in the first sentence and is an adjective, modifying *meet*, in the second sentence.**)

2 Proceed to page 53. Say, spell, and say each Pattern, Content, and Vocabulary Word. Provide this week's Challenge Words and have students write them in the spaces provided. Students complete the page.

3 Proceed to page 54. Encourage students to use the table as an aid in building each Vocabulary Word. For example, the root *fin* goes with the suffixes *-al* and *-ly* to build the word *finally.* Allow students to complete the page independently.

4 Homework suggestion: Students use their Spelling Dictionary to write the definition of each word on the back of the corresponding flash card that was suggested for homework on Day 1.

Day 3 Word Study Strategies

Objective

The students will utilize dictionary skills by answering questions about the different components of a dictionary entry. They will underline conjunctions and locate and write list words from given sentences.

Introduction

Before class, write the following on the board:

- Belle and Sheila are substitute players on the varsity water-polo team. (**The conjunction *and* is joining two subjects—*Belle* and *Sheila*.**)
- The locker room was crowded, but the gymnasium was sparsely populated. (**The conjunction *but* is joining two sentences.**)
- Paige is handling and controlling the ball very well. (**The conjunction *and* is joining a verb phrase and a verb—*is handling* and *controlling*.**)

Remind students of the following: A *conjunction* is a word that is used to join words or groups of words. A *coordinating conjunction* is a word that is used to join words that have the same function. Some coordinating conjunctions are *and, so, or,* and *but.* Students identify what the conjunctions are joining in each sentence.

Directed Instruction

1 Challenge students to locate list words used in the sentences. (**substitute; locker room; handling**)

2 Proceed to page 55. Encourage students to work in pairs to complete the page.

3 Select a volunteer to read Philippians 4:8. Discuss the importance of thinking and pondering on things that are praiseworthy.

Day 4 Writing

Objective

The students will complete captions on a scrapbook page in the context of a cloze activity using pattern, content, and vocabulary words.

Introduction

Share a few PHOTOGRAPHS from a vacation experience or a recent class field trip. Invite students to assist in collating the photographs and writing caption labels. Display photographs and captions on a large sheet of construction paper.

Directed Instruction

1 Ask students if they have ever designed a scrapbook page. Explain that a scrapbook is a great way of noting memorable events through pictures and captions. Inform students that today's lesson contains a scrapbook page.

2 Proceed to page 56. Select volunteers to read the captions below the photographs aloud. Allow students to work in pairs or trios to reread each caption and locate list words to complete sentences.

3 Homework suggestion: Distribute a copy of **BLM SP6-14A Lesson 14 Homework** to each student.

Day 5 Posttest

Objective

The students will correctly write dictated spelling words and sentences.

Introduction

Review by using flash cards noted in Day 1 and Day 2 Homework suggestion.

Directed Assessment

1 Dictate the list words by using the Pretest sentences or developing original ones. Reserve *well-conditioned, praiseworthy, refine, buoyant, handling,* and *swimming pool* for the dictation sentences.

2 Read each sentence. Repeat as needed.

- Pam is a well-conditioned athlete in water polo.
- She also has an attitude that is praiseworthy.
- Pam continually chooses to refine her throwing technique.
- She can throw the buoyant ball with great force.
- She only uses one hand when handling the ball.
- Pam's ability in the swimming pool is brilliant.

3 If assigned, dictate Extra Challenge Words.

4 Score the test, counting each misspelled word as an error. Correct the dictation sentences by grading only the spelling words or grading the complete sentences.

Notes

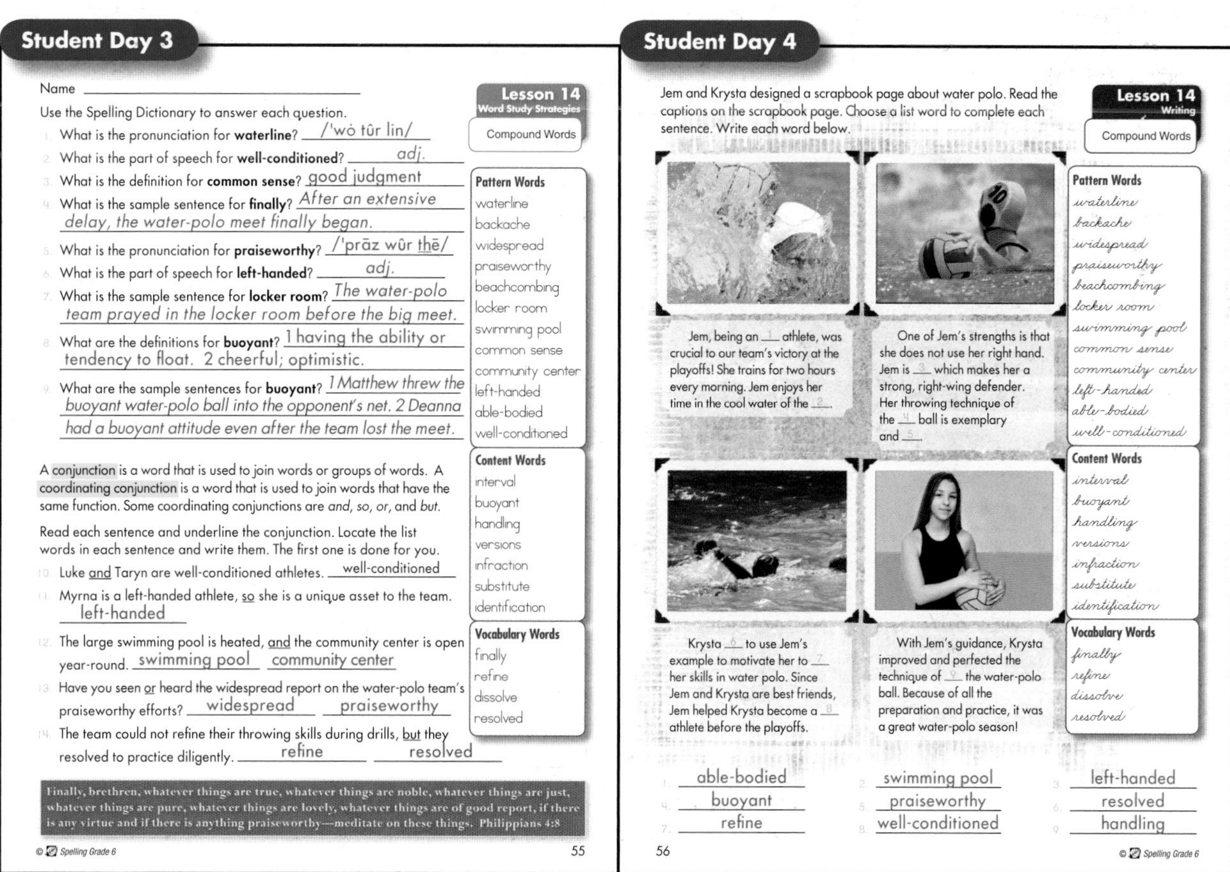

Student Day 3

Name ______________________

Lesson 14 Word Study Strategies — Compound Words

Use the Spelling Dictionary to answer each question.

1. What is the pronunciation for **waterline**? /ˈwȯ tûr līn/
2. What is the part of speech for **well-conditioned**? adj.
3. What is the definition for **common sense**? good judgment
4. What is the sample sentence for **finally**? After an extensive delay, the water-polo meet finally began.
5. What is the pronunciation for **praiseworthy**? /ˈprāz wûr thē/
6. What is the part of speech for **left-handed**? adj.
7. What is the sample sentence for **locker room**? The water-polo team prayed in the locker room before the big meet.
8. What are the definitions for **buoyant**? 1 having the ability or tendency to float. 2 cheerful; optimistic.
9. What are the sample sentences for **buoyant**? 1 Matthew threw the buoyant water-polo ball into the opponent's net. 2 Deanna had a buoyant attitude even after the team lost the meet.

A conjunction is a word that is used to join words or groups of words. A coordinating conjunction is a word that is used to join words that have the same function. Some coordinating conjunctions are *and*, *so*, *or*, and *but*.

Read each sentence and underline the conjunction. Locate the list words in each sentence and write them. The first one is done for you.

10. Luke and Taryn are well-conditioned athletes. well-conditioned
11. Myrna is a left-handed athlete, so she is a unique asset to the team. left-handed
12. The large swimming pool is heated, and the community center is open year-round. swimming pool community center
13. Have you seen or heard the widespread report on the water-polo team's praiseworthy efforts? widespread praiseworthy
14. The team could not refine their throwing skills during drills, but they resolved to practice diligently. refine resolved

Pattern Words: waterline, backache, widespread, praiseworthy, beachcombing, locker room, swimming pool, common sense, community center, left-handed, able-bodied, well-conditioned

Content Words: interval, buoyant, handling, versions, infraction, substitute, identification

Vocabulary Words: finally, refine, dissolve, resolved

Finally, brethren, whatever things are true, whatever things are noble, whatever things are just, whatever things are pure, whatever things are lovely, whatever things are of good report, if there is any virtue and if there is anything praiseworthy—meditate on these things. Philippians 4:8

© Spelling Grade 6 55

Student Day 4

Lesson 14 Writing — Compound Words

Jem and Krysta designed a scrapbook page about water polo. Read the captions on the scrapbook page. Choose a list word to complete each sentence. Write each word below.

Jem, being an __1__ athlete, was crucial to our team's victory at the playoffs! She trains for two hours every morning. Jem enjoys her time in the cool water of the __2__.

One of Jem's strengths is that she does not use her right hand. Jem is __3__ which makes her a strong, right-wing defender. Her throwing technique of the __4__ ball is exemplary and __5__.

Krysta __6__ to use Jem's example to motivate her to __7__ her skills in water polo. Since Jem and Krysta are best friends, Jem helped Krysta become a __8__ athlete before the playoffs.

With Jem's guidance, Krysta improved and perfected the technique of __9__ the water-polo ball. Because of all the preparation and practice, it was a great water-polo season!

1. able-bodied
2. swimming pool
3. left-handed
4. buoyant
5. praiseworthy
6. resolved
7. refine
8. well-conditioned
9. handling

Pattern Words: waterline, backache, widespread, praiseworthy, beachcombing, locker room, swimming pool, common sense, community center, left-handed, able-bodied, well-conditioned

Content Words: interval, buoyant, handling, versions, infraction, substitute, identification

Vocabulary Words: finally, refine, dissolve, resolved

56 © Spelling Grade 6

Lesson 15

Endings

Student Pages

Pages 57–60

Lesson Materials

BLM SP6-01B
Card stock
Index cards
T-11
BLM SP6-15A
BLM SP6-15B

Sports

The theme of this lesson is waterskiing. Waterskiing is a sport in which skiers are towed across the surface of a body of water by a motorboat. Water-skiers may ski either barefoot or mounted on specialized skis. There are many different forms of waterskiing, including traditional, kneeboard, barefoot, show, speed, disabled, and collegiate.

Day 1 Pretest

Objective

The students will accurately spell and write words with the **endings nce** and **nse**. They will spell and write content, vocabulary, and challenge words.

Introduction

Before class, select Challenge Words for numbers 24 and 25 from a cross-curricular subject, words misspelled on previous assignments, or words that interest your students. The word *obedience* has the ending **nce** and is suggested for number 24. Administer the Pretest.

Directed Instruction

1 Say each word, use it in a sentence, and then repeat the word.

Pattern Words

1. We required assistance to restart the stalled boat.
2. I will try to condense my narrative into a few paragraphs.
3. Can you convince your friends to rent a motorboat?
4. It is important to study God's Word with diligence.
5. To glorify God in all we do, we should strive for excellence.
6. Robin learned better ways to ski through experience.
7. Freestyle waterskiing provides independence from strict rules.
8. The motorboat was an intense shade of blue.
9. Nan joined the team on the pretense that she could water-ski.
10. The water offered little resistance to the skier.
11. April used her sense of hearing to tell when to shift the gears.
12. Neal learned to water-ski as a boy, and he has loved it ever since.

Content Words

13. The skier rises on her skis as the boat accelerates.
14. Spencer performed an aerial trick on his wakeboard.
15. Nate is balancing on only one ski.
16. The waterskiing competition was held on Lake Powell.
17. Waterskiing involves hydroplaning over the surface of the water.
18. The water-skiers were perpendicular to the surface of the water.
19. The beginning water-skier gripped the towrope tightly.

Vocabulary Words

20. The powerboat's engine was functional.
21. I could tell by the inflection in her voice that she was excited.
22. The motorboat suffered an engine malfunction.
23. The sunlight reflected off the surface of the lake.

Challenge Words

24. ______________________
25. ______________________

2 Allow students to self-correct their Pretest. Write each word on the board. Point out the *nce* or *nse* spelling pattern in each Pattern Word. Note the roots *flect* and *funct* in the Vocabulary Words. The Vocabulary Word *functional* has two suffixes, *-ion* and *-al*.

3 As a class, read, spell, and read each word. Direct students to highlight misspelled words and rewrite them correctly.

4 Proof each student's Pretest. This becomes an individualized study sheet that can be used at school or at home.

5 Homework suggestion: Duplicate **BLM SP6-01B Flash Cards Template** on CARD STOCK for students to write the list words, using the flash cards as a study aid. Another option is to use INDEX CARDS.

Day 2 Word Analysis and Vocabulary

Objective

The students will sort pattern words according to their **endings**. They will complete sentences with content words. Students will use a table to write vocabulary words, complete sentences, and choose list words that match definitions.

Introduction

Write the endings *nce* and *nse* on the board. Invite students to refer to the list words, found on page 57. As you read each Pattern Word, ask students to raise their left hand for words ending in *nce* and their right hand for words ending in *nse*. (***nce*—since, diligence, convince, assistance, resistance, excellence, experience, independence; *nse*—sense, intense, pretense, condense**) Write the words under the appropriate spelling. Instruct students to highlight or underline the **endings** in each Pattern Word on the flash cards, using a different color for each ending.

Directed Instruction

1 Select seven students to locate the definition of each Content Word from this lesson in their Spelling Dictionary. Students read the definitions aloud.

2 Proceed to page 57. Say, spell, and say each Pattern, Content, and Vocabulary Word. Provide this week's Challenge Words and have students write them in the spaces provided. Select a student to read 1 Corinthians 6:20 and discuss the fact that we belong to the Lord. Students complete the page.

3 Proceed to page 58. Remind students to use the table to assist in building each Vocabulary Word. For example, the prefix *in-* goes with

Differentiated Instruction

- For students who spelled all the words correctly on the Pretest, select and assign Extra Challenge Words from the following list: efficiency, displacement, portmanteau, psephology, biopsy, staccato.
- For students who spelled less than half correctly, assign the following Pattern, Content, and Vocabulary Words: since, diligence, convince, assistance, excellence, experience, towrope, balancing, accelerates, perpendicular, reflected, functional. On the Posttest, evaluate these students on the twelve words assigned; however, encourage them to attempt to spell all the list words to the best of their ability. They are also responsible for writing the dictated sentences.

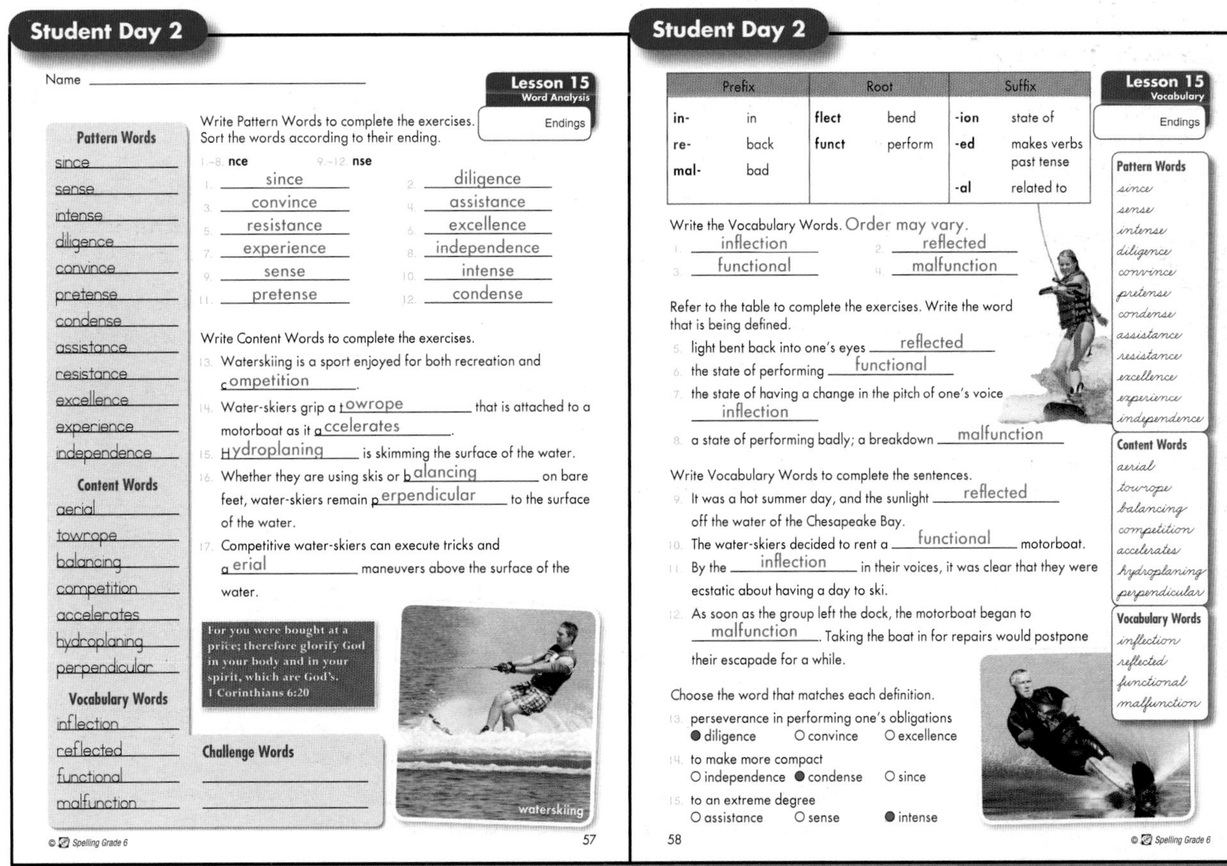

Student Day 2

Name

Lesson 15 Word Analysis — Endings

Pattern Words: since, sense, intense, diligence, convince, pretense, condense, assistance, resistance, excellence, experience, independence

Content Words: aerial, towrope, balancing, competition, accelerates, hydroplaning, perpendicular

Vocabulary Words: inflection, reflected, functional, malfunction

Write Pattern Words to complete the exercises. Sort the words according to their ending.

1–8 **nce** / 9–12 **nse**

1. since
2. diligence
3. convince
4. assistance
5. resistance
6. excellence
7. experience
8. independence
9. sense
10. intense
11. pretense
12. condense

Write Content Words to complete the exercises.

13. Waterskiing is a sport enjoyed for both recreation and competition.
14. Water-skiers grip a towrope that is attached to a motorboat as it accelerates.
15. Hydroplaning is skimming the surface of the water.
16. Whether they are using skis or balancing on bare feet, water-skiers remain perpendicular to the surface of the water.
17. Competitive water-skiers can execute tricks and aerial maneuvers above the surface of the water.

For you were bought at a price; therefore glorify God in your body and in your spirit, which are God's. 1 Corinthians 6:20

Challenge Words

waterskiing

© Spelling Grade 6 — 57

Student Day 2

Lesson 15 Vocabulary — Endings

Prefix		Root		Suffix	
in-	in	**flect**	bend	**-ion**	state of
re-	back	**funct**	perform	**-ed**	makes verbs past tense
mal-	bad			**-al**	related to

Write the Vocabulary Words. Order may vary.

1. inflection
2. reflected
3. functional
4. malfunction

Refer to the table to complete the exercises. Write the word that is being defined.

5. light bent back into one's eyes reflected
6. the state of performing functional
7. the state of having a change in the pitch of one's voice inflection
8. a state of performing badly; a breakdown malfunction

Write Vocabulary Words to complete the sentences.

9. It was a hot summer day, and the sunlight reflected off the water of the Chesapeake Bay.
10. The water-skiers decided to rent a functional motorboat.
11. By the inflection in their voices, it was clear that they were ecstatic about having a day to ski.
12. As soon as the group left the dock, the motorboat began to malfunction. Taking the boat in for repairs would postpone their escapade for a while.

Choose the word that matches each definition.

13. perseverance in performing one's obligations ● diligence ○ convince ○ excellence
14. to make more compact ○ independence ● condense ○ since
15. to an extreme degree ○ assistance ○ sense ● intense

Pattern Words: since, sense, intense, diligence, convince, pretense, condense, assistance, resistance, excellence, experience, independence

Content Words: aerial, towrope, balancing, competition, accelerates, hydroplaning, perpendicular

Vocabulary Words: inflection, reflected, functional, malfunction

58 — © Spelling Grade 6

Student Spelling Support Materials

BLM SP6-01A

Student Spelling Support

1. Use **BLM SP6-01A A Spelling Study Strategy** in instructional groups to provide assistance with some or all of the words.
2. Invite students to write the Challenge Words, numbers 24 and 25, in the Word Bank, in the back of their textbook.
3. Challenge students to research and compare wakeboarding to traditional waterskiing. Compile information in the progressive, sport journal that was started in Lesson 1.
4. Write this week's words, categorize the Pattern, Content, and Vocabulary Words, and attach them to the Word Wall.
5. Read 1 Corinthians 6:20: "For you were bought at a price; therefore glorify God in your body and in your spirit, which are God's." Remind students that the price paid for their salvation was Jesus' death on the cross. Invite students to brainstorm ways in which they can glorify God in their body, for example, by staying fit, by eating well, and by using their body in service to others.

Cont. on page 61

the root *flect* and the suffix *-ion* to build the word *inflection*. Choose volunteers to use each Vocabulary Word in an original sentence. Allow students to complete the page independently.

4 Homework suggestion: Students use their Spelling Dictionary to write the definition of each word on the back of the corresponding flash card that was suggested for homework on Day 1.

Day 3 Word Study Strategies

Objective

The students will write related forms of list words. They will change verbs to their noun form. Students will utilize the Spelling Dictionary to identify the part of speech and the definition for words with multiple meanings.

Introduction

Write the following words that are related forms on the board: reflection, reflect; balance, balancing. Write the following sentences, leaving blanks where indicated:

- A mirror will _______ light. (**reflect**; *v.*)
- I see a _______ in the mirror. (**reflection**; *n.*)
- Todd is _______ on the wakeboard. (**balancing**; *v.*)
- He has a good sense of _______. (**balance**; *n.*)

Select students to complete each sentence and to identify the part of speech for the word that they chose to complete the sentence. Note that the inflection of each word is a clue as to the part of speech. However, sentence context is the determining factor for a word's part of speech.

Directed Instruction

1 To reinforce multiple meanings of list words, choose volunteers to locate *sense* and *reflected* in the Spelling Dictionary and read the part(s) of speech and both definitions for the words. Request volunteers to use each word in two separate sentences, demonstrating that they understand both meanings of each word.

2 Proceed to page 59. Allow students to complete the page.

Day 4 Writing

Objective

The students will use proofreading marks to identify mistakes in a narrative. They will correctly write misspelled words and rewrite a run-on sentence as two complete sentences. The students will choose a solution for the problem presented in the narrative and write an ending to the narrative.

Introduction

Share a problem that you have faced with a mechanical breakdown. Discuss the steps that you took to solve the problem. Ask students to narrate similar situations. Explain that today's activity is a narrative, a story told from the narrator's viewpoint. This narrative involves a problem with a motorboat.

Directed Instruction

1 Write the following run-on sentence on the board: Glenna loves waterskiing she spends most of her summer vacation on the lake. Remind students that a run-on sentence is an incorrect combination of two or more complete sentences. Choose a volunteer to correctly punctuate the sentence so that it reads as two separate sentences. (**Glenna loves waterskiing. She spends most of her summer vacation on the lake.**)

2 Display **T-11 Proofreading a Narrative** on the overhead, keeping the bottom portion of the transparency covered. Read the text aloud. Correct the identified mistakes using the appropriate proofreading marks. Challenge students to identify the run-on sentence. Use **BLM SP6-15A T-11 Answer Key** as a guide. Uncover the bottom of the transparency and read the corrected version of the text.

3 Proceed to page 60. Assist students as needed while they independently proofread the narrative and solutions. Review all the necessary proofreading marks and corrections. (**9 misspellings; 2 capital letters needed; 3 periods needed; 2 deletes; 1 add something—*the*; 1 small letter needed; 1 new paragraph**)

4 Students complete the narrative, assigned at the bottom of page 60, on a separate piece of paper. Encourage students to proofread their work.

5 Homework suggestion: Distribute a copy of **BLM SP6-15B Lesson 15 Homework** to each student.

Day 5 Posttest

Objective

The students will correctly write dictated spelling words and sentences.

Introduction

Review by using flash cards noted in Day 1 and Day 2 Homework suggestion.

Directed Assessment

1 Dictate the list words by using the Pretest sentences or developing original ones. Reserve *convince, assistance, experience, accelerates, towrope,* and *reflected* for the dictation sentences.

2 Read each sentence. Repeat as needed.

- Mike tried to convince Carla to try waterskiing.
- Carla needed a little assistance to get her balance on the water skis.
- Her first experience on water skis was difficult.
- Carla did not realize how quickly a boat accelerates.
- She was startled, so she let go of the towrope.
- Carla laughed when she reflected on her adventure.

3 If assigned, dictate Extra Challenge Words.

4 Score the test, counting each misspelled word as an error. Correct the dictation sentences by grading only the spelling words or grading the complete sentences.

Student Spelling Support

Cont. from page 60

6. Spellings with identical sounds, such as the final syllable in several of this week's Pattern Words, can be challenging. Using the flash cards that were suggested for homework on Day 1, help students to develop their study skills by applying the following suggestions:
   - Sort the Pattern Words into two groups, one with *nce* endings and one with *nse* endings. Compose silly sentences for sets of Pattern Words, for example, Sally edits on the *pretense* that she can *sense* where to *condense*, because her focus is *intense*.
   - Circle the vowel before each *nce* or *nse* ending to reinforce its spelling.

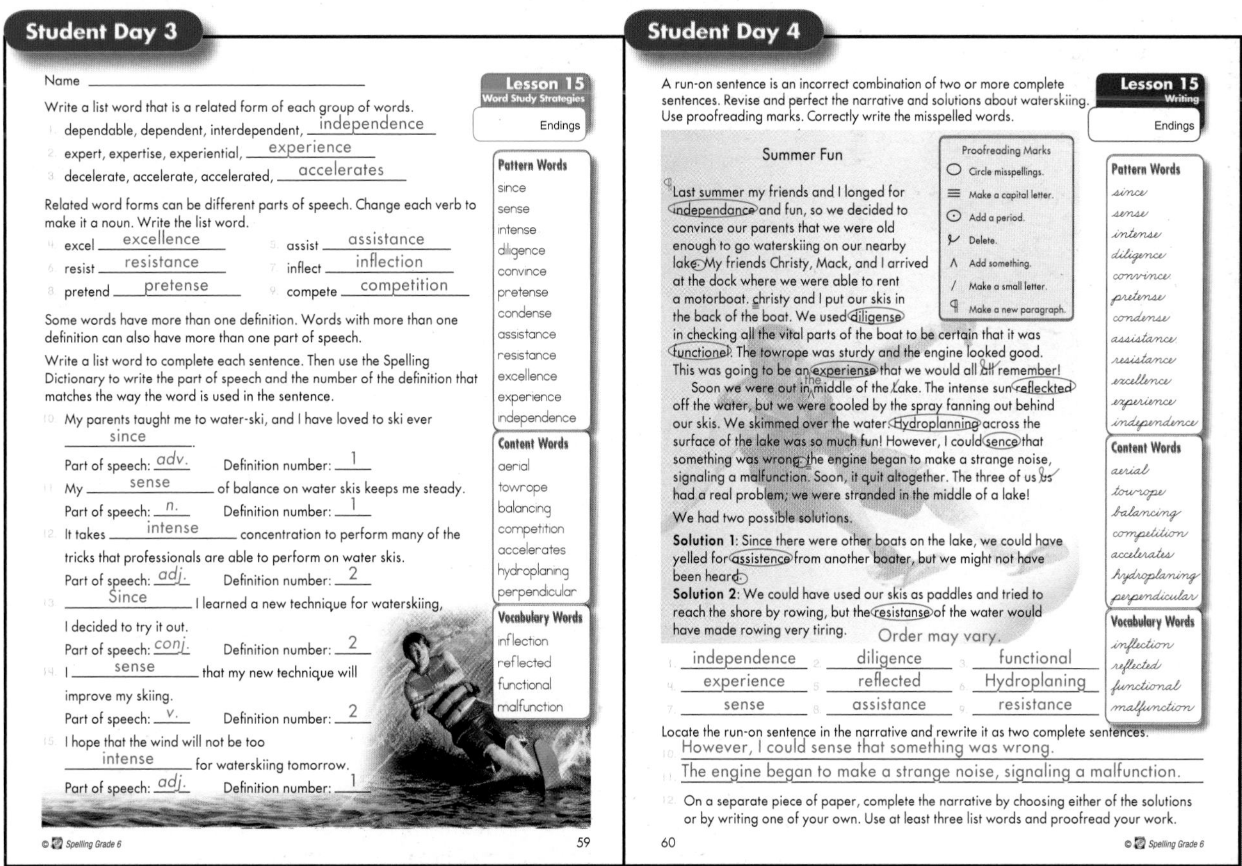

Student Day 3

Lesson 15 Word Study Strategies — Endings

Name ____________

Write a list word that is a related form of each group of words.

1. dependable, dependent, interdependent, independence
2. expert, expertise, experiential, experience
3. decelerate, accelerate, accelerated, accelerates

Related word forms can be different parts of speech. Change each verb to make it a noun. Write the list word.

4. excel excellence
5. assist assistance
6. resist resistance
7. inflect inflection
8. pretend pretense
9. compete competition

Some words have more than one definition. Words with more than one definition can also have more than one part of speech.

Write a list word to complete each sentence. Then use the Spelling Dictionary to write the part of speech and the number of the definition that matches the way the word is used in the sentence.

10. My parents taught me to water-ski, and I have loved to ski ever since. Part of speech: adv. Definition number: 1
11. My sense of balance on water skis keeps me steady. Part of speech: n. Definition number: 1
12. It takes intense concentration to perform many of the tricks that professionals are able to perform on water skis. Part of speech: adj. Definition number: 2
13. Since I learned a new technique for waterskiing, I decided to try it out. Part of speech: conj. Definition number: 2
14. I sense that my new technique will improve my skiing. Part of speech: v. Definition number: 2
15. I hope that the wind will not be too intense for waterskiing tomorrow. Part of speech: adj. Definition number: 1

Pattern Words: since, sense, intense, diligence, convince, pretense, condense, assistance, resistance, excellence, experience, independence

Content Words: aerial, towrope, balancing, competition, accelerates, hydroplaning, perpendicular

Vocabulary Words: inflection, reflected, functional, malfunction

© Spelling Grade 6 — 59

Student Day 4

Lesson 15 Writing — Endings

A run-on sentence is an incorrect combination of two or more complete sentences. Revise and perfect the narrative and solutions about waterskiing. Use proofreading marks. Correctly write the misspelled words.

Summer Fun

Proofreading Marks: Circle misspellings. Make a capital letter. Add a period. Delete. Add something. Make a small letter. Make a new paragraph.

Last summer my friends and I longed for independance and fun, so we decided to convince our parents that we were old enough to go waterskiing on our nearby lake My friends Christy, Mack, and I arrived at the dock where we were able to rent a motorboat. christy and I put our skis in the back of the boat. We used diligense in checking all the vital parts of the boat to be certain that it was functionel. The towrope was sturdy and the engine looked good. This was going to be an experiense that we would all all remember!

Soon we were out in middle of the Lake. The intense sun reflleckted off the water, but we were cooled by the spray fanning out behind our skis. We skimmed over the water. Hydroplanning across the surface of the lake was so much fun! However, I could sence that something was wrong the engine began to make a strange noise, signaling a malfunction. Soon, it quit altogether. The three of us us had a real problem; we were stranded in the middle of a lake!

We had two possible solutions.

Solution 1: Since there were other boats on the lake, we could have yelled for assistence from another boater, but we might not have been heard

Solution 2: We could have used our skis as paddles and tried to reach the shore by rowing, but the resistanse of the water would have made rowing very tiring.

Order may vary.

1. independence
2. diligence
3. functional
4. experience
5. reflected
6. Hydroplaning
7. sense
8. assistance
9. resistance

Locate the run-on sentence in the narrative and rewrite it as two complete sentences.

10. However, I could sense that something was wrong.
11. The engine began to make a strange noise, signaling a malfunction.
12. On a separate piece of paper, complete the narrative by choosing either of the solutions or by writing one of your own. Use at least three list words and proofread your work.

Pattern Words: since, sense, intense, diligence, convince, pretense, condense, assistance, resistance, excellence, experience, independence

Content Words: aerial, towrope, balancing, competition, accelerates, hydroplaning, perpendicular

Vocabulary Words: inflection, reflected, functional, malfunction

60 — © Spelling Grade 6

Lesson
16 Endings

Student Pages

Pages 61–64

Lesson Materials

BLM SP6-01B
Card stock
Index cards
BLM SP6-16A

Sports

The theme of this lesson is rowing and canoeing. Competitive rowing is one of the oldest and most traditional sports. The Doggett's Coat and Badge Race held on the Thames River in England has been an annual event since 1715. Canoeing includes kayaking, and they are both popular recreational activities for many outdoor enthusiasts. Oars are used to propel rowboats while paddles are used to propel canoes and kayaks.

Day 1 Pretest

Objective

The students will accurately spell and write words with the **endings ant** and **ent**. They will spell and write content, vocabulary, and challenge words.

Introduction

Before class, select Challenge Words for numbers 24 and 25 from a cross-curricular subject, words misspelled on previous assignments, or words that interest your students. The word *omnipotent* has the ending **ent** and is suggested for number 24. Administer the Pretest.

Directed Instruction

1 Say each word, use it in a sentence, and then repeat the word.

Pattern Words

1. Wearing a life vest is significant to one's safety on a boat.
2. Tamara was reluctant to go white-water rafting.
3. After the canoe tipped over, resilient Gerron climbed right back in.
4. Our campsite was adjacent to the dock.
5. Myra used an absorbent towel to soak up the water on the seats.
6. Grandpa walked down the short gradient to get into the kayak.
7. Stan and Kaden enjoy talking about things relevant to boating.
8. The boys are confident they will be able to go kayaking in June.
9. The applicant turned in his application for the new position.
10. It is always pleasant to spend time reading God's Word.
11. The constant love of our Savior is unending.
12. The Fry family takes frequent trips to the river to go kayaking.

Content Words

13. Oars are used to propel a boat.
14. Strokes used in rowing consist of recovery, catch, drive, and release.
15. It can be difficult to negotiate around rocks while rafting.
16. Sculling is a type of rowing that does not have a navigator.
17. The framework for the new boat is almost finished.
18. Will is using wood for the construction of the canoe.
19. It is important to have rhythm when paddling a kayak.

Vocabulary Words

20. Newer boat designs supersede older models.
21. Is the race confined to the area north or south of the bridge?
22. There is an area in the marina for the confinement of the boats.
23. Everyone should live an active lifestyle and not be sedentary.

Challenge Words

24. ______________________
25. ______________________

2 Allow students to self-correct their Pretest. Write each word on the board. Point out that this week's list contains Pattern Words with the **endings** *ant* and *ent*. Note the roots *fin* and *sed* in the Vocabulary Words. The word *sedentary* contains two suffixes, *-ent* and *-ary*.

3 As a class, read, spell, and read each word. Direct students to highlight misspelled words and rewrite them correctly.

4 Proof each student's Pretest. This becomes an individualized study sheet that can be used at school or at home.

5 Homework suggestion: Duplicate **BLM SP6-01B Flash Cards Template** on CARD STOCK for students to write the list words, using the flash cards as a study aid. Another option is to use INDEX CARDS.

Day 2 Word Analysis and Vocabulary

Objective

The students will sort and write pattern words containing **endings** with *ant* and *ent*. They will write content words to complete sentences. Students will use a table to write vocabulary words and complete sentences in context. They will choose the best meaning for underlined words.

Introduction

Write the **endings** *ant* and *ent* on the board. Have students refer to their flash cards for this activity. Dictate the Pattern words and select volunteers to identify the words ending with *ant* (**relevant, pleasant, constant, reluctant, applicant, significant**) and the Pattern Words ending with *ent* (**resilient, gradient, adjacent, frequent, confident, absorbent**). To assist students in memorizing the **endings**, instruct students to highlight or underline the **endings** of each Pattern Word on the flash cards.

Directed Instruction

1 Generate original silly sentences containing all the words with one of the spellings, such as *ant*. For example, The applic<u>ant</u> was reluct<u>ant</u> to apply for the signific<u>ant</u> and relev<u>ant</u> position since he knew it would not be const<u>ant</u> or pleas<u>ant</u>. Write the student-generated silly sentences on the board and underline the endings.

2 Explain that this week's Content Words relate to the theme of rowing, canoeing, and kayaking. *Sculling* is *a type of sport rowing that does not have a navigator sitting at the stern or back of the boat.* The most common type of sport rowing is called crew or sweep-oar racing. This is where a nonrowing navigator sits at the stern of the boat and steers the boat, decides tactics, and helps rowers establish and maintain speed and rhythm of their strokes. Select a volunteer to read the Content Words found on page 61. Refer to the Spelling Dictionary and discuss the meaning of any unfamiliar words.

Differentiated Instruction

- For students who spelled all the words correctly on the Pretest, select and assign Extra Challenge Words from the following list: empirical, electromagnetic, exaggeration, oligopoly, communicable, syncopation.
- For students who spelled less than half correctly, assign the following Pattern, Content, and Vocabulary Words: pleasant, constant, adjacent, frequent, reluctant, confident, propel, sculling, strokes, construction, confined, supersede. On the Posttest, evaluate these students on the twelve words assigned; however, encourage them to attempt to spell all the list words to the best of their ability. They are also responsible for writing the dictated sentences.

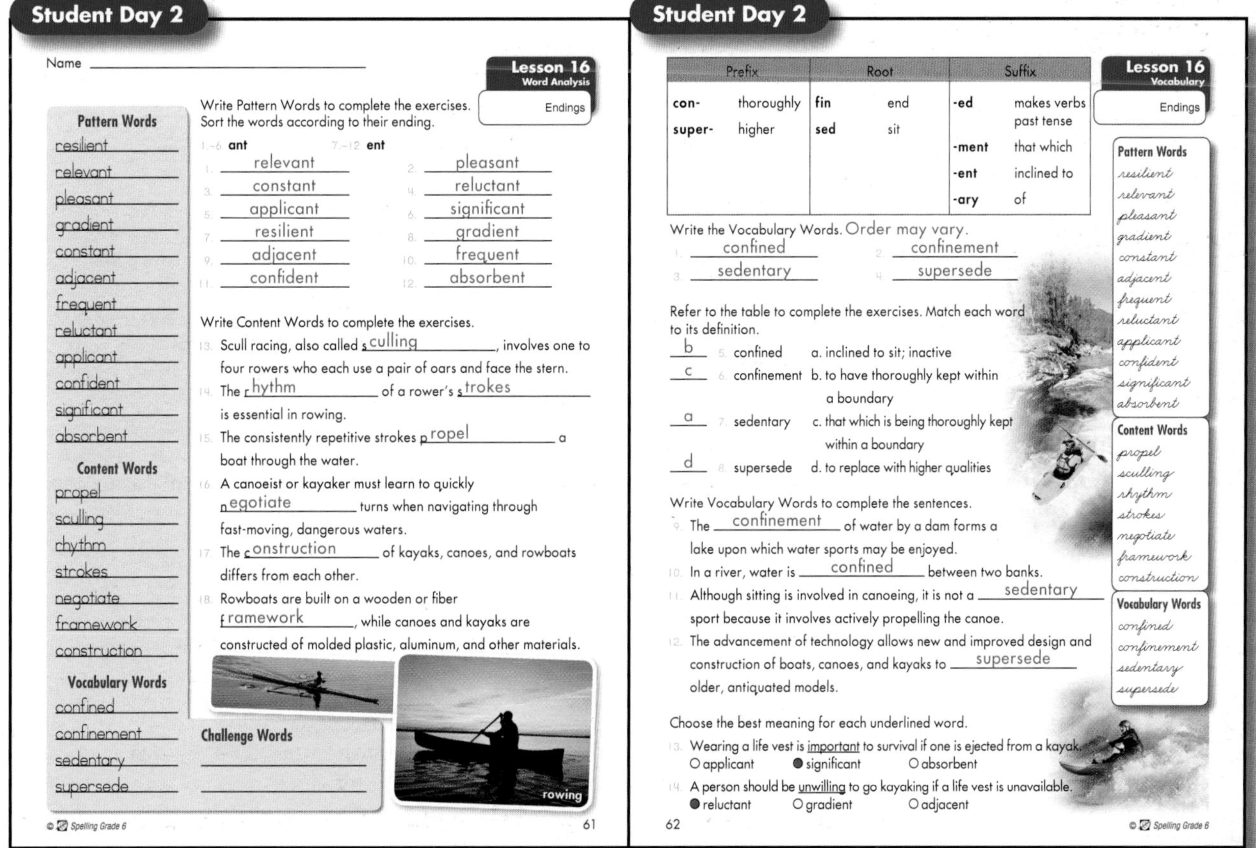

Student Day 2

Name ______

Lesson 16 Word Analysis — Endings

Pattern Words: resilient, relevant, pleasant, gradient, constant, adjacent, frequent, reluctant, applicant, confident, significant, absorbent

Content Words: propel, sculling, rhythm, strokes, negotiate, framework, construction

Vocabulary Words: confined, confinement, sedentary, supersede

Challenge Words

Write Pattern Words to complete the exercises. Sort the words according to their ending.

1.–6. ant	7.–12. ent
1. relevant	2. pleasant
3. constant	4. reluctant
5. applicant	6. significant
7. resilient	8. gradient
9. adjacent	10. frequent
11. confident	12. absorbent

Write Content Words to complete the exercises.

13. Scull racing, also called sculling, involves one to four rowers who each use a pair of oars and face the stern.
14. The rhythm of a rower's strokes is essential in rowing.
15. The consistently repetitive strokes propel a boat through the water.
16. A canoeist or kayaker must learn to quickly negotiate turns when navigating through fast-moving, dangerous waters.
17. The construction of kayaks, canoes, and rowboats differs from each other.
18. Rowboats are built on a wooden or fiber framework, while canoes and kayaks are constructed of molded plastic, aluminum, and other materials.

rowing

© Spelling Grade 6 — 61

Student Day 2

Lesson 16 Vocabulary — Endings

Prefix		Root		Suffix	
con-	thoroughly	fin	end	-ed	makes verbs past tense
super-	higher	sed	sit	-ment	that which
				-ent	inclined to
				-ary	of

Write the Vocabulary Words. Order may vary.

1. confined 2. confinement
3. sedentary 4. supersede

Refer to the table to complete the exercises. Match each word to its definition.

b 5. confined — a. inclined to sit; inactive
c 6. confinement — b. to have thoroughly kept within a boundary
a 7. sedentary — c. that which is being thoroughly kept within a boundary
d 8. supersede — d. to replace with higher qualities

Write Vocabulary Words to complete the sentences.

9. The confinement of water by a dam forms a lake upon which water sports may be enjoyed.
10. In a river, water is confined between two banks.
11. Although sitting is involved in canoeing, it is not a sedentary sport because it involves actively propelling the canoe.
12. The advancement of technology allows new and improved design and construction of boats, canoes, and kayaks to supersede older, antiquated models.

Choose the best meaning for each underlined word.

13. Wearing a life vest is <u>important</u> to survival if one is ejected from a kayak.
○ applicant ● significant ○ absorbent
14. A person should be <u>unwilling</u> to go kayaking if a life vest is unavailable.
● reluctant ○ gradient ○ adjacent

62 — © Spelling Grade 6

Pattern Words: resilient, relevant, pleasant, gradient, constant, adjacent, frequent, reluctant, applicant, confident, significant, absorbent

Content Words: propel, sculling, rhythm, strokes, negotiate, framework, construction

Vocabulary Words: confined, confinement, sedentary, supersede

Student Spelling Support Materials

BLM SP6-01A

Student Spelling Support

1. Use **BLM SP6-01A A Spelling Study Strategy** in instructional groups to provide assistance with some or all of the words.
2. Invite students to write the Challenge Words, numbers 24 and 25, in the Word Bank, in the back of their textbook.
3. As a class, compose one or two paragraphs of an original narrative, omitting the ending of the story. Ask students to complete the narrative with their own idea for the ending. Select students to share their narratives and display the narratives on a bulletin board.
4. Write this week's words, categorize the Pattern, Content, and Vocabulary Words, and attach them to the Word Wall.
5. Read Philippians 1:6: "Being **confident** of this very thing, that He who has begun a good work in you will complete it until the day of Jesus Christ." Discuss that from the very moment God, our Heavenly Father, created us, He began a good work in us. He gave each one unique talents and abilities, likes and dislikes, and goals and dreams. We certainly can be **confident**, knowing that the Lord God is working in us and through us and that He will continue to do so until we meet Him face-to-face. Ask students to write down their abilities and to record a prayer, asking God to develop their abilities for use in His kingdom. Challenge students to imagine the future and write a narrative, describing how they might use their gifts for kingdom work.

3 Proceed to page 61. Say, spell, and say each Pattern, Content, and Vocabulary Word. Provide this week's Challenge Words and have students write them in the spaces provided before completing the page.

4 Proceed to page 62. Remind students to use the table to assist in building each Vocabulary Word. For example, the prefix *con-* goes with the root *fin* and the suffix *-ed* to get the word *confined*. Note that silent *e* in the words *confined* and *confinement* is not included in the original root spelling of *fin*. Note that *sedentary* contains two suffixes. In *supersede*, silent e is not in the original root *sed*. Students complete the page.

5 Homework suggestion: Students use their Spelling Dictionary to write the definition of each word on the back of the corresponding flash card that was suggested for homework on Day 1.

Day 3 Word Study Strategies

Objective

The students will write list words that are antonyms of given words. They will write compound sentences from two simple sentences using a comma and a coordinating conjunction.

Introduction

Write the word *inapplicable* on the board. Solicit a volunteer to name the word that means the opposite of another word. (**antonym**) Review that an *antonym* is a word that means the opposite of another word. Direct students to the list words on page 63 and ask a volunteer to state a word that is the opposite of *inapplicable*. (**relevant**)

Directed Instruction

1 Write the following simple sentences on the board: Asher fell into the river when the canoe tipped over. Resilient Asher climbed right back in. Remind students that a simple sentence expresses a complete thought. Teach that a *compound sentence* is made up of two or more simple sentences that are linked with a comma and a coordinating conjunction. Some coordinating conjunctions are *and*, *so*, *or*, and *but*.

2 Use the simple sentences to write a compound sentence. (**Asher fell into the river when the canoe tipped over, but resilient Asher climbed right back in.**) Teach students the following facts about compound sentences:

- Although a compound sentence has a coordinating conjunction linking simple sentences, each simple sentence still has a subject, a verb, and is a complete thought.
- Simple sentences are linked by a comma at the end of the first sentence, and a coordinating conjunction at the beginning of the second sentence.
- The simple sentences within a compound sentence are equally important.
- Some coordinating conjunctions are *and*, *so*, *or*, and *but*. Teach the following: *and* is used to show the same kind of idea, *so* is used to show the equally important outcome, *or* is used when there is an equal choice, *but* is used to show there is an equal but opposite idea.

3 Proceed to page 63. Students complete the page. Select volunteers to read the compound sentences and state each list word in the sentences. (**confident, negotiate, reluctant; pleasant, sculling; propel, constant, rhythm, strokes, significant; confined**)

Day 4 Writing

Objective

The students will read a narrative. They will write list words to replace the bold word or words. They will write a different ending to the narrative.

Introduction

Instruct students to lay their flash cards suggested for homework on Day 1 and Day 2 on top of their desk so that each word is visible. Read a definition of one list word. The first student to hold up the flash card with the word that matches the given definition, reads the definition and states a definition for another word. Repeat the process.

Directed Instruction

1 Proceed to page 64. Students will read a narrative and write a different ending to the narrative on a separate piece of paper. Remind students to check their sentences for fluency and correct use of conventions.

2 Homework suggestion: Distribute a copy of **BLM SP6-16A Lesson 16 Homework** to each student.

Day 5 Posttest

Objective

The students will correctly write dictated spelling words and sentences.

Introduction

Review by using flash cards noted in Day 1 and Day 2 Homework suggestion.

Directed Assessment

1 Dictate the list words by using the Pretest sentences or developing original ones. Reserve *adjacent, construction, confined, sculling, frequent,* and *pleasant* for the dictation sentences.

2 Read each sentence. Repeat as needed.

- Mark bought property adjacent to a lake.
- His new house is under construction.
- He plans to keep his boat confined to the dock.
- Sculling is Mark's hobby, and he is on a boating team.
- He plans frequent boating trips each month.
- Mark always has a pleasant time when he is on his boat.

3 If assigned, dictate Extra Challenge Words.

4 Score the test, counting each misspelled word as an error. Correct the dictation sentences by grading only the spelling words or grading the complete sentences.

Notes

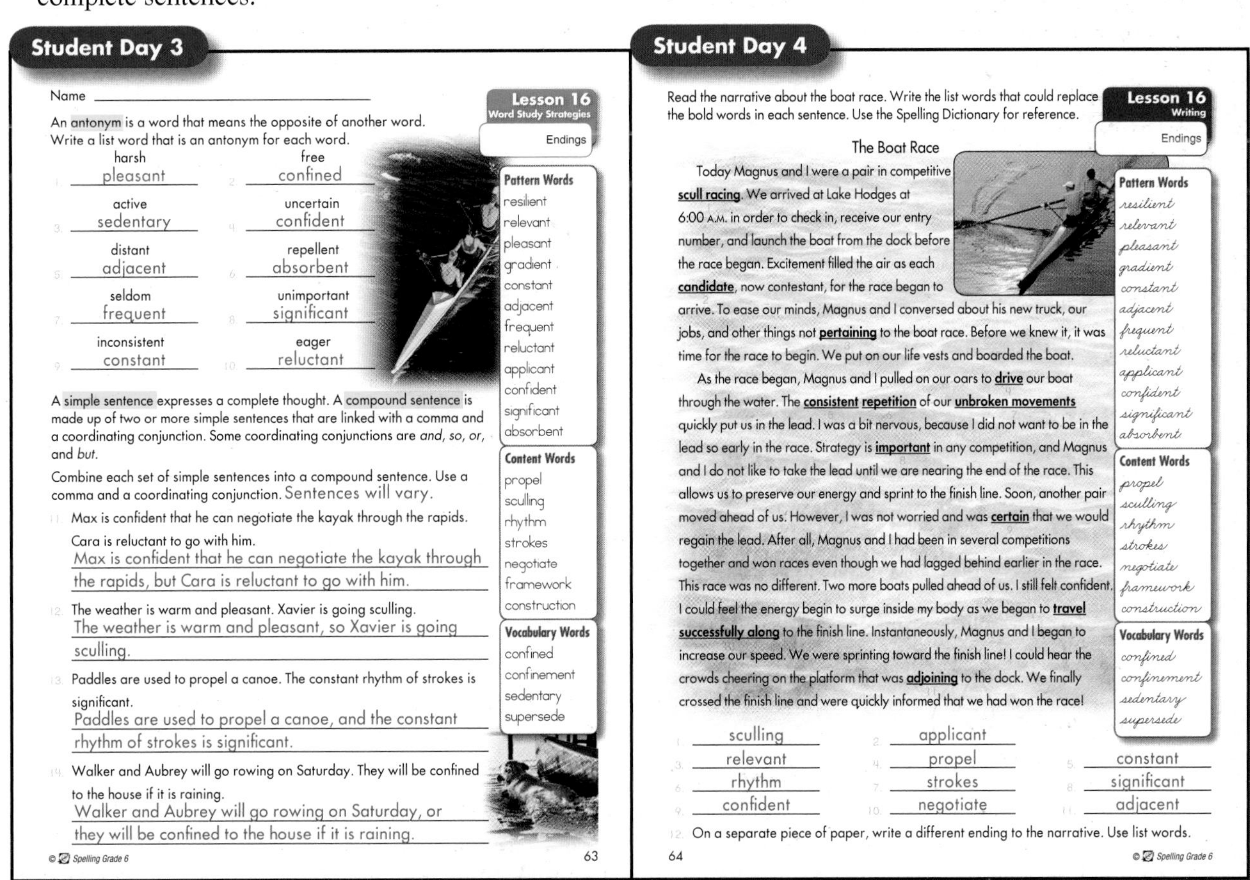

Student Day 3

Name ____________

Lesson 16
Word Study Strategies
Endings

An antonym is a word that means the opposite of another word. Write a list word that is an antonym for each word.

1. harsh — pleasant
2. free — confined
3. active — sedentary
4. uncertain — confident
5. distant — adjacent
6. repellent — absorbent
7. seldom — frequent
8. unimportant — significant
9. inconsistent — constant
10. eager — reluctant

A simple sentence expresses a complete thought. A compound sentence is made up of two or more simple sentences that are linked with a comma and a coordinating conjunction. Some coordinating conjunctions are *and, so, or,* and *but*.

Combine each set of simple sentences into a compound sentence. Use a comma and a coordinating conjunction. Sentences will vary.

11. Max is confident that he can negotiate the kayak through the rapids. Cara is reluctant to go with him.
Max is confident that he can negotiate the kayak through the rapids, but Cara is reluctant to go with him.
12. The weather is warm and pleasant. Xavier is going sculling.
The weather is warm and pleasant, so Xavier is going sculling.
13. Paddles are used to propel a canoe. The constant rhythm of strokes is significant.
Paddles are used to propel a canoe, and the constant rhythm of strokes is significant.
14. Walker and Aubrey will go rowing on Saturday. They will be confined to the house if it is raining.
Walker and Aubrey will go rowing on Saturday, or they will be confined to the house if it is raining.

Pattern Words: resilient, relevant, pleasant, gradient, constant, adjacent, frequent, reluctant, applicant, confident, significant, absorbent

Content Words: propel, sculling, rhythm, strokes, negotiate, framework, construction

Vocabulary Words: confined, confinement, sedentary, supersede

© Spelling Grade 6 63

Student Day 4

Lesson 16
Writing
Endings

Read the narrative about the boat race. Write the list words that could replace the bold words in each sentence. Use the Spelling Dictionary for reference.

The Boat Race

Today Magnus and I were a pair in competitive **scull racing**. We arrived at Lake Hodges at 6:00 A.M. in order to check in, receive our entry number, and launch the boat from the dock before the race began. Excitement filled the air as each **candidate**, now contestant, for the race began to arrive. To ease our minds, Magnus and I conversed about his new truck, our jobs, and other things not **pertaining** to the boat race. Before we knew it, it was time for the race to begin. We put on our life vests and boarded the boat.

As the race began, Magnus and I pulled on our oars to **drive** our boat through the water. The **consistent** **repetition** of our **unbroken movements** quickly put us in the lead. I was a bit nervous, because I did not want to be in the lead so early in the race. Strategy is **important** in any competition, and Magnus and I do not like to take the lead until we are nearing the end of the race. This allows us to preserve our energy and sprint to the finish line. Soon, another pair moved ahead of us. However, I was not worried and was **certain** that we would regain the lead. After all, Magnus and I had been in several competitions together and won races even though we had lagged behind earlier in the race. This race was no different. Two more boats pulled ahead of us. I still felt confident. I could feel the energy begin to surge inside my body as we began to **travel successfully along** to the finish line. Instantaneously, Magnus and I began to increase our speed. We were sprinting toward the finish line! I could hear the crowds cheering on the platform that was **adjoining** to the dock. We finally crossed the finish line and were quickly informed that we had won the race!

1. sculling
2. applicant
3. relevant
4. propel
5. constant
6. rhythm
7. strokes
8. significant
9. confident
10. negotiate
11. adjacent
12. On a separate piece of paper, write a different ending to the narrative. Use list words.

Pattern Words: resilient, relevant, pleasant, gradient, constant, adjacent, frequent, reluctant, applicant, confident, significant, absorbent

Content Words: propel, sculling, rhythm, strokes, negotiate, framework, construction

Vocabulary Words: confined, confinement, sedentary, supersede

64 © Spelling Grade 6

Lesson 17 Endings

Student Pages

Pages 65–68

Lesson Materials

BLM SP6-01B
Card stock
Index cards
T-12
BLM SP6-17A
BLM SP6-17B

Sports

The theme of this lesson is surfing. Surfing is the sport of using a surfboard to ride waves as they break. The sport of surfing is believed to have originated on islands in the Pacific Ocean, and in the Hawaiian Islands, surfing has historically been not only a sport, but a part of the culture. Surfing can be enjoyed virtually anywhere that there are breaking waves.

Day 1 Pretest

Objective

The students will accurately spell and write words with the **endings cial**, **sion**, **tial**, and **tion**. They will spell and write content, vocabulary, and challenge words.

Introduction

Before class, select Challenge Words for numbers 24 and 25 from a cross-curricular subject, words misspelled on previous assignments, or words that interest your students. The word *comprehension* has the ending **sion** and is suggested for number 24. Administer the Pretest.

Directed Instruction

1 Say each word, use it in a sentence, and then repeat the word.

Pattern Words

1. Zeke's ambition is to become a champion surfer.
2. Faith in Jesus is crucial for salvation.
3. No exception will be made for anyone arriving late.
4. Shay voiced an exclamation when her name was called.
5. The reflection of the sun on the water gave the illusion of fire.
6. Judges at surfing competitions must be impartial.
7. The surfing competition had a brief intermission at noon.
8. On one occasion, Jamie was tossed off her board by a huge wave.
9. Few surfers are able to surf as a profession.
10. We had substantial time to practice our surfing skills.
11. Shawn's board received a superficial scratch.
12. I approached my first surfing lesson with much trepidation.

Content Words

13. Surfing requires agility.
14. Surfing was an extremely challenging assignment.
15. What are the dimensions of your long board?
16. Surfers can maintain their equilibrium during a long ride.
17. Surfers use speed and momentum to ride up the face of a wave.
18. Alex was paddling out into the surf, hoping for a wave to break.
19. Ten surfboards were stuck in the sand.

Vocabulary Words

20. Kelly remained flexible about the idea of learning to surf.
21. A good surfboard must be inflexible.
22. Will Collette need to refinish her surfboard?
23. Phil's surfboard is still in the garage because it is unfinished.

Challenge Words

24. ______________________________
25. ______________________________

2 Allow students to self-correct their Pretest. Write each word on the board. Point out the endings *cial, sion, tial,* and *tion* in the Pattern Words. Remind students that the letters *ci, si,* and *ti,* make the /sh/ sound. Because the sounds of *cial* and *tial* are identical, and the sounds of *sion* and *tion* are identical, these spellings must be memorized. Note the roots *fin* and *flex* in the Vocabulary Words. The Vocabulary Word *unfinished* has two suffixes, *-ish* and *-ed*.

3 As a class, read, spell, and read each word. Direct students to highlight misspelled words and rewrite them correctly.

4 Proof each student's Pretest. This becomes an individualized study sheet that can be used at school or at home.

5 Homework suggestion: Duplicate **BLM SP6-01B Flash Cards Template** on CARD STOCK for students to write the list words, using the flash cards as a study aid. Another option is to use INDEX CARDS.

Day 2 Word Analysis and Vocabulary

Objective

The students will sort pattern words according to their **endings**. They will complete sentences with content words. Students will use a table to write vocabulary words, complete sentences, and choose the best meaning for underlined list words.

Introduction

Write the **endings** *cial, sion, tial,* and *tion* on the board. Invite students to refer to the list words, found on page 65. Choose four volunteers to come to the board and write the Pattern Words with the corresponding spellings under each heading. (***cial*—crucial, superficial; *sion*—illusion, occasion, profession, intermission; *tial*—impartial, substantial; *tion*—ambition, exception, trepidation, exclamation**) Instruct students to highlight or underline the **endings** in each word on the flash cards, suggested for homework on Day 1, using a different color for each ending.

Directed Instruction

1 Select seven students to locate the definition of each Content Word from this lesson in the Spelling Dictionary. Students read the definitions aloud.

2 Proceed to page 65. Say, spell, and say each Pattern, Content, and Vocabulary Word. Provide this week's Challenge Words and have students write them in the spaces provided. Select a student to read Exodus 15:2 and discuss God as our source of strength as well as our freedom to praise the Lord at all times and in all places. Students complete the page.

3 Proceed to page 66. Remind students to use the table to assist in

Differentiated Instruction

- For students who spelled all the words correctly on the Pretest, select and assign Extra Challenge Words from the following list: inequalities, elliptical, parody, totalitarianism, degenerative, synthesizer.
- For students who spelled less than half correctly, assign the following Pattern, Content, and Vocabulary Words: crucial, ambition, profession, trepidation, intermission, exclamation, agility, dimensions, challenging, surfboards, refinish, flexible. On the Posttest, evaluate these students on the twelve words assigned; however, encourage them to attempt to spell all the list words to the best of their ability. They are also responsible for writing the dictated sentences.

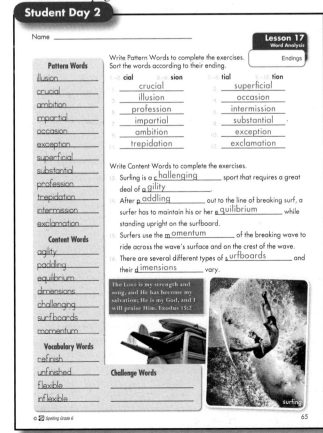

Student Day 2

Name ______________________

Lesson 17 Word Analysis — Endings

Pattern Words: illusion, crucial, ambition, impartial, occasion, exception, superficial, substantial, profession, trepidation, intermission, exclamation

Content Words: agility, paddling, equilibrium, dimensions, challenging, surfboards, momentum

Vocabulary Words: refinish, unfinished, flexible, inflexible

Write Pattern Words to complete the exercises. Sort the words according to their ending.

1.–2. cial	3.–6. sion	7.–8. tial	9.–12. tion
1. crucial	2. superficial		
3. illusion	4. occasion		
5. profession	6. intermission		
7. impartial	8. substantial		
9. ambition	10. exception		
11. trepidation	12. exclamation		

Write Content Words to complete the exercises.

13. Surfing is a challenging sport that requires a great deal of agility.
14. After paddling out to the line of breaking surf, a surfer has to maintain his or her equilibrium while standing upright on the surfboard.
15. Surfers use the momentum of the breaking wave to ride across the wave's surface and on the crest of the wave.
16. There are several different types of surfboards and their dimensions vary.

The LORD is my strength and song, and He has become my salvation; He is my God, and I will praise Him. Exodus 15:2

surfing

Challenge Words

© Spelling Grade 6 — 65

Student Day 2

Lesson 17 Vocabulary — Endings

Prefix		Root		Suffix	
re-	again	fin	end	-ish	process of
un-	not	flex	bend	-ed	makes verbs past tense
in-	not			-ible	is able

Write the Vocabulary Words. Order may vary.

1. refinish 2. unfinished
3. flexible 4. inflexible

Refer to the table to complete the exercises. Write the word that is being defined.

5. not yet at an end; incomplete unfinished
6. not able to be bent; unbendable inflexible
7. the process of finishing again; redo refinish
8. able to be bent; adaptable flexible

Write Vocabulary Words to complete the sentences.

9. I have always preferred body surfing, so my brother Daron encouraged me to be flexible and try surfing on a surfboard.
10. Daron had his own board, but we had to refinish one of our dad's old boards for me to use.
11. The board was made of a foam core with added fiberglass and resin to make it stiff and inflexible.
12. Daron gave me a few surfing lessons before we went out on the water, but my surfing education is still unfinished.

Choose the best meaning for each underlined word.

13. Rachael approached learning to surf with trepidation.
● fear ○ delay ○ balance
14. Her ambition is to become an excellent surfer.
○ honesty ● desire to achieve ○ role
15. Rachael's surfboard has decals and other superficial designs.
○ ordinary ○ engraved ● on the surface
16. She enjoys surfing but would not choose it as a profession.
● career ○ hobby ○ substitute

66 — © Spelling Grade 6

Student Spelling Support Materials

BLM SP6-01A
Index cards

Student Spelling Support

1. Use **BLM SP6-01A A Spelling Study Strategy** in instructional groups to provide assistance with some or all of the words.
2. Invite students to write the Challenge Words, numbers 24 and 25, in the Word Bank, in the back of their textbook.
3. As a writing activity, challenge students to research various types of surfboards. Students illustrate each surfboard and write a one-paragraph caption for each illustration. They may add their surfboards to their progressive, sport journal that was started in Lesson 1.
4. Write this week's words, categorize the Pattern, Content, and Vocabulary Words, and attach them to the Word Wall.
5. Read Exodus 15:2: "The LORD is my strength and song, and He has become my salvation; He is my God, and I will praise Him." Brainstorm a list of times, places, and ways to praise the Lord outside of the traditional settings of church or chapel.
6. Reinforce the various **endings** in the Pattern Words by providing each student with a set of sixteen INDEX CARDS. On twelve cards, students write the Pattern Words, omitting the endings. On the four remaining cards, students write each ending—*cial, sion, tial,* and *tion.* Students are to match the card with the beginning part of each word to its ending. Each ending card is used more than once. Emphasize checking each word against the current word list to insure accuracy.

building each Vocabulary Word. For example, the prefix *re-* goes with the root *fin* and the suffix *-ish* to build the word *refinish*. Allow students to complete the page independently.

4 Homework suggestion: Students use their Spelling Dictionary to write the definition of each word on the back of the corresponding flash card that was suggested for homework on Day 1.

Day 3 Word Study Strategies

Objective

The students will write list words to complete analogies. The students will combine three simple sentences into a compound sentence.

Introduction

Invite students to turn to the list words on page 67. Write the following incomplete analogies on the board:

- Always is to never as reality is to ______. **(illusion)**
- Jumping is to leaping as rowing is to ______. **(paddling)**

An analogy is made up of two word pairs. Both pairs of words have the same kind of relationship. Read the first analogy and ask a volunteer to state how the words *always* and *never* are related. (***Always* and *never* are antonyms.**) Apply the same relationship to the second part of the analogy by asking students which list word is the antonym of *reality*. (**illusion**) Select a volunteer to complete the analogies.

Directed Instruction

1 Write the following sentences on the board: Oscar used his agility to stand up on his surfboard. He maintained his equilibrium. He did not fall. Remind students that a compound sentence is made up of two or more simple sentences that are linked with a comma and a coordinating conjunction, such as *and, so, or,* and *but.* Choose a volunteer to read each simple sentence and to rewrite the sentences as a compound sentence. (**Possible answer: Oscar used his agility to stand up on his surfboard, and he maintained his equilibrium, so he did not fall.**)

2 Proceed to page 67. Assist students as necessary to complete the page.

Day 4 Writing

Objective

The students will write list words to replace synonyms in a narrative. They will use a graphic organizer to write a personal narrative.

Introduction

Invite students to refer to the list words, found on page 68, as you display **T-12 Graphic Organizer for a Narrative** on the overhead. Cover the top section and answers at the bottom. Explain that the underlined words in the text are synonyms for list words. Read the entire text aloud, asking students to supply each synonym needed. Record the synonyms in the spaces provided at the bottom of the transparency. Uncover the answers to check.

Directed Instruction

1 Uncover the top section and refer to the transparency as you remind students that a graphic organizer is a drawing that shows how words or ideas fit together. This graphic organizer shows the elements that an author used to write the narrative shown. Each section of the text is colored to correspond to one of the elements shown in the graphic organizer. Select a volunteer to read the first element, indicated in orange, and the corresponding text. Explain that the text follows the directions indicated on each division of the graphic organizer.

2 Proceed to page 68 and read the text aloud. Ask students to identify each element of a narrative present in the text. Note that there may be more than one way to describe the problem or the resolution to the problem in the narrative. (**Possible answer: The problem is that the surfer faces a**

huge wave; the resolution is that he had adaptable skills and the younger brother prays. The conculsion is that the surfer is successful.) Allow students to independently complete the page.

3 Distribute a copy of **BLM SP6-17A Graphic Organizer for a Narrative** to each student. This graphic organizer is designed for students to jot down notes in preparation for writing a narrative. Students complete the graphic organizer and the narrative, assigned at the bottom of page 68.

4 Homework suggestion: Distribute a copy of **BLM SP6-17B Lesson 17 Homework** to each student.

Day 5 Posttest

Objective

The students will correctly write dictated spelling words and sentences.

Introduction

Review by using flash cards noted in Day 1 and Day 2 Homework suggestion.

Directed Assessment

1 Dictate the list words by using the Pretest sentences or developing original ones. Reserve *crucial, ambition, trepidation, surfboards, agility*, and *refinish* for the dictation sentences.

2 Read each sentence. Repeat as needed.

- It is crucial to know all the safety rules before you learn to surf.
- Many surfers have an ambition to ride huge waves.
- If you feel trepidation at the size of the waves, do not surf.
- Surfboards are designed to be lightweight.
- It takes agility to surf well.
- It is possible to refinish a damaged surfboard.

3 If assigned, dictate Extra Challenge Words.

4 Score the test, counting each misspelled word as an error. Correct the dictation sentences by grading only the spelling words or grading the complete sentences.

Notes

Student Day 3

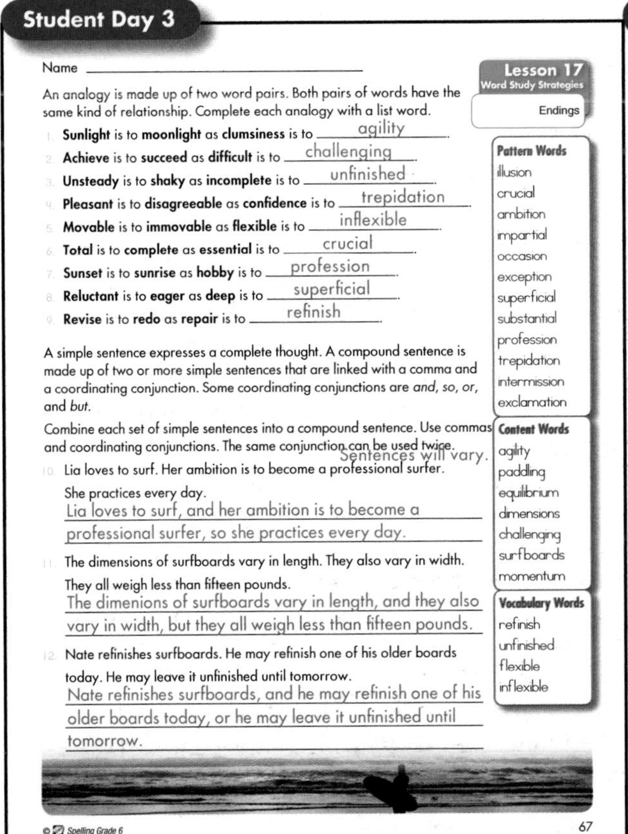

Name ______

Lesson 17
Word Study Strategies
Endings

An analogy is made up of two word pairs. Both pairs of words have the same kind of relationship. Complete each analogy with a list word.

1. **Sunlight** is to **moonlight** as **clumsiness** is to agility.
2. **Achieve** is to **succeed** as **difficult** is to challenging.
3. **Unsteady** is to **shaky** as **incomplete** is to unfinished.
4. **Pleasant** is to **disagreeable** as **confidence** is to trepidation.
5. **Movable** is to **immovable** as **flexible** is to inflexible.
6. **Total** is to **complete** as **essential** is to crucial.
7. **Sunset** is to **sunrise** as **hobby** is to profession.
8. **Reluctant** is to **eager** as **deep** is to superficial.
9. **Revise** is to **redo** as **repair** is to refinish.

A simple sentence expresses a complete thought. A compound sentence is made up of two or more simple sentences that are linked with a comma and a coordinating conjunction. Some coordinating conjunctions are *and, so, or*, and *but*.

Combine each set of simple sentences into a compound sentence. Use commas and coordinating conjunctions. The same conjunction can be used twice. Sentences will vary.

10. Lia loves to surf. Her ambition is to become a professional surfer. She practices every day.
Lia loves to surf, and her ambition is to become a professional surfer, so she practices every day.

11. The dimensions of surfboards vary in length. They also vary in width. They all weigh less than fifteen pounds.
The dimenions of surfboards vary in length, and they also vary in width, but they all weigh less than fifteen pounds.

12. Nate refinishes surfboards. He may refinish one of his older boards today. He may leave it unfinished until tomorrow.
Nate refinishes surfboards, and he may refinish one of his older boards today, or he may leave it unfinished until tomorrow.

Pattern Words
illusion
crucial
ambition
impartial
occasion
exception
superficial
substantial
profession
trepidation
intermission
exclamation

Content Words
agility
paddling
equilibrium
dimensions
challenging
surfboards
momentum

Vocabulary Words
refinish
unfinished
flexible
inflexible

© Spelling Grade 6 67

Student Day 4

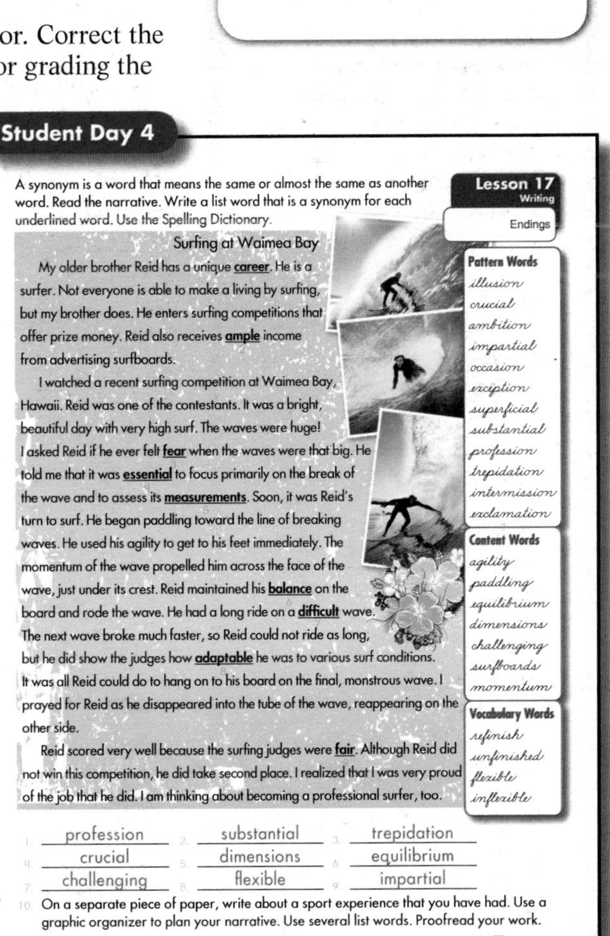

Lesson 17
Writing
Endings

A synonym is a word that means the same or almost the same as another word. Read the narrative. Write a list word that is a synonym for each underlined word. Use the Spelling Dictionary.

Surfing at Waimea Bay

My older brother Reid has a unique career. He is a surfer. Not everyone is able to make a living by surfing, but my brother does. He enters surfing competitions that offer prize money. Reid also receives ample income from advertising surfboards.

I watched a recent surfing competition at Waimea Bay, Hawaii. Reid was one of the contestants. It was a bright, beautiful day with very high surf. The waves were huge! I asked Reid if he ever felt fear when the waves were that big. He told me that it was essential to focus primarily on the break of the wave and to assess its measurements. Soon, it was Reid's turn to surf. He began paddling toward the line of breaking waves. He used his agility to get to his feet immediately. The momentum of the wave propelled him across the face of the wave, just under its crest. Reid maintained his balance on the board and rode the wave. He had a long ride on a difficult wave. The next wave broke much faster, so Reid could not ride as long, but he did show the judges how adaptable he was to various surf conditions. It was all Reid could do to hang on to his board on the final, monstrous wave. I prayed for Reid as he disappeared into the tube of the wave, reappearing on the other side.

Reid scored very well because the surfing judges were fair. Although Reid did not win this competition, he did take second place. I realized that I was very proud of the job that he did. I am thinking about becoming a professional surfer, too.

1. profession 2. substantial 3. trepidation
4. crucial 5. dimensions 6. equilibrium
7. challenging 8. flexible 9. impartial

10. On a separate piece of paper, write about a sport experience that you have had. Use a graphic organizer to plan your narrative. Use several list words. Proofread your work.

Pattern Words
illusion
crucial
ambition
impartial
occasion
exception
superficial
substantial
profession
trepidation
intermission
exclamation

Content Words
agility
paddling
equilibrium
dimensions
challenging
surfboards
momentum

Vocabulary Words
refinish
unfinished
flexible
inflexible

68 © Spelling Grade 6

Lesson 18 Review Lessons 13–17

Student Pages

Pages 69–72

Lesson Materials

T-13
BLM SP6-18A
BLM SP6-18B
BLM SP6-18C
P-2
P-3
BLM SP6-18D
BLMs SP6-18E–F
BLM SP6-06G
BLM SP6-18G

Day 1 Homophones and Homographs

Objective

The students will spell, identify, and sort **homophones and homographs**. They will write **homographs** from pronunciations and complete a sentence with correct **homophones**.

Introduction

Teacher Note: This week's lesson incorporates the Pattern, Content, and Vocabulary Words taught in Lessons 13–17 using a variety of activities such as sorting, pronunciations, a cloze sentence, combining words, filling in the correct answer circle, an acrostic, unscrambling syllables, riddles, and writing words from given roots.

Review the following: **Homophones** are words that sound the same but have different meanings and spellings. **Homographs** are words that are spelled alike but have different meanings. They may also be pronounced differently. The pronunciation of the homograph depends upon the way the word is used in context.

Directed Instruction

1 Display **T-13 Lessons 13–17 Study Sheet** on the overhead to review Lesson 13 words in unison, using the say-spell-say technique. Invite volunteers to identify homophone pairs. Challenge students to correctly use and pronounce **homographs** in sentence context.

2 Proceed to page 69. Explain that the box contains all the Pattern, Content, and Vocabulary Words in Lessons 13–17. This list is the same list of words that was previously displayed on the overhead. Encourage students to use this list as a review tool. Instruct students to read the directions and independently complete the page.

3 Distribute a copy of **BLM SP6-18A Lessons 13–17 Study Sheet** to each student to take home for study.

4 Homework suggestion: Distribute a copy of **BLM SP6-18B Lesson 18 Homework I** to each student to practice with **homophones and homographs**, **compound words**, and **endings**. Remind students to review their weekly sets of flash cards from Lessons 13–17.

Day 2 Compound Words and Endings

Objective

The students will combine two smaller words to form **compound words** that are closed, open, or hyphenated. They will select the appropriate answer circle to indicate if words with the **endings nce** and **nse** are spelled correctly. They will correctly write each word.

Introduction

Display **T-13 Lessons 13–17 Study Sheet** to review Lesson 14 words in unison, using the say-spell-say technique. Remind students that a compound word is made of two or more smaller words. **Compound words** can be closed, open, or hyphenated. Review the following:

- A closed compound word is a single closed word.
- An open compound word is two separate words. Open compound words are usually nouns.
- A hyphenated compound word can contain two or more words joined by hyphens. Hyphenated compound words are usually adjectives.

Directed Instruction

1 Write the following column headings on the board: closed compound words, open compound words, hyphenated compound words. Invite students to come to the board to do the following: identify the two smaller words in each compound list word, name the number of syllables in each smaller word, write the compound word under the correct column heading. Assist as needed.

2 Display **T-13 Lessons 13–17 Study Sheet** to review Lesson 15 words in unison, using the say-spell-say technique. Point out the *nce* or *nse* spelling pattern in each word. Invite students to circle the vowel preceding each *nce* or *nse* ending.

3 Proceed to page 70. Students complete the page.

4 Homework suggestion: Distribute a copy of **BLM SP6-18C Lesson 18 Homework II** to each student to practice with **endings**, Content Words, and Vocabulary Words.

Day 3 Endings

Objective

The students will write words with the **endings ant** and **ent** to complete an acrostic. They will rearrange and eliminate syllables to write words with the **endings cial**, **sion**, **tial**, and **tion**.

Introduction

Display **T-13 Lessons 13–17 Study Sheet** to review Lesson 16 words in unison, using the say-spell-say technique. Write the following acrostic, with missing letters, on the board:

a _ _ o _ **b**◯n t
_ **o** n _ _ d◯_ t
p _ e **a** _◯n t
c _ n _ **t**◯n _

Invite students to come to the board and fill in the missing letters to write words from Lesson 16 to complete the acrostic that uses the word *boat*. (**absorbent; confident; pleasant; constant**) When complete, circle the indicated vowels to point out the correct ending spelling pattern.

Directed Instruction

1 Display **T-13 Lessons 13–17 Study Sheet** to review Lesson 17 words in unison, using the say-spell-say technique. Write the following on the board:

- ca cial sion oc (**occasion; extra syllable is *cial***)
- cep ex tial tion (**exception; extra syllable is *tial***)
- sub sion tial stan (**substantial; extra syllable is *sion***)

Inform students that the syllables need to be rearranged to spell a Pattern Word from Lesson 17. Students cross out the extra, unnecessary syllable before writing the word.

2 Proceed to page 71. Select a student to state the words formed in the acrostic at the top of the page. (**oars and paddles**) Students complete the page independently.

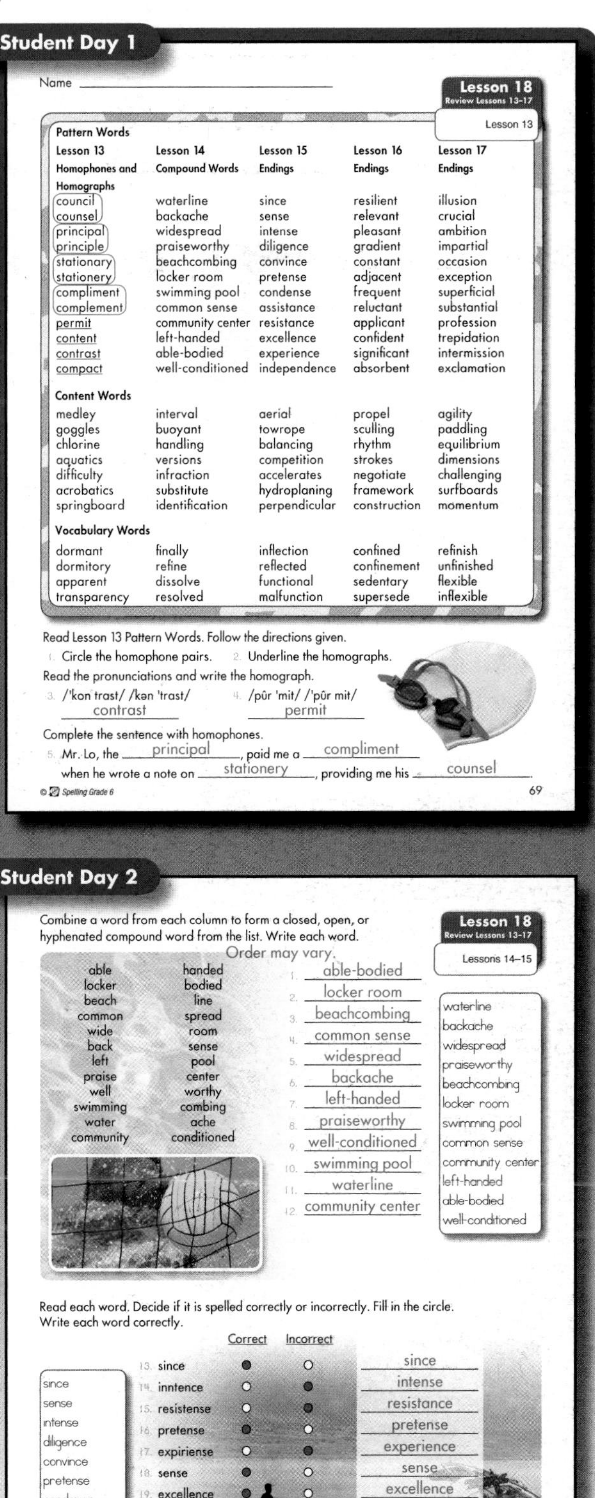

Student Day 1

Name ______________________

Lesson 18
Review Lessons 13–17

Lesson 13

Pattern Words

Lesson 13 Homophones and Homographs	Lesson 14 Compound Words	Lesson 15 Endings	Lesson 16 Endings	Lesson 17 Endings
council	waterline	since	resilient	illusion
counsel	backache	sense	relevant	crucial
principal	widespread	intense	pleasant	ambition
principle	praiseworthy	diligence	gradient	impartial
stationary	beachcombing	convince	constant	occasion
stationery	locker room	pretense	adjacent	exception
compliment	swimming pool	condense	frequent	superficial
complement	common sense	assistance	reluctant	substantial
permit	community center	resistance	applicant	profession
content	left-handed	excellence	confident	trepidation
contrast	able-bodied	experience	significant	intermission
compact	well-conditioned	independence	absorbent	exclamation

Content Words

medley	interval	aerial	propel	agility
goggles	buoyant	towrope	sculling	paddling
chlorine	handling	balancing	rhythm	equilibrium
aquatics	versions	competition	strokes	dimensions
difficulty	infraction	accelerates	negotiate	challenging
acrobatics	substitute	hydroplaning	framework	surfboards
springboard	identification	perpendicular	construction	momentum

Vocabulary Words

dormant	finally	inflection	confined	refinish
dormitory	refine	reflected	confinement	unfinished
apparent	dissolve	functional	sedentary	flexible
transparency	resolved	malfunction	supersede	inflexible

Read Lesson 13 Pattern Words. Follow the directions given.

1. Circle the homophone pairs. 2. Underline the homographs.

Read the pronunciations and write the homograph.

3. /'kon trast/ /kən 'trast/ contrast
4. /pûr 'mit/ /'pûr mit/ permit

Complete the sentence with homophones.

5. Mr. Lo, the principal, paid me a compliment when he wrote a note on stationery, providing me his counsel.

© Spelling Grade 6 69

Student Day 2

Combine a word from each column to form a closed, open, or hyphenated compound word from the list. Write each word.

Lesson 18
Review Lessons 13–17

Lessons 14–15

Order may vary.

able	handed
locker	bodied
beach	line
common	spread
wide	room
back	sense
left	pool
praise	center
well	worthy
swimming	combing
water	ache
community	conditioned

1. able-bodied
2. locker room
3. beachcombing
4. common sense
5. widespread
6. backache
7. left-handed
8. praiseworthy
9. well-conditioned
10. swimming pool
11. waterline
12. community center

waterline
backache
widespread
praiseworthy
beachcombing
locker room
swimming pool
common sense
community center
left-handed
able-bodied
well-conditioned

Read each word. Decide if it is spelled correctly or incorrectly. Fill in the circle. Write each word correctly.

since
sense
intense
diligence
convince
pretense
condense
assistance
resistance
excellence
experience
independence

	Correct	Incorrect	
13. since	●	○	since
14. inntence	○	●	intense
15. resistense	○	●	resistance
16. pretense	●	○	pretense
17. expiriense	○	●	experience
18. sense	●	○	sense
19. excellence	●	○	excellence
20. kondence	○	●	condense
21. diligence	●	○	diligence
22. indipendance	○	●	independence
23. convince	●	○	convince
24. asistense	○	●	assistance

70 © Spelling Grade 6

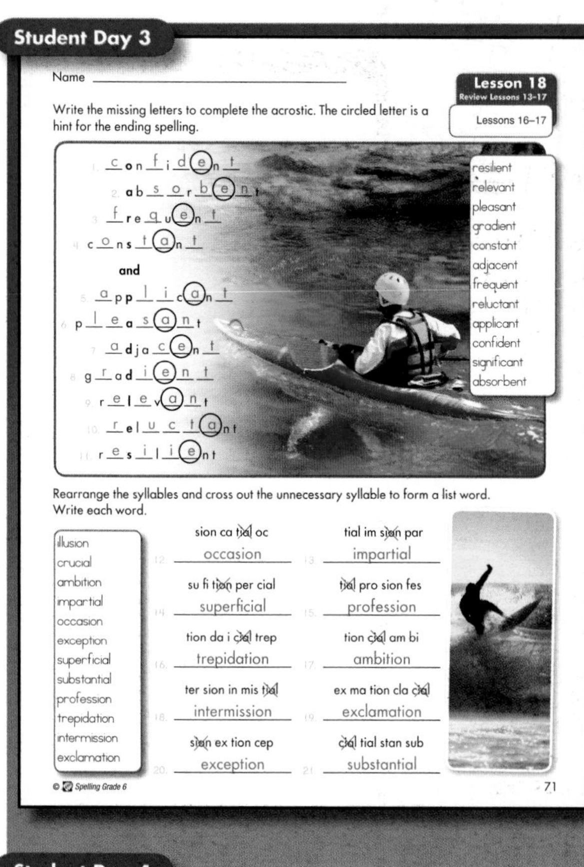

Student Day 3

Name ______________________

Lesson 18 Review Lessons 13–17

Lessons 16–17

Write the missing letters to complete the acrostic. The circled letter is a hint for the ending spelling.

1. confident
2. absorbent
3. frequent
4. constant

and

5. applicant
6. pleasant
7. adjacent
8. gradient
9. relevant
10. reluctant
11. resilient

resilient, relevant, pleasant, gradient, constant, adjacent, frequent, reluctant, applicant, confident, significant, absorbent

Rearrange the syllables and cross out the unnecessary syllable to form a list word. Write each word.

illusion, crucial, ambition, impartial, occasion, exception, superficial, substantial, profession, trepidation, intermission, exclamation

sion ca tial oc
12. occasion

tial im sion par
13. impartial

su fi tion per cial
14. superficial

tial pro sion fes
15. profession

tion da i cial trep
16. trepidation

tion cial am bi
17. ambition

ter sion in mis tial
18. intermission

ex ma tion cla cial
19. exclamation

sion ex tion cep
20. exception

cial tial stan sub
21. substantial

© Spelling Grade 6 71

Student Day 4

Write the Content Word that answers each riddle.

Lesson 18 Review Lessons 13–17

Content and Vocabulary Words

1. Which word is a contest? competition
2. Which word implies balance? equilibrium
3. Which word is being built? construction
4. Which word is a chemical? chlorine
5. Which word skims the water? hydroplaning
6. Which word occurs in the air? aerial
7. Which word is a replacement? substitute
8. Which word is a failure to obey? infraction
9. Which word protects your eyes? goggles
10. Which word proves who you are? identification
11. Which word is a skeletal structure? framework
12. Which word is not easy to achieve? difficulty
13. Which word is able to move quickly? agility
14. Which word provides measurements? dimensions
15. Which word moves you forward by force? propel

goggles, chlorine, difficulty, infraction, substitute, identification, aerial, competition, hydroplaning, propel, framework, construction, agility, equilibrium, dimensions

Read the meaning of each root. Write the Vocabulary Words that contain the given root.

dormant, dormitory, apparent, finally, dissolve, resolved, inflection, reflected, functional, confined, sedentary, supersede, refinish, flexible, inflexible

16. The root **solv** means **loosen** or **solve**. Order may vary.
dissolve resolved

17. The root **dorm** means **sleep**.
dormant dormitory

18. The root **sed** means **sit**.
sedentary supersede

19. The root **flect** or **flex** means **bend**.
inflection reflected
flexible inflexible

20. The root **fin** means **end**.
finally confined
refinish

21. The root **par** means **appear**.
apparent

72 © Spelling Grade 6

Day 4 Content Words and Vocabulary Words

Objective

The students will write content words to answer riddles. They will write vocabulary words from given roots and their meanings.

Introduction

Display **T-13 Lessons 13–17 Study Sheet** to review Content Words in unison, using the say-spell-say technique. Circle the following Content Words on the transparency: springboard, buoyant, towrope. Read the following riddles aloud:

- Which word floats? (**buoyant**)
- Which word pulls you? (**towrope**)
- Which word is flexible? (**springboard**)

Challenge students to identify the Content Word that answers each riddle.

Directed Instruction

1 Display **T-13 Lessons 13–17 Study Sheet** to review Vocabulary Words in unison, using the say-spell-say technique. Refer to **P-2** and **P-3 Latin Roots** to review the meanings of the following roots:

- *dorm* means *sleep*
- *par* means *appear*
- *solv* means *loosen* or *solve*
- *funct* means *perform*
- *flex* means *bend*
- *it* means *to go*
- *fin* means *end*
- *flect* means *bend*
- *sed* means *sit*

2 Proceed to page 72. Allow students to complete the page independently.

3 Homework suggestion: Distribute a copy of **BLM SP6-18D Lessons 13–17 Test Prep** to each student to practice with many of the words that may appear on the Assessment. Prepare for the Assessment by studying the words on **BLM SP6-18A Lessons 13–17 Study Sheet** that was sent home on Day 1 or by using their flash card sets.

Day 5 Assessment

Objective

The students will accurately select the appropriate answer within the context of a sentence. They will fill in the corresponding answer circle.

Introduction

Teacher Note: The Test makes provision for Differentiated Instruction. The first twelve sentences include the words assigned to students with shortened lists. Encourage these students to try all the sentences, but only grade the first twelve sentences. The Test is found on two blackline masters.

Duplicate a copy of **BLMs SP6-18E–F Lessons 13–17 Test I** and **II** and distribute to each student. Duplicate **BLM SP6-06G Student Answer Form** and cut apart. Distribute one answer form to each student. Remind students to fill in each answer circle completely and to erase completely if they wish to change an answer.

Directed Assessment

1 Instruct students to listen as you dictate the following Sample:

Sample

As the boat <u>acellerates</u>, it is <u>crucial</u> to hold the <u>towrope</u> tightly. <u>All correct</u>

A B C D

Say, "Are any of the first three underlined words misspelled?" Pause for replies. Inform students that the letter *A* is below the underlined word that is misspelled. (**accelerates**) Guide students to the answer form that was previously distributed. Lead students to find the Sample box and fill in the appropriate answer circle containing the same letter. Say, "You will continue in the same way. You will read each sentence, choose the word that you think is misspelled, and fill in the corresponding circle on the answer form. If all the words are spelled correctly, fill in the fourth circle, labeled *D*, for *All correct*."

2 Assist students as needed while they read the sentences and complete the Test on their own.

1. The well-conditioned athlete was content in her new profession.
2. The principal wrote a pleasant note on his personal stationery.
3. It is apparent that diligence and experience helped the surfer win.
4. Since aquatics are very challenging, one should be focused.
5. The substitute player had ambition and resolved to perform well.
6. Frequent dives helped Sondra to be confident, not reluctant.
7. A constant backache gave Quentin some trepidation about skiing.
8. The construction of the swimming pool required a permit.
9. Contrast the dimensions of the new locker room with the old one.
10. With Ray's assistance, Collin will refinish his surfboards.
11. The left-handed player was skillfully handling the buoyant ball.
12. Without difficulty, Darcy used powerful strokes to propel the kayak.
13. A stationary bike gives one a substantial or significant workout.
14. Aaden's acrobatics and intense focus will complement the team.
15. Kate felt a sense of independence during her aerial maneuvers.
16. During the competition, Joel was paddling and keeping rhythm.
17. To negotiate rough waters, it is relevant to use common sense.
18. The swimming medley finally started after a lengthy interval.
19. The athletic council will condense old rules in the new framework.
20. The able-bodied applicant walked into the athletic dormitory.
21. The chlorine stung the superficial cut through the absorbent bandage.
22. The compact engine's malfunction stopped the boat's momentum.
23. During intermission, an impartial decision was made about the infraction.
24. Brad reflected on Dewey's surfing agility and good equilibrium.
25. The perpendicular springboard at the community center was broken.

3 Refer to **BLM SP6-18G Lessons 13–17 Answer Key** when correcting the Test.

Notes

Lesson

19 Greek Roots

Student Pages

Pages 73–76

Lesson Materials

BLM SP6-01B
Card stock
Index cards
P-4
BLM SP6-19A

Sports

Lessons 19–23 utilize the theme of racket and paddle sports. Lesson 19 begins with tennis. Tennis was invented in England and originally played on grass. International tournaments are still played on grass. Each year, professional tennis players compete in four major tournaments called the grand slam events. They are the Australian Open, French Open, United States Open, and the Wimbledon Championships. The term *open* refers to the tournament being open to amateurs, as well as professionals.

Day 1 Pretest

Objective

The students will accurately spell and write words with **Greek roots**. They will spell and write content, vocabulary, and challenge words.

Introduction

Before class, select Challenge Words for numbers 24 and 25 from a cross-curricular subject, words misspelled on previous assignments, or words that interest your students. The word *thermodynamics* has the **Greek roots thermo** and **dynam** and is suggested for number 24. Administer the Pretest.

Directed Instruction

1 Say each word, use it in a sentence, and then repeat the word.

Pattern Words

1. Zane thanked the Lord that a cardiogram showed a normal heartbeat.
2. The patient was connected to the cardiograph by wires.
3. Dr. Froelig studied cardiology in order to become a cardiologist.
4. Can a healthy diet and routine exercise prevent cardiopathy?
5. Hydropathy was a method to cure disease in the nineteenth century.
6. Tyrone is a pipeline inspector who uses a hydroscope to detect leaks.
7. Hydrotherapy baths are often used to relieve headaches and stress.
8. A hydrothermal vent spewed water through a crack in the ocean floor.
9. A thermogenic sport, such as tennis, raises one's body temperature.
10. Thermography is a printing process that produces raised images.
11. The outdoor thermometer read 98 degrees Fahrenheit.
12. The thermostat at the indoor tennis club read 68 degrees Fahrenheit.

Content Words

13. Lena's confidence rose when she earned the advantage in tennis.
14. The velocity of a tennis serve can be over one hundred miles per hour.
15. Shelby finally won the tennis game after the deuce with Ian.
16. Line judges determine if the ball lands outside the boundaries.
17. When Edwin served the ball, it went diagonally into the service box.
18. The doctor suggested that Kaylin begin an aerobic sport such as tennis.
19. A few tennis professionals have won all four major tournaments.

Vocabulary Words

20. Line judges arbitrate disputes over where the ball landed.
21. Perspiration is noticeable when players are actively engaged in a game.
22. One's respiration will increase when aggressively involved in a sport.
23. In recreational tennis, players make arbitrary decisions.

Challenge Words

24. ______________________
25. ______________________

2 Allow students to self-correct their Pretest. Write each word on the board. Point out that each Pattern Word contains two **Greek roots**. *Cardio, hydro,* and *thermo* are the **Greek roots** that appear at the beginning of each Pattern Word. Note the roots *arbitr* and *spir* in the Vocabulary Words. Teach that a *root* is the part of a word that gives the basic meaning. It is suggested to use the Spelling Dictionary as a reference for the accurate pronunciation of the Pattern Words.

3 As a class, read, spell, and read each word. Direct students to highlight misspelled words and rewrite them correctly.

4 Proof each student's Pretest. This becomes an individualized study sheet that can be used at school or at home.

5 Homework suggestion: Duplicate **BLM SP6-01B Flash Cards Template** on CARD STOCK for students to write the list words, using the flash cards as a study aid. Another option is to use INDEX CARDS.

Day 2 Word Analysis and Vocabulary

Objective

The students will sort and write words that have **Greek roots** and complete sentences with content words. They will use a table to write vocabulary words, select words to match definitions, complete sentences in context, and choose the best meaning for given words.

Introduction

Teacher Note: This week's lesson contains suff
or "rooted" in the Greek and Latin languages.
Display **P-4 Greek Roots** for students to use as
students to fold a piece of notebook paper leng
labeling the first column *root* and the second *su*
turn to page 73 to refer to the list words. Expla
hydroscope is not in the original spelling of the
each Pattern Word contains two **Greek roots**. I
segment and write each Pattern Word. Allow st
activity. Assist as needed.

The psychologist prescribed lots of rest for her client.
Because the dog was being irrational, they had him checked for rabies.

Root	Suffix	Root	
cardio, logy		hydro, therap	
cardio, path	-y	hydro, therm	-al
cardio, gram		thermo, stat	
cardio, graph		thermo, gen	-ic
hydro, path	-y	thermo, meter	
hydro, scop		thermo, graph	-y

Differentiated Instruction

- For students who spelled all the words correctly on the Pretest, select and assign Extra Challenge Words from the following list: irrational, exothermic, soliloquy, profiteering, psychologist, ukulele.
- For students who spelled less than half correctly, assign the
Content,
Words:
diogram,
othermal,
ometer,
advantage,
rary,
e Posttest,
dents on
assigned;
ge them
l all the
est of
are also responsible for writing the dictated sentences.

57 pts.

Student Day 2

Name ______________________

Lesson 19 Word Analysis

Greek Roots

Pattern Words
cardiology
cardiopathy
cardiogram
cardiograph
hydropathy
hydroscope
hydrotherapy
hydrothermal
thermostat
thermogenic
thermometer
thermography
Content Words
deuce
velocity
aerobic
diagonally
advantage
boundaries
professionals
Vocabulary Words
arbitrate
arbitrary
perspiration
respiration

Greek roots are used to build many words in the English language. A root is the part of a word that gives the basic meaning. Knowledge of word origins helps in building spelling and vocabulary skills.

Write Pattern Words to complete the exercises. Sort by Greek roots.

1.–4. **hydro** 5.–8. **cardio** 9.–12. **thermo**

1. hydropathy
2. hydroscope
3. hydrotherapy
4. hydrothermal
5. cardiology
6. cardiopathy
7. cardiogram
8. cardiograph
9. thermostat
10. thermogenic
11. thermometer
12. thermography

Write Content Words to complete the exercises.

13. A tennis court has sideline boundaries for singles and doubles play.
14. The server must hit the ball so that it lands in the service box, diagonally opposite of the server.
15. The velocity of a tennis serve by some professionals has reached over one hundred miles per hour.
16. When the score is deuce, the player who wins the next point has the advantage.
17. Tennis is an aerobic sport because it is an action-filled game and increases your heart rate.

Challenge Words

____
____

tennis

© Spelling Grade 6 73

Student Day 2

Lesson 19 Vocabulary

Greek Roots

Prefix		Root		Suffix	
per-	through	**arbitr**	judge	**-ate**	to act
re-	again	**spir**	breathe	**-ary**	related to
				-ation	state of

Write the Vocabulary Words. Order may vary.

1. arbitrate
2. arbitrary
3. perspiration
4. respiration

Refer to the table to complete the exercises. Write the word that is being defined.

5. related to a personal decision or judgment; random arbitrary
6. the state of secreting sweat through the skin; sweat perspiration
7. to act as a judge to make a decision arbitrate
8. the state of breathing respiration

Write Vocabulary Words to complete the sentences.

9. Claire will arbitrate Annie and Ida's tennis match to ensure the line calls are fair.
10. Claire is known for making fair, not arbitrary decisions.
11. Ida could hear Annie's heavy respiration during the exciting, close match.
12. During Ida and Annie's tennis match, their exertion resulted in perspiration.

Choose the best meaning for each word.

13. velocity
- ● speed
- ○ volume
- ○ length

14. hydrothermal
- ○ relating to cold water
- ○ relating to salt water
- ● relating to hot water

15. boundaries
- ○ results
- ● limits
- ○ objects

16. cardiopathy
- ● a disease or disorder of the heart
- ○ a disease or disorder of the eye
- ○ a disease or disorder of the liver

Pattern Words
cardiology
cardiopathy
cardiogram
cardiograph
hydropathy
hydroscope
hydrotherapy
hydrothermal
thermostat
thermogenic
thermometer
thermography
Content Words
deuce
velocity
aerobic
diagonally
advantage
boundaries
professionals
Vocabulary Words
arbitrate
arbitrary
perspiration
respiration

74 © Spelling Grade 6

Student Spelling Support Materials

BLM SP6-01A

Student Spelling Support

1. Use **BLM SP6-01A A Spelling Study Strategy** in instructional groups to provide assistance with some or all of the words.
2. Invite students to write the Challenge Words, numbers 24 and 25, in the Word Bank, in the back of their textbook.
3. Have students write a persuasive essay about a sport or activity that they enjoy doing, for example, tennis or playing the piano. Instruct students to include facts and the reasons to persuade someone to become involved in the sport or activity.
4. Write this week's words, categorize the Pattern, Content, and Vocabulary Words, and attach them to the Word Wall.
5. Read I Corinthians 6:19–20: "Or do you not know that your body is the temple of the Holy Spirit who is in you, whom you have from God, and you are not your own? For you were bought at a price; therefore glorify God in your body and in your spirit, which are God's." Discuss with students that God created each one of us, and we should take care of our body. Many diseases can be prevented by proper exercise and diet. Invite students to keep a log of their activities and food consumed for an entire week and formulate one goal for increasing a healthy lifestyle. Discuss how healthy lifestyles can begin at an early age.

Directed Instruction

1 Invite students to refer to their chart to identify the following: words without a suffix (**cardiology, cardiogram, cardiograph, hydroscope, thermostat, thermometer**); words with a suffix (**cardiopathy, hydropathy, hydrotherapy, hydrothermal, thermogenic, thermography**); a word with silent *e* added to the root (**hydroscope**).

2 Proceed to page 73. Say, spell, and say each Pattern, Content, and Vocabulary Word. Provide this week's Challenge Words and have students write them in the spaces provided before completing the page.

3 Proceed to page 74. Remind students to use the table to assist in building each Vocabulary Word. For example, the root *arbitr* goes with the suffix *-ate* to build the word *arbitrate.* Students complete the page.

4 Homework suggestion: Students use their Spelling Dictionary to write the definition of each word on the back of the corresponding flash card that was suggested for homework on Day 1.

Day 3 Word Study Strategies

Objective

The students will circle common **Greek roots** in sets of words and write the roots according to their definitions. They will write pattern words by combining the meanings of two roots. They will write complete sentences from sentence fragments.

Introduction

Remind students to reference **P-4 Greek Roots**. Write the following words and incomplete sentence on the board:

- cardiology, cardiopathy, cardiogram, cardiograph

The root _______ means *heart.* (**cardio**)

Invite volunteers to circle and write the common root in the set of words.

Directed Instruction

1 Invite students to refer to page 75 for the list words. Write the following on the board and select students to build list words:

• water + treatment	• heat + write	• heart + write
(hydro) (therap)	(thermo) (graph)	(cardio) (gram or graph)
(**hydrotherapy**)	(**thermography**)	(**cardiogram**) (**cardiograph**)

Point out that the **Greek roots** *gram* and *graph* mean *write.*

2 Write the following phrase on the board: Diagonally over the net. Read the phrase and ask students if it expressed a complete thought. (**No.**) Explain that the phrase is a sentence fragment. Define *sentence fragment* as an incomplete sentence that does not express a complete thought. A fragment is missing the subject, predicate, or both. Explain that the sentence fragment is missing the subject and the predicate. Select a volunteer to change the sentence fragment into a complete sentence. (**Possible answer: Andre hit the ball diagonally over the net.**)

3 Proceed to page 75. Students complete the page. Assist as needed.

Day 4 Writing

Objective

The students will read a persuasive essay and replace definitions with list words.

Introduction

Teacher Note: The persuasive domain is the focus for the writing pages in Lessons 19–23.

Explain that today's writing page is a persuasive essay about tennis. Persuasive writing involves the writer giving facts about a topic with the intent to convince the reader to agree with the author's point of view. Select a student to orally persuade classmates to read a book he or she has read.

Directed Instruction

1. Read the definition of a selected Pattern Word from this lesson out of the Spelling Dictionary. Students determine which word is being defined from the list of words on page 76, look it up in their Spelling Dictionary, and identify the word. Repeat the process.
2. Proceed to page 76. Encourage students to use their Spelling Dictionary. When finished, select a volunteer to orally read the essay with the replaced list words.
3. Homework suggestion: Distribute a copy of **BLM SP6-19A Lesson 19 Homework** to each student.

Day 5 Posttest

Objective

The students will correctly write dictated spelling words and sentences.

Introduction

Review by using flash cards noted in Day 1 and Day 2 Homework suggestion.

Directed Assessment

1. Dictate the list words by using the Pretest sentences or developing original ones. Reserve *cardiogram, cardiopathy, aerobic, arbitrary, boundaries,* and *thermometer* for the dictation sentences.
2. Read each sentence. Repeat as needed.
   - Dean's doctor looked at his cardiogram with him.
   - He was glad there were no signs of cardiopathy.
   - Dean knows that aerobic exercise helps him to stay healthy.
   - He makes the arbitrary decision to play tennis three times a week.
   - He is learning to hit the tennis ball within the boundaries.
   - If the thermometer shows an unpleasant temperature, Dean stays home.
3. If assigned, dictate Extra Challenge Words.
4. Score the test, counting each misspelled word as an error. Correct the dictation sentences by grading only the spelling words or grading the complete sentences.

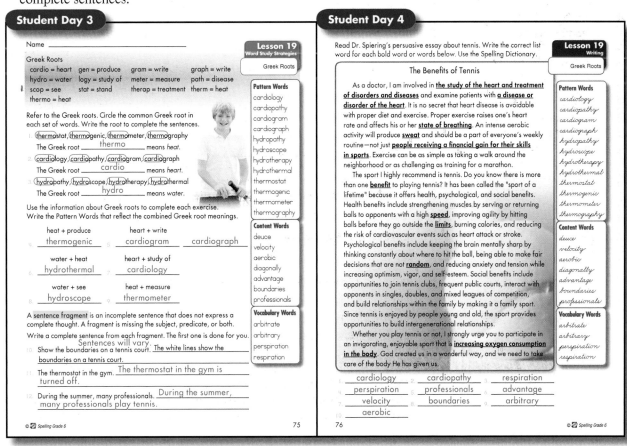

Student Day 3

Name ____________________

Lesson 19 Word Study Strategies — Greek Roots

Greek Roots

cardio = heart	gen = produce	gram = write	graph = write
hydro = water	logy = study of	meter = measure	path = disease
scop = see	stat = stand	therap = treatment	therm = heat
thermo = heat			

Refer to the Greek roots. Circle the common Greek root in each set of words. Write the root to complete the sentences.

1. thermostat, thermogenic, thermometer, thermography
   The Greek root thermo means *heat*.
2. cardiology, cardiopathy, cardiogram, cardiograph
   The Greek root cardio means *heart*.
3. hydropathy, hydroscope, hydrotherapy, hydrothermal
   The Greek root hydro means *water*.

Use the information about Greek roots to complete each exercise. Write the Pattern Words that reflect the combined Greek root meanings.

4. heat + produce: thermogenic
5. heart + write: cardiogram, cardiograph
6. water + heat: hydrothermal
7. heart + study of: cardiology
8. water + see: hydroscope
9. heat + measure: thermometer

A sentence fragment is an incomplete sentence that does not express a complete thought. A fragment is missing the subject, predicate, or both.

Write a complete sentence from each fragment. The first one is done for you. Sentences will vary.

10. Show the boundaries on a tennis court. The white lines show the boundaries on a tennis court.
11. The thermostat in the gym. The thermostat in the gym is turned off.
12. During the summer, many professionals. During the summer, many professionals play tennis.

Pattern Words: cardiology, cardiopathy, cardiogram, cardiograph, hydropathy, hydroscope, hydrotherapy, hydrothermal, thermostat, thermogenic, thermometer, thermography

Content Words: deuce, velocity, aerobic, diagonally, advantage, boundaries, professionals

Vocabulary Words: arbitrate, arbitrary, perspiration, respiration

© Spelling Grade 6 75

Student Day 4

Read Dr. Spiering's persuasive essay about tennis. Write the correct list word for each bold word or words below. Use the Spelling Dictionary.

Lesson 19 Writing — Greek Roots

The Benefits of Tennis

As a doctor, I am involved in **the study of the heart and treatment of disorders and diseases** and examine patients with **a disease or disorder of the heart**. It is no secret that heart disease is avoidable with proper diet and exercise. Proper exercise raises one's heart rate and affects his or her **state of breathing**. An intense aerobic activity will produce **sweat** and should be a part of everyone's weekly routine—not just **people receiving a financial gain for their skills in sports**. Exercise can be as simple as taking a walk around the neighborhood or as challenging as training for a marathon.

The sport I highly recommend is tennis. Do you know there is more than one **benefit** to playing tennis? It has been called the "sport of a lifetime" because it offers health, psychological, and social benefits. Health benefits include strengthening muscles by serving or returning balls to opponents with a high **speed**, improving agility by hitting balls before they go outside the **limits**, burning calories, and reducing the risk of cardiovascular events such as heart attack or stroke. Psychological benefits include keeping the brain mentally sharp by thinking constantly about where to hit the ball, being able to make fair decisions that are not **random**, and reducing anxiety and tension while increasing optimism, vigor, and self-esteem. Social benefits include opportunities to join tennis clubs, frequent public courts, interact with opponents in singles, doubles, and mixed leagues of competition, and build relationships within the family by making it a family sport. Since tennis is enjoyed by people young and old, the sport provides opportunities to build intergenerational relationships.

Whether you play tennis or not, I strongly urge you to participate in an invigorating, enjoyable sport that is **increasing oxygen consumption in the body**. God created us in a wonderful way, and we need to take care of the body He has given us.

1. cardiology
2. cardiopathy
3. respiration
4. perspiration
5. professionals
6. advantage
7. velocity
8. boundaries
9. arbitrary
10. aerobic

Pattern Words: cardiology, cardiopathy, cardiogram, cardiograph, hydropathy, hydroscope, hydrotherapy, hydrothermal, thermostat, thermogenic, thermometer, thermography

Content Words: deuce, velocity, aerobic, diagonally, advantage, boundaries, professionals

Vocabulary Words: arbitrate, arbitrary, perspiration, respiration

76 © Spelling Grade 6

Lesson
20 Greek Roots

Student Pages

Pages 77–80

Lesson Materials

BLM SP6-01B
Card stock
Index cards
P-4
Newspaper advertisement
T-14
BLM SP6-20A
BLM SP6-20B

Sports

The theme of this lesson is badminton. Badminton is a sport for two or four players, utilizing lightweight rackets and a shuttlecock. Players volley the shuttlecock from one side of the net to the other, trying to keep the shuttlecock from hitting the ground. Badminton dates back to ancient times where it was played in Asia and Greece. British officers brought the modern version of badminton from India to England in the mid-nineteenth century. Badminton has been an Olympic medal sport since 1992.

Day 1 Pretest

Objective

The students will accurately spell and write words with **Greek roots.** They will spell and write content, vocabulary, and challenge words.

Introduction

Before class, select Challenge Words for numbers 24 and 25 from a cross-curricular subject, words misspelled on previous assignments, or words that interest your students. The word *microbiologist* has the **Greek roots macro**, **bio**, and **logy** and is suggested for number 24. Administer the Pretest.

Directed Instruction

1 Say each word, use it in a sentence, and then repeat the word.

Pattern Words

1. God is the creator and ruler of the macrocosm, the universe.
2. Some algae are macroscopic.
3. A drop of pond water may contain a microcosm of life.
4. Scientists use micrograph images to study viruses.
5. The referee used a microphone to announce the badminton score.
6. Many animal and plant cells are microscopic.
7. The team selected a monochromatic color scheme for uniforms.
8. Stuart has his monogram embroidered above his shirt pocket.
9. Defeating the badminton champs seemed to be a monolithic task.
10. A tournament photographer used a monopod to support her camera.
11. Can an optometrist test the optokinetic ability of the eyes?
12. Kendall will study optometry to become an eye doctor.

Content Words

13. Many players use aluminum badminton rackets.
14. Shuttlecocks, used in badminton, are conical in shape.
15. A quick game of badminton will be energizing.
16. Badminton rackets are lightweight.
17. Only two teams in our league will be qualifying to move up.
18. Our team follows the requirements for tournament play.
19. In badminton, the shuttlecock is always volleyed over the net.

Vocabulary Words

20. Candice made an alteration to the length of her sleeves.
21. The girls' team altered their uniforms by hemming their shorts.
22. An inspector checked the gymnasium floor before the match.
23. From Mack's perspective, today's game would be an easy win.

Challenge Words

24. ____________________
25. ____________________

2 Allow students to self-correct their Pretest. Write each word on the board. Point out that each Pattern Word contains two **Greek roots.** *Macro, micro, mono,* and *opto* are the **Greek roots** that appear at the beginning of each Pattern Word. Note the roots *alter* and *spect* in the Vocabulary Words. Remind students that a root is the part of a word that gives the basic meaning.

3 As a class, read, spell, and read each word. Direct students to highlight misspelled words and rewrite them correctly.

4 Proof each student's Pretest. This becomes an individualized study sheet that can be used at school or at home.

5 Homework suggestion: Duplicate **BLM SP6-01B Flash Cards Template** on CARD STOCK for students to write the list words, using the flash cards as a study aid. Another option is to use INDEX CARDS.

Day 2 Word Analysis and Vocabulary

Objective

The students will sort and write words with **Greek roots** and complete sentences with content words. They will use a table to write vocabulary words, select words to match definitions, and complete sentences in context. They will choose the best meaning for the given words.

Introduction

Teacher Note: This w… or "rooted" in the Gre…

Display **P-4 Greek Ro…** students to fold a piec… Invite students to labe… Direct students to turn… that the silent *e* in *mic…* of the root *phon*. Indic… roots. Demonstrate ho… students to complete th…

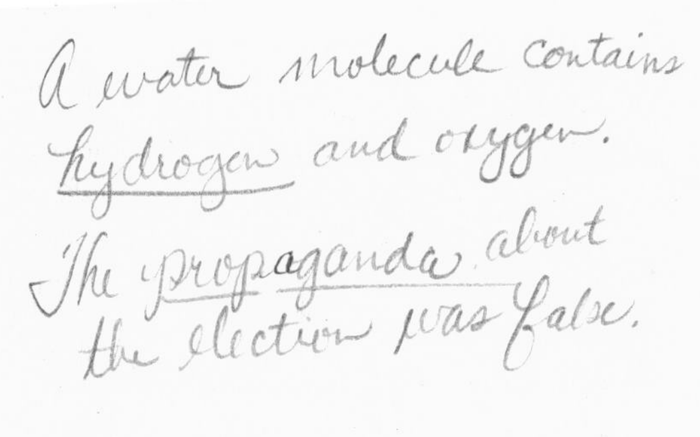

A water molecule contains
hydrogen and oxygen.
The propaganda about
the election was false.

Root	Suf…		…uffix
macro, cosm		mono, pod	
macro, scop	-ic	mono, lith	-ic
micro, cosm		mono, gram	
micro, graph		mono, chrom	-atic
micro, phon		opto, kin	-etic
micro, scop	-ic	opto, metr	-y

Directed Instruction

1 Select twelve students to find the definition of each Pattern Word in

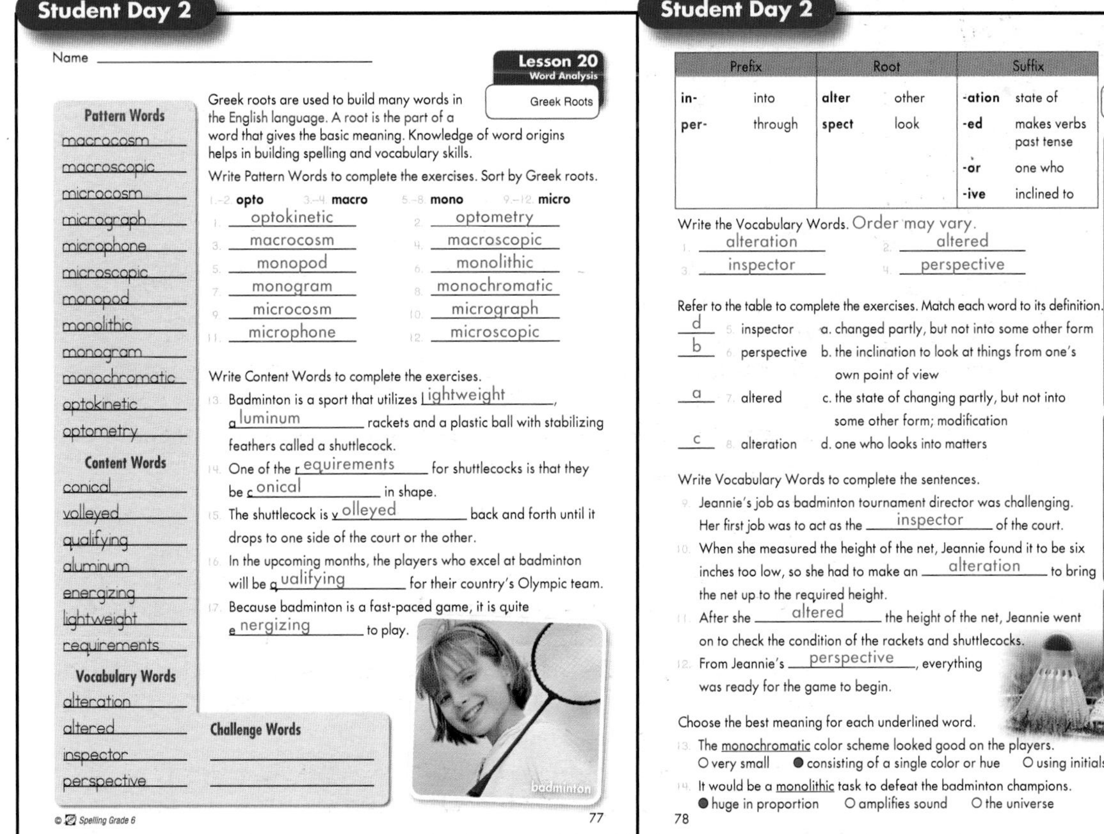

Student Day 2

Name ______________

Lesson 20 Word Analysis — Greek Roots

Pattern Words: macrocosm, macroscopic, microcosm, micrograph, microphone, microscopic, monopod, monolithic, monogram, monochromatic, optokinetic, optometry

Content Words: conical, volleyed, qualifying, aluminum, energizing, lightweight, requirements

Vocabulary Words: alteration, altered, inspector, perspective

Challenge Words

Greek roots are used to build many words in the English language. A root is the part of a word that gives the basic meaning. Knowledge of word origins helps in building spelling and vocabulary skills.

Write Pattern Words to complete the exercises. Sort by Greek roots.

1–2 **opto** 3–4 **macro** 5–8 **mono** 9–12 **micro**

1. optokinetic
2. optometry
3. macrocosm
4. macroscopic
5. monopod
6. monolithic
7. monogram
8. monochromatic
9. microcosm
10. micrograph
11. microphone
12. microscopic

Write Content Words to complete the exercises.

13. Badminton is a sport that utilizes lightweight, aluminum rackets and a plastic ball with stabilizing feathers called a shuttlecock.
14. One of the requirements for shuttlecocks is that they be conical in shape.
15. The shuttlecock is volleyed back and forth until it drops to one side of the court or the other.
16. In the upcoming months, the players who excel at badminton will be qualifying for their country's Olympic team.
17. Because badminton is a fast-paced game, it is quite energizing to play.

badminton

© Spelling Grade 6 — 77

Student Day 2

Lesson 20 Vocabulary — Greek Roots

Prefix		Root		Suffix	
in-	into	**alter**	other	**-ation**	state of
per-	through	**spect**	look	**-ed**	makes verbs past tense
				-or	one who
				-ive	inclined to

Write the Vocabulary Words. Order may vary.

1. alteration
2. altered
3. inspector
4. perspective

Refer to the table to complete the exercises. Match each word to its definition.

5. d inspector
6. b perspective
7. a altered
8. c alteration

a. changed partly, but not into some other form
b. the inclination to look at things from one's own point of view
c. the state of changing partly, but not into some other form; modification
d. one who looks into matters

Write Vocabulary Words to complete the sentences.

9. Jeannie's job as badminton tournament director was challenging. Her first job was to act as the inspector of the court.
10. When she measured the height of the net, Jeannie found it to be six inches too low, so she had to make an alteration to bring the net up to the required height.
11. After she altered the height of the net, Jeannie went on to check the condition of the rackets and shuttlecocks.
12. From Jeannie's perspective, everything was ready for the game to begin.

Choose the best meaning for each underlined word.

13. The monochromatic color scheme looked good on the players.
○ very small ● consisting of a single color or hue ○ using initials
14. It would be a monolithic task to defeat the badminton champions.
● huge in proportion ○ amplifies sound ○ the universe

78 — © Spelling Grade 6

Student Spelling Support Materials

BLM SP6-01A
Laminated paper

Student Spelling Support

1. Use **BLM SP6-01A A Spelling Study Strategy** in instructional groups to provide assistance with some or all of the words.
2. Invite students to write the Challenge Words, numbers 24 and 25, in the Word Bank, in the back of their textbook.
3. Challenge students to research and write a brief report on the differences between tennis and badminton, including the history, equipment, scoring, and rules. Compile information in the progressive, sport journal that was started in Lesson 1.
4. Write this week's words, categorize the Pattern, Content, and Vocabulary Words, and attach them to the Word Wall.
5. For a Bible connection, read Proverbs 16:3: "Commit your works to the LORD, and your thoughts will be established." It is interesting to see how our actions and our thoughts are connected. When we commit our work to the Lord, He will keep our thoughts centered on Him as well. Challenge students to find and share other verses that show how our thoughts, attitudes, and actions are interconnected.
6. Provide additional study for a small group of students by playing a version of Tic-Tac-Toe. Prepare a list of the Pattern Words with their definitions for use by a moderator. Use the diagram shown to draw the game board on a large piece of LAMINATED PAPER or the chalkboard. Mark x's and

Cont. on page 81

the Spelling Dictionary. Students raise their hand when each word is located and read each definition and sample sentence aloud. Challenge students to use each word in an original sentence.

2 Proceed to page 77. Say, spell, and say each Pattern, Content, and Vocabulary Word. Provide this week's Challenge Words and have students write them in the spaces provided before completing the page.

3 Proceed to page 78. Remind students to use the table to assist in building each Vocabulary Word. For example, the root *alter* goes with the suffix *-ation* to build the word *alteration*. Choose volunteers to use each Vocabulary Word in an original sentence. Allow students to complete the page independently.

4 Homework suggestion: Students use their Spelling Dictionary to write the definition of each word on the back of the corresponding flash card that was suggested for homework on Day 1.

Day 3 Word Study Strategies

Objective

The students will identify and circle common **Greek roots** in sets of words and write roots to complete sentences. They will write pattern words using combined Greek root meanings and complete sentences.

Introduction

Greek roots are used to build many words in the English language. Remind students to refer to **P-4 Greek Roots** as they complete the activity that follows. Write the following sets of words on the board, and select volunteers to underline the root that is common to the words in each set and state its meaning:

- monopod, monolithic, monogram, monochromatic (**mono; one**)
- optokinetic, optometry (**opto; see**)

Challenge students to share other words with the same roots. (**Possible answers: monocot, monopoly; optometric, optometrist.**) Knowledge of the root meaning aides in determining the definition of a word.

Directed Instruction

1 Invite students to use the list words on page 79 as a reference. Write the following on the board and select a volunteer to form a list word:
- one (mono) + write (gram) = ______ (**monogram**)
- small (micro) + universe (cosm) = ______ (**microcosm**)
- large (macro) + see (scop) = ______ (**macroscopic**)

2 Write the following on the board. Have volunteers complete the exercises:
- (lith) Is that enormous boulder ______? (**monolithic**)
- (scop) Are viruses and bacteria ______? (**macroscopic or microscopic**)
- (pod) Can a camera operator use a ______? (**monopod**)

3 Proceed to page 79. Students complete the page.

Day 4 Writing

Objective

The students will use proofreading marks to identify mistakes in an advertisement. They will correctly write misspelled words.

Introduction

Remind students that the persuasive writing domain is the focus for this lesson. Display an advertisement for a sporting goods store from a local NEWSPAPER ADVERTISEMENT. Invite volunteers to tell why an advertisement is an example of persuasive writing. Explain that today's activity involves proofreading an advertisement.

Directed Instruction

1 Display **T-14 Proofreading an Advertisement** on the overhead, keeping the bottom portion of the transparency covered. Read the text aloud.

Correct the identified mistakes using the appropriate proofreading marks. Use **BLM SP6-20A T-14 Answer Key** as a guide. Uncover the bottom of the transparency and read the corrected version of the text.

2 Proceed to page 80 and assist students as needed while they independently proofread the advertisement. Review all the necessary proofreading marks and corrections. (**10 misspellings; 1 capital letter needed; 2 periods needed; 2 deletes; 2 add something—*comma, on*; 1 small letter needed; 1 new paragraph**)

3 Homework suggestion: Distribute a copy of **BLM SP6-20B Lesson 20 Homework** to each student.

Day 5 Posttest

Objective

The students will correctly write dictated spelling words and sentences.

Introduction

Review by using flash cards noted in Day 1 and Day 2 Homework suggestion.

Directed Assessment

1 Dictate the list words by using the Pretest sentences or developing original ones. Reserve *microphone, monogram, optokinetic, volleyed, lightweight,* and *perspective* for the dictation sentences.

2 Read each sentence. Repeat as needed.

- Before the match, Noah heard his name spoken into the microphone.
- He found his racket by looking for his monogram on the cover.
- Noah used his sharp optokinetic abilities to return his opponent's serve.
- Noah volleyed the shuttlecock over the net.
- His lightweight racket moved quickly through the air.
- From Noah's perspective, the match was an easy win.

3 If assigned, dictate Extra Challenge Words.

4 Score the test, counting each misspelled word as an error. Correct the dictation sentences by grading only the spelling words or grading the complete sentences.

Student Spelling Support

Cont. from page 80

o's with erasable pen, whiteboard marker, or chalk. To earn a square, a player must state the number of the square desired, say a Pattern Word with the Greek root shown on the square, and correctly spell and define that word. It is up to the moderator to decide if the student has both correctly spelled and defined the word. The moderator then crosses that word off the list so that words may only be used once.

1. micro	2. mono	3. opto
4. macro	5. micro	6. mono
7. opto	8. micro	9. macro

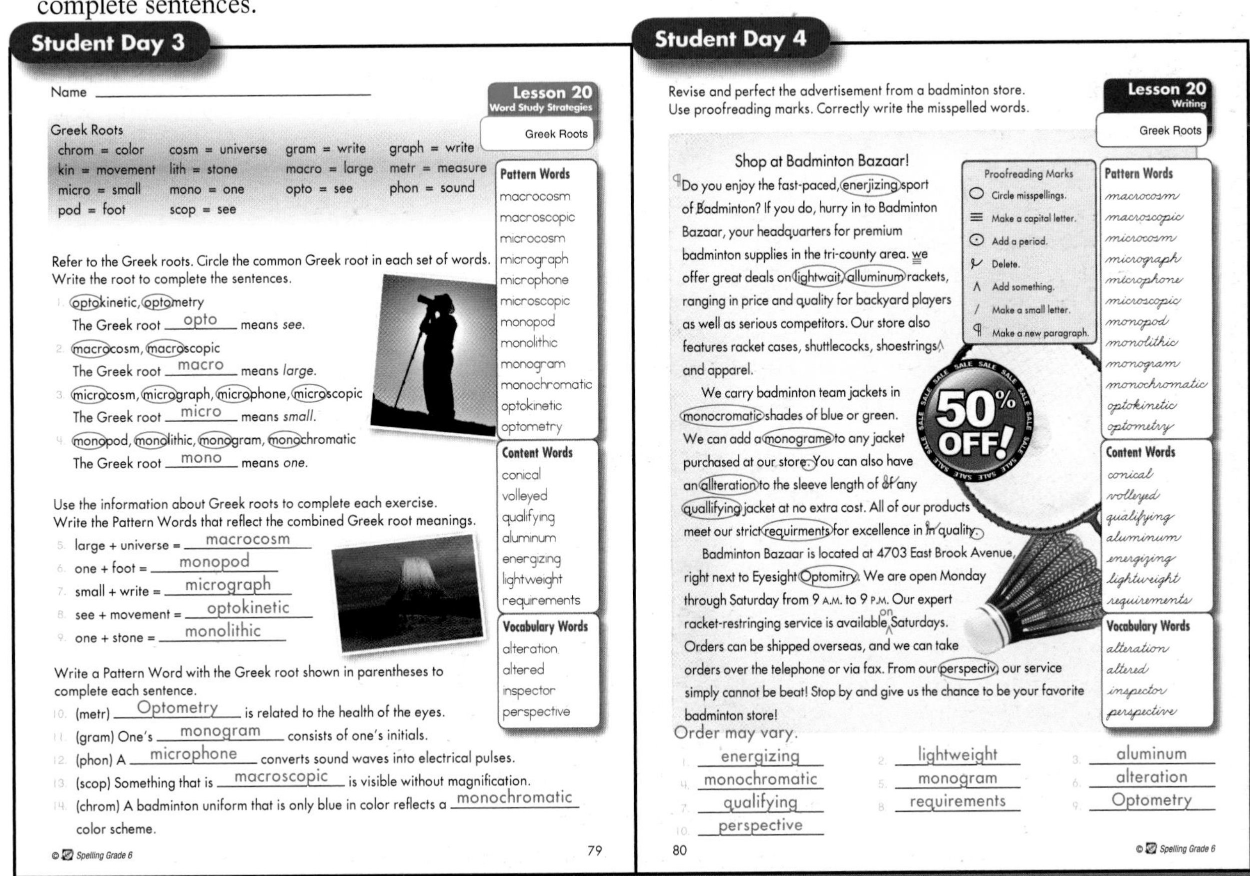

Student Day 3

Name ____________

Lesson 20 — Word Study Strategies — Greek Roots

Greek Roots
chrom = color, cosm = universe, gram = write, graph = write, kin = movement, lith = stone, macro = large, metr = measure, micro = small, mono = one, opto = see, phon = sound, pod = foot, scop = see

Refer to the Greek roots. Circle the common Greek root in each set of words. Write the root to complete the sentences.

1. optokinetic, optometry — The Greek root opto means *see.*
2. macrocosm, macroscopic — The Greek root macro means *large.*
3. microcosm, micrograph, microphone, microscopic — The Greek root micro means *small.*
4. monopod, monolithic, monogram, monochromatic — The Greek root mono means *one.*

Use the information about Greek roots to complete each exercise. Write the Pattern Words that reflect the combined Greek root meanings.

5. large + universe = macrocosm
6. one + foot = monopod
7. small + write = micrograph
8. see + movement = optokinetic
9. one + stone = monolithic

Write a Pattern Word with the Greek root shown in parentheses to complete each sentence.

10. (metr) Optometry is related to the health of the eyes.
11. (gram) One's monogram consists of one's initials.
12. (phon) A microphone converts sound waves into electrical pulses.
13. (scop) Something that is macroscopic is visible without magnification.
14. (chrom) A badminton uniform that is only blue in color reflects a monochromatic color scheme.

Pattern Words: macrocosm, macroscopic, microcosm, micrograph, microphone, microscopic, monopod, monolithic, monogram, monochromatic, optokinetic, optometry
Content Words: conical, volleyed, qualifying, aluminum, energizing, lightweight, requirements
Vocabulary Words: alteration, altered, inspector, perspective

© Spelling Grade 6 — 79

Student Day 4

Lesson 20 — Writing — Greek Roots

Revise and perfect the advertisement from a badminton store. Use proofreading marks. Correctly write the misspelled words.

Shop at Badminton Bazaar!

Do you enjoy the fast-paced, enerjizing sport of Badminton? If you do, hurry in to Badminton Bazaar, your headquarters for premium badminton supplies in the tri-county area. we offer great deals on lightwait, alluminum rackets, ranging in price and quality for backyard players as well as serious competitors. Our store also features racket cases, shuttlecocks, shoestrings and apparel.

We carry badminton team jackets in monocromatic shades of blue or green. We can add a monograme to any jacket purchased at our store. You can also have an allteration to the sleeve length of of any quallifying jacket at no extra cost. All of our products meet our strict requirments for excellence in In quality

Badminton Bazaar is located at 4703 East Brook Avenue, right next to Eyesight Optomitry. We are open Monday through Saturday from 9 A.M. to 9 P.M. Our expert racket-restringing service is available on Saturdays. Orders can be shipped overseas, and we can take orders over the telephone or via fax. From our perspectiv, our service simply cannot be beat! Stop by and give us the chance to be your favorite badminton store!

Proofreading Marks: Circle misspellings. / Make a capital letter. / Add a period. / Delete. / Add something. / Make a small letter. / Make a new paragraph.

50% OFF!

Order may vary.

1. energizing
2. lightweight
3. aluminum
4. monochromatic
5. monogram
6. alteration
7. qualifying
8. requirements
9. Optometry
10. perspective

80 — © Spelling Grade 6

Lesson 21

Greek and Latin Roots

Student Pages

Pages 81–84

Lesson Materials

BLM SP6-01B
Card stock
Index cards
P-2
P-3
P-4
Newspaper page
BLM SP6-21A

Sports

The theme of this lesson is racquetball. Racquetball is a fast-paced game that can be played on an indoor or outdoor court. The court must be enclosed on at least three sides. The court's floor, walls, and ceiling are legal playing surfaces. Racquetball is played with a hollow rubber ball and a racquet that is a shorter version of the one used in tennis. The sport was devised from rules based on the sports of squash, handball, and paddleball.

Day 1 Pretest

Objective

The students will accurately spell and write words with **Greek and Latin roots**. They will spell and write content, vocabulary, and challenge words.

Introduction

Before class, select Challenge Words for numbers 24 and 25 from a cross-curricular subject, words misspelled on previous assignments, or words that interest your students. The word *photogram* has the **Greek roots photo** and **gram** and is suggested for number 24. Administer the Pretest.

Directed Instruction

1 Say each word, use it in a sentence, and then repeat the word.

Pattern Words

1. Micah autographed the fan's racquetball program after the match.
2. Lorell rode in an antique automobile to the game banquet.
3. The attendees of the automotive convention played racquetball daily.
4. Do you know the circumstances of the game cancellation?
5. As a result of living in different countries, Meiko was multilingual.
6. Sylvia spoke to the paralegal after her car accident.
7. Bev wanted to be a paramedic and studied diligently.
8. A true relationship with Jesus is a matter of paramount importance.
9. The photographer took some action shots of Keegan during the match.
10. Mason sprained his ankle during the semifinal match.
11. The final match was televised to millions of viewers.
12. Vance watched the World Championship on the television.

Content Words

13. Gloria was dominating the racquetball court and winning.
14. Abe and Cristiano were finalists in the World Championship match.
15. Quinn had quick footwork during the racquetball game.
16. The rubber ball was irretrievable after it bounced into the thick hedge.
17. The impact of the ball did reverberate loudly in the enclosed court.
18. The rubber ball will quickly ricochet off the court walls.
19. Grace won the tiebreaker after scoring the final point.

Vocabulary Words

20. Geoff can repel the ball forcefully with his new racquet.
21. Yuri did expel a loud breath when the rubber ball hit him.
22. It was a corporate decision to donate funds for the new athletic club.
23. The new racquetball corporation was headed by Ed and Gigi.

Challenge Words

24. ______________________
25. ______________________

2 Allow students to self-correct their Pretest. Write each word on the board. Point out that the **Greek and Latin roots** in the Pattern Words are *auto, circum, fin, graph, leg, lingu, medic, mob, mot, mount, multi, para, photo, semi, stanc, tele,* and *vis*. The Latin roots in the Vocabulary Words are *corpor* and *pel*. Remind students that a root is the part of a word that gives the basic meaning.

3 As a class, read, spell, and read each word. Direct students to highlight misspelled words and rewrite them correctly.

4 Proof each student's Pretest. This becomes an individualized study sheet that can be used at school or at home.

5 Homework suggestion: Duplicate **BLM SP6-01B Flash Cards Template** on CARD STOCK for students to write the list words, using the flash cards as a study aid. Another option is to use INDEX CARDS.

Day 2 Word Analysis and Vocabulary

Objective

The students will sort words with **Greek and Latin roots** and complete sentences v… ocabulary words and …

His interpretation was confusing.

The choir sang the decrescendo with feeling.

Introduc…

Display **P-2**… t students to have their f… ity. Dictate each Patter… r flash card pile, highli… ted that students us… **nd Latin roots.** Note… cabulary Words con… ived from both Greek…

Prefix	Root	Suffix	Prefix	Root	Suffix
	auto, mob	-ile		photo, graph	-er
	auto, mot	-ive		semi, fin	-al
	auto, graph	-ed		tele, vis	-ed
	circum, stanc	-es		tele, vis	-ion
	multi, lingu	-al		corpor	-ate
	para, leg	-al		corpor	-ation
	para, medic		ex-	pel	
	para, mount		re-	pel	

Directed Instruction

1 Select students to look up the Content Words *ricochet* and *reverberate* in the Spelling Dictionary. Students read the dictionary information aloud.

Differentiated Instruction

- For students who spelled all the words correctly on the Pretest, select and assign Extra Challenge Words from the following list: iterative, interpretation, baccalaureate, redistribution, chromosomal, decrescendo.
- For students who spelled less than half correctly, assign the following Pattern, Content, and Vocabulary Words: automotive, circumstances, multilingual, paramedic, photographer, televised, finalists, footwork, tiebreaker, dominating, corporate, repel. On the Posttest, evaluate these students on the twelve words assigned; however, encourage them to attempt to spell all the list words to the best of their ability. They are also responsible for writing the dictated sentences.

61 pts.

Student Day 2

Name ______________________

Lesson 21 Word Analysis — Greek and Latin Roots

Pattern Words: automobile, automotive, autographed, circumstances, multilingual, paralegal, paramedic, paramount, photographer, semifinal, televised, television

Content Words: finalists, ricochet, footwork, tiebreaker, dominating, irretrievable, reverberate

Vocabulary Words: corporate, corporation, expel, repel

Challenge Words

Greek and Latin roots and affixes are used to build many words in the English language.
A root is the part of a word that gives the basic meaning. Affixes expand the meaning or function of a word. Knowledge of word origins helps in building spelling and vocabulary skills.

Write Pattern Words to complete the exercises. Sort by Greek and Latin roots.

1 multi · 2 circum · 3 photo · 4 semi · 5–6 tele · 7–9 auto · 10–12 para

1. multilingual
2. circumstances
3. photographer
4. semifinal
5. televised
6. television
7. automobile
8. automotive
9. autographed
10. paralegal
11. paramedic
12. paramount

Write Content Words to complete the exercises.

13. The team finalists were dominating the racquetball competition.
14. The sport of racquetball requires speed, racquet control, and quick footwork.
15. The hollow rubber ball did ricochet or reverberate and reverberate or ricochet loudly during the match tiebreaker.
16. The rubber ball was irretrievable after it bounced off the court and into the thick hedges around the playground.

racquetball

© Spelling Grade 6 · 81

Student Day 2

Prefix		Root		Suffix	
ex-	out of	**corpor**	body	**-ate**	to act
re-	back	**pel**	push	**-ation**	state of

Lesson 21 Vocabulary — Greek and Latin Roots

Pattern Words: automobile, automotive, autographed, circumstances, multilingual, paralegal, paramedic, paramount, photographer, semifinal, televised, television
Content Words: finalists, ricochet, footwork, tiebreaker, dominating, irretrievable, reverberate
Vocabulary Words: corporate, corporation, expel, repel

Write the Vocabulary Words. Order may vary.

1. corporate
2. corporation
3. expel
4. repel

Refer to the table to complete the exercises. Write the word that is being defined.

5. to push or force out expel
6. to act as one unified body of individuals corporate
7. to push, drive back, or exert an opposing force repel
8. the state of a group of individuals acting as one unified body corporation

Write Vocabulary Words to complete the sentences.

9. A local corporation donated money for the racquetball competition prize.
10. The corporate decision to donate money was made after the organization realized that many of its employees were competition participants.
11. One participant did expel a loud breath when the hollow rubber ball ricocheted and hit her in the stomach.
12. She determined to rally back by choosing to repel the rubber ball forcefully with her racquet as she used quick footwork.

Choose the word that matches each definition.

13. related to speaking several languages — ○ semifinal ○ televised ● multilingual
14. the way something happens — ○ paramedic ○ photographer ● circumstances
15. greatest — ○ television ● paramount ○ automotive

82 · © Spelling Grade 6

Student Spelling Support Materials

BLM SP6-01A
BLM SP6-08B
P-2
P-3
P-4
Index cards

Student Spelling Support

1. Use **BLM SP6-01A A Spelling Study Strategy** in instructional groups to provide assistance with some or all of the words.
2. Invite students to write the Challenge Words, numbers 24 and 25, in the Word Bank, in the back of their textbook.
3. Challenge students to work in groups to research and compare the similarities and differences between racquetball and tennis. Provide a copy of **BLM SP6-08B Venn Diagram** for student groups to use the graphic organizer to compare and contrast the two sports. Students may compile information in the progressive, sport journal that was started in Lesson 1.
4. Write this week's words, categorize the Pattern, Content, and Vocabulary Words, and attach them to the Word Wall.
5. Invite students to refer to **P-2** and **P-3 Latin Roots** and **P-4 Greek Roots** to compile flash cards of **Greek and Latin roots** and their meanings from this lesson. Students write the root on one side of an INDEX CARD and the meaning on the other side. Challenge students to highlight or color code their flash cards to differentiate between **Greek and Latin roots**. Students use the flash cards as a study aid to memorize root meanings. Knowledge of word origins helps in building spelling and vocabulary skills.

2 Proceed to page 81. Say, spell, and say each Pattern, Content, and Vocabulary Word. Provide this week's Challenge Words and have students write them in the spaces provided. Encourage students to add the Challenge Words to their flash card study pile and use their flash cards as a reference tool when completing the page.

3 Proceed to page 82. Build each Vocabulary Word before students complete the page. For example, the root *corpor* goes with the suffix *-ate* to build the word *corporate.* Provide assistance as needed.

4 Homework suggestion: Students use their Spelling Dictionary to write the definition of each word on the back of the corresponding flash card that was suggested for homework on Day 1.

Day 3 Word Study Strategies

Objective

The students will write **Greek and Latin roots** to complete sentences. They will use combined root meanings to write list words. The students will write a missing root or affix to complete pattern and vocabulary words. They will locate and circle content words.

Introduction

Refer to **P-2** and **P-3 Latin Roots** and **P-4 Greek Roots.** Invite students to have their flash card pile, from Day 2 Introduction, on hand for this activity. Remind students that each Greek and Latin root was highlighted on the Pattern and Vocabulary Word flash cards. Challenge students to locate the **Greek and Latin roots** on the posters and their meanings. Students write the root meanings underneath each highlighted root on the front of their flash cards. Remind students that the Greek root *para* means *almost* in *paralegal* and *paramedic,* but is a Latin root in *paramount* and means *by.*

Directed Instruction

1 Write the following on the board:

- Greek roots found in Pattern Words: auto, graph, para, photo, tele
- Latin roots found in Pattern Words: circum, fin, leg, lingu, medic, mob, mot, mount, multi, para, semi, stanc, vis
- Latin roots found in Vocabulary Words: corpor, pel
  Cover up or take down **P-2** and **P-3 Latin Roots** and **P-4 Greek Roots.** Dictate the roots from this lesson. Challenge students to verbalize the root meanings. Students may reference their flash cards.

2 Students continue to use their flash cards as a reference. Write the following on the board and select volunteers to form list words:

- half + end = ______ **(semifinal)**
- around + stand = ______ **(circumstances)**

3 Write the following and select volunteers to complete the sentence:

- Did the large, athletic corpor______ send their personal photo______ to take pictures of the racquetball tiebreaker? **(ation; grapher)**

4 Proceed to page 83. Students complete the page independently.

Day 4 Writing

Objective

The students will complete a cloze activity in the context of a letter to the editor of a newspaper.

Introduction

Display a NEWSPAPER PAGE that features letters to the editor. Select a letter to read aloud. When finished, ask students to state the purpose or intent of the letter. Explain that many people write letters to the editor of their local newspaper when a personal viewpoint or a community problem is important enough to be shared. Ask students to share about any issues that concern them.

Directed Instruction

1 Discuss with students possible benefits of having a letter printed in the newspaper, including bringing attention to a specific cause. (**Possible answers: garner attention for a specific cause; provide another viewpoint toward a specific issue**)

2 Proceed to page 84. Encourage students to work in groups to complete the page. Students may take alternating turns reading the letter aloud.

3 Homework suggestion: Distribute a copy of **BLM SP6-21A Lesson 21 Homework** to each student.

Day 5 Posttest

Objective

The students will correctly write dictated spelling words and sentences.

Introduction

Review by using flash cards noted in Day 1 and Day 2 Homework suggestion.

Directed Assessment

1 Dictate the list words by using the Pretest sentences or developing original ones. Reserve *automotive, corporate, dominating, finalists, televised,* and *photographer* for the dictation sentences.

2 Read each sentence. Repeat as needed.

- The automotive group decided to play racquetball.
- It was a corporate decision to enter a competition.
- Tony's team was dominating the entire match.
- They played very well and were match finalists.
- The qualifying matches were televised on the weekend.
- A company photographer took pictures of the competition.

3 If assigned, dictate Extra Challenge Words.

4 Score the test, counting each misspelled word as an error. Correct the dictation sentences by grading only the spelling words or grading the complete sentences.

Notes

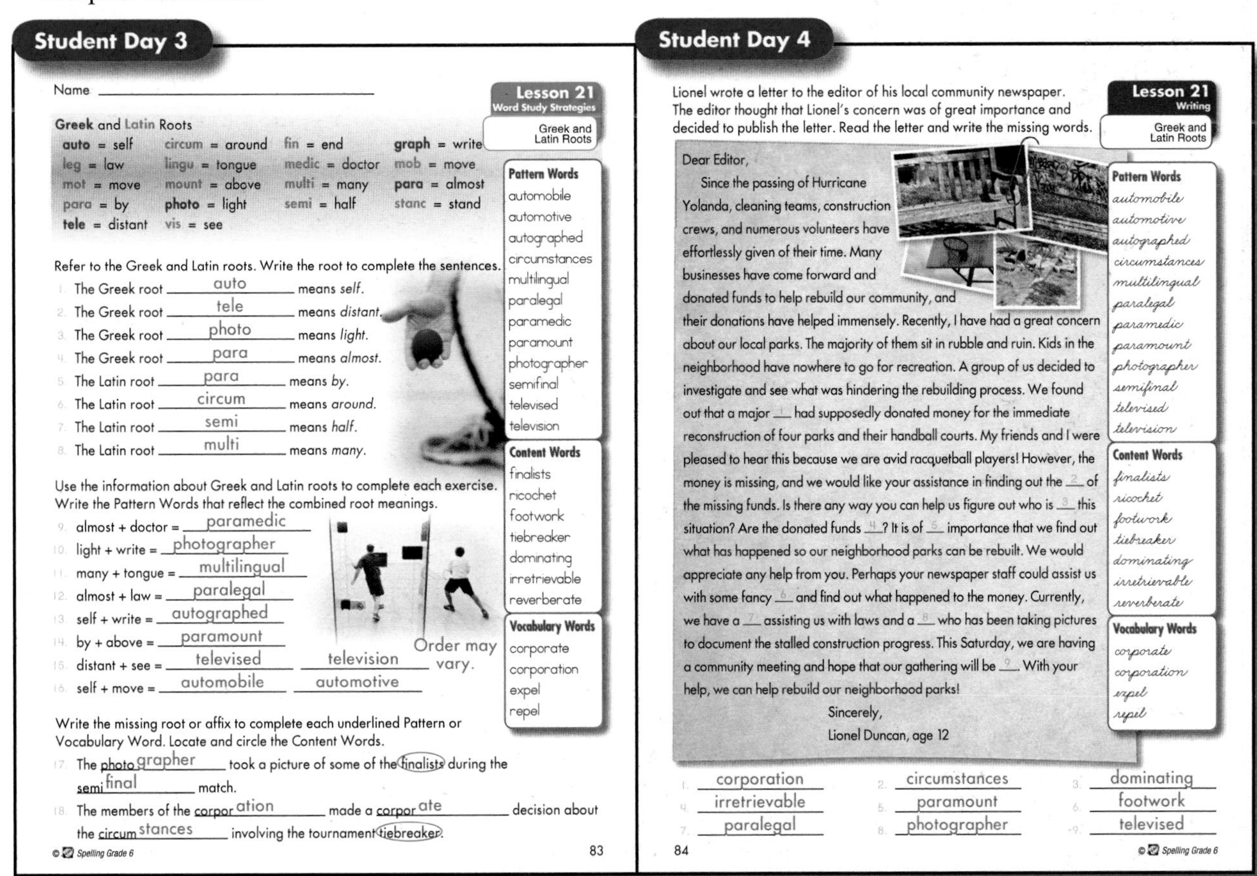

Student Day 3

Name ____________________

Lesson 21 Word Study Strategies — Greek and Latin Roots

Greek and **Latin** Roots

auto = self	circum = around	fin = end	graph = write
leg = law	lingu = tongue	medic = doctor	mob = move
mot = move	mount = above	multi = many	para = almost
para = by	photo = light	semi = half	stanc = stand
tele = distant	vis = see		

Refer to the Greek and Latin roots. Write the root to complete the sentences.

1. The Greek root auto means *self*.
2. The Greek root tele means *distant*.
3. The Greek root photo means *light*.
4. The Greek root para means *almost*.
5. The Latin root para means *by*.
6. The Latin root circum means *around*.
7. The Latin root semi means *half*.
8. The Latin root multi means *many*.

Use the information about Greek and Latin roots to complete each exercise. Write the Pattern Words that reflect the combined root meanings.

9. almost + doctor = paramedic
10. light + write = photographer
11. many + tongue = multilingual
12. almost + law = paralegal
13. self + write = autographed
14. by + above = paramount
15. distant + see = televised television
16. self + move = automobile automotive

Order may vary.

Write the missing root or affix to complete each underlined Pattern or Vocabulary Word. Locate and circle the Content Words.

17. The photographer took a picture of some of the finalists during the semifinal match.
18. The members of the corporation made a corporate decision about the circumstances involving the tournament tiebreaker.

Pattern Words: automobile, automotive, autographed, circumstances, multilingual, paralegal, paramedic, paramount, photographer, semifinal, televised, television

Content Words: finalists, ricochet, footwork, tiebreaker, dominating, irretrievable, reverberate

Vocabulary Words: corporate, corporation, expel, repel

© Spelling Grade 6 83

Student Day 4

Lesson 21 Writing — Greek and Latin Roots

Lionel wrote a letter to the editor of his local community newspaper. The editor thought that Lionel's concern was of great importance and decided to publish the letter. Read the letter and write the missing words.

Dear Editor,

Since the passing of Hurricane Yolanda, cleaning teams, construction crews, and numerous volunteers have effortlessly given of their time. Many businesses have come forward and donated funds to help rebuild our community, and their donations have helped immensely. Recently, I have had a great concern about our local parks. The majority of them sit in rubble and ruin. Kids in the neighborhood have nowhere to go for recreation. A group of us decided to investigate and see what was hindering the rebuilding process. We found out that a major _1_ had supposedly donated money for the immediate reconstruction of four parks and their handball courts. My friends and I were pleased to hear this because we are avid racquetball players! However, the money is missing, and we would like your assistance in finding out the _2_ of the missing funds. Is there any way you can help us figure out who is _3_ this situation? Are the donated funds _4_? It is of _5_ importance that we find out what has happened so our neighborhood parks can be rebuilt. We would appreciate any help from you. Perhaps your newspaper staff could assist us with some fancy _6_ and find out what happened to the money. Currently, we have a _7_ assisting us with laws and a _8_ who has been taking pictures to document the stalled construction progress. This Saturday, we are having a community meeting and hope that our gathering will be _9_. With your help, we can help rebuild our neighborhood parks!

Sincerely,

Lionel Duncan, age 12

1. corporation
2. circumstances
3. dominating
4. irretrievable
5. paramount
6. footwork
7. paralegal
8. photographer
9. televised

Pattern Words: automobile, automotive, autographed, circumstances, multilingual, paralegal, paramedic, paramount, photographer, semifinal, televised, television

Content Words: finalists, ricochet, footwork, tiebreaker, dominating, irretrievable, reverberate

Vocabulary Words: corporate, corporation, expel, repel

84 © Spelling Grade 6

Lesson 22 Hard and Soft c, g

Student Pages

Pages 85–88

Lesson Materials

BLM SP6-01B
Card stock
Index cards
BLM SP6-22A

Sports

The theme of this lesson is table tennis. Table tennis is a popular recreational and competitive sport all over the world. The sport, similar to tennis, involves hitting a ball back and forth over a net. However, in table tennis, the ball is made of lightweight plastic and the "court" is a tabletop. Table tennis is believed to have English origins and was first played with rubber or cork balls on dining tables.

Day 1 Pretest

Objective

The students will accurately spell and write words with **hard and soft c** and **g**. They will spell and write content, vocabulary, and challenge words.

Introduction

Before class, select Challenge Words for numbers 24 and 25 from a cross-curricular subject, words misspelled on previous assignments, or words that interest your students. The word *conspicuous* has two **hard c** spellings and is suggested for number 24. Administer the Pretest.

Directed Instruction

1 Say each word, use it in a sentence, and then repeat the word.

Pattern Words

1. Know certainly that the Lord, our God, hears our prayers.
2. Table tennis is a popular, cultural sport in Asia.
3. Matches of odd numbers are customary in tournament table tennis.
4. Dave could not disguise his disappointment after losing the match.
5. Malia shared that her ethnicity was Asian-American.
6. John took his car to three different garages for repair quotes.
7. A good competitor can gauge his opponent's next move.
8. Javier is knowledgeable about the rules of table tennis.
9. Sharon spoke four different languages by the age of twenty.
10. An unexpected occurrence caused us to be late to the match.
11. Original table-tennis games were played on dining tables.
12. The European team played a successful tournament and won the title.

Content Words

13. In table tennis, each player alternates hitting the ball.
14. A table-tennis ball is made of white or orange celluloid.
15. Ann was in deep concentration during the table-tennis game.
16. There are many contenders in the competitive sport of table tennis.
17. The game of table tennis requires a lot of coordination.
18. Table tennis is a recreational activity in many countries.
19. Garrison's reflexes were superb during the tournament.

Vocabulary Words

20. Did Derrell write a composition about the rules of table tennis?
21. Gwen had a cheerful disposition during the tournament.
22. Joyce spoke the Cantonese dialect fluently during her visit to China.
23. Malachi gave a lecture about table tennis to the university students.

Challenge Words

24. ______________________
25. ______________________

2 Allow students to self-correct their Pretest. Write each word on the board. Point out that the Pattern Words consist of one or more **hard and soft c** and **g**. The letters *c* and *g* usually make the soft sounds /s/ and /j/ when followed by the letters *e*, *i*, or *y*. Both *c* and *g* make the hard sounds, /k/ or /g/, when followed by any other letter. The spelling pattern *dge* makes the **soft g** sound /j/, usually follows a short vowel, and has a silent *d*. Note the roots *lect* and *posit* in the Vocabulary Words.

3 As a class, read, spell, and read each word. Direct students to highlight misspelled words and rewrite them correctly.

4 Proof each student's Pretest. This becomes an individualized study sheet that can be used at school or at home.

5 Homework suggestion: Duplicate **BLM SP6-01B Flash Cards Template** on CARD STOCK for students to write the list words, using the flash cards as a study aid. Another option is to use INDEX CARDS.

Day 2 Word Analysis and Vocabulary

Objective

The students will sort and write words with **hard and soft c** and **g** and complete sentences with content words. They will use a table to write vocabulary words, match given definitions in context, and complete sentences.

Introduction

Instruct students to have their flash card pile from this lesson on hand for this activity. Dictate each Pattern Word slowly. Students look through their flash card pile, locate the dictated words, and highlight or underline the letter or letters for each **hard and soft c** and **g**. Remind students that some Pattern Words may contain both **hard and soft c** and **g**.

Directed Instruction

1 Invite students to work in pairs or trios to assist one another in quickly sorting their Pattern Word flash cards into the following categories:
- both hard and soft *c* (**successful, occurrence**)
- only hard *c* (**cultural, customary**)
- only soft *c* (**ethnicity, certainly**)
- both hard and soft *g* (**gauge, garages, languages**)
- only hard *g* (**disguise**)
- only soft *g* (**original, knowledgeable**)

Encourage students to check one another's flash cards for accuracy in highlighting or underlining the identified **hard and soft c** and **g**. Assist as needed. When complete, select volunteers to read Pattern Words from each category aloud.

2 Challenge students to locate the definition(s) and part(s) of speech

Differentiated Instruction

- For students who spelled all the words correctly on the Pretest, select and assign Extra Challenge Words from the following list: monomial, isotope, parentheses, renaissance, ambulatory, ostinato.
- For students who spelled less than half correctly, assign the following Pattern, Content, and Vocabulary Words: cultural, disguise, certainly, languages, successful, knowledgeable, reflexes, contenders, recreational, concentration, dialect, disposition. On the Posttest, evaluate these students on the twelve words assigned; however, encourage them to attempt to spell all the list words to the best of their ability. They are also responsible for writing the dictated sentences.

Student Day 2

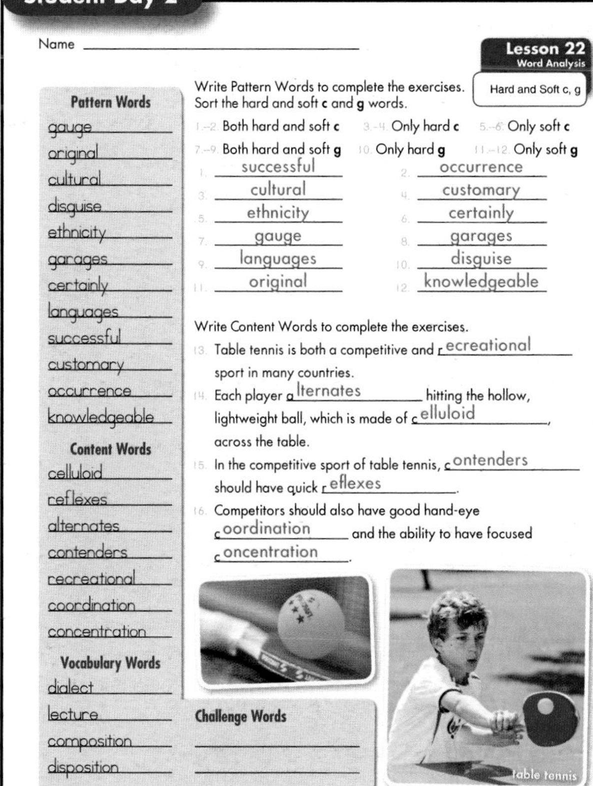

Student Day 2

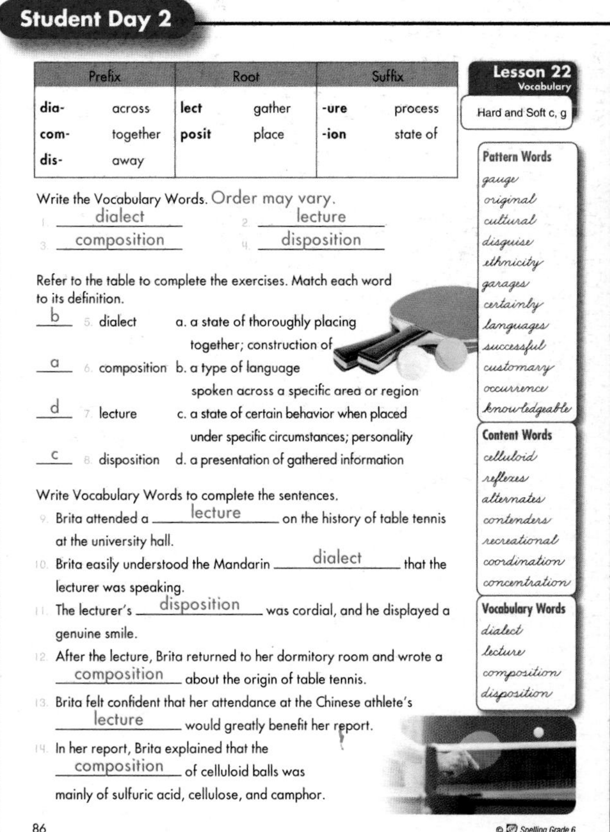

Student Spelling Support Materials

BLM SP6-01A

Student Spelling Support

1. Use **BLM SP6-01A A Spelling Study Strategy** in instructional groups to provide assistance with some or all of the words.
2. Invite students to write the Challenge Words, numbers 24 and 25, in the Word Bank, in the back of their textbook.
3. Challenge students to work in groups to research the history of table tennis as a recognized, Olympic sport. Students may also choose a professional player of the sport and write a short biography of the athlete. Add the information to the progressive, sport journal that was started in Lesson 1.
4. Write this week's words, categorize the Pattern, Content, and Vocabulary Words, and attach them to the Word Wall.
5. Read Psalm 100:4–5 and ask volunteers to name any words they hear that begin with **hard** and **soft c** and **g**, and then write the words on the board. "Enter into His **g**ates with thanksgiving, and into His **c**ourts with praise. Be thankful to Him, and bless His name. For the LORD is **g**ood; His mercy is everlasting, and His truth endures to all **g**enerations."

for the following Content Words in the Spelling Dictionary: celluloid, reflexes, alternates, contenders.

3 Proceed to page 85. Say, spell, and say each Pattern, Content, and Vocabulary Word. Provide this week's Challenge Words and have students write them in the spaces provided. Encourage students to use their flash cards as a reference tool when completing the page.

4 Proceed to page 86. Build each Vocabulary Word before students complete the page. For example, the prefix *dia-* goes with the root *lect* to build the word *dialect.* Provide assistance as needed. When complete, select a volunteer to read exercises 9–14 aloud.

5 Homework suggestion: Students use their Spelling Dictionary to write the definition of each word on the back of the corresponding flash card that was suggested for homework on Day 1.

Day 3 Word Study Strategies

Objective

The students will write list words to match their pronunciations. They will write words that are related forms of given words.

Introduction

Write the following pronunciations on the board:

- /'lek chûr/ (**lecture**)
- /'ȯl tûr nāts/ (**alternates**)
- /dis pə 'zi shən/ (**disposition**)
- /ə 'rij ə nəl/ (**original**)
- /'kus tə mâr ē/ (**customary**)
- /kont sən 'trā shən/ (**concentration**)

Challenge students to sound out the pronunciations and identify the words. Select volunteers to write the correct spelling next to each pronunciation. Students may refer to the list words, found on page 87, for this activity.

Directed Instruction

1 Write the following sentences on the board, underlining words and leaving a blank space as shown:

- <u>Dialectology</u> is the study of regional varieties of language.
- <u>Dialectical</u> is related to the study of regional varieties of language.
- A _______ is a type of language spoken across a specific area or region. (**dialect**)

The underlined words are related forms of the Pattern Word needed to complete the final sentence. Chorally read each sentence. Select a volunteer to locate the correct list word, found on page 87, and write the word in the blank.

2 Proceed to page 87. Students independently complete the page.

Day 4 Writing

Objective

The students will read a persuasive speech and replace synonyms with list words.

Introduction

Instruct students to listen carefully as you dictate the following short, persuasive speech:

Table tennis is unquestionably the most popular sport in the world. <u>Contestants</u> must be in top form and have quick <u>responses</u> to an opponent's move. The sport of table tennis is also a great source of exercise. One <u>definitely</u> works up a sweat while trying to keep up with the rally of small <u>plastic</u> balls! Anyone can play a game of table tennis for recreation. These many factors show why table tennis is considered the world's most popular sport.

Invite students to refer to the list words, found on page 88, for this activity. Students may also use their Spelling Dictionary. Reread the speech and pause after each underlined word. Challenge students to locate list words that are synonyms for the identified words in the speech. Read each sentence again while replacing synonyms with list words. (**Contenders; reflexes; certainly; celluloid**)

Directed Instruction

1 Proceed to page 88. Allow students to work in collaborative groups as they complete the page. When complete, chorally read the speech while replacing synonyms with list words.

2 Homework suggestion: Distribute a copy of **BLM SP6-22A Lesson 22 Homework** to each student.

Day 5 Posttest

Objective

The students will correctly write dictated spelling words and sentences.

Introduction

Review by using flash cards noted in Day 1 and Day 2 Homework suggestion.

Directed Assessment

1 Dictate the list words by using the Pretest sentences or developing original ones. Reserve *certainly, knowledgeable, successful, reflexes, contenders,* and *disposition* for the dictation sentences.

2 Read each sentence. Repeat as needed.

- Deb was certainly excited to play table tennis.
- She was knowledgeable about the rules of the game.
- Deb was successful in qualifying for a tournament.
- Deb's reflexes were excellent during the final match.
- She was one of the most experienced contenders.
- Deb had a joyful disposition and terrific attitude.

3 If assigned, dictate Extra Challenge Words.

4 Score the test, counting each misspelled word as an error. Correct the dictation sentences by grading only the spelling words or grading the complete sentences.

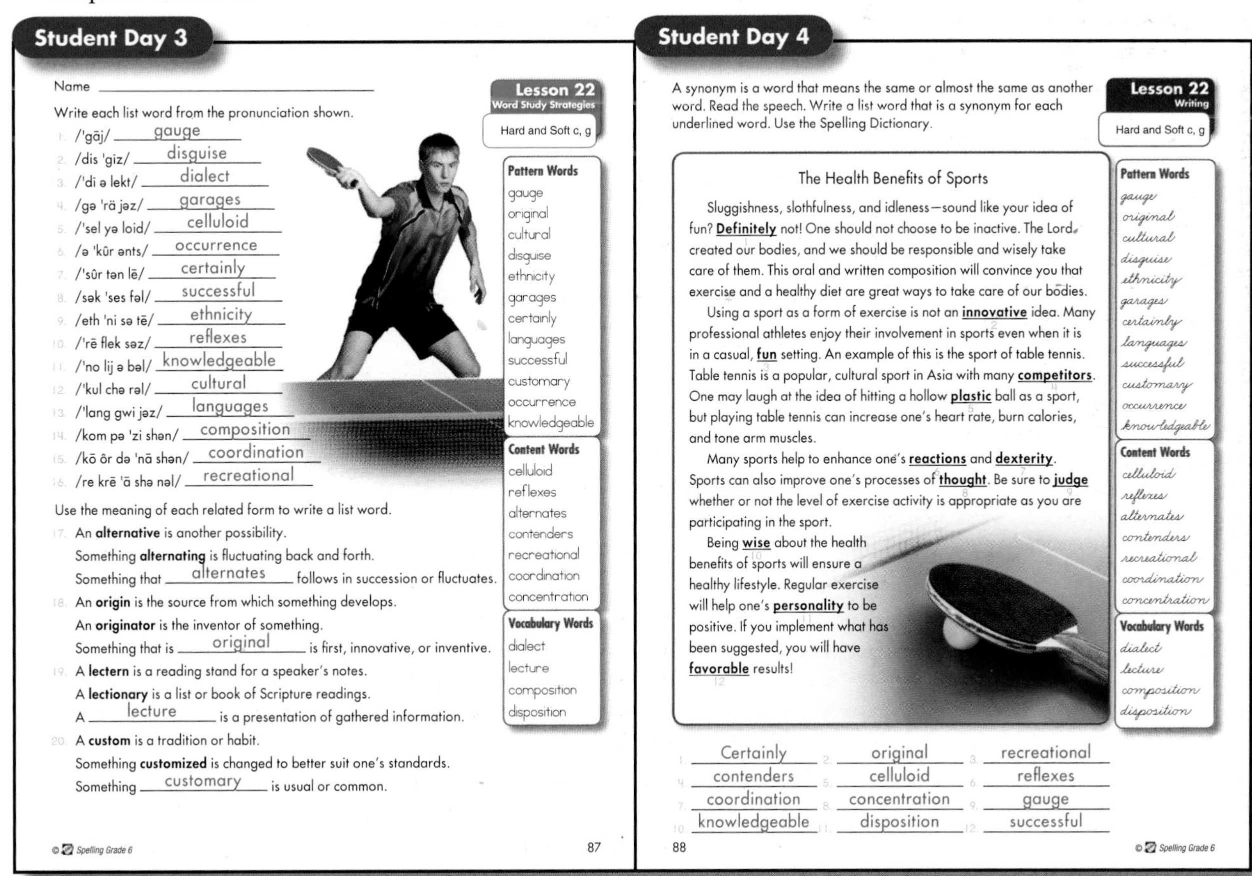

Student Day 3

Lesson 22
Word Study Strategies
Hard and Soft c, g

Name ______

Write each list word from the pronunciation shown.

1. /ˈgāj/ gauge
2. /dis ˈgiz/ disguise
3. /ˈdi ə lekt/ dialect
4. /gə ˈrä jəz/ garages
5. /ˈsel yə loid/ celluloid
6. /ə ˈkûr ənts/ occurrence
7. /ˈsûr tən lē/ certainly
8. /sək ˈses fəl/ successful
9. /eth ˈni sə tē/ ethnicity
10. /ˈrē flek səz/ reflexes
11. /ˈno lij ə bəl/ knowledgeable
12. /ˈkul chə rəl/ cultural
13. /ˈlang gwi jəz/ languages
14. /kom pə ˈzi shən/ composition
15. /kō ôr də ˈnā shən/ coordination
16. /re krē ˈā shə nəl/ recreational

Use the meaning of each related form to write a list word.

17. An **alternative** is another possibility.
Something **alternating** is fluctuating back and forth.
Something that alternates follows in succession or fluctuates.
18. An **origin** is the source from which something develops.
An **originator** is the inventor of something.
Something that is original is first, innovative, or inventive.
19. A **lectern** is a reading stand for a speaker's notes.
A **lectionary** is a list or book of Scripture readings.
A lecture is a presentation of gathered information.
20. A **custom** is a tradition or habit.
Something **customized** is changed to better suit one's standards.
Something customary is usual or common.

Pattern Words: gauge, original, cultural, disguise, ethnicity, garages, certainly, languages, successful, customary, occurrence, knowledgeable
Content Words: celluloid, reflexes, alternates, contenders, recreational, coordination, concentration
Vocabulary Words: dialect, lecture, composition, disposition

© Spelling Grade 6 87

Student Day 4

Lesson 22
Writing
Hard and Soft c, g

A synonym is a word that means the same or almost the same as another word. Read the speech. Write a list word that is a synonym for each underlined word. Use the Spelling Dictionary.

The Health Benefits of Sports

Sluggishness, slothfulness, and idleness—sound like your idea of fun? **Definitely** not! One should not choose to be inactive. The Lord created our bodies, and we should be responsible and wisely take care of them. This oral and written composition will convince you that exercise and a healthy diet are great ways to take care of our bodies.

Using a sport as a form of exercise is not an **innovative** idea. Many professional athletes enjoy their involvement in sports even when it is in a casual, **fun** setting. An example of this is the sport of table tennis. Table tennis is a popular, cultural sport in Asia with many **competitors**. One may laugh at the idea of hitting a hollow **plastic** ball as a sport, but playing table tennis can increase one's heart rate, burn calories, and tone arm muscles.

Many sports help to enhance one's **reactions** and **dexterity**. Sports can also improve one's processes of **thought**. Be sure to **judge** whether or not the level of exercise activity is appropriate as you are participating in the sport.

Being **wise** about the health benefits of sports will ensure a healthy lifestyle. Regular exercise will help one's **personality** to be positive. If you implement what has been suggested, you will have **favorable** results!

1. Certainly	2. original	3. recreational
4. contenders	5. celluloid	6. reflexes
7. coordination	8. concentration	9. gauge
10. knowledgeable	11. disposition	12. successful

Pattern Words: gauge, original, cultural, disguise, ethnicity, garages, certainly, languages, successful, customary, occurrence, knowledgeable
Content Words: celluloid, reflexes, alternates, contenders, recreational, coordination, concentration
Vocabulary Words: dialect, lecture, composition, disposition

88 © Spelling Grade 6

Lesson **23**

Variant Consonant Spellings

Student Pages

Pages 89–92

Lesson Materials

BLM SP6-01B
Card stock
Index cards
BLM SP6-23A

Sports

The theme of this lesson is field hockey and ice hockey. The term *hockey* is believed to have been adapted into English from the French word *hoquet,* meaning *shepherd's crook.* Modern field hockey is believed to have been played since the 1800s in England. Modern ice hockey was developed in Canada in the mid 1850s and is still a very popular sport.

Day 1 Pretest

Objective

The students will accurately spell and write words with **variant consonant spellings**. They will spell and write content, vocabulary, and challenge words.

Introduction

Before class, select Challenge Words for numbers 24 and 25 from a cross-curricular subject, words misspelled on previous assignments, or words that interest your students. The word *presumptuous* has a **variant consonant spelling** for the /z/ sound, spelled *s*, and is suggested for number 24. Administer the Pretest.

Directed Instruction

1 Say each word, use it in a sentence, and then repeat the word.

Pattern Words

1. Coach Wright used the whiteboard as a visual aid to explain the play.
2. Laughter ensued when the winning goal was scored.
3. Building an ice rink can be an architectural challenge.
4. A face mask is advisable when playing goalkeeper.
5. Zoe is a phenomenal ice-hockey goalie.
6. Smart hockey parents emphasize the fun of the game.
7. The machinery that resurfaces the ice in a rink is indispensable.
8. Extra training gave the team a measurable edge this season.
9. Our coach gave my teammates and me a brochure for hockey camp.
10. All players must be insured before they are allowed to play.
11. Did you see the advertisement for field hockey in today's newspaper?
12. Two players were roughhousing and put into the penalty box.

Content Words

13. Hockey players wear protective gear to prevent injuries.
14. All players and coaches must wear regulation helmets on the ice.
15. Good hockey players are always in their correct positions.
16. Playing hockey makes one quite muscular.
17. The Hawks played a very aggressive team last week.
18. Too much fighting leads to many stoppages during a game.
19. Collisions between players are common in hockey.

Vocabulary Words

20. The player in the penalty box kept protesting his innocence.
21. We receive absolution when we confess our sins to the Lord.
22. Randy innocently swept the puck into his own net.
23. A shoot-out is the resolution to a tied game in ice hockey.

Challenge Words

24. ______________________________
25. ______________________________

2 Allow students to self-correct their Pretest. Write each word on the board. Point out that each Pattern Word contains a consonant sound that is represented by a **variant consonant spelling**. A *variant consonant spelling* is an uncommon spelling for a consonant sound. The **variant consonant spellings** are as follows: /f/ spelled *gh* or *ph*, /k/ spelled *ch*, /sh/ spelled *ch* or *s*, /z/ spelled *s*, and /zh/ spelled *s*. Clearly differentiate between the sounds and spellings of *ch* and *s*. Review each spelling and its sound. Note the roots *noc* and *solut* in the Vocabulary Words.

3 As a class, read, spell, and read each word. Direct students to highlight misspelled words and rewrite them correctly.

4 Proof each student's Pretest. This becomes an individualized study sheet that can be used at school or at home.

5 Homework suggestion: Duplicate **BLM SP6-01B Flash Cards Template** on CARD STOCK for students to write the list words, using the flash cards as a study aid. Another option is to use INDEX CARDS.

Day 2 Word Analysis and Vocabulary

Objective

The students will sort words with **variant consonant spellings** and complete sentences with content words. They will use a table to write vocabulary words and complete sentences. They will choose words to match definitions.

Introduction

Write the following consonant sounds and **variant consonant spellings** on the board: /f/ spelled *gh* or *ph*, /k/ spelled *ch*, /sh/ spelled *ch* or *s*, /z/ spelled *s*, /zh/ spelled *s*. Instruct students to lay the Pattern Words from their stack of flash cards on their desk. Dictate each Pattern Word emphasizing the consonant sound that has a unique spelling. Select a volunteer to identify the spelling that corresponds with the consonant sound. Instruct students to highlight the variant consonant spelling. For example, pronounce /'vi zhə wəl/, isolating the sound /zh/ that is spelled *s* in *visual.* Students should identify *s* as the variai
flash card.

The dress fit well after a slight modification.
Mr. Smith wrote a memorandum to call his client.

Directed Instruction

1 Explain that the Content
ice hockey. Select volunte
Words in the Spelling Di

2 Proceed to page 89. Say, s
Vocabulary Word. Provid
students write them in the

3 Proceed to page 90. Rem
building each Vocabulary

Differentiated Instruction

- For students who spelled all the words correctly on the Pretest, select and assign Extra Challenge Words from the following list: nonlinear, modification, memorandum, self-sufficiency, arrhythmia, violoncello.
- For students who spelled less than half correctly, assign the following Pattern, Content, and Vocabulary Words: visual, insured, laughter, machinery, emphasize, roughhousing, injuries, collisions, positions, stoppages, innocently, resolution. On the Posttest, evaluate these students on the twelve words assigned; however, encourage them to attempt to spell all the list words to the best of their ability. They are also responsible for writing the dictated sentences.

66 pts.

Student Day 2

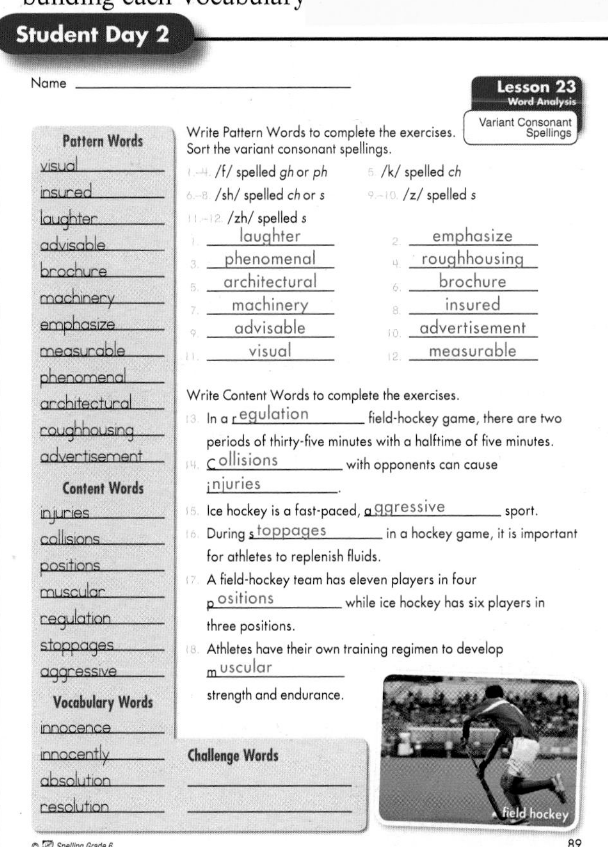

Name

Lesson 23 Word Analysis
Variant Consonant Spellings

Pattern Words: visual, insured, laughter, advisable, brochure, machinery, emphasize, measurable, phenomenal, architectural, roughhousing, advertisement

Content Words: injuries, collisions, positions, muscular, regulation, stoppages, aggressive

Vocabulary Words: innocence, innocently, absolution, resolution

Challenge Words

Write Pattern Words to complete the exercises. Sort the variant consonant spellings.

1–4. /f/ spelled *gh* or *ph*
5. /k/ spelled *ch*
6–8. /sh/ spelled *ch* or *s*
9–10. /z/ spelled *s*
11–12. /zh/ spelled *s*

1. laughter
2. emphasize
3. phenomenal
4. roughhousing
5. architectural
6. brochure
7. machinery
8. insured
9. advisable
10. advertisement
11. visual
12. measurable

Write Content Words to complete the exercises.

13. In a regulation field-hockey game, there are two periods of thirty-five minutes with a halftime of five minutes.
14. Collisions with opponents can cause injuries.
15. Ice hockey is a fast-paced, aggressive sport.
16. During stoppages in a hockey game, it is important for athletes to replenish fluids.
17. A field-hockey team has eleven players in four positions while ice hockey has six players in three positions.
18. Athletes have their own training regimen to develop muscular strength and endurance.

field hockey

© Spelling Grade 6 89

Student Day 2

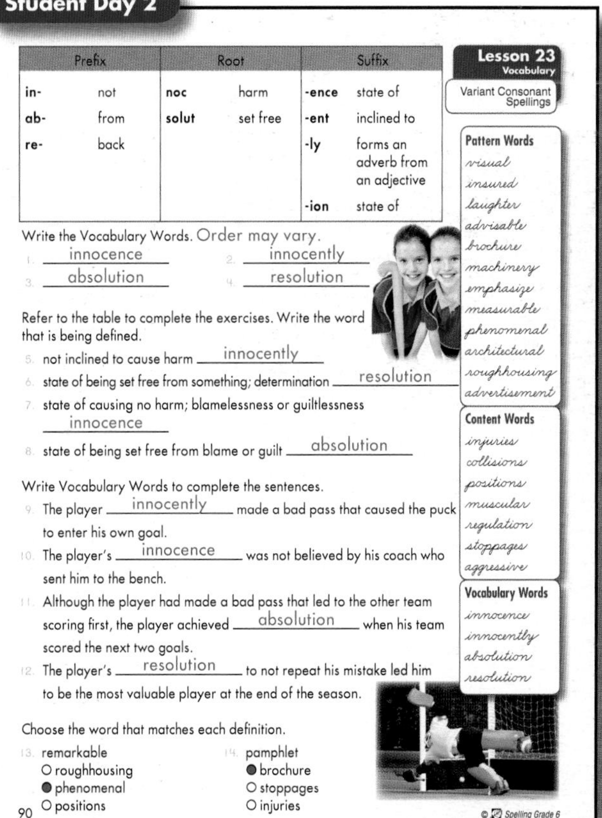

Lesson 23 Vocabulary
Variant Consonant Spellings

Prefix		Root		Suffix	
in-	not	noc	harm	-ence	state of
ab-	from	solut	set free	-ent	inclined to
re-	back			-ly	forms an adverb from an adjective
				-ion	state of

Pattern Words: visual, insured, laughter, advisable, brochure, machinery, emphasize, measurable, phenomenal, architectural, roughhousing, advertisement

Content Words: injuries, collisions, positions, muscular, regulation, stoppages, aggressive

Vocabulary Words: innocence, innocently, absolution, resolution

Write the Vocabulary Words. Order may vary.

1. innocence
2. innocently
3. absolution
4. resolution

Refer to the table to complete the exercises. Write the word that is being defined.

5. not inclined to cause harm innocently
6. state of being set free from something; determination resolution
7. state of causing no harm; blamelessness or guiltlessness innocence
8. state of being set free from blame or guilt absolution

Write Vocabulary Words to complete the sentences.

9. The player innocently made a bad pass that caused the puck to enter his own goal.
10. The player's innocence was not believed by his coach who sent him to the bench.
11. Although the player had made a bad pass that led to the other team scoring first, the player achieved absolution when his team scored the next two goals.
12. The player's resolution to not repeat his mistake led him to be the most valuable player at the end of the season.

Choose the word that matches each definition.

13. remarkable
○ roughhousing
● phenomenal
○ positions

14. pamphlet
● brochure
○ stoppages
○ injuries

90 © Spelling Grade 6

Student Spelling Support Materials

BLM SP6-01A

Student Spelling Support

1. Use **BLM SP6-01A A Spelling Study Strategy** in instructional groups to provide assistance with some or all of the words.
2. Invite students to write the Challenge Words, numbers 24 and 25, in the Word Bank, in the back of their textbook.
3. Invite students to research the dates that men's and women's field hockey and ice hockey became Olympic sports. Instruct them to write facts about each sport followed by a personal opinion about why it took longer for the women's teams to become Olympic sports than the men's teams.
4. Write this week's words, categorize the Pattern, Content, and Vocabulary Words, and attach them to the Word Wall.
5. Read Philippians 2:14–15: "Do all things without complaining and disputing, that you may become blameless and harmless, children of God without fault in the midst of a crooked and perverse generation, among whom you shine as lights in the world." Discuss how our hurtful words and actions can be discouraging to others. Challenge students to encourage classmates, siblings, teachers, and parents. Invite students to write an essay describing how they can be a light in their school or home.

the root *noc* and the suffix *-ence* to get the word *innocence*. Allow students to complete the page independently.

4 Homework suggestion: Students use their Spelling Dictionary to write the definition of each word on the back of the corresponding flash card that was suggested for homework on Day 1.

Day 3 Word Study Strategies

Objective

The students will write list words to match pronunciations and identify words that have the same consonant sound as the underlined letter or letters in given words. They will write complete sentences from fragments.

Introduction

Write the following pronunciations on the board:

• /'ruf hou zing/ (**roughhousing**) • /är kə 'tek chə rəl/ (**architectural**)

Challenge students to read the pronunciations and identify the Pattern Words.

Directed Instruction

1 Write the following words on the board, underlining the **variant consonant spellings**: vi<u>s</u>ual, in<u>s</u>ured, lau<u>gh</u>ter, bro<u>ch</u>ure, mea<u>s</u>urable, <u>ph</u>enomenal. Instruct students to identify the words that contain the same underlined sounds. Challenge the students to identify the letter or letters that share the same pronunciation in each pair of words. (**vi<u>s</u>ual, mea<u>s</u>urable—Each underlined *s* is pronounced /zh/; in<u>s</u>ured, bro<u>ch</u>ure—The underlined *s* and *ch* are pronounced /sh/; lau<u>gh</u>ter, <u>ph</u>enomenal—The underlined *gh* and *ph* are pronounced /f/.**)

2 Write the following phrase on the board: Oliver's innocence. Read the phrase and ask students if it is a complete sentence. (**No.**) Solicit a volunteer to identify this type of error. (**a sentence fragment**) Remind students that a sentence fragment is an incomplete sentence that does not express a complete thought. A fragment is missing the subject, predicate, or both. Explain that the sentence fragment on the board is missing the predicate. Although the phrase begins with a capital letter and ends with a period, it is still a sentence fragment. Select a volunteer to change the sentence fragment into a complete sentence. (**Possible answer: Oliver's innocence in receiving the penalty caused him to be more focused on the game.**)

3 Proceed to page 91. Students complete the page. When complete, select volunteers to read their complete sentences in exercises 16–19.

Day 4 Writing

Objective

The students will read facts about field hockey and ice hockey and write list words in the context of a cloze activity. They will write a personal opinion about which form of hockey that they would rather play.

Introduction

Instruct students to refer to the list words on page 92 for this activity. Slowly read the story and select volunteers to complete the sentences.

Tamah is a goalie for her hockey team, the Hawks. Her God-given talent for athletics and her __1__ to always do her best make her a __2__ player. During games, Tamah wears her __3__ helmet and uniform and is __4__ so that opponents find it difficult to score. Tamah is such a talented athlete that she was voted the Most Valuable Player.

Directed Instruction

1 Reread the story, supplying each correct answer. (**1—resolution; 2—phenomenal; 3—regulation; 4—aggressive**)

2 Select volunteers to state the facts in the story. (**Tamah is a goalie; her team name is the Hawks; she has God-given talent for athletics; she wears a helmet and uniform; she was voted the Most Valuable**

Player.) Choose other volunteers to state a personal opinion about Tamah. (**Possible answers: Tamah is the best goalie in the league; everyone voted for Tamah to be the Most Valuable Player.**)

3 Proceed to page 92. Select a volunteer to read the sentences at the top of the page. Instruct students to complete the page, including writing their opinion. When completed, solicit a volunteer to orally read the story with list words inserted.

4 Homework suggestion: Distribute a copy of **BLM SP6-23A Lesson 23 Homework** to each student.

Day 5 Posttest

Objective

The students will correctly write dictated spelling words and sentences.

Introduction

Review by using flash cards noted in Day 1 and Day 2 Homework suggestion.

Directed Assessment

1 Dictate the list words by using the Pretest sentences or developing original ones. Reserve *insured, collisions, injuries, roughhousing, emphasize,* and *resolution* for the dictation sentences.

2 Read each sentence. Repeat as needed.

- Hockey players are required to be insured.
- Collisions are common between opponents.
- Injuries often occur during games.
- Players who are roughhousing are sent to the penalty box.
- Time spent in the penalty box is to emphasize the importance of fair play.
- A team's resolution to play fairly reduces the number of penalties given.

3 If assigned, dictate Extra Challenge Words.

4 Score the test, counting each misspelled word as an error. Correct the dictation sentences by grading only the spelling words or grading the complete sentences.

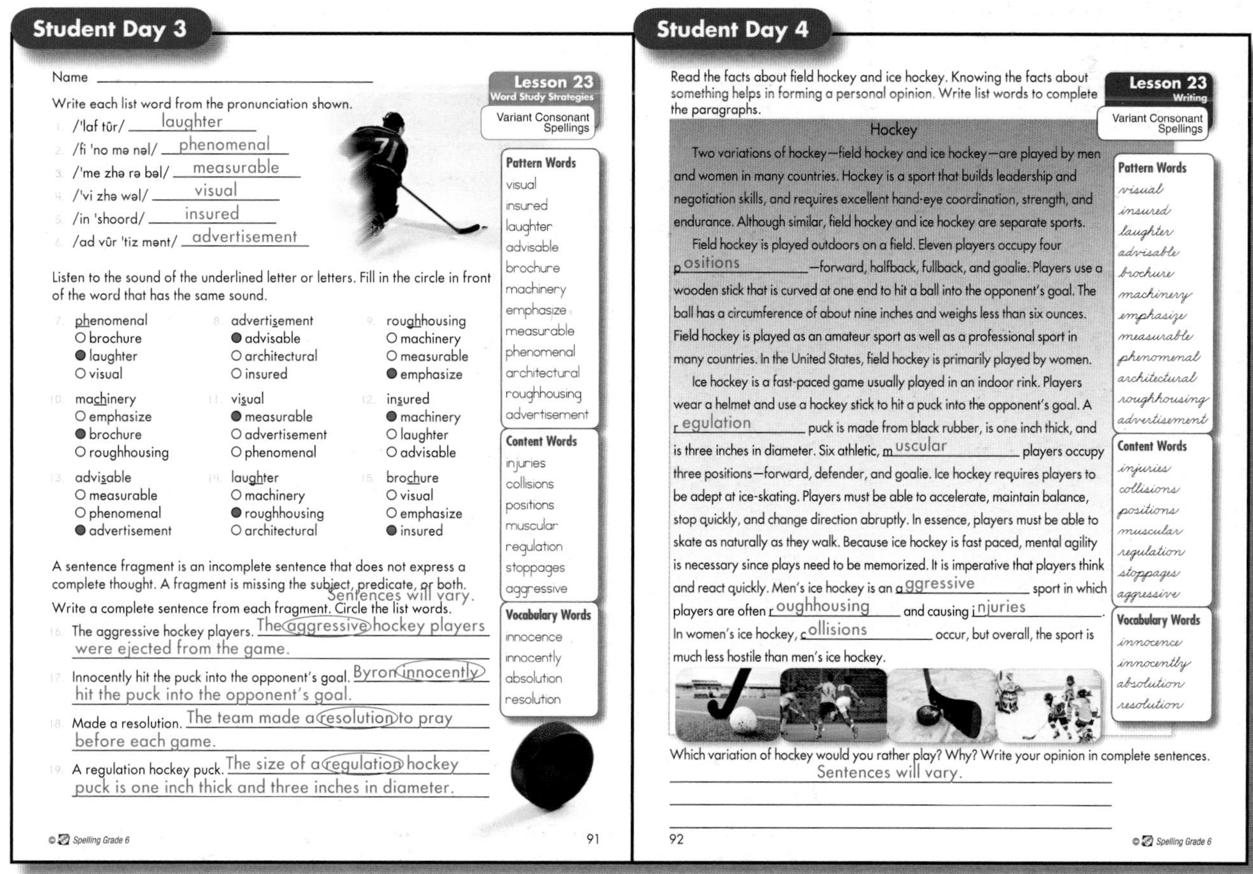

Student Day 3

Name ________________

Lesson 23 Word Study Strategies
Variant Consonant Spellings

Write each list word from the pronunciation shown.

1. /'laf tûr/ laughter
2. /fi 'no mə nəl/ phenomenal
3. /'me zhə rə bəl/ measurable
4. /'vi zhə wəl/ visual
5. /in 'shoord/ insured
6. /ad vûr 'tiz mənt/ advertisement

Listen to the sound of the underlined letter or letters. Fill in the circle in front of the word that has the same sound.

7. phenomenal — ○ brochure ● laughter ○ visual
8. advertisement — ● advisable ○ architectural ○ insured
9. roughhousing — ○ machinery ○ measurable ● emphasize
10. machinery — ○ emphasize ● brochure ○ roughhousing
11. visual — ● measurable ○ advertisement ○ phenomenal
12. insured — ● machinery ○ laughter ○ advisable
13. advisable — ○ measurable ○ phenomenal ● advertisement
14. laughter — ○ machinery ● roughhousing ○ architectural
15. brochure — ○ visual ○ emphasize ● insured

A sentence fragment is an incomplete sentence that does not express a complete thought. A fragment is missing the subject, predicate, or both. Sentences will vary.

Write a complete sentence from each fragment. Circle the list words.

16. The aggressive hockey players. The aggressive hockey players were ejected from the game.
17. Innocently hit the puck into the opponent's goal. Byron innocently hit the puck into the opponent's goal.
18. Made a resolution. The team made a resolution to pray before each game.
19. A regulation hockey puck. The size of a regulation hockey puck is one inch thick and three inches in diameter.

Pattern Words: visual, insured, laughter, advisable, brochure, machinery, emphasize, measurable, phenomenal, architectural, roughhousing, advertisement

Content Words: injuries, collisions, positions, muscular, regulation, stoppages, aggressive

Vocabulary Words: innocence, innocently, absolution, resolution

© Spelling Grade 6 91

Student Day 4

Read the facts about field hockey and ice hockey. Knowing the facts about something helps in forming a personal opinion. Write list words to complete the paragraphs.

Lesson 23 Writing
Variant Consonant Spellings

Hockey

Two variations of hockey—field hockey and ice hockey—are played by men and women in many countries. Hockey is a sport that builds leadership and negotiation skills, and requires excellent hand-eye coordination, strength, and endurance. Although similar, field hockey and ice hockey are separate sports.

Field hockey is played outdoors on a field. Eleven players occupy four positions—forward, halfback, fullback, and goalie. Players use a wooden stick that is curved at one end to hit a ball into the opponent's goal. The ball has a circumference of about nine inches and weighs less than six ounces. Field hockey is played as an amateur sport as well as a professional sport in many countries. In the United States, field hockey is primarily played by women.

Ice hockey is a fast-paced game usually played in an indoor rink. Players wear a helmet and use a hockey stick to hit a puck into the opponent's goal. A regulation puck is made from black rubber, is one inch thick, and is three inches in diameter. Six athletic, muscular players occupy three positions—forward, defender, and goalie. Ice hockey requires players to be adept at ice-skating. Players must be able to accelerate, maintain balance, stop quickly, and change direction abruptly. In essence, players must be able to skate as naturally as they walk. Because ice hockey is fast paced, mental agility is necessary since plays need to be memorized. It is imperative that players think and react quickly. Men's ice hockey is an aggressive sport in which players are often roughhousing and causing injuries. In women's ice hockey, collisions occur, but overall, the sport is much less hostile than men's ice hockey.

Which variation of hockey would you rather play? Why? Write your opinion in complete sentences.

Sentences will vary.

Pattern Words: visual, insured, laughter, advisable, brochure, machinery, emphasize, measurable, phenomenal, architectural, roughhousing, advertisement

Content Words: injuries, collisions, positions, muscular, regulation, stoppages, aggressive

Vocabulary Words: innocence, innocently, absolution, resolution

92 © Spelling Grade 6

Lesson 24

Review Lessons 19–23

Student Pages

Pages 93–96

Lesson Materials

T-15
P-4
BLM SP6-24A
BLM SP6-24B
P-2
P-3
BLM SP6-24C
T-5
BLM SP6-24D
BLMs SP6-24E–F
BLM SP6-06G
BLM SP6-24G

Day 1 Greek Roots

Objective

The students will spell, identify, and sort words with **Greek roots.**

Introduction

Teacher Note: This week's lesson incorporates the Pattern, Content, and Vocabulary Words taught in Lessons 19–23 using a variety of activities such as sorting, combining **Greek roots**, writing words in shape boxes, filling in the correct answer circle, finding words in a word search, unscrambling words in context, and using a coordinate grid to write words.

Display **T-15 Lessons 19–23 Study Sheet** on the overhead to review Lesson 19 words in unison, using the say-spell-say technique. Select three students to participate in a word guessing game. Choose a Pattern Word from Lesson 19 and draw one short line on the board for each letter in the word. Invite the first student to suggest a letter that may be in the word. If the suggested letter is in the word, write that letter above the corresponding short line. If the letter is not present, write the letter in another area of the board. Students may guess the word if they have discovered a letter within the word. Students alternate turns until one of the participants correctly guesses the word. Write the completed word. Continue with additional words to provide sufficient review.

Directed Instruction

1 Refer to **P-4 Greek Roots** and invite volunteers to identify the two **Greek roots** in each Pattern Word. Challenge students to use one word with each of the following beginning roots in an original sentence: cardio, hydro, thermo.

2 Proceed to page 93. Explain that the box contains all the Pattern, Content, and Vocabulary Words in Lessons 19–23. This list is the same list of words that was previously displayed on the overhead. Encourage students to use this list as a review tool. Instruct students to read the directions and independently complete the page.

3 Distribute a copy of **BLM SP6-24A Lessons 19–23 Study Sheet** to each student to take home for study.

4 Homework suggestion: Distribute a copy of **BLM SP6-24B Lesson 24 Homework I** to each student to practice with **Greek roots**, **Greek and Latin roots**, and **hard and soft c** and **g**. Remind students to review their weekly sets of flash cards from Lessons 19–23.

Day 2 Greek Roots and Greek and Latin Roots

Objective

The students will write words that reflect the combined meanings of two **Greek roots**. Students will write words with **Greek and Latin roots** in shape boxes.

Introduction

Display **T-15 Lessons 19–23 Study Sheet** to review Lesson 20 words in unison, using the say-spell-say technique. Remind students that each Pattern Word has two **Greek roots**. Refer to **P-4 Greek Roots** to review the meaning of the following roots that appear at the beginning of each

Pattern Word:

- *macro* means *large* • *micro* means *small*
- *mono* means *one* • *opto* means *see*

Review the following roots that appear as final syllables:

- *chrom* means *color* • *cosm* means *universe*
- *phon* means *sound* • *pod* means *foot*

Invite students to state the word that has the following combined root meanings: *one foot* (**monopod**), *one color* (**monochromatic**), *small sound* (**microphone**), *small universe* (**microcosm**).

Directed Instruction

1 Display **T-15 Lessons 19–23 Study Sheet** to review Lesson 21 words in unison, using the say-spell-say technique. Refer to **P-2** and **P-3 Latin Roots** and **P-4 Greek Roots.** Invite a volunteer to circle the **Greek roots** and the **Latin roots** of each Pattern Word with two different transparency pens, reserving one color for the **Greek roots** and the second color for the **Latin roots.**

2 Proceed to page 94. Students complete the page.

3 Homework suggestion: Distribute a copy of **BLM SP6-24C Lesson 24 Homework II** to each student to practice **variant consonant spellings**, Content Words, and Vocabulary Words.

Day 3 Hard and Soft c, g and Variant Consonant Spellings

Objective

The students will select an appropriate answer circle to indicate if words with **hard and soft c** and **g** are spelled correctly or incorrectly and correctly write each word. They will find and write words with **variant consonant spellings** in a word search.

Introduction

Display **T-15 Lessons 19–23 Study Sheet.** Direct students' attention to Lesson 22 Pattern Words. Write the following activity on the board to provide practice for the exercises on the student page:

	Correct	Incorrect	
guage	○	○	**(incorrect; gauge)**
disgise	○	○	**(incorrect; disguise)**
occurrence	○	○	**(correct; occurrence)**

Read each word and select volunteers to identify if each word is spelled correctly or incorrectly. Fill in each appropriate answer circle. Write each word correctly.

Directed Instruction

1 Display **T-5 Word Search Grid.** Select a volunteer to write the following Pattern Words from Lesson 23 in the squares of the grid: visual,

i	i	x	z	q	p	r	z	l	x	d
n	d	a	d	v	i	s	a	b	l	e
s	v	l	v	z	j	u	r	z	n	v
u	q	z	i	n	s	r	r	e	d	s
r	i	e	x	i	b	r	t	v	j	s
e	r	v	v	t	a	n	q	r	g	n
d	e	l	b	a	r	u	s	a	e	m

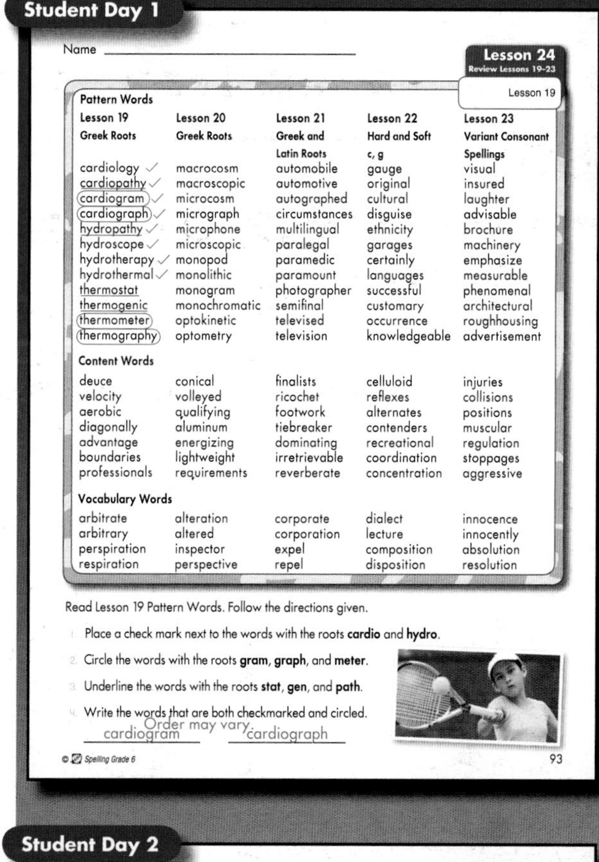

Student Day 1

Name ______________________

Lesson 24
Review Lessons 19-23

Lesson 19

Pattern Words

Lesson 19 Greek Roots	Lesson 20 Greek Roots	Lesson 21 Greek and Latin Roots	Lesson 22 Hard and Soft c, g	Lesson 23 Variant Consonant Spellings
cardiology ✓	macrocosm	automobile	gauge	visual
cardiopathy ✓	macroscopic	automotive	original	insured
cardiogram ✓	microcosm	autographed	cultural	laughter
cardiograph ✓	micrograph	circumstances	disguise	advisable
hydropathy ✓	microphone	multilingual	ethnicity	brochure
hydroscope ✓	microscopic	paralegal	garages	machinery
hydrotherapy ✓	monopod	paramedic	certainly	emphasize
hydrothermal ✓	monolithic	paramount	languages	measurable
thermostat	monogram	photographer	successful	phenomenal
thermogenic	monochromatic	semifinal	customary	architectural
thermometer	optokinetic	televised	occurrence	roughhousing
thermography	optometry	television	knowledgeable	advertisement

Content Words

deuce	conical	finalists	celluloid	injuries
velocity	volleyed	ricochet	reflexes	collisions
aerobic	qualifying	footwork	alternates	positions
diagonally	aluminum	tiebreaker	contenders	muscular
advantage	energizing	dominating	recreational	regulation
boundaries	lightweight	irretrievable	coordination	stoppages
professionals	requirements	reverberate	concentration	aggressive

Vocabulary Words

arbitrate	alteration	corporate	dialect	innocence
arbitrary	altered	corporation	lecture	innocently
perspiration	inspector	expel	composition	absolution
respiration	perspective	repel	disposition	resolution

Read Lesson 19 Pattern Words. Follow the directions given.

1. Place a check mark next to the words with the roots **cardio** and **hydro**.
2. Circle the words with the roots **gram**, **graph**, and **meter**.
3. Underline the words with the roots **stat**, **gen**, and **path**.
4. Write the words that are both checkmarked and circled.

cardiogram Order may vary. cardiograph

© Spelling Grade 6 93

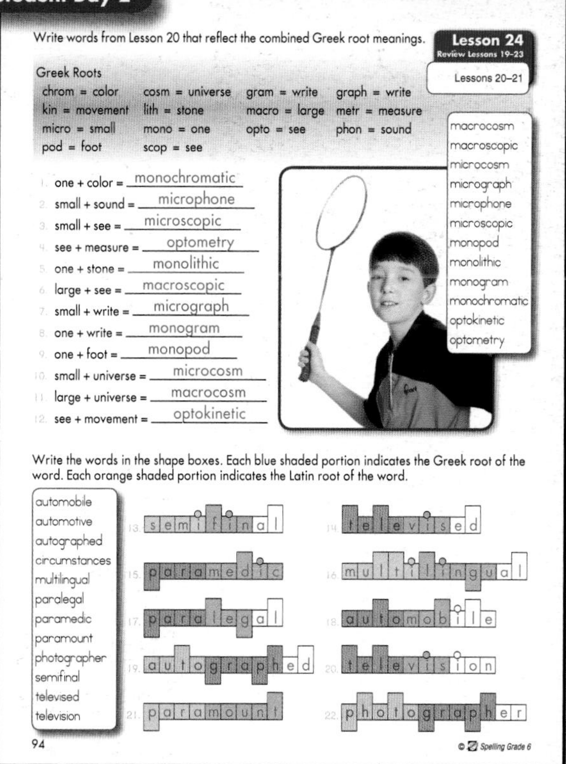

Student Day 2

Write words from Lesson 20 that reflect the combined Greek root meanings.

Lesson 24
Review Lessons 19-23

Lessons 20–21

Greek Roots

chrom = color, cosm = universe, gram = write, graph = write
kin = movement, lith = stone, macro = large, metr = measure
micro = small, mono = one, opto = see, phon = sound
pod = foot, scop = see

macrocosm, macroscopic, microcosm, micrograph, microphone, microscopic, monopod, monolithic, monogram, monochromatic, optokinetic, optometry

1. one + color = monochromatic
2. small + sound = microphone
3. small + see = microscopic
4. see + measure = optometry
5. one + stone = monolithic
6. large + see = macroscopic
7. small + write = micrograph
8. one + write = monogram
9. one + foot = monopod
10. small + universe = microcosm
11. large + universe = macrocosm
12. see + movement = optokinetic

Write the words in the shape boxes. Each blue shaded portion indicates the Greek root of the word. Each orange shaded portion indicates the Latin root of the word.

automobile, automotive, autographed, circumstances, multilingual, paralegal, paramedic, paramount, photographer, semifinal, televised, television

13. semifinal
14. televised
15. paramedic
16. multilingual
17. paralegal
18. automobile
19. autographed
20. television
21. paramount
22. photographer

94 © Spelling Grade 6

Student Day 3

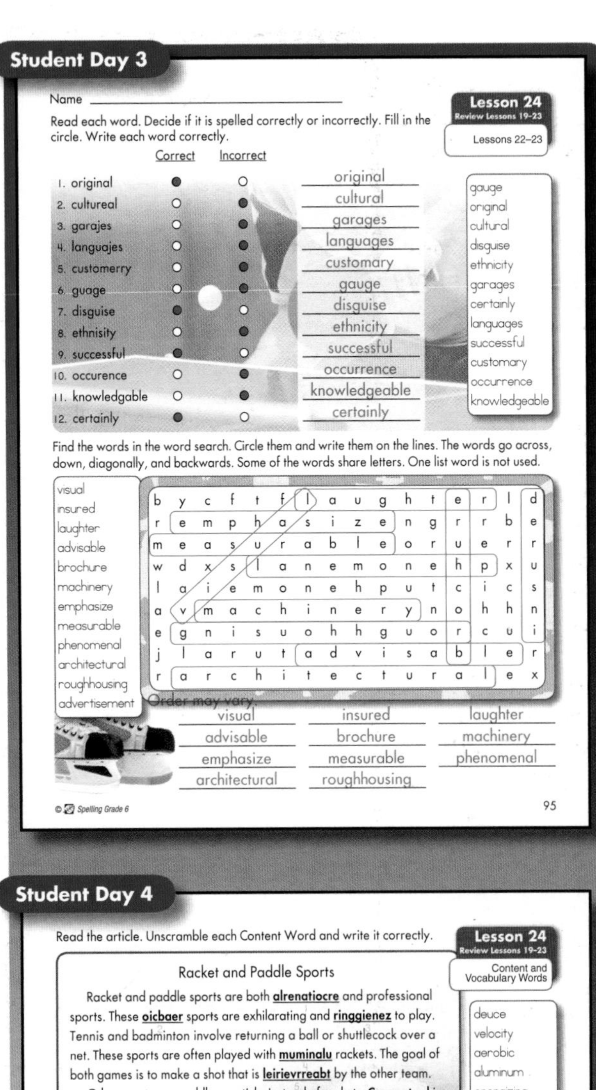

Name ______________________

Lesson 24 Review Lessons 19–23

Lessons 22–23

Read each word. Decide if it is spelled correctly or incorrectly. Fill in the circle. Write each word correctly.

	Correct	Incorrect	
1. original	●	○	original
2. cultureal	○	●	cultural
3. garajes	○	●	garages
4. languajes	○	●	languages
5. customerry	○	●	customary
6. guage	○	●	gauge
7. disguise	●	○	disguise
8. ethnisity	○	●	ethnicity
9. successful	●	○	successful
10. occurence	○	●	occurrence
11. knowledgable	○	●	knowledgeable
12. certainly	●	○	certainly

gauge
original
cultural
disguise
ethnicity
garages
certainly
languages
successful
customary
occurrence
knowledgeable

Find the words in the word search. Circle them and write them on the lines. The words go across, down, diagonally, and backwards. Some of the words share letters. One list word is not used.

visual
insured
laughter
advisable
brochure
machinery
emphasize
measurable
phenomenal
architectural
roughhousing
advertisement

b	y	c	f	t	f	l	a	u	g	h	t	e	r	l	d
r	e	m	p	h	a	s	i	z	e	n	g	r	r	b	e
m	e	a	s	u	r	a	b	l	e	o	r	u	e	r	r
w	d	x	s	l	a	n	e	m	o	n	e	h	p	x	u
l	a	i	e	m	o	n	e	h	p	u	t	c	i	c	s
a	v	m	a	c	h	i	n	e	r	y	n	o	h	h	n
e	g	n	i	s	u	o	h	h	g	u	o	r	c	u	i
j	l	a	r	u	t	a	d	v	i	s	a	b	l	e	r
r	a	r	c	h	i	t	e	c	t	u	r	a	l	e	x

Order may vary.

visual, insured, laughter
advisable, brochure, machinery
emphasize, measurable, phenomenal
architectural, roughhousing

© Spelling Grade 6 95

Student Day 4

Lesson 24 Review Lessons 19–23

Content and Vocabulary Words

Read the article. Unscramble each Content Word and write it correctly.

Racket and Paddle Sports

Racket and paddle sports are both **alrenatiocre** and professional sports. These **oicbaer** sports are exhilarating and **ringgienez** to play. Tennis and badminton involve returning a ball or shuttlecock over a net. These sports are often played with **muminalu** rackets. The goal of both games is to make a shot that is **leirievrreabt** by the other team.

Other sports use paddles or sticks instead of rackets. **Ceonentrsd** in table tennis play with a **igwethtligh** ball and paddles. Hockey players use hockey sticks to propel a ball or a puck at a high **ctyveloi**. Racket and paddle sports can be challenging and **agsivresge** sports to play.

deuce
velocity
aerobic
aluminum
energizing
lightweight
dominating
irretrievable
reverberate
alternates
contenders
recreational
regulation
stoppages
aggressive

1. recreational 2. aerobic 3. energizing
4. aluminum 5. irretrievable 6. Contenders
7. lightweight 8. velocity 9. aggressive

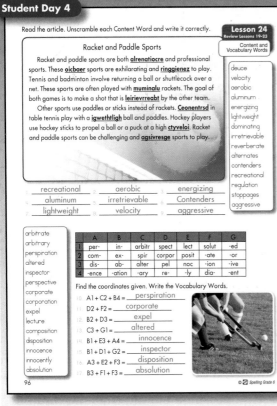

arbitrate
arbitrary
perspiration
altered
inspector
perspective
corporate
corporation
expel
lecture
composition
disposition
innocence
innocently
absolution

	A	B	C	D	E	F	G
1	per-	in-	arbitr	spect	lect	solut	-ed
2	com-	ex-	spir	corpor	posit	-ate	-or
3	dis-	ab-	alter	pel	noc	-ion	-ive
4	-ence	-ation	-ary	re-	-ly	dia-	-ent

Find the coordinates given. Write the Vocabulary Words.

10. A1 + C2 + B4 = perspiration
11. D2 + F2 = corporate
12. B2 + D3 = expel
13. C3 + G1 = altered
14. B1 + E3 + A4 = innocence
15. B1 + D1 + G2 = inspector
16. A3 + E2 + F3 = disposition
17. B3 + F1 + F3 = absolution

96 © Spelling Grade 6

insured, advisable, measurable. Assist the volunteer in positioning the words across, down, diagonally, and backwards. Fill in the surrounding squares with letters to conceal the words. When completed, display the transparency on the overhead and challenge students to find the Pattern Words, referring to the list words on the bottom of page 95. Circle each word as it is found. An example word search is shown.

2 Refer to **T-15 Lessons 19–23 Study Sheet** to review Lessons 22–23 words in unison, using the say-spell-say technique.

3 Proceed to page 95. Allow students to complete the exercises independently.

Day 4 Content Words and Vocabulary Words

Objective

The students will unscramble content words written in the context of an article and write the words correctly. Students will write vocabulary words by locating the word parts found within a coordinate grid.

Introduction

Display **T-15 Lessons 19–23 Study Sheet** to review Content Words in unison, using the say-spell-say technique. Choose a pair of volunteers to work collaboratively to select ten different Content Words and to write the words in scrambled form on the board. Allow the pair of volunteers to select other students to come to the board to unscramble, write the Content Words correctly, and use each unscrambled word in a sentence.

Directed Instruction

1 Display **T-15 Lessons 19–23 Study Sheet** to review Vocabulary Words in unison, using the say-spell-say technique. Refer to **P-2** and **P-3 Latin Roots** to review the meanings of the following roots:

- *alter* means *other*
- *corpor* means *body*
- *noc* means *harm*
- *posit* means *place*
- *spect* means *look*
- *arbitr* means *judge*
- *lect* means *gather*
- *pel* means *push*
- *solut* means *set free*
- *spir* means *breathe*

2 Proceed to page 96. Allow students to independently complete the page.

3 Homework suggestion: Distribute a copy of **BLM SP6-24D Lessons 19–23 Test Prep** to each student to practice with many of the words that may appear on the Assessment. Prepare for the Assessment by studying the words on **BLM SP6-24A Lessons 19–23 Study Sheet** that was sent home on Day 1 or by using their flash card sets.

Day 5 Assessment

Objective

The students will accurately select the appropriate answer within the context of a sentence. They will fill in the corresponding answer circle.

Introduction

Teacher Note: The Test makes provision for Differentiated Instruction. The first twelve sentences include the words assigned to students with shortened lists. Encourage these students to try all the sentences, but only grade the first twelve sentences. The Test is found on two blackline masters.

Duplicate a copy of **BLMs SP6-24E–F Lessons 19–23 Test I** and **II** and distribute to each student. Duplicate **BLM SP6-06G Student Answer Form** and cut apart. Distribute one answer form to each student. Remind students to fill in each answer circle completely and to erase completely if they wish to change an answer.

Directed Assessment

1 Instruct students to listen as you dictate the following Sample:

Sample

A visual image from a cardiogram gives doctors an advantige. All correct
(A: visual; B: cardiogram; C: advantige; D: All correct)

Say, "Are any of the first three underlined words misspelled?" Pause for replies. Inform students that the letter *C* is below the underlined word that is misspelled. (**advantage**) Guide students to the answer form that was previously distributed. Lead students to find the Sample box and fill in the appropriate answer circle containing the same letter. Say, "You will continue in the same way. You will read each sentence, choose the word that you think is misspelled, and fill in the corresponding circle on the answer form. If all the words are spelled correctly, fill in the fourth circle, labeled *D*, for *All correct*."

2 Assist students as needed while they read the sentences and complete the Test on their own.

1. The tennis contenders all had good reflexes and great footwork.
2. All qualifying jackets must have a monogram and be lightweight.
3. As a paramedic, Sam saw instances of cardiopathy and poor respiration.
4. Our family's cars are insured against collisions by an automotive policy.
5. Players need concentration and optokinetic skill to repel a shuttlecock.
6. A multilingual announcer spoke several languages into the microphone.
7. Recreational players know the tennis requirements and boundaries.
8. The badminton finalists volleyed the shuttlecock at a high velocity.
9. Li made a resolution to check the thermometer and adjust the thermostat.
10. As the children were roughhousing, there was laughter but no injuries.
11. It was certainly no surprise that Kit was dominating the tiebreaker.
12. Since she wasn't knowledgeable, Mia innocently questioned the positions.
13. A brochure may contain an advertisement for machinery.
14. Many tennis professionals are both muscular and aggressive.
15. In my perspective, a phenomenal game should be televised.
16. It is customary for the semifinal game to be shown on television.
17. The photographer used an aluminum monopod.
18. Mechanics at some garages gauge the tire pressure of each automobile.
19. AhJung hit the conical shuttlecock diagonally, making it irretrievable.
20. An architectural regulation delay hurt the progress of the corporation.
21. A successful table-tennis player autographed a ball made of celluloid.
22. Perspiration flowed when the energizing tennis game went to deuce.
23. In the lecture, Dr. Perez explained the microscopic composition of cells.
24. Doctors of cardiology emphasize the benefits of aerobic exercise.
25. Her client's innocence was of paramount importance to the paralegal.

3 Refer to **BLM SP6-24G Lessons 19–23 Answer Key** when correcting the Test.

Notes

Lesson 25

Prefixes

Student Pages

Pages 97–100

Lesson Materials

BLM SP6-01B
Card stock
Index cards
Whiteboards
Laminated card stock
Erasable markers
BLM SP6-25A

Sports

Lessons 25–29 utilize the theme of track-and-field sports. The theme of this lesson is short-distance running. Short-distance running events are called sprints or dashes. Outdoor sprints include the 100-meter, 200-meter, and 400-meter events. Indoor events include the 50- and 60-meter dashes as well as the 200- and 400-meter events. Eric Liddell, a famous Christian sprinter who was also a missionary, took the gold medal for Britain in the 400-meter dash in the 1924 Olympics.

Day 1 Pretest

Objective

The students will accurately spell and write words with **prefixes**. They will spell and write content, vocabulary, and challenge words.

Introduction

Before class, select Challenge Words for numbers 24 and 25 from a cross-curricular subject, words misspelled on previous assignments, or words that interest your students. The word *dissatisfaction* has the **prefix dis-** and is suggested for number 24. Administer the Pretest.

Directed Instruction

1 Say each word, use it in a sentence, and then repeat the word.

Pattern Words

1. Some running shoes have a soft, supportive midsole.
2. Antibiotics are sometimes prescribed for infections.
3. Proper rest and nutrition are antistress strategies for health.
4. An athlete with a disability ran in the Paralympics.
5. DeVon ran the race even with a dislocation to one of his fingers.
6. Dana embodied all the qualities of a fine Christian athlete.
7. Luis' father embraced him when he completed his first race.
8. Immovable hurdles would be dangerous to runners.
9. Allie made an improvement in her time in the 100-meter dash.
10. The coach was incredulous at his athletes' results.
11. Derek practiced hard and invariably took first place.
12. The medal ceremony was held in the midfield.

Content Words

13. The champions received gold medals.
14. Track-and-field races are run counterclockwise.
15. The runners began by crouching in the starting blocks.
16. Runners will elongate their stride to cover more ground.
17. The multilane track had staggered starting lines.
18. All the runners began racing simultaneously.
19. Eric Liddell was a Christian missionary as well as a sprinter.

Vocabulary Words

20. A flash of lightning was a disruption to the event at the meet.
21. The track meet was ended abruptly by a sudden thunderstorm.
22. Water revived the dehydrated runner.
23. Does Stephanie have a vivacious personality?

Challenge Words

24. ______________________
25. ______________________

2 Allow students to self-correct their Pretest. Write each word on the board. Point out the following **prefixes** in the Pattern Words: anti-, dis-, em-, im-, in-, mid-. Note the roots *rupt* and *viv* in the Vocabulary Words.

3 As a class, read, spell, and read each word. Direct students to highlight misspelled words and rewrite them correctly.

4 Proof each student's Pretest. This becomes an individualized study sheet that can be used at school or at home.

5 Homework suggestion: Duplicate **BLM SP6-01B Flash Cards Template** on CARD STOCK for students to write the list words, using the flash cards as a study aid. Another option is to use INDEX CARDS.

Day 2 Word Analysis and Vocabulary

Objective

The students will sort and write words with **prefixes** and complete sentences with content words. Students will use a table to write vocabulary words, match vocabulary words to their definitions, complete sentences, and choose the best meaning for underlined words.

Introduction

Review the following definition: A *prefix* is a word part that is added to the beginning of a root or a root with a suffix. A prefix is an *affix*. Affixes expand the meaning or function of a word. Invite students to refer to the list words, found on page 97. Dictate the following word parts: ability, biotic ... field, location, movable, provement, sole, st... d list for the missing ... d part, identify the m...

The President's ideas of socialism were not well recieved.
A deficiency in iron makes you feel tired.

Directed Instru...

1 Select six Patter... he board. Invite a ... in each word. Poin... g of a root or root w... ents to suggest word... **es** *anti-, dis-, em-,* ...

2 Choose volunteers to look up the ... Spelling Dictionary and share the definitions with the class: sprinter, elongate, crouching, simultaneously.

3 Proceed to page 97. Say, spell, and say each Pattern, Content, and Vocabulary Word. Provide this week's Challenge Words and have students write them in the spaces provided. Students complete the page.

4 Proceed to page 98. Remind students to use the table to assist in building each Vocabulary Word. For example, the prefix *ab-* goes

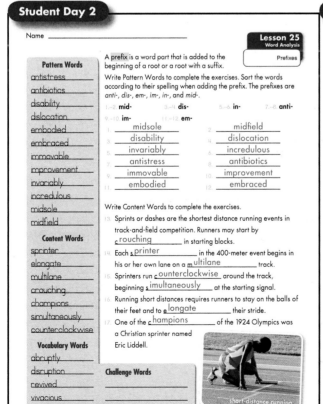

Differentiated Instruction

- For students who spelled all the words correctly on the Pretest, select and assign Extra Challenge Words from the following list: overestimation, phylogenetics, mythological, socialism, deficiency, piccolo.
- For students who spelled less than half correctly, assign the following Pattern, Content, and Vocabulary Words: antibiotics, disability, embodied, improvement, invariably, midfield, sprinter, champions, simultaneously, counterclockwise, abruptly, vivacious. On the Posttest, evaluate these students on the twelve words assigned; however, encourage them to attempt to spell all the list words to the best of their ability. They are also responsible for writing the dictated sentences.

52 pts.

Student Day 2

Name ______________

Lesson 25 Word Analysis — Prefixes

Pattern Words: antistress, antibiotics, disability, dislocation, embodied, embraced, immovable, improvement, invariably, incredulous, midsole, midfield

Content Words: sprinter, elongate, multilane, crouching, champions, simultaneously, counterclockwise

Vocabulary Words: abruptly, disruption, revived, vivacious

A prefix is a word part that is added to the beginning of a root or a root with a suffix.

Write Pattern Words to complete the exercises. Sort the words according to their spelling when adding the prefix. The prefixes are *anti-, dis-, em-, im-, in-,* and *mid-*.

1.–2. **mid-** 3.–4. **dis-** 5.–6. **in-** 7.–8. **anti-** 9.–10. **im-** 11.–12. **em-**

1. midsole 2. midfield
3. disability 4. dislocation
5. invariably 6. incredulous
7. antistress 8. antibiotics
9. immovable 10. improvement
11. embodied 12. embraced

Write Content Words to complete the exercises.

13. Sprints or dashes are the shortest distance running events in track-and-field competition. Runners may start by crouching in starting blocks.
14. Each sprinter in the 400-meter event begins in his or her own lane on a multilane track.
15. Sprinters run counterclockwise around the track, beginning simultaneously at the starting signal.
16. Running short distances requires runners to stay on the balls of their feet and to elongate their stride.
17. One of the champions of the 1924 Olympics was a Christian sprinter named Eric Liddell.

short-distance running

Challenge Words
____
____

© Spelling Grade 6 — 97

Student Day 2

Lesson 25 Vocabulary — Prefixes

Prefix		Root		Suffix	
ab-	away	rupt	break	-ly	forms an adverb from an adjective
dis-	off	viv	life	-ion	state of
re-	again			-ed	makes verbs past tense
				-acious	quality of

Write the Vocabulary Words. Order may vary.

1. abruptly 2. disruption
3. revived 4. vivacious

Refer to the table to complete the exercises. Write the word that is being defined.

5. in a sudden breaking away; suddenly abruptly
6. brought back to life revived
7. having the quality of liveliness; perky; lively vivacious
8. the state of breaking something apart or interrupting disruption

Write Vocabulary Words to complete the sentences.

9. At the track meet, Eva competed in the 200- and 400-meter races. Her competitors enjoyed meeting her because she has a vivacious personality.
10. Before the start of the 400-meter race, Eva abruptly stopped stretching and grasped her calf.
11. A slight cramp in her leg had caused a momentary disruption in her preparation for the race.
12. Eva massaged the cramp and drank some water, which revived her in time for the race.

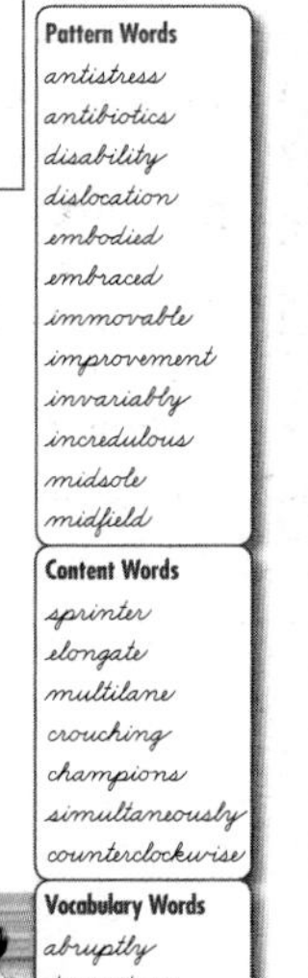

Choose the best meaning for each underlined word.

13. Marco invariably arrived early for practice.
● always ○ never ○ soon
14. He embodied the qualities of a dedicated sprinter.
○ embraced ● personified ○ revived

Pattern Words: antistress, antibiotics, disability, dislocation, embodied, embraced, immovable, improvement, invariably, incredulous, midsole, midfield
Content Words: sprinter, elongate, multilane, crouching, champions, simultaneously, counterclockwise
Vocabulary Words: abruptly, disruption, revived, vivacious

98 — © Spelling Grade 6

with the root *rupt* and the suffix *-ly* to build the word *abruptly*. Allow students to complete the page independently.

5 Homework suggestion: Students use their Spelling Dictionary to write the definition of each word on the back of the corresponding flash card that was suggested for homework on Day 1.

Day 3 Word Study Strategies

Objective

The students will write pattern words with **prefixes** to match definitions. The students will combine two short sentences into one sentence having a compound predicate.

Introduction

Provide each student with a WHITEBOARD or a piece of LAMINATED CARD STOCK and an ERASABLE MARKER. Direct students to turn to page 99 to refer to the meanings of the **prefixes** located in the shaded area. Ask the following riddles and invite students to write and hold up their response to each riddle:

- Which word describes a bone that is not in its right location? (**dislocation**)
- Which word fights against harmful biological organisms? (**antibiotics**)
- Which word is put into bodily form? (**embodied**)

Directed Instruction

1 To practice and improve sentence fluency in the students' writing, write the following short sentences on the board:

- Felicia had a dislocation to her knee.
- Felicia suffered a temporary disability.

(**Felicia had a dislocation to her knee and suffered a temporary disability.**)

Explain that short, choppy sentences that share the same subject can be combined into a single longer sentence that has a compound predicate. Ask students to identify the subject that is shared in the two short sentences by making a circle around both subjects. Invite a volunteer to underline the complete predicates in both sentences. Rewrite the two sentences as one sentence, using a conjunction to add the second complete predicate to the first sentence. Challenge students to state the list words in the sentence. (**dislocation, disability**)

2 Proceed to page 99. Assist students as needed to complete the page.

Day 4 Writing

Objective

The students will read a brief biography about Eric Liddell, an Olympic champion who was a missionary. They will write list words that could replace the bold word or words.

Introduction

Teacher Note: The informative domain is the focus for the writing pages in Lessons 25–29.

Review the following definition: A biography is a written account of someone's life. Explain that biographies are usually organized in chronological order. Biographies include details such as important dates, events, achievements, contributions, and major challenges in the person's life. Today's lesson includes a brief biography of Eric Liddell.

Directed Instruction

1 Instruct students to lay their flash cards suggested for homework on Day 1 and Day 2 on top of their desk, keeping the list words faceup. Read the following definitions and challenge students to find a list word with the matching definition in the flash cards:

- occurring at the same time as something else (**simultaneously**)
- having the quality of liveliness; perky; lively (**vivacious**)

Student Spelling Support Materials

BLM SP6-01A

Student Spelling Support

1. Use **BLM SP6-01A A Spelling Study Strategy** in instructional groups to provide assistance with some or all of the words.
2. Invite students to write the Challenge Words, numbers 24 and 25, in the Word Bank, in the back of their textbook.
3. Challenge students to research and write a brief biography of a Christian athlete, beginning with a graphic organizer such as a time line. Discuss the organization of the biography and relevant details that should be included in biographical sketches including the subject's life events, achievements, goals, and contributions.
4. Write this week's words, categorize the Pattern, Content, and Vocabulary Words, and attach them to the Word Wall.
5. For a Bible connection, read the second part of 1 Samuel 16:7: "For the LORD does not see as man sees; for man looks at the outward appearance, but the LORD looks at the heart." Explain that Eric Liddell's contemporaries may have looked at his refusal to run races held on Sundays as a lack of dedication to his sport or to his country, but that God saw Eric's heart. Invite students to share instances in Scripture where the people only regarded someone's outward appearance or actions, but where God commended the heart of the believer. (**Possible answers: Even though David did not appear**

Cont. on page 101

Students turn each card to the definition side to check their response.

2 Proceed to page 100. Encourage students to read the biography silently and to provide an example of chronological order in the organization and the type of details included in the text. (**important dates, major challenges, achievements, and contributions**) Students complete the page independently. Choose a volunteer to reread the biography orally, inserting the correct list word in place of each definition.

3 Homework suggestion: Distribute a copy of **BLM SP6-25A Lesson 25 Homework** to each student.

Day 5 Posttest

Objective

The students will correctly write dictated spelling words and sentences.

Introduction

Review by using flash cards noted in Day 1 and Day 2 Homework suggestion.

Directed Assessment

1 Dictate the list words by using the Pretest sentences or developing original ones. Reserve *sprinter, improvement, embodied, champions, vivacious,* and *invariably* for the dictation sentences.

2 Read each sentence. Repeat as needed.
- Beth was the best sprinter on the track team.
- She listened to her coach to make an improvement in her form.
- Beth embodied the ideals of fair play.
- She took advice from former champions.
- Beth has a vivacious and outgoing personality that others noticed.
- She was invariably admired by her peers.

3 If assigned, dictate Extra Challenge Words.

4 Score the test, counting each misspelled word as an error. Correct the dictation sentences by grading only the spelling words or grading the complete sentences.

Student Spelling Support

Cont. from page 100

to be the strongest choice for king, God chose him because of his godly heart; Paul was not the most eloquent speaker, but God saw his faith and zeal for preaching the Gospel.)

6. To enhance study skills, instruct students who need additional practice to use colored pencils to write the Pattern Words from this lesson. Students use a different color to differentiate the prefix from the root or root with a suffix. The following are some examples: **antistress, disability, embodied**.

Student Day 3

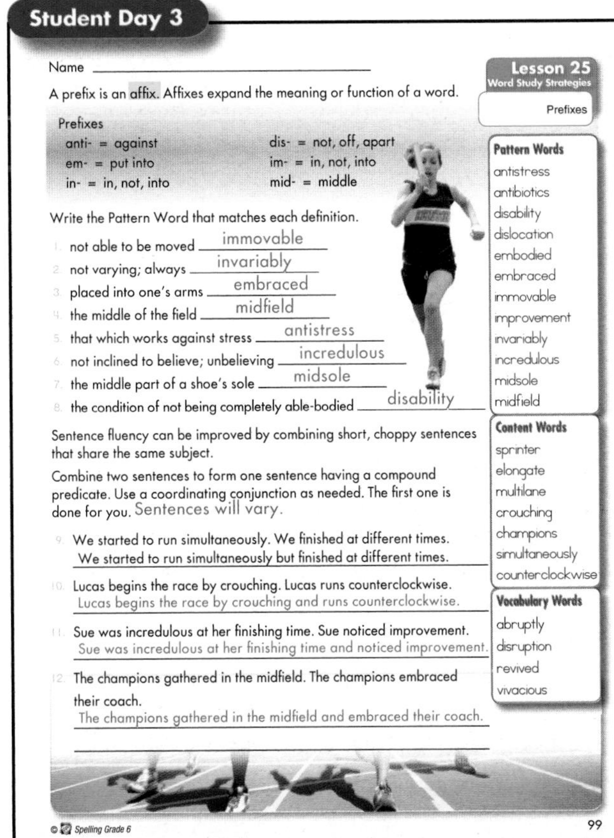
Name ______

Lesson 25 Word Study Strategies — Prefixes

A prefix is an affix. Affixes expand the meaning or function of a word.

Prefixes
anti- = against
em- = put into
in- = in, not, into
dis- = not, off, apart
im- = in, not, into
mid- = middle

Write the Pattern Word that matches each definition.

1. not able to be moved immovable
2. not varying; always invariably
3. placed into one's arms embraced
4. the middle of the field midfield
5. that which works against stress antistress
6. not inclined to believe; unbelieving incredulous
7. the middle part of a shoe's sole midsole
8. the condition of not being completely able-bodied disability

Sentence fluency can be improved by combining short, choppy sentences that share the same subject.

Combine two sentences to form one sentence having a compound predicate. Use a coordinating conjunction as needed. The first one is done for you. Sentences will vary.

9. We started to run simultaneously. We finished at different times.
We started to run simultaneously but finished at different times.
10. Lucas begins the race by crouching. Lucas runs counterclockwise.
Lucas begins the race by crouching and runs counterclockwise.
11. Sue was incredulous at her finishing time. Sue noticed improvement.
Sue was incredulous at her finishing time and noticed improvement.
12. The champions gathered in the midfield. The champions embraced their coach.
The champions gathered in the midfield and embraced their coach.

Pattern Words: antistress, antibiotics, disability, dislocation, embodied, embraced, immovable, improvement, invariably, incredulous, midsole, midfield

Content Words: sprinter, elongate, multilane, crouching, champions, simultaneously, counterclockwise

Vocabulary Words: abruptly, disruption, revived, vivacious

© Spelling Grade 6 99

Student Day 4

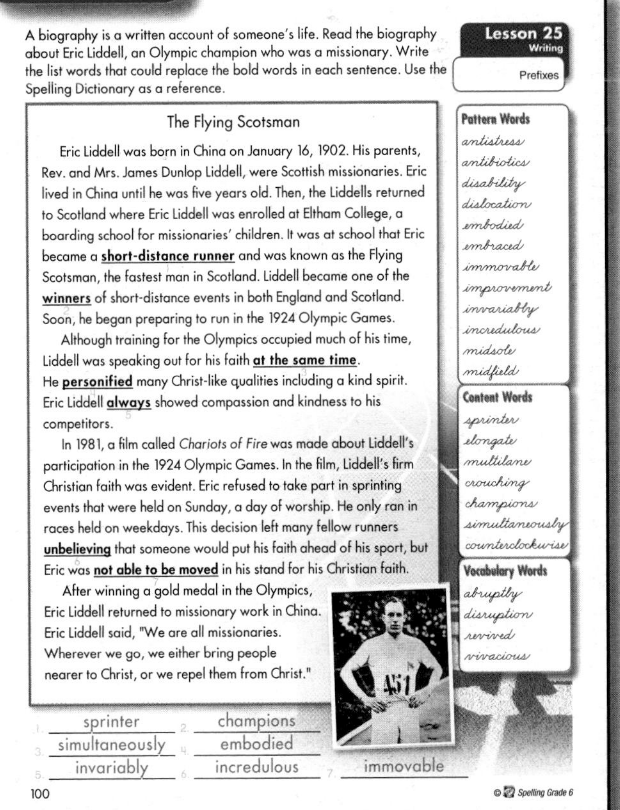
Lesson 25 Writing — Prefixes

A biography is a written account of someone's life. Read the biography about Eric Liddell, an Olympic champion who was a missionary. Write the list words that could replace the bold words in each sentence. Use the Spelling Dictionary as a reference.

The Flying Scotsman

Eric Liddell was born in China on January 16, 1902. His parents, Rev. and Mrs. James Dunlop Liddell, were Scottish missionaries. Eric lived in China until he was five years old. Then, the Liddells returned to Scotland where Eric Liddell was enrolled at Eltham College, a boarding school for missionaries' children. It was at school that Eric became a **short-distance runner** and was known as the Flying Scotsman, the fastest man in Scotland. Liddell became one of the **winners** of short-distance events in both England and Scotland. Soon, he began preparing to run in the 1924 Olympic Games.

Although training for the Olympics occupied much of his time, Liddell was speaking out for his faith **at the same time**. He **personified** many Christ-like qualities including a kind spirit. Eric Liddell **always** showed compassion and kindness to his competitors.

In 1981, a film called *Chariots of Fire* was made about Liddell's participation in the 1924 Olympic Games. In the film, Liddell's firm Christian faith was evident. Eric refused to take part in sprinting events that were held on Sunday, a day of worship. He only ran in races held on weekdays. This decision left many fellow runners **unbelieving** that someone would put his faith ahead of his sport, but Eric was **not able to be moved** in his stand for his Christian faith.

After winning a gold medal in the Olympics, Eric Liddell returned to missionary work in China. Eric Liddell said, "We are all missionaries. Wherever we go, we either bring people nearer to Christ, or we repel them from Christ."

1. sprinter 2. champions
3. simultaneously 4. embodied
5. invariably 6. incredulous 7. immovable

Pattern Words: antistress, antibiotics, disability, dislocation, embodied, embraced, immovable, improvement, invariably, incredulous, midsole, midfield

Content Words: sprinter, elongate, multilane, crouching, champions, simultaneously, counterclockwise

Vocabulary Words: abruptly, disruption, revived, vivacious

100 © Spelling Grade 6

Lesson 26

Prefixes

Student Pages

Pages 101–104

Lesson Materials

BLM SP6-01B
Card stock
Index cards
T-16
BLM SP6-26A
BLM SP6-26B

Sports

The theme of this lesson is long-distance running. Long-distance running surged in the United States in the 1970s after American Frank Shorter won a gold medal in the marathon at the 1972 Olympics. Long-distance running has been firmly established as a recreational activity as well as part of a training regimen. Millions of people participate each year in a 5K, 10K, half marathon, marathon, and other cross-country running events.

Day 1 Pretest

Objective

The students will accurately spell and write words with **prefixes**. They will spell and write content, vocabulary, and challenge words.

Introduction

Before class, select Challenge Words for numbers 24 and 25 from a cross-curricular subject, words misspelled on previous assignments, or words that interest your students. The word *superambitious* has the **prefix super-** and is suggested for number 24. Administer the Pretest.

Directed Instruction

1 Say each word, use it in a sentence, and then repeat the word.

Pattern Words

1. Carlota is proactive in living a healthy lifestyle.
2. The multicultural team included five nationalities.
3. People should never underestimate the power of prayer.
4. Shad mistreated his body by continuing to run with a stress fracture.
5. A superathlete has the ability to play several sports well.
6. A postexercise activity allows the body to cool down after exercising.
7. Since Art broke his ankle, it prolonged his inability to compete.
8. Gina is multitalented since she sings, paints, and runs well.
9. The athlete volunteered his time to help undernourished children.
10. Sal mismanaged his money and could not pay the entrance fees.
11. Calvin received excellent postoperative care from the nurses.
12. The coach's supereffective techniques assist the cross-country team.

Content Words

13. Dehydration from lack of fluids in the body is very dangerous.
14. Stella disciplined herself to run fifteen miles a week.
15. Antoni is strategizing ways to improve his running time.
16. Daily workouts build one's stamina.
17. Have you surpassed a previous personal running record?
18. The conditioning of muscles assists in one's overall performance.
19. Mona collapsed with fatigue at the end of the race.

Vocabulary Words

20. Mitchell was opposed to drinking soda before working out.
21. Reporters waited for the duration of the marathon to see the winner.
22. Kiley is enduring the training to be in a cross-country race.
23. Hallie is supposing she will do well since she has trained hard.

Challenge Words

24. ______________________
25. ______________________

2 Allow students to self-correct their Pretest. Write each word on the board. Point out that the following **prefixes** are in the Pattern Words: mis-, multi-, post-, pro-, super-, under-. Note the roots *dur* and *pos* in the Vocabulary Words.

3 As a class, read, spell, and read each word. Direct students to highlight misspelled words and rewrite them correctly.

4 Proof each student's Pretest. This becomes an individualized study sheet that can be used at school or at home.

5 Homework suggestion: Duplicate **BLM SP6-01B Flash Cards Template**

on CARD STOCK for students to write the list words, using the flash cards as a study aid. Another option is to use INDEX CARDS.

Day 2 W… …ary

Justin learned how to find the area of a parallelogram.

The orchestra hired a new percussionist.

Objective

The students will … with content words. Th… …ch definitions, compl… …ing for given words.

Introduction

Remind students … beginning of a roo… …es expand the meani… …ern Word aloud and select a volunteer to identify and spell the prefix. Explain that the following four prefixes are also used as independent words: post, pro, super, under.

Directed Instruction

1 Challenge students to brainstorm additional words that begin with the following prefixes: mis-, multi-, post-, pro-, super-, under-. Write the words on the board and circle the prefixes.

2 Explain that this week's Content Words relate to the theme of long-distance running. Select seven volunteers to find a Content Word in the Spelling Dictionary and read the definition aloud.

3 Proceed to page 101. Say, spell, and say each Pattern, Content, and Vocabulary Word. Provide this week's Challenge Words and have students write them in the spaces provided before completing the page.

4 Proceed to page 102. Remind students to use the table to assist in building each Vocabulary Word. For example, the root *dur* goes with the suffix *-ation* to get the word *duration*. Teach that the prefix *sup-* in *supposing* is derived from the prefix *sub-*. The prefix *sub-* has a tendency to drop the letter *b*, pick up the first letter of the root *pos*,

Differentiated Instruction

- For students who spelled all the words correctly on the Pretest, select and assign Extra Challenge Words from the following list: parallelogram, polymers, archetype, socioeconomic, neurasthenia, percussionist.
- For students who spelled less than half correctly, assign the following Pattern, Content, and Vocabulary Words: mistreated, multitalented, postoperative, prolonged, supereffective, undernourished, fatigue, stamina, disciplined, strategizing, duration, opposed. On the Posttest, evaluate these students on the twelve words assigned; however, encourage them to attempt to spell all the list words to the best of their ability. They are also responsible for writing the dictated sentences.

62 pts.

Student Day 2

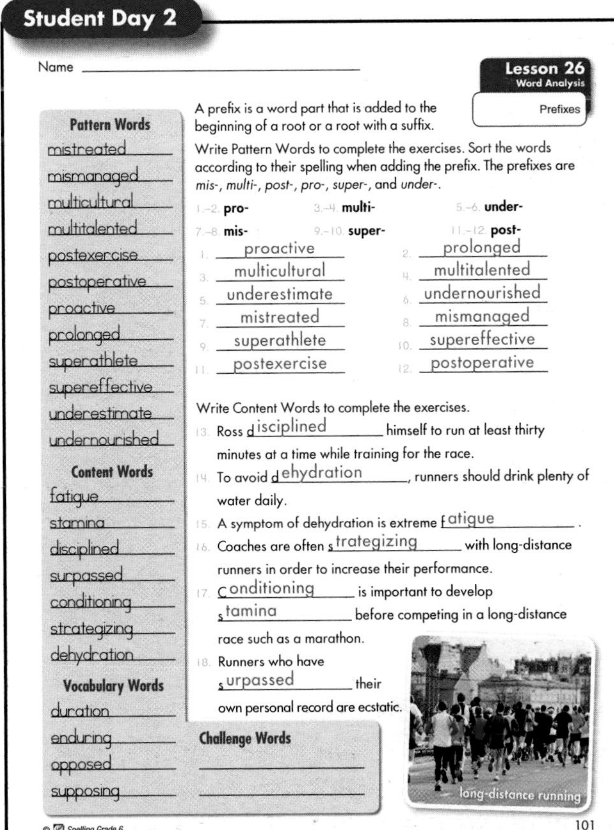

Name ______

Lesson 26 Word Analysis

Prefixes

Pattern Words: mistreated, mismanaged, multicultural, multitalented, postexercise, postoperative, proactive, prolonged, superathlete, supereffective, underestimate, undernourished

Content Words: fatigue, stamina, disciplined, surpassed, conditioning, strategizing, dehydration

Vocabulary Words: duration, enduring, opposed, supposing

Challenge Words ______ ______

A prefix is a word part that is added to the beginning of a root or a root with a suffix.

Write Pattern Words to complete the exercises. Sort the words according to their spelling when adding the prefix. The prefixes are *mis-, multi-, post-, pro-, super-,* and *under-*.

1.–2. pro- 3.–4. multi- 5.–6. under- 7.–8. mis- 9.–10. super- 11.–12. post-

1. proactive 2. prolonged
3. multicultural 4. multitalented
5. underestimate 6. undernourished
7. mistreated 8. mismanaged
9. superathlete 10. supereffective
11. postexercise 12. postoperative

Write Content Words to complete the exercises.

13. Ross disciplined himself to run at least thirty minutes at a time while training for the race.
14. To avoid dehydration, runners should drink plenty of water daily.
15. A symptom of dehydration is extreme fatigue.
16. Coaches are often strategizing with long-distance runners in order to increase their performance.
17. Conditioning is important to develop stamina before competing in a long-distance race such as a marathon.
18. Runners who have surpassed their own personal record are ecstatic.

long-distance running

© Spelling Grade 6 101

Student Day 2

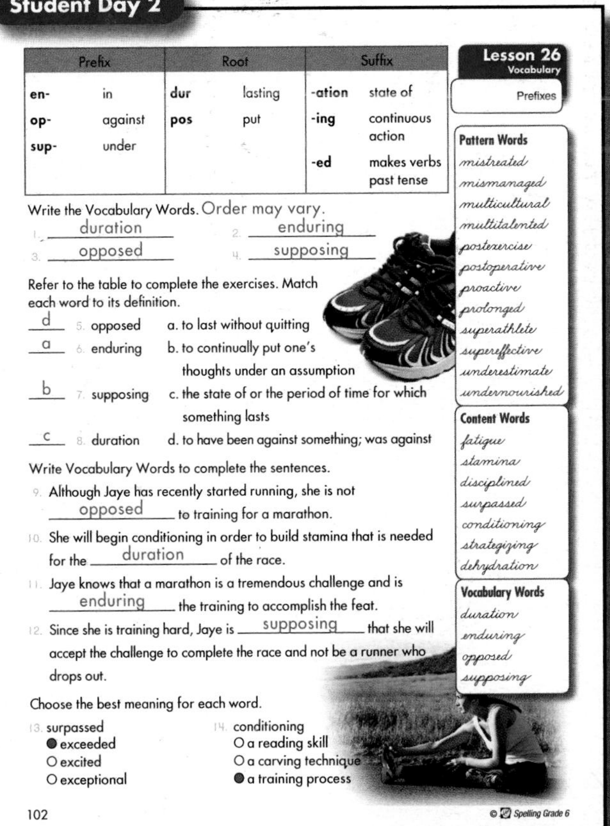

Lesson 26 Vocabulary

Prefixes

Prefix		Root		Suffix	
en-	in	dur	lasting	-ation	state of
op-	against	pos	put	-ing	continuous action
sup-	under			-ed	makes verbs past tense

Write the Vocabulary Words. Order may vary.

1. duration 2. enduring
3. opposed 4. supposing

Refer to the table to complete the exercises. Match each word to its definition.

d 5. opposed — a. to last without quitting
a 6. enduring — b. to continually put one's thoughts under an assumption
b 7. supposing — c. the state of or the period of time for which something lasts
c 8. duration — d. to have been against something; was against

Write Vocabulary Words to complete the sentences.

9. Although Jaye has recently started running, she is not opposed to training for a marathon.
10. She will begin conditioning in order to build stamina that is needed for the duration of the race.
11. Jaye knows that a marathon is a tremendous challenge and is enduring the training to accomplish the feat.
12. Since she is training hard, Jaye is supposing that she will accept the challenge to complete the race and not be a runner who drops out.

Choose the best meaning for each word.

13. surpassed
● exceeded
○ excited
○ exceptional

14. conditioning
○ a reading skill
○ a carving technique
● a training process

Pattern Words: mistreated, mismanaged, multicultural, multitalented, postexercise, postoperative, proactive, prolonged, superathlete, supereffective, underestimate, undernourished

Content Words: fatigue, stamina, disciplined, surpassed, conditioning, strategizing, dehydration

Vocabulary Words: duration, enduring, opposed, supposing

102 © Spelling Grade 6

Student Spelling Support Materials

BLM SP6-01A

Student Spelling Support

1. Use **BLM SP6-01A A Spelling Study Strategy** in instructional groups to provide assistance with some or all of the words.
2. Invite students to write the Challenge Words, numbers 24 and 25, in the Word Bank, in the back of their textbook.
3. Have students write an informational report about a long-distance runner of their choice. Since running is a popular sport, students may personally know a marathoner or cross-country runner. Students may interview a person or research a long-distance runner. Instruct students to research information about the runner, such as the age when he or she started running, participation in any competitions, personal record achievements, his or her training regimen, training with a coach, and favorite place to run.
4. Write this week's words, categorize the Pattern, Content, and Vocabulary Words, and attach them to the Word Wall.
5. Read I Corinthians 9:24: "Do you not know that those who run in a race all run, but one receives the prize? Run in such a way that you may obtain it." Explain that the apostle Paul is comparing Christians to runners. Runners are **disciplined**, motivated people who exercise self-control. A serious runner will diligently concentrate on winning. This involves a training regimen, proper rest,

Cont. on page 105

and double that letter. This accounts for the doubling of the letter *p* in *supposing*. Allow students to complete the page independently.

5 Homework suggestion: Students use their Spelling Dictionary to write the definition of each word on the back of the corresponding flash card that was suggested for homework on Day 1.

Day 3 Word Study Strategies

Objective

The students will write pattern words with **prefixes** to match definitions. They will write list words that are a related form to a group of words.

Introduction

Write the following meanings of prefixes from this lesson on the board:

• wrong, bad • more, better, higher • below, less than

Read the following sentences and select volunteers to deduce the meaning of the prefix:

- Since *undernourished* means *having less than the minimum amount of food for proper nourishment,* the prefix *under-* means ______. **(below, less than**)
- Since *supereffective* means *better results than anticipated,* the prefix *super-* means ______. **(more, better, higher)**
- Since *mistreated* means *to have treated badly,* the prefix *mis-* means ______. **(wrong, bad)**

Directed Instruction

1 Write *strategizing* and *opposed* on the board. Challenge students to name related forms of each of the words *strategizing* and *opposed.* **(Possible answers: strategizes, strategize, strategized; opposition, suppose, opposing)**

2 Proceed to page 103. Allow students to work independently. Assist as needed.

Day 4 Writing

Objective

The students will use proofreading marks to identify mistakes in an informative summary.

Introduction

Display **T-16 Proofreading an Informative Article** on the overhead, keeping the bottom portion covered. Explain that this article is an example of informative writing. Read the article and challenge students to identify the information contained within the paragraph. **(Possible answers: how the competitive race, the marathon, was named; the marathon as a men's Olympic sport; the first women's marathon race; the name of the first woman to win a marathon; characteristics of marathoners)** Orally read the text again and challenge students to locate the mistakes. Correct the mistakes on the overhead using the appropriate proofreading mark. Use **BLM SP6-26A T-16 Answer Key** as a guide. Uncover the bottom portion of the transparency, so students can see a corrected version.

Directed Instruction

1 Proceed to page 104. Select a student to read the sentences at the top of the page. Allow students to work independently, assisting as needed. **(9 misspellings; 3 capital letters; 2 periods needed; 2 deletes; 2 add something—*are, are*; 3 small letters needed; 1 new paragraph)**

2 Homework suggestion: Distribute a copy of **BLM SP6-26B Lesson 26 Homework** to each student.

Day 5 Posttest

Objective

The students will correctly write dictated spelling words and sentences.

Introduction

Review by using flash cards noted in Day 1 and Day 2 Homework suggestion.

Directed Assessment

1 Dictate the list words by using the Pretest sentences or developing original ones. Reserve *postoperative, prolonged, undernourished, strategizing, stamina,* and *opposed* for the dictation sentences.

2 Read each sentence. Repeat as needed.

- Lonnie received excellent postoperative care at the hospital.
- Having surgery prolonged his inability to enter a half marathon.
- His eating habits are healthy, so he will not be undernourished.
- Lonnie is strategizing new running techniques.
- He knows he will need to build up his stamina again.
- The doctor is opposed to Lonnie running until he has fully recovered.

3 If assigned, dictate Extra Challenge Words.

4 Score the test, counting each misspelled word as an error. Correct the dictation sentences by grading only the spelling words or grading the complete sentences.

Student Spelling Support

Cont. from page 104

nutrition, and abstaining from things that will hinder performance. As Christians, we need to be just as focused on the upward call of Christ Jesus. The race set before us is to live in such a way that honors God. The prize waiting for Christians is eternal life. It is human nature to want to fall into worldly habits, but with self-control, resolution, conscious effort, and the Holy Spirit, Christians can live a victorious life. Brainstorm ways in which one can use self-control and make a conscious effort to live a Christian life. (**Possible answers: maintaining good morals; having daily devotions; monitoring choices of music, movies, and television shows; and keeping one's word**)

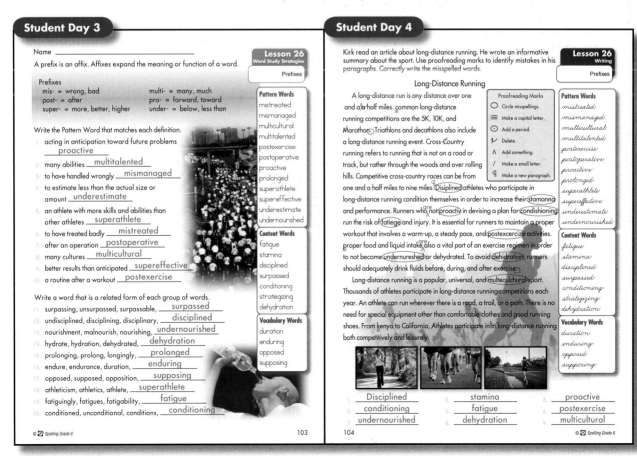

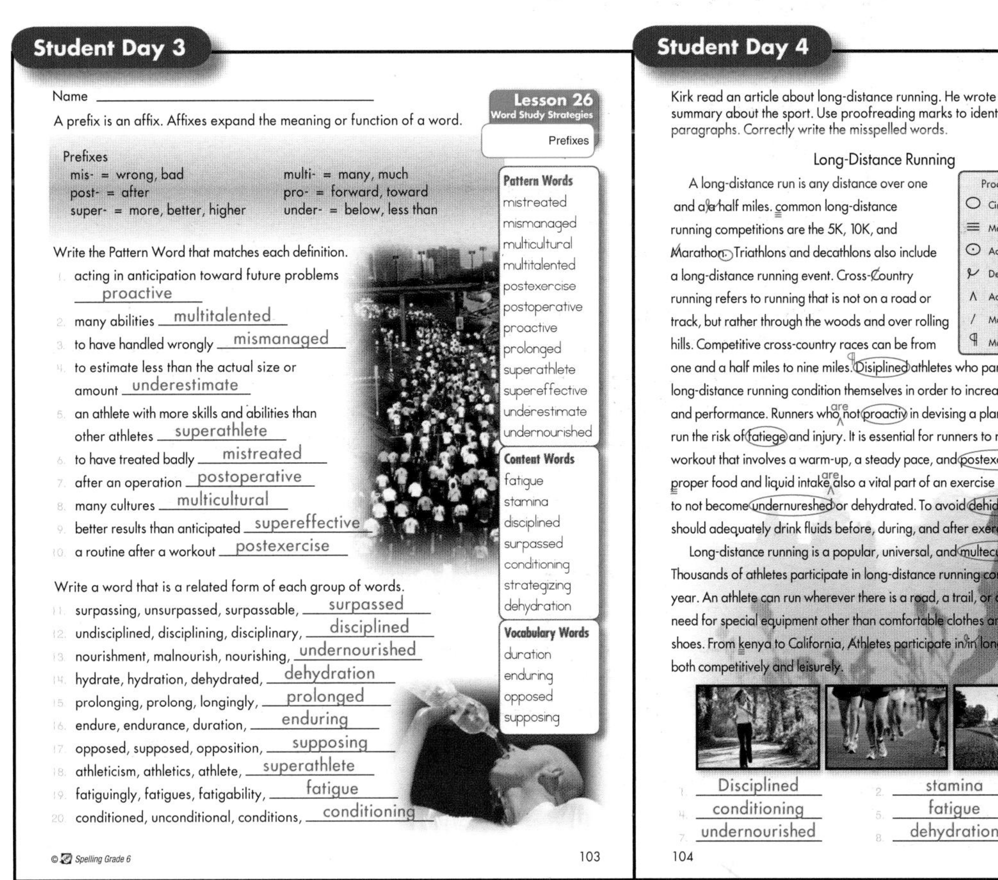

Student Day 3

Name ______

Lesson 26 — Word Study Strategies — Prefixes

A prefix is an affix. Affixes expand the meaning or function of a word.

Prefixes
mis- = wrong, bad; post- = after; super- = more, better, higher; multi- = many, much; pro- = forward, toward; under- = below, less than

Write the Pattern Word that matches each definition.

1. acting in anticipation toward future problems proactive
2. many abilities multitalented
3. to have handled wrongly mismanaged
4. to estimate less than the actual size or amount underestimate
5. an athlete with more skills and abilities than other athletes superathlete
6. to have treated badly mistreated
7. after an operation postoperative
8. many cultures multicultural
9. better results than anticipated supereffective
10. a routine after a workout postexercise

Write a word that is a related form of each group of words.

11. surpassing, unsurpassed, surpassable, surpassed
12. undisciplined, disciplining, disciplinary, disciplined
13. nourishment, malnourish, nourishing, undernourished
14. hydrate, hydration, dehydrated, dehydration
15. prolonging, prolong, longingly, prolonged
16. endure, endurance, duration, enduring
17. opposed, supposed, opposition, supposing
18. athleticism, athletics, athlete, superathlete
19. fatiguingly, fatigues, fatigability, fatigue
20. conditioned, unconditional, conditions, conditioning

Pattern Words: mistreated, mismanaged, multicultural, multitalented, postexercise, postoperative, proactive, prolonged, superathlete, supereffective, underestimate, undernourished

Content Words: fatigue, stamina, disciplined, surpassed, conditioning, strategizing, dehydration

Vocabulary Words: duration, enduring, opposed, supposing

© Spelling Grade 6 — 103

Student Day 4

Lesson 26 — Writing — Prefixes

Kirk read an article about long-distance running. He wrote an informative summary about the sport. Use proofreading marks to identify mistakes in his paragraphs. Correctly write the misspelled words.

Long-Distance Running

A long-distance run is any distance over one and a a half miles. common long-distance running competitions are the 5K, 10K, and Marathon Triathlons and decathlons also include a long-distance running event. Cross-Country running refers to running that is not on a road or track, but rather through the woods and over rolling hills. Competitive cross-country races can be from one and a half miles to nine miles. Disiplined athletes who participate in long-distance running condition themselves in order to increase their stamanna and performance. Runners who are not proactiv in devising a plan for condishioning run the risk of fatiege and injury. It is essential for runners to maintain a proper workout that involves a warm-up, a steady pace, and postexcercize activities. proper food and liquid intake are also a vital part of an exercise regimen in order to not become undernureshed or dehydrated. To avoid dehidration, runners should adequately drink fluids before, during, and after exercise

Long-distance running is a popular, universal, and multeculchural sport. Thousands of athletes participate in long-distance running competitions each year. An athlete can run wherever there is a road, a trail, or a path. There is no need for special equipment other than comfortable clothes and good running shoes. From kenya to California, Athletes participate in in long-distance running both competitively and leisurely.

Proofreading Marks: Circle misspellings. Make a capital letter. Add a period. Delete. Add something. Make a small letter. Make a new paragraph.

1. Disciplined 2. stamina 3. proactive 4. conditioning 5. fatigue 6. postexercise 7. undernourished 8. dehydration 9. multicultural

104 — © Spelling Grade 6

Lesson

27 Suffixes

Student Pages

Pages 105–108

Lesson Materials

BLM SP6-01B
Card stock
Index cards
T-17
BLM SP6-27A
BLM SP6-27B

Sports

The theme of this lesson is the pole vault and high jump. Pole vaulting involves an attempt to clear a crossbar that is elevated very high into the air. A pole vaulter uses a flexible pole to propel his or her body into the air and over the crossbar. High jumping is similar to pole vaulting except that the athlete uses a strong running approach and the strength of his or her legs to leap over an elevated crossbar. Both sports require a cushioned area for the athlete to land on.

Day 1 Pretest

Objective

The students will accurately spell and write words with **suffixes**. They will spell and write content, vocabulary, and challenge words.

Introduction

Before class, select Challenge Words for numbers 24 and 25 from a cross-curricular subject, words misspelled on previous assignments, or words that interest your students. The word *occasionally* has the final **suffix -ly** and is suggested for number 24. Administer the Pretest.

Directed Instruction

1 Say each word, use it in a sentence, and then repeat the word.

Pattern Words

1. Wendy's technical achievement in the high jump was admirable.
2. Rita noticed the arrangement of the landing mats in the pole-vault pit.
3. What is your availability for track-and-field practice this week?
4. The team doctor recommended a dosage of aspirin for pain relief.
5. Corrina immediately began to prepare for the pole-vault event.
6. J.J. thought it was an impossibility to jump over the high crossbar.
7. What percentage of high-jump athletes uses the Fosbury Flop method?
8. Christian athletes have the responsibility to share Christ's love.
9. Lois received a full athletic scholarship to her college of choice.
10. Brody displayed great sportsmanship during the pole-vault competition.
11. The history of track-and-field events statistically shows Greek origins.
12. Cyril was asked to take the vaulting poles out of storage.

Content Words

13. Foam mats cushioned Malik's fall after his pole-vault attempt.
14. The high-jump crossbar was elevated to a record height.
15. Pole vaulters use poles that are made of fiberglass.
16. The flexion of the pole used for pole vaulting is very important.
17. Lee's body dislodged the transverse crossbar during his high jump.
18. Janelle successfully vaulted over the high crossbar.
19. Vertical posts hold a crossbar during pole-vault or high-jump events.

Vocabulary Words

20. Heavy athletic wear is impractical during track-and-field competition.
21. Rose was very inquisitive about the history of the pole vault.
22. Rex does train and practice his vaulting techniques six days a week.
23. Principal Brady put in a requisition for new track-and-field equipment.

Challenge Words

24. ____________________
25. ____________________

2 Allow students to self-correct their Pretest. Write each word on the board. Point out the following **suffixes** in the Pattern Words: -age, -ility, -ly, -ment, -ship. The following generalization applies to this lesson: Drop silent *e* when adding a suffix that begins with a vowel. Note the roots *pract* and *quisit* in the Vocabulary Words.

3 As a class, read, spell, and read each word. Direct students to highlight misspelled words and rewrite them correctly.

4 Proof each student's Pretest. This becomes an individualized study sheet that can be used at school or at home.

5 Homework suggestion: Duplicate **BLM SP6-01B Flash Cards**

Template on CARD STOCK for students to write the list words, using the flash cards as a study aid. Another option is to use INDEX CARDS.

We need protein to help our bodies grow.

Because of his paralysis, he was unable to participate in the games.

Day … abulary

Objec…

The stu… …ntences with content … …ords, match given de…

Introd…

Instruct… …on hand for this acti… …following **suffixes:** … …ir flash card pile and … …uct students to spread out the twelve Pattern Word flash cards on their desk. As a class, sort the flash cards into the following categories: words that keep silent *e* before adding the suffix (**immediately, achievement, arrangement**), words that do not change before adding the suffix (**percentage, statistically, scholarship, sportsmanship**), words that drop *-le* before adding a suffix (**availability, impossibility, responsibility**), words that drop silent *e* before adding the suffix (**dosage, storage**).

Directed Instruction

1 Students refer to the list words on page 105 for this activity. Challenge students to quickly locate the definition of each Content Word in their Spelling Dictionary. Students read the definitions aloud.

2 Proceed to page 105. Say, spell, and say each Pattern, Content, and Vocabulary Word. Provide this week's Challenge Words and have students write them in the spaces provided before completing the page.

3 Proceed to page 106. Encourage students to use the table as an aid in building each Vocabulary Word. For example, the prefix *im-* goes with the root *pract* and the suffix *-ical* to build the word *impractical*. Allow students to complete the page independently.

Differentiated Instruction

- For students who spelled all the words correctly on the Pretest, select and assign Extra Challenge Words from the following list: parametric, protein, correlative, specialization, paralysis, orchestrated.
- For students who spelled less than half correctly, assign the following Pattern, Content, and Vocabulary Words: storage, percentage, availability, responsibility, scholarship, achievement, vaulted, vertical, elevated, cushioned, practice, inquisitive. On the Posttest, evaluate these students on the twelve words assigned; however, encourage them to attempt to spell all the list words to the best of their ability. They are also responsible for writing the dictated sentences.

64 pts.

Student Day 2

Name ______________________

Lesson 27
Word Analysis
Suffixes

Pattern Words
dosage
storage
percentage
availability
impossibility
responsibility
statistically
immediately
scholarship
sportsmanship
achievement
arrangement

Content Words
flexion
vaulted
vertical
elevated
cushioned
fiberglass
transverse

Vocabulary Words
impractical
practice
inquisitive
requisition

A suffix is a word part that is added to the ending of a root or a root with a prefix.

Write Pattern Words to complete the exercises. Sort the words according to their spelling when adding the suffix. The suffixes are *-age, -ility, -ly, -ment,* and *-ship.*

1.–3. Words that keep **silent e**
4.–7. Words that do not change
8.–10. Words that drop **-le**
11.–12. Words that drop **silent e**

1. immediately
2. achievement
3. arrangement
4. percentage
5. statistically
6. scholarship
7. sportsmanship
8. availability
9. impossibility
10. responsibility
11. dosage
12. storage

Write Content Words to complete the exercises.

13. The flexion of one's body during the track-and-field events of pole vault and high jump is crucial to success.
14. The pole vaulter elevated herself over the crossbar by using a pole made of fiberglass.
15. A soft pit cushioned the athlete's landing during the high-jump event.
16. Dom vaulted over the transverse crossbar that was set upon two vertical posts.

high jump

pole vault

Challenge Words
____
____

© Spelling Grade 6 105

Student Day 2

Lesson 27
Vocabulary
Suffixes

Prefix		Root		Suffix	
im-	not	**pract**	to do	**-ical**	related to
in-	into	**quisit**	seek	**-ice**	state of
re-	back			**-ive**	inclined to
				-ion	state of

Write the Vocabulary Words. Order may vary.

1. impractical
2. practice
3. inquisitive
4. requisition

Refer to the table to complete the exercises. Write the word that is being defined.

5. related to doing something that is not useful impractical
6. inclined to seek out knowledge; curious inquisitive
7. a state of seeking or requesting something that is required requisition
8. the state of doing something repeatedly so as to become proficient or to improve practice

Write Vocabulary Words to complete the sentences.

9. Tyler will practice his vaulting technique numerous times before perfecting his style.
10. During a meeting with an Olympic pole vaulter, Maya was very inquisitive and asked an abundance of questions.
11. Coach Williams put in a requisition for new pit cushions and vaulting poles.
12. Since high-jump shoes include spikes for increased traction, regular track shoes can be impractical for high jumpers to use.
13. A high-jump technique, called the straddle, seemed to be impractical, so athletes tried to alter their jumping techniques.
14. Dick Fosbury began to practice a new technique of leaping sideways across the transverse crossbar, and he successfully revolutionized the high-jump event with his new technique called the Fosbury Flop.

Pattern Words
dosage
storage
percentage
availability
impossibility
responsibility
statistically
immediately
scholarship
sportsmanship
achievement
arrangement

Content Words
flexion
vaulted
vertical
elevated
cushioned
fiberglass
transverse

Vocabulary Words
impractical
practice
inquisitive
requisition

106 © Spelling Grade 6

Student Spelling Support Materials

BLM SP6-01A
BLM SP6-08B

Student Spelling Support

1. Use **BLM SP6-01A A Spelling Study Strategy** in instructional groups to provide assistance with some or all of the words.
2. Invite students to write the Challenge Words, numbers 24 and 25, in the Word Bank, in the back of their textbook.
3. Challenge students to research and write about the history of pole vaulting and high jumping. Interesting facts such as the progression of various jumping techniques, sport mechanics, and equipment guidelines should be covered. Provide a copy of **BLM SP6-08B Venn Diagram** for students to compare and contrast the mechanics of the two sports. Students may compile information in the progressive, sport journal that was started in Lesson 1.
4. Write this week's words, categorize the Pattern, Content, and Vocabulary Words, and attach them to the Word Wall.

4 Homework suggestion: Students use their Spelling Dictionary to write the definition of each word on the back of the corresponding flash card that was suggested for homework on Day 1.

Day 3 Word Study Strategies

Objective

The students will write words with **suffixes** to match definitions. They will add or subtract letters to write list words. Students will write list words to match their pronunciations.

Introduction

Write the following **suffixes** on the board: -age, -ility, -ly, -ment, -ship. Instruct students to have their flash card pile from this lesson on hand for this activity. Students sort the Pattern Word flash cards according to **suffixes**. (**-age: dosage, storage, percentage; -ility: availability, impossibility, responsibility; -ly: statistically, immediately; -ment: achievement, arrangement; -ship: scholarship, sportsmanship**)

Directed Instruction

1 Write the following meanings for **suffixes** on the board:

- -age = place of, state of
- -ly = characteristic of, forms an adverb from an adjective
- -ility = forms a noun
- -ment = state of, process of
- -ship = state of, quality of

Challenge students to work in groups, for a brief amount of time, to study and quiz one another on the meanings of each word from the Pattern Word flash cards.

2 Write the following on the board:

- impossible – le + ility = _______ (**impossibility**)
- store – e + age = _______ (**storage**)

Invite volunteers to add or subtract letters to write list words.

3 Write the following pronunciations on the board:

- /'prak təs/ (**practice**)
- /'fī bûr glas/ (**fiberglass**)

Challenge students to sound out the pronunciations and identify the words.

4 Proceed to page 107. Students independently complete the page.

Day 4 Writing

Objective

The students will write list words to complete sentences in a graphic organizer for a process essay. They will use a graphic organizer to write an informative process essay.

Introduction

Display **T-17 Flow Chart Graphic Organizer**. Cover the answers at the bottom. Remind students that a graphic organizer is a drawing that shows how words or ideas fit together. A *flow chart* shows the flow or process of a particular activity. This week's lesson incorporates using a flow chart to write a process essay. A *process essay* provides information and gives direction to the reader. Explain that examples of transition words that can be used in a process essay are *first, next, then, while, after, finally,* and *last*. Select a volunteer to read the text aloud. Challenge students to raise their hand when they have located the correct list word to complete the sentences. Correctly write list words while referring to the answers at the bottom. Ask volunteers to identify the transition words in the flow chart. Chorally read the completed text.

Directed Instruction

1 Ask students to identify what made the information in the flow chart helpful. (**The information included each step of the high-jump process, the steps were described in order, and each step was accurate.**) Explain that a process essay should contain information that is pertinent in order to perform or understand a complete process.

2 Proceed to page 108 and read the text aloud. Ask students to identify the transition words in the informative flow chart. (**First, Next, Then, While, Finally**) Allow students to work in groups to complete the page.

3 Distribute a copy of **BLM SP6-27A Flow Chart** to each student. Students use this graphic organizer to jot down process essay ideas, in sequence, while using transition words. These notes will assist them in writing an informative process essay for exercise number 7 on page 108.

4 Homework suggestion: Distribute a copy of **BLM SP6-27B Lesson 27 Homework** to each student.

Day 5 Posttest

Objective

The students will correctly write dictated spelling words and sentences.

Introduction

Review by using flash cards noted in Day 1 and Day 2 Homework suggestion.

Directed Assessment

1 Dictate the list words by using the Pretest sentences or developing original ones. Reserve *vaulted, elevated, scholarship, responsibility, percentage,* and *inquisitive* for the dictation sentences.

2 Read each sentence. Repeat as needed.

- Toby easily vaulted over the high bar during the meet.
- He was told that the bar was elevated to a new record height.
- Toby wanted to apply for an athletic scholarship to college.
- He took the responsibility to research all of his options.
- Toby read that a high percentage of athletes apply for aid.
- He was very inquisitive and asked his coach for advice.

3 If assigned, dictate Extra Challenge Words.

4 Score the test, counting each misspelled word as an error. Correct the dictation sentences by grading only the spelling words or grading the complete sentences.

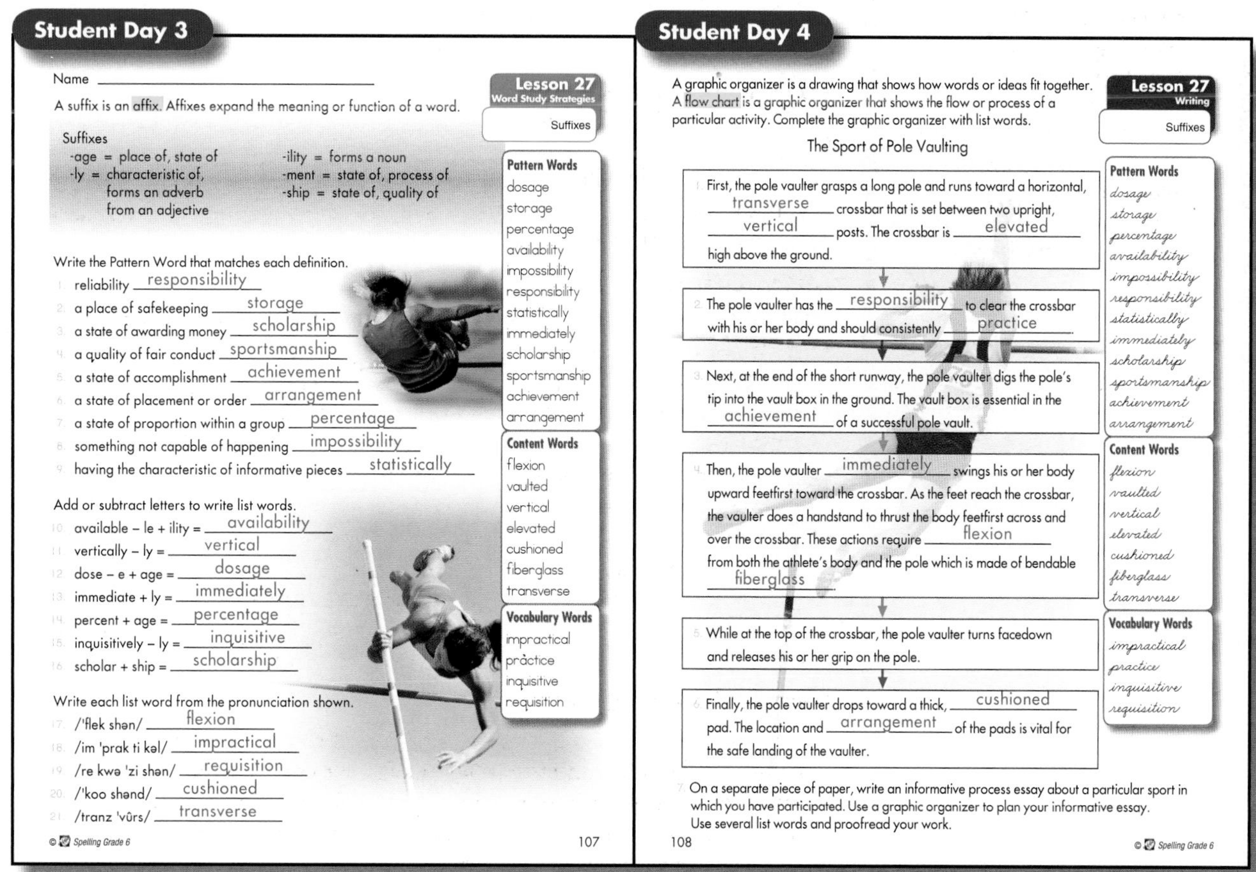

Student Day 3

Lesson 27 — Word Study Strategies — Suffixes

Name ______

A suffix is an affix. Affixes expand the meaning or function of a word.

Suffixes
- -age = place of, state of
- -ly = characteristic of, forms an adverb from an adjective
- -ility = forms a noun
- -ment = state of, process of
- -ship = state of, quality of

Write the Pattern Word that matches each definition.
1. reliability responsibility
2. a place of safekeeping storage
3. a state of awarding money scholarship
4. a quality of fair conduct sportsmanship
5. a state of accomplishment achievement
6. a state of placement or order arrangement
7. a state of proportion within a group percentage
8. something not capable of happening impossibility
9. having the characteristic of informative pieces statistically

Add or subtract letters to write list words.
10. available – le + ility = availability
11. vertically – ly = vertical
12. dose – e + age = dosage
13. immediate + ly = immediately
14. percent + age = percentage
15. inquisitively – ly = inquisitive
16. scholar + ship = scholarship

Write each list word from the pronunciation shown.
17. /'flek shən/ flexion
18. /im 'prak ti kəl/ impractical
19. /re kwə 'zi shən/ requisition
20. /'koo shənd/ cushioned
21. /tranz 'vûrs/ transverse

Pattern Words: dosage, storage, percentage, availability, impossibility, responsibility, statistically, immediately, scholarship, sportsmanship, achievement, arrangement

Content Words: flexion, vaulted, vertical, elevated, cushioned, fiberglass, transverse

Vocabulary Words: impractical, practice, inquisitive, requisition

© Spelling Grade 6 — 107

Student Day 4

Lesson 27 — Writing — Suffixes

A graphic organizer is a drawing that shows how words or ideas fit together. A flow chart is a graphic organizer that shows the flow or process of a particular activity. Complete the graphic organizer with list words.

The Sport of Pole Vaulting

1. First, the pole vaulter grasps a long pole and runs toward a horizontal, transverse crossbar that is set between two upright, vertical posts. The crossbar is elevated high above the ground.
2. The pole vaulter has the responsibility to clear the crossbar with his or her body and should consistently practice.
3. Next, at the end of the short runway, the pole vaulter digs the pole's tip into the vault box in the ground. The vault box is essential in the achievement of a successful pole vault.
4. Then, the pole vaulter immediately swings his or her body upward feetfirst toward the crossbar. As the feet reach the crossbar, the vaulter does a handstand to thrust the body feetfirst across and over the crossbar. These actions require flexion from both the athlete's body and the pole which is made of bendable fiberglass.
5. While at the top of the crossbar, the pole vaulter turns facedown and releases his or her grip on the pole.
6. Finally, the pole vaulter drops toward a thick, cushioned pad. The location and arrangement of the pads is vital for the safe landing of the vaulter.
7. On a separate piece of paper, write an informative process essay about a particular sport in which you have participated. Use a graphic organizer to plan your informative essay. Use several list words and proofread your work.

Pattern Words: dosage, storage, percentage, availability, impossibility, responsibility, statistically, immediately, scholarship, sportsmanship, achievement, arrangement

Content Words: flexion, vaulted, vertical, elevated, cushioned, fiberglass, transverse

Vocabulary Words: impractical, practice, inquisitive, requisition

108 — © Spelling Grade 6

Lesson

28 Suffixes

Student Pages

Pages 109–112

Lesson Materials

BLM SP6-01B
Card stock
Index cards
T-18
BLM SP6-28A
BLM SP6-28B

Sports

The theme of this lesson is the shot put, javelin, and discus throw. These three events, along with the hammer throw, make up the throwing events in many track-and-field competitions, including Olympic competition. The objects used in these competitions are called *weights*. The distance that a weight travels determines the winner of the event. The javelin and discus throws are also included in the decathlon and heptathlon competitions.

Day 1 Pretest

Objective

The students will accurately spell and write words with **suffixes**. They will spell and write content, vocabulary, and challenge words.

Introduction

Before class, select Challenge Words for numbers 24 and 25 from a cross-curricular subject, words misspelled on previous assignments, or words that interest your students. The word *elitism* has the **suffix -ism** and is suggested for number 24. Administer the Pretest.

Directed Instruction

1 Say each word, use it in a sentence, and then repeat the word.

Pattern Words

1. The bronze medal was acceptable to the track coach.
2. Olympic athletes participate in continuous training sessions.
3. Despite injuries, the courageous athlete kept going.
4. Athletes often follow their coaches' dietary advice.
5. Even veteran competitors feel nervous before a track meet.
6. I practiced with an imaginary discus before trying actual throws.
7. Heaven's glory is incomparable to anything on the earth.
8. Our resurrected bodies will be incorruptible.
9. God's forgiveness and grace are inexhaustible.
10. Russ did not consider his disability to be insurmountable.
11. Hope wanted to try journalism, so she wrote for the school paper.
12. I admire the heroism of athletes who have spoken out for Christ.

Content Words

13. Centrifugal force is required to throw a discus.
14. The entire midfield expanse was dedicated to throwing events.
15. The gold medalist won by hurling the javelin over twenty meters.
16. The men's discus weighs two kilograms.
17. The winner had the longest discus throw in linear meters.
18. The measurement of Andrea's throw in the shot put was ten meters.
19. Will the new stadium be completed before the track meet?

Vocabulary Words

20. After the throwing events, Loni had an impulse to try the discus.
21. Javelin throwers use momentum as the propulsion for the javelin.
22. The weight of a javelin is in subjection to federation rules.
23. The discus is a disk-shaped projectile.

Challenge Words

24. ______________________________
25. ______________________________

2 Allow students to self-correct their Pretest. Write each word on the board. Point out the following **suffixes** in the Pattern Words: -able, -ary, -ible, -ism, -ous. Note the roots *ject* and *puls* in the Vocabulary Words. In *impulse,* silent *e* is not in the original root *puls*.

3 As a class, read, spell, and read each word. Direct students to highlight misspelled words and rewrite them correctly.

4 Proof each student's Pretest. This becomes an individualized study sheet that can be used at school or at home.

5 Homework suggestion: Duplicate **BLM SP6-01B Flash Cards**

Template on CARD STOCK for students to write the list words, using the flash cards as a study aid. Another option is to use INDEX CARDS.

Day 2 W… …lary

Objective

The students wi… sentences with … vocabulary wor… …nplete sentences, and c…

Introduction

Write the words … the board. Expl… word prior to ad… …ing generalization fo… silent *e* when ad… …ix that begins with a vowel. Ask students to identify the word that follows the generalization and the word that does not follow the generalization. (***Continuous* drops silent *e* before the suffix *-ous*, but *courageous* retains silent *e* before *-ous*.**) Explain that words ending in *ce* or *ge* retain silent *e* unless the suffix begins with *e*, *i*, or *y*. Invite students to refer to the list words on page 109 as you dictate each Pattern Word while emphasizing the following **suffixes**: -able, -ary, -ible, -ism, -ous. Invite students to state and spell each Pattern Word as it would be spelled if it did not have an affix. (**diet, imagine, nerve, continue, courage, hero, journal, accept, compare, surmount, corrupt, exhaust**) Encourage students to state whether the silent *e* was dropped or retained for words originally ending in silent *e*. (**Silent *e* is dropped in *imaginary*, *nervous*, *continuous*, and *incomparable*. It is retained in *courageous* to maintain the soft *g* sound.**)

Because the glue was old it was not very cohesive.

A metropolitan area often has a lot of polution.

Directed Instruction

1 Challenge students to refer to page 109 and to quickly locate the definition of each Content Word in the Spelling Dictionary.

Differentiated Instruction

- For students who spelled all the words correctly on the Pretest, select and assign Extra Challenge Words from the following list: polynomial, quantum, cohesive, metropolitan, specificity, symphonically.
- For students who spelled less than half correctly, assign the following Pattern, Content, and Vocabulary Words: imaginary, nervous, continuous, journalism, insurmountable, inexhaustible, linear, stadium, kilograms, measurement, projectile, impulse. On the Posttest, evaluate these students on the twelve words assigned; however, encourage them to attempt to spell all the list words to the best of their ability. They are also responsible for writing the dictated sentences.

53 pts.

Student Day 2

Name ____________________

Lesson 28 Word Analysis — Suffixes

Pattern Words: dietary, imaginary, nervous, continuous, courageous, heroism, journalism, acceptable, incomparable, insurmountable, incorruptible, inexhaustible

Content Words: linear, hurling, stadium, expanse, kilograms, centrifugal, measurement

Vocabulary Words: projectile, subjection, impulse, propulsion

A suffix is a word part that is added to the ending of a root or a root with a prefix.

Write Pattern Words to complete the exercises. Sort the words according to their spelling when adding the suffix. The suffixes are *-able*, *-ary*, *-ible*, *-ism*, and *-ous*.

1.–8. Words that do not change	9.–12. Words that drop **silent e**
1. dietary	2. courageous
3. heroism	4. journalism
5. acceptable	6. insurmountable
7. incorruptible	8. inexhaustible
9. imaginary	10. nervous
11. continuous	12. incomparable

Write Content Words to complete the exercises.

13. The shot put, javelin, and discus are throwing events in track-and-field competitions that consist of h<u>urling</u> objects over an e<u>xpanse</u>.
14. In throwing events, the winner is determined by a l<u>inear</u> m<u>easurement</u> of the length of the longest throw.
15. The shot used in the shot put is a heavy metal ball. The women's shot is 4 kilograms and the men's shot weighs 7.26 k<u>ilograms</u>.
16. To throw the discus or to put the shot, the athlete generates c<u>entrifugal</u> force by spinning his or her body before throwing.
17. Throwing events are held in the midfield area of the s<u>tadium</u>.

shot put

discus

javelin

Challenge Words

____

____

© Spelling Grade 6 109

Student Day 2

Prefix		Root		Suffix	
pro-	forward	**ject**	throw	**-ile**	related to
sub-	under	**puls**	drive	**-ion**	state of
im-	in				

Lesson 28 Vocabulary — Suffixes

Pattern Words: dietary, imaginary, nervous, continuous, courageous, heroism, journalism, acceptable, incomparable, insurmountable, incorruptible, inexhaustible

Content Words: linear, hurling, stadium, expanse, kilograms, centrifugal, measurement

Vocabulary Words: projectile, subjection, impulse, propulsion

Write the Vocabulary Words. Order may vary.

1. projectile 2. subjection
3. impulse 4. propulsion

Refer to the table to complete the exercises. Match each word to its definition.

a 5. subjection — a. the state of bringing under control
c 6. projectile — b. the state of driving something forward by force
d 7. impulse — c. an object that is thrown forward
b 8. propulsion — d. a sudden drive to act

Write Vocabulary Words to complete the sentences.

9. Sonia researched the history of the javelin throw in the Olympics. She learned that a javelin is a projectile since it is thrown forward.
10. Participants in the javelin throw provide the driving force, or propulsion, by first running several meters to gain momentum and then throwing the javelin.
11. Sonia learned that the weight and length of a javelin are in subjection to federation rules.
12. While researching the javelin throw, Sonia had a sudden impulse to try throwing a javelin.

Choose the best meaning for each underlined word.

13. Sonia found throwing the javelin to be an <u>insurmountable</u> task.
   - ○ not able to be understood
   - ● not able to be overcome
14. She decided to pursue a career in <u>journalism</u>.
   - ● the act of writing journals or periodicals
   - ○ the act of writing poems

110 © Spelling Grade 6

Student Spelling Support Materials

BLM SP6-01A
Index cards

Student Spelling Support

1. Use **BLM SP6-01A A Spelling Study Strategy** in instructional groups to provide assistance with some or all of the words.
2. Invite students to write the Challenge Words, numbers 24 and 25, in the Word Bank, in the back of their textbook.
3. Challenge students to research one of the following throwing events in the Olympic Games: shot put, discus, hammer, javelin. Provide INDEX CARDS for each student to write notes in preparation for an oral presentation. Choose volunteers to present their research to the class.
4. Write this week's words, categorize the Pattern, Content, and Vocabulary Words, and attach them to the Word Wall.
5. For a Bible connection, read Psalm 19:14: "Let the words of my mouth and the meditation of my heart be **acceptable** in Your sight, O LORD, my strength and my Redeemer." Explain that the *meditation of my heart* is describing one's attitude or thought life and that the psalmist is praying that both his words and his thought life would be **acceptable** to the Lord. Encourage students to provide examples of how one's attitude or thought life affects one's words.

2 Proceed to page 109. Say, spell, and say each Pattern, Content, and Vocabulary Word. Provide this week's Challenge Words and have students write them in the spaces provided before completing the page.

3 Proceed to page 110. Encourage students to use the table as an aid in building each Vocabulary Word. For example, the prefix *pro-* goes with the root *ject* and the suffix *-ile* to build the word *projectile.* Allow students to complete the page independently. When complete, choose volunteers to state other words with the roots *ject* and *puls.* (**Possible answers: reject, object, compulsion, impulsive**)

4 Homework suggestion: Students use their Spelling Dictionary to write the definition of each word on the back of the corresponding flash card that was suggested for homework on Day 1.

Day 3 Word Study Strategies

Objective

The students will write words with **suffixes** to match definitions. Students will use the meaning of related word forms to define list words.

Introduction

Write the following **suffixes** on the board as headings: -able, -ary, -ible, -ism, -ous. Invite students to refer to the Pattern Words on page 111. Choose five students, one for each column, to write the Pattern Words that contain each suffix. (**-able: acceptable, incomparable, insurmountable; -ary: dietary, imaginary; -ible: incorruptible, inexhaustible; -ism: heroism, journalism; -ous: nervous, continuous, courageous**)

Directed Instruction

1 Write the following meanings for suffixes on the board:
- -able = is able
- -ary = of, related to
- -ible = is able
- -ism = act of, state of
- -ous = quality of

Invite pairs of students to study the Pattern Word flash cards, locate the words that contain each suffix and quiz each other on the definitions.

2 Write the following sentences on the board, underlining words and leaving a blank space as shown:
- To <u>surmount</u> means to overcome.
- Something <u>surmountable</u> is able to be overcome.
- Something _______ is not able to be overcome. (**insurmountable**)

Explain that the underlined words are related forms of the Pattern Word needed to complete the final sentence. Choose a volunteer to write the word on the blank. Note that the meaning of each related form provides a clue to the meaning of the Pattern Word.

3 Proceed to page 111. Before students independently complete the page, select a volunteer to read Psalm 19:14. Share that God is not only interested in what we say, but also in the attitude behind our words.

Day 4 Writing

Objective

The students will write list words used in an informative oral report.

Introduction

Display **T-18 Shot Put and Javelin**. Explain that the information shown on the transparency is similar to what would appear in an encyclopedia entry or another reference source. When writing notes in preparation for an oral report, students summarize and paraphrase information found in reference materials, emphasizing the main ideas. To *summarize* is <u>to write a shortened version of the main idea and supporting details</u>. To *paraphrase* is <u>to retell information in one's own words</u>. Choose volunteers to paraphrase the information found in each paragraph and to write their ideas on the lines provided. Challenge students to underline the list words. (**expanse, centrifugal, propulsion; subjection, acceptable, linear, measurement**) Refer to **BLM SP6-28A T-18 Answer Key**.

Directed Instruction

1 Explain that one method for organizing and presenting an oral report is to research and paraphrase the material by writing notes on index cards. Paraphrasing is necessary to avoid plagiarism and to reduce the volume of information in order to keep the report as brief as possible.

2 Proceed to page 112 and read the text aloud. Allow students to complete the page.

3 Homework suggestion: Distribute a copy of **BLM SP6-28B Lesson 28 Homework** to each student.

Day 5 Posttest

Objective

The students will correctly write dictated spelling words and sentences.

Introduction

Review by using flash cards noted in Day 1 and Day 2 Homework suggestion.

Directed Assessment

1 Dictate the list words by using the Pretest sentences or developing original ones. Reserve *impulse, kilograms, imaginary, nervous, measurement,* and *continuous* for the dictation sentences.

2 Read each sentence. Repeat as needed.

- Lou had an impulse to try one of the throwing events.
- He chose a discus that weighed two kilograms.
- Lou tried a few imaginary throws before he threw the discus.
- Lou felt a bit nervous as he released the discus.
- He felt that the measurement would be quite short.
- Lou knew that a continuous series of exercises would help him.

3 If assigned, dictate Extra Challenge Words.

4 Score the test, counting each misspelled word as an error. Correct the dictation sentences by grading only the spelling words or grading the complete sentences.

Notes

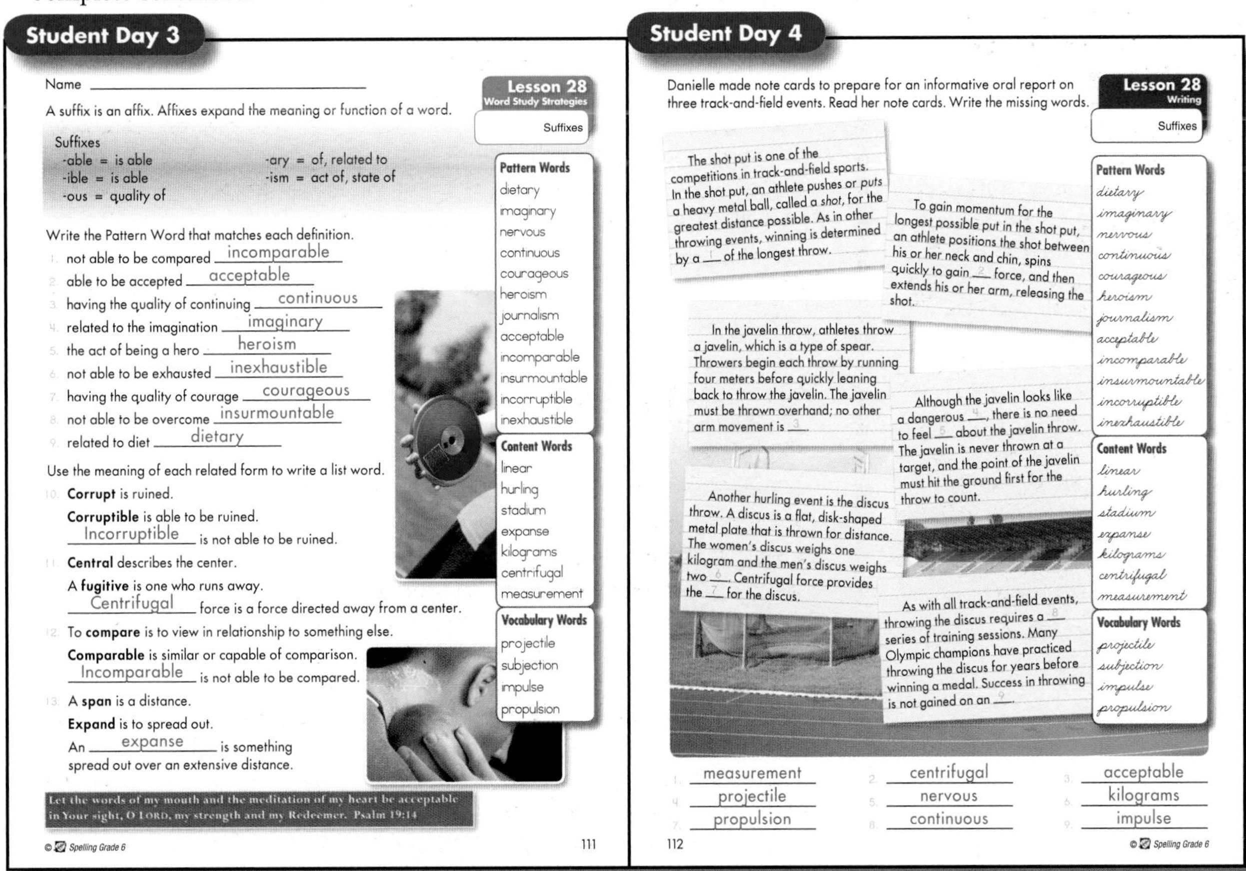

Student Day 3

Name ____________________

Lesson 28 Word Study Strategies — Suffixes

A suffix is an affix. Affixes expand the meaning or function of a word.

Suffixes
-able = is able
-ible = is able
-ous = quality of
-ary = of, related to
-ism = act of, state of

Write the Pattern Word that matches each definition.

1. not able to be compared incomparable
2. able to be accepted acceptable
3. having the quality of continuing continuous
4. related to the imagination imaginary
5. the act of being a hero heroism
6. not able to be exhausted inexhaustible
7. having the quality of courage courageous
8. not able to be overcome insurmountable
9. related to diet dietary

Use the meaning of each related form to write a list word.

10. **Corrupt** is ruined. **Corruptible** is able to be ruined. Incorruptible is not able to be ruined.
11. **Central** describes the center. A **fugitive** is one who runs away. Centrifugal force is a force directed away from a center.
12. To **compare** is to view in relationship to something else. **Comparable** is similar or capable of comparison. Incomparable is not able to be compared.
13. A **span** is a distance. **Expand** is to spread out. An expanse is something spread out over an extensive distance.

Pattern Words: dietary, imaginary, nervous, continuous, courageous, heroism, journalism, acceptable, incomparable, insurmountable, incorruptible, inexhaustible

Content Words: linear, hurling, stadium, expanse, kilograms, centrifugal, measurement

Vocabulary Words: projectile, subjection, impulse, propulsion

Let the words of my mouth and the meditation of my heart be acceptable in Your sight, O LORD, my strength and my Redeemer. Psalm 19:14

© Spelling Grade 6 111

Student Day 4

Lesson 28 Writing — Suffixes

Danielle made note cards to prepare for an informative oral report on three track-and-field events. Read her note cards. Write the missing words.

The shot put is one of the competitions in track-and-field sports. In the shot put, an athlete pushes or *puts* a heavy metal ball, called a *shot*, for the greatest distance possible. As in other throwing events, winning is determined by a __1__ of the longest throw.

To gain momentum for the longest possible put in the shot put, an athlete positions the shot between his or her neck and chin, spins quickly to gain __2__ force, and then extends his or her arm, releasing the shot.

In the javelin throw, athletes throw a javelin, which is a type of spear. Throwers begin each throw by running four meters before quickly leaning back to throw the javelin. The javelin must be thrown overhand; no other arm movement is __3__.

Although the javelin looks like a dangerous __4__, there is no need to feel __5__ about the javelin throw. The javelin is never thrown at a target, and the point of the javelin must hit the ground first for the throw to count.

Another hurling event is the discus throw. A discus is a flat, disk-shaped metal plate that is thrown for distance. The women's discus weighs one kilogram and the men's discus weighs two __6__. Centrifugal force provides the __7__ for the discus.

As with all track-and-field events, throwing the discus requires a __8__ series of training sessions. Many Olympic champions have practiced throwing the discus for years before winning a medal. Success in throwing is not gained on an __9__.

Pattern Words: dietary, imaginary, nervous, continuous, courageous, heroism, journalism, acceptable, incomparable, insurmountable, incorruptible, inexhaustible

Content Words: linear, hurling, stadium, expanse, kilograms, centrifugal, measurement

Vocabulary Words: projectile, subjection, impulse, propulsion

1. measurement 2. centrifugal 3. acceptable
4. projectile 5. nervous 6. kilograms
7. propulsion 8. continuous 9. impulse

112 © Spelling Grade 6

Lesson 29 R-Controlled Vowels

Student Pages

Pages 113–116

Lesson Materials

BLM SP6-01B
Card stock
Index cards
BLM SP6-29A

Sports

The theme of this lesson is the long jump. Long jumping is a track-and-field event that measures who can jump the farthest horizontal distance. The athlete runs down a runway toward a takeoff board. Once takeoff has occurred, the athlete sails through the air and lands, feetfirst, in a sandpit. The indentation of the feet in the sand is measured for jump distance. The sport of the long jump requires quickness in running. For this reason, many athletes who are sprinters also compete as long jumpers.

Day 1 Pretest

Objective

The students will accurately spell and write words with **r-controlled vowels.** They will spell and write content, vocabulary, and challenge words.

Introduction

Before class, select Challenge Words for numbers 24 and 25 from a cross-curricular subject, words misspelled on previous assignments, or words that interest your students. The word *discouraged* has the **r-controlled vowel** sound /ûr/, spelled *our,* and is suggested for number 24. Administer the Pretest.

Directed Instruction

1 Say each word, use it in a sentence, and then repeat the word.

Pattern Words

1. Coach Preston was the school administrator for sporting events.
2. Many track-and-field athletes are lean and have angular features.
3. The bus departed from the stadium after the competition.
4. Coach Judy told the team to not be disheartened after losing the meet.
5. Brady's parents were worried about his domineering attitude.
6. The sudden downpour drenched the field and caused a long delay.
7. Laney watched her brother's long-jump attempts for entertainment.
8. Aaron showed formidable skills with his new long-jump record.
9. The healthy meal of protein nourished the athlete's body.
10. Jesus should be highly revered for His great love toward us.
11. Charley bought a souvenir after the track-and-field finals.
12. Violet was told that her entry fee payment was unnecessary.

Content Words

13. Brock was among the fifty long-jump contestants at the meet.
14. Helen's elimination from the meet was due to illness.
15. Was Eliza focused during the long-jump training sessions?
16. The long jump measures one's ability to jump a horizontal distance.
17. The long-jump official measured the indentation in the sand.
18. The precise long-jump distance was twenty feet, seven inches.
19. Tremendous applause erupted after the record-breaking jump.

Vocabulary Words

20. In retrospect, the long-jump event ran smoothly and was a success.
21. Janeen shared her introspective viewpoint about the meet results.
22. Chelsea was concerned about the weather during the long-jump event.
23. Darby used discernment as she gauged her long-jump approach.

Challenge Words

24. ______________________________
25. ______________________________

2 Allow students to self-correct their Pretest. Write each word on the board. Point out that *r-controlled vowels* are vowels or combinations of vowels that precede *r.* The letter *r* affects the sound of the vowel or vowels. The following vowel sounds are heard in the Pattern Words in this lesson: the /âr/ sound in *unnecessary,* the /är/ sound in *departed,* the /îr/ sound in *revered,* the /ôr/ sound in *downpour,* the /ûr/ sound in *angular.* Note the roots *cern* and *spect* in the Vocabulary Words.

3 As a class, read, spell, and read each word. Direct students to highlight misspelled words and rewrite them correctly.

4 Proof each student's Pretest. This becomes an individualized study sheet that can be used at school or at home.

5 Homework suggestion: Duplicate **BLM SP6-01B Flash Cards Template** on CARD STOCK for students to write the list words, using the flash cards as a study aid. Another option is to use INDEX CARDS.

Day 2 Word Analysis and Vocabulary

Objective

The students will sort words with **r-controlled vowels** and complete sentences with content words. They will use a table to write vocabulary words, match given definitions in context, and choose list words that match definitions.

Introduction

Instruct students to have their flash card pile from this lesson on hand for this activity. Students may also refer to the list words on page 113 for assistance. Dictate each Pattern Word while emphasizing the following r-controlled vowel sounds: /âr/, /är/, /îr/, /ôr/, /ûr/. Students look through their flash card pile and highlight or underline each spelling for each sound. (**/âr/—unnecessary; /är/—departed, disheartened; /îr/—revered, souvenir, domineering; /ôr/—downpour, formidable; /ûr/—angular, nourished, administrator, entertainment**)

Directed Instruction

1 Students refer to the list words on page 113 for this activity. Challenge students to quickly locate the definition of each Content Word in the Spelling Dictionary. Students read the definitions aloud.

2 Proceed to page 113. Say, spell, and say each Pattern, Content, and Vocabulary Word. Provide this week's Challenge Words and have students write them in the spaces provided before completing the page.

3 Proceed to page 114. Encourage students to use the table as an aid in building each Vocabulary Word. For example, the prefix *con-* goes with the root *cern* and the suffix *-ed* to build the word *concerned*.

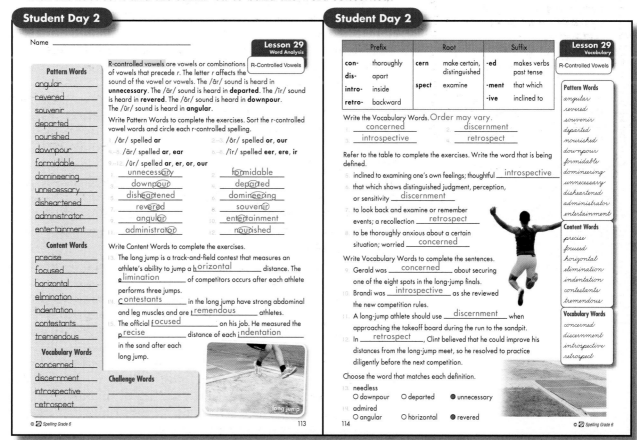

Differentiated Instruction

- For students who spelled all the words correctly on the Pretest, select and assign Extra Challenge Words from the following list: proportional, radioactive, denotative, disenfranchise, abrasion, tonality.
- For students who spelled less than half correctly, assign the following Pattern, Content, and Vocabulary Words: revered, departed, formidable, unnecessary, administrator, entertainment, precise, focused, contestants, tremendous, concerned, introspective. On the Posttest, evaluate these students on the twelve words assigned; however, encourage them to attempt to spell all the list words to the best of their ability. They are also responsible for writing the dictated sentences.

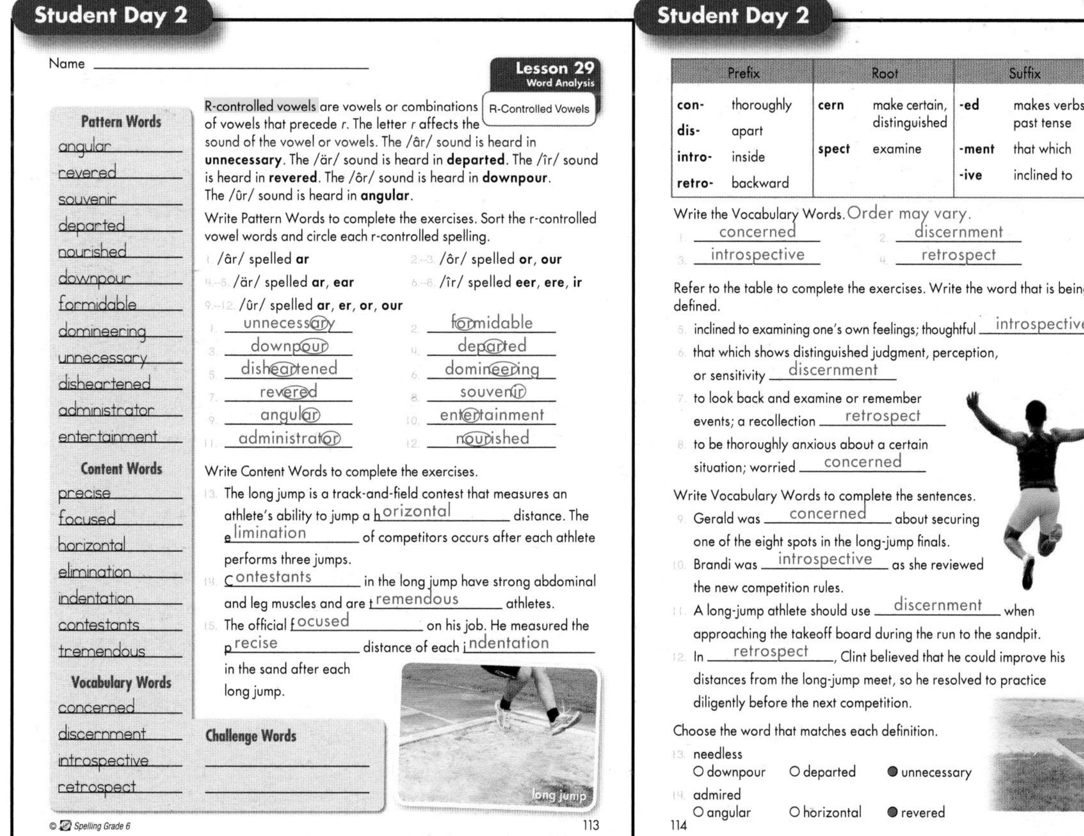

Student Spelling Support Materials

BLM SP6-01A

Student Spelling Support

1. Use **BLM SP6-01A A Spelling Study Strategy** in instructional groups to provide assistance with some or all of the words.
2. Invite students to write the Challenge Words, numbers 24 and 25, in the Word Bank, in the back of their textbook.
3. Challenge students to research a famous track-and-field athlete who excelled in the event of the long jump. Students may compile information in the progressive, sport journal that was started in Lesson 1.
4. Write this week's words, categorize the Pattern, Content, and Vocabulary Words, and attach them to the Word Wall.
5. Read Galatians 5:22–23: "But the fruit of the Spirit is love, joy, peace, longsuffering, kindness, goodness, faithfulness, gentleness, self-control." Invite students to share about a time that they displayed the behaviors of the Spirit during a difficult situation. Discuss the benefits and rewards of displaying these behaviors. Ask, "How can athletes display these behaviors during practice and competition?"

Allow students to complete the page independently. When complete, select a volunteer to read exercises 9–12 aloud.

4 Homework suggestion: Students use the Spelling Dictionary to write the definition of each word on the back of the corresponding flash card that was suggested for homework on Day 1.

Day 3 Word Study Strategies

Objective

The students will utilize dictionary skills by answering questions about the different components of a dictionary entry. They will write list words to complete sentences with inferences.

Introduction

Select a few Pattern, Content, and Vocabulary Words from this lesson. Dictate them and instruct students to turn to the Spelling Dictionary. Challenge students to locate the following components for each word: entry word, pronunciation, part of speech, definition, sample sentence. Ask students to verbalize different components of each word.

Directed Instruction

1 Write the following list words on the board: angular, downpour, indentation. Remind students that an inference is a conclusion reached by looking at facts. Read the following sentences aloud:

- A strong wind began to blow, and the sky looked ominous and threatening. Martina ran inside just as the _______ occurred.

Students listen to the facts in each sentence to infer the missing list word. Select a volunteer to identify the missing word. (**downpour**)

2 Proceed to page 115. Students independently complete the page.

3 Chorally read Galatians 5:22–23. Discuss the importance of displaying behaviors that are representative of the Holy Spirit.

Day 4 Writing

Objective

The students will complete sentences in an informative dialogue with list words that match pronunciations.

Introduction

Write the following pronunciations on the board in this order: /pri 'sīs/, /in trə 'spek tiv/, /tri 'men dəs/, /fôr 'mi də bəl/. Remind students that a dialogue is a conversation between two or more people. Inform students that you will be reading a dialogue between two friends, Kirk and Nanette. Read the following dialogue aloud while pausing at each pronunciation:

KIRK: Hi, Nanette! Are you ready to learn about the /pri 'sīs/ dynamics of the track-and-field event of the long jump? (**precise**)

NANETTE: Yes, Kirk. I am glad that Coach Discoll asked me to get your /in trə 'spek tiv/ viewpoint about the subtleties of the sport before I decided to participate. It will be neat to learn about how an athlete successfully performs the long jump. (**introspective**)

KIRK: I can tell you that a long-jump athlete needs to have strong leg muscles, /tri 'men dəs/ running speed, and good bodily flexion. All of these factors help the long jumper to sprint, throw his or her body into the air, land feetfirst, and pivot the body forward in the sandpit. (**tremendous**)

NANETTE: Wow! I never knew that a long jumper had to do all of that! Long jumping sounds like a /fôr 'mi də bəl/ sport! (**formidable**)

Invite volunteers to come to the board to write a list word that matches each pronunciation. Read the entire dialogue aloud.

Directed Instruction

1 Proceed to page 116. Students independently complete the page.

2 Homework suggestion: Distribute a copy of **BLM SP6-29A Lesson 29 Homework** to e

Day 5 Po

Objective

The students will ... ces.

Introduction

Review by using fl ... stion.

Directed Asse

1 Dictate the list ... original ones. I ... ary, *formidable*, an

Radium and uranium are radioactive metallic elements.

He had an abrasion on his knee from falling on the gravel.

2 Read each sentence. Repeat as needed.

- Roger was very focused during the long jump.
- He was one of thirty contestants in the meet.
- Roger was concerned about placing in the finals.
- However, Roger's concerns were unnecessary.
- He showed a great display of formidable skills.
- Roger departed the stadium with a happy disposition.

3 If assigned, dictate Extra Challenge Words.

4 Score the test, counting each misspelled word as an error. Correct the dictation sentences by grading only the spelling words or grading the complete sentences.

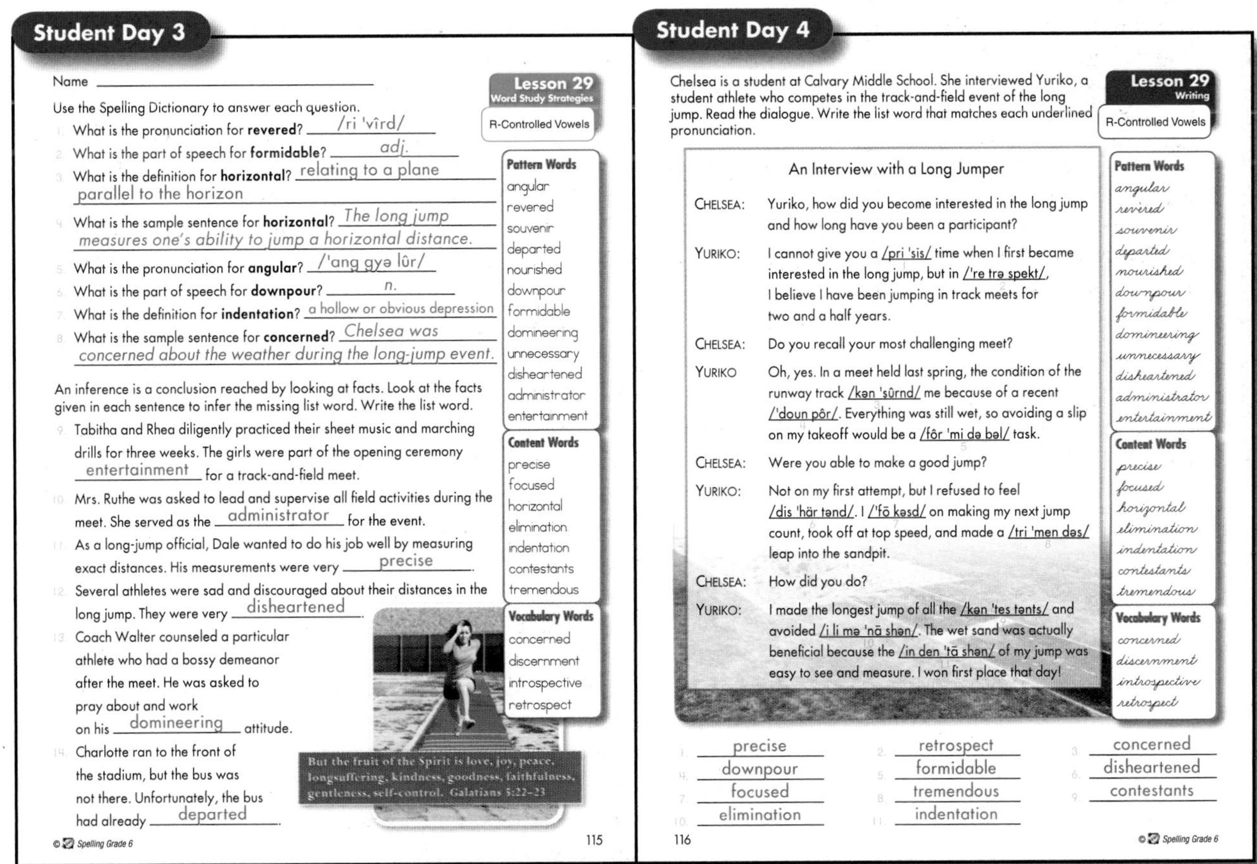

Student Day 3

Name ____________

Lesson 29 — Word Study Strategies — R-Controlled Vowels

Use the Spelling Dictionary to answer each question.

1. What is the pronunciation for **revered**? /ri 'vîrd/
2. What is the part of speech for **formidable**? adj.
3. What is the definition for **horizontal**? relating to a plane parallel to the horizon
4. What is the sample sentence for **horizontal**? The long jump measures one's ability to jump a horizontal distance.
5. What is the pronunciation for **angular**? /'ang gyə lûr/
6. What is the part of speech for **downpour**? n.
7. What is the definition for **indentation**? a hollow or obvious depression
8. What is the sample sentence for **concerned**? Chelsea was concerned about the weather during the long-jump event.

An inference is a conclusion reached by looking at facts. Look at the facts given in each sentence to infer the missing list word. Write the list word.

9. Tabitha and Rhea diligently practiced their sheet music and marching drills for three weeks. The girls were part of the opening ceremony entertainment for a track-and-field meet.
10. Mrs. Ruthe was asked to lead and supervise all field activities during the meet. She served as the administrator for the event.
11. As a long-jump official, Dale wanted to do his job well by measuring exact distances. His measurements were very precise.
12. Several athletes were sad and discouraged about their distances in the long jump. They were very disheartened.
13. Coach Walter counseled a particular athlete who had a bossy demeanor after the meet. He was asked to pray about and work on his domineering attitude.
14. Charlotte ran to the front of the stadium, but the bus was not there. Unfortunately, the bus had already departed.

Pattern Words: angular, revered, souvenir, departed, nourished, downpour, formidable, domineering, unnecessary, disheartened, administrator, entertainment

Content Words: precise, focused, horizontal, elimination, indentation, contestants, tremendous

Vocabulary Words: concerned, discernment, introspective, retrospect

But the fruit of the Spirit is love, joy, peace, longsuffering, kindness, goodness, faithfulness, gentleness, self-control. Galatians 5:22–23

© Spelling Grade 6 — 115

Student Day 4

Lesson 29 — Writing — R-Controlled Vowels

Chelsea is a student at Calvary Middle School. She interviewed Yuriko, a student athlete who competes in the track-and-field event of the long jump. Read the dialogue. Write the list word that matches each underlined pronunciation.

An Interview with a Long Jumper

CHELSEA: Yuriko, how did you become interested in the long jump and how long have you been a participant?

YURIKO: I cannot give you a /pri 'sis/ time when I first became interested in the long jump, but in /'re trə spekt/, I believe I have been jumping in track meets for two and a half years.

CHELSEA: Do you recall your most challenging meet?

YURIKO: Oh, yes. In a meet held last spring, the condition of the runway track /kən 'sûrnd/ me because of a recent /'doun pôr/. Everything was still wet, so avoiding a slip on my takeoff would be a /fôr 'mi də bəl/ task.

CHELSEA: Were you able to make a good jump?

YURIKO: Not on my first attempt, but I refused to feel /dis 'här tənd/. I /'fō kəsd/ on making my next jump count, took off at top speed, and made a /tri 'men dəs/ leap into the sandpit.

CHELSEA: How did you do?

YURIKO: I made the longest jump of all the /kən 'tes tənts/ and avoided /i li mə 'nā shən/. The wet sand was actually beneficial because the /in den 'tā shən/ of my jump was easy to see and measure. I won first place that day!

Pattern Words: angular, revered, souvenir, departed, nourished, downpour, formidable, domineering, unnecessary, disheartened, administrator, entertainment

Content Words: precise, focused, horizontal, elimination, indentation, contestants, tremendous

Vocabulary Words: concerned, discernment, introspective, retrospect

1. precise
2. retrospect
3. concerned
4. downpour
5. formidable
6. disheartened
7. focused
8. tremendous
9. contestants
10. elimination
11. indentation

116 — © Spelling Grade 6

Lesson 30

Review Lessons 25–29

Student Pages

Pages 117–120

Lesson Materials

T-19
BLM SP6-30A
BLM SP6-30B
T-5
BLM SP6-30C
BLM SP6-30D
BLMs SP6-30E–F
BLM SP6-06G
BLM SP6-30G

Day 1 Prefixes

Objective

The students will spell, identify, and sort words with **prefixes**.

Introduction

Teacher Note: This week's lesson incorporates the Pattern, Content, and Vocabulary Words taught in Lessons 25–29 using a variety of activities such as sorting, filling in the correct answer circle, a word search, incorporating definitions into an acrostic, circling the correct spelling, shape boxes, and a coordinate grid.

On one area of the board, write the following **prefixes**: anti-, dis-, em-, im-, in-, mid-. On another area of the board, write the following word parts: sole, braced, movable, location, stress, credulous. Have students refer to page 117 and use the Pattern Words in Lesson 25 for this activity. Select volunteers to choose a prefix and a word part to correctly spell the words. (**antistress, dislocation, embraced, immovable, incredulous, midsole**)

Directed Instruction

1 Display **T-19 Lessons 25–29 Study Sheet** on the overhead to review Lesson 25 words in unison, using the say-spell-say technique.

2 Proceed to page 117. Explain that the box contains all the Pattern, Content, and Vocabulary Words in Lessons 25–29. This list is the same list of words that was previously displayed on the overhead. Encourage students to use this list as a review tool. Instruct students to read the directions and independently complete the page.

3 Distribute a copy of **BLM SP6-30A Lessons 25–29 Study Sheet** to each student to take home for study.

4 Homework suggestion: Distribute a copy of **BLM SP6-30B Lesson 30 Homework I** to each student to practice **prefixes** and **suffixes**. Remind students to review their weekly sets of flash cards from Lessons 25–29.

Day 2 Prefixes and Suffixes

Objective

The students will select the appropriate answer circle to indicate if words with **prefixes** are spelled correctly or incorrectly, and correctly write the words. They will find and circle words with **suffixes** in a word search.

Introduction

Write the following on the board:

	Correct	Incorrect	
multitalented	O	O	(**correct; multitalented**)
undrestimate	O	O	(**incorrect; underestimate**)
superathlete	O	O	(**correct; superathlete**)

Display **T-19 Lessons 25–29 Study Sheet** to review Lessons 26–27 words in unison, using the say-spell-say technique. Select volunteers to identify if each word on the board is spelled correctly or incorrectly. Fill in each appropriate answer circle and write each word correctly.

Directed Instruction

1 Before class, select a volunteer to write the following Pattern Words from Lesson 27 in the squares of **T-5 Word Search Grid**: dosage, storage, percentage, achievement. Assist the volunteer in positioning the words across, down, and backwards. Fill in the surrounding

squares with letters to conceal the words. When complete, display the transparency on the overhead and challenge students to find the Pattern Words, referring to the list words on the bottom of page 118. Circle each word as it is found. An example word search is shown.

u	j	x	h	i	c	t	w	a	r
c	x	j	k	m	i	i	a	c	k
e	k	e	x	b	g	k	r	h	w
p	g	g	c	k	e	f	y	i	i
e	g	a	t	n	e	c	r	e	p
o	e	s	r	a	h	f	q	v	r
s	e	o	h	o	c	f	o	e	t
j	b	d	d	j	t	q	s	m	d
f	n	s	t	o	r	a	g	e	z
s	s	t	t	z	l	p	l	n	i
f	x	c	t	v	s	c	b	t	k

2 Proceed to page 118. Allow students to complete the exercises independently.

3 Homework suggestion: Distribute a copy of **BLM SP6-30C Lesson 30 Homework II** to each student to practice **r-controlled vowels**, Content Words, and Vocabulary Words.

Day 3 Suffixes and R-Controlled Vowels

Objective

The students will identify and write words with **suffixes** in an acrostic. They will select the correct spelling for words with **r-controlled vowels**, and write the words correctly.

Introduction

Display **T-19 Lessons 25–29 Study Sheet** to review Lessons 28–29 words in unison, using the say-spell-say technique.

Directed Instruction

1 Read the definitions below and challenge students to find a Pattern Word from Lesson 28 that matches each definition. Write each word on the board, underlining the letters shown.

- having the quality of continuing (**continuous**)
- jumpy (**nervous**)
- having the quality of courage (**courageous**)
- the act of writing journals or periodicals (**journalism**)
- not able to be compared (**incomparable**)

2 Ask the following question: What shape do a shot put and discus have in common? (**They each have a circular shape.**) Inform students that the underlined letters, when put in order, spell the answer word *circular.*

3 Write the following on the board, and challenge students to circle the correct r-controlled spelling and correctly spell the word:

- n ___ ished — er — (our) — (**nourished**)
- dish ___ tened — (ear) — are — (**disheartened**)
- administrat ___ — (or) — ir — (**administrator**)
- rev ___ d — eer — (ere) — (**revered**)

4 Proceed to page 119. Students complete the page independently. Assist as needed. When finished, select a volunteer to read the sentence in exercise 12. Inform students that the word *Paralympians* begins with a capital letter since it is a proper noun.

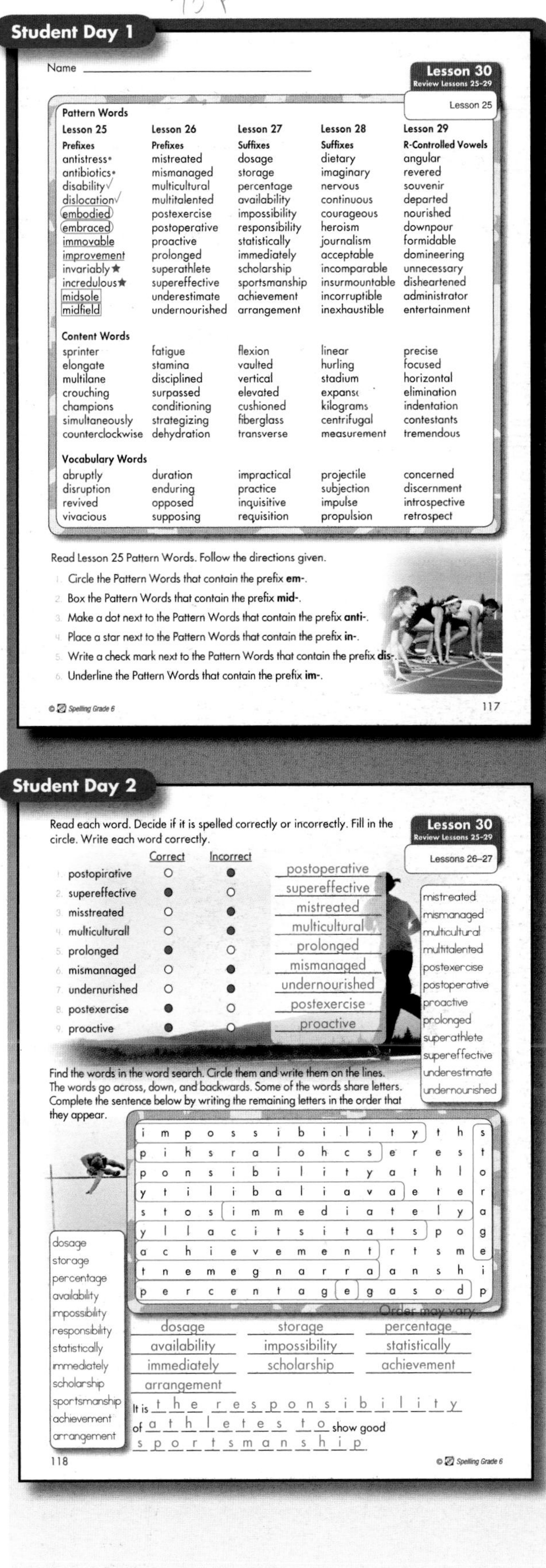

73 pts.

Student Day 1

Name ____________________

Lesson 30
Review Lessons 25–29

Lesson 25

Pattern Words

Lesson 25	Lesson 26	Lesson 27	Lesson 28	Lesson 29
Prefixes	Prefixes	Suffixes	Suffixes	R-Controlled Vowels
antistress•	mistreated	dosage	dietary	angular
antibiotics•	mismanaged	storage	imaginary	revered
disability√	multicultural	percentage	nervous	souvenir
dislocation√	multitalented	availability	continuous	departed
embodied	postexercise	impossibility	courageous	nourished
embraced	postoperative	responsibility	heroism	downpour
immovable	proactive	statistically	journalism	formidable
improvement	prolonged	immediately	acceptable	domineering
invariably★	superathlete	scholarship	incomparable	unnecessary
incredulous★	supereffective	sportsmanship	insurmountable	disheartened
midsole	underestimate	achievement	incorruptible	administrator
midfield	undernourished	arrangement	inexhaustible	entertainment

Content Words

sprinter	fatigue	flexion	linear	precise
elongate	stamina	vaulted	hurling	focused
multilane	disciplined	vertical	stadium	horizontal
crouching	surpassed	elevated	expanse	elimination
champions	conditioning	cushioned	kilograms	indentation
simultaneously	strategizing	fiberglass	centrifugal	contestants
counterclockwise	dehydration	transverse	measurement	tremendous

Vocabulary Words

abruptly	duration	impractical	projectile	concerned
disruption	enduring	practice	subjection	discernment
revived	opposed	inquisitive	impulse	introspective
vivacious	supposing	requisition	propulsion	retrospect

Read Lesson 25 Pattern Words. Follow the directions given.

1. Circle the Pattern Words that contain the prefix **em-**.
2. Box the Pattern Words that contain the prefix **mid-**.
3. Make a dot next to the Pattern Words that contain the prefix **anti-**.
4. Place a star next to the Pattern Words that contain the prefix **in-**.
5. Write a check mark next to the Pattern Words that contain the prefix **dis-**.
6. Underline the Pattern Words that contain the prefix **im-**.

© Spelling Grade 6 117

Student Day 2

Lesson 30
Review Lessons 25–29

Lessons 26–27

Read each word. Decide if it is spelled correctly or incorrectly. Fill in the circle. Write each word correctly.

	Correct	Incorrect	
1. postopirative	○	●	postoperative
2. supereffective	●	○	supereffective
3. misstreated	○	●	mistreated
4. multiculturall	○	●	multicultural
5. prolonged	●	○	prolonged
6. mismannaged	○	●	mismanaged
7. undernurished	○	●	undernourished
8. postexercise	●	○	postexercise
9. proactive	●	○	proactive

mistreated
mismanaged
multicultural
multitalented
postexercise
postoperative
proactive
prolonged
superathlete
supereffective
underestimate
undernourished

Find the words in the word search. Circle them and write them on the lines. The words go across, down, and backwards. Some of the words share letters. Complete the sentence below by writing the remaining letters in the order that they appear.

i	m	p	o	s	s	i	b	i	l	i	t	y	t	h	s
p	i	h	s	r	a	l	o	h	c	s	e	r	e	s	t
p	o	n	s	i	b	i	l	i	t	y	a	t	h	l	o
y	t	i	l	i	b	a	l	i	a	v	a	e	t	e	r
s	t	o	s	i	m	m	e	d	i	a	t	e	l	y	a
y	l	l	a	c	i	t	s	i	t	a	t	s	p	o	g
a	c	h	i	e	v	e	m	e	n	t	r	t	s	m	e
t	n	e	m	e	g	n	a	r	r	a	a	n	s	h	i
p	e	r	c	e	n	t	a	g	e	g	a	s	o	d	p

dosage
storage
percentage
availability
impossibility
responsibility
statistically
immediately
scholarship
sportsmanship
achievement
arrangement

Order may vary.

dosage — storage — percentage
availability — impossibility — statistically
immediately — scholarship — achievement
arrangement

It is t h e r e s p o n s i b i l i t y of a t h l e t e s t o show good s p o r t s m a n s h i p.

118 © Spelling Grade 6

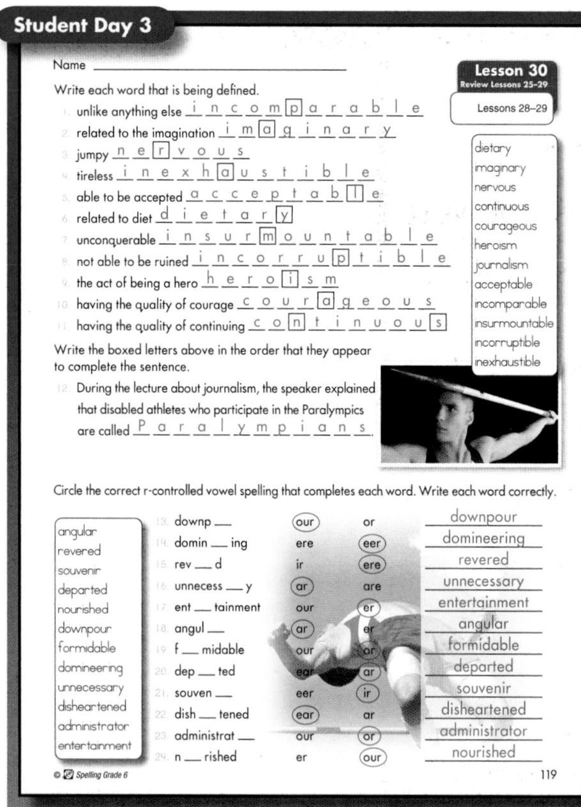

Student Day 3

Name ______

Lesson 30 Review Lessons 25–29

Lessons 28–29

Write each word that is being defined.

1. unlike anything else incomparable
2. related to the imagination imaginary
3. jumpy nervous
4. tireless inexhaustible
5. able to be accepted acceptable
6. related to diet dietary
7. unconquerable insurmountable
8. not able to be ruined incorruptible
9. the act of being a hero heroism
10. having the quality of courage courageous
11. having the quality of continuing continuous

dietary, imaginary, nervous, continuous, courageous, heroism, journalism, acceptable, incomparable, insurmountable, incorruptible, inexhaustible

Write the boxed letters above in the order that they appear to complete the sentence.

12. During the lecture about journalism, the speaker explained that disabled athletes who participate in the Paralympics are called Paralympians.

Circle the correct r-controlled vowel spelling that completes each word. Write each word correctly.

angular, revered, souvenir, departed, nourished, downpour, formidable, domineering, unnecessary, disheartened, administrator, entertainment

13. downp__	our	or	downpour
14. domin__ing	ere	eer	domineering
15. rev__d	ir	ere	revered
16. unneces__y	ar	are	unnecessary
17. ent__tainment	our	er	entertainment
18. angul__	ar	er	angular
19. f__midable	our	or	formidable
20. dep__ted	ear	ar	departed
21. souven__	eer	ir	souvenir
22. dish__tened	ear	ar	disheartened
23. administrat__	our	or	administrator
24. n__rished	er	our	nourished

© Spelling Grade 6 119

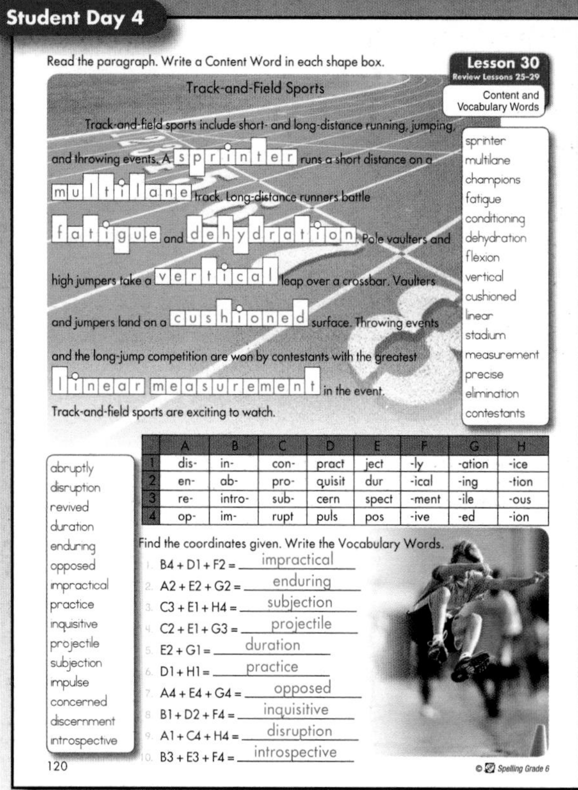

Student Day 4

Read the paragraph. Write a Content Word in each shape box.

Lesson 30 Review Lessons 25–29

Content and Vocabulary Words

Track-and-Field Sports

Track-and-field sports include short- and long-distance running, jumping, and throwing events. A sprinter runs a short distance on a multilane track. Long-distance runners battle fatigue and dehydration. Pole vaulters and high jumpers take a vertical leap over a crossbar. Vaulters and jumpers land on a cushioned surface. Throwing events and the long-jump competition are won by contestants with the greatest linear measurement in the event. Track-and-field sports are exciting to watch.

sprinter, multilane, champions, fatigue, conditioning, dehydration, flexion, vertical, cushioned, linear, stadium, measurement, precise, elimination, contestants

	A	B	C	D	E	F	G	H
1	dis-	in-	con-	pract	ject	-ly	-ation	-ice
2	en-	ob-	pro-	quisit	dur	-ical	-ing	-tion
3	re-	intro-	sub-	cern	spect	-ment	-ile	-ous
4	op-	im-	rupt	puls	pos	-ive	-ed	-ion

abruptly, disruption, revived, duration, enduring, opposed, impractical, practice, inquisitive, projectile, subjection, impulse, concerned, discernment, introspective

Find the coordinates given. Write the Vocabulary Words.

1. B4 + D1 + F2 = impractical
2. A2 + E2 + G2 = enduring
3. C3 + E1 + H4 = subjection
4. C2 + E1 + G3 = projectile
5. E2 + G1 = duration
6. D1 + H1 = practice
7. A4 + E4 + G4 = opposed
8. B1 + D2 + F4 = inquisitive
9. A1 + C4 + H4 = disruption
10. B3 + E3 + F4 = introspective

120 © Spelling Grade 6

Day 4 Content Words and Vocabulary Words

Objective

The students will write content words in shape boxes in the context of a paragraph. They will write vocabulary words by locating the word parts found within a coordinate grid.

Introduction

Display **T-19 Lessons 25–29 Study Sheet** to review Content and Vocabulary Words in unison, using the say-spell-say technique.

Directed Instruction

1 Write the following Content Words on the board and select volunteers to draw shape boxes around them:

- champions
- flexion
- precise
- elimination

Studying the shape of a word promotes visual memory.

2 On the board, draw the grid as shown and invite volunteers to find the Vocabulary Word using the following coordinates:

	A	B	C
1	con-	puls	-ed
2	re-	cern	-ing
3	im-	viv	-ive

- A2 + B3 + C1 = ______ **(revived)**
- A1 + B2 + C1 = ______ **(concerned)**
- A3 + B1 = ______ **(impulse)**

Remind students that silent *e* does not always appear in original root spellings.

3 Proceed to page 120. Students independently complete the page.

4 Homework suggestion: Distribute a copy of **BLM SP6-30D Lessons 25–29 Test Prep** to each student to practice with many of the words that may appear on the Assessment. Students prepare for the Assessment by studying the words on **BLM SP6-30A Lessons 25–29 Study Sheet** that was sent home on Day 1 or by using their flash card sets.

Day 5 Assessment

Objective

The students will accurately select the appropriate answer within the context of a sentence. They will fill in the corresponding answer circle.

Introduction

Teacher Note: The Test makes provision for Differentiated Instruction. The first twelve sentences include the words assigned to students with shortened lists. Encourage these students to try all the sentences, but only grade the first twelve sentences. The Test is found on two blackline masters.

Duplicate a copy of **BLMs SP6-30E–F Lessons 25–29 Test I** and **II** and distribute to each student. Duplicate **BLM SP6-06G Student Answer Form** and cut apart. Distribute one answer form to each student. Remind students to fill in each answer circle completely and to erase completely if they wish to change an answer.

Directed Assessment

1 Instruct students to listen as you dictate the following Sample:

Sample

Brandt <u>abrubtly</u> <u>departed</u> and <u>elevated</u> himself over the bar. <u>All correct</u>
A B C D

Say, "Are any of the first three underlined words misspelled?" Pause for replies. Inform students that the letter *A* is below the underlined word that is misspelled. (**abruptly**) Guide students to the answer form that was previously distributed. Lead students to find the Sample box and fill in the appropriate answer circle containing the same letter. Say, "You will continue in the same way. You will read each sentence, choose the word that you think is misspelled, and fill in the corresponding circle on the answer form. If all the words are spelled correctly, fill in the fourth circle, labeled *D*, for *All correct*."

2 Assist students as needed while they read the sentences and complete the Test on their own.

1. The multitalented sprinter ran counterclockwise around the track.
2. Ellery's jump was a tremendous linear improvement.
3. Champions invariably practice hard.
4. The contestants ran simultaneously around the stadium.
5. It is the responsibility of the administrator to award the scholarship.
6. The team revered their coach's continuous stamina for marathons.
7. The inquisitive and introspective student is studying journalism.
8. The athlete was nervous, but he focused on throwing the projectile.
9. Was there entertainment for the duration of her postoperative care?
10. Huge mats cushioned the disciplined athlete after he vaulted.
11. The illness was not prolonged due to supereffective antibiotics.
12. Cal's achievement is formidable despite his disability.
13. The superathlete was incredulous when she surpassed her record.
14. Never underestimate conditioning drills and postexercise tactics.
15. Jean was immediately disheartened over her elimination.
16. The vivacious team members embraced each other at the midfield.
17. God's devotion to us is inexhaustible, immovable, and incomparable.
18. Are you opposed to running on a multilane track after a downpour?
19. Dehydration and fatigue quickly affect undernourished runners.
20. In retrospect, Andy wishes he had not departed without a souvenir.
21. The proactive athlete shows good sportsmanship and discernment.
22. It is not impractical to have a daily dosage of dietary supplements.
23. Del was enduring his domineering coach's unnecessary comments.
24. It's acceptable to use centrifugal force for the propulsion of a shot.
25. The arrangement of the transverse pole is not an impossibility.

3 Refer to **BLM SP6-30G Lessons 25–29 Answer Key** when correcting the Test.

Notes

Lesson 31

Frequently Misspelled Words

Student Pages

Pages 121–124

Lesson Materials

BLM SP6-01B
Card stock
Index cards
Plastic cups
Plastic or foam golf balls
T-20
BLM SP6-31A
BLM SP6-31B

Sports

Lessons 31–35 utilize the theme of individual sports. The theme of this lesson is golf. The sport of golf is played outdoors on an area of grass known as a golf course. Golfers advance a small, hard ball around the course using as few strokes as possible. The advancement of the ball is done by using golf clubs. A round of golf is typically divided into eighteen sections, called holes. Each hole of golf is assigned a par score, the number of strokes achieved by a very good player. Most professionals score below par.

Day 1 Pretest

Objective

The students will accurately spell and write **frequently misspelled words.** They will spell and write content, vocabulary, and challenge words.

Introduction

Before class, select Challenge Words for numbers 24 and 25 from a cross-curricular subject, words misspelled on previous assignments, or words that interest your students. The word *pronunciation* is a **frequently misspelled word** and is suggested for number 24. Administer the Pretest.

Directed Instruction

1 Say each word, use it in a sentence, and then repeat the word.

Pattern Words

1. Numerous fans expressed their congratulations after the golf game.
2. Jacques was conscientious as he focused on the putting green.
3. Chrissy definitely had the advantage in the last golf tournament.
4. Old stories about Bart's beginning attempts at golf embarrassed him.
5. Margot was meticulous in the landscaping of the golf course.
6. Carlo bought a miniature version of golf clubs for his son, Ajay.
7. Diligent practice is necessary if one wants to improve in golf.
8. Trials in competition produce perseverance in Christ.
9. Lorena had the privilege of praying for the golf team.
10. Wyatt and Alexa ate lunch at the club restaurant after their golf game.
11. Bryce and Reggie arrived separately for the golf tournament.
12. Paloma was sincerely honored when named golf team captain.

Content Words

13. Vern used accuracy in his putting stroke and won the golf tournament.
14. Emmi replaced each divot after teeing off in her golf game.
15. The newly designed golf course contained many water hazards.
16. Theresa was the head of lawn maintenance for the private club.
17. Brenda's new golf clubs were made of titanium.
18. During a golf swing, torque is a twisting movement of the club's shaft.
19. The golf ball's trajectory determines how far it goes down the fairway.

Vocabulary Words

20. Golf does dignify the character of many people who play the game.
21. Arturo had dignity and did not cheat while writing his golf score.
22. The sport of golf allows participants to be sociable with fellow players.
23. Angela gives back to society by teaching children how to play golf.

Challenge Words

24. ______________________
25. ______________________

2 Allow students to self-correct their Pretest. Write each word on the board. Point out that the Pattern Words are **frequently misspelled words** and that spellings need to be memorized. Enunciate each syllable in each Pattern Word. Note the roots *dign* and *soci* in the Vocabulary Words.

3 As a class, read, spell, and read each word. Direct students to highlight misspelled words and rewrite them correctly.

4 Proof each student's Pretest. This becomes an individualized study sheet that can be used at school or at home.

5 Homework suggestion: Duplicate **BLM SP6-01B Flash Cards Template** on CARD STOCK for students to write the list words, using the flash cards as a study aid. Another option is to use INDEX CARDS.

Day 2 Word Analysis and Vocabulary

Objective

The students will sort **frequently misspelled words** according to their pronunciation and complete sentences with content words. They will use a table to write vocabulary words, match given definitions in context, and choose list words that match definitions.

Introduction

Pair students together for the following activity: Provide each pair with a PLASTIC CUP and a PLASTIC OR FOAM GOLF BALL. One student holds the cup while the other holds the golf ball. Dictate each Pattern Word and direct students to stand three feet apart while taking turns tossing the golf ball into the cup and spelling a word. If the word is spelled correctly, the student gets two throws. If the word is spelled incorrectly, the student must correct the word, and then he gets one throw only. After each student has spelled the word, write the correct spelling of the word on the board. Be sure to enunciate each Pattern Word clearly.

Directed Instruction

1 Instruct students to have their flash card pile from this lesson on hand for this activity. Have students refer to the list of Pattern Words on the board and to locate the corresponding flash cards. Discuss and instruct students to highlight the following unique aspects:

- *privilege*—Latin root *leg*
- *sincerely*—soft *c*
- *necessary*—soft *c*, double *s*
- *meticulous*—*ous* ending
- *definitely*—Latin root *fin*
- *miniature*—letter *a* in the third syllable
- *separately*—Latin root *par*
- *restaurant*—*aur* spelling
- *conscientious*—Latin root *sci*, *ious* ending
- *embarrassed*—double *r*, double *s*
- *perseverance*—prefix *per*, *ance* ending
- *congratulations*—Latin root *grat*

Differentiated Instruction

- For students who spelled all the words correctly on the Pretest, select and assign Extra Challenge Words from the following list: representation, recessive, circumlocution, telecommunication, allergenic, libretto.
- For students who spelled less than half correctly, assign the following Pattern, Content, and Vocabulary Words: privilege, definitely, necessary, separately, perseverance, congratulations, torque, hazards, accuracy, maintenance, dignity, sociable. On the Posttest, evaluate these students on the twelve words assigned; however, encourage them to attempt to spell all the list words to the best of their ability. They are also responsible for writing the dictated sentences.

Student Day 2

79 pts.

Name ______

Lesson 31 Word Analysis — Frequently Misspelled Words

Pattern Words: privilege, definitely, sincerely, miniature, necessary, separately, meticulous, restaurant, conscientious, embarrassed, perseverance, congratulations

Content Words: divot, torque, titanium, hazards, accuracy, trajectory, maintenance

Vocabulary Words: dignify, dignity, sociable, society

Challenge Words

Write Pattern Words to complete the exercises. Sort the frequently misspelled words according to their pronunciation.

1. /ˈpri və lij/ privilege
2. /sin ˈsîr lē/ sincerely
3. /im ˈbâr əsd/ embarrassed
4. /kont shē ˈent shəs/ conscientious
5. /ˈne sə sâr ē/ necessary
6. /pûr sə ˈvîr ənts/ perseverance
7. /ˈres tə ränt/ restaurant
8. /kən gra chə ˈlā shənz/ congratulations
9. /ˈde fə nit lē/ definitely
10. /mə ˈti kyə ləs/ meticulous
11. /ˈmi nē ə choor/ miniature
12. /ˈse pə rət lē/ separately

Write Content Words to complete the exercises.

13. The sport of golf requires accuracy in swinging clubs to advance a small, hard ball over a course of play.
14. Many popular golf clubs are made of a strong, lightweight metal called titanium. The angle of a golf club and the torque of its shaft are necessary for a good path, or trajectory, of the golf ball.
15. The maintenance of water hazards and each divot that is dug out of the green is an industrious job.

golf

© Spelling Grade 6 121

Student Day 2

Lesson 31 Vocabulary — Frequently Misspelled Words

Prefix	Root		Suffix	
	dign	worthy	-ify	to make
	soci	companion	-ity	state of
			-able	is able
			-ety	state of

Write the Vocabulary Words. Order may vary.

1. dignify
2. dignity
3. sociable
4. society

Refer to the table to complete the exercises. Write the word that is being defined.

5. a state of being worthy; self-respect dignity
6. to make worthy of; to honor, distinguish, or give distinction dignify
7. able to seek out the company of other people or engage in social interaction; friendly; outgoing sociable
8. a state of companionship; a group of people, generally with a common interest or role society

Write Vocabulary Words to complete the sentences.

9. Arthur joined a golf club that was a big part of the local society.
10. Arthur and Franco were sociable with the newest members of the golf association.
11. Arthur and Franco kept dignity during the long tournament and did not cheat while keeping record of their score.
12. Arthur chose to dignify the various sponsors of the golf tournament by acknowledging each one during his closing speech.

Choose the word that matches each definition.

13. conscientious; thorough; careful
○ divot ● meticulous ○ privilege
14. persistence; determination
○ sincerely ● perseverance ○ torque

Pattern Words: privilege, definitely, sincerely, miniature, necessary, separately, meticulous, restaurant, conscientious, embarrassed, perseverance, congratulations

Content Words: divot, torque, titanium, hazards, accuracy, trajectory, maintenance

Vocabulary Words: dignify, dignity, sociable, society

122 © Spelling Grade 6

Student Spelling Support Materials

BLM SP6-01A

Student Spelling Support

1. Use **BLM SP6-01A A Spelling Study Strategy** in instructional groups to provide assistance with some or all of the words.
2. Invite students to write the Challenge Words, numbers 24 and 25, in the Word Bank, in the back of their textbook.
3. Challenge students to research and write a biography of a famous golfer. Students may compile information in the progressive, sport journal that was started in Lesson 1.
4. Write this week's words, categorize the Pattern, Content, and Vocabulary Words, and attach them to the Word Wall.
5. Read Romans 5:3–4: "We also glory in tribulations, knowing that tribulation produces **perseverance**; and **perseverance**, character; and character, hope." Invite students to share about a time that a difficulty in their life produced **perseverance** —persistence and determination—in their walk with the Lord. Discuss how the admonition at the beginning of the verse seems contrary to what we want to do when trials arise. However, it is proven true when we solely allow the trial to bring us closer to the Lord and the hope that is found in Him. Invite students to share about a trial, orally or in writing, and detail how it built **perseverance** in their lives.

2 Select a volunteer to look up the Pattern Words *meticulous* and *perseverance* in the Spelling Dictionary and read the definitions aloud.

3 Students refer to the list words on page 121 for this activity. Challenge students to quickly locate the definition of each Content Word in the Spelling Dictionary. Students read the definitions aloud.

4 Proceed to page 121. Say, spell, and say each Pattern, Content, and Vocabulary Word. Provide this week's Challenge Words and have students write them in the spaces provided before completing the page. Note the number of syllables in each Pattern Word according to their pronunciation.

5 Proceed to page 122. Encourage students to use the table as an aid in building each Vocabulary Word. For example, the root *dign* goes with the suffix *-ify* to build the word *dignify*. Point out that there are no prefixes in this week's Vocabulary Words. Allow students to complete the page independently. When complete, select a volunteer to read exercises 9–12 aloud.

6 Homework suggestion: Students use their Spelling Dictionary to write the definition of each word on the back of the corresponding flash card that was suggested for homework on Day 1.

Day 3 Word Study Strategies

Objective

The students will write list words that relate to an idiom. Students will alphabetize list words.

Introduction

Teach that *idioms* are <u>fun ways to talk about everyday things</u>. Read the following idioms aloud and ask students to explain what they mean: a piece of cake (**a task that can be accomplished very easily**), pulling your leg (**tricking someone as a joke**), under the weather (**feeling ill or sick**).

Directed Instruction

1 Dictate the following words and invite a volunteer to write them on the board in alphabetical order: embarrassed, divot, accuracy, sociable. (**accuracy, divot, embarrassed, sociable**)

2 Proceed to page 123. Students work in groups to complete the page.

Day 4 Writing

Objective

The students will use proofreading marks to identify mistakes in a descriptive blog. They will locate and correct sentence fragments. Students will correctly write misspelled words.

Introduction

Teacher Note: The descriptive domain is the focus for the writing pages in Lessons 31–35.

Display **T-20 Proofreading a Blog** on the overhead, keeping the bottom portion of the transparency covered. Read the text aloud. Correct the identified mistakes using the appropriate proofreading marks. Remind students that a sentence fragment is an incomplete sentence that does not express a complete thought. A fragment is missing the subject, predicate, or both. Challenge students to identify the sentence fragments. Use **BLM SP6-31A T-20 Answer Key** as a guide. Uncover the bottom of the transparency and read the corrected version of the text.

Directed Instruction

1 Proceed to page 124 and assist students as needed while they independently proofread the blog. Review all necessary proofreading marks and corrections. (**12 misspellings; 3 capital letters needed; 2 periods needed; 3 deletes; 2 add something—*the, question mark*;**

4 small letters needed; 1 new paragraph) Have students identify the sentence fragments in the blog. (**I had the privilege of spending the day. With many children who suffer from this disease.; Then things started to fall apart. For the governor.**)

2 Select a volunteer to read Romans 5:3–4. Discuss how trials cause us to become more determined in Christ when we allow them to.

3 Homework suggestion: Distribute a copy of **BLM SP6-31B Lesson 31 Homework** to each student.

Day 5 Posttest

Objective

The students will correctly write dictated spelling words and sentences.

Introduction

Review by using flash cards noted in Day 1 and Day 2 Homework suggestion.

Directed Assessment

1 Dictate the list words by using the Pretest sentences or developing original ones. Reserve *sociable, privilege, definitely, accuracy, hazards,* and *perseverance* for the dictation sentences.

2 Read each sentence. Repeat as needed.

- The sport of golf allows Ralph to be sociable with many people.
- He had the privilege of playing with a professional golfer.
- Ralph was definitely nervous, but he asked the Lord to give him peace.
- During play, Ralph wanted to focus on the accuracy of his golf shots.
- Ralph successfully avoided the hazards on the golf course.
- He showed a lot of perseverance and played very well.

3 If assigned, dictate Extra Challenge Words.

4 Score the test, counting each misspelled word as an error. Correct the dictation sentences by grading only the spelling words or grading the complete sentences.

Notes

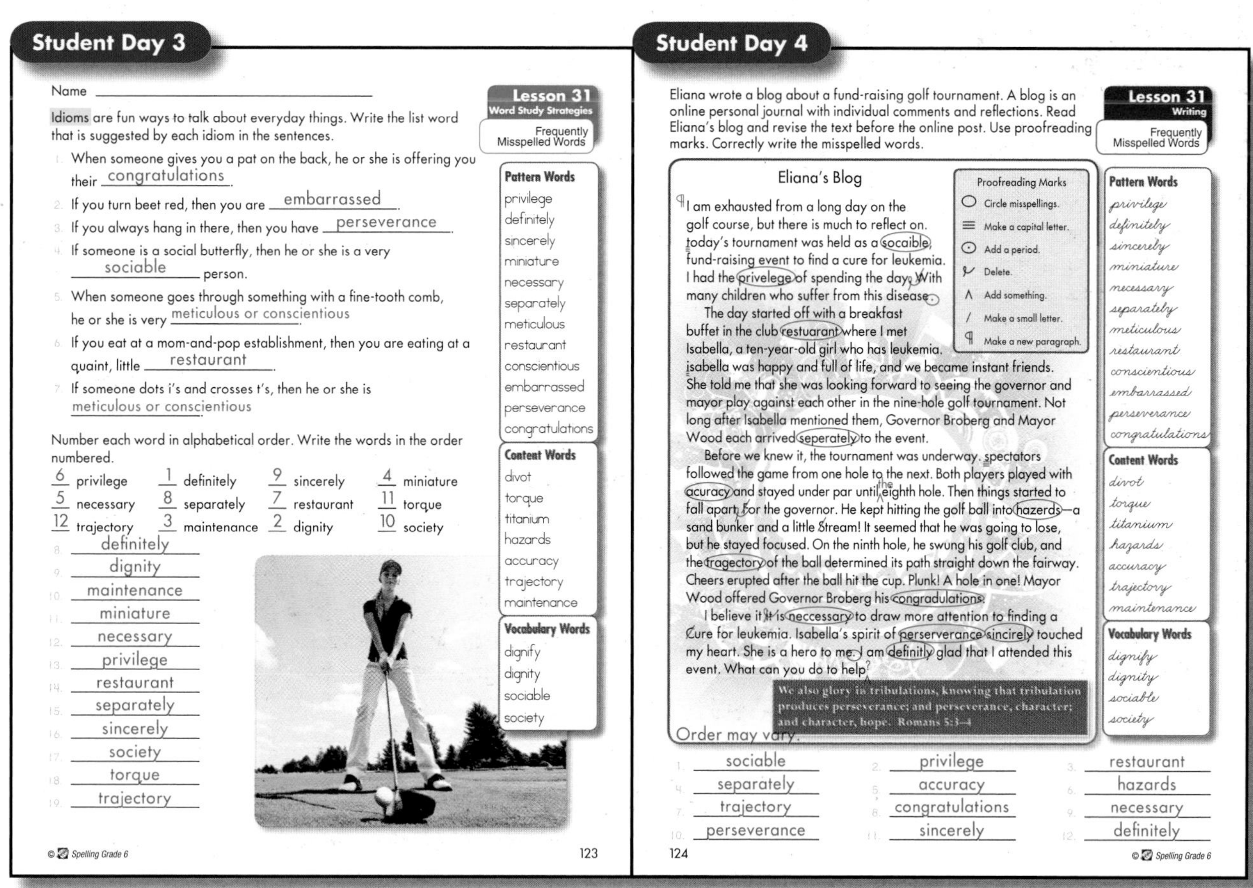

Lesson 32 Words from French and Italian

Student Pages

Pages 125–128

Lesson Materials

BLM SP6-01B
Card stock
Index cards
T-21
BLM SP6-32A

Sports

The theme of this lesson is horseback riding. Horseback riding is one of the equestrian sports. Equestrian sports involve both riding and driving horses, and they include rodeo competitions, horse racing, harness racing, and dressage. *Dressage* is a competition of show horses that have trained to make particular movements. Horseback riding is both an amateur and a professional sport. Riding can be done in competition or as a relaxing hobby.

Day 1 Pretest

Objective

The students will accurately spell and write **words from French and Italian.** They will spell and write content, vocabulary, and challenge words.

Introduction

Before class, select Challenge Words for numbers 24 and 25 from a cross-curricular subject, words misspelled on previous assignments, or words that interest your students. The word *picturesque* is from the **French** language and is suggested for number 24. Administer the Pretest.

Directed Instruction

1 Say each word, use it in a sentence, and then repeat the word.

Pattern Words

1. As the organist played an adagio, Carmen bowed her head to pray.
2. The gait of the Tennessee walking horse resembles ballet.
3. Nina presented a bouquet to the winner of the steeplechase.
4. A crystal chandelier hung in the grand ballroom.
5. The chauffeur drove the heiress to her riding lessons.
6. It is good etiquette for a rider to signal he is ready to begin.
7. The gaited Paso Fino performed the finale of the horse show.
8. Gourmet cheeses were served at the riding academy's open house.
9. Macaroni and cheese was available at the rodeo.
10. Avril's horse avoided the parapet near the crevice in the road.
11. The ceiling of the rotunda had beautiful paintings of horses.
12. A plate of spaghetti was a welcome sight to the hungry riders.

Content Words

13. Horses were domesticated centuries ago.
14. Marie trains horses in dressage.
15. Steeplechase and harness racing are both equestrian sports.
16. The exhibition by horses with beautiful gaits intrigued Aimee.
17. In barrel racing, horses need to turn quickly to avoid obstacles.
18. Was Chloe a poised, well-prepared rider?
19. Henri had a prestigious reputation for training Lipizzaners.

Vocabulary Words

20. The thoroughbred was sold at auction to the highest bidder.
21. Judges at the horse show surveyed the field circumspectly.
22. The auctioneer sold a palomino to Mrs. Chavez.
23. Hugh tried to circumvent the obstacle by reining in his horse.

Challenge Words

24. ______________________
25. ______________________

2 Allow students to self-correct their Pretest. Write each word on the board. Point out that the Pattern Words originally came from either French or Italian. The **words from French** are *ballet, bouquet, gourmet, etiquette, chauffeur,* and *chandelier.* The **words from Italian** are *finale, adagio, rotunda, parapet, spaghetti,* and *macaroni.* Note the roots *auct, circum, spect,* and *vent* in the Vocabulary Words. The word *auctioneer* has two suffixes, *-ion* and *-eer*; *circumspectly* contains two roots *circum* and *spect*; and *circumvent* contains two roots, *circum* and *vent.*

3 As a class, read, spell, and read each word. Direct students to highlight misspelled words and rewrite them correctly.

4 Proof each student's Pretest. This becomes an individualized study sheet that can be used at school or at home.

5 Homework suggestion: Duplicate **BLM SP6-01B Flash Cards Template** on CARD STOCK for students to write the list words, using the flash cards as a study aid. Another option is to use INDEX CARDS.

Day 2 Word Analysis and Vocabulary

Objective

The students will sort and write **words from French and Italian** and complete sentences with content words. Students will use a table to write vocabulary words, match vocabulary words to their definition, complete sentences, and choose the best meaning for underlined words.

Introduction

Remind students that the Pattern Words are derived from the French and Italian languages. *Derivation* is the act of determining the source or origin of a word. Etymology, or studying word origins, helps in developing spelling and vocabulary skills. Display **T-21 Words from French and Italian** on the overhead. Ask the following questions:

- Which words from French have /ā/ spelled *et*? (**ballet, bouquet, gourmet**)
- Which words from French have /sh/ spelled *ch*? (**chauffeur, chandelier**)
- Which words from Italian have /ē/ spelled *i*? (**adagio, spaghetti, macaroni**)

Directed Instruction

1 Instruct students to have the flash cards on hand for this activity. Review that the first six Pattern Words, found on page 125, are derived from French, and the second six are from Italian. Invite students to work in pairs to find and pronounce each Pattern Word in the Spelling Dictionary. Students sort the Pattern Word flash cards into **words from French** and **words from Italian**, and underline each group in a separate color.

2 Proceed to page 125. Say, spell, and say each Pattern, Content, and Vocabulary Word. Provide this week's Challenge Words and have students write them in the spaces provided. Students complete the page.

Differentiated Instruction

- For students who spelled all the words correctly on the Pretest, select and assign Extra Challenge Words from the following list: scalar, scientific, summation, incorporation, arthroscopy, virtuoso.
- For students who spelled less than half correctly, assign the following Pattern, Content, and Vocabulary Words: ballet, bouquet, etiquette, finale, adagio, rotunda, exhibition, dressage, equestrian, prestigious, auction, circumvent. On the Posttest, evaluate these students on the twelve words assigned; however, encourage them to attempt to spell all the list words to the best of their ability. They are also responsible for writing the dictated sentences.

Student Day 2

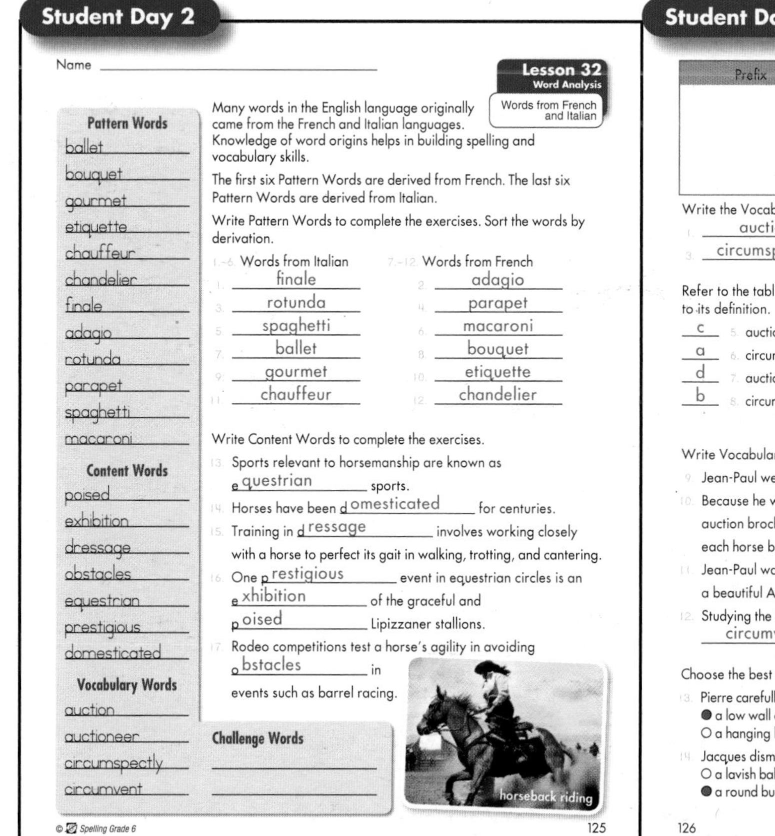

Name ______

Lesson 32 Word Analysis

Pattern Words: ballet, bouquet, gourmet, etiquette, chauffeur, chandelier, finale, adagio, rotunda, parapet, spaghetti, macaroni

Content Words: poised, exhibition, dressage, obstacles, equestrian, prestigious, domesticated

Vocabulary Words: auction, auctioneer, circumspectly, circumvent

Words from French and Italian

Many words in the English language originally came from the French and Italian languages. Knowledge of word origins helps in building spelling and vocabulary skills.

The first six Pattern Words are derived from French. The last six Pattern Words are derived from Italian.

Write Pattern Words to complete the exercises. Sort the words by derivation.

1–6 Words from Italian	7–12 Words from French
1. finale	2. adagio
3. rotunda	4. parapet
5. spaghetti	6. macaroni
7. ballet	8. bouquet
9. gourmet	10. etiquette
11. chauffeur	12. chandelier

Write Content Words to complete the exercises.

13. Sports relevant to horsemanship are known as equestrian sports.
14. Horses have been domesticated for centuries.
15. Training in dressage involves working closely with a horse to perfect its gait in walking, trotting, and cantering.
16. One prestigious event in equestrian circles is an exhibition of the graceful and poised Lipizzaner stallions.
17. Rodeo competitions test a horse's agility in avoiding obstacles in events such as barrel racing.

Challenge Words

______

______

horseback riding

© Spelling Grade 6 125

Student Day 2

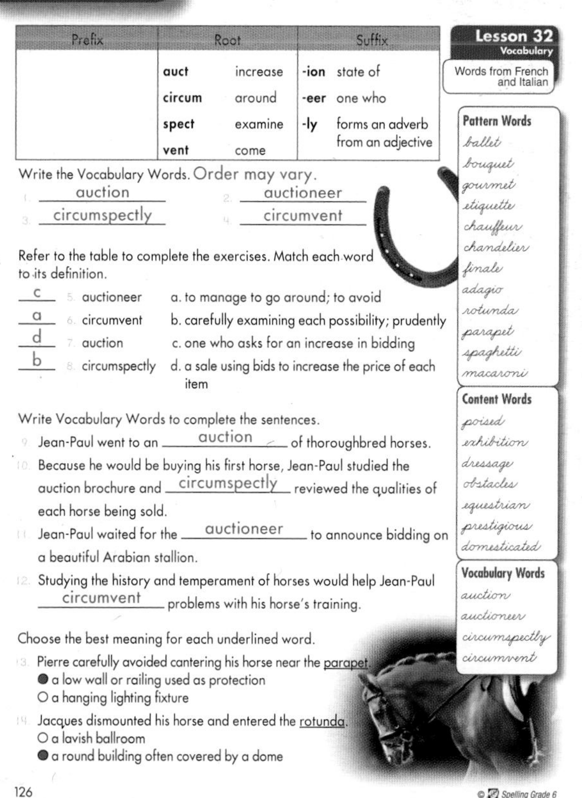

Lesson 32 Vocabulary

Words from French and Italian

Prefix	Root		Suffix	
	auct	increase	-ion	state of
	circum	around	-eer	one who
	spect	examine	-ly	forms an adverb from an adjective
	vent	come		

Write the Vocabulary Words. Order may vary.

1. auction 2. auctioneer
3. circumspectly 4. circumvent

Refer to the table to complete the exercises. Match each word to its definition.

c 5. auctioneer — a. to manage to go around; to avoid
a 6. circumvent — b. carefully examining each possibility; prudently
d 7. auction — c. one who asks for an increase in bidding
b 8. circumspectly — d. a sale using bids to increase the price of each item

Write Vocabulary Words to complete the sentences.

9. Jean-Paul went to an auction of thoroughbred horses.
10. Because he would be buying his first horse, Jean-Paul studied the auction brochure and circumspectly reviewed the qualities of each horse being sold.
11. Jean-Paul waited for the auctioneer to announce bidding on a beautiful Arabian stallion.
12. Studying the history and temperament of horses would help Jean-Paul circumvent problems with his horse's training.

Choose the best meaning for each underlined word.

13. Pierre carefully avoided cantering his horse near the parapet.
● a low wall or railing used as protection
○ a hanging lighting fixture

14. Jacques dismounted his horse and entered the rotunda.
○ a lavish ballroom
● a round building often covered by a dome

Pattern Words: ballet, bouquet, gourmet, etiquette, chauffeur, chandelier, finale, adagio, rotunda, parapet, spaghetti, macaroni

Content Words: poised, exhibition, dressage, obstacles, equestrian, prestigious, domesticated

Vocabulary Words: auction, auctioneer, circumspectly, circumvent

126 © Spelling Grade 6

Student Spelling Support Materials

BLM SP6-01A

Student Spelling Support

1. Use **BLM SP6-01A A Spelling Study Strategy** in instructional groups to provide assistance with some or all of the words.
2. Invite students to write the Challenge Words, numbers 24 and 25, in the Word Bank, in the back of their textbook.
3. Challenge students to research and write about equestrian sports, such as horse racing, rodeo riding, and dressage. Students may compile information in the progressive, sport journal that was started in Lesson 1.
4. Write this week's words, categorize the Pattern, Content, and Vocabulary Words, and attach them to the Word Wall.
5. Read James 3:2–3: "For we all stumble in many things. If anyone does not stumble in word, he is a perfect man, able also to bridle the whole body. Indeed, we put bits in horses' mouths that they may obey us, and we turn their whole body." Discuss how we as Christians must bring our words under control, just as a rider controls a horse. Invite students to brainstorm ways to gain control over their speech. Write ideas on the board.
6. Challenge students to use the dictionary to collect additional English words with a French or Italian origin. Post several words ending in the French spelling *et* that makes the sound /ā/ on your classroom word wall. (**Possible words: crochet, ricochet, parquet, cachet, duvet**) Post several words ending in

Cont. on page 129

3 Proceed to page 126. Remind students to use the table to assist in building each Vocabulary Word. For example, the root *auct* goes with the suffix *-ion* to build the word *auction*. Lead students to conclude that there are no prefixes in the Vocabulary Words in this list. Allow students to complete the page independently.

4 Homework suggestion: Students use their Spelling Dictionary to write the definition of each word on the back of the corresponding flash card that was suggested for homework on Day 1.

Day 3 Word Study Strategies

Objective

The students will write clauses to complete complex sentences, underline subordinating conjunctions, and identify types of clauses.

Introduction

Write the following subordinating conjunctions on the board: after, although, as, because, since, when, where, while. A *subordinating conjunction* is a conjunction that joins two clauses, an independent clause and a dependent clause, into one sentence. An independent clause can stand alone because it contains both a subject and a predicate and expresses a complete thought. A dependent clause may begin with a subordinating conjunction, but does not express a complete thought. A *complex sentence* is a combination of an independent and a dependent clause. Write the following complex sentence on the board:

- While Phil was adjusting his horse's stirrups, he checked the girth to circumvent problems with the saddle.

Choose volunteers to circle the subordinating conjunction, underline the independent clause once, and the dependent clause twice.

Directed Instruction

1 Remind students that when the dependent clause in a complex sentence begins the sentence, a comma is used after the dependent clause.

2 Proceed to page 127. Assist students to complete the page. When completed, select volunteers to read the sentences in exercises 1–5. Choose volunteers to read exercises 7–9 and make any necessary corrections.

Day 4 Writing

Objective

The students will write list words to complete stanzas in a quatrain poem.

Introduction

Write the following short poem on the board:

An auction is the best place to go,
To buy a horse at a price that's low.
When the auctioneer calls for your bid,
Be sure to speak; you'll be glad you did.

Select a volunteer to read the poem. Explain that this poem is a *quatrain*. A *quatrain* is a poem with four lines that rhyme. Note that the first and second lines rhyme, and the third and fourth lines rhyme. This is an AABB rhyme scheme.

Directed Instruction

1 Invite students to refer to the list words, found on page 128. Challenge students to underline the list words in the poem. (**auction, auctioneer**)

2 Introduce students to a *cinquain*. A *cinquain* is a poem with five lines that do not rhyme. The cinquain form of poerty always follows a pattern. This type of poem uses various parts of speech. The pattern for a cinquain is as follows:

- Line 1: the subject of the poem
- Line 2: two adjectives that describe the subject
- Line 3: three action verbs that relate to the subject

- Line 4: a sentence about the subject
- Line 5: a synonym of the subject

3 Proceed to page 128 and read the definition at the top of the page. Students write the missing words on the lines. Choose volunteers to tell the words that rhyme and identify the rhyme scheme. (**AABB**)

4 Review the format for a cinquain poem and read the example together before inviting students to write a poem to share.

5 Homework suggestion: Distribute a copy of **BLM SP6-32A Lesson 32 Homework** to each student.

Student Spelling Support

Cont. from page 128

the Italian spelling *i* that makes the sound /ē/. (**Possible words: pepperoni, manicotti, fettuccini, broccoli, zucchini**)

Day 5 Posttest

Objective

The students will correctly write dictated spelling words and sentences.

Introduction

Review by using flash cards noted in Day 1 and Day 2 Homework suggestion.

Directed Assessment

1 Dictate the list words by using the Pretest sentences or developing original ones. Reserve *exhibition, rotunda, ballet, circumvent, bouquet,* and *equestrian* for the dictation sentences.

2 Read each sentence. Repeat as needed.
- Diane took riding lessons to prepare for an exhibition.
- The riders would be performing in the rotunda near the stables.
- Diane and her horse trained to perform a leap as in ballet.
- Diane hoped to circumvent any missteps by training hard.
- The winner of the show would receive a bouquet of roses.
- Diane will participate in future equestrian events.

3 If assigned, dictate Extra Challenge Words.

4 Score the test, counting each misspelled word as an error. Correct the dictation sentences by grading only the spelling words or grading the complete sentences.

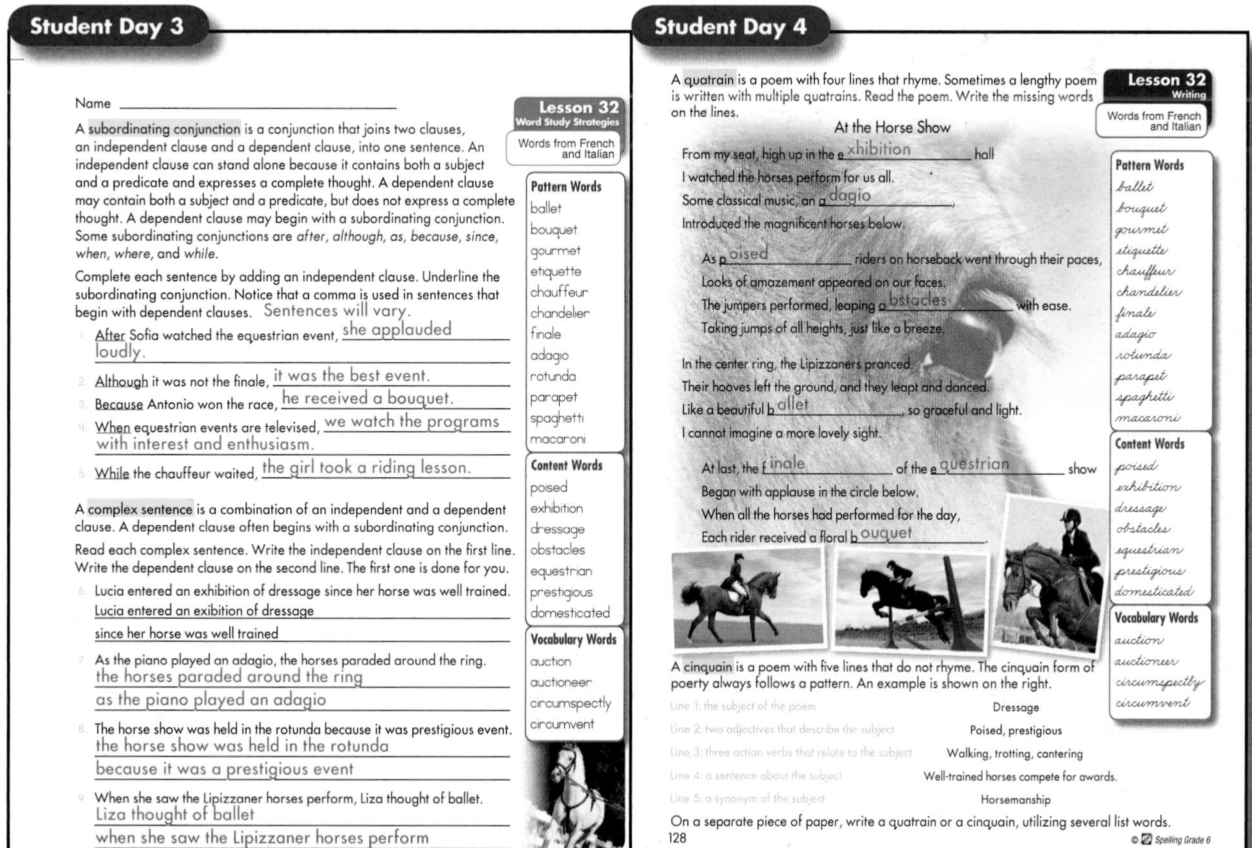

Student Day 3

Name ______________________

Lesson 32 Word Study Strategies — Words from French and Italian

A subordinating conjunction is a conjunction that joins two clauses, an independent clause and a dependent clause, into one sentence. An independent clause can stand alone because it contains both a subject and a predicate and expresses a complete thought. A dependent clause may contain both a subject and a predicate, but does not express a complete thought. A dependent clause may begin with a subordinating conjunction. Some subordinating conjunctions are *after, although, as, because, since, when, where,* and *while.*

Complete each sentence by adding an independent clause. Underline the subordinating conjunction. Notice that a comma is used in sentences that begin with dependent clauses. Sentences will vary.

1. After Sofia watched the equestrian event, she applauded loudly.
2. Although it was not the finale, it was the best event.
3. Because Antonio won the race, he received a bouquet.
4. When equestrian events are televised, we watch the programs with interest and enthusiasm.
5. While the chauffeur waited, the girl took a riding lesson.

A complex sentence is a combination of an independent and a dependent clause. A dependent clause often begins with a subordinating conjunction.

Read each complex sentence. Write the independent clause on the first line. Write the dependent clause on the second line. The first one is done for you.

6. Lucia entered an exhibition of dressage since her horse was well trained.
Lucia entered an exhibition of dressage
since her horse was well trained
7. As the piano played an adagio, the horses paraded around the ring.
the horses paraded around the ring
as the piano played an adagio
8. The horse show was held in the rotunda because it was prestigious event.
the horse show was held in the rotunda
because it was a prestigious event
9. When she saw the Lipizzaner horses perform, Liza thought of ballet.
Liza thought of ballet
when she saw the Lipizzaner horses perform

Pattern Words: ballet, bouquet, gourmet, etiquette, chauffeur, chandelier, finale, adagio, rotunda, parapet, spaghetti, macaroni

Content Words: poised, exhibition, dressage, obstacles, equestrian, prestigious, domesticated

Vocabulary Words: auction, auctioneer, circumspectly, circumvent

Student Day 4

Lesson 32 Writing — Words from French and Italian

A quatrain is a poem with four lines that rhyme. Sometimes a lengthy poem is written with multiple quatrains. Read the poem. Write the missing words on the lines.

At the Horse Show

From my seat, high up in the exhibition hall
I watched the horses perform for us all.
Some classical music, an adagio,
Introduced the magnificent horses below.

As poised riders on horseback went through their paces,
Looks of amazement appeared on our faces.
The jumpers performed, leaping obstacles with ease.
Taking jumps of all heights, just like a breeze.

In the center ring, the Lipizzaners pranced.
Their hooves left the ground, and they leapt and danced.
Like a beautiful ballet, so graceful and light.
I cannot imagine a more lovely sight.

At last, the finale of the equestrian show
Began with applause in the circle below.
When all the horses had performed for the day,
Each rider received a floral bouquet.

A cinquain is a poem with five lines that do not rhyme. The cinquain form of poetry always follows a pattern. An example is shown on the right.

Line 1: the subject of the poem	Dressage
Line 2: two adjectives that describe the subject	Poised, prestigious
Line 3: three action verbs that relate to the subject	Walking, trotting, cantering
Line 4: a sentence about the subject	Well-trained horses compete for awards.
Line 5: a synonym of the subject	Horsemanship

On a separate piece of paper, write a quatrain or a cinquain, utilizing several list words.

Pattern Words: ballet, bouquet, gourmet, etiquette, chauffeur, chandelier, finale, adagio, rotunda, parapet, spaghetti, macaroni

Content Words: poised, exhibition, dressage, obstacles, equestrian, prestigious, domesticated

Vocabulary Words: auction, auctioneer, circumspectly, circumvent

128 © Spelling Grade 6

Lesson 33

Words from Spanish

Student Pages

Pages 129–132

Lesson Materials

BLM SP6-01B
Card stock
Index cards
T-22
BLM SP6-33A

Sports

The theme of this lesson is fencing. In the Middle Ages, fencing was a form of attack and defense using a sword and a shield. Today, fencing is a recreational and competitive sport. Fencing was a sport in the ancient Olympic Games in Greece and is one of only four sports that have been played in every modern Olympic game since 1896.

Day 1 Pretest

Objective

The students will accurately spell and write **words from Spanish**. They will spell and write content, vocabulary, and challenge words.

Introduction

Before class, select Challenge Words for numbers 24 and 25 from a cross-curricular subject, words misspelled on previous assignments, or words that interest your students. The word *guacamole* is from the **Spanish** language and is suggested for number 24. Administer the Pretest.

Directed Instruction

1 Say each word, use it in a sentence, and then repeat the word.

Pattern Words

1. Eugene ate a quesadilla for a snack.
2. While we ate at the Mexican restaurant, a mariachi band played.
3. The waitress asked Aria if she wanted chicken or beef in her burrito.
4. Juan asked for one more tortilla to eat with his fajitas.
5. My fencing club celebrated Cinco de Mayo with a fiesta.
6. The wide brim of a sombrero shaded Hector's face from the sun.
7. Greg enjoys playing the guitar and singing praises to the Lord.
8. Papá Valdez feeds alfalfa to the livestock on his farm.
9. The enchilada that Aunt Rosa served was warm and delicious.
10. The teacher instructed the class to line up for lunch, pronto.
11. Mamá Negrete bought maize at the store today.
12. Have you ever eaten an anchovy?

Content Words

13. Jorge initiated the duel by moving his back foot.
14. Correct posture is important in fencing.
15. Do all fencing clubs teach the same tactics?
16. By using a feint, I was able to score the winning point.
17. Felipe touched Hunter's torso with his blade and scored a point.
18. Martin's dexterity in fencing is remarkable.
19. Mahera played a three-minute bout with Tamar.

Vocabulary Words

20. All fencers must be protected by a fencing uniform.
21. The judge made a declaration that unfair play results in elimination.
22. In fencing, a machine scores the detection of a touch to an opponent.
23. Concentration and clarity of mind are vital when competing.

Challenge Words

24. ____________________
25. ____________________

2 Allow students to self-correct their Pretest. Write each word on the board. Point out that each Pattern Word has been adopted into the English language from the Spanish language. Note the roots *clar* and *tect* in the Vocabulary Words.

3 As a class, read, spell, and read each word. Direct students to highlight misspelled words and rewrite them correctly.

4 Proof each student's Pretest. This becomes an individualized study sheet that can be used at school or at home.

5 Homework suggestion: Duplicate **BLM SP6-01B Flash Cards Template**

on CARD STOCK for students to write the list words, using the flash cards as a study aid. Another option is to use INDEX CARDS.

Day 2 Word Analysis and Vocabulary

Objective

The students will alphabetize **words from Spanish** and complete sentences with content words. Students will use a table to write vocabulary words, match given definitions, and complete sentences. Students will choose list words that match definitions.

Introduction

Remind students that this week's Pattern Words originated as Spanish words. The **words from Spanish** have become common words used in the English language. Display **T-22 Words from Spanish** on the overhead to familiarize students with the Pattern Words. Select volunteers to identify the pictures with **words from Spanish** and answer the following questions:

- Which words end with the /ō/ sound? (**pronto, burrito, sombrero**)
- Which word ends with an r-controlled vowel? (**guitar**)
- Which words end with /ē/ spelled *i* or *y*? (**anchovy, mariachi**)
- Which words end with a schwa sound? (**fiesta, tortilla, alfalfa, enchilada, quesadilla**)
- Which word is one syllable? (**maize**)
- What is the alphabetical order of the words? (**alfalfa, anchovy, burrito, enchilada, fiesta, guitar, maize, mariachi, pronto, quesadilla, sombrero, tortilla**)

Directed Instruction

1 Inform students that the theme of this lesson is fencing. Select seven volunteers, one for each Content Word, to find and read the definition.

2 Proceed to page 129. Say, spell, and say each Pattern, Content, and Vocabulary Word. Provide this week's Challenge Words and have students write them in the spaces provided before completing the page.

Differentiated Instruction

- For students who spelled all the words correctly on the Pretest, select and assign Extra Challenge Words from the following list: sigma, semiconductor, interpretation, privatization, hemoglobin, accompanist.
- For students who spelled less than half correctly, assign the following Pattern, Content, and Vocabulary Words: fiesta, guitar, tortilla, burrito, enchilada, sombrero, bout, torso, tactics, posture, declaration, protected.

On the Posttest, evaluate these students on the twelve words assigned; however, encourage them to attempt to spell all the list words to the best of their ability. They are also responsible for writing the dictated sentences.

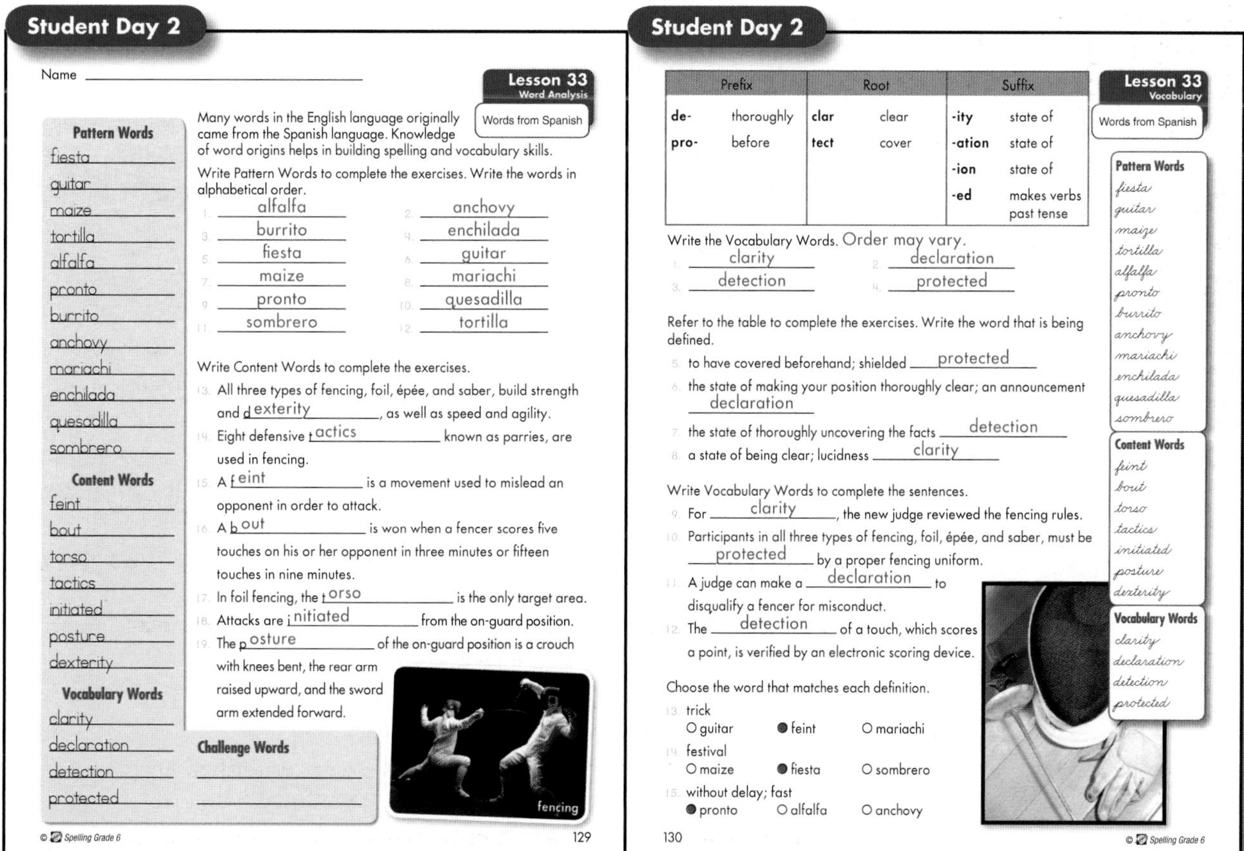

Student Day 2

Name ____________________

Lesson 33 Word Analysis — Words from Spanish

Pattern Words: fiesta, guitar, maize, tortilla, alfalfa, pronto, burrito, anchovy, mariachi, enchilada, quesadilla, sombrero

Content Words: feint, bout, torso, tactics, initiated, posture, dexterity

Vocabulary Words: clarity, declaration, detection, protected

Challenge Words: ____________________

Many words in the English language originally came from the Spanish language. Knowledge of word origins helps in building spelling and vocabulary skills.

Write Pattern Words to complete the exercises. Write the words in alphabetical order.

1. alfalfa
2. anchovy
3. burrito
4. enchilada
5. fiesta
6. guitar
7. maize
8. mariachi
9. pronto
10. quesadilla
11. sombrero
12. tortilla

Write Content Words to complete the exercises.

13. All three types of fencing, foil, épée, and saber, build strength and dexterity, as well as speed and agility.
14. Eight defensive tactics known as parries, are used in fencing.
15. A feint is a movement used to mislead an opponent in order to attack.
16. A bout is won when a fencer scores five touches on his or her opponent in three minutes or fifteen touches in nine minutes.
17. In foil fencing, the torso is the only target area.
18. Attacks are initiated from the on-guard position.
19. The posture of the on-guard position is a crouch with knees bent, the rear arm raised upward, and the sword arm extended forward.

fencing

© Spelling Grade 6 — 129

Student Day 2

Prefix		Root		Suffix	
de-	thoroughly	clar	clear	-ity	state of
pro-	before	tect	cover	-ation	state of
				-ion	state of
				-ed	makes verbs past tense

Lesson 33 Vocabulary — Words from Spanish

Pattern Words: fiesta, guitar, maize, tortilla, alfalfa, pronto, burrito, anchovy, mariachi, enchilada, quesadilla, sombrero

Content Words: feint, bout, torso, tactics, initiated, posture, dexterity

Vocabulary Words: clarity, declaration, detection, protected

Write the Vocabulary Words. Order may vary.

1. clarity
2. declaration
3. detection
4. protected

Refer to the table to complete the exercises. Write the word that is being defined.

5. to have covered beforehand; shielded protected
6. the state of making your position thoroughly clear; an announcement declaration
7. the state of thoroughly uncovering the facts detection
8. a state of being clear; lucidness clarity

Write Vocabulary Words to complete the sentences.

9. For clarity, the new judge reviewed the fencing rules.
10. Participants in all three types of fencing, foil, épée, and saber, must be protected by a proper fencing uniform.
11. A judge can make a declaration to disqualify a fencer for misconduct.
12. The detection of a touch, which scores a point, is verified by an electronic scoring device.

Choose the word that matches each definition.

13. trick
○ guitar ● feint ○ mariachi
14. festival
○ maize ● fiesta ○ sombrero
15. without delay; fast
● pronto ○ alfalfa ○ anchovy

130 — © Spelling Grade 6

Student Spelling Support Materials

BLM SP6-01A

Student Spelling Support

1. Use **BLM SP6-01A A Spelling Study Strategy** in instructional groups to provide assistance with some or all of the words.
2. Invite students to write the Challenge Words, numbers 24 and 25, in the Word Bank, in the back of their textbook.
3. Challenge students to write a descriptive essay describing one of the three styles of fencing—foil, épée, or saber. Students may compile information in the progressive, sport journal that was started in Lesson 1.
4. Write this week's words, categorize the Pattern, Content, and Vocabulary Words, and attach them to the Word Wall.
5. Read Hebrews 4:12: "For the word of God is living and powerful, and sharper than any two-edged sword, piercing even to the division of soul and spirit, and of joints and marrow, and is a discerner of the thoughts and intents of the heart." Discuss ways in which God's Word is active in the hearts, minds, and actions of believers. List these ideas on the board.
6. Invite students to imagine their own fencing match with a classmate and ask them to write their own descriptive journal entry, utilizing three to five list words. Post the journal entries on a bulletin board entitled "On Guard!"

3 Proceed to page 130. Remind students to use the table to assist in building each Vocabulary Word. For example, the root *clar* goes with the suffix *-ity* to build the word *clarity.* Challenge students to state other words with the roots *clar* and *tect.* (**Possible answers: clarify, declare, detective, tectonic**) Allow students to complete the page independently.

4 Homework suggestion: Students use their Spelling Dictionary to write the definition of each word on the back of the corresponding flash card that was suggested for homework on Day 1.

Day 3 Word Study Strategies

Objective

The students will write list words that fit a category and complete riddles.

Introduction

Write the following groups of words on the board:

- kernels, crop, husks (**maize**)
- began, started, commenced (**initiated**)
- shielded, covered, guarded (**protected**)
- methods, maneuvers, strategies (**tactics**)

Have students refer to the list words on page 131 for this activity. Select volunteers to identify the list words that fit each category.

Directed Instruction

1 Read the following riddles aloud and choose volunteers to identify the list word.

- It does not lag behind. (**pronto**)
- It has a neck, but no head. (**guitar**)
- It is always safe. (**protected**)
- It can be rolled up or placed flat. (**tortilla**)

2 Write *maze* and *faint* on the board and ask students to find a list word, found on page 131, that is a homophone for each of the words. Remind students that homophones are words that sound the same but have different meanings and spellings.

- *maze* which means *in a daze; a confusing path* (***maize* which means *Indian corn***)
- *faint* which means *lacking courage; lacking strength* (***feint* which means *a mock attack to distract from what was really intended; a trick***)

3 Proceed to page 131. Provide assistance as students complete the page independently. Choose a volunteer to read Hebrews 4:12 and discuss the power of God's Word to change lives.

Day 4 Writing

Objective

The students will complete sentences in a descriptive journal by writing list words in shape boxes.

Introduction

Invite students to refer to their list words on page 132. Challenge students to listen for the list words as you read the following journal entry:

> Today, I had a three-minute bout with Jody. When I initiated the duel, he struck back. With dexterity, I quickly blocked with a parry and protected my torso. I was able to use several tactics and was excited to be pronounced the winner.

Directed Instruction

1 Select volunteers to name each list word used in the paragraph, write each word on the board, and draw shape boxes around each word. (**bout, initiated, dexterity, protected, torso, tactics**)

2 Proceed to page 132. Students complete the page. Select a volunteer to orally read the journal entry.

3 Homework suggestion: Distribute a copy of **BLM SP6-33A Lesson 33 Homework** to each student.

Day 5 Posttest

Objective

The students will correctly write dictated spelling words and sentences.

Introduction

Review by using flash cards noted in Day 1 and Day 2 Homework suggestion.

Directed Assessment

1 Dictate the list words by using the Pretest sentences or developing original ones. Reserve *declaration, fiesta, guitar, burrito, tactics,* and *bout* for the dictation sentences.

2 Read each sentence. Repeat as needed.

- Our teacher made a declaration to the class.
- The class is to help plan a fiesta.
- Mr. Perez will play his guitar for musical entertainment.
- Alma will make a burrito for each guest.
- Julio and Ramon will demonstrate tactics in fencing.
- Partners can use fake swords to have a bout.

3 If assigned, dictate Extra Challenge Words.

4 Score the test, counting each misspelled word as an error. Correct the dictation sentences by grading only the spelling words or grading the complete sentences.

Notes

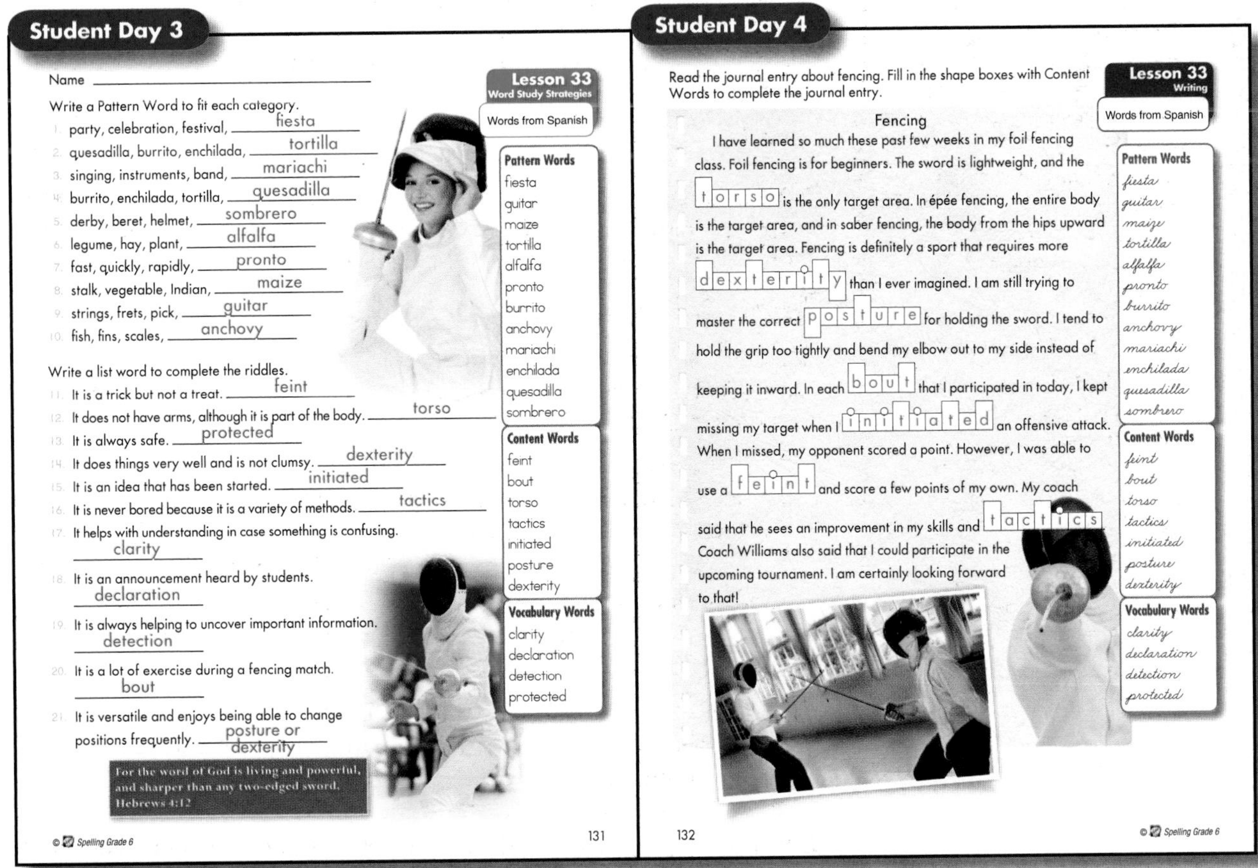

Student Day 3
Name
Lesson 33
Word Study Strategies
Words from Spanish
Write a Pattern Word to fit each category.
1. party, celebration, festival, fiesta
2. quesadilla, burrito, enchilada, tortilla
3. singing, instruments, band, mariachi
4. burrito, enchilada, tortilla, quesadilla
5. derby, beret, helmet, sombrero
6. legume, hay, plant, alfalfa
7. fast, quickly, rapidly, pronto
8. stalk, vegetable, Indian, maize
9. strings, frets, pick, guitar
10. fish, fins, scales, anchovy
Write a list word to complete the riddles.
11. It is a trick but not a treat. feint
12. It does not have arms, although it is part of the body. torso
13. It is always safe. protected
14. It does things very well and is not clumsy. dexterity
15. It is an idea that has been started. initiated
16. It is never bored because it is a variety of methods. tactics
17. It helps with understanding in case something is confusing. clarity
18. It is an announcement heard by students. declaration
19. It is always helping to uncover important information. detection
20. It is a lot of exercise during a fencing match. bout
21. It is versatile and enjoys being able to change positions frequently. posture or dexterity
Pattern Words
fiesta
guitar
maize
tortilla
alfalfa
pronto
burrito
anchovy
mariachi
enchilada
quesadilla
sombrero
Content Words
feint
bout
torso
tactics
initiated
posture
dexterity
Vocabulary Words
clarity
declaration
detection
protected
For the word of God is living and powerful, and sharper than any two-edged sword. Hebrews 4:12
© Spelling Grade 6
131
Student Day 4
Read the journal entry about fencing. Fill in the shape boxes with Content Words to complete the journal entry.
Lesson 33
Writing
Words from Spanish
Fencing
I have learned so much these past few weeks in my foil fencing class. Foil fencing is for beginners. The sword is lightweight, and the torso is the only target area. In épée fencing, the entire body is the target area, and in saber fencing, the body from the hips upward is the target area. Fencing is definitely a sport that requires more dexterity than I ever imagined. I am still trying to master the correct posture for holding the sword. I tend to hold the grip too tightly and bend my elbow out to my side instead of keeping it inward. In each bout that I participated in today, I kept missing my target when I initiated an offensive attack. When I missed, my opponent scored a point. However, I was able to use a feint and score a few points of my own. My coach said that he sees an improvement in my skills and tactics. Coach Williams also said that I could participate in the upcoming tournament. I am certainly looking forward to that!
Pattern Words
fiesta
guitar
maize
tortilla
alfalfa
pronto
burrito
anchovy
mariachi
enchilada
quesadilla
sombrero
Content Words
feint
bout
torso
tactics
initiated
posture
dexterity
Vocabulary Words
clarity
declaration
detection
protected
132
© Spelling Grade 6

Lesson **34**

Words from German

Student Pages

Pages 133–136

Lesson Materials

BLM SP6-01B
Card stock
Index cards
T-23
T-24
BLM SP6-34A

Sports

The theme of this lesson is archery. Archery involves the skill of using a bow and arrow. Ancient Egyptians were the first known society to use archery for hunting and for military defense. The Old Testament refers to the Hebrews as skilled archers. With the invention of gunpowder, archery ceased being the most important military defense and is presently enjoyed by many as an amateur sport. However, in parts of Africa and South America, archery is still used for hunting and defense.

Day 1 Pretest

Objective

The students will accurately spell and write **words from German**. They will spell and write content, vocabulary, and challenge words.

Introduction

Before class, select Challenge Words for numbers 24 and 25 from a cross-curricular subject, words misspelled on previous assignments, or words that interest your students. The word *glockenspiel* is from the **German** language and is suggested for number 24. Administer the Pretest.

Directed Instruction

1 Say each word, use it in a sentence, and then repeat the word.

Pattern Words

1. Sunny ate a cherry strudel for dessert.
2. Phillip ordered sauerkraut and sausage from the menu.
3. Josie enjoyed a big soft pretzel as she watched the archers practice.
4. Uncle Delmar drove his diesel to the archery tournament.
5. Seltzer is used in carbonated beverages such as soda pop.
6. After I sneezed, Delaney said, "Gesundheit!"
7. After archery practice, our family ate lunch at a delicatessen.
8. Laura ordered a turkey sandwich with pumpernickel bread.
9. Kurt likes to eat his hamburger with mustard and ketchup.
10. Did you know that liverwurst is high in iron and vitamin A?
11. An edelweiss grows in high altitudes above the tree line.
12. Corinne ordered a frankfurter when her team went out to eat.

Content Words

13. Dena bought a bow made of graphite at the sporting goods store.
14. The tension of the bow propelled the arrow toward the target.
15. Jackson placed ten arrows in the quiver.
16. Sadie placed the notch at the end of the arrow into the bowstring.
17. How many categories are in archery competitions?
18. The bull's eye is in the middle of concentric circles.
19. The bowstring must be taut before the arrow is released.

Vocabulary Words

20. The retired archer will regenerate his skills by practicing.
21. Each generation must teach others about the good news of Jesus.
22. The archery team demonstrated their skills at the county exposition.
23. The coach's proposition to have a pizza party excited the archers.

Challenge Words

24. ______________________
25. ______________________

2 Allow students to self-correct their Pretest. Write each word on the board. Point out that each Pattern Word has been adopted into the English language from the German language. Note the roots *gen* and *posit* in the Vocabulary Words. *Generation* contains two suffixes, *-er* and *-ation*. *Regenerate* contains two suffixes, *-er* and *-ate*.

3 As a class, read, spell, and read each word. Direct students to highlight misspelled words and rewrite them correctly.

4 Proof each student's Pretest. This becomes an individualized study sheet that can be used at school or at home.

5 Homework suggestion: Duplicate **BLM SP6-01B Flash Cards Template** on CARD STOCK for students to write the list words, using the flash cards as a study aid. Another option is to use INDEX CARDS.

Day 2 Word Analysis and Vocabulary

Objective

The students will sort **words from German** by the number of syllables and complete sentences with content words. Students will use a table to write vocabulary words, select words to match definitions, and complete sentences in context. They will choose the best meaning for words.

Introduction

Remind students that this week's Pattern Words originated as German words. The **words from German** have become common words used in the English language. Display **T-23 Words from German** on the overhead to familiarize students with the Pattern Words. Select volunteers to identify the pictures and answer the following questions:

- Which words contain an r-controlled vowel? (**seltzer, liverwurst, sauerkraut, hamburger, frankfurter, pumpernickel**)
- Which words end with schwa plus *l*? (**diesel, strudel, pretzel, pumpernickel**)
- Which word begins with the letter *e* but is pronounced /ā/? (**edelweiss**)
- Which words contain the letter *s* pronounced /z/? (**diesel, gesundheit**)
- Which words contain the letter *z* pronounced /s/? (**seltzer, pretzel**)
- Which five-syllable word contains two schwas spelled *a* and *e*? (**delicatessen**)
- Which word is more commonly known by its first four letters? (**delicatessen**)

Directed Instruction

1 Inform students that the theme of this lesson is archery. Select seven volunteers to each read the definition of an assigned Content Word from the Spelling Dictionary. Challenge students to name a

Differentiated Instruction

- For students who spelled all the words correctly on the Pretest, select and assign Extra Challenge Words from the following list: sinusoidal, solubility, literary, referendum, neural, beauteous.
- For students who spelled less than half correctly, assign the following Pattern, Content, and Vocabulary Words: diesel, strudel, pretzel, sauerkraut, hamburger, frankfurter, taut, notch, quiver, concentric, generation, exposition. On the Posttest, evaluate these students on the twelve words assigned; however, encourage them to attempt to spell all the list words to the best of their ability. They are also responsible for writing the dictated sentences.

Student Day 2

Name ______________________

Lesson 34 Word Analysis — Words from German

Pattern Words: diesel, seltzer, strudel, pretzel, edelweiss, liverwurst, gesundheit, sauerkraut, hamburger, frankfurter, delicatessen, pumpernickel

Content Words: taut, notch, quiver, tension, graphite, concentric, categories

Vocabulary Words: generation, regenerate, exposition, proposition

Challenge Words

Many words in the English language originally came from the German language. Knowledge of word origins helps in building spelling and vocabulary skills.

Write Pattern Words to complete the exercises. Sort the words by the number of syllables.

1–4 Two Syllables	5–10 Three Syllables
1. diesel	2. seltzer
3. strudel	4. pretzel
5. edelweiss	6. liverwurst
7. gesundheit	8. sauerkraut
9. hamburger	10. frankfurter
11 Four Syllables	**12 Five Syllables**
11. pumpernickel	12. delicatessen

Write Content Words to complete the exercises.

13. Arrows are made of aluminum or carbon graphite and are kept in a quiver.
14. A notch at the end of the arrow allows the arrow to be fitted to the bowstring.
15. The string or cord on a bow must be taut so that when tension is applied, the arrow is propelled forward.
16. Archers shoot arrows at a target that usually consists of a bull's eye and a series of concentric circles.
17. Target, field, and flight shooting are categories in archery competitions.

archery

© Spelling Grade 6 133

Student Day 2

Lesson 34 Vocabulary — Words from German

Prefix		Root		Suffix	
re-	again	gen	birth	-er	that which, action
ex-	out of	posit	place	-ation	state of
pro-	for			-ate	to make
				-ion	state of

Write the Vocabulary Words. Order may vary.

1. generation 2. regenerate
3. exposition 4. proposition

Refer to the table to complete the exercises. Match each word to its definition.

d 5. exposition — a. to make or produce again
b 6. generation — b. the state of time between the birth of parents and their offspring
a 7. regenerate — c. the state of something being placed or offered for consideration; proposal
c 8. proposition — d. the state of placing items out in the view of the public; a fair or exhibition

Write Vocabulary Words to complete the sentences.

9. The archery coach offered Terrell and the team a proposition to perform at the Kern County Fair.
10. The exposition will be at the fairground in two weeks.
11. Because they had been on vacation, the team will practice daily in order to regenerate their championship archery skills.
12. Terrell's parents were also archery champions, making Terrell an archer for the second generation.

Choose the best meaning for each word.

13. pumpernickel
- ● a dark sourdough bread
- ○ a glazed donut
- ○ a long twisted pastry

14. edelweiss
- ○ a pastry
- ● a flower
- ○ an animal

Pattern Words: diesel, seltzer, strudel, pretzel, edelweiss, liverwurst, gesundheit, sauerkraut, hamburger, frankfurter, delicatessen, pumpernickel
Content Words: taut, notch, quiver, tension, graphite, concentric, categories
Vocabulary Words: generation, regenerate, exposition, proposition

134 © Spelling Grade 6

Student Spelling Support Materials

BLM SP6-01A
Pretzels

Student Spelling Support

1. Use **BLM SP6-01A A Spelling Study Strategy** in instructional groups to provide assistance with some or all of the words.
2. Invite students to write the Challenge Words, numbers 24 and 25, in the Word Bank, in the back of their textbook.
3. Instruct students to research the origin of the **pretzel** and write a descriptive paragraph about why it was made to resemble praying hands. Share the research in class while eating PRETZELS.
4. Write this week's words, categorize the Pattern, Content, and Vocabulary Words, and attach them to the Word Wall.
5. Read I Chronicles 12:1–2: "Now these were the men who came to David at Ziklag while he was still a fugitive from Saul the son of Kish; and they were among the mighty men, helpers in the war, armed with bows, using both the right hand and the left in hurling stones and shooting arrows with the bow. They were of Benjamin, Saul's brethren." Explain that in the midst of David fleeing from and being persecuted by Saul, men came to assist David during this trying time. As a believer in Christ, one needs to not fear in times of personal trials. The Lord is one's help in time of need. He will provide assistance when one least expects it. God knows the needs of His people and provides for them exactly what is needed in due time. Ask students to write a prayer in letter

Cont. on page 137

homophone for *taut*, give the correct spelling, and state its meaning. (**taught—past tense of TEACH; to have imparted knowledge**)

2 Proceed to page 133. Say, spell, and say each Pattern, Content, and Vocabulary Word. Provide this week's Challenge Words and have students write them in the spaces provided before completing the page. When complete, select volunteers to orally read exercises 13–17.

3 Proceed to page 134. Remind students to use the table to assist in building each Vocabulary Word. For example, the root *gen* goes with the suffix *-er* and the suffix *-ation* to build the word *generation*. Remind students that *generation* and *regenerate* each have two suffixes. Allow students to complete the page independently.

4 Homework suggestion: Students use their Spelling Dictionary to write the definition of each word on the back of the corresponding flash card that was suggested for homework on Day 1.

Day 3 Word Study Strategies

Objective

The students will utilize dictionary skills by answering questions about the different components of a dictionary entry. They will write list words that match descriptions of sets of words.

Introduction

Select a variety of Pattern, Content, and Vocabulary Words from this lesson. As each one is pronounced, instruct students to locate the word in the Spelling Dictionary. Select volunteers to name the following components for each word: entry word, pronunciation, part of speech, definition, sample sentence.

Directed Instruction

1 Write the following words and descriptions on the board: strudel, pumpernickel, tension.
- sourdough, rye, flour, _______ (**pumpernickel**)
- pastry, rolled, filling, _______ (**strudel**)
- stretched, stiffness, tautness, _______ (**tension**)

2 Invite three volunteers to locate *strudel, pumpernickel,* and *tension* in the Spelling Dictionary, read the definitions aloud, and write the list word next to the correct description.

3 Proceed to page 135. Instruct students to independently complete the page. Assist as needed.

Day 4 Writing

Objective

The students will write list words to replace definitions in a descriptive friendly letter, as well as compose their own letter using list words.

Introduction

Display **T-24 A Friendly Letter About Archery** on the overhead. Cover the answers at the bottom of the page. Have students refer to the list words and to the Spelling Dictionary for this activity. Select a volunteer to read the letter in its entirety to familiarize students with the content. Read the letter a second time, stopping at each bold definition. Invite students to determine which list word is defined and look it up in the Spelling Dictionary. If the list word matches the definition given, write the answer on the board. Reread the letter replacing each definition with the list word.

Directed Instruction

1 Proceed to page 136. Select a volunteer to read the sentences at the top of the page. Instruct students to refer to the Spelling Dictionary as needed. When completed, select a volunteer to read the letter, inserting the list word for each definition.

2 As a writing extension, invite students to write a letter home describing their own imaginative adventures at an archery camp. Encourage students to use several list words. Select volunteers to orally read their letters.

3 Homework suggestion: Distribute a copy of **BLM SP6-34A Lesson 34 Homework** to each student.

Day 5 Posttest

Objective

The students will correctly write dictated spelling words and sentences.

Introduction

Review by using flash cards noted in Day 1 and Day 2 Homework suggestion.

Directed Assessment

1 Dictate the list words by using the Pretest sentences or developing original ones. Reserve *diesel, exposition, quiver, taut, hamburger,* and *pretzel* for the dictation sentences.

2 Read each sentence. Repeat as needed.

- Mel drove his diesel to the archery contest.
- The contest was at the county's summer exposition.
- When he arrived, he took his bow and quiver with him.
- Before it was his turn to compete, Mel made sure the bowstring was taut.
- Mel ate a hamburger while he waited for his turn to compete.
- Mel celebrated his win by buying each teammate a large soft pretzel.

3 If assigned, dictate Extra Challenge Words.

4 Score the test, counting each misspelled word as an error. Correct the dictation sentences by grading only the spelling words or grading the complete sentences.

Student Spelling Support

Cont. from page 136

format, describing one personal trial and how He met their needs.

Student Day 3

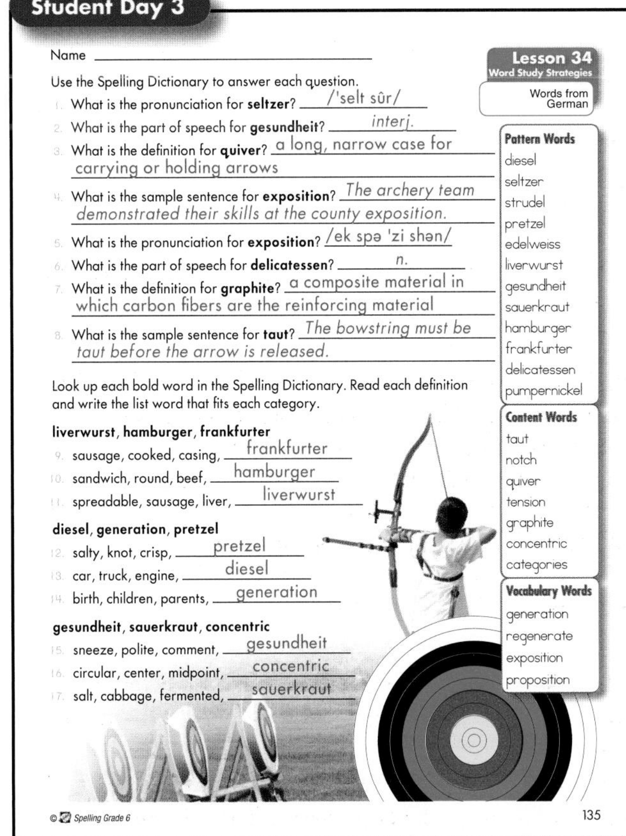

Name ______________

Lesson 34
Word Study Strategies
Words from German

Use the Spelling Dictionary to answer each question.

1. What is the pronunciation for **seltzer**? /'selt sûr/
2. What is the part of speech for **gesundheit**? interj.
3. What is the definition for **quiver**? a long, narrow case for carrying or holding arrows
4. What is the sample sentence for **exposition**? The archery team demonstrated their skills at the county exposition.
5. What is the pronunciation for **exposition**? /ek spə 'zi shən/
6. What is the part of speech for **delicatessen**? n.
7. What is the definition for **graphite**? a composite material in which carbon fibers are the reinforcing material
8. What is the sample sentence for **taut**? The bowstring must be taut before the arrow is released.

Look up each bold word in the Spelling Dictionary. Read each definition and write the list word that fits each category.

liverwurst, hamburger, frankfurter

9. sausage, cooked, casing, frankfurter
10. sandwich, round, beef, hamburger
11. spreadable, sausage, liver, liverwurst

diesel, generation, pretzel

12. salty, knot, crisp, pretzel
13. car, truck, engine, diesel
14. birth, children, parents, generation

gesundheit, sauerkraut, concentric

15. sneeze, polite, comment, gesundheit
16. circular, center, midpoint, concentric
17. salt, cabbage, fermented, sauerkraut

Pattern Words: diesel, seltzer, strudel, pretzel, edelweiss, liverwurst, gesundheit, sauerkraut, hamburger, frankfurter, delicatessen, pumpernickel

Content Words: taut, notch, quiver, tension, graphite, concentric, categories

Vocabulary Words: generation, regenerate, exposition, proposition

© Spelling Grade 6 135

Student Day 4

Lesson 34
Writing
Words from German

Phillip wrote a descriptive, friendly letter to his parents. Read the letter. Write the list words that could replace the bold word or words in each sentence. Use the Spelling Dictionary.

Dear Mom and Dad,

I am having a lot of fun at camp this summer. All the counselors and campers have Native American names. My counselor, Sitting Bull, suggested three names that he thought I might like to be called. His **proposal** for *White Cloud* intrigued me, so I chose that one. There is so much to do here that I am never bored. My favorite activity is archery. The campers were divided into **classifications**, depending on their experience. I am in the novice group, called Papoose. At first, I just shot arrows toward the target. Sitting Bull helped me realize that there is actual skill involved. I learned how to place the **V-shaped cut** at the end of the arrow into the bowstring, pull back until the bowstring is **stretched tightly**, let my fingers roll off the string, and remain still until the arrow reaches the target. I am amazed at how the **act of being stretched to stiffness** of the bow is what propels the arrow forward. It is amazing how much strength it actually takes to do archery! When everyone's **long, narrow case for carrying or holding arrows** is empty, then we are allowed to take a closer look at our targets and collect our arrows. I hope I can get a bull's eye before camp is over on Saturday!

The food has been really good here at camp. For dinner, I ate a **sandwich consisting of a ground beef patty on a round bun**, and enjoyed a **rolled pastry made from thin dough that contains a filling** for dessert. Tonight we are going to roast marshmallows around a campfire and make s'mores. I really enjoy the campfire each night because we share about how God is working in each of our lives. There have been three campers who gave their lives to Christ. It is so awesome to see the next **group of people born at approximately the same time** become believers. I will see you on Saturday.

Love,
Phillip

1. proposition
2. categories
3. notch
4. taut
5. tension
6. quiver
7. hamburger
8. strudel
9. generation
10. On a separate piece of paper, write a letter home describing your imaginative adventures at an archery camp.

Pattern Words: diesel, seltzer, strudel, pretzel, edelweiss, liverwurst, gesundheit, sauerkraut, hamburger, frankfurter, delicatessen, pumpernickel

Content Words: taut, notch, quiver, tension, graphite, concentric, categories

Vocabulary Words: generation, regenerate, exposition, proposition

136 © Spelling Grade 6

Lesson 35

Words from Asian Languages

Student Pages

Pages 137–140

Lesson Materials

BLM SP6-01B
Card stock
Index cards
T-25
BLM SP6-35A

Sports

The theme of this lesson is martial arts. Martial arts is a broad group of sports that involve combat. Martial arts is grouped into two main categories, those involving striking, such as karate and kung fu, and those involving wrestling, such as aikido. Most martial arts originated in East Asia, but they are now popular in many countries throughout the world. Martial arts is practiced for the purposes of self-defense, exercise, competition, and enjoyment.

Day 1 Pretest

Objective

The students will accurately spell and write **words from Asian languages.** They will spell and write content, vocabulary, and challenge words.

Introduction

Before class, select Challenge Words for numbers 24 and 25 from a cross-curricular subject, words misspelled on previous assignments, or words that interest your students. The word *origami* is from the **Japanese** language and is suggested for number 24. Administer the Pretest.

Directed Instruction

1 Say each word, use it in a sentence, and then repeat the word.

Pattern Words

1. Jia trains her bonsai to look like a windblown cypress tree.
2. The Katakias vacation in their bungalow in India.
3. Jung dropped the chopsticks on the table.
4. Chow mein is a simple dish to make.
5. We use a futon as a bed for our guests.
6. When we learned of a Bible study, we were gung ho to get started.
7. Valerie went to study karate at a dojo.
8. Aikido is a martial art that originated in Japan.
9. A wooden staff may be used for sparring in kung fu.
10. Tasvee wore her silk pajamas from India to bed.
11. Anjali loves teriyaki beef over rice.
12. The veranda was the coolest place to be on a hot summer night.

Content Words

13. Students must demonstrate competency to receive a black belt.
14. Karishma faced a dilemma with courage.
15. A distinctive feature of kendo is the use of bamboo sticks as swords.
16. Excellence in martial arts requires methodical training.
17. Nathan's participation in martial arts has helped his balance.
18. Practitioners of martial arts are skilled in self-defense.
19. Are many of the movements in martial arts rhythmic?

Vocabulary Words

20. Soon-Yee did not want to disgrace her family by behaving badly.
21. The sixth grade class is known for its gracious behavior.
22. Ravinder hopes to specialize in New Testament history.
23. Hong Choi's specialty is tae kwon do.

Challenge Words

24. ______________________________
25. ______________________________

2 Allow students to self-correct their Pretest. Write each word on the board. Point out that the Pattern Words originally came from Japanese, Chinese, or Hindi. The words from Japanese are *futon, aikido, bonsai, karate,* and *teriyaki.* The words from Chinese are *kung fu, gung ho, chopsticks,* and *chow mein.* The words from Hindi, spoken in India, are *veranda, pajamas,* and *bungalow.* Note the roots *grac* and *spec* in the Vocabulary Words. The silent *e* in the word *disgrace* is not included in the original root spelling of *grac. Specialize* has two suffixes, *-ial* and *-ize. Specialty* has two suffixes, *-ial* and *-ty.*

3 As a class, read, spell, and read each word. Direct students to highlight misspelled words and rewrite them correctly.

4 Proof each student's Pretest. This becomes an individualized study sheet that can be used at school or at home.

5 Homework suggestion: Duplicate **BLM SP6-01B Flash Cards Template** on CARD STOCK for students to write the list words, using the flash cards as a study aid. Another option is to use INDEX CARDS.

Day 2 Word Analysis and Vocabulary

Objective

The students will sort **words from Asian languages** and complete sentences with content words. They will use a table to write vocabulary words, match given definitions in context, and choose the best meaning for underlined words.

Introduction

Remind students that the Pattern Words are derived from the Japanese, Chinese, and Hindi languages. Etymology, or studying word origins, helps in developing spelling and vocabulary skills. Display **T-25 Words from Asian Languages** on the overhead to familiarize students with the Pattern Words. Ask the following questions:

- Which **words from Asian languages** end in vowels? (**aikido, bonsai, karate, teriyaki, kung fu, gung ho, veranda**) Do you hear the vowels in these words or are they silent? (**They are heard.**)
- Which words from Chinese are open compound words? (**kung fu, gung ho, chow mein**)
- Which words from Hindi relate to architecture? (**veranda, bungalow**)

Directed Instruction

1 Instruct students to have the flash cards on hand for this activity. Review that the first five Pattern Words, found on page 137, are derived from Japanese, the next four words are from Chinese, and the last three words are from Hindi. Invite students to work in pairs to find each Pattern Word in the Spelling Dictionary and to pronounce the word to their partner. Instruct students to sort the Pattern Word

Differentiated Instruction

- For students who spelled all the words correctly on the Pretest, select and assign Extra Challenge Words from the following list: spurious, subatomic, juxtaposition, constituency, athleticism, decibel.
- For students who spelled less than half correctly, assign the following Pattern, Content, and Vocabulary Words: futon, karate, gung ho, veranda, pajamas, bungalow, dilemma, distinctive, methodical, participation, gracious, specialty. On the Posttest, evaluate these students on the twelve words assigned; however, encourage them to attempt to spell all the list words to the best of their ability. They are also responsible for writing the dictated sentences.

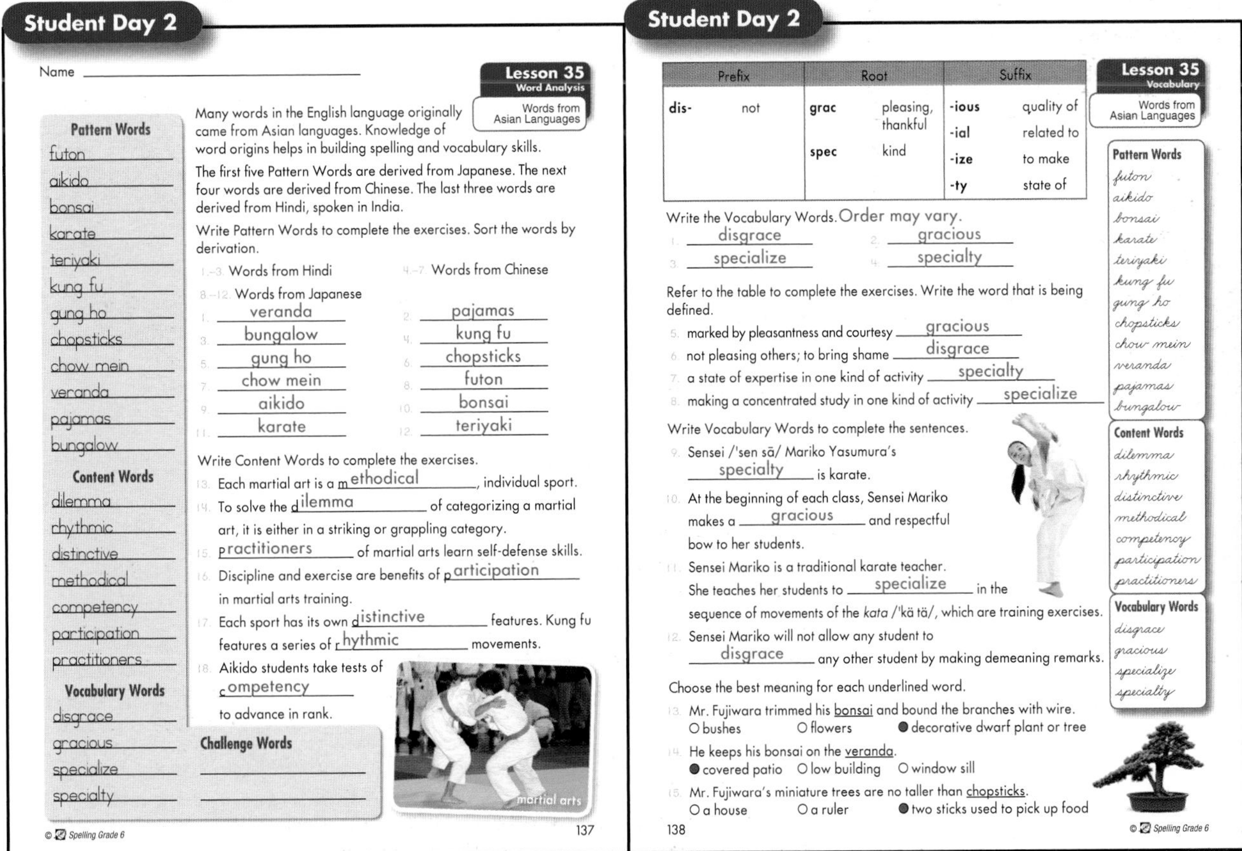

Student Day 2

Name ____________

Lesson 35 Word Analysis

Words from Asian Languages

Pattern Words: futon, aikido, bonsai, karate, teriyaki, kung fu, gung ho, chopsticks, chow mein, veranda, pajamas, bungalow

Content Words: dilemma, rhythmic, distinctive, methodical, competency, participation, practitioners

Vocabulary Words: disgrace, gracious, specialize, specialty

Many words in the English language originally came from Asian languages. Knowledge of word origins helps in building spelling and vocabulary skills.

The first five Pattern Words are derived from Japanese. The next four words are derived from Chinese. The last three words are derived from Hindi, spoken in India.

Write Pattern Words to complete the exercises. Sort the words by derivation.

1–3 Words from Hindi 4–7 Words from Chinese 8–12 Words from Japanese

1. veranda 2. pajamas
3. bungalow 4. kung fu
5. gung ho 6. chopsticks
7. chow mein 8. futon
9. aikido 10. bonsai
11. karate 12. teriyaki

Write Content Words to complete the exercises.

13. Each martial art is a methodical, individual sport.
14. To solve the dilemma of categorizing a martial art, it is either in a striking or grappling category.
15. practitioners of martial arts learn self-defense skills.
16. Discipline and exercise are benefits of participation in martial arts training.
17. Each sport has its own distinctive features. Kung fu features a series of rhythmic movements.
18. Aikido students take tests of competency to advance in rank.

Challenge Words

martial arts

© Spelling Grade 6 137

Student Day 2

Prefix		Root		Suffix	
dis-	not	grac	pleasing, thankful	-ious	quality of
		spec	kind	-ial	related to
				-ize	to make
				-ty	state of

Write the Vocabulary Words. Order may vary.

1. disgrace 2. gracious
3. specialize 4. specialty

Refer to the table to complete the exercises. Write the word that is being defined.

5. marked by pleasantness and courtesy gracious
6. not pleasing others; to bring shame disgrace
7. a state of expertise in one kind of activity specialty
8. making a concentrated study in one kind of activity specialize

Write Vocabulary Words to complete the sentences.

9. Sensei /'sen sā/ Mariko Yasumura's specialty is karate.
10. At the beginning of each class, Sensei Mariko makes a gracious and respectful bow to her students.
11. Sensei Mariko is a traditional karate teacher. She teaches her students to specialize in the sequence of movements of the *kata* /'kä tä/, which are training exercises.
12. Sensei Mariko will not allow any student to disgrace any other student by making demeaning remarks.

Choose the best meaning for each underlined word.

13. Mr. Fujiwara trimmed his bonsai and bound the branches with wire.
○ bushes ○ flowers ● decorative dwarf plant or tree
14. He keeps his bonsai on the veranda.
● covered patio ○ low building ○ window sill
15. Mr. Fujiwara's miniature trees are no taller than chopsticks.
○ a house ○ a ruler ● two sticks used to pick up food

Lesson 35 Vocabulary

Words from Asian Languages

Pattern Words: futon, aikido, bonsai, karate, teriyaki, kung fu, gung ho, chopsticks, chow mein, veranda, pajamas, bungalow

Content Words: dilemma, rhythmic, distinctive, methodical, competency, participation, practitioners

Vocabulary Words: disgrace, gracious, specialize, specialty

138 © Spelling Grade 6

Student Spelling Support Materials

BLM SP6-01A
BLM SP6-08B

Student Spelling Support

1. Use **BLM SP6-01A A Spelling Study Strategy** in instructional groups to provide assistance with some or all of the words.
2. Invite students to write the Challenge Words, numbers 24 and 25, in the Word Bank, in the back of their textbook.
3. Challenge students to research and write about two different martial arts such as **kung fu** and **karate**. Provide a copy of **BLM SP6-08B Venn Diagram** for students to compare and contrast various elements of the two sports. Students may compile information in the progressive, sport journal that was started in Lesson 1. As a culminating activity for the year, invite students to share their sport journal with a classmate.
4. Write this week's words, categorize the Pattern, Content, and Vocabulary Words, and attach them to the Word Wall.

flash cards into three groups, words from Japanese, from Chinese, and from Hindi. Students underline each group in a separate color.

2 Proceed to page 137. Say, spell, and say each Pattern, Content, and Vocabulary Word. Provide this week's Challenge Words and have students write them in the spaces provided before completing the page.

3 Proceed to page 138. Remind students to use the table to assist in building each Vocabulary Word. For example, the prefix *dis-* goes with the root *grac* to build the word *disgrace*. Remind students that silent *e* in the word *disgrace* is not in the original root spelling of *grac*. Allow students to complete the page independently.

4 Homework suggestion: Students use their Spelling Dictionary to write the definition of each word on the back of the corresponding flash card that was suggested for homework on Day 1.

Day 3 Word Study Strategies

Objective

The students will use the Spelling Dictionary to correctly place words in sentence context. They will combine independent and dependent clauses into complex sentences, using subordinating conjunctions.

Introduction

Write the following words and incomplete sentence on the board, leaving blanks where indicated: practitioners, dilemma.

- Choosing which martial art to study is a _______ that I hope to solve by asking _______ of each sport for their opinion of the best sport to study. (**dilemma, practitioners**)

Select a student to find the definition of the words in the Spelling Dictionary and to fill in the blanks.

Directed Instruction

1 Review that a complex sentence is a combination of an independent and a dependent clause. Write the following complex sentence on the board:

- Although they are skilled in kung fu, they specialize in aikido.

Explain that this complex sentence begins with the subordinating conjunction *although*. The subordinating conjunction precedes the dependent clause, so there is a comma after the dependent clause. When an independent clause begins the sentence, no comma is needed. Encourage students to list several subordinating conjunctions, such as *after, although, as, because, since, when, where,* and *while*. Choose a volunteer to circle the subordinating conjunction, underline the independent clause once, and underline the dependent clause twice.

2 Proceed to page 139. Students complete the page. When completed, invite students to read exercises 3–6 and make corrections as needed.

Day 4 Writing

Objective

The students will write Pattern Words to complete two imaginary tales and a fable.

Introduction

Read the following imaginary tale aloud:

Li was a poor child from a tiny village. She had no playmates and often felt lonely. One day as she ate chow mein, a tear rolled down her cheek and fell onto her chopsticks. The chopsticks quivered and began to sing a funny little song. Li giggled with delight, and soon her loneliness melted away.

Invite students to share the element of the tale that classifies it as an imaginary tale. (**The chopsticks quivered and began to sing a funny little song.**) This literary element is called personification. *Personification* is giving human qualities to something nonhuman.

Directed Instruction

1 Proceed to page 140. Explain that the first and third selections are imaginary tales, and that the second is a fable, a story with a moral. Challenge students to identify exaggeration, personification, and the moral within the three selections. (**Selection one: exaggeration—The wind lifts the child; selection two: moral—Jun helps others; selection three: personification—The cricket tries to obey a command.**)

2 Homework suggestion: Distribute a copy of **BLM SP6-35A Lesson 35 Homework** to each student.

Day 5 Posttest

Objective

The students will correctly write dictated spelling words and sentences.

Introduction

Review by using flash cards noted in Day 1 and Day 2 Homework suggestion.

Directed Assessment

1 Dictate the list words by using the Pretest sentences or developing original ones. Reserve *gung ho, karate, pajamas, distinctive, participation,* and *specialty* for the dictation sentences.

2 Read each sentence. Repeat as needed.

- Kang was gung ho to go to the gym after school.
- His mother had enrolled him in karate.
- Kang put on a uniform that looked like pajamas.
- He knew many of the distinctive movements of the sport.
- Kang was sure his participation in class would help him learn.
- He wanted this sport to become his specialty.

3 If assigned, dictate Extra Challenge Words.

4 Score the test, counting each misspelled word as an error. Correct the dictation sentences by grading only the spelling words or grading the complete sentences.

Notes

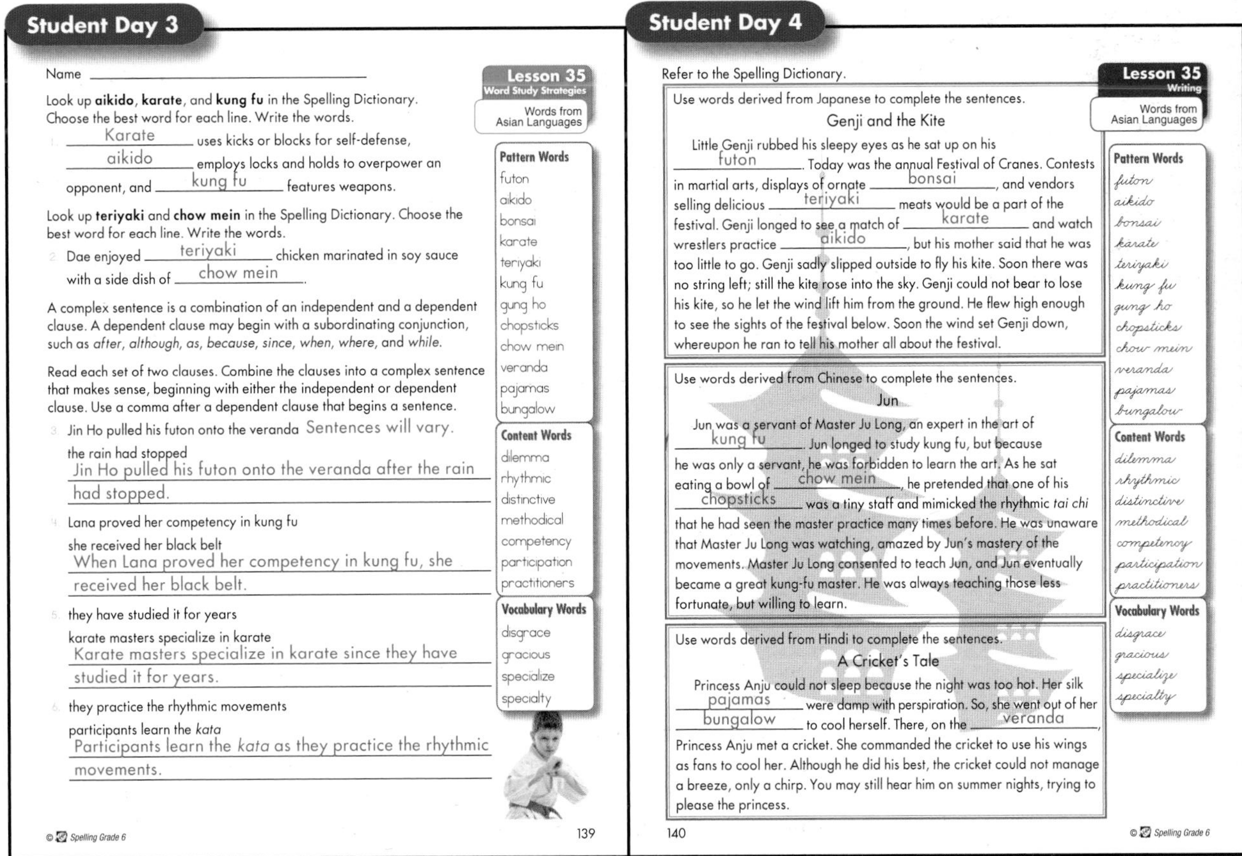

Lesson 36 Review Lessons 31–35

Student Pages

Pages 141–144

Lesson Materials

T-26
BLM SP6-36A
BLM SP6-36B
T-5
BLM SP6-36C
3" × 5" Index cards
BLM SP6-36D
BLMs SP6-36E–F
BLM SP6-06G
BLM SP6-36G

Day 1 Frequently Misspelled Words

Objective

The students will spell, identify, sort, and write **frequently misspelled words**.

Introduction

Teacher Note: This week's lesson incorporates the Pattern, Content, and Vocabulary Words taught in Lessons 31–35 using a variety of activities such as sorting, filling in missing letters, a word search, filling in the correct answer circle, shape boxes, unscrambling words, and writing missing affixes or roots.

Display **T-26 Lessons 31–35 Study Sheet** on the overhead to review Lesson 31 words in unison using the say-spell-say technique. To assist students, review the unique aspects of the following **frequently misspelled words**:

- *privilege*—Latin root *leg*
- *sincerely*—soft *c*
- *necessary*—soft *c*, double *s*
- *meticulous*—*ous* ending
- *definitely*—Latin root *fin*
- *miniature*—letter *a* in the third syllable
- *separately*—Latin root *par*
- *restaurant*—*aur* spelling
- *conscientious*—Latin root *sci, ious* ending
- *embarrassed*—double *r,* double *s*
- *perseverance*—prefix *per, ance* ending
- *congratulations*—Latin root *grat*

Directed Instruction

1 Invite students to identify the following from Lesson 31 words: words that contain three syllables (**privilege, sincerely, restaurant, embarrassed**), words that contain four syllables (**definitely, miniature, necessary, separately, meticulous, conscientious, perseverance**), word that contains five syllables (**congratulations**).

2 Proceed to page 141. Explain that the box contains all the Pattern, Content, and Vocabulary Words in Lessons 31–35. This list is the same list of words that was previously displayed on the overhead. Encourage students to use this list as a review tool. Instruct students to read the directions and independently complete the page.

3 Distribute a copy of **BLM SP6-36A Lessons 31–35 Study Sheet** to each student to take home for study.

4 Homework suggestion: Distribute a copy of **BLM SP6-36B Lesson 36 Homework I** to each student to practice **frequently misspelled words, words from French and Italian, words from Spanish**, and **words from German**. Remind students to review their weekly sets of flash cards from Lessons 31–35.

Day 2 Words from French and Italian and Words from Spanish

Objective

The students will write missing letters to complete **words from French and Italian**. They will find and circle **words from Spanish** in a word search.

Introduction

Display **T-26 Lessons 31–35 Study Sheet** to review Lessons 32–33 words in unison, using the say-spell-say technique. Remind students that these words are derived from French, Italian, and Spanish. Derivation is the act of determining the source or origin of a word. Etymology, or studying word origins, helps in developing spelling and vocabulary skills.

Directed Instruction

1 Write the following incomplete words from Lesson 32 on the board:

- b ___ ___ ___ ___ e t **(bouquet)**
- ___ o ___ ___ n d ___ **(rotunda)**

Select volunteers to refer to Lesson 32 words on **T-26 Lessons 31–35 Study Sheet** to complete the words by filling in the missing letters. Point out the following derivations: *bouquet* is derived from French; *rotunda* is derived from Italian.

2 Write the following Pattern Words from Lesson 33 on the board: fiesta, guitar, maize, alfalfa. Note that the words are derived from Spanish. Select a volunteer to make a word search on **T-5 Word Search Grid**, using the words on the board. Assist the volunteer in positioning the words across, down, diagonally, and backwards. Fill in each remaining square on the grid with a letter. Display the transparency on the overhead. Challenge students to find the Pattern Words from the board. An example word search is shown.

m	g	z	t	e	f	z	g
a	r	a	t	i	u	g	t
i	t	m	e	g	m	t	r
z	r	s	z	t	g	r	z
e	t	f	r	z	m	f	m
a	l	f	a	l	f	a	f

3 Proceed to page 142. Students complete the page.

4 Homework suggestion: Distribute a copy of **BLM SP6-36C Lesson 36 Homework II** to each student to practice **words from Asian languages**, Content Words, and Vocabulary Words.

Day 3 Words from German and Words from Asian Languages

Objective

The students will select the appropriate answer circle to indicate if **words from German** are spelled correctly. They will correctly write each word. Students will write **words from Asian languages** in shape boxes that are shaded to indicate the word origins.

Introduction

Display **T-26 Lessons 31–35 Study Sheet** to review Lessons 34–35 words in unison, using the say-spell-say technique. Note that these words are derived from the German, Japanese, Chinese, and Hindi languages.

Directed Instruction

1 Write the bulleted words from Lesson 34 on the board:

- d i e s e l **(correct; diesel)**
- s a u r k r a u t **(incorrect; sauerkraut)**

Dictate each word and invite students to identify whether each dictated word was spelled correctly or incorrectly. Ask students to correct the spelling of their word or leave it as is. Challenge students to identify the derivation of the words. **(German)**

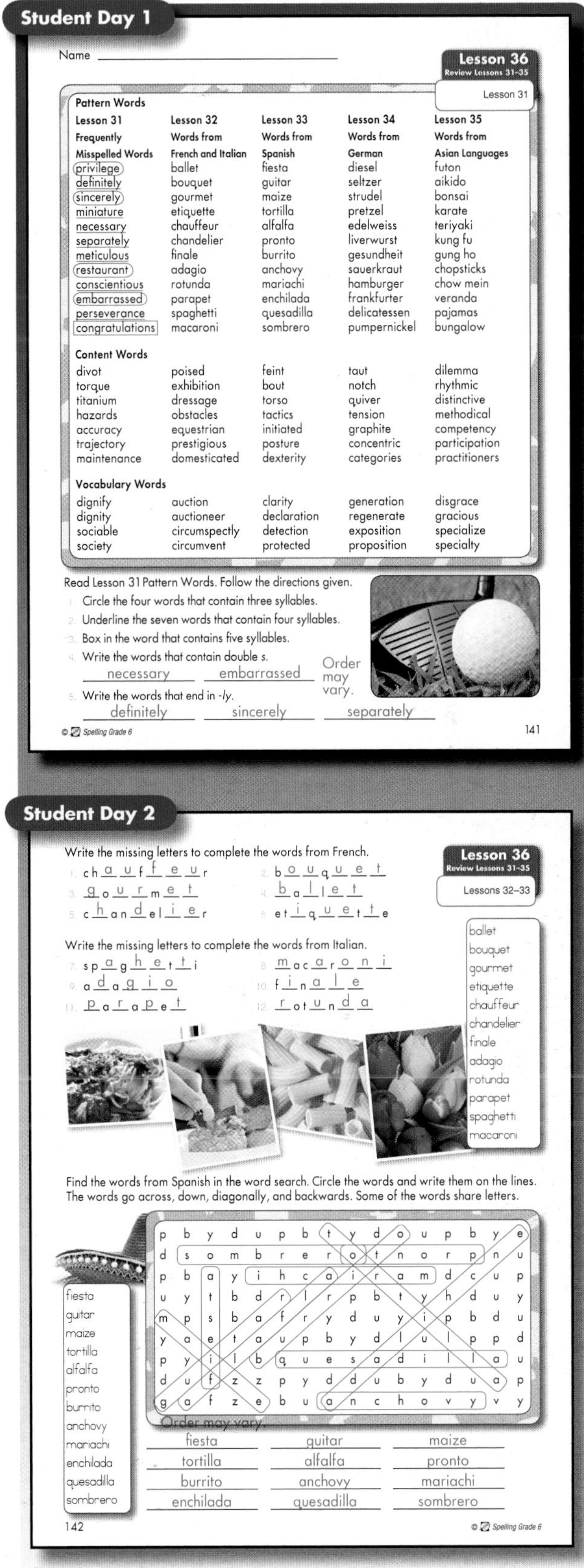

Student Day 1

Name ____________________

Lesson 36
Review Lessons 31–35

Lesson 31

Pattern Words

Lesson 31 Frequently Misspelled Words	Lesson 32 Words from French and Italian	Lesson 33 Words from Spanish	Lesson 34 Words from German	Lesson 35 Words from Asian Languages
privilege	ballet	fiesta	diesel	futon
definitely	bouquet	guitar	seltzer	aikido
sincerely	gourmet	maize	strudel	bonsai
miniature	etiquette	tortilla	pretzel	karate
necessary	chauffeur	alfalfa	edelweiss	teriyaki
separately	chandelier	pronto	liverwurst	kung fu
meticulous	finale	burrito	gesundheit	gung ho
restaurant	adagio	anchovy	sauerkraut	chopsticks
conscientious	rotunda	mariachi	hamburger	chow mein
embarrassed	parapet	enchilada	frankfurter	veranda
perseverance	spaghetti	quesadilla	delicatessen	pajamas
congratulations	macaroni	sombrero	pumpernickel	bungalow

Content Words

divot	poised	feint	taut	dilemma
torque	exhibition	bout	notch	rhythmic
titanium	dressage	torso	quiver	distinctive
hazards	obstacles	tactics	tension	methodical
accuracy	equestrian	initiated	graphite	competency
trajectory	prestigious	posture	concentric	participation
maintenance	domesticated	dexterity	categories	practitioners

Vocabulary Words

dignify	auction	clarity	generation	disgrace
dignity	auctioneer	declaration	regenerate	gracious
sociable	circumspectly	detection	exposition	specialize
society	circumvent	protected	proposition	specialty

Read Lesson 31 Pattern Words. Follow the directions given.

1. Circle the four words that contain three syllables.
2. Underline the seven words that contain four syllables.
3. Box in the word that contains five syllables.
4. Write the words that contain double *s*.
   necessary embarrassed Order may vary.
5. Write the words that end in *-ly*.
   definitely sincerely separately

© Spelling Grade 6 141

Student Day 2

Lesson 36
Review Lessons 31–35

Lessons 32–33

Write the missing letters to complete the words from French.

1. chauffeur
2. bouquet
3. gourmet
4. ballet
5. chandelier
6. etiquette

Write the missing letters to complete the words from Italian.

7. spaghetti
8. macaroni
9. adagio
10. finale
11. parapet
12. rotunda

ballet
bouquet
gourmet
etiquette
chauffeur
chandelier
finale
adagio
rotunda
parapet
spaghetti
macaroni

Find the words from Spanish in the word search. Circle the words and write them on the lines. The words go across, down, diagonally, and backwards. Some of the words share letters.

p	b	y	d	u	p	b	t	y	d	o	u	p	b	y	e
d	s	o	m	b	r	e	r	o	t	n	o	r	p	n	u
p	b	a	y	i	h	c	a	i	r	a	m	d	c	u	p
u	y	t	b	d	r	l	r	p	b	t	y	h	d	u	y
m	p	s	b	a	f	r	y	d	u	y	i	p	b	d	u
y	a	e	t	a	u	p	b	y	d	l	u	l	p	p	d
p	y	i	l	b	q	u	e	s	a	d	i	l	l	a	u
d	u	f	z	z	p	y	d	d	u	b	y	d	u	a	p
g	a	f	z	e	b	u	a	n	c	h	o	v	y	v	y

fiesta
guitar
maize
tortilla
alfalfa
pronto
burrito
anchovy
mariachi
enchilada
quesadilla
sombrero

Order may vary.

fiesta	guitar	maize
tortilla	alfalfa	pronto
burrito	anchovy	mariachi
enchilada	quesadilla	sombrero

142 © Spelling Grade 6

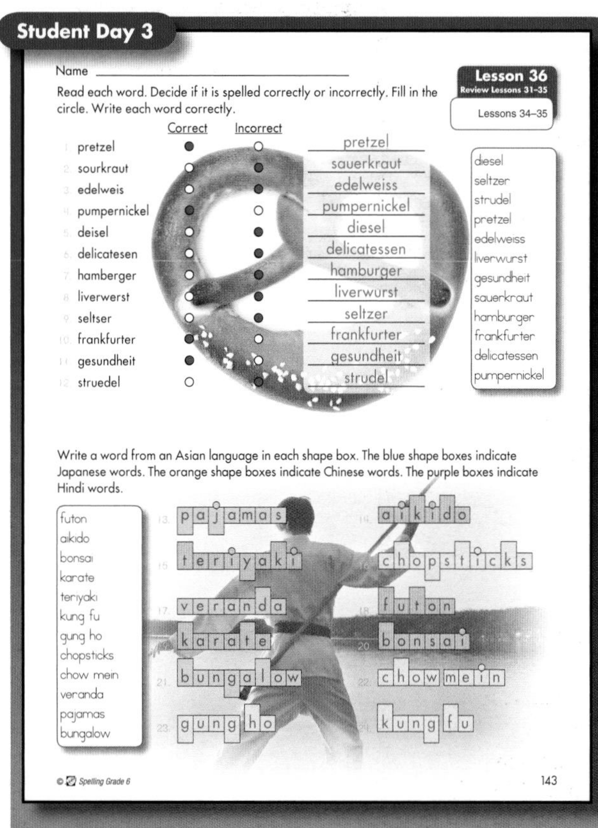
Student Day 3

Name ______________________

Lesson 36
Review Lessons 31–35

Lessons 34–35

Read each word. Decide if it is spelled correctly or incorrectly. Fill in the circle. Write each word correctly.

		Correct	Incorrect	
1	pretzel	●	○	pretzel
2	sourkraut	○	●	sauerkraut
3	edelweis	○	●	edelweiss
4	pumpernickel	●	○	pumpernickel
5	deisel	○	●	diesel
6	delicatesen	○	●	delicatessen
7	hamberger	○	●	hamburger
8	liverwerst	○	●	liverwurst
9	seltser	○	●	seltzer
10	frankfurter	●	○	frankfurter
11	gesundheit	●	○	gesundheit
12	struedel	○	●	strudel

diesel, seltzer, strudel, pretzel, edelweiss, liverwurst, gesundheit, sauerkraut, hamburger, frankfurter, delicatessen, pumpernickel

Write a word from an Asian language in each shape box. The blue shape boxes indicate Japanese words. The orange shape boxes indicate Chinese words. The purple boxes indicate Hindi words.

futon, aikido, bonsai, karate, teriyaki, kung fu, gung ho, chopsticks, chow mein, veranda, pajamas, bungalow

13. pajamas
14. aikido
15. teriyaki
16. chopsticks
17. veranda
18. futon
19. karate
20. bonsai
21. bungalow
22. chow mein
23. gung ho
24. kung fu

© Spelling Grade 6 143

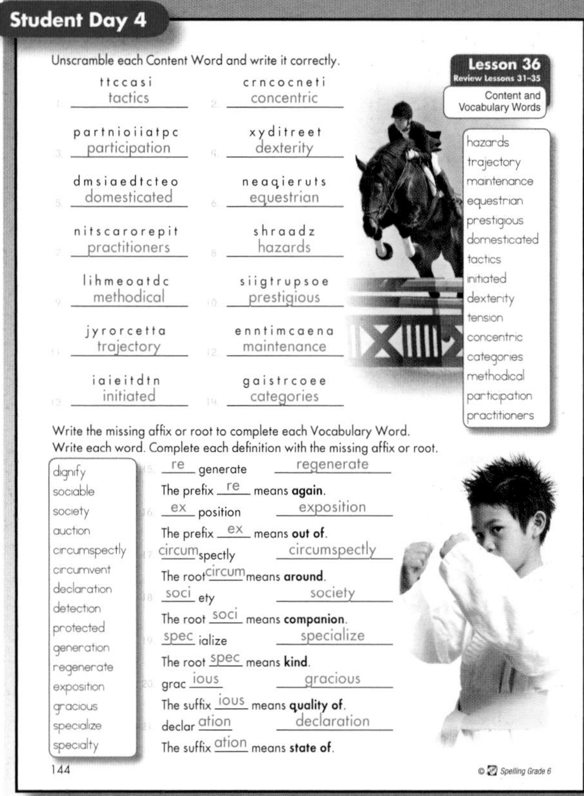
Student Day 4

Lesson 36
Review Lessons 31–35

Content and Vocabulary Words

Unscramble each Content Word and write it correctly.

1. ttccasi — tactics
2. crncocneti — concentric
3. partnioiiatpc — participation
4. xyditreet — dexterity
5. dmsiaedtcteo — domesticated
6. neaqieruts — equestrian
7. nitscarorepit — practitioners
8. shraadz — hazards
9. lihmeoatdc — methodical
10. siigtrupsoe — prestigious
11. jyrorcetta — trajectory
12. enntimcaena — maintenance
13. iaieitdtn — initiated
14. gaistrcoee — categories

hazards, trajectory, maintenance, equestrian, prestigious, domesticated, tactics, initiated, dexterity, tension, concentric, categories, methodical, participation, practitioners

Write the missing affix or root to complete each Vocabulary Word. Write each word. Complete each definition with the missing affix or root.

dignify, sociable, society, auction, circumspectly, circumvent, declaration, detection, protected, generation, regenerate, exposition, gracious, specialize, specialty

15. re generate — regenerate
The prefix re means **again**.
16. ex position — exposition
The prefix ex means **out of**.
17. circum spectly — circumspectly
The root circum means **around**.
18. soci ety — society
The root soci means **companion**.
19. spec ialize — specialize
The root spec means **kind**.
20. grac ious — gracious
The suffix ious means **quality of**.
21. declar ation — declaration
The suffix ation means **state of**.

144 © Spelling Grade 6

2 Select three other volunteers and invite them to the board. Dictate the following Lesson 35 words, and assign a word for each volunteer to write on the board: futon, kung fu, bungalow. Instruct volunteers to draw shape boxes around their word. Note that *kung fu* is an open compound word and should have a space between the shape boxes for *kung* and *fu*. Point out the following derivations: *Futon* is derived from Japanese, *kung fu* is derived from Chinese, *bungalow* is derived from Hindi, spoken in India.

3 Proceed to page 143. Students complete the page.

Day 4 Content Words and Vocabulary Words

Objective

The students will unscramble and write content words. They will write missing affixes or roots and write vocabulary words.

Introduction

Display **T-26 Lessons 31–35 Study Sheet** to review Content Words in unison, using the say-spell-say technique. Write the following Content Words on 3" × 5" INDEX CARDS and pass them out to five volunteers: accuracy, poised, feint, quiver, rhythmic. Invite the volunteers to the board and instruct them to scramble and write their word. Challenge students to unscramble and correctly write the Content Words.

Directed Instruction

1 Continue to refer to **T-26 Lessons 31–35 Study Sheet** to review Vocabulary Words in unison, using the say-spell-say technique. Review the following:

- A root is the part of a word that gives the basic meaning. Some words contain more than one root.
- Prefixes and suffixes are affixes. Affixes expand the meaning or function of a word.

Select volunteers to circle the following affixes or roots in the Vocabulary Words on the transparency as you dictate them: pro, re, circum, gen, able, ation. **(pro—protected, proposition; re—regenerate; circum—circumspectly, circumvent; gen—generation, regenerate; able—sociable; ation—declaration, generation)**

2 Review the following meanings for the dictated affixes and roots:

- *pro* means *before* or *for*
- *circum* means *around*
- *able* means *is able*
- *re* means *again*
- *gen* means *birth*
- *ation* means *state of*

3 Proceed to page 144. Students independently complete the page. Select volunteers to read exercises 15–21 aloud to reinforce the definitions of affixes and roots.

4 Homework suggestion: Distribute a copy of **BLM SP6-36D Lessons 31–35 Test Prep** to each student to practice with many of the words that may appear on the Assessment. Prepare for the Assessment by studying the words on **BLM SP6-36A Lessons 31–35 Study Sheet** that was sent home on Day 1 or by using their flash card sets.

Day 5 Assessment

Objective

The students will accurately select the appropriate answer within the context of a sentence. They will fill in the corresponding answer circle.

Introduction

Teacher Note: The Test makes provision for Differentiated Instruction. The first twelve sentences include the words assigned to students with shortened lists. Encourage these students to try all the sentences, but only grade the first twelve sentences. The Test is found on two blackline masters.

Duplicate a copy of **BLMs SP6-36E–F Lessons 31–35 Test I** and **II** and distribute to each student. Duplicate **BLM SP6-06G Student Answer Form** and cut apart. Distribute one answer form to each student. Remind students to fill in each answer circle completely and to erase completely if they wish to change an answer.

Directed Instruction

1 Instruct students to listen as you dictate the following Sample:

Sample

You can buy a hamberger (A) or a frankfurter (B) at the exhibition (C) hall. All correct (D)

Say, "Are any of the first three underlined words misspelled?" Pause for replies. Inform students that the letter *A* is below the underlined word that is misspelled. (**hamburger**) Guide students to the answer form that was previously distributed. Lead students to find the Sample box and fill in the appropriate answer circle containing the same letter. Say, "You will continue in the same way. You will read each sentence, choose the word that you think is misspelled, and fill in the corresponding circle on the answer form. If all the words are spelled correctly, fill in the fourth circle, labeled *D*, for *All correct*."

2 Assist students as needed while they read the sentences and complete the Test on their own.

1. Dressage is an equestrian event that requires dignity and poise.
2. The finale of the ballet was definitely the high point.
3. Katie is both sociable and gracious, always using good etiquette.
4. Erica had a burrito and an enchilada at the fiesta.
5. Mrs. Pham's specialty was the methodical *kata* of karate.
6. We gave Inez a bouquet and our congratulations on a beautiful adagio.
7. Klaus ordered sauerkraut, a pretzel, and a strudel at the Oktoberfest.
8. Eve considered it necessary maintenance to keep the diesel oiled.
9. It was a prestigious privilege to be invited into the rotunda.
10. One of the challenges of golf is to circumvent hazards with accuracy.
11. At the exposition, a man in a sombrero strolled by, strumming his guitar.
12. Back in her bungalow, Anh put on her pajamas and slept on the futon.
13. While at the gourmet restaurant, I ordered their finest spaghetti.
14. The girls ate chow mein and teriyaki chicken with their chopsticks.
15. At the delicatessen, Stu ordered liverwurst on pumpernickel bread.
16. Shou and Riku specialize in cultivating miniature bonsai.
17. Posture, dexterity, and mastery of tactics are keys to good fencing.
18. To make a quesadilla, one starts with a tortilla made from maize.
19. Aikido and kung fu are in different categories of martial arts.
20. Participation in the auction will benefit the society helping the poor.
21. Do golf clubs made of graphite or titanium produce more torque?
22. The parapet protected the horses from dangerous obstacles.
23. Since she was conscientious, Jill was sincerely embarrassed by an error.
24. Practitioners of *tai chi* demonstrate competency in rhythmic exercises.
25. A declaration by the auctioneer showed that he was gung ho to start.

3 Refer to **BLM SP6-36G Lessons 31–35 Answer Key** when correcting the Test.

Notes

Name ____________________

Word Bank

A *a*

B *b*

basketball

C *C*

canoeing

D *D*

E *E*

F 𝓕
G 𝓖
H 𝓗
horseback riding

I *I*

J *J*

K *K*

karate

L *L*

M *m*

motocross

N *n*

O *O*

P *P*

pole vault

Q *Q*

R *R*

S *S*

surfing

T *T*

U *u*

V *v*

W *w*

water polo

X *x*

Y *y*

Z *z*

Pronunciation Key

Letters written within slashes on this key represent common phonemes, the smallest units of distinct sound in English. Listed to the right are variant spellings for these sounds.

Consonants

/b/	**b**i**b**, **b**a**b**y, **b**u**bb**le
/ch/	**ch**ild, mu**ch**, pa**tch**, na**t**ure, ques**t**ion
/d/	**d**ay, sa**d**, la**dd**er
/f/	**f**ish, o**f**ten, o**ff**, **ph**one, cou**gh**
/g/	**g**o, bi**g**, wi**gg**le, **gh**ost, lea**gue**
/h/	**h**ot, **h**urry, **wh**o
/j/	**j**ump, ju**dge**, **g**ym, ran**ge**
/k/	**k**eep, **c**up, si**ck**, ti**ck**le, pi**c**ni**c**, anti**que**, s**ch**ool
/l/	**l**ook, ta**ll**, **l**i**l**y, a**ll**ey, penci**l**
/m/	**m**y, co**m**e, **m**o**mm**y
/n/	**n**o, **n**i**n**e, wi**nn**er, **kn**ow
/ng/	ri**ng**, si**ng**i**ng**
/p/	**p**ie, ho**p**e, a**pp**le
/kw/	**qu**een, **qu**iet, **ch**oir
/r/	**r**ed, **r**ose, nea**r**, a**rr**ow
/s/	**s**ee, le**ss**on, mi**ss**, **c**ity, dan**ce**
/sh/	**sh**e, wi**sh**, **s**ugar, ma**ch**ine, na**ti**on, spe**ci**al
/t/	**t**ie, ea**t**, **t**a**tt**le, walk**ed**
/th/	**th**ink, bo**th** (breath)
/<u>th</u>/	**th**is, ei**th**er (voice)
/v/	**v**ase, sa**v**e
/w/	**w**e, **w**ell
/hw/ or /w/	**wh**at, **wh**y, **wh**ether
/y/	**y**es, **y**ellow, on**i**on, mill**i**on
/z/	**z**oo, fu**zz**y, ma**z**e, ha**s**
/zh/	mea**s**ure, vi**s**ion

Vowels

/ā/	**a**ble, d**a**t**e**, **ai**d, p**ay**, **eigh**t, gr**ea**t
/a/	p**a**t, **a**pple
/ä/	f**a**ther (same sound as /o/)
/är/	f**ar**m, **ar**m, sp**ar**kle, h**ear**t
/ē/	m**e**, b**ee**, m**ea**t, chi**e**f, c**ei**ling, lad**y**, vall**ey**
/e/	b**e**t, **e**dge, m**e**ss, r**ea**dy, fr**ie**nd
/ī/	**I**, f**i**n**e**, n**igh**t, p**ie**, b**y**
/i/	h**i**s, **i**t, g**y**m
/ō/	b**o**n**e**, **o**pen, c**oa**t, sh**ow**, s**ou**l
/o/	t**o**p, **o**tter, b**o**ther (same sound as /ä/)
/ȯ/	s**o**ft, **o**ften, **a**lso, h**au**l, c**augh**t, dr**aw**, b**ough**t
/oi/	j**oy**, f**oi**l, r**oy**al
/oo/	b**oo**k, p**u**ll, sh**ou**ld
/o͞o/	p**oo**l, t**u**b**e**, t**o**, st**ew**, fr**ui**t, gr**ou**p
/yo͞o/	**u**s**e**, f**ue**l, p**ew**, **you**, b**eau**ty
/ou/	**ou**t, n**ow**, t**ow**el
/u/	h**u**t, l**o**ve, c**ou**ple, an**o**ther (used in stressed syllables)
/âr/	**air**, c**are**, b**ear**, Janu**ary**
/ôr/	f**or**, t**or**n, c**or**n, ch**ore**, w**ar**m
/îr/	**ear**, p**ier**ce, w**eir**d
/ûr/	t**ur**n, w**or**d, th**ir**d, t**ur**tle, f**er**tile, h**ear**d (used in stressed syllables) furth**er**, col**or** (used in unstressed syllables)
/ə/	schwa—the /u/ sound in unstressed syllables: **a**like sudd**e**n penc**i**l cott**o**n circ**u**s

Spelling Dictionary

The Guide Words are two words at the top of the page in a dictionary. These two words are the first and last words defined on a page.

broaden	**celluloid**

broaden celluloid

An Entry Word is a word being defined. A dot is used to show syllable division. Multisyllable words are separated into syllables. Syllable division and pronunciation can differ.

buoy·ant

bul·le·tin /'boo lə tən/ *n.* a newsletter; a short news broadcast. *The news bulletin informed the viewers of the winning team.*

bun·ga·low /'bung gə lō/ *n.* derived from HINDI; a one-story house with a low r... *The Katakias vacation in thei... in India.*

buoy·ant /'boi ənt/ *adj.* **1** having the ability or tendency to float. *...thew threw the buoyant water-polo ... the opponent's net.* **2** cheerful; o... *Deanna had a buoyant attitude ... after the team lost the meet.*

bur·ri·to /bə 'rē tō/ *n.* derived from SPANISH; a flour tortilla wrapp... around a filling of meat, beans, and c...ese. *The waitress asked Aria if she want... chicken or beef in her burrito.*

C

cap·i·tal·is·m /'ka pə tə liz əm/ *n.* condition of a free-market, ec...mic system. *Capitalism is characte... as a free, competitive market.*

cap·i·tal·ize /'ka pə tə liz/ *v.* to make ... fit or benefit by turning something to ... advantage. *An athlete may capital...*

...in order to become a cardiologist.

cat·e·... CATEGORY; divisions within a system;

The Pronunciation shows how to say the word.

/'boi ənt/

The Part of Speech follows the pronunciation. An entry word may have more than one part of speech.

buoy·ant /'boi ənt/ *adj.* **1** having the ability or tendency to float. *Matthew threw the buoyant water-polo ball into the opponent's net.* **2** cheerful; optimistic. *Deanna had a buoyant attitude even after the team lost the meet.*

A Sample Sentence helps in understanding the definition.

buoy·ant /'boi ənt/ *adj.* **1** having the ability or tendency to float. *Matthew threw the buoyant water-polo ball into the opponent's net.* **2** cheerful; optimistic. *Deanna had a buoyant attitude even after the team lost the meet.*

A Definition is the meaning of the word. A word may have more than one definition.

buoy·ant /'boi ənt/ *adj.* **1** having the ability or tendency to float. *Matthew threw the buoyant water-polo ball into the opponent's net.* **2** cheerful; optimistic. *Deanna had a buoyant attitude even after the team lost the meet.*

A

a·ble-bod·ied /ā bəl 'bo dēd/ *adj.* being healthy and physically strong. *Marlene was an able-bodied athlete and played in the entire game.*

a·brupt·ly /ə 'brupt lē/ *adv.* in a sudden breaking away; suddenly. *The track meet was ended abruptly by a sudden thunderstorm.*

ab·so·lu·tion /ab sə 'lo͞o shən/ *n.* state of being set free from blame or guilt. *We receive absolution when we confess our sins to the Lord.*

ab·sorb·ent /əb 'sôr bənt/ *adj.* the tendency to soak up. *Myra used an absorbent towel to soak up the water on the seats.*

ac·cel·er·ates /ik 'se lə rāts/ *v.* increases in speed. *The skier rises on her skis as the boat accelerates.*

ac·cept·a·ble /ik 'sep tə bəl/ *adj.* able to be accepted. *The bronze medal was acceptable to the track coach.*

ac·co·lades /'a kə lādz/ *n. pl.* plural of ACCOLADE; praises. *Could you hear the announcer over the accolades of the fans?*

ac·cu·ra·cy /'a kyə rə sē/ *n.* precision. *Vern used accuracy in his putting stroke and won the golf tournament.*

ac·cus·tomed /ə 'kus təmd/ *adj.* being in the habit; usual. *The team is accustomed to playing on their home field.*

a·chieve·ment /ə 'chēv mənt/ *n.* a state of accomplishment; an accomplishment, especially as a result of unusual effort or skill. *Wendy's technical achievement in the high jump was admirable.*

ac·ro·ba·tics /a krə 'ba tiks/ *n.* a spectacular performance demonstrating agility or complexity. *A diver implements acrobatics into his or her routine.*

a·da·gi·o /ə 'dä zhē ō/ *n.* derived from ITALIAN; a musical composition usually performed at a slow tempo. *As the organist played an adagio, Carmen bowed her head to pray.*

ad·ja·cent /ə 'jā sənt/ *adj.* nearby; connected at a point; adjoining. *Our campsite was adjacent to the dock.*

ad·join·ing /ə 'joi ning/ *adj.* joining at a point or a line. *The soccer field and the skate park are adjoining.*

ad·min·is·tra·tor /əd 'mi nə strā tûr/ *n.* director; supervisor. *Coach Preston was the school administrator for sporting events.*

ad·van·tage /əd 'van tij/ *n.* **1** the first point in tennis after a deuce. *Lena's confidence rose when she earned the advantage in tennis.* **2** a benefit. *An advantage to playing tennis is that it is great exercise.*

ad·ver·tise·ment /ad vûr 'tīz mənt/ *n.* a public notice promoting something in a newspaper, on television, or on radio. *Did you see the advertisement for field hockey in today's newspaper?*

ad·vis·a·ble /əd 'vī zə bəl/ *adj.* worth doing; recommendable. *A face mask is advisable when playing goalkeeper.*

ae·ri·al /'âr ē əl/ *adj.* occurring in the air above the surface. *Spencer performed an aerial trick on his wakeboard.*

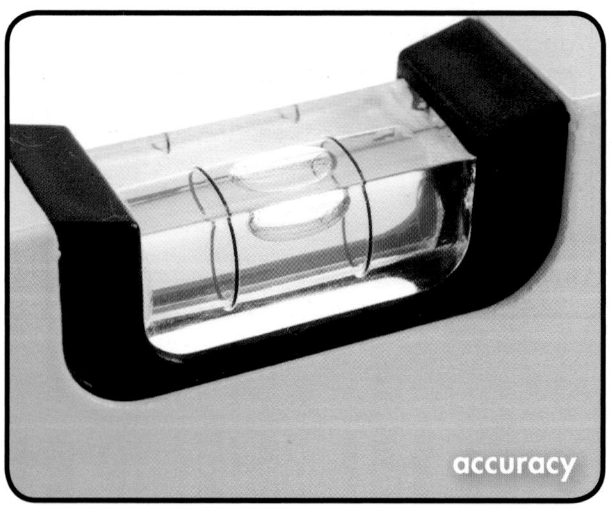
accuracy

aer·o·bic /er 'ō bik/ *adj.* increasing oxygen consumption in the body. *The doctor suggested that Kaylin begin an aerobic sport such as tennis.*

ag·gres·sive /ə 'gre siv/ *adj.* hostile. *The Hawks played a very aggressive team last week.*

a·ghast /ə 'gast/ *adj.* horrified; astonished. *The crowd was aghast when the soccer player broke her ankle.*

a·gile /'a jəl/ *adj.* having the ability to move quickly; able to move quickly. *The agile rider could maneuver her bike around sharp corners.*

a·gil·i·ty /ə 'ji lə tē/ *n.* the ability to move quickly. *Surfing requires agility.*

ai·ki·do /ī ki 'dō/ *n.* derived from JAPANESE; a martial art using locks and holds. *Aikido is a martial art that originated in Japan.*

al·fal·fa /al 'fal fə/ *n.* derived from SPANISH; a plant from the pea family that is grown for hay and forage; a legume. *Papá Valdez feeds alfalfa to the livestock on his farm.*

al·ge·bra /'al jə brə/ *adj.* the branch of mathematics where symbols are used to represent unknown numbers. *Tavonia did her algebra homework before soccer practice.*

al·ter·a·tion /ȯl tə 'rā shən/ *n.* the state of changing partly, but not into some other form; modification. *Candice made an alteration to the length of her sleeves.*

al·tered /'ȯl tûrd/ *v.* past tense of ALTER; changed partly, but not into some other form. *The girls' team altered their uniforms by hemming their shorts.*

al·ter·nates /'ȯl tûr nāts/ *v.* follows in succession; fluctuates. *In table tennis, each player alternates hitting the ball.*

a·lu·mi·num /ə 'lo͞o mə nəm/ *adj.* a soft, silver-white metal. *Many players use aluminum badminton rackets.*

am·a·teur /'a mə chûr/ *adj.* lacking in experience. *Ivan is an amateur player who is dreaming of becoming a professional.*

am·bi·tion /am 'bi shən/ *n.* the desire to achieve. *Zeke's ambition is to become a champion surfer.*

an·chored /'ang kûrd/ *v.* past tense of ANCHOR; to have secured firmly. *A portaledge is a tent that is anchored to the side of a rock.*

an·cho·vy /'an chō vē/ *n.* derived from SPANISH; a small fish. *Have you ever eaten an anchovy?*

an·gu·lar /'ang gyə lûr/ *adj.* sharply defined; thin. *Many track-and-field athletes are lean and have angular features.*

an·nounce·ments /ə 'nount smənts/ *n. pl.* plural of ANNOUNCEMENT; public statements; written notices. *Al heard the announcements about the Nordic skiing event.*

an·ti·bi·ot·ics /an tī bī 'o tiks/ *n. pl.* plural of ANTIBIOTIC; medication against harmful biological organisms. *Antibiotics are sometimes prescribed for infections.*

an·tic·i·pate /an 'ti sə pāt/ *v.* to expect or look forward to; to deal with something beforehand. *A motocross racer should anticipate racing in all types of weather.*

an·ti·quat·ed /'an tə kwā təd/ *v.* past tense of ANTIQUATE; to cause to be old or outdated. *The new soccer stadium's layout antiquated the older stadium's design.*

an·ti·stress /an tī 'stres/ *adj.* that which works against stress. *Proper rest and nutrition are antistress strategies for health.*

anx·ious /'angk shəs/ *adj.* worried. *The teammates were anxious when one of the players was injured.*

a·pol·o·gy /ə 'po lə jē/ *n.* a statement expressing remorse and regret. *An apology was due after unsportsmanlike conduct was exhibited.*

ap·par·ent /ə 'pâr ənt/ *adj.* inclined to appear; visible; obvious. *It is apparent that Marcus has a God-given talent for swimming.*

ap·pli·cant /'a pli kənt/ *n.* a person who applies for a job; candidate. *The applicant turned in his application for the new position.*

a·qua·tics /ə 'kwä tiks/ *n. pl.* plural of AQUATIC; water sports. *Aquatics include swimming and diving.*

ar·bi·trar·y /'är bə trâr ē/ *adj.* related to a personal decision or judgment; random. *In recreational tennis, players make arbitrary decisions.*

ar·bi·trate /'är bə trāt/ *v.* to act as a judge to make a decision. *Line judges arbitrate disputes over where the ball landed.*

ar·chi·tec·tur·al /är kə 'tek chə rəl/ *adj.* relating to a single design, form, or structure. *Building an ice rink can be an architectural challenge.*

a·re·nas /ə 'rē nəz/ *n. pl.* plural of ARENA; enclosed stadiums. *Basketball is played in arenas throughout the world.*

ar·range·ment /ə 'rānj mənt/ *n.* a state of placement or order. *Rita noticed the arrangement of the landing mats in the pole-vault pit.*

as·cend·ing /ə 'sen ding/ *v.* rising to a higher level. *The climbers will be ascending the mountain for two days.*

as·pi·ra·tion /as pə 'rā shən/ *n.* a state of desiring to achieve a goal; a hope. *My aspiration is to become like Jesus.*

as·sis·tance /ə 'sis tənts/ *n.* help. *We required assistance to restart the stalled boat.*

as·so·ci·a·tion /ə sō sē 'ā shən/ *n.* organization; group. *The amateur soccer association voted on the yearly budget.*

ath·lete /'ath lēt/ *n.* a person skilled in playing sports. *An athlete trains hard to improve his or her skills.*

at·ti·tude /'a tə to͞od/ *n.* one's thoughts or feelings about something. *Ryan's attitude improved when he took time to pray.*

auc·tion /'ȯk shən/ *n.* a sale using bids to increase the price of each item. *The thoroughbred was sold at auction to the highest bidder.*

auc·tion·eer /ȯk shə 'nîr/ *n.* one who asks for an increase in bidding. *The auctioneer sold a palomino to Mrs. Chavez.*

au·to·graphed /'ȯ tə grafd/ *v.* past tense of AUTOGRAPH; to have written a signature with one's own hand. *Micah autographed the fan's racquetball program after the match.*

au·to·mo·bile /'ȯ tə mō bēl/ *n.* a vehicle designed to transport passengers. *Lorell rode in an antique automobile to the game banquet.*

au·to·mo·tive /ȯ tə 'mō tiv/ *adj.* relating to automobiles. *The attendees of the automotive convention played racquetball daily.*

a·vail·a·bil·i·ty /ə vā lə 'bi lə tē/ *n.* accessibility; the condition of being accessible or available. *What is your availability for track-and-field practice this week?*

awe·some /'ȯ səm/ *adj.* terrific. *Our God is absolutely awesome!*

awk·ward /'ȯ kwûrd/ *adj.* clumsy, not graceful; embarrassing. *Sometimes rock climbers have awkward maneuvers.*

ax·les /'ak səlz/ *n. pl.* plural of AXLE; bars with bearings at their ends on which wheels revolve. *The axles help hold the wheels on skateboards and in-line skates.*

B

back·ache /'bak āk/ *n.* a pain affecting the back. *Becka had a backache after being kicked by another player.*

bal·an·cing /'ba lənt sing/ *v.* maintaining physical equilibrium. *Nate is balancing on only one ski.*

bal·let /ba 'lā/ *n.* derived from FRENCH; a form of dance originating in France. *The gait of the Tennessee walking horse resembles ballet.*

ba·sis /'bā səs/ *n.* the foundation. *Motorcycle cross-country riding became the basis for BMX.*

beach·comb·ing /'bēch kō ming/ *v.* looking for or collecting useful items from the beach. *Reno and Austin are beachcombing in Laguna Niguel.*

beau·ti·ful·ly /'byo͞o ti fə lē/ *adv.* attractively. *Our wonderful world was beautifully designed by our loving God.*

be·hav·ior /bi 'hā vyûr/ *n.* the manner or way of conducting oneself; conduct. *The volleyball player's behavior was exemplary.*

be·liev·ers /bə 'lē vûrz/ *n. pl.* plural of BELIEVER; people who have strong firm opinions as in religious beliefs. *Believers in Christ have the promise of eternal salvation.*

ben·e·fi·cial /be nə 'fi shəl/ *adj.* that which improves one's well-being. *Basketball and other aerobic sports are beneficial to one's health.*

ben·e·fit·ted /'be nə fi təd/ *v.* past tense of BENEFIT; to have given someone help or an advantage. *Tarah benefitted from hours of practice on the racecourse.*

bi·lin·gual /bī 'ling gwəl/ *adj.* related to speaking two languages. *The new coach was bilingual and was able to communicate effectively.*

bon·sai /'bon sī/ *n.* **1** derived from JAPANESE; a decorative dwarf plant or tree. *Jia trains her bonsai to look like a windblown cypress tree.* *n. pl.* **2** plural of BONSAI; decorative dwarf plants or trees. *Mr. Yamamoto has a display of ten bonsai in the window of his flower shop.*

boul·der·ing /'bōl də ring/ *n.* rock climbing. *Lani and her family enjoy bouldering on weekends.*

bound·a·ries /'boun də rēz/ *n. pl.* plural of BOUNDARY; limits. *Line judges determine if the ball lands outside the boundaries.*

bou·quet /bō 'kā/ *n.* derived from FRENCH; a grouping of flowers often held in one's hand. *Nina presented a bouquet to the winner of the steeplechase.*

bout /'bout/ *n.* an athletic match. *Mahera played a three-minute bout with Tamar.*

bril·liant /'bril yənt/ *adj.* having great ability; very smart; talented. *Misty exhibitedbrilliant technique on the court.*

bouldering

broad·en /ˈbrȯ dən/ *v.* to widen. *The game was so close that the coach wanted to broaden the score.*

bro·chure /brō ˈshoor/ *n.* pamphlet. *Our coach gave my teammates and me a brochure for hockey camp.*

bul·le·tin /ˈboo lə tən/ *n.* a newsletter; a short news broadcast. *The news bulletin informed the viewers of the winning team.*

bun·ga·low /ˈbung gə lō/ *n.* derived from HINDI; a one-story house with a low roof. *The Katakias vacation in their bungalow in India.*

buoy·ant /ˈboi ənt/ *adj.* **1** having the ability or tendency to float. *Matthew threw the buoyant water-polo ball into the opponent's net.* **2** cheerful; optimistic. *Deanna had a buoyant attitude even after the team lost the meet.*

bur·ri·to /bə ˈrē tō/ *n.* derived from SPANISH; a flour tortilla wrapped around a filling of meat, beans, and cheese. *The waitress asked Aria if she wanted chicken or beef in her burrito.*

C

cap·i·tal·is·m /ˈka pə tə liz əm/ *n.* the condition of a free-market, economic system. *Capitalism is characterized as a free, competitive market.*

cap·i·tal·ize /ˈka pə tə līz/ *v.* to make a profit or benefit by turning something to an advantage. *An athlete may capitalize on an opponent's mistake during a game.*

car·di·o·gram /ˈkär dē ə gram/ *n.* the tracing made by a cardiograph. *Zane thanked the Lord that a cardiogram showed a normal heartbeat.*

car·di·o·graph /ˈkär dē ə graf/ *n.* an instrument that measures the movements of the heart. *The patient was connected to the cardiograph by wires.*

car·di·ol·o·gy /kär dē ˈo lə jē/ *n.* the study of the heart and treatment of disorders and diseases. *Dr. Froelig studied cardiology in order to become a cardiologist.*

car·di·op·a·thy /kär dē ˈo pə thē/ *n.* a disease or disorder of the heart. *Can a healthy diet and routine exercise prevent cardiopathy?*

ca·su·al /ˈka zhə wəl/ *adj.* relaxed; informal. *Kevin played a casual game of beach volleyball yesterday.*

cat·e·go·ries /ˈka tə gôr ēz/ *n. pl.* plural of CATEGORY; divisions within a system; classifications. *How many categories are in archery competitions?*

cel·e·brate /ˈse lə brāt/ *v.* to commemorate a notable occasion with festivities. *Donavan will celebrate the victory with his teammates.*

cel·lu·loid /ˈsel yə loid/ *n.* **1** a transparent, plastic material. *A table-tennis ball is made of white or orange celluloid.* *adj.* **2** having the qualities of a transparent, plastic material. *The celluloid ball was hollow and very light.*

bungalow

cen·trif·u·gal /sen 'tri fyə gəl/ *adj.* directed away from a center. *Centrifugal force is required to throw a discus.*

cer·tain·ly /'sûr tən lē/ *adv.* definitely. *Know certainly that the Lord, our God, hears our prayers.*

chal·leng·ing /'cha lən jing/ *adj.* presenting a challenge; difficult. *Surfing was an extremely challenging assignment.*

cham·pi·ons /'cham pē ənz/ *n. pl.* plural of CHAMPION; more than one champion; winners. *The champions received gold medals.*

cham·pi·on·ship /'cham pē ən ship/ *n.* a contest to determine a champion. *The best football team won the championship.*

chan·de·lier /shan də 'lîr/ *n.* derived from FRENCH; a decorative lighting fixture with multiple bulbs or candles, hung from a ceiling. *A crystal chandelier hung in the grand ballroom.*

chan·nel /'cha nəl/ *n.* a specific band of frequencies that broadcast a television or radio program. *Uncle Ted and I watched the World Series on the sports channel.*

char·i·ty /'châr ə tē/ *n.* impartial, Christian love. *The Lord wants us to have fervent charity toward each other.*

chauf·feur /shō 'fûr/ *n.* derived from FRENCH; a hired driver. *The chauffeur drove the heiress to her riding lessons.*

chlo·rine /'klôr ēn/ *n.* a chemical used for water purification. *Can you smell the chlorine in a swimming pool?*

chop·sticks /'chop stiks/ *n. pl.* derived from CHINESE; plural of CHOPSTICK; two sticks used to pick up food. *Jung dropped the chopsticks on the table.*

chow mein /'chou mān/ *n.* derived from CHINESE; a seasoned stew of meat and vegetables served with fried noodles. *Chow mein is a simple dish to make.*

cir·cuit /'sûr kət/ *n.* a circular course or path. *Chad maintained good form as he followed the challenging circuit.*

cir·cum·spect·ly /'sûr kəm spekt lē/ *adv.* carefully examining each possibility; prudently. *Judges at the horse show surveyed the field circumspectly.*

cir·cum·stan·ces /'sûr kəm stant səz/ *n. pl.* plural of CIRCUMSTANCE; conditions or events surrounding a particular situation; the way something happens. *Do you know the circumstances of the game cancellation?*

cir·cum·vent /sûr kəm 'vent/ *v.* to manage to go around; to avoid. *Hugh tried to circumvent the obstacle by reining in his horse.*

clar·i·ty /'klâr ə tē/ *n.* a state of being clear; lucidness. *Concentration and clarity of mind are vital when competing.*

close·ly /'klōs lē/ *adv.* in close proximity. *Each of the BMX riders followed closely behind the other.*

col·le·giate /kə 'lē jət/ *adj.* relating to college. *Players in the collegiate conference are university students.*

col·lide /kə 'līd/ *v.* to crash. *Offensive and defensive players often collide.*

col·li·sions /kə 'li zhənz/ *n. pl.* plural of COLLISION; crashes. *Collisions between players are common in hockey.*

com·mit·tee /kə 'mi tē/ *n.* a group convened for a specific purpose and goal. *The committee will seek land to build a new stadium.*

com·mon sense /'ko mən sents/ *n.* good judgment. *One should use common sense when playing in or around water.*

com·mu·ni·ty /kə 'myōō nə tē/ *n.* neighborhood. *Our community has an indoor football stadium.*

com·mu·ni·ty cen·ter /kə 'myo͞o nə tē sen tûr/ *n.* a building used for community activities. *During renovations, the team used the pool at the community center.*

¹com·pact /kəm 'pakt/ *v.* combine; to press together. *Michaella began to compact the swim gear into her bag.*

²com·pact /kom 'pakt/ *adj.* occupying a small space. *The swim team could not fit into the coach's compact car.*

com·pan·ion /kəm 'pan yən/ *n.* one who shares in what the other is doing; friend. *Jesus is our ever faithful and loyal companion.*

com·pe·ten·cy /'kom pə tənt sē/ *n.* an adequate ability to perform a task. *Students must demonstrate competency to receive a black belt.*

com·pe·ti·tion /kom pə 'ti shən/ *n.* a contest between opponents. *The waterskiing competition was held on Lake Powell.*

com·pet·i·tive /kəm 'pe tə tiv/ *adj.* desiring to compete; aggressive. *Competitive athletes enjoy the thrill of a competition.*

com·ple·ment /'kom plə mənt/ *v.* to fill up, complete, or perfect something else. *Judd's skills complement the swim team.*

com·pli·ment /'kom plə mənt/ *n.* an expression of admiration or praise. *Rae received a compliment from Bonnie for her improved time.*

com·pos·ite /kom 'po zət/ *adj.* made up of different parts; combination. *Skateboard decks made of wood are preferred over composite ones.*

com·po·si·tion /kom pə 'zi shən/ *n.* a state of thoroughly placing together; construction of. *Did Derrell write a composition about the rules of table tennis?*

con·ceit /kən 'sēt/ *n.* too high an opinion of oneself or of one's ability to do things; egotism. *Bragging about one's own abilities shows conceit.*

con·cen·tra·tion /kont sən 'trā shən/ *n.* the direction of focused attention to a particular task; thought. *Ann was in deep concentration during the table-tennis game.*

con·cen·tric /kən 'sen trik/ *adj.* having a common center or midpoint; circular shaped. *The bull's eye is in the middle of concentric circles.*

con·cerned /kən 'sûrnd/ *v.* past tense of CONCERN; to be thoroughly anxious about a certain situation; worried. *Chelsea was concerned about the weather during the long-jump event.*

con·ces·sions /kən 'se shənz/ *n. pl.* plural of CONCESSION; smaller businesses on the premises of larger businesses. *Hal visited the concessions to get some snacks during the game.*

con·cludes /kən 'klo͞odz/ *v.* ends. *When the game concludes, we will celebrate.*

con·dense /kən 'dents/ *v.* to make more compact. *I will try to condense my narrative into a few paragraphs.*

con·di·tion·ing /kən 'di shə ning/ *n.* a training process. *The conditioning of muscles assists in one's overall performance.*

con·fi·dent /'kon fə dənt/ *adj.* certain. *The boys are confident they will be able to go kayaking in June.*

con·fig·ured /kən 'fi gyûrd/ *v.* past tense of CONFIGURE; set up in a particular way. *The coach configured the plays on a chalkboard.*

con·fined /kən 'fīnd/ *v.* past tense of CONFINE; to have thoroughly kept within a boundary. *Is the race confined to the area north or south of the bridge?*

con·fine·ment /kən 'fīn mənt/ *n.* that which is being thoroughly kept within a boundary. *There is an area in the marina for the confinement of the boats.*

con·grat·u·la·tions /kən gra chə 'lā shənz/ *n. pl.* plural of CONGRATULATION; expressions of praise, good wishes, or compliments. *Numerous fans expressed their congratulations after the golf game.*

con·i·cal /'ko ni kəl/ *adj.* having the shape of a cone; cone shaped. *Shuttlecocks, used in badminton, are conical in shape.*

con·sci·en·tious /kont shē 'ent shəs/ *adj.* meticulous; thorough; careful. *Jacques was conscientious as he focused on the putting green.*

con·stant /'kont stənt/ *adj.* faithfulness; consistent. *The constant love of our Savior is unending.*

con·struc·tion /kən 'struk shən/ *n.* the process of building something. *Will is using wood for the construction of the canoe.*

con·tact /'kon takt/ *n.* a state of interaction. *Alisa came into contact with many professional racers at Supercross.*

con·tend·ers /kən 'ten dûrz/ *n. pl.* plural of CONTENDER; competitors or contestants. *There are many contenders in the competitive sport of table tennis.*

[1]**con·tent** /kən 'tent/ *adj.* satisfied. *Wade did his best at the meet, so he is content with his diving score.*

[2]**con·tent** /'kon tent/ *n.* something contained. *The content of your character depicts your attitude and personality.*

con·tes·tants /kən 'tes tənts/ *n. pl.* plural of CONTESTANT; competitors; participants. *Brock was among the fifty long-jump contestants at the meet.*

con·tin·u·ous /kən 'tin yōō əs/ *adj.* having the quality of continuing. *Olympic athletes participate in continuous training sessions.*

[1]**con·trast** /'kon trast/ *n.* a sharp or striking difference. *The contrast of colors on the swimsuits was striking.*

[2]**con·trast** /kən 'trast/ *v.* to compare the differences of. *Can you contrast synchronized swimmers and competitive swimmers?*

con·vince /kən 'vints/ *v.* to persuade. *Can you convince your friends to rent a motorboat?*

co·op·er·ate /kō 'o pə rāt/ *v.* to collaborate. *BMX riders need to cooperate with each other.*

co·op·er·a·tion /kō o pə 'rā shən/ *n.* the act of working together to achieve a common goal; collaboration or compliance. *Team cooperation is necessary for a successful outcome.*

co·or·di·na·tion /kō ôr də 'nā shən/ *n.* the skillful movement of parts for effective results; dexterity. *The game of table tennis requires a lot of coordination.*

cor·dial /'kôr jəl/ *adj.* sincere; friendly. *Gabe gave a cordial smile to his new teammate.*

cor·po·rate /'kôr pə rət/ *adj.* to act as one unified body of individuals. *It was a corporate decision to donate funds for the new athletic club.*

construction

cor·po·ra·tion /kôr pə 'rā shən/ *n.* the state of a group of individuals acting as one unified body. *The new racquetball corporation was headed by Ed and Gigi.*

coun·cil /'kount səl/ *n.* a club; a group that makes rules and takes care of other matters for a larger group. *The swim council meets every Tuesday.*

coun·sel /'kount səl/ *v.* **1** to advise. *A good coach will counsel athletes to help improve their skills. n.* **2** advice. *My coach's counsel helped me improve my breathing technique.*

coun·ter·clock·wise /koun tûr 'klok wīz/ *adv.* the circular direction that is opposite of the way the hands on a clock move. *Track-and-field races are run counterclockwise.*

cou·ple /'ku pəl/ *v.* to fasten, link, or join. *Selena will couple her boots to her skis before riding the ski lift.*

cou·ra·geous /kə 'rā jəs/ *adj.* having the quality of courage. *Despite injuries, the courageous athlete kept going.*

crouch·ing /'krou ching/ *n.* **1** the lowering of one's body position by bending the legs. *The runners began by crouching in the starting blocks. v.* **2** lowering one's body by bending the legs. *Karl was crouching in readiness for the start of the race.*

cru·cial /'kro͞o shəl/ *adj.* very important; essential. *Faith in Jesus is crucial for salvation.*

cul·tur·al /'kul chə rəl/ *adj.* relating to a culture. *Table tennis is a popular, cultural sport in Asia.*

cush·ioned /'koo shənd/ *v.* **1** past tense of CUSHION; to have protected against impact. *Foam mats cushioned Malik's fall after his pole-vault attempt. adj.* **2** soft. *The cushioned, landing pad was very plush.*

cus·tom·ar·y /'kus tə mâr ē/ *adj.* usual; common. *Matches of odd numbers are customary in tournament table tennis.*

cy·cling /'sī kə ling/ *n.* shortened form of BICYCLING. *Is BMX cycling an Olympic sport?*

D

dan·ger·ous /'dān jə rəs/ *adj.* hazardous; unsafe. *The sport of motocross racing is very dangerous.*

day·dream /'dā drēm/ *n.* a pleasant waking thought. *Alana was lost in a daydream about a bike race.*

dec·la·ra·tion /de klə 'rā shən/ *n.* the state of making your position thoroughly clear; an announcement. *The judge made a declaration that unfair play results in elimination.*

de·coy /'dē koi/ *n.* someone or something used to divert the attention of another person. *The decoy was used to help the climber to not be fearful.*

de·fense /'dē fents/ *n.* the sports team members who defend and carry out methods to prevent the other team from scoring. *Celeste played on defense during the last four games.*

cycling

def·i·nite·ly /ˈde fə nit lē/ *adv.* certainly; clearly; without a doubt. *Chrissy definitely had the advantage in the last golf tournament.*

de·flect /di ˈflekt/ *v.* to bend away from a fixed direction. *Sunglasses deflect light rays from a rider's eyes.*

de·hy·dra·tion /dē hī ˈdrā shən/ *n.* a depletion of body fluids. *Dehydration from lack of fluids in the body is very dangerous.*

del·i·ca·tes·sen /de li kə ˈte sən/ *n.* derived from GERMAN; a store where ready-to-eat food products are sold. *After archery practice, our family ate lunch at a delicatessen.*

de·part·ed /di ˈpär təd/ *v.* past tense of DEPART; to have left or proceeded. *The bus departed from the stadium after the competition.*

de·scrib·ing /di ˈskrī bing/ *v.* giving a thorough account. *Matthias wrote a story describing his rock-climbing adventure.*

de·scrip·tion /di ˈskrip shən/ *n.* the state or process of explanation; an explanation. *The announcer gave a detailed description of the game's highlights.*

de·signed /di ˈzīnd/ *v.* past tense of DESIGN; to have planned. *The BMX bike was designed with smaller wheels than other bikes.*

de·signs /di ˈzīnz/ *n. pl.* plural of DESIGN; something's structure and form; models. *Regan submitted her snowboard designs into the competition.*

de·tec·tion /di ˈtek shən/ *n.* the state of thoroughly uncovering the facts. *In fencing, a machine scores the detection of a touch to an opponent.*

deuce /ˈdo͞os/ *n.* a tie at 40 in tennis that requires two consecutive points by one side to win. *Shelby finally won the tennis game after the deuce with Ian.*

de·vel·op·ment /di ˈve ləp mənt/ *n.* a result of planning. *An improvement to the equipment was a positive development.*

dex·ter·i·ty /dek ˈstâr ə tē/ *n.* physical and mental skill. *Martin's dexterity in fencing is remarkable.*

di·ag·o·nal·ly /dī ˈa gə nə lē/ *adv.* in a diagonal manner. *When Edwin served the ball, it went diagonally into the service box.*

di·a·gram /ˈdī ə gram/ *n.* a drawing that shows relations of parts. *Coach Sid drew a diagram of the new play strategy.*

di·a·lect /ˈdī ə lekt/ *n.* a type of language spoken across a specific area or region. *Joyce spoke the Cantonese dialect fluently during her visit to China.*

di·am·e·ter /dī ˈa mə tûr/ *n.* a line segment passing through the center of a circle having end points on the circle. *A circle's diameter passes through its midpoint.*

die·sel /ˈdē zəl/ *n.* derived from GERMAN; a vehicle with a diesel engine. *Uncle Delmar drove his diesel to the archery tournament.*

di·e·tar·y /ˈdī ə târ ē/ *adj.* related to diet. *Athletes often follow their coaches' dietary advice.*

dif·fi·cult /ˈdi fi kəlt/ *adj.* complex; complicated. *Carrie maneuvered through the difficult course on her motorcycle.*

dif·fi·cul·ty /ˈdi fi kəl tē/ *n.* not easy to achieve. *Each dive is assigned a level of difficulty.*

dig·ni·fy /ˈdig nə fī/ *v.* to make worthy of; to honor, distinguish, or give distinction. *Golf does dignify the character of many people who play the game.*

dig·ni·ty /ˈdig nə tē/ *n.* a state of being worthy; self-respect. *Arturo had dignity and did not cheat while writing his golf score.*

di·lem·ma /də 'le mə/ *n.* an unwanted choice. *Karishma faced a dilemma with courage.*

dil·i·gence /'di lə jənts/ *n.* perseverance in performing one's obligations. *It is important to study God's Word with diligence.*

di·men·sions /də 'ment shənz/ *n. pl.* plural of DIMENSION; measurements. *What are the dimensions of your long board?*

dis·a·bil·i·ty /dis ə 'bi lə tē/ *n.* the condition of not being completely able-bodied. *An athlete with a disability ran in the Paralympics.*

dis·be·lief /dis bə 'lēf/ *n.* mental rejection as if untrue; incredulous. *Joe was in disbelief when he qualified for the competition.*

dis·cern·ment /di 'sûrn mənt/ *n.* that which shows distinguished judgment, perception, or sensitivity. *Darby used discernment as she gauged her long-jump approach.*

dis·ci·plined /'di sə plənd/ *v.* **1** past tense of DISCIPLINE; to have exercised self-control; to have made oneself do something regularly. *Stella disciplined herself to run fifteen miles a week.* *adj.* **2** self-controlled. *Disciplined athletes have regular workouts.*

dis·cus·sion /di 'sku shən/ *n.* an oral consideration of a question or idea. *Was there a discussion held about wheelchair basketball?*

dis·grace /dis 'grās/ *v.* not pleasing others; to bring shame. *Soon-Yee did not want to disgrace her family by behaving badly.*

dis·guise /dis 'gīz/ *v.* to conceal. *Dave could not disguise his disappointment after losing the match.*

dis·heart·ened /dis 'här tənd/ *adj.* discouraged; dismayed. *Coach Judy told the team to not be disheartened after losing the meet.*

dis·lo·ca·tion /dis lō 'kā shən/ *n.* a separation of a bone at a joint. *DeVon ran the race even with a dislocation to one of his fingers.*

dis·po·si·tion /dis pə 'zi shən/ *n.* a state of certain behavior when placed under specific circumstances; personality. *Gwen had a cheerful disposition during the tournament.*

dis·re·spect·ful /dis ri 'spekt fəl/ *adj.* not showing proper honor. *Todd did not want to appear disrespectful and interrupt a game.*

dis·rup·tion /dis 'rup shən/ *n.* the state of breaking something apart or interrupting. *A flash of lightning was a disruption to the event at the meet.*

dis·solve /di 'zolv/ *v.* to loosen or melt apart. *The added pool chemicals should dissolve after a few minutes.*

dis·tinc·tion /di 'stingk shən/ *n.* the state of standing out from others. *Kareema had the distinction of being the tallest player on the team.*

dis·tinc·tive /di 'stingk tiv/ *adj.* standing out from others. *A distinctive feature of kendo is the use of bamboo sticks as swords.*

div·ot /'di vət/ *n.* a loose lump of grass and dirt that is dug out of the ground during a sport such as golf. *Emmi replaced each divot after teeing off in her golf game.*

do·mes·ti·ca·ted /də 'mes ti kā təd/ *adj.* adapted to live in association with humans; tamed. *Horses were domesticated centuries ago.*

dom·i·nate /'do mə nāt/ *v.* to be the master over something or someone. *The Eagles sought to dominate the competition.*

dom·i·nat·ing /'do mə nā ting/ *v.* mastering, controlling, or having power over others. *Gloria was dominating the racquetball court and winning.*

dom·i·neer·ing /do mə 'nîr ing/ *adj.* bossy. *Brady's parents were worried about his domineering attitude.*

do·min·ion /də 'mi nyən/ *n.* the state of supreme authority. *Jesus has dominion over all the earth.*

dor·mant /'dôr mənt/ *adj.* the state of being asleep; inactive. *The flowers that had been dormant began to bloom.*

dor·mi·to·ry /'dôr mə tôr ē/ *n.* a place to go to sleep; a residence hall usually without private bathrooms. *The boys slept in a dormitory during sports camp.*

dos·age /'dō sij/ *n.* the frequency and amount of the dispensation of a drug. *The team doctor recommended a dosage of aspirin for pain relief.*

down·pour /'doun pôr/ *n.* a heavy, sustained shower of rain. *The sudden downpour drenched the field and caused a long delay.*

dres·sage /drə 'säzh/ *n.* the precise movements of a thoroughly trained horse; horsemanship. *Marie trains horses in dressage.*

drought /'drout/ *n.* a long period of dry weather. *Falling snow was a welcome sight after the period of drought.*

dur·a·tion /doo 'rā shən/ *n.* the state of or the period of time for which something lasts. *Reporters waited for the duration of the marathon to see the winner.*

E

ec·lect·ic /e 'klek tik/ *adj.* related to a gathering of various sources; diverse. *There was an eclectic selection of ski equipment at the store.*

e·del·weiss /'ā dəl vīs/ *n.* derived from GERMAN; a flower with woolly leaves native to central or southeast Europe. *An edelweiss grows in high altitudes above the tree line.*

el·e·vat·ed /'e lə vā təd/ *v.* past tense of ELEVATE; to have raised, lifted, or advanced. *The high-jump crossbar was elevated to a record height.*

e·lim·i·na·tion /i li mə 'nā shən/ *n.* removal; exclusion. *Helen's elimination from the meet was due to illness.*

e·lon·gate /i 'lòng gāt/ *v.* to make longer; lengthen. *Runners will elongate their stride to cover more ground.*

el·o·quent /'e lə kwənt/ *adj.* expressive. *Coach's halftime speech was not eloquent, but it was effective.*

em·bar·rassed /im 'bâr əsd/ *v.* past tense of EMBARRASS; humiliated; to have caused an uneasy feeling. *Old stories about Bart's beginning attempts at golf embarrassed him.*

em·bod·ied /im 'bo dēd/ *v.* past tense of EMBODY; to be in bodily form; personified. *Dana embodied all the qualities of a fine Christian athlete.*

em·braced /im 'brāsd/ *v.* past tense of EMBRACE; placed into one's arms. *Luis' father embraced him when he completed his first race.*

downpour

em·pha·size /ˈemp fə sīz/ *v.* to place an importance on something; stress. *Smart hockey parents emphasize the fun of the game.*

en·chi·la·da /en chə ˈlä də/ *n.* derived from SPANISH; a tortilla wrapped around a mixture, covered with chili sauce, and baked. *The enchilada that Aunt Rosa served was warm and delicious.*

en·coun·ter /in ˈkoun tûr/ *v.* coming up against something unexpectedly. *A snowboarder should be ready to encounter numerous hazards.*

en·dur·ance /in ˈdoor ənts/ *n.* the ability to tolerate prolonged exertion or activity; stamina. *Volleyball players need to have a lot of endurance.*

en·dur·ing /in ˈdoor ing/ *v.* to last without quitting. *Kiley is enduring the training to be in a cross-country race.*

en·er·gi·zing /ˈe nûr jī zing/ *adj.* invigorating. *A quick game of badminton will be energizing.*

en·gine /ˈen jən/ *n.* a machine for powering equipment. *Jake's motorcycle has a modified and powerful engine.*

en·ter·tain·ment /en tûr ˈtān mənt/ *n.* **1** enjoyment; recreation. *Laney watched her brother's long-jump attempts for entertainment.* **2** performance; production. *Kent enjoyed the opening ceremony entertainment before the final meet.*

e·ques·tri·an /i ˈkwes trē ən/ *adj.* relating to horsemanship. *Steeplechase and harness racing are both equestrian sports.*

e·qui·lib·ri·um /ē kwə ˈli brē əm/ *n.* a state of being in balance; balance. *Surfers can maintain their equilibrium during a long ride.*

e·quip·ment /i ˈkwip mənt/ *n.* the apparatus used in an activity or operation. *Motocross racers wear safety equipment such as body armor and boots.*

er·rant /ˈâr ənt/ *adj.* inclined to wander. *An errant climber greeted Ty when he reached the summit.*

er·ror /ˈâr ûr/ *n.* state of straying from what is correct. *Drew was very careful and did not make an error.*

es·pe·cial·ly /is ˈpesh lē/ *adv.* particularly. *It is especially important to practice free throws.*

es·sen·tial /i ˈsent shəl/ *adj.* absolutely necessary. *It is essential to warm up before practice.*

eth·nic·i·ty /eth ˈni sə tē/ *n.* background; ethnic origin. *Malia shared that her ethnicity was Asian-American.*

et·i·quette /ˈe ti kət/ *n.* derived from FRENCH; proper manners. *It is good etiquette for a rider to signal he is ready to begin.*

eu·phor·ic /yo͞o ˈfôr ik/ *adj.* extremely happy; overjoyed. *The team was euphoric after reaching the summit of the rock.*

ex·cel·lence /ˈek sə lənts/ *n.* superiority. *To glorify God in all we do, we should strive for excellence.*

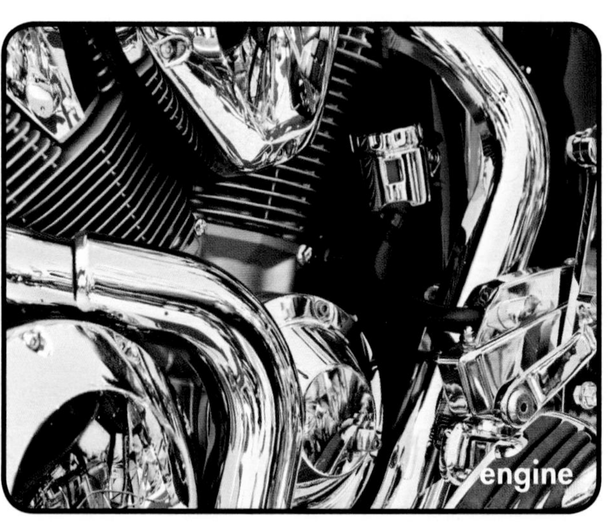
engine

ex·cep·tion /ik 'sep shən/ *n.* something excluded. *No exception will be made for anyone arriving late.*

ex·cla·ma·tion /eks klə 'mā shən/ *n.* a sharp utterance; a cry. *Shay voiced an exclamation when her name was called.*

ex·haust·ed /ig 'zȯ stəd/ *adj.* extremely tired. *Our Lord is always ready to help us and is never exhausted.*

ex·hi·bi·tion /ek sə 'bi shən/ *n.* **1** a display; a show. *The exhibition by horses with beautiful gaits intrigued Aimee.* *adj.* **2** related to a display or show. *The exhibition hall on Fairfield Street was used for the annual charity horse show.*

ex·panse /ik 'spants/ *n.* something spread out over an extensive distance. *The entire midfield expanse was dedicated to throwing events.*

ex·pel /ik 'spel/ *v.* to push or force out. *Yuri did expel a loud breath when the rubber ball hit him.*

ex·pe·ri·ence /ik 'spîr ē ənts/ *n.* direct observation and participation. *Robin learned better ways to ski through experience.*

ex·plo·sion /ik 'splō zhən/ *n.* a sudden, powerful burst. *A basket was accompanied by an explosion of applause.*

ex·po·si·tion /ek spə 'zi shən/ *n.* the state of placing items out in the view of the public; a fair or exhibition. *The archery team demonstrated their skills at the county exposition.*

ex·po·sure /ik 'spō zhûr/ *n.* the process of being made known. *Soccer players receive a lot of exposure due to the sport's popularity.*

ex·tra·or·di·nar·y /ik 'strôr də nâr ē/ *adj.* remarkable; unusual. *Erich completed an extraordinary feat when he ski jumped 400 feet!*

fa·cil·i·tate /fə 'si lə tāt/ *v.* assist with; aid. *Mel will facilitate the freestyle skiing competition as a judge.*

fa·mil·iar /fə 'mil yûr/ *adj.* well-known; easily recognized. *A spike is a familiar offensive technique in volleyball.*

fas·ten·ers /'fa sən ûrz/ *n. pl.* plural of FASTENER; connective devices. *Felix secured the fasteners on his boot before riding the half-pipe.*

fa·tigue /fə 'tēg/ *n.* weariness from exertion. *Mona collapsed with fatigue at the end of the race.*

feint /'fānt/ *n.* a mock attack to distract from what was really intended; a trick. *By using a feint, I was able to score the winning point.*

fi·ber·glass /'fī bûr glas/ *n.* a combination of glass fibers and plastic. *Pole vaulters use poles that are made of fiberglass.*

fi·es·ta /fē 'es tə/ *n.* derived from SPANISH; a festival. *My fencing club celebrated Cinco de Mayo with a fiesta.*

fi·nal /'fī nəl/ *adj.* related to an ending competition. *Lauren qualified for the final Pro Motocross event.*

fi·na·le /fə 'na lē/ *n.* derived from ITALIAN; the final portion of a performance. *The gaited Paso Fino performed the finale of the horse show.*

fi·nal·ist /'fī nə list/ *n.* one who is qualified for an ending competition. *Curtis was a finalist in the Motocross World Championship.*

fi·nal·ists /'fi nə lists/ *n. pl.* plural of FINALIST; contestants who are qualified for an ending competition. *Abe and Cristiano were finalists in the World Championship match.*

fi·nal·ly /'fi nəl ē/ *adv.* related to the end of a series or process; at last. *After an extensive delay, the water-polo meet finally began.*

fis·sures /'fi shûrz/ *n. pl.* plural of FISSURE; long narrow cracks or openings; crevices. *Climbers often put their hands into fissures when climbing.*

flex·i·bil·i·ty /flek sə 'bi lə tē/ *n.* the capability of bending easily; elasticity. *Experienced skaters have flexibility to perform stunts.*

flex·i·ble /'flek sə bəl/ *adj.* able to be bent; adaptable. *Kelly remained flexible about the idea of learning to surf.*

flex·ion /'flek shən/ *n.* a bending. *The flexion of the pole used for pole vaulting is very important.*

fo·cused /'fō kəsd/ *v.* past tense of FOCUS; to have concentrated thoughts. *Was Eliza focused during the long-jump training sessions?*

foot·work /'foot wûrk/ *n.* skillful movement or maneuvering. *Quinn had quick footwork during the racquetball game.*

for·eign·er /'fôr ə nûr/ *n.* a person from or of another country than one's own; outsider. *A foreigner was a spectator at an international skating competition.*

for·ma·tions /fôr 'mā shənz/ *n. pl.* plural of FORMATION; shapes or patterns. *Yosemite National Park is known for its beautiful rock formations.*

for·mi·da·ble /fôr 'mi də bəl/ *adj.* remarkable; impressive. *Aaron showed formidable skills with his new long-jump record.*

frame·work /'frām wûrk/ *n.* a skeletal structure. *The framework for the new boat is almost finished.*

frank·furt·er /'frangk fûr tûr/ *n.* derived from GERMAN; a cured, cooked sausage that is either skinless or stuffed in a casing. *Corinne ordered a frankfurter when her team went out to eat.*

free·style /'frē stī əl/ *adj.* with free choice of style. *Britt competed in the freestyle, half-pipe event.*

fre·quent /'frē kwənt/ *adj.* happening often. *The Fry family takes frequent trips to the river to go kayaking.*

func·tion /'fungk shən/ *n.* a purpose, action, or role. *What is the function of large wheels on a race motorcycle?*

func·tion·al /'fungk shə nəl/ *adj.* the state of performing. *The powerboat's engine was functional.*

fu·ton /'fo͞o ton/ *n.* derived from JAPANESE; a cotton mattress often used with a frame. *We use a futon as a bed for our guests.*

G

ga·ra·ges /gə 'rä jəz/ *n. pl.* plural of GARAGE; buildings for parking, storing, or repairing vehicles. *John took his car to three different garages for repair quotes.*

gauge /'gāj/ *v.* to estimate or judge. *A good competitor can gauge his opponent's next move.*

gen·er·a·tion /je nə 'rā shən/ *n.* **1** the state of time between the birth of parents and their offspring. *Each generation must teach others about the good news of Jesus.* **2** a group of people born at approximately the same time. *Hillary was interested in researching the history of her grandparent's generation.*

ge·sund·heit /gə 'zoont hīt/ *interj.* derived from GERMAN; a polite comment to wish someone good health after he or she has sneezed. *After I sneezed, Delaney said, "Gesundheit!"*

goal·keep·er /'gōl kē pûr/ *n.* a player who defends a goal in a sport. *The goalkeeper dove and successfully blocked the kick.*

gog·gles /'go gəlz/ *n.* protective glasses in a plastic or rubber frame that fits snugly against the face to protect the eyes. *Do you wear goggles when you swim?*

gour·met /goor 'mā/ *adj.* derived from FRENCH; relating to a refined taste in food. *Gourmet cheeses were served at the riding academy's open house.*

gra·cious /'grā shəs/ *adj.* marked by pleasantness and courtesy. *The sixth grade class is known for its gracious behavior.*

gra·di·ent /'grā dē ənt/ *n.* a slope. *Grandpa walked down the short gradient to get into the kayak.*

grad·u·al·ly /'gra jə wə lē/ *adv.* slowly; steadily. *Kari noticed that the day was gradually getting warmer.*

graph·ite /'gra fīt/ *n.* a composite material in which carbon fibers are the reinforcing material. *Dena bought a bow made of graphite at the sporting goods store.*

grate·ful /'grāt fəl/ *adj.* full of thanks; thankful. *I am grateful that God forgives me of my sins.*

grat·i·fy /'gra tə fī/ *v.* to do something that makes someone pleased. *Does it gratify you that the Lord provides for our needs?*

grief /'grēf/ *n.* deep sadness caused by trouble or loss; sorrow. *The team experienced grief when it was disqualified last year.*

gui·tar /gə 'tär/ *n.* derived from SPANISH; a stringed musical instrument. *Greg enjoys playing the guitar and singing praises to the Lord.*

gung ho /'gung hō/ *adj.* derived from CHINESE; overly enthusiastic. *When we learned of a Bible study, we were gung ho to get started.*

gym·na·si·um /jim 'nā zē əm/ *n.* a large, exercise room. *The college volleyball match was held in the gymnasium.*

ham·burg·er /'ham bûr gûr/ *n.* derived from GERMAN; ground beef; a sandwich consisting of a ground beef patty on a round bun. *Kurt likes to eat his hamburger with mustard and ketchup.*

hand·ling /'hand ling/ *v.* touching; managing. *Goalkeepers may use two hands when handling the ball in water polo.*

haz·ards /'ha zûrdz/ *n. pl.* plural of HAZARD; obstacles on a golf course, such as a lake or sand trap, that are either naturally or artificially constructed. *The newly designed golf course contained many water hazards.*

goalkeeper

height /ˈhīt/ *n.* the distance from top to bottom of someone or something standing upright. *Because of her height, Nicole played center.*

hel·met /ˈhel mət/ *n.* protective headgear. *It is important to wear a sturdy helmet when riding a bike.*

her·o·ism /ˈhîr ə wi zəm/ *n.* the act of being a hero. *I admire the heroism of athletes who have spoken out for Christ.*

hic·cup /ˈhi kəp/ *v.* **1** to make an involuntary gulp. *Simon heard Matt hiccup after the championship Grand Prix.* *n.* **2** an involuntary gulp. *A loud hiccup came from Jeremy's mouth.*

high·lights /ˈhī līts/ *n. pl.* plural of HIGHLIGHT; featured items of interest. *One of the race highlights was a spectacular jump.*

hor·i·zon·tal /hôr ə ˈzon təl/ *adj.* relating to a plane parallel to the horizon. *The long jump measures one's ability to jump a horizontal distance.*

hurl·ing /ˈhûr ling/ *n.* throwing forward forcefully. *The gold medalist won by hurling the javelin over twenty meters.*

hy·brid /ˈhī brəd/ *adj.* something formed by merging two original designs. *Hybrid bikes are a cross between motorcycles and mountain bikes.*

hy·drop·a·thy /hī ˈdro pə thē/ *n.* a method of treating disease by the frequent use of water both internally and externally. *Hydropathy was a method to cure disease in the nineteenth century.*

hy·dro·pla·ning /ˈhī drə plā ning/ *n.* skimming across water. *Waterskiing involves hydroplaning over the surface of the water.*

hy·dro·scope /ˈhī drə skōp/ *n.* an instrument used for viewing objects deep below the surface of water. *Tyrone is a pipeline inspector who uses a hydroscope to detect leaks.*

hy·dro·ther·a·py /hī drə ˈthâr ə pē/ *adj.* the use of water for healing. *Hydrotherapy baths are often used to relieve headaches and stress.*

hy·dro·ther·mal /hī drə ˈthûr məl/ *adj.* relating to hot water. *A hydrothermal vent spewed water through a crack in the ocean floor.*

I

i·de·al·ly /ī ˈdē ə lē/ *adv.* optimally; perfectly. *Ideally, one should remove the kickstand on a BMX bike.*

i·den·ti·fi·ca·tion /ī den tə fə ˈkā shən/ *n.* evidence or proof of identity. *Different colored caps provide identification in water polo.*

il·lu·sion /i ˈlo͞o zhən/ *n.* something that is not real. *The reflection of the sun on the water gave the illusion of fire.*

im·ag·i·nar·y /i ˈma jə nâr ē/ *adj.* related to the imagination. *I practiced with an imaginary discus before trying actual throws.*

im·i·tate /ˈi mə tāt/ *v.* copy. *Many children try to imitate the athletic style of their favorite athlete.*

im·me·di·ate·ly /i ˈmē dē ət lē/ *adv.* directly; at once; without delay. *Corrina immediately began to prepare for the pole-vault event.*

helmet

im·mi·grant /ˈi mə grənt/ *n.* one who has moved from one country to another. *Natasha was an immigrant from Russia.*

im·mov·a·ble /im ˈmo͞o və bəl/ *adj.* not able to be moved. *Immovable hurdles would be dangerous to runners.*

im·par·tial /im ˈpär shəl/ *adj.* free from bias; fair. *Judges at surfing competitions must be impartial.*

im·pose /im ˈpōz/ *v.* to put down, insist upon, or enforce. *Reina did impose her rules about penalties during the game.*

im·pos·si·bil·i·ty /im po sə ˈbi lə tē/ *n.* something not capable of happening. *J.J. thought it was an impossibility to jump over the high crossbar.*

im·prac·ti·cal /im ˈprak ti kəl/ *adj.* related to doing something that is not useful. *Heavy athletic wear is impractical during track-and-field competition.*

im·prove·ment /im ˈpro͞ov mənt/ *n.* the state of being improved; an advancement. *Allie made an improvement in her time in the 100-meter dash.*

im·pulse /ˈim pəls/ *n.* a sudden drive to act. *After the throwing events, Loni had an impulse to try the discus.*

in·com·pa·ra·ble /in ˈkom pə rə bəl/ *adj.* not able to be compared; unlike anything else. *Heaven's glory is incomparable to anything on the earth.*

in·cor·rupt·i·ble /in kə ˈrup tə bəl/ *adj.* not able to be ruined; not subject to corruption. *Our resurrected bodies will be incorruptible.*

in·cred·u·lous /in ˈkre jə ləs/ *adj.* not inclined to believe; unbelieving. *The coach was incredulous at his athletes' results.*

in·den·ta·tion /in den ˈtā shən/ *n.* a hollow or obvious depression. *The long-jump official measured the indentation in the sand.*

in·de·pen·dence /in də ˈpen dənts/ *n.* freedom. *Freestyle waterskiing provides independence from strict rules.*

in·de·scrib·a·ble /in di ˈskrī bə bəl/ *adj.* not able to give a thorough account; indefinable. *The feeling of success in reaching the top was indescribable.*

in·di·vid·u·al /in də ˈvi jə wəl/ *n.* a person. *Each individual on a soccer team is responsible for his or her actions.*

in·ex·haust·i·ble /i nig ˈzȯ stə bəl/ *adj.* not able to be exhausted; tireless. *God's forgiveness and grace are inexhaustible.*

in·flec·tion /in ˈflek shən/ *n.* **1** the state of having a change in the pitch of one's voice. *I could tell by the inflection in her voice that she was excited.* **2** a suffix that changes the part of speech or function of a word. *The suffix* -ed *is an inflection that makes verbs past tense.*

in·flex·i·ble /in ˈflek sə bəl/ *adj.* not able to be bent; unbendable. *A good surfboard must be inflexible.*

in·frac·tion /in ˈfrak shən/ *n.* a violation; a failure to obey. *An infraction was called when Allison took the ball underwater.*

i·ni·ti·at·ed /i ˈni shē ā təd/ *v.* past tense of INITIATE; to have begun. *Jorge initiated the duel by moving his back foot.*

in·ju·ries /ˈin jə rēz/ *n. pl.* plural of INJURY; hurts or damages. *Hockey players wear protective gear to prevent injuries.*

in·no·cence /ˈi nə sənts/ *n.* state of causing no harm; blamelessness or guiltlessness. *The player in the penalty box kept protesting his innocence.*

in·no·cent·ly /ˈi nə sənt lē/ *adv.* not inclined to cause harm. *Randy innocently swept the puck into his own net.*

in·quire /in ˈkwī ûr/ *v.* to seek information. *Hank began to inquire about the new skate park hours.*

in·quir·y /in 'kwī ûr ē/ *n.* the state of seeking information; a request for information. *Ethan's inquiry helped him plan his weekend schedule.*

in·quis·i·tive /in 'kwi zə tiv/ *adj.* inclined to seek out knowledge; curious. *Rose was very inquisitive about the history of the pole vault.*

in·sist /in 'sist/ *v.* to take a stand and refuse to change; to persist and maintain. *The motorcycling federation does insist on strict safety measures.*

in·spec·tion /in 'spek shən/ *n.* state of looking into or closely observing. *A detailed inspection of ski equipment should be performed regularly.*

in·spec·tor /in 'spek tûr/ *n.* one who looks into matters. *An inspector checked the gymnasium floor before the match.*

in·spire /in 'spī ûr/ *v.* to have a positive influence in someone's life. *Does the life of the apostle Paul inspire you?*

in·spir·ing /in 'spī ûr ing/ *v.* having a continuously motivating influence on someone. *The faith of our forefathers is inspiring.*

in·sured /in 'shoord/ *adj.* to have obtained insurance for. *All players must be insured before they are allowed to play.*

in·sur·mount·a·ble /int sûr 'moun tə bəl/ *adj.* not able to be overcome; unconquerable. *Russ did not consider his disability to be insurmountable.*

in·tense /in 'tents/ *adj.* **1** to an extreme degree. *The motorboat was an intense shade of blue.* **2** showing great determination or zeal. *Vince's intense concentration showed on his face.*

in·ter·cep·tion /in tûr 'sep shən/ *n.* a pass intended for an offensive receiver that is caught by a defender. *A defender caught a pass for an interception.*

in·ter·fer·ence /in tûr 'fîr ənts/ *n.* interposing in a way that impedes a play. *A penalty was called for offensive interference.*

in·ter·mis·sion /in tûr 'mi shən/ *n.* a short break between the parts of an activity. *The surfing competition had a brief intermission at noon.*

in·ter·val /'in tûr vəl/ *n.* a period of time between two events. *Jocelyn rested during the interval and encouraged her teammates.*

in·tra·mu·ral /in trə 'myoor əl/ *adj.* occurring with the members of a single school. *Callie is the pitcher on her intramural softball team.*

in·tro·spec·tive /in trə 'spek tiv/ *adj.* inclined to examining one's own feelings; thoughtful. *Janeen shared her introspective viewpoint about the meet results.*

in·var·i·ab·ly /in 'vâr ē ə blē/ *adv.* not varying; always. *Derek practiced hard and invariably took first place.*

ir·re·triev·a·ble /ir i 'trē və bəl/ *adj.* incapable of recovering, regaining, or repairing. *The rubber ball was irretrievable after it bounced into the thick hedge.*

J

jour·nal·ism /'jûr nə li zəm/ *n.* the act of writing journals or periodicals. *Hope wanted to try journalism, so she wrote for the school paper.*

K

ka·ra·te /kə 'rä tē/ *n.* derived from JAPANESE; an unarmed martial art using kicks, punches, or blocks primarily for self-defense. *Valerie went to study karate at a dojo.*

ki·lo·grams /'ki lə gramz/ *n. pl.* plural of KILOGRAM; one thousand grams. *The men's discus weighs two kilograms.*

knowl·edge·a·ble /'no lij ə bəl/ *adj.* possessing a great deal of intelligence or awareness; wise. *Javier is knowledgeable about the rules of table tennis.*

kung fu /kəng 'fo͞o/ *n.* derived from CHINESE; a martial art using open-handed techniques as well as weapons. *A wooden staff may be used for sparring in kung fu.*

L

lan·gua·ges /'lang gwi jəz/ *n. pl.* plural of LANGUAGE; the speech of races or nations; the means of expressing thoughts and feelings. *Sharon spoke four different languages by the age of twenty.*

laugh·ter /'laf tûr/ *n.* the sound of laughing. *Laughter ensued when the winning goal was scored.*

league /'lēg/ *n.* a group of sports teams that play one another. *Keith's baseball team is in the south central league.*

lec·ture /'lek chûr/ *n.* a presentation of gathered information. *Malachi gave a lecture about table tennis to the university students.*

left-hand·ed /left 'han dəd/ *adj.* using the left hand. *Jeb is unique because he is the only left-handed player on the team.*

lei·sure /'lē zhûr/ *n.* free time not taken up with work or duties. *At his leisure, Grandpa watches professional skaters on television.*

lieu·ten·ant /lo͞o 'te nənt/ *n.* a person who acts in place of someone above him in authority; an officer. *The young lieutenant enjoys in-line skating during his free time.*

light·weight /'līt wāt/ *adj.* having the quality of being light in weight. *Badminton rackets are lightweight.*

lin·e·ar /'li nē ûr/ *adj.* having the quality of a line; straight. *The winner had the longest discus throw in linear meters.*

lin·guis·tics /ling 'gwis tiks/ *n.* related to the study of language. *Lester is proficient in the area of linguistics.*

li·ver·wurst /'li vûr wûrst/ *n.* derived from GERMAN; sausage made from ground liver that is spreadable. *Did you know that liverwurst is high in iron and vitamin A?*

lock·er room /'lo kûr ro͞om/ *n.* a room used by sports players to store equipment and change clothes. *The water-polo team prayed in the locker room before the big meet.*

M

mac·a·ro·ni /ma kə 'rō nē/ *n.* derived from ITALIAN; a pasta that is shaped in the form of a tube. *Macaroni and cheese was available at the rodeo.*

ma·chin·er·y /mə 'shē nə rē/ *n.* machines in general. *The machinery that resurfaces the ice in a rink is indispensible.*

mac·ro·cosm /'ma krə ko zəm/ *n.* the universe. *God is the creator and ruler of the macrocosm, the universe.*

kung fu

mac·ro·scop·ic /ma krə 'sko pik/ *adj.* large enough to be seen without magnification. *Some algae are macroscopic.*

main·te·nance /'mān tə nənts/ *n.* upkeep of equipment or property. *Theresa was the head of lawn maintenance for the private club.*

maize /'māz/ *n.* derived from SPANISH; Indian corn. *Mamá Negrete bought maize at the store today.*

mal·func·tion /mal 'fungk shən/ *n.* **1** a state of performing badly; a breakdown. *The motorboat suffered an engine malfunction. v.* **2** to perform badly; to break down. *No sooner had the group left the dock than the engine began to malfunction.*

ma·neu·vers /mə 'nōō vûrz/ *n. pl.* plural of MANEUVER; movement involving skill and expert physical movement; tricks. *Can you perform any maneuvers on in-line skates?*

ma·ri·a·chi /mär ē 'ä chē/ *adj.* derived from SPANISH; a Mexican street band. *While we ate at the Mexican restaurant, a mariachi band played.*

mea·sur·a·ble /'me zhə rə bəl/ *adj.* capable of being measured. *Extra training gave the team a measurable edge this season.*

mea·sure·ment /'me zhûr mənt/ *n.* the dimension obtained by measuring. *The measurement of Andrea's throw in the shot put was ten meters.*

me·di·um /'mē dē əm/ *adj.* average; intermediate. *Cindi chose a track of medium length.*

med·ley /'med lē/ *n.* an assortment or mixture. *A medley relay consists of swimmers doing different strokes.*

meth·od /'me thəd/ *n.* an approach to doing something; an orderly system. *Sherri followed a specific training method when preparing to race.*

me·thod·i·cal /mə 'tho di kəl/ *adj.* following a method; thorough. *Excellence in martial arts requires methodical training.*

me·tic·u·lous /mə 'ti kyə ləs/ *adj.* conscientious; thorough; careful. *Margot was meticulous in the landscaping of the golf course.*

mi·cro·cosm /'mī krə ko zəm/ *n.* a diminished size or scale. *A drop of pond water may contain a microcosm of life.*

mi·cro·graph /'mī krə graf/ *adj.* a reproduction of an image of an object formed through a microscope. *Scientists use micrograph images to study viruses.*

mi·cro·phone /'mī krə fōn/ *n.* a device used to change sound waves into electrical impulses for the purpose of recording or amplifying the sounds. *The referee used a microphone to announce the badminton score.*

mi·cro·scop·ic /mī krə 'sko pik/ *adj.* too small to be seen without magnification under a microscope. *Many animal and plant cells are microscopic.*

mid·field /'mid fēld/ *n.* the middle of the field. *The medal ceremony was held in the midfield.*

maize

mid·sole /'mid sōl/ *n.* the middle part of a shoe's sole. *Some running shoes have a soft, supportive midsole.*

mi·grate /'mī grāt/ *v.* to move from one country to another. *The Petrov family wanted to migrate to North America.*

mil·lion·aire /mil yə 'nâr/ *n.* a very wealthy person whose wealth is estimated at a million dollars, pounds, or another currency unit; tycoon. *An athlete can become a millionaire through product endorsements.*

min·i·a·ture /'mi nē ə choor/ *adj.* small; tiny. *Carlo bought a miniature version of golf clubs for his son, Ajay.*

mis·man·aged /mis 'ma nijd/ *v.* past tense of MISMANAGE; to have handled wrongly. *Sal mismanaged his money and could not pay the entrance fees.*

mis·treat·ed /mis 'trē təd/ *v.* past tense of MISTREAT; to have treated badly. *Shad mistreated his body by continuing to run with a stress fracture.*

mois·ture /'mois chûr/ *n.* dampness; liquid spread out or concentrated in small drops. *Moisture on rocks can cause a climber to slip.*

mo·men·tous /mō 'men təs/ *adj.* important. *It was a momentous occasion when the Vipers defeated the Lions.*

mo·men·tum /mō 'men təm/ *n.* a force gained by motion. *Surfers use speed and momentum to ride up the face of a wave.*

mon·o·chro·mat·ic /mo nə krō 'ma tik/ *adj.* consisting of a single color or hue. *The team selected a monochromatic color scheme for uniforms.*

mon·o·gram /'mo nə gram/ *n.* a simple graphic formed by combining the initials in one's name. *Stuart has his monogram embroidered above his shirt pocket.*

mon·o·lith·ic /mo nə 'li thik/ *adj.* having the quality of being formed from a single stone block; huge in proportion. *Defeating the badminton champs seemed to be a monolithic task.*

mon·o·pod /'mo nə pod/ *n.* a one-legged support. *A tournament photographer used a monopod to support her camera.*

mo·to·cross /'mō tō kròs/ *n.* motorcycle cross-country racing. *The sport of motocross was the inspiration for BMX.*

mul·ti·cul·tur·al /məl tī 'kul chə rəl/ *adj.* many cultures. *The multicultural team included five nationalities.*

mul·ti·lane /'mul tī lān/ *adj.* a track with more than one lane. *The multilane track had staggered starting lines.*

mul·ti·lin·gual /məl tē 'ling gwəl/ *adj.* related to speaking several languages. *As a result of living in different countries, Meiko was multilingual.*

mul·ti·tal·ent·ed /məl tī 'ta lən təd/ *adj.* many abilities. *Gina is multitalented since she sings, paints, and runs well.*

mus·cu·lar /'mus kyə lûr/ *adj.* relating to physical strength; brawny. *Playing hockey makes one quite muscular.*

N

nec·es·sar·y /'ne sə sâr ē/ *adj.* required; essential. *Diligent practice is necessary if one wants to improve in golf.*

ne·go·ti·ate /ni 'gō shē āt/ *v.* to travel successfully along; to navigate. *It can be difficult to negotiate around rocks while rafting.*

ner·vous /'nûr vəs/ *adj.* relating to the nerves; jumpy. *Even veteran competitors feel nervous before a track meet.*

neu·tral /'nōō trəl/ *adj.* without hue; lacking vivid color. *The colorful flowers surrounded the neutral hue of the rocks.*

news·wor·thy /'nōōz wûr thē/ *adj.* interesting enough to warrant reporting to the public. *The blind man's ascent up the granite rock was a newsworthy event.*

notch /'noch/ *n.* a V-shaped cut. *Sadie placed the notch at the end of the arrow into the bowstring.*

nour·ished /'nûr ishd/ *v.* past tense of NOURISH; sustained. *The healthy meal of protein nourished the athlete's body.*

nu·mer·i·cal /noo 'mâr i kəl/ *adj.* relating to numbers. *Racers do not always line up in numerical order.*

ob·nox·ious /ob 'nok shəs/ *adj.* rudely annoying. *The crowd's behavior during the game was obnoxious.*

ob·sta·cles /'ob sti kəlz/ *n. pl.* plural of OBSTACLE; that which impedes the progress of something; barriers. *In barrel racing, horses need to turn quickly to avoid obstacles.*

ob·sti·nate /'ob stə nət/ *adj.* resisting change; stubborn. *The obstinate player would not quit despite being injured.*

oc·ca·sion /ə 'kā zhən/ *n.* an occurrence. *On one occasion, Jamie was tossed off her board by a huge wave.*

oc·cur·rence /ə 'kûr ənts/ *n.* a happening; an event or incident. *An unexpected occurrence caused us to be late to the match.*

of·fense /'o fents/ *n.* the sports team members who attempt to score in a game. *Jerry led the offense to a victory in the final game.*

of·fi·cial /ə 'fi shəl/ *n.* one whose duty is to act as a referee. *The official began the game with a jump ball.*

om·ni·scient /om 'ni shənt/ *adj.* all-knowing. *God is omniscient, omnipotent, and omnipresent.*

op·po·nents /ə 'pō nənts/ *n. pl.* plural of OPPONENT; competitors. *The athletes were opponents on the court, but friends elsewhere.*

op·posed /ə 'pōzd/ *v.* past tense of OPPOSE; to have been against something; was against. *Mitchell was opposed to drinking soda before working out.*

op·po·site /'o pə zət/ *adj.* something opposed or against another specified thing. *The teams lined up on opposite sides of the field.*

op·to·ki·net·ic /op tō kə 'ne tik/ *adj.* relating to the movement of the eyes. *Can an optometrist test the optokinetic ability of the eyes?*

op·tom·e·try /op 'to mə trē/ *n.* the health care profession concerned with assisting patients to see clearly. *Kendall will study optometry to become an eye doctor.*

o·ri·gi·nal /ə 'rij ə nəl/ *adj.* first; innovative; inventive. *Original table-tennis games were played on dining tables.*

out·crop·pings /'out kro pingz/ *n. pl.* plural of OUTCROPPING; parts of rock formations that jut out of the ground. *Sloan rested on one of the outcroppings along the trail.*

out·field·ers /'out fēl dûrz/ *n. pl.* plural of OUTFIELDER; the players in baseball or softball who play the defensive positions of left field, center field, and right field. *Two outfielders collided when they tried to catch the fly ball.*

P

pad·dling /'pad ling/ *v.* rowing with one's arms. *Alex was paddling out into the surf, hoping for a wave to break.*

pa·ja·mas /pə 'jä məz/ *n. pl.* derived from HINDI; plural of PAJAMA; loose clothing worn for sleeping. *Tasvee wore her silk pajamas from India to bed.*

par·a·le·gal /pa rə 'lē gəl/ *n.* a trained aide who assists a lawyer. *Sylvia spoke to the paralegal after her car accident.*

par·a·med·ic /pa rə 'me dik/ *n.* a trained medical technician who performs emergency medical procedures in the absence of a doctor. *Bev wanted to be a paramedic and studied diligently.*

par·a·mount /'pâr ə mount/ *adj.* greatest. *A true relationship with Jesus is a matter of paramount importance.*

par·a·pet /'pa rə pət/ *n.* derived from ITALIAN; a low wall or railing used as protection. *Avril's horse avoided the parapet near the crevice in the road.*

par·tic·i·pa·tion /pär ti sə 'pā shən/ *n.* taking part in an activity. *Nathan's participation in martial arts has helped his balance.*

ped·es·tal /'pe dəs təl/ *n.* the supporting base of a column. *The team manager placed the trophy on the pedestal.*

pen·al·ties /'pe nəl tēz/ *n. pl.* plural of PENALTY; disadvantages imposed upon a person or team for a violation of the rules. *Numerous penalties caused the home team to lose.*

per·cent·age /pûr 'sen tij/ *n.* a state of proportion within a group. *What percentage of high-jump athletes uses the Fosbury Flop method?*

¹per·mit /pûr 'mit/ *v.* to allow; give consent; authorize. *The community pool director does not permit swimming alone.*

²per·mit /'pûr mit/ *n.* written permission; license. *Kelsi is excited to get her driver's permit.*

per·pen·dic·u·lar /pûr pən 'di kyə lûr/ *adj.* standing at right angles to a given plane or surface. *The water-skiers were perpendicular to the surface of the water.*

per·se·ver·ance /pûr sə 'vîr ənts/ *n.* persistence; determination. *Trials in competition produce perseverance in Christ.*

per·spec·tive /pûr 'spek tiv/ *n.* the inclination to look at things from one's own point of view. *From Mack's perspective, today's game would be an easy win.*

per·spi·ra·tion /pûr spə 'rā shən/ *n.* the state of secreting sweat through the skin; sweat. *Perspiration is noticeable when players are actively engaged in a game.*

per·spire /pûr 'spī ûr/ *v.* to secrete sweat through the skin. *The heat of the race caused many riders to perspire.*

per·suade /pûr 'swād/ *v.* to convince by reasoning or pleading; to convince. *Trisha tried to persuade the referee to change his decision.*

phe·nom·e·nal /fi 'no mə nəl/ *adj.* remarkable. *Zoe is a phenomenal ice-hockey goalie.*

paddling

pho·tog·ra·pher /fə 'to grə fûr/ *n.* a person who practices or makes a business of taking pictures. *The photographer took some action shots of Keegan during the match.*

phys·i·cal /'fi zi kəl/ *adj.* involving a lot of bodily strength. *Motocross racing involves intense, physical demands.*

pleas·ant /'ple zənt/ *adj.* agreeable; enjoyable. *It is always pleasant to spend time reading God's Word.*

poised /'poizd/ *adj.* showing confidence and graciousness. *Was Chloe a poised, well-prepared rider?*

pop·u·lar·i·ty /po pyə 'la rə tē/ *n.* the state of being popular. *The popularity of winter sports has risen in the last few years.*

po·si·tions /pə 'zi shənz/ *n. pl.* plural of POSITION; the areas occupied by someone or something; locations. *Good hockey players are always in their correct positions.*

pos·ses·sion /pə 'ze shən/ *n.* a period of controlling the ball. *The rebound changed the possession of the basketball.*

post·ex·er·cise /pōst 'ek sûr siz/ *adj.* a routine after a workout. *A postexercise activity allows the body to cool down after exercising.*

post·op·er·a·tive /pōst 'o pə rə tiv/ *adj.* after an operation. *Calvin received excellent postoperative care from the nurses.*

pos·ture /'pos chûr/ *n.* the position of the body. *Correct posture is important in fencing.*

po·ten·tial /pə 'tent shəl/ *adj.* showing great promise. *Did the coach feel the team had a lot of potential ability?*

poul·try /'pōl trē/ *n.* domesticated birds such as chicken or turkey. *After the competition, contestants were served poultry for dinner.*

prac·tice /'prak təs/ *v.* the state of doing something repeatedly so as to become proficient or to improve. *Rex does train and practice his vaulting techniques six days a week.*

prac·ti·tion·ers /prak 'ti shə nûrz/ *n. pl.* plural of PRACTITIONER; those who practice an art or skill; experts. *Practitioners of martial arts are skilled in self-defense.*

praise·wor·thy /'prāz wûr t͟hē/ *adj.* admirable; deserving praise. *Kaitlin's sportsmanlike and respectful behavior was praiseworthy.*

pre·cau·tion /pri 'kò shən/ *n.* caution or care taken beforehand. *Crash pads are used as a precaution to avoid injuries.*

pre·cise /pri 'sīs/ *adj.* exact. *The precise long-jump distance was twenty feet, seven inches.*

pres·ti·gious /pre 'stē jəs/ *adj.* having prestige; honored. *Henri had a prestigious reputation for training Lipizzaners.*

pre·tense /'prē tents/ *n.* a claim made that is not supported by fact. *Nan joined the team on the pretense that she could water-ski.*

photographer

pret·zel /'pret səl/ *n.* derived from GERMAN; a slender, crisp or soft bread shaped like a stick or a knot, and usually salty. *Josie enjoyed a big soft pretzel as she watched the archers practice.*

prin·ci·pal /'print sə pəl/ *n.* a person who has authority in a leading position. *The principal congratulated the team for its winning performance.*

prin·ci·ple /'print sə pəl/ *n.* a rule of action or conduct. *Judges at a swim and diving meet must be people of principle.*

priv·i·lege /'pri və lij/ *n.* honor; pleasure. *Lorena had the privilege of praying for the golf team.*

pro·ac·tive /prō 'ak tiv/ *adj.* acting in anticipation toward future problems. *Carlota is proactive in living a healthy lifestyle.*

pro·ce·dure /prə 'sē jûr/ *n.* method; way of doing things. *The team doctor followed the proper procedure to treat the injury.*

pro·fes·sion /prə 'fe shən/ *n.* a calling or vocation; a career. *Few surfers are able to surf as a profession.*

pro·fes·sion·als /prə 'fe shə nəlz/ *n. pl.* plural of PROFESSIONAL; people receiving a financial gain for their skills in sports. *A few tennis professionals have won all four major tennis tournaments.*

prog·ress /'pro grəs/ *n.* a development toward achieving a goal. *Kirsten made significant progress in the latest motocross race.*

pro·jec·tile /prə 'jek tī əl/ *n.* an object that is thrown forward. *The discus is a disk-shaped projectile.*

pro·longed /prō 'lôngd/ *v.* past tense of PROLONG; to have lengthened the time to do something. *Since Art broke his ankle, it prolonged his inability to compete.*

pron·to /'pron tō/ *adv.* derived from SPANISH; without delay; fast. *The teacher instructed the class to line up for lunch, pronto.*

pro·pel /prə 'pel/ *v.* to move forward by a force; drive. *Oars are used to propel a boat.*

prop·o·si·tion /pro pə 'zi shən/ *n.* the state of something being placed or offered for consideration; proposal. *The coach's proposition to have a pizza party excited the archers.*

pro·pul·sion /prə 'pul shən/ *n.* the state of driving something forward by force. *Javelin throwers use momentum as the propulsion for the javelin.*

pro·tect·ed /prə 'tek təd/ *v.* past tense of PROTECT; to have covered beforehand; shielded. *All fencers must be protected by a fencing uniform.*

pum·per·nick·el /'pum pûr ni kəl/ *adj.* derived from GERMAN; a dark sourdough bread made with coarse rye flour. *Laura ordered a turkey sandwich with pumpernickel bread.*

qual·i·fied /'kwä lə fīd/ *v.* **1** past tense of QUALIFY; to have been made eligible. *The best teams qualified for the World Cup competition.* **2** modified. *Mrs. Davis qualified the rules during our meeting.*

qual·i·fy·ing /'kwä lə fī ing/ *v.* **1** to meet the requirements to advance in a competition. *Only two teams in our league will be qualifying to move up.* *adj.* **2** that which meets the requirements. *The players will play a qualifying round before the match.*

quar·ter·back /'kwôr tûr bak/ *n.* the offensive back who calls and directs the plays. *Michelle plays quarterback for her flag football team.*

que·sa·dil·la /kā sə 'dē ə/ *n.* derived from SPANISH; a tortilla filled with cheese and other ingredients and grilled. *Eugene ate a quesadilla for a snack.*

qui·ver /'kwi vûr/ *n.* a long, narrow case for carrying or holding arrows. *Jackson placed ten arrows in the quiver.*

R

ran·dom /'ran dəm/ *adj.* lacking a definite pattern. *In a random sequence of errors, the home team scored three runs.*

rap·pel /rə 'pel/ *v.* to descend down a rope. *Thea began to slowly rappel to the ground.*

rau·cous /'rò kəs/ *adj.* loud; disorderly. *In a raucous voice, the coach objected to the umpire's call.*

rea·sons /'rē zənz/ *n. pl.* plural of REASON; sensible explanations. *There are good reasons for every rule in BMX racing.*

re·ceipt /ri 'sēt/ *n.* a written statement that something has been received. *Kyle took the receipt from the clerk when he paid for the skateboard.*

re·ceived /ri 'sēvd/ *v.* past tense of RECEIVE; to have taken something that was given, paid, or sent; accepted. *Have you received Jesus Christ as your Savior?*

rec·ol·lect /re kə 'lekt/ *v.* to remember. *I recollect the score from last year's final game.*

rec·om·mend /re kə 'mend/ *v.* to advise favorably. *Experts recommend that you warm up before playing football.*

rec·re·a·tion·al /re krē 'ā shə nəl/ *adj.* relating to relaxation; entertaining or fun. *Table tennis is a recreational activity in many countries.*

rect·an·gu·lar /rek 'tang gyə lûr/ *adj.* shaped like a rectangle; quadrilateral. *The sand court was rectangular and bordered by bleachers.*

ref·er·ee /re fə 'rē/ *n.* a sports official who governs play. *Did you know that there is only one referee in a soccer game?*

re·fine /ri 'fīn/ *v.* to improve or perfect again. *Coach David asked the team to refine their throwing techniques.*

re·fin·ish /rē 'fi nish/ *v.* the process of finishing again; redo. *Will Collette need to refinish her surfboard?*

re·flec·ted /ri 'flek təd/ *v.* **1** past tense of REFLECT; light bent back into one's eyes. *The sunlight reflected off the surface of the lake.* **2** to think about a past event. *Jonathan reflected on the enjoyment he had experienced at summer camp.*

re·flec·tive /ri 'flek tiv/ *adj.* having the ability to bend light back into one's eyes. *Owen wore a jacket with a reflective stripe down each sleeve.*

re·flex·es /'rē flek səz/ *n. pl.* plural of REFLEX; reactions or responses. *Garrison's reflexes were superb during the tournament.*

re·gen·er·ate /ri 'je nə rāt/ *v.* to make or produce again. *The retired archer will regenerate his skills by practicing.*

re·gu·la·tion /re gyə 'lā shən/ *adj.* relating to a rule dealing with details or procedures. *All players and coaches must wear regulation helmets on the ice.*

re·joined /ri 'joind/ *v.* past tense of REJOIN; to have joined again. *Cole rejoined his friends after attending his sister's soccer game.*

rel·e·vant /'re lə vənt/ *adj.* pertaining to the matter at hand. *Stan and Kaden enjoy talking about things relevant to boating.*

re·luc·tant /ri 'luk tənt/ *adj.* unwilling. *Tamara was reluctant to go white-water rafting.*

re·new·a·ble /ri 'no͞o ə bəl/ *adj.* capable of being replaced. *Permits to rock climb are renewable every year.*

re·pel /ri 'pel/ *v.* to push, drive back, or exert an opposing force. *Geoff can repel the ball forcefully with his new racquet.*

re·po·si·tion /rē pə 'zi shən/ *v.* to change the place of an item. *Did the placekicker need to reposition the ball?*

re·quire·ments /ri 'kwī ûr mənts/ *n. pl.* plural of REQUIREMENT; regulations. *Our team follows the requirements for tournament play.*

req·ui·si·tion /re kwə 'zi shən/ *n.* a state of seeking or requesting something that is required. *Principal Brady put in a requisition for new track-and-field equipment.*

re·sil·ient /ri 'zil yənt/ *adj.* capable of recovering from misfortune. *After the canoe tipped over, resilient Gerron climbed right back in.*

re·sis·tance /ri 'zis tənts/ *n.* an opposing or slowing force. *The water offered little resistance to the skier.*

res·o·lu·tion /re zə 'lo͞o shən/ *n.* state of being set free from something; determination. *A shoot-out is the resolution to a tied game in ice hockey.*

re·solved /ri 'zolvd/ *v.* past tense of RESOLVE; to have determined, solved, or settled. *The arguing teammates resolved to put aside their differences.*

re·sound·ing /ri 'zoun ding/ *adj.* resonating; echoing. *With resounding joy, Eloise sang a worship song of praise.*

re·spect·a·ble /ri 'spek tə bəl/ *adj.* capable of being viewed favorably. *It is important to demonstrate respectable conduct at all times.*

re·spec·ted /ri 'spek təd/ *v.* past tense of RESPECT; esteemed. *Professional athletes are respected when they make wise choices.*

res·pi·ra·tion /res pə 'rā shən/ *n.* the state of breathing. *One's respiration will increase when aggressively involved in a sport.*

re·spon·si·bil·i·ty /ri spont sə 'bi lə tē/ *n.* reliability; state of being responsible. *Christian athletes have the responsibility to share Christ's love.*

res·tau·rant /'res tə ränt/ *n.* a business establishment where meals or refreshments can be purchased. *Wyatt and Alexa ate lunch at the club restaurant after their golf game.*

ret·ro·spect /'re trə spekt/ *n.* to look back and examine or remember events; a recollection. *In retrospect, the long-jump event ran smoothly and was a success.*

re·ver·ber·ate /ri 'vûr bə rāt/ *v.* to echo repeatedly. *The impact of the ball did reverberate loudly in the enclosed court.*

re·vered /ri 'vîrd/ *v.* past tense of REVERE; admired; respected. *Jesus should be highly revered for His great love toward us.*

re·versed /ri 'vûrsd/ *v.* past tense of REVERSE; to have turned something to the opposite direction, order, or position. *Due to the weather, the judges reversed the order of race events.*

restaurant

re·vived /ri 'vīvd/ *v.* past tense of REVIVE; brought back to life. *Water revived the dehydrated runner.*

rhy·thm /'ri t͟həm/ *n.* a movement with a recurring pattern of elements; repetition. *It is important to have rhythm when paddling a kayak.*

rhyth·mic /'rit͟h mik/ *adj.* having a rhythm. *Are many of the movements in martial arts rhythmic?*

ric·o·chet /'ri kə shā/ *v.* to hit a surface and bounce back; rebound. *The rubber ball will quickly ricochet off the court walls.*

ro·ta·tion /rō 'tā shən/ *n.* a turn around an axis. *I could tell that the wheel was bent from its wobbly rotation.*

ro·tun·da /rō 'tun də/ *n.* derived from ITALIAN; a round building often covered by a dome. *The ceiling of the rotunda had beautiful paintings of horses.*

rough·hous·ing /'ruf hou zing/ *v.* behaving in a rough, boisterous manner. *Two players were roughhousing and put into the penalty box.*

route /'ro͞ot/ *n.* a path; a course. *Martin carved a route in the fresh snow as he descended the mountain.*

S

sat·el·lite /'sa tə līt/ *n.* a device put into orbit around Earth or another planet to relay information or transmit communications signals. *Billions of people received the World Cup broadcast via satellite.*

sau·er·kraut /'sou ûr krout/ *n.* derived from GERMAN; shredded cabbage fermented in its own juice with salt. *Phillip ordered sauerkraut and sausage from the menu.*

sched·ules /'ske jəlz/ *n. pl.* plural of SCHEDULE; lists of commitments or appointments; plans. *The coach checked all of the time schedules before the big meet.*

schol·ar·ship /'sko lûr ship/ *n.* a state of awarding money; money given to help a worthy student continue his or her educational studies; a grant. *Lois received a full athletic scholarship to her college of choice.*

scrim·mage /'skri mij/ *n.* practice play. *Our offensive and defensive teams practice during a scrimmage.*

scul·ling /'sku ling/ *n.* a form of rowing; scull racing. *Sculling is a type of rowing that does not have a navigator.*

sed·en·tar·y /'se dən târ ē/ *adj.* inclined to sit; inactive. *Everyone should live an active lifestyle and not be sedentary.*

seize /'sēz/ *v.* to take possession of; to take hold of suddenly; grab. *The team is working diligently to seize the championship this year.*

se·lec·tion /sə 'lek shən/ *n.* the state of gathering or choosing something from among others. *There was a large selection of ski apparel to purchase.*

selt·zer /'selt sûr/ *n.* derived from GERMAN; artificially carbonated water. *Seltzer is used in carbonated beverages such as soda pop.*

sem·i·fi·nal /se mē 'fi nəl/ *adj.* the last round before the ending match of a competition. *Mason sprained his ankle during the semifinal match.*

rotunda

se·nior /'sē nyûr/ *adj.* leading; superior; higher ranking. *Franklin is a senior member of the volleyball team.*

sense /'sents/ *n.* **1** a function of perception such as sight, hearing, touch, smell, or taste. *April used her sense of hearing to tell when to shift the gears. v.* **2** to become conscious of. *Perhaps you can sense when the Lord is leading you.*

sep·a·rat·ed /'se pə rā təd/ *v.* past tense of SEPARATE; divided. *A tall net separated the two volleyball teams.*

sep·a·rate·ly /'se pə rət lē/ *adv.* distinctly; on their own. *Bryce and Reggie arrived separately for the golf tournament.*

sig·nif·i·cant /sig 'ni fi kənt/ *adj.* important. *Wearing a life vest is significant to one's safety on a boat.*

sim·u·lat·ed /'sim yə lā təd/ *v.* past tense of SIMULATE; to have replicated the effect or features of something. *The computerized game effectively simulated motocross events.*

si·mul·ta·ne·ous·ly /sī məl 'tā nē əs lē/ *adv.* occurring at the same time as something else. *All the runners began racing simultaneously.*

since /'sints/ *adv.* **1** from a definite time in the past until now. *Neal learned to water-ski as a boy, and he has loved it ever since. conj.* **2** because. *Since Isaac was not paying attention, he fell from the boat.*

sin·cere·ly /sin 'sîr lē/ *adv.* genuinely; truly. *Paloma was sincerely honored when named golf team captain.*

sla·lom /'slä ləm/ *n.* a timed race over a zigzag course. *Hannah entered the competition for the women's giant slalom.*

so·cia·ble /'sō shə bəl/ *adj.* able to seek out the company of other people or engage in social interaction; friendly; outgoing. *The sport of golf allows participants to be sociable with fellow players.*

so·ci·e·ty /sə 'sī ə tē/ *n.* a state of companionship; a group of people, generally with a common interest or role. *Angela gives back to society by teaching children how to play golf.*

som·bre·ro /səm 'brâr ō/ *n.* derived from SPANISH; a high crowned hat with a very wide brim. *The wide brim of a sombrero shaded Hector's face from the sun.*

sought /'sȯt/ *v.* past tense of SEEK; looked for. *Nick eagerly sought the results of the men's big air competition.*

sou·ve·nir /'so͞o və nîr/ *n.* a keepsake. *Charley bought a souvenir after the track-and-field finals.*

sov·er·eign /'so və rən/ *n.* above all others; supreme; greatest. *Our God is loving, just, and sovereign.*

spa·ghet·ti /spə 'ge tē/ *n.* derived from ITALIAN; long, thin strips of pasta. *A plate of spaghetti was a welcome sight to the hungry riders.*

spe·cial·ize /'spe shə līz/ *v.* making a concentrated study in one kind of activity. *Ravinder hopes to specialize in New Testament history.*

spe·cial·ty /'spe shəl tē/ *n.* a state of expertise in one kind of activity. *Hong Choi's specialty is tae kwon do.*

spec·ta·tor /'spek tā tûr/ *n.* one who watches. *Being a spectator is not as much fun as playing in a baseball game.*

spher·i·cal /'sfîr i kəl/ *adj.* shaped like a sphere; round. *The inflated, spherical volleyball was white and black.*

sports·man·ship /'spôrts mən ship/ *n.* a quality of fair conduct; fair behavior during participation in a sport. *Brody displayed great sportsmanship during the pole-vault competition.*

spring·board /'spring bôrd/ *n.* a flexible board secured at one end for diving. *A diver can dive off of a springboard or platform.*

sprint·er /'sprin tûr/ *n.* one who sprints; a short-distance runner. *Eric Liddell was a Christian missionary as well as a sprinter.*

sta·di·um /'stā dē əm/ *n.* a venue for spectators at sporting events. *Will the new stadium be completed before the track meet?*

stam·i·na /'sta mə nə/ *n.* endurance. *Daily workouts build one's stamina.*

sta·tion·ar·y /'stā shə nâr ē/ *adj.* immobile. *A diving board is stationary since it is bolted to the concrete.*

sta·tion·er·y /'stā shə nâr ē/ *n.* materials used for writing such as paper, pens, and envelopes. *The captain used stationery to write thank-you notes to the team.*

sta·tis·ti·cal·ly /stə 'tis ti kə lē/ *adv.* having the characteristic of informative pieces; precisely. *The history of track-and-field events statistically shows Greek origins.*

sta·tis·tics /stə 'tis tiks/ *n. pl.* plural of STATISTIC; a collection of data. *Kim's statistics are so impressive that scouts are watching her.*

sta·tus /'sta təs/ *n.* position in relation to others. *A softball player's status depends on his or her performance.*

stop·pa·ges /'sto pi jəz/ *n. pl.* plural of STOPPAGE; the act of stopping; obstructions. *Too much fighting leads to many stoppages during a game.*

stor·age /'stôr ij/ *n.* a place of safekeeping; a space in which items are placed for safekeeping and storing. *Cyril was asked to take the vaulting poles out of storage.*

strat·e·giz·ing /'stra tə jī zing/ *v.* devising a plan. *Antoni is strategizing ways to improve his running time.*

strat·e·gy /'stra tə jē/ *n.* a careful plan or method. *Strategy and skill are vital to playing basketball.*

strik·ers /'strī kûrz/ *n. pl.* plural of STRIKER; players on a soccer team whose main responsibility is to score goals. *Tammy warmed up by stretching with other strikers on the team.*

strokes /'strōks/ *n. pl.* plural of STROKE; unbroken movements. *Strokes used in rowing consist of recovery, catch, drive, and release.*

stru·del /'strōō dəl/ *n.* derived from GERMAN; a rolled pastry made from thin dough that contains a filling. *Sunny ate a cherry strudel for dessert.*

sub·jec·tion /səb 'jek shən/ *n.* the state of bringing under control. *The weight of a javelin is in subjection to federation rules.*

sub·scrip·tion /səb 'skrip shən/ *n.* the state of agreement to sign for something and pay for it. *Jesse renewed his sport's magazine subscription last week.*

sub·stan·tial /səb 'stant shəl/ *adj.* ample. *We had substantial time to practice our surfing skills.*

sub·sti·tute /'sub stə tōōt/ *adj.* **1** temporary replacement. *Was Theo the only substitute player for the team in last week's game? n.* **2** a replacement. *Having only one substitute for the match, the players pushed through the game.*

sub·to·tal /'sub tō təl/ *n.* the sum of a partial set of figures. *The subtotal came to fifty-five dollars, before tax.*

suc·cess·ful /sək 'ses fəl/ *adj.* favorable; effective. *The European team played a successful tournament and won the title.*

suc·ces·sion /sək 'se shən/ *n.* a sequence. *A volleyball player is not allowed to hit the ball twice in succession.*

suf·fi·cient /sə 'fi shənt/ *adj.* enough. *Players who do not drink sufficient water risk dehydration.*

su·per·ath·lete /'so͞o pûr ath lēt/ *n.* an athlete with more skills and abilities than other athletes. *A superathlete has the ability to play several sports well.*

su·per·ef·fec·tive /'so͞o pûr i fek tiv/ *adj.* better results than anticipated. *The coach's supereffective techniques assist the cross-country team.*

su·per·fi·cial /so͞o pûr 'fi shəl/ *adj.* on the surface; not deep. *Shawn's board received a superficial scratch.*

su·per·sede /so͞o pûr 'sēd/ *v.* to replace with higher qualities. *Newer boat designs supersede older models.*

sup·pos·ing /sə 'pō zing/ *v.* to continually put one's thoughts under an assumption. *Hallie is supposing she will do well since she has trained hard.*

surf·boards /'sûrf bôrdz/ *n. pl.* plural of SURFBOARD; more than one surfboard. *Ten surfboards were stuck in the sand.*

sur·passed /sûr 'pasd/ *v.* past tense of SURPASS; exceeded; to have gone beyond. *Have you surpassed a previous personal running record?*

swim·ming pool /'swi ming po͞ol/ *n.* a structure filled with water for recreational or competitive use. *Jennifer jumped into the swimming pool and began to warm up.*

T

tac·tics /'tak tiks/ *n. pl.* plural of TACTIC; methods used in combat. *Do all fencing clubs teach the same tactics?*

taut /'tȯt/ *adj.* having no slack; stretched tightly. *The bowstring must be taut before the arrow is released.*

tech·ni·cal /'tek ni kəl/ *adj.* relating to a specific subject. *A technical foul was called for poor sportsmanship.*

tech·nique /tek 'nēk/ *n.* a method. *In-line skaters and skateboarders develop their own technique.*

tech·nol·o·gy /tek 'no lə jē/ *n.* application and method of applying technical knowledge. *Modern engineering technology enables motorcycles to run faster.*

tel·e·vised /'te lə vīzd/ *v.* past tense of TELEVISE; to have broadcasted a far distance to be seen. *The final match was televised to millions of viewers.*

tel·e·vi·sion /'te lə vi zhən/ *n.* an electronic device that receives and projects pictures and sounds. *Vance watched the World Championship on the television.*

ten·sion /'tent shən/ *n.* the act of being stretched to stiffness; tautness. *The tension of the bow propelled the arrow toward the target.*

surfboards

ter·i·ya·ki /târ ē 'yä kē/ *adj.* derived from JAPANESE; a dish of meat or fish marinated in a seasoned soy sauce marinade. *Anjali loves teriyaki beef over rice.*

ter·rain /tə 'rān/ *n.* landscape; ground. *Jerome felt confident as he raced along the bumpy terrain.*

ther·mo·gen·ic /thûr mə 'je nik/ *adj.* relating to the production of heat. *A thermogenic sport, such as tennis, raises one's body temperature.*

ther·mog·ra·phy /thûr 'mo grə fē/ *n.* a process of printing or writing using heat. *Thermography is a printing process that produces raised images.*

ther·mom·e·ter /thûr 'mo mə tûr/ *n.* a device to measure heat. *The outdoor thermometer read 98 degrees Fahrenheit.*

ther·mo·stat /'thûr mə stat/ *n.* a device that automatically regulates heat. *The thermostat at the indoor tennis club read 68 degrees Fahrenheit.*

thor·ough·ly /'thûr ō lē/ *adv.* done fully. *Justin thoroughly practiced before the finals competition.*

though /'th̲ō/ *conj.* even if; although. *Though it was snowing, the Alpine events continued.*

thought·less·ly /'thôt ləs lē/ *adv.* carelessly. *The ski jumper thoughtlessly broke form and landed awkwardly.*

through·out /thro͞o 'out/ *prep.* during the whole time. *Dimitri had a positive attitude throughout the competition.*

tie·break·er /'tī brā kûr/ *n.* a method used to decide the winner of a competition with a tied score. *Grace won the tiebreaker after scoring the final point.*

ti·ta·ni·um /tī 'tā nē əm/ *n.* a strong, lightweight, metallic element. *Brenda's new golf clubs were made of titanium.*

torque /'tôrk/ *n.* a rotating force that causes turning and twisting. *During a golf swing, torque is a twisting movement of the club's shaft.*

tor·so /'tôr sō/ *n.* the upper part of the body, not including the head and the arms. *Felipe touched Hunter's torso with his blade and scored a point.*

tor·til·la /tôr 'tē ə/ *n.* derived from SPANISH; a round, thin bread made from cornmeal or wheat flour. *Juan asked for one more tortilla to eat with his fajitas.*

touch·down /'tuch doun/ *n.* a score of six points in American football. *The Mountain Goats scored a touchdown!*

tour·na·ment /'toor nə mənt/ *n.* a series of games. *The soccer tournament began with a parade of athletes.*

tow·rope /'tō rōp/ *n.* a line used in towing a water-skier behind a boat; a line used for towing. *The beginning water-skier gripped the towrope tightly.*

trac·tion /'trak shən/ *n.* adhesive friction that causes a thing to hold firmly to a surface; grip. *It is difficult for wheels to have traction on wet surfaces.*

tra·jec·to·ry /trə 'jek tə rē/ *n.* the path or route of a flying object. *The golf ball's trajectory determines how far it goes down the fairway.*

titanium

tran·si·tion·al /tran 'zi shə nəl/ *adj.* moves from one stage to another. *Is this a transitional period for the Paralympics?*

trans·par·en·cy /trants 'pâr ənt sē/ *n.* the quality of light passing through objects so they can be seen from one side to the other side. *The transparency of the water allowed Seth to see the sunken rings.*

trans·verse /tranz 'vûrs/ *adj.* extending across; horizontal. *Lee's body dislodged the transverse crossbar during his high jump.*

tra·versed /trə 'vûrsd/ *v.* past tense of TRAVERSE; to have traveled across, over, or through a particular location. *Meika successfully traversed the course during the women's event.*

tre·men·dous /tri 'men dəs/ *adj.* incredible. *Tremendous applause erupted after the record-breaking jump.*

trep·i·da·tion /tre pə 'dā shən/ *n.* fear. *I approached my first surfing lesson with much trepidation.*

tri·vi·a /'tri vē ə/ *n. pl.* unimportant information or details. *Do you know any trivia about baseball?*

U

un·au·tho·rized /'un ȯ thə rīzd/ *adj.* not warranted by proper authority; not duly commissioned. *Climbers should always avoid wandering into unauthorized areas.*

un·con·vinced /ən kən 'vinst/ *adj.* doubtful. *We were unconvinced that the scoreboard was accurate.*

un·der·es·ti·mate /ən dûr 'es tə māt/ *v.* to estimate less than the actual size or amount. *People should never underestimate the power of prayer.*

un·der·nour·ished /ən dûr 'nûr isht/ *adj.* having less than the minimum amount of food for proper nourishment. *The athlete volunteered his time to help undernourished children.*

un·fin·ished /ən 'fi nisht/ *adj.* not yet at an end; incomplete. *Phil's surfboard is still in the garage because it is unfinished.*

u·ni·fy /'yo͞o nə fī/ *v.* to unite. *Working together will unify the team.*

un·nec·es·sar·y /ən 'ne sə sâr ē/ *adj.* needless. *Violet was told that her entry fee payment was unnecessary.*

V

vault·ed /'vȯl təd/ *v.* past tense of VAULT; to have executed a leap with the aid of the hands or a pole. *Janelle successfully vaulted over the high crossbar.*

ve·loc·i·ty /və 'lo sə tē/ *n.* speed. *The velocity of a tennis serve can be over one hundred miles per hour.*

ve·ran·da /və 'ran də/ *n.* derived from HINDI; a roofed portico attached to the exterior of a building; a covered patio. *The veranda was the coolest place to be on a hot summer night.*

ver·sa·tile /'vûr sə təl/ *adj.* easily turning from one thing to another; changeable. *A versatile player is very good at batting and also at fielding.*

ver·sions /'vûr zhənz/ *n. pl.* plural of VERSION; forms or types of. *Different versions of water polo can involve variations in play area.*

ver·ti·cal /'vûr ti kəl/ *adj.* upright at a right angle to the horizon. *Vertical posts hold a crossbar during pole-vault or high-jump events.*

vi·sor /'vī zûr/ *n.* the upper, front piece of a helmet. *Renee's visor shields her eyes from the sun.*

vi·su·al /ˈvi zhə wəl/ *adj.* relating to vision. *Coach Wright used the whiteboard as a visual aid to explain the play.*

vi·va·cious /vī ˈvā shəs/ *adj.* having the quality of liveliness; perky; lively. *Does Stephanie have a vivacious personality?*

vol·leyed /ˈvo lēd/ *v.* past tense of VOLLEY; to have hit a ball or shuttlecock in succession without allowing it to hit the ground. *In badminton, the shuttlecock is always volleyed over the net.*

W

wa·ter·line /ˈwȯ tûr līn/ *n.* a line to which a body of water rises. *The floating water-polo nets touched the waterline in the pool.*

weird /ˈwîrd/ *adj.* odd; unusual; strange. *Many skateboards have weird designs on their decks.*

well-con·di·tioned /wel kən ˈdi shənd/ *adj.* being in good physical condition or shape. *The well-conditioned athlete effortlessly swam laps.*

wide·spread /ˈwīd spred/ *adj.* happening in many places; prevalent. *After a major win, the news of the team's success was widespread.*

Index

Note: Page numbers refer to the student page inserts in the Teacher Edition. Lesson numbers preceded by TE *refer to Teacher Edition content.*

Note: Page numbers refer to the student page inserts in the Teacher Edition. Lesson numbers preceded by TE refer to Teacher Edition content.

Note: Page numbers refer to the student page inserts in the Teacher Edition. Lesson numbers preceded by TE refer to Teacher Edition content.

Q

R

Note: Page numbers refer to the student page inserts in the Teacher Edition. Lesson numbers preceded by TE refer to Teacher Edition content.

S

Note: Page numbers refer to the student page inserts in the Teacher Edition. Lesson numbers preceded by TE *refer to Teacher Edition content.*

T

V

Note: Page numbers refer to the student page inserts in the Teacher Edition. Lesson numbers preceded by TE *refer to Teacher Edition content.*

W

Note: Page numbers refer to the student page inserts in the Teacher Edition. Lesson numbers preceded by TE *refer to Teacher Edition content.*

SILVER EDITION

Teacher's Edition with Tests

Mosaic 1

LISTENING/SPEAKING

Jami Hanreddy
Elizabeth Whalley
Teacher's Edition by Becky Tarver Chase

Mosaic 1 Listening/Speaking Teacher's Edition with Tests, Silver Edition

Published by McGraw-Hill ESL/ELT, a business unit of The McGraw-Hill Companies, Inc. 1221 Avenue of the Americas, New York, NY 10020.

ISBN 13: 978-0-07-329409-4 (Teacher's Edition)
ISBN 10: 0-07-329409-8 (Teacher's Edition)
2 3 4 5 6 7 8 9 10 EUS 11 10 09 08 07

Editorial director: Erik Gundersen
Series editor: Valerie Kelemen
Developmental editor: Jenny Petrow
Production manager: Juanita Thompson
Production coordinator: Vanessa Nuttry
Cover designer: Robin Locke Monda
Interior designer: Nesbitt Graphics, Inc.

Cover photo: David Samuel Robbins/CORBIS

www.esl-elt.mcgraw-hill.com

The McGraw·Hill Companies

Table of Contents

Introduction

Student Book Teaching Notes and Answer Keys

Welcome to the Teacher's Edition

The Teacher's Edition of *Interactions/Mosaic* Silver Edition provides support and flexibility to teachers using the *Interactions/Mosaic* Silver Edition 18-book academic skills series. The Teacher's Edition provides step-by-step guidance for implementing each activity in the Student Book. The Teacher's Edition also provides expansion activities with photocopiable masters of select expansion activities, identification of activities that support a Best Practice, valuable notes on content, answer keys, audioscripts, end-of-chapter tests, and placement tests. Each chapter in the Teacher's Edition begins with an overview of the content, vocabulary, and teaching goals in that chapter. Each chapter in the Student Book begins with an engaging photo and related discussion questions that strengthen the educational experience and connect students to the topic.

- **Procedural Notes**
  The procedural notes are useful for both experienced and new teachers. Experienced teachers can use the bulleted, step-by step procedural notes as a quick guide and refresher before class, while newer or substitute teachers can use the notes as a more extensive guide to assist them in the classroom. The procedural notes guide teachers through each strategy and activity; describe what materials teachers might need for an activity; and help teachers provide context for the activities.

- **Answer Keys**
  Answer keys are provided for all activities that have definite answers. For items that have multiple correct answers, various possible answers are provided. The answer key follows the procedural note for the relevant activity. Answer keys are also provided for the Chapter Tests and the Placement Tests.

- **Expansion Activities**
  A number of expansion activities with procedural notes are included in each chapter. These activities offer teachers creative ideas for reinforcing the chapter content while appealing to different learning styles. Activities include games, conversation practice, presentations, and projects. These expansion activities often allow students to practice integrated language skills, not just the skills that the student book focuses on. Some of the expansion activities include photocopiable black line masters included in the back of the book.

- **Content Notes**
  Where appropriate, content notes are included in the Teacher's Edition. These are notes that might illuminate or enhance a learning point in the activity and might help teachers answer student questions about the content. These notes are provided at the logical point of use, but teachers can decide if and when to use the information in class.

- **Chapter Tests**
  Each chapter includes a chapter test that was designed to test the vocabulary, reading, writing, grammar, and/or listening strategies taught in the chapter, depending on the language skill strand being used. Teachers can simply copy and distribute the tests, then use the answer keys found in the Teacher's Edition. The purpose of the chapter tests is not only to assess students' understanding of material covered in the chapter but also to give students an idea of how they are doing and what they need to work on. Each chapter test has four parts with items totaling 100 points. Item types include multiple choice, fill-in-the blank, and true/false. Audioscripts are provided when used.

- **Black Line Masters (Photocopiable Masters)**
  Each chapter includes a number of expansion activities with black line masters, or master worksheets, that teachers can copy and distribute. These activities and black line masters are optional. They can help reinforce and expand on chapter material in an engaging way. Activities include games;

conversation practice; working with manipulatives such as sentence strips; projects; and presentations. Procedural notes and answer keys (when applicable) are provided in the Teacher's Edition.

- **Placement Tests**
  Each of the four language skill strands has a placement test designed to help assess in which level the student belongs. Each test has been constructed to be given in under an hour. Be sure to go over the directions and answer any questions before the test begins. Students are instructed not to ask questions once the test begins. Following each placement test, you'll find a scoring placement key that suggests the appropriate book to be used based on the number of items answered correctly. Teachers should use judgment in placing students and selecting texts.

The Interactions/Mosaic Silver Edition Program

Interactions/Mosaic Silver Edition is a fully-integrated, 18-book academic skills series. Language proficiencies are articulated from the beginning through advance levels <u>within</u> each of the four language skill strands. Chapter themes articulate <u>across</u> the four skill strands to systematically recycle content, vocabulary, and grammar.

- **Reading Strand**
  Reading skills and strategies are strategically presented and practiced through a variety of themes and reading genres in the five Reading books. Pre-reading, reading, and post-reading activities include strategies and activities that aid comprehension, build vocabulary, and prepare students for academic success. Each chapter includes at least two readings that center around the same theme, allowing students to deepen their understanding of a topic and command of vocabulary related to that topic. Readings include magazine articles, textbook passages, essays, letters, and website articles. They explore, and guide the student to explore, stimulating topics. Vocabulary is presented before each reading and is built on throughout the chapter. High-frequency words and words from the Academic Word List are focused on and pointed out with asterisks (*) in each chapter's Self-Assessment Log.

- **Listening/Speaking Strand**
  A variety of listening input, including lectures, academic discussions, and conversations help students explore stimulating topics in the five Listening/Speaking books. Activities associated with the listening input, such as pre-listening tasks, systematically guide students through strategies and critical thinking skills that help prepare them for academic achievement. In the Interactions books, the activities are coupled with instructional photos featuring a cast of engaging, multi-ethnic students participating in North American college life. Across the strand, lectures and dialogues are broken down into manageable parts giving students an opportunity to predict, identify main ideas, and effectively manage lengthy input. Questions, guided discussion activities, and structured pair and group work stimulate interest and interaction among students, often culminating in organizing their information and ideas in a graphic organizer, writing, and/or making a presentation to the class. Pronunciation is highlighted in every chapter, an aid to improving both listening comprehension and speaking fluency. Enhanced focus on vocabulary building is developed throughout and a list of target words for each chapter is provided so students can interact meaningfully with the material. Finally, Online Learning Center features MP3 files from the Student Book audio program for students to download onto portable digital audio players.

- **Writing Strand**
  Activities in each of the four Writing books are systematically structured to culminate in a *Writing Product* task. Activities build on key elements of writing from sentence development to writing single

paragraphs, articles, narratives, and essays of multiple lengths and genres. Connections between writing and grammar tie the writing skill in focus with the grammar structures needed to develop each writing skill. Academic themes, activities, writing topics, vocabulary development, and critical thinking strategies prepare students for university life. Instructional photos are used to strengthen engagement and the educational experience. Explicit pre-writing questions and discussions activate prior knowledge, help organize ideas and information, and create a foundation for the writing product. Each chapter includes a self-evaluation rubric which supports the learner as he or she builds confidence and autonomy in academic writing. Finally, the Writing Articulation Chart helps teachers see the progression of writing strategies both in terms of mechanics and writing genres.

- **Grammar Strand**
  Questions and topical quotes in the four Grammar books, coupled with instructional photos stimulate interest, activate prior knowledge, and launch the topic of each chapter. Engaging academic topics provide context for the grammar and stimulate interest in content as well as grammar. A variety of activity types, including individual, pair, and group work, allow students to build grammar skills and use the grammar they are learning in activities that cultivate critical thinking skills. Students can refer to grammar charts to review or learn the form and function of each grammar point. These charts are numbered sequentially, formatted consistently, and indexed systematically, providing lifelong reference value for students.

- **Focus on Testing for the TOEFL® iBT**
  The all-new TOEFL® iBT *Focus on Testing* sections prepare students for success on the TOEFL® iBT by presenting and practicing specific strategies for each language skill area. The Focus on Testing sections are introduced in Interactions 1 and are included in all subsequent levels of the Reading, Listening/Speaking, and Writing strands. These strategies focus on what The Educational Testing Service (ETS) has identified as the target skills in each language skill area. For example, "reading for basic comprehension" (identifying the main idea, understanding pronoun reference) is a target reading skill and is presented and practiced in one or more *Focus on Testing* sections. In addition, this and other target skills are presented and practiced in chapter components outside the *Focus on Testing* sections and have special relevance to the TOEFL® iBT. For example, note-taking is an important test-taking strategy, particularly in the listening section of the TOEFL® iBT, and is included in activities within each of the Listening/Speaking books. All but two of the *Interactions/Mosaic* titles have a *Focus on Testing* section. Although *Interactions Access Reading* and *Interaction Access Listening/Speaking* don't include these sections because of their level, they do present and develop skills that will prepare students for the TOEFL® iBT.

- **Best Practices**
  In each chapter of this Teacher's Edition, you'll find Best Practices boxes that highlight a particular activity and show how this activity is tied to a particular Best Practice. The Interactions/Mosaic Silver Edition team of writers, editors, and teacher consultants has identified the following six interconnected Best Practices.

* TOEFL is a registered trademark of Educational Testing Services (ETS). This publication is not endorsed or approved by ETS.

Interactions Mosaic/Best Practices

Best Practices

Each chapter identifies at least six different activities that support six Best Practices, principles that contribute to excellent language teaching and learning. Identifying Best Practices helps teachers to see, and make explicit for students, how a particular activity will aid the learning process.

Making Use of Academic Content

Materials and tasks based on academic content and experiences give learning real purpose. Students explore real world issues, discuss academic topics, and study content-based and thematic materials.

Organizing Information

Students learn to organize thoughts and notes through a variety of graphic organizers that accommodate diverse learning and thinking styles.

Scaffolding Instruction

A scaffold is a physical structure that facilitates construction of a building. Similarly, scaffolding instruction is a tool used to facilitate language learning in the form of predictable and flexible tasks. Some examples include oral or written modeling by the teacher or students, placing information in a larger framework, and reinterpretation.

Activating Prior Knowledge

Students can better understand new spoken or written material when they connect to the content. Activating prior knowledge allows students to tap into what they already know, building on this knowledge, and stirring a curiosity for more knowledge.

Interacting with Others

Activities that promote human interaction in pair work, small group work, and whole class activities present opportunities for real world contact and real world use of language.

Cultivating Critical Thinking

Strategies for critical thinking are taught explicitly. Students learn tools that promote critical thinking skills crucial to success in the academic world.

Chapter

1

New Challenges

In this chapter, students will think about language learning and how languages affect the people who speak them. In Part 1, they will prepare for the topic by getting in touch with their own ideas about languages and language learning, and by previewing useful vocabulary. In Part 2, they will listen to a lecture about the nature of language and how a language can affect the worldview of its speakers. They will also learn how making predictions while listening can help them maintain their focus and improve their comprehension. In Part 3, students will learn about offering and requesting clarification, as well as polite ways to interrupt a speaker. In Part 4, they will examine TOEFL® iBT questions dealing with pragmatic understanding.

Chapter Opener

- ❑ Direct students' attention to the photo and ask questions: *Who are these people? Where do you think they are? Which language are they using to talk to each other?*
- ❑ Divide students into groups to discuss the "Connecting to the Topic" questions.
- ❑ Discuss the quotation from Italian film director Federico Fellini. What does it mean? How can a language affect the way we experience life?

"A different language is a different vision of life."

—Federico Fellini
Italian filmmaker (1920–1993)

Chapter Overview

Lecture: Learning to Speak Someone Else's Language

Learning Strategy: Making Predictions

Language Function: Offering and Requesting Clarification

Part 1: Building Background Knowledge

Did You Know?

Sharing Your Experience

Vocabulary Preview

Part 2: Making Predictions

Predicting What an Instructor Will Say Next

After You Listen

Talk It Over

Part 3: Offering and Requesting Clarification

Ways to Offer Clarification

Understanding a Lecturer's Style of Offering Clarification

Ways to Request Clarification

Talk It Over

Part 4: Focus on Testing

Self-Assessment Log

Did You Know?

- ❑ Have students read the "Did You Know?" points.
- ❑ Compare the statistics with the students' own languages. Ask, for example, "How many languages have you learned to speak fluently?" or "How many letters does the alphabet for your language have?"

1 What Do You Think?

Best Practice

Interacting with Others

This activity is an example of collaborative learning intended to promote fluency and confidence. In this pairs activity, communication is more important than grammar. Students begin to discuss languages and language learning in pairs, and when they discuss the topic as a class they should feel more confident in their use of the new language.

- ❑ Divide students into pairs to discuss the questions. Set a time limit for the discussion.
- ❑ Go over each question as a class and ask students to volunteer ideas from their pair discussions. Note key words and ideas on the board.

Sharing Your Experience

2 Discussing Changes

- ❑ Give students time to read the questions and take brief notes on their ideas.
- ❑ Divide students into small groups to discuss the questions. Ask each student to be responsible for reading one of the questions aloud to the group. Make sure every group member has the opportunity express an opinion about the question.

Vocabulary Preview

3 Determining Meaning from Context

Best Practice

Scaffolding Instruction

This activity raises an awareness of learning strategies. In real life, we use context clues to work out the meanings of unfamiliar words. This activity isolates potentially unfamiliar words from the lecture and asks students to use the surrounding words in each sentence to get a sense of the new vocabulary.

- ❑ Instruct students to look for clues in the sentences. Tell them that this will help them understand the meanings of the underlined words.
- ❑ Have students work individually to match the underlined words with their definitions.
- ❑ Go over the answers. Refer to the sentences and their context clues. Say for item 1, for example, "All right, if collage means 'an artistic arrangement of a variety of materials and objects', what examples of materials or objects can we find in this sentence?" The students should indicate paper, wood, leaves, and glue.

ANSWER KEY

1. c 2. f 3. e 4. h 5. i 6. a 7. j 8. b 9. d 10. g

Content Note: the /ʒ/ or /ž/ sound

- The final sound in the word *collage*, or the one in the middle of *déjà*, is transcribed in the International Phonetic Alphabet as /ʒ/ or /ž/, and is one of the rarest sounds in the English language. Sometimes occurring in words borrowed from French, including *rouge* and *beige*, the /ʒ/ or /ž/ sound also occurs in English words like *division* and *measure*. It is formed with the same mouth position as the /ʃ/ or /š/ sound in *wish* and *fish*, but with the vibration of the vocal chords added.

4 Categorizing 

Best Practice

Organizing Information

This activity uses a graphic organizer to arrange information visually. Creating a chart that presents new vocabulary from the lecture encourages students to process and organize the words and concepts, and also provides a record for them to refer to when reviewing their notes. This type of graphic organizer emphasizes vocabulary categorizing skills. Other types of graphic organizers are used throughout this book.

- ❑ Explain to students that this chart is a tool to help them study new vocabulary.
- ❑ Divide students into pairs to brainstorm ideas to complete the chart. Go over the categories and examples together to see if there are any questions.

REPRODUCIBLE EXPANSION ACTIVITY

- The goal of this activity is for students to become more familiar with their classmates as well as the ideas in the chapter.
- Photocopy and distribute BLM 1, "Language Learning Survey" on page BLM 1 of this Teacher's Edition.
- Ask students to move around the classroom and talk to three classmates as they fill in their charts.
- Finish the activity by asking the class what they learned about each student; for example, "What did you find out about Se-Hee?"

Strategy

Predicting What an Instructor Will Say Next

- Go over the steps for making predictions while listening to a lecture.
- Point out that learning is the process of making new connections in the brain. When students think about a topic they are already familiar with, their brains are ready to form connections between that familiar information and new information.
- Tell students that making predictions during a lecture gives them something to listen for. This keeps them actively focused on content and means they will learn more!

Before You Listen

1 Considering the Topic

Best Practice

Activating Prior Knowledge

The pre-listening sections activate students' prior knowledge. This activity helps students relate their own experiences with languages and language learning to the material in this chapter. When students activate their prior knowledge before learning new material, they are better able to use that knowledge to understand new concepts about language and communication presented in the chapter.

- ❑ Point out that *brainstorm* means to think of as many ideas as possible in the shortest time possible.
- ❑ Divide students into small groups to brainstorm ideas for each question using the graphic organizers on page 9 of the Student Book.
- ❑ Ask the note-takers in each group to write members' ideas in the smaller circles of the graphic organizer.
- ❑ Call on note-takers to report on their groups' brainstorming sessions.

Listen

2 Listening to Make Predictions

- ❑ Remind students of the guidelines for making predictions on page 8 of the Student Book.
- ❑ Play the audio of the lecture, stopping after each sentence indicated in the activity. Ask students to write down their predictions and then share them with a partner.
- ❑ Continue listening to check predictions and change those that are not correct.

AUDIOSCRIPT

Lecture: Learning to Speak Someone Else's Language

Professor: Good morning! I am James Munro, and this is Linguistics 101.

Students: Good morning. Hello. Hi.

Professor: Our topic today is "Learning to Speak Someone Else's Language." Before I begin, I'd like to hear your questions on the topic. What does the title "Learning to Speak Someone Else's Language" bring to mind? What does it make you think about? Just call out your questions.

Student 1: What is language? I mean, where does it come from?

Professor: Good question. Any others?

Student 2: Who uses language? Is it only humans?

Professor: Interesting. Next?

Student 3: When does language develop? At what age?

Professor: Good, got that. Yes, go ahead.

Student 4: How many languages are there in the world? And can we ever really learn to speak someone else's language?

Professor: Hmm. Any more? No? Then let's begin with that last question. Can we ever really learn to speak another person's language? Well, I think that we must at least try. You see, language is the only window we have to see into someone else's mind. But this presents us with a paradox. On the one hand, language helps us communicate with each other. On the other hand, communication is almost impossible when we don't understand the words and symbols that someone else is using. OK so far?

Communication can fail even when two people have the same native language. You see, in addition to their usual meanings, words and concepts have very personal meanings for each person based on memories and experiences. Does that make sense to you?

Student 2: I think so. Is it like when I hear the word *dog*, I might think of the little beagle named Sarge that I had when I was a kid, but my friend, who is afraid of dogs, might think of Cujo? You know, that huge dog that attacked people in that old Stephen King movie?

Professor: That's right! Exactly! Here's another example: A rose may be just a beautiful object to me, but it may remind you of a lovely summer in England or a romantic birthday present. So you can see the problem, right?

Students: Sure. Right. Uh-huh.

Professor: Also, there are between 3,000 and 6,000 public languages in the world and we must add approximately five billion private languages since each of us has one. Did you get that? With this many languages, it's amazing that we understand each other at all.

However, sometimes we *do* communicate successfully. We *do* learn to speak other languages. But learning to speak a language seems to be a very mysterious process. Now this brings us back to the first question on our list: Where does language come from? And how does it develop?

For a long time, people thought that we learned language only by imitation and association. For example, a baby touches a hot pot and starts to cry. The mother says, "Hot, hot!" and the baby—when it stops crying—imitates the mother and says, "Hot, hot." The baby then associates the word "hot" with the burning feeling. However, Noam Chomsky, a famous linguist, said that although children do learn *some* words by imitation and association, they also combine words to make sentences in ways they have never heard before. Chomsky suggested that this is possible because human babies have an innate ability to learn any language in the world. Are you following me?

Student 5: Maybe.

Professor: Chomsky says that children are born with the ability to learn language, but this does not explain how children begin to use language in different ways. For example, as children develop their language skills, they quickly learn that language is used for more than stating facts such as "The ball is red." They learn to make requests, to give commands, to agree, to disagree, to explain, to excuse, and even to lie. The uses of language seem endless. This is the positive side of the paradox. Did you get that?

Students: Maybe. Not exactly. I'm not sure.

Professor: In other words, language is a wonderful way of communicating our ideas to other people. The negative side of the paradox is that not all people speak the same language, and therefore we cannot understand each other.

So we're back to where we started. Can we ever really learn to speak someone else's language?

For now, let's assume that we can learn to speak someone else's language, not just a few polite phrases, but really learn to speak it fluently. We know that we will be able to communicate with other people who speak that language. But something else happens as well. I think that learning another language can transform us as individuals—it can change our world view and even our personalities. For example, if we speak French fluently, we can begin to see the world in a way that is typically French. That is, we can view the world from an entirely different point of view, which might change our personalities dramatically. Are you following me?

Student 3: Not exactly. Professor Munro, I'm not sure that I buy the idea that I would actually become someone else just because I learned to speak another language.

Professor: OK, consider this. A linguist named Benjamin Lee Whorf said that our native language actually determines the way we see the world. I believe he meant something like this: Imagine a language that has no words for anger, fear, or jealousy. Does that mean that we won't experience these emotions if we are native speakers of that language?

Or, imagine a language that has 25 words for love. Will we be able to love more deeply if we are native speakers of that language?

Student 3: Well, maybe. But I think there's a problem with that point of view.

Professor: OK. What do you think that might be?.

Student 3: Well, for one thing, that point of view ignores the fact that languages change and that they borrow words from other languages. For example, English sometimes uses words from other languages to express a thought or name a thing in a better way.

Professor: Yes, of course! As I sat at home preparing for this lecture, I looked up at the collage on my wall and took a bite out of my croissant. Later I experienced a moment of déjà-vu. So, to describe my activities this morning, I have just used three words borrowed from French—*collage, croissant,* and *déjà-vu*—because they describe certain things and experiences better than any English words.

Student 3: So English is transformed by words from other languages that express things that really cannot be expressed very well in English!

Professor: Right! In a way, this transformation is what happens to us when we learn to speak someone else's language. We learn, perhaps, to express things that could not be expressed as well—or even at all—in our own languages. We may also learn to understand things in ways that we could not before. Does that make sense to you? We can begin to experience what it must be like to be born into another culture.

Oh, my. Our time seems to be up. Next time, be prepared to talk about your own experiences in learning about another culture as you learned to speak a second language. Also, please read Chapters 1 and 2 in your textbook and think about this question: If we learn one language so easily as children, why is it such a challenge to learn a second language as adults?

Content Notes

- Noam Chomsky is Professor Emeritus of linguistics at the Massachusetts Institute of Technology (MIT). In *Syntactic Structures*, published in 1957, Chomsky challenged behavioral theories of language learning, which emphasized imitating others and responding to positive or negative feedback. Chomsky presented the idea that human beings are born with the ability to learn the patterns of a language and generate an unlimited number of sentences based on those patterns. This idea became known as Transformational (or Generative) Grammar. Chomsky also writes and speaks on political topics.
- Benjamin Whorf (1897–1941) was another American linguist who is remembered most for his contribution to the Sapir-Whorf Hypothesis, which states that languages are shaped by the cultures that create them, and that languages affect the thoughts of the people who speak them. Modern linguists have mixed views about this hypothesis.

After You Listen

3 Comparing Predictions 

- ❑ Play the audio of the lecture again, stopping at the points indicated in the "Listening to Make Predictions" section to compare predictions.
- ❑ Conduct a class discussion about the students' predictions, how they made their predictions, and what they learned from their classmates' predictions and reasons for them. Ask students what they learned from the activity that they can use in future listening situations.

Talk It Over

4 Making Predictions 

Best Practice

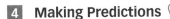

Making Use of Academic Content

This small group discussion involves real-world issues. This type of activity encourages students to relate the topic of the chapter to the authentic world of their own experiences. Asking students to discuss their predictions creates an authentic framework through which they can interpret the topic and contribute real examples from their own lives.

- ❑ Go over the directions and the example situation from the student book.
- ❑ Ask students to read the situations and write their predictions about what will happen. Set a time limit for this part of the activity.
- ❑ Divide students into small groups to share their predictions. Encourage them to explain the reasons behind their predictions; for example, ask whether they considered details about the characters, their own past experiences, or some other criteria.

Content Notes

- In Activity 4, item 3, a young man and woman are interested in getting married and are trying to think of a way to broach the subject with each other. As in many cultures, young people in the U.S. often choose a spouse themselves without the help of a matchmaker or family.
- While the independence of American young people is well known, the 16-year-old boy from item 2 in the activity who wants his mother's permission to get his nose pierced is also typical. Both the young couple and the young man want to make their own decisions, but they may also want their families' approval.

5 Role-Plays 

- ❑ Divide students into pairs and ask them to choose one of the situations from Activity 4 "Making Predictions" to perform in front of the class. Alternatively, have each pair take a numbered slip of paper to speed up the selection process.
- ❑ Instruct students to talk about what they will say in their role-play rather than write a script. This will make the role-plays easier to understand and give students time to rehearse.
- ❑ Notify the students when the preparation time is almost up. Then ask them to give their classmates their undivided attention during the presentations.
- ❑ After each role-play, conduct a brief discussion using the questions provided.

REPRODUCIBLE

EXPANSION ACTIVITY

- The aim of this activity is for students to use the Internet to learn about famous linguists, and then share their information and reactions with classmates.
- Photocopy and distribute BLM 2, "Learning About Linguists" on page BLM 2 of this Teacher's Edition and divide the class into groups of four. (If your class is not divisible by four, ask one student to research two linguists, or two students to research the same linguist.)
- Ask the groups to assign one linguist to each member. Students will go online and find out about one of the linguists so that they can tell their classmates about her or him. This can be done in a computer lab during class time or assigned for homework.
- Have the groups reassemble and share the information they need to complete their charts, as well as their reactions to the linguists' ideas. Encourage discussion.

Strategy

Ways to Offer Clarification

- Read the introductory paragraph as a class. Ask students if they have ever experienced similar "symptoms" when they didn't understand a speaker, or ask them to describe what they do when they don't understand a speaker.
- Have the whole class repeat after you as you say each of the "Expressions to Offer Clarification." Use a friendly tone of voice with rising intonation.
- Practice the expressions by calling on individual students and asking for either a formal or informal expression. Allow them to choose any expression from that category.

Content Note

- Not all of the "Expressions to Offer Clarification" are complete grammatical sentences. "OK so far?" is a way to ask a listener, "Are you OK so far?" and "Got it?" comes from "Have you got it?" (To "get it" means "to understand.")

1 Listening for Intonation 

- Play the audio and ask for volunteers to answer the questions that follow each conversation.
- Practice the expressions again, prompting the whole class to repeat after you. This time, model the difference between the helpful tone of voice and the critical tone of voice, using a scolding tone of voice and falling intonation to demonstrate the angry or critical way of saying these expressions.

ANSWER KEY

Conversation 1:

Question 1: *Is that clear?*

Question 2: She is being helpful; offering clarification.

Conversation 2:

Question: She is scolding her son.

AUDIOSCRIPT

Conversation 1

Ms. Garcia: To figure out the daily costs, you'll have to add up all the numbers in column A, divide by 30, and then multiply by the number of days you'll be there. Is that clear?

Conversation 2

Mrs. Smith: No, you can't watch TV. First, you have to clean up your room, write a thank-you note to your grandmother for your birthday present, put your bicycle away, take your model airplane project off the kitchen table, put your library books in the car so we can return them tomorrow, finish your homework, and take out the garbage. Is that clear?

Strategy

Understanding a Lecturer's Style of Offering Clarification

Read or have a volunteer read the paragraph aloud. Call on students to describe the different lecturing styles they experience in their own classes.

2 Listening for Expressions That Offer Clarification 

- ❑ Play the audio again as students listen for and check off the listed expressions. If students have trouble hearing the expressions, stop the audio and re-play sections.

ANSWER KEY

Students should check: *Are you following me?; Did you get that?; Does that make sense to you?; OK so far?; Right?*

3 Sharing Your Data

- ❑ Call on students to read the discussion questions aloud. This will help to build their independence and ownership of class discussions.

Strategy

Ways to Request Clarification

- Read or ask for a volunteer to read the introductory paragraph aloud. Ask students if they feel comfortable interrupting a speaker to request clarification and whether they know how to do it politely.
- Review the "Polite Expressions for Interrupting to Request Clarification." Point out that interrupting politely has two steps. Ask for volunteers to read aloud any of the polite expressions for interrupting in the first column, followed by any of the expressions in the second column.
- Model the "Informal Expressions for Requesting Clarification" and have the class repeat after you. Explain that these expressions do the same job as the polite expressions.
- Ask students for examples of situations in which they might hear polite or informal expressions like these. For example, an employee might use a polite expression with an employer, while two siblings might use informal expressions when talking together.

4 Requesting Clarification During a Lecture 

- ❑ Make sure that students have the lists of expressions for interrupting and requesting clarification available as they listen to the lecture.
- ❑ Encourage students to try to clarify parts of the lecture their classmates did not understand.

EXPANSION ACTIVITY

- The aim of this activity is to practice predicting test questions, which is useful when studying and taking notes.
- After students have heard the lecture several times, divide them into pairs or small groups to brainstorm questions the professor might include on a test.
- Ask the pairs or groups to write four or five test questions.
- Have the pairs or groups exchange their "tests" with another pair or group. Set a time limit for the groups to discuss and write their answers to the questions.
- Ask students to return the "tests" to the pair or group that wrote them, and to join them in discussing all of the questions and answers.
- Explain that students can use this technique alone or with a study group when preparing

for an exam. They can also keep potential test questions in mind as they listen to a lecture and decide which information to take notes on.

Content Note

- In some cultures, students would never be so bold as to interrupt a teacher or professor, but interrupting can be done politely in English-speaking countries. Most educators in the West consider it an exchange that makes communication possible, and they would rather be interrupted than not be understood. As long as the student uses a polite expression for interrupting and a friendly tone of voice, the interruption is not likely to be considered rude.

Talk It Over

5 Brain Teasers 

Best Practice

Cultivating Critical Thinking

This is a collaborative partner activity requiring students to apply the concept of requesting clarification to new situations. This activity involves the reinterpretation, synthesis, and application of concepts presented in the chapter. The process of manipulating language and concepts in this way creates deeper processing of new material, which allows students to evaluate whether they understand new material and helps them remember it better.

- ❑ Go over the directions for the activity and make sure that students understand them.
- ❑ As the partners work, make sure that the listeners are requesting clarification appropriately and are listening with books closed.

ANSWER KEY

1. Zero, because 0 times *anything* is 0.
2. The answer is a nine-digit number that is a string of the number you choose to multiply by before you multiply by 9. For example, if you multiply by 4, the answer will be 444,444,444.
3. Marcy is only five years old and cannot reach the button for the twelfth floor.
4. None. Hens can't talk.
5. The letter *m*.
6. Just divide the answer by 4 and you will have the number your partner started with.
7. a. The man first takes the sheep across the river and leaves it there.
   b. He then returns and takes the lion across the river.
   c. He leaves the lion on the other side and takes the sheep back to the first side.
   d. Then he takes the hay over to the other side and leaves it with the lion.
   e. Finally, he returns for the sheep and the job is done.

TOEFL® IBT

QUESTIONS ABOUT PRAGMATIC UNDERSTANDING

- Ask students to read the information about pragmatic-understanding questions.
- Write the words *attitudes, opinions, strategies,* and *goals* on the board.
- For each sample prompt, ask students whether they think the question is about the speaker's attitudes, opinions, strategies, or goals. Write each sample prompt number under the appropriate word on the board.

ANSWER KEY

Possible answers

Sample Prompt 1 asks about the professor's purpose, so it is a question about the speaker's strategies or goals.

Sample Prompt 2 asks directly about the speaker's attitude.

Sample Prompt 3 asks what the professor's remarks imply, so it is probably a question about the speaker's attitudes or opinions.

1 Pragmatic Understanding: Lecture 

- ❑ Play the audio of the complete lecture from Part 2 once more and have students take notes with their books closed.
- ❑ Play the audio of the lecture segments and instruct students to choose the best multiple-choice answer for each question. Pause for 20 seconds between questions.
- ❑ Discuss how students can determine the answers to pragmatic understanding questions. Ask whether thinking about the professor's *attitudes, opinions, strategies,* and *goals* helped them answer the questions.

ANSWER KEY

1. c 2. c 3. b 4. b 5. a

AUDIOSCRIPT

Narrator: Question 1. Listen again to part of the lecture.

Student 3: How many languages are there in the world? And can we ever really learn to speak someone else's language?

Professor: Hmmm. Any more? No?

Narrator: Why does the professor say, "Any more? No?"

Narrator: Question 2. Listen again to part of the lecture.

Professor: For a long time, people thought that we learned language only by imitation and association... However, Noam Chomsky, a famous linguist, said that although children do learn *some* language through imitation and association, they also combine words to make sentences in ways they have never heard before.

Narrator: What is the professor's opinion about learning languages through imitation and association?

Narrator: Question 3. How would the professor answer the student's question, "Can we ever really learn to speak someone else's language?"

Narrator: Question 4. Listen again to part of the lecture.

Professor: As I sat at home preparing for this lecture, I looked up at the collage on my wall and took a bite out of my croissant. Later, I experienced a moment of déjà vu. So, to describe my activities this morning, I have just used three words borrowed from French—*collage, croissant,* and *déjà vu*—because they describe certain things and experiences better than any English words.

Narrator: Why does the professor mention three French words?

Narrator: Question 5. Listen again to part of the lecture.

Professor: We may also begin to understand things in ways that we could not before.

Narrator: What is the professor implying in this statement?

EXPANSION ACTIVITY

- Students can try samples of the TOEFL® iBT test online at www.toefl.org. Visit the site yourself first so that you can direct students to useful links such as "Learn About TOEFL® iBT," "TOEFL® iBT Tour," and "TOEFL® Practice Online."

Self-Assessment Log

- ❑ Explain to students that thinking about their learning can help them decide what to focus on in their lessons and homework and can help them chart their progress.
- ❑ The Self-Assessment Log at the end of each chapter helps students track their own strengths and weaknesses and also encourages them to take ownership of their own learning.
- ❑ Read the directions aloud and have students check vocabulary they learned in the chapter and are prepared to use.
- ❑ Tell students to find definitions in the chapter for any words they did not check.
- ❑ Have students check the degree to which they learned the strategies practiced in the chapter. Put students in small groups. Ask students to find the information or an activity related to each strategy in the chapter.
- ❑ If possible, meet privately with each student on a regular basis and review his or her assessment log. This provides an opportunity for the student to ask key questions and for you to see where additional help may be needed and to offer one-on-one encouragement.

Chapter 2

Cooperation and Competition

In this chapter, students will learn about cooperation and competition among penguins in Antarctica. In Part 1, they will encounter useful vocabulary along with interactive pair and group activities that will help prepare them for the topic. In Part 2, they will listen to a lecture about the behavior of penguins and complete outlines to help them both process information while listening and organize their ideas for a presentation. In Part 3, students will learn expressions used to confirm understanding. In Part 4, they will continue to evaluate pragmatic understanding test material similar to that used on the TOEFL® iBT.

Chapter Opener

- ❑ Direct students' attention to the photo and ask the following questions: What kind of animal is pictured? Where does it live? How does the photo relate to the chapter title?
- ❑ Divide students into groups to discuss the "Connecting to the Topic" questions. For the third question, draw a T-chart (a chart with two columns and two headings) on the board with "animals cooperate" written on one side and "animals compete" on the other. Ask students for situations in which animals might cooperate or compete. Would the chart be similar or different for humans?
- ❑ Discuss the quotation from Cicero. Ask students to express the same idea using simpler language. Ask students if they agree or disagree with the quotation.

" Do not have the delusion that your advancement is accomplished by crushing others. "

—Marcus Tullius Cicero
Roman philosopher (106 B.C.–43 A.D.)

Chapter Overview

Lecture: Penguin Partners at the Pole

Learning Strategy: Distinguishing Main Ideas and Supporting Details

Language Function: Asking for Confirmation of Understanding

Part 1: Building Background Knowledge

Did You Know?

Sharing Your Experience

Vocabulary Preview

Part 2: Distinguishing Main Ideas and Supporting Details

Identifying Main Ideas and Supporting Details

Making a Basic Outline of Main Ideas and Details

Listen

After You Listen

Talk It Over

Part 3: Asking for Confirmation of Understanding

Using Appropriate Intonation and Expressions when Asking for Confirmation of Understanding

Talk It Over

Asking for Confirmation to Challenge Excuses

Part 4: Focus on Testing

Developing Your Pragmatic-Understanding Skills

Self-Assessment Log

Did You Know?

- ❑ Have students read the "Did You Know?" points.
- ❑ Ask them to think of or find examples of cooperation among animals.

Content Note

- In 2006, the documentary film *March of the Penguins*, which depicts the life cycle of Antarctica's emperor penguin, won the Academy Award for Best Documentary Feature.

1 What Do You Think? 

Best Practice

Activating Prior Knowledge

Pre-listening pair discussions activate students' prior knowledge. This activity helps students relate their own experiences with human and animal cooperation and competition to the material in this chapter. When students activate their prior knowledge before learning new material, they are better able to use that knowledge in understanding new concepts.

- ❑ Divide students into pairs to discuss the questions. Encourage them to expand on the discussion in the Chapter Opener about cooperation and competition among animals and humans.
- ❑ Ask each pair of students to talk to another pair about their ideas.

Sharing Your Experience

2 A Scientific Collaboration 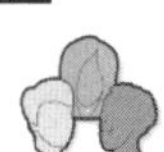

Best Practice

Cultivating Critical Thinking

This activity is an example of a collaborative team activity resulting in a final product. This type of activity requires students to apply their previous planning experience to the new situation of an Antarctic expedition. This involves reinterpretation, synthesis, and the application of concepts, and requires communication with classmates in English.

- ❑ Divide the class into small groups of 3–4 students.
- ❑ Go over the directions together to see if there are questions. Set a time limit for the activity.
- ❑ Ask the small groups to share and reach an agreement on their ideas, and then write them in the boxes under the appropriate category.
- ❑ Instruct the small groups to transfer their charts in the book to poster paper.
- ❑ When students have completed their charts, ask them to tape them to the classroom walls. Have the rest of the class gather around as each group presents its ideas. If the class is large, have more than one group present at the same time to different classmates.

Vocabulary Preview

3 Vocabulary in Context

- ❑ Instruct students to read through the vocabulary words and sentences without using a dictionary, and then fill in the blanks with any words from the list they know or can guess will fit.
- ❑ After they have attempted the activity on their own, allow students to use dictionaries to look up unknown words.
- ❑ Put students in pairs to compare answers. Tell them they can ask you about the meanings and usage of any words they are unsure of.

ANSWER KEY

1. desolate 2. beachfront 3. Catastrophic 4. migratory 5. ecosystem 6. Fahrenheit/Celsius 7. to fast 8. to teem 9. disposition/battle 10. ferocious 11. awkward

Content Notes

- The difference between degrees Celsius and degrees Fahrenheit when discussing temperature commonly causes problems. Fortunately, it is fairly easy to convert degrees Celsius to Fahrenheit by multiplying by 1.8 and then adding 32. For example, 30 degrees Celsius times 1.8 equals 54, plus 32 equals 86. So 30 degrees Celsius equals 86 degrees Fahrenheit. Converting Fahrenheit to Celsius is the same process in reverse. Simply subtract 32 from degrees Fahrenheit and divide that number by 1.8.
- The word *chick* refers to a baby bird, but it also has the slang meaning *young woman*. Because most young women consider being called a chick insulting, it is best to discourage the use of this slang term.

REPRODUCIBLE

EXPANSION ACTIVITY

- The aim of this activity is to give students an organizational tool that will help them learn and remember new vocabulary.
- Photocopy and distribute BLM 3, "Vocabulary Table" on page BLM 3 of this Teacher's Edition.
- Tell students that a vocabulary table is a good way to keep a record of new words they want to remember.
- Have students complete the table using words from the "Vocabulary in Context" section, or let them choose unfamiliar words from the chapter.

❑ Read or ask for a volunteer to read aloud the information in the box. You may want to clarify the ideas of overall main idea, other main ideas, and supporting details by listing these phrases on the board in outline fashion. Explain that the overall idea is the most general information, and that the supporting details are the most specific.

Strategy

Identifying Main Ideas and Supporting Details

- Go over the information in this strategy. It might be helpful to use the following arithmetic analogy to explain the deductive and inductive methods. With the deductive method, the main idea comes first, followed by the details that support it, which is similar to saying that 12 = 4 + 4 + 4. With the inductive method, the details come first and lead to the main idea, which is similar to saying that 4 + 4 + 4 = 12.
- Ask students if and when they have used outlines in the past. To take lecture notes? To rewrite notes after a lecture?

Strategy

Making a Basic Outline of Main Ideas and Details

- Review the basic outline form with students. Point out that the main ideas in an outline are represented by Roman numerals on the far left. The farther to the right an outline item is, the more specific the detail is.
- BLM 4, "Making an Outline" on page BLM 4 of this Teacher's Edition includes the Roman numerals 1–10 in case students need a review.

Before You Listen

1 What's Happening? 

❑ Divide students into small groups to discuss the photos and report their ideas to the class.

❑ Make sure they talk about the ideas of cooperation and competition and situations in which animals might cooperate or compete.

ANSWER KEY

Answers will vary.

The male and female penguin both spend time sitting on their egg, so they must cooperate in order to keep it warm. On the other hand, male penguins may fight (compete) to get a mate. It's interesting that the same goal, reproduction, can require both cooperation and competition.

2 Predicting Main Ideas and Supporting Information 

Best Practice

Organizing Information

This activity uses a graphic organizer, in this case an outline, to categorize information. Using an outline encourages students to process and organize information while they are listening, and also provides a record for them to refer to when reviewing their notes. This type of graphic organizer emphasizes listing and categorizing skills. Other types of graphic organizers are used throughout the book.

❑ Divide students into pairs to look over the partial outline and discuss the missing information.

❑ Explain that students should first identify what's missing in terms of category (main idea, major supporting example, minor supporting example, or detail), then in terms of possible content.

ANSWER KEY

The numbered items are minor supporting examples or details. The lettered item C is a major supporting example or detail. Answers will vary for possible content.

Listen

Best Practice

Making Use of Academic Content

The lecture, an example of a real-world model, encourages students to develop listening skills they can use in real-world academic settings. As students listen to a professor talk about penguins in Antarctica, they experience an authentic context in which they can interpret the ideas and language from the chapter.

3 Listening for Main Ideas and Supporting Information 

- ❑ Tell students they will hear the first half of a lecture on penguins and should pay special attention to the part about mating habits.
- ❑ Play the audio of the first half of the lecture.
- ❑ Play the first half of the audio a second time and have students fill in the missing outline information in Activity 2 as they listen.
- ❑ Divide students into the same pairs as in Activity 2 to compare outlines.

ANSWER KEY

I. Mating habits of penguins

A. Need for order leads penguins to build nests in rows

B. Order often interrupted by small wars between penguins

1. two males may fight over a female
2. a male and female may fight over when and how to mate and where to build a nest

C. Winners begin relationships with females

D. Losers move to edge of nesting ground

1. Steal unguarded eggs
2. Disturb nests and play jokes

AUDIOSCRIPT

Lecture: Penguin Partners at the Pole, Part 1

Professor Gill: Good Morning.

Students: Good morning. Hello. Hi.

Professor Gill: Well, to continue with our study of the ecosystem of Antarctica, I have invited a special guest to speak to you today. My colleague, Professor Byrd, has just returned from a two-year field study in Antarctica and he's going to share a few things about a part-time polar resident—the penguin.

Professor Byrd: Hello. I see that you're all smiling. It never fails! Every time people hear that my lecture will be about penguins, everyone immediately seems happier. This is not surprising. No one can resist these awkward little creatures that appear to be dressed in black and white suits.

Well, to begin. Antarctica is like a huge and desolate icy desert and only the strongest forms of life survive there. It seems strange that this hard land could be the spring and summer home of a migratory bird—the penguin.

Did I say bird? It also seems strange to call something that cannot fly a bird. But that's not all! The penguin is a tireless swimmer and is also affectionate, considerate, and loyal—rare qualities in the bird kingdom. Because of their warm, friendly, and cooperative natures, these lovely birds are thought of as the treasure of Antarctica.

The penguin is an extremely important part of a very limited ecosystem. In the Antarctic, all of the activity of the ecosystem takes place on a thin shelf of land next to the great dome of ice that covers most of the region. It is here, to this little bit of beachfront, that one species of penguin comes to mate and raise babies. It would be a little cold for us at this beach, though.

Students: (*laughter*) That's for sure. Absolutely.

Professor Byrd: Today I'm going to talk about only one type of penguin, the adelie penguin. The adelie penguin arrives in the relative warmth of spring, when the temperature rises above zero degrees Fahrenheit—that would be about minus 17 degrees Celsius. Right away, the penguin begins a long fast, a time when it does not eat. During the previous months, the penguins continuously eat krill—small, shrimp-like animals—and small fish in warmer waters, and in the spring, they have a store of fat to help them survive the months ahead. Using these fat reserves, they are able to swim hundreds of miles through freezing waters back to the familiar shore of Antarctica each spring.

When the penguins arrive at the nesting ground, their first task is to pair up—to mate—and to begin a kind of "civilized" life. Since as many as 50,000 birds may gather at a time, there is definitely a need for order and neatness. Because of this need for order, penguins build nests in perfect rows and the nesting area looks very much like the streets of a city.

This organization and order, however, is often interrupted by battles or fights between birds. For example, two male birds may fight a small war over a particularly adorable female that they think will make a good "wife." Or a male and a female may battle as they settle the marriage contract and reach agreement on when and how they will mate and where they will build their nest. These little battles can go on constantly for several weeks until all of the pairs have settled down. The penguins never actually kill one another, but it is not unusual to see bloodstains and broken wings.

The male winner of the love battle over a female wins a relationship with the female that is one of the most extraordinary in the animal world. There seems to be a

	wonderful understanding between mates. I've observed the delicate and kind way they treat each other, standing very close and swaying back and forth as if they are dancing to celebrate their marriage. The losers, the males that fail to find a suitable mate, move to the edge of the nesting ground. These birds become the hooligans, or minor troublemakers, of the group. They steal unguarded eggs, disturb nests, and play jokes on the happy couples.
Student 1:	I think we have a few of those hooligan types in this class.
All Students:	(*laughter*)

4 Constructing an Outline 

- Play the audio of the second half of the lecture, asking students to pay special attention to information about nesting, feeding, and taking care of chicks.
- Have students fill in the missing outline information on page 32 of the Student Book as you play the audio a second time.
- Instruct the same pairs of students to compare and combine outlines so that they both have the same completed outline.

ANSWER KEY

II. Penguin nesting

Eggs are laid in stone nests but up to 75 percent of them are lost to climate, death of parents, or predatory birds.

III. Penguin feeding

A. Long marches

Parents take turns feeding chicks by going off to feed in large groups, walking or sliding in single file lines on their way from their nesting ground to the ocean.

B. Danger of predators

The sea leopard feeds on swimming penguins.

IV. Care of orphaned chicks

Food is shared with the orphaned chicks and adult penguins share babysitting duties.

AUDIOSCRIPT

Lecture: Penguin Partners at the Pole, Part 2

Professor Byrd:	Yes, I've seen that behavior myself. So … after nearly a month of fasting, the eggs are laid in little nests made of stones by the males. Then family life begins. Although the parenting instinct is very strong and parental care is truly dedicated and careful, as many as 75 percent of the eggs are lost due to catastrophic floods, death of the parents, destruction of the nests by landslides or heavy snows, bad behavior of the hooligan males I mentioned before, and, of course, there are the skuas—the predatory birds that come down from the sky to eat the eggs and even baby penguins.
Students:	That's awful! That's so sad! Oh, no!
Professor Byrd:	Yes, that's sad, but some eggs do survive, of course, and once the chicks, the baby penguins, begin to hatch out of the eggs, the penguin colony teems with life. The long fast is over, and the parents take turns feeding and bringing back food for their new penguin chick.

It is during this period that we can see the comical character of the penguin. They often go off to feed in large groups, walking or sliding in single file lines on their way from their nesting ground to the ocean. At the shoreline, they dare one another to jump into the water. They often approach the edge of a cliff and then retreat over and over again, until finally one brave penguin dives in. Then the others follow almost at once, jumping into the water from exactly the same spot on the shore. In the water, they play various water sports that they've invented while they fill themselves up with krill and other small sea animals.

It's not all fun and games, however. Even though their black and white color helps hide them, there is not very much the penguins can do to protect themselves from the jaws of the sea leopard. This scary creature looks like a cross between a seal and a great white shark. Some of you might remember the movie *Jaws*?

Students: Yeah! Sure! Right!

Student 1: Sure we do! Dah-dum, dah-dum, dah-dum!

Students: (*laughter*)

Professor Byrd: Well, the sea leopard's jaw is just as tough as the white shark's. The sea leopard is really a large seal with many large, sharp teeth, an aggressive disposition, and a taste for penguin meat. Even though penguins are excellent swimmers, it is difficult for them to escape these ferocious predators.

For this reason, the group of feeding penguins is smaller when it returns to the nesting ground. But penguins are generous creatures and food is shared with the orphaned chicks—the chicks whose parents have been killed. Adult penguins also share babysitting duties. One bird will watch over several chicks while the others play.

Student 2: Even the males?

Professor Byrd: Especially the males!

Student 2: Hear that, you guys?

Students: (*laughter*)

Professor Byrd: Oh, yes. Penguins share everything. And they love to visit with neighbors, explore nearby ice floes or islands, and even climb mountains, following the leader in long lines up the mountainside.

When the mating season finally ends, the penguins line up in rows like little black and white soldiers and prepare to march to the sea. Responding to a signal that humans cannot perceive, the penguins suddenly begin their highly organized and orderly walk. At the edge of the sea, they stand as if at attention again, waiting for another signal. When it is given, they begin their swim back to their winter home on another part of the continent.

	Well, I think I'm keeping you a bit late. If Professor Gill will invite me back, maybe we can continue talking about penguins another time.
Students:	Yes! That would be great! Please do come back, Professor.
Professor Gill:	Definitely. Please do come back. Thank you so much, Professor Byrd. We all enjoyed your talk tremendously.

After You Listen

Best Practice

Interacting with Others

This activity is an example of collaborative learning used to encourage fluency and confidence. In this activity, based on the students' outlines, communication is more important than grammar. Students discuss their outlines in pairs before presenting them to the whole class. By the time they discuss their outlines with the class, they should feel more confident in their use of the new language.

5 Comparing Outlines

- ❑ Instruct the pairs of students to transfer their outlines to poster paper or the board, if there is enough space.
- ❑ Have the class look for and discuss similarities and differences in the outlines. Are the outlines equally effective at organizing important information? Do the students prefer one over another?

Talk It Over

Best Practice

Scaffolding Instruction

Activities 6–10 provide scaffolded support to students as they develop and express their views on the topic of endangered species. Students slowly form their opinions on the topic, beginning by discussing it within the group context and then continuing on their own with individual research. The activities culminate with an individual presentation by each student. This scaffolded instruction provides support to students and builds confidence as they move from group work to individual accountability.

6 Sharing Prior Knowledge of a Topic 

- ❑ Explain to students that they are going to prepare for individual presentations through small group discussions.
- ❑ Divide students into small groups to discuss the questions about whale hunting. Set a time limit for the discussion.

7 Choosing a Position 

- ❑ Have students continue to discuss the questions and come to a consensus as a group. Later they will have an opportunity to expand on their personal opinions.
- ❑ Tell students that they can choose a different endangered species if their group agrees.

8 Researching a Topic of Study 

- ❑ As homework, have students do an Internet search to gather more information on their topic and to further their own ideas about the topic they chose.

9 Making an Outline to Discuss Your Views

- ❑ Instruct students to work individually to make an outline of their views along with the reasons for them. Tell students that they will use the outlines as a guide in presenting their views to their groups.

10 Presenting Your Views to a Group

- ❑ Give students a time limit for their presentations and allow time for practice and preparation.
- ❑ Have students present their ideas to the class.
- ❑ If time allows, prompt students to compare and contrast their views as a class.
- ❑ If the class is large, consider having students work in the same groups created for activities 6 and 7.

EXPANSION ACTIVITY

- The goal of this activity is for students to make a formal outline of an article.
- Photocopy and distribute BLM 4, "Making an Outline" on page BLM 4 of this Teacher's Edition.
- Explain that in addition to being useful for listening and speaking, students can also use outlines to analyze and take notes on a reading or to plan their own writing.
- Give students a short, interesting article on penguins, whale hunting, endangered species, or another topic that has come up during discussion.
- Have students outline the article using formal outline style.
- Have students compare their outlines in pairs and discuss why they organized their outlines the way they did.

Strategy

Using Appropriate Intonation and Expressions when Asking for Confirmation of Understanding

- Have students read the opening paragraph about tone of voice when asking for confirmation of understanding.
- Ask students how this speaking skill is related to the chapter topic of cooperation and competition. Elicit intonation that can make a speaker sound either cooperative and polite or competitive and impolite.
- Direct students' attention to the list of expressions to use when asking for confirmation of understanding.
- Point out that the expressions have two parts: an expression of doubt: "I'm not sure I'm getting this." followed by a question restating of the main topic: "Are you saying that the sun actually moves around the earth?"
- Practice the expressions by preparing several strange or confusing statements and prompting students to ask for confirmation of understanding when you say them. Create your own statements or consider these: "I'm terribly afraid of butterflies," "We haven't had any rain in weeks, so my flowers are growing well," or "I wouldn't say that I don't feel unfriendly toward him."

1 Listening for Appropriate Expressions and Intonation 

- ❑ Play the audio of each conversation.
- ❑ Stop the audio after each conversation and discuss the question or questions.

AUDIOSCRIPT

Conversation 1

Driver: Pardon me. How do I get to the university library?

Police officer: You make a U-turn, go back on Washington until you hit Jefferson, then make a right turn, and it's the second white building on your left.

Driver: Could you repeat that, please?

Police officer: Sure. You make a U-turn, go back on Washington until you hit Jefferson, about three blocks, then make a right turn, and it's the second white building on your left.

Driver: You mean I turn around and stay on Washington until I get to Jefferson and then make a right?

Police officer: Yeah, that's right.

Driver: And did you say it's a white building on the left?

Police officer: Uh-huh.

Driver: Thanks a lot.

Police officer: You're welcome.

Conversation 2

Student: I didn't get the directions on the test. That's why I didn't do well.

Professor: Well, Tim, the directions say, "Answer 1A and then choose and answer 1B, 1C, or 1D."

Student: Do you mean to say that we had to do A and then choose either B or C or D?

Professor: Yes, you had a choice for the second half of the question.

Student: Oh, OK.

Conversation 3

Student: Professor Thompson, I'm not sure I understand the directions on this test.

Professor: Well, Tim, the directions say, "Answer IA and then choose and answer 1B, 1C, or 1D."

Student: You mean that we all do 1A, but then we each could do any one of 1B, C, or D?

Professor: That's right, Tim.

Student: Oh, now I see. Thank you.

Conversation 4

Student: What do I do now?

Assistant: You take that white sheet and the blue card. You fill out the white sheet with the courses you want. Then you have your advisor sign the white sheet and the blue card, and you turn them in to the first-floor office in Building Four and pay your fees.

Student: You mean I've got to have my advisor sign both the sheet and the card, and then I've got to stand in line again?

Conversation 5

Student: Excuse me, could you tell me what I must do next to pre-register?

Assistant: You take that white sheet and the blue card. You fill out the white sheet with the courses you want. Then you have your advisor sign the white sheet and the blue card, and you turn them in to the first-floor office in Building Four and pay your fees.

Student: I'm not sure I understand. Do you mean that the advisor must sign both forms? And that I take the forms to Building Four and pay my fees there?

Assistant: Yes, that's right.

Student: Oh, OK. Now I understand. Thank you.

ANSWER KEY

1. Yes. The driver used confirmation expressions and follow-up questions.
2. No. The confirmation question was not very polite.
3. Yes. The confirmation strategy used was appropriate.
4. The student used rude, inappropriate language. The administrative assistant likely felt hurt and angry.
5. In this conversation, the student's confirmation strategy was much more polite and appropriate.

2 Asking for Confirmation During a Lecture 

- ❑ Divide students into pairs and review the directions.
- ❑ Play the audio of the lecture from Part 2 again. Stop after the sentences indicated.
- ❑ Have pairs try different expressions asking for confirmation of understanding.
- ❑ Listen to the partners. Check that they are using both parts of the expressions, and that their intonation is polite and cooperative. Answers will vary.

3 Asking for Confirmation of Understanding During a Presentation

- ❑ Go over the directions and answer any questions that arise. Point out that group members can work cooperatively in both the planning and presentation stages of the activity.
- ❑ Provide poster paper or let students use the board if they would like to add a visual component to their presentations.
- ❑ Conduct the presentations like a business meeting. Encourage listeners to act as co-workers, interrupting politely to ask for clarification or confirmation of understanding. Consider assigning one listener to be the boss who will decide whether or not the company will make the product. Answers will vary.

Strategy

Asking for Confirmation to Challenge Excuses

- Go over the information in the strategy as a class.
- Ask students to give examples of situations in which they have made or challenged excuses. Ask for volunteers to read the example dialogues aloud for the class.

Talk It Over

4 Making and Challenging Excuses

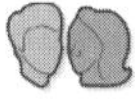

- ❑ Divide students into pairs and ask them to follow the pattern in planning their dialogues. Set a time limit for planning.
- ❑ When the planning time is up, ask students to give each pair their undivided attention as they role-play their dialogue for the class.

Content Note

- For Americans, "The dog ate my homework" is an excuse that is so well known that it is almost a joke. (Few teachers would believe a child who used this excuse!)

REPRODUCIBLE

EXPANSION ACTIVITY

- The aim of this activity is for students to share information about themselves and their cultures as they brainstorm excuses for different situations.
- Photocopy and distribute BLM 5, "Making Excuses" on BLM 5 of this Teacher's Edition.
- Divide the class into small groups and ask students to discuss the questions in relation to each situation. Encourage them to share their own thoughts along with information about their cultures.

DEVELOPING YOUR PRAGMATIC-UNDERSTANDING SKILLS

- Have students read or follow along as you read aloud the paragraph.

1 Pragmatic Understanding: Brief Conversations 

- Play the audio of the brief conversations all the way through and have students answer the multiple-choice questions. There will be a 20-second pause between each question.
- Play the audio again, stopping after each conversation to discuss the correct answer and how students chose it.

ANSWER KEY

1. b 2. c

AUDIOSCRIPT

Conversation 1

Speaker: Wow, Frank! You mean you're taking French 4, Biology 2, Intro to Economics, Eastern Religions, Music Appreciation, and Beginning Acting? That's a really heavy load for your first semester.

Narrator: Question: What is the speaker implying?

Conversation 2

Speaker: I can't believe this! I'm spending over $2,000 a year for this meal plan, and it doesn't include meals on Saturdays and Sundays!

Narrator: Question: How is this student feeling and why?

EXPANSION ACTIVITY

- The goal of this activity is for students to gain a deeper understanding of the TOEFL® iBT pragmatic-understanding questions by writing a sample test item themselves.
- Have each student write a test item similar to those in the short conversations they just heard. The test item should include a short conversation script, a question that requires pragmatic understanding, and four multiple-choice answers.
- Collect the test items and create an answer sheet for the class with everyone's questions and multiple-choice answers, but no conversation scripts. Alternatively, divide students into small groups to create answer sheets with only their questions and multiple-choice answers to be used by another group. The answer sheets should be similar to those on pages 39 and 40 in the student book.
- Read the conversation scripts and questions aloud, or have groups read the scripts and questions to each other, allowing time for students to answer questions.
- Go over the "tests," allowing the person who wrote each item to explain the correct answer.
- Ask students what they learned about pragmatic-understanding questions by writing test items themselves.

2 Pragmatic Understanding: Lecture 

- Play the audio of the lecture from Part 2 "Penguin Partners at the Pole" once more as students take notes with books closed.
- Have students open their books to page 40 as you play the audio of the questions all the way through and have them choose the answers. Pause 20 seconds between questions to allow students time to answer.
- Discuss how students can determine the answers to pragmatic-understanding questions,

for example, by thinking about the situation and the speaker's intention.

AUDIOSCRIPT

Narrator: **Question 1.** Listen again to part of the lecture.

Professor: It seems strange that this hard land could be the spring and summer home of a migratory bird—the penguin. Did I say bird? It also seems strange to call something that cannot fly a bird.

Narrator: Why does the professor say, "Did I say bird?"

Narrator: **Question 2.** Listen again to part of the lecture.

Professor: In the Antarctic, all of the activity of the ecosystem takes place on a thin shelf of land next to the great dome of ice that covers most of the region. It is here, to this little bit of beachfront, that one species of penguin comes to mate and raise babies. It would be a little cold for us at this beach, though.

Narrator: What is the professor's opinion about the penguins' choice of a home site?

Narrator: **Question 3.** Listen again to part of the lecture.

Professor: The losers, the males that fail to find a suitable mate, move to the edge of the nesting ground. These birds become the "hooligans," or minor troublemakers of the group. They steal unguarded eggs, disturb nests, and play jokes on the happy couples.

Student: I think we have a few of those hooligan types in this class.

Narrator: What is the student implying by saying "I think we have a few of those hooligan types in this class"?

Narrator: **Question 4.** Why does the professor mention the movie *Jaws*?

Narrator: **Question 5.** Listen again to part of the lecture.

Professor: Adult penguins also share babysitting duties. One bird will watch over several chicks while the others play.

Student: Even the males?

Professor: Especially the males.

Student: Hear that, you guys?

Narrator: Why does the student say, "Hear that, you guys?"

ANSWER KEY

1. c 2. b 3. d 4. d 5. a & c

Self-Assessment Log

- ❑ Read the directions aloud and have students check vocabulary they learned in the chapter and are prepared to use.
- ❑ Tell students to find definitions in the chapter for any words they did not check.
- ❑ Have students check the degree to which they learned the strategies practiced in the chapter. Put students in small groups. Ask students to find the information or an activity related to each strategy in the chapter.

Chapter

3

Relationships

In this chapter, students will discuss family relationships and the elderly. In Part 1, they will share their ideas about marriage, life expectancy, and the lifestyles of elderly people. They will also use new vocabulary in meaningful contexts. Part 2 includes information about straw-man arguments and a lecture in which a professor uses such arguments to challenge students' assumptions about families and the elderly in the United States. In Part 3, students will learn about making generalizations, which often include adverbs of frequency. Part 4 presents test questions involving pragmatic understanding of brief informal speeches and conversations.

Chapter Opener

- ❑ Have students read the quotation from Elbert Hubbard and write a one-sentence paraphrase of it.
- ❑ Divide the class into small groups and ask students to share with one another their paraphrases as well as their personal reactions to the quotation.
- ❑ Direct students' attention to the photo and in the same small groups have them discuss the questions in the "Connecting to the Topic" section.

"No matter what you've done for yourself or for humanity, if you can't look back on having given love and attention to your own family, what have you really accomplished?"

—Elbert Hubbard
U.S. writer, editor, and printer (1865–1915)

Chapter Overview

Lecture: Family Networks and the Elderly

Learning Strategy: Understanding Straw-Man Arguments

Language Function: Making Generalizations

Part 1: Building Background Knowledge

Did You Know?

Sharing Your Experience

Vocabulary Preview

Part 2: Making Predictions

Distinguishing Man Arguments from Main Points

Using an Anticipatory Guide to Test Assumptions and Predict Straw-Man Arguments

Listen

After You Listen

Talk It Over

Doing Research to Check Assumptions

Part 3: Making Generalizations

Generalizing with Adverbs of Time

Talk It Over

Part 4: Focus on Testing

Self-Assessment Log

Did You Know?

- ❑ Go over the surprising facts presented in the first two bullet points.
- ❑ Ask students about some of the numbers in the life expectancy chart to see if they need help saying numbers with decimals. Say, for example, "What is the life expectancy for men in Japan?" Students should respond, "seventy-seven point zero (or 'oh') two years."
- ❑ Ask students whether they know or can guess the life expectancies of men and women in their own countries if they are not listed in this chart.

Content Note

- Sir Temulji Bhicaji Nariman and Lady Nariman, a couple married for 86 years, were from India, and they were first cousins. Sir Nariman was nearly 92 years old when he died.

1 What Do You Think? 

- ❑ Divide students into pairs. Ask partners to take turns reading the questions aloud before discussing them.
- ❑ Monitor the pairs and encourage thoughtful discussion. For example, if students think that people in the five countries listed in the chart have high life expectancies due to wealth, point out that Mexico, Russia, and China are not particularly wealthy countries. What other factors might contribute to long life spans?
- ❑ Call on pairs to share their ideas with the class.

Sharing Your Experience

2 Considering Lifestyles of the Elderly 

- ❑ Have students fill out the chart individually.
- ❑ Divide the class into small groups to compare ideas. If your class has students from different countries, make each group as diverse as possible.

Vocabulary Preview

3 Vocabulary in Context

- ❑ Ask students to read the vocabulary words and definitions, and then fill in as many blanks as possible without using a dictionary.
- ❑ Divide students into pairs to compare answers.
- ❑ Answer any questions about vocabulary items students are still unsure about.

ANSWER KEY

1. siblings 2. household 3. Statistics 4. data 5. assumption 6. extended family 7. disjointed 8. isolated

Content Note

- Students are usually interested to learn that the word *sibling* is a gender-neutral alternative to *sister* or *brother*, just as a spouse can be either a wife or husband, and a child can be either a girl or boy.

4 Using Vocabulary 

Best Practice

Interacting with Others

This small group activity promotes collaborative learning to encourage fluency and confidence. When students share the personal information they have written in their charts, communication with classmates is more important than grammar. Students can practice the vocabulary in context, enriching their understanding of the meanings of words. By the time they encounter the new vocabulary again, they should feel more confident that they understand it well.

- ❑ Give students time to think and fill out the chart individually.

- ❑ Divide the class into small groups different from those in "Sharing Your Experience," Activity 2, to encourage interaction among students.
- ❑ Ask students to read the questions from the chart aloud and discuss the answers in their groups.

EXPANSION ACTIVITY

- The aim of this activity is for students to consider the topic of aging and to practice speaking as they dictate and discuss quotations on aging by famous people.
- Divide the class into pairs. Give one person in each pair a copy of BLM 6, "Words on Aging: Partner A" and the other person a copy of BLM 7, "Words on Aging: Partner B" on pages BLM 6 and BLM 7 of this Teacher's Edition.
- Instruct partners to dictate their quotations to each other so that both write down all of the quotations.
- Ask students to discuss the meaning of each quotation and express their opinions about the idea or ideas it conveys.
- Go over the quotations as a class and ask students to share their ideas about them.

Strategy

Distinguishing Straw-Man Arguments from Main Points

- Ask students if they have heard of *straw-man arguments*.
- Explain that an academic argument is an idea or assertion that can usually be proved or disproved. (It is not the same as when people disagree and quarrel over matters of opinion.)
- Have students follow along as you read the strategy aloud.
- Check for comprehension. Ask, for example, "If straw-man arguments are based on assumptions that someone wants to disprove, whose assumptions might a professor want to disprove?" Students should indicate that the professor might want to disprove their own assumptions.

Before You Listen

Strategy

Using an Anticipatory Guide to Test Assumptions and Predict Straw-Man Arguments

- Go over the strategy and explain that the anticipatory guide is a tool to help students consider their assumptions about the elderly and families.

1 Considering Your Assumptions 

Best Practice

Activating Prior Knowledge

Using the anticipatory guide to examine assumptions about the elderly and families, and to predict the content of the lecture, activates students' prior knowledge. This activity helps students relate their own ideas about the elderly and families to the material in this chapter. When students activate their prior knowledge before learning new material, they are better able to understand the new language and concepts they encounter.

- ❑ Give students time to think and fill out the chart individually.
- ❑ Divide students into small groups to share their assumptions.

2 Predicting Straw-Man Arguments 

- ❑ Consider providing an example before having students predict possible straw-man arguments. For instance, if students assume that the elderly spend most of their time at home, the straw-man argument might be that the elderly are not very involved in the community. The professor might disprove this argument with statistics about elderly people's involvement in churches, businesses, and volunteer organizations, for example.
- ❑ Have students think about their assumptions and those of their classmates as they predict which straw-man arguments the professor might use.
- ❑ Divide students into small groups to share their predictions.

Listen

3 Listening for Straw-Man Arguments 

Best Practice

Making Use of Academic Content

The handout used in this activity is an example of real-world academic content. This activity allows students to experience the sort of material they will encounter in academic settings. When students look at a course handout as they listen to a lecture, they experience an authentic context in which they can interpret the language and concepts presented in this chapter.

- ❑ Have students read the directions and look over the handout.
- ❑ Ask students what type of course the handout is used in. They should respond that it was used in a sociology seminar.
- ❑ Play the audio of the lecture all the way through so students can get the gist and note any straw-man arguments they hear.
- ❑ Give students a moment to jot down any questions they have.
- ❑ Ask for volunteers to share some of their questions with the class. Ask, for example, "What questions do you have that you hope will be answered the second time we listen?"

4 Listening for Data Refuting Straw-Man Arguments 

- ❑ Give students time to read the directions and questions. Review the example and make sure students understand the activity.
- ❑ Play the audio of the lecture a second time all the way through as students listen for data and straw-man arguments.
- ❑ Give students time to answer questions 1–3 and write down the straw-man arguments and their respective counterarguments.
- ❑ Go over the answers as a class, encouraging students to supply information for classmates who might have missed something.
- ❑ Ask students whether their questions from the first part of the exercise were answered when they listened a second time.

ANSWER KEY

1. c 2. b 3. d

Straw-man argument 1: Americans move a great deal, so the elderly typically live far away from their children.

Information used to defeat argument 1: Sixty-one percent of American elderly live with or within ten minutes of their children.

Straw-man argument 2: Americans live in small households and not in extended families, so the elderly seldom see their relatives.

Information used to defeat argument 2: Forty-three percent of women and thirty-four percent of men had seen a sibling within the past week.

Straw-man argument 3: The high divorce rate and number of single-parent homes means that American families are disjointed and the elderly rarely see their children.

Information used to defeat argument 3: Over 50 percent of the elderly had seen their children that day or the day before; 78 percent had seen their children within the past week.

AUDIOSCRIPT

Lecture: Family Networks and the Elderly

Professor: Good morning. We've got twelve people signed up for this seminar on families and aging. I'm really glad to see so much interest in this topic.

Well, to begin, I'm going to present some statistics on the family in the United States. Then I'll introduce four assumptions some people make about families in the

United States based on those statistics. Finally, I'm going to present some cross-cultural data, facts, and statistics on the elderly, from research done back in the 1970s. I haven't found any studies that duplicate this particular cross-cultural data more recent than that. Maybe one of you will do a research project on this topic and present more recent cross-cultural data. OK?

Students: Great. Sure. Sounds good.

Professor: Good. First of all, let's define *the elderly*. How old do you have to be to be considered elderly?

Student 1: 75?

Student 2: 65?

Student 3: 70?

Professor: Well, the elderly are generally defined as people over 65. But now that people are living and working much longer, that age is closer to 75. Let me tell you some interesting facts and statistics about family patterns in the United States. These statistics are often reported in magazines or newspapers to show that family life in the United States is not very good. Let's take a closer look at these statistics.

The first fact that is often reported is that Americans move a great deal. Believe it or not, about 18 percent of American households moved last year.

Second, since the beginning of the twentieth century, there has been a decline in the average size of households and a dramatic increase in the percentage of one-person households—that means people living alone.

Third, today in the United States, one in every two marriages ends in divorce—that's 50 percent.

And fourth, you may be surprised to find that over 60 percent of the children born in 1997 will spend some time in single-parent households by the time they are 18. That's nearly two out of every three children.

Student 1: I'm surprised that it isn't higher.

Professor: Higher?

Student 1: Yes. I mean, I don't know very many people whose parents are still married.

Professor: Well, your perception of American lifestyles is based on what you've observed. And these statistics certainly *do* indicate that there have been changes in lifestyles over the last 50 years. But looking at these changes has led some people to make assumptions about the elderly and how they might feel isolated in the United States. Let's consider three assumptions based on these changes, and then let's look at the research to decide whether they are true or false.

The first assumption is that since Americans move a great deal, the elderly typically live far away from their children.

The second assumption is that because most Americans live in small households and do not live in extended families, the elderly hardly ever see their relatives, including their siblings.

And the third assumption is that because of the high number of divorces and single-parent homes, the American family is disjointed and the elderly rarely see their children.

All three assumptions could lead you to believe that in the United States, the elderly might feel isolated. But is there any truth to these assumptions about the elderly and their families? Is there any data—any statistics—that can really support this thinking?

Student 2: It seems logical.

Professor: Well, it may seem logical, but let's look at these three beliefs—these three assumptions—again and see just how true they are according to research that was done in the 1970s. Let's see if the data—the statistics—from this research supports these assumptions. This research was done by Ethel Shanas at the University of Illinois, Chicago Circle.

Let's look at the first assumption. It says that because Americans move so often, the elderly typically live very far from their children. Well, let's see if this is true. Shanas found that in the United States, 61 percent of the elderly live with their children or within ten minutes of their children. Shanas's study also included some European countries, and on your handout, you can see that more elderly people in the United States live with their children or within ten minutes of their children than in Denmark. However, it is interesting to note that for the most part, the elderly in the United States interviewed for a more recent survey preferred to live in their own homes or apartments rather than with their children.

Student 3: So the first assumption is not true.

Professor: Right. Now let's look at the second assumption that because people do not live in extended families, the elderly hardly ever see their siblings—brothers and sisters—or other relatives. As you can see on the handout, 43 percent of women and 34 percent of men had seen a sibling within the past week.

Student 1: And the second assumption is not true either.

Professor: Exactly. So how about the third assumption: that because of the high number of divorces and single-parent homes, the American family is disjointed and the elderly rarely see their children. Look at Table 2 on the handout. You can see that over 50 percent of the elderly had seen their children that day or the day before. In any case, 78 percent of the elderly had seen their children within the last week. Also on the handout, you can see how the United States compares with some other European countries.

Student 2: Gee, the third assumption is not even close to being true.

Professor: I agree. Now, let's review what we have learned today about the elderly. First, the truth is that most of the elderly do not live far from their children. Second, the elderly do see their siblings and other relatives fairly frequently. And third, by and large, the elderly do see their children. Since this data indicates that the elderly actually do spend quite a bit of time with their families, they probably do not feel isolated. So from my point of view, we can, in general, feel good about how the elderly are treated in the United States.

Student 3: At least according to the statistics from Shanas's study in the 70s!

Professor: Yes, Molly. And that's why I thought it would be a good idea for students in this class to do a research project and get more recent data. What do you think we'll find? Do you think things have changed in the last 30 years? Do you think these assumptions are still false, or might they be true now? Let's take a break, and then we'll begin to develop our research plan.

EXPANSION ACTIVITY

- The goal of this activity is for students to use the Internet to find interesting statistics about the lifestyles of the elderly in the U.S. or their own countries.
- Instruct students to use a search engine such as Google (www.google.com) or Yahoo (www.yahoo.com) and search for one or two interesting statistics about the lifestyles of the elderly in the U.S. or in students' own countries. Suggest that they visit government websites or free online encyclopedias such as Wikipedia (www.wikipedia.org) to get reliable information.
- Tell students that possible search keywords include "elderly," "aging," "lifestyle," "statistics," "data," and the name of the country they are interested in.
- Have students present the data they found in class. Explain that they should be ready to speak for about one minute and present the statistics they found along with an explanation of why they found them interesting.
- Tell students to practice their note-taking skills by writing down the data their classmates present and asking for clarification of any information they don't understand during the presentation.

After You Listen

5 Examining Ways to Defeat Straw-Man Arguments

Best Practice

Organizing Information

This activity uses a graphic organizer to categorize information. Using a T-chart encourages students to process and organize information while thinking about the lecture and their assumptions. It also provides a record for them to refer to when reviewing their notes. This type of graphic organizer emphasizes listing and categorizing skills. Other types of graphic organizers are used throughout the book.

- ❑ Divide the class into small groups and ask students to discuss their answers to the questions and their ideas about the lecture content in general.
- ❑ Give students time to think and fill out the chart individually.

Talk It Over

6 Sharing Ideas Based on Assumptions

Best Practice

Cultivating Critical Thinking

This activity asks students to examine their assumptions about other people's lifestyles. This type of activity requires students to process the information they have learned and apply it to a new situation. The analysis of existing assumptions involves reinterpretation, synthesis, and application of concepts. The process of manipulating language and concepts in this way creates deeper processing of new material, which allows students to evaluate whether they have understood the new material and helps them remember it better.

- ❑ Divide the class into small groups and have each group member choose one of the living situations; two people may choose the same situation.
- ❑ Give students two minutes to close their eyes and think about the daily lives of the people they have chosen.
- ❑ Tell students when time is up, and then have them write about their person's daily life in the left-hand column of the chart provided for five minutes. Encourage students to write freely without worrying about grammar or spelling.
- ❑ Have students tell their group about their ideas by reading their writing or simply speaking.
- ❑ Ask group members to listen carefully and say whether they agree or disagree with each person's ideas. If they disagree, they should explain why their classmate's assumptions about the person's lifestyle may not be correct.
- ❑ Give students time to reflect on their group discussions and fill out the right-hand column of the chart.
- ❑ Ask for volunteers to talk about their guesses or assumptions with the entire class and explain whether or not their classmates agreed with them.

Strategy

Doing Research to Check Assumptions

Read the strategy aloud. Using sources to confirm the accuracy of assumptions is crucial in an academic setting. If students want their views to be taken seriously, they must be ready to cite either primary sources, which include interviews with people who actually experienced an event or the diaries and letters written by those people, or secondary sources such as articles and books written by authors who investigated a subject. The following activity gives students practice using a personal interview as a primary method of checking their assumptions about other people's lifestyles.

7 Checking Your Assumptions

- ❑ As a class, brainstorm where to find people to interview. Talking to neighbors or to people on campus are good ideas; politely approaching people in public places like the library or a coffee shop can work well, though tell your students to exercise caution and bring a friend or classmate, if possible. Students can also contact local neighborhood centers or other social organizations and ask if they can talk to people there.
- ❑ Discuss techniques for conducting a good interview:

  1. Plan and write down interview questions. Ask specific questions about things you want to know, but also ask open-ended questions that allow the interviewee to talk freely.
  2. Tell the person you want to interview who you are and why you want to do an interview.
  3. Relax and try to have fun while doing the interview. This should be an enjoyable experience for both the interviewer and interviewee.
  4. Be sure to thank the interviewee for their time and for helping you with your assignment.

- ❑ Instruct students to take notes during and after the interview and be prepared to share with the class what they learned in their interviews.
- ❑ Discuss the ways in which incorrect assumptions the students held before doing the interviews could be used as straw-man arguments in lectures or conversations.

Strategy

Generalizing with Adverbs of Time

- Go over the introductory information about making generalizations, as well as the adverbs of time often used in generalizations.
- Ask students whether any of the adverbs or adverbial phrases in the list are unfamiliar to them. Provide example sentences using familiar topics, such as, "For the most part, students in this class are unmarried."

Content Note

- When the negative adverbs *rarely, seldom, hardly ever,* and others appear at the beginnings of sentences, they trigger subject-verb or subject-auxiliary inversion in the sentence. Because of this inversion, we find sentences such as these:
  - I have seldom heard more beautiful music.
  - Seldom have I heard more beautiful music.
- In the second sentence, the word *seldom* at the beginning of the sentence causes the subject *I* to come after the auxiliary *have*.
- In another example we see a similar inversion:
  - Liza is rarely at home.
  - Rarely is Liza at home.
- In this case, the subject *Liza* comes after the verb *is* when *rarely* moves to the beginning of the sentence. This inversion is a common stumbling block for students since the inverted statements appear to have question word order.

1 Paraphrasing Generalizations 

- ❑ Divide students into small groups to write the paraphrases. Then assign students from four different groups to each write their paraphrase of one of the sentences in the exercise on the board.
- ❑ Go over each sentence on the board. Ask students if its meaning is the same as in the original sentence and whether there are other ways to paraphrase it.

ANSWER KEY

Answers will vary.

Sentence 1: Substitute *rarely* or *seldom* for *hardly ever* in the sentence. Alternatively, use one of the expressions from the first column in a negative statement, such as, "Rock concerts are typically not performed in homes for the elderly."

Sentence 2: Any word or phrase in the first column can be used at the beginning of the sentence: "By and large, we don't think of the elderly playing in a rock and roll band." Alternatively, *normally* or *typically* can be substituted for *generally* in the sentence. The words and phrases in the second column can also be used as part of an affirmative statement, such as, "Rarely do we think of the elderly playing in a rock and roll band."

Sentence 3: Substitute *hardly ever* or *seldom* for *rarely* in the sentence. Alternatively, use an expression from the first column in a negative statement, such as, "For the most part, elderly women did not compete in races in the 1950s."

Sentence 4: Substitute any other expression from the first column for *In general* at the beginning of the sentence, or use an expression from the second column with *single* men as the main focus: "Single men rarely live longer than married men."

2 Listening for Generalizations 

- ❑ Give students time to read the directions and the statements. Tell them that they will mark the statements *T* (true) or *F* (false) as they listen again to the lecture.
- ❑ Play the audio of the lecture from Part 2 again and have students complete the activity. Remind them to pay special attention to the way the professor uses adverbs of time to make generalizations.
- ❑ Divide students into pairs to compare answers.

ANSWER KEY

Answers may vary.

1. T
2. F
3. F
4. F
5. T
6. T
7. F
8. F
9. T

3 Correcting False Statements 

- ❑ Divide students into pairs.
- ❑ Ask the pairs to correct the incorrect statements. Collect these sentences to check for accuracy.
- ❑ Answer any questions about using adverbs of time to make generalizations.

ANSWER KEY

Answers may vary.

2. By and large, Americans do not move every year. About 18 percent of Americans moved last year.
3. In the United States, 50 percent of marriages end in divorce.
4. Generally speaking, the elderly live close to their children. Sixty-one percent live with or within ten minutes of their children.
7. Despite the high number of divorces and single-parent homes in the United States, the elderly typically see their children frequently. Seventy-eight percent had seen their children within the past week.
8. Although elderly people don't live with their extended families, they see their siblings fairly often. Forty-three percent of women and thirty-four percent of men had seen a sibling within the past week.

Talk It Over

4 Using Generalizations 

- ❑ Divide the class into groups of four and make sure students have available the list of adverbs of time for making generalizations.
- ❑ Set a time limit for the activity so that every group member has a chance to make a generalization about every topic.

Reproducible — EXPANSION ACTIVITY

- ■ The aim of this activity is for students to practice making generalizations using a Venn diagram. In this activity, students will compare and contrast the lifestyles of young people in the U.S. and in their own countries.
- ■ Photocopy and distribute BLM 8 "Venn Diagram" on page BLM 8 of this Teacher's Edition.
- ■ Ask students to label one of the circles "United States," and label the other with the name of their own country.
- ■ In the "United States" circle, have students write two or three generalizations about the

lifestyles of young people that are only true for the United States. Make sure they use the adverbs of time from the chapter.

- Tell students to do the same with the other circle, writing generalizations that are only true for their own countries.
- Where the circles overlap, tell students to write two or three generalizations about the lifestyles of young people that are true in both countries.
- Divide the class into small groups. If students are from different countries, make the groups as diverse as possible.
- Prompt students to share their generalizations with their classmates.
- Note that unless these generalizations are based on reliable research, they are based on students' assumptions. If possible, follow through with the chapter theme of questioning the accuracy of assumptions by having the students ask Americans whether their generalizations about the lifestyles of young people in the United States are correct. (See the "Doing Research to Check Assumptions" strategy box on page 54 in Part 2 for suggestions on conducting interviews.)

PRAGMATIC-UNDERSTANDING QUESTIONS IN CONVERSATION

- Ask students to read the information about pragmatic-understanding questions.
- Remind students that the Focus on Testing section in Chapters 1 and 2 were also on pragmatic-understanding questions.

Best Practice

Scaffolding Instruction

This activity provides scaffolded support to students. In the student book, students are provided multiple opportunities to participate in activities that are both predictable and flexible as they progress from their current performance levels toward realizing their full potential. As students repeatedly practice test items requiring pragmatic understanding throughout the book, they are guided through the steps of developing this necessary test-taking skill.

1 Pragmatic Understanding: Brief Informal Speeches 

- ❑ Play the audio of the brief informal speeches once all the way through and have students answer the multiple-choice questions. Pause for 20 seconds between the two conversations.
- ❑ Play each speech again and discuss any generalizations the students hear. Point out that in each case, there is a special scenario that contrasts with the usual situation. Understanding this contrast is one key to choosing the correct answer.

ANSWER KEY

1. d 2. a

AUDIOSCRIPT

Pragmatic Understanding: Brief Informal Speeches

Speaker 1

Mother: OK kids, listen up. Normally, we divide up the housework equally, but this week Dad has to help Grandpa and Grandma paint their house. So, James and Ruth, you're both going to have to pitch in more around here.

Narrator: Question: What is the speaker's main point?

Speaker 2

Father: We hardly ever take the dog on our summer vacation, but she's getting so old and looks so sad when we leave her. I can't bear to think of her in a kennel again. You think she'll like the Grand Canyon?

Narrator: Question: What is the father trying to say to the family?

2 Pragmatic Understanding: A Conversation 

- ❑ Play the audio all the way through as students listen and take notes with books closed. Let them know they are permitted to take notes during the TOEFL® iBT test.
- ❑ Play the audio of the questions. Have students open their books to page 58 and answer the multiple-choice questions they hear. Pause for 20 seconds between each question.
- ❑ Discuss the conversation and the test questions. What do the questions ask about? Remind students that pragmatic-understanding questions ask about speakers' attitudes and intentions.

ANSWER KEY

1. c 2. a 3. d 4. a 5. d

AUDIOSCRIPT

Pragmatic Understanding: A Conversation

Man: Sorry I couldn't be at band practice on Thursday. I had a family emergency.

Woman: Really? I'm so sorry. If you don't mind saying, what happened?

Man: No, no, it's OK. I just had to help move my grandfather into a nursing home.

Woman: Are you upset about it?

Man: No. I'm OK.

Woman: When old people can't live by themselves, a nursing home is the best place to go, right?

Man: Sorry?

Woman: If he can't take care of himself at home, he'd better go to an institution.

Man: Wait a minute. That's a little cold. This is my grandfather. I love the guy. I've loved spending time at his house. I'm not happy about moving him out.

Woman: But why not? You can't take care of him.

Man: Well, not by myself. I have classes, band practice, homework, late-night study sessions.

Woman: Right. And for your grandfather's care, it's either you or nobody.

Man: Why are you being so hard-hearted about this? It wasn't an easy decision.

Woman: But it's for his own good. He'll fit in better there, and he'll have a lot of friends.

Man: Yeah. But to be honest, he didn't look as bad off as most of those people. I wonder if he'll really make any friends.

Woman: Still, he'd be all alone if he stayed at home.

Man: OK, OK. We could probably piece something together if we really worked on it. Maybe my parents could juggle their work schedules. My sister has four kids, but maybe she could drop in on him once or twice a week.

Woman: So you don't really believe this nursing home is the best place for him, do you?

Man: Well, to be honest, not really.

Narrator: Question 1. Listen again to part of the conversation.

Woman: Really? I'm so sorry. If you don't mind saying, what happened?

Man: No, no, it's OK. I just had to help move my grandfather into a nursing home.

Narrator: What does the man mean by saying, "No, no."?

Narrator: Question 2. Why does the man mention his family emergency?

Narrator: Question 3. Listen again to part of the conversation.

Woman: But why not? You can't take care of him.

Man: Well, not by myself. I have classes, band practice, homework, late-night study sessions.

Woman: Right. And it's either you or nobody.

Man: Why are you being so hard-hearted about this? It wasn't an easy decision.

Narrator: Why does the man think the woman is being hard-hearted (unconcerned about his feelings)?

Narrator: Question 4. Listen again to part of the conversation.

Woman: Still, he'd be all alone if he stayed home.

Narrator: Why does the woman mention a lack of other people to care for the grandfather?

Narrator: Question 5. Why did the woman use straw-man arguments throughout the conversation?

EXPANSION ACTIVITY

- The aim of this activity is for students to practice cloze listening skills and to examine the language used in a conversation.
- Photocopy and distribute BLM 9 "Cloze Passage" on page BLM 9 of this Teacher's Edition.
- Have students read through the passage to see if they can fill in any of the blanks from memory.
- Play the audio of the conversation from Activity 2 of the Focus on Testing section on Student Book page 58 at least two times as students fill in the missing information.
- Divide students into pairs to compare answers and ask you about any language they are unsure of.
- Ask students what they notice about the conversation and the straw-man arguments the woman uses, and ask if they have any questions.

Self-Assessment Log

- ❑ Read the directions aloud and have students check vocabulary they learned in the chapter and are prepared to use.
- ❑ Tell students to find definitions in the chapter for any words they did not check.
- ❑ Have students check the degree to which they learned the strategies practiced in the chapter. Put students in small groups. Ask students to find the information or an activity related to each strategy in the chapter.

Chapter

4

Health and Leisure

This chapter focuses on the human heart and introduces students to analogies. In Part 1, students will prepare for the listening by sharing their existing knowledge about the heart. They will also consider how some parts of the body are similar to familiar objects, and learn new vocabulary in context. Part 2 presents expressions for making analogies as well as graphic organizers that help students as they listen to a group study session. In Part 3, students will learn ways to express opinions appropriately. Part 4 gives them a chance to express their opinions as they practice the type of speaking tasks required on the TOEFL® iBT.

Chapter Opener

- ❑ Direct students' attention to the photo and ask them to explain how it illustrates the chapter title, "Health and Leisure."
- ❑ Divide students into groups to brainstorm answers to the questions in the "Connecting to the Topic" section. Call on groups to report on their answers and list students' ideas on the board.
- ❑ Discuss the Spanish proverb. Ask questions such as, "Why are tools important to a mechanic? What happens if a mechanic doesn't take care of them? How is a person's health similar to a mechanic's tools?"

“A man too busy to take care of his health is like a mechanic too busy to take care of his tools.”

—Spanish proverb

Chapter Overview

Lecture: What Makes Us Tick: The Cardiac Muscle

Learning Strategy: Understanding and Using Analogies

Language Function: Expressing Opinions

Part 1: Building Background Knowledge

Did You Know?

Sharing Your Experience

Vocabulary Preview

Part 2: Making Predictions

Listening for Analogies

Before You Listen

Listen

After You Listen

Talk It Over

Part 3: Expressing Opinions

Introducing Your Opinion Appropriately

Talk It Over

Part 4: Focus on Testing

Self-Assessment Log

Did You Know?

- Go over the heart rate statistics and ask students if they think any of the numbers are surprising. Ask if they can explain why animals' heart rates might differ so much. For example, "Canaries' hearts beat quickly because of their small size and the demands of their activities."

1 What Do You Think? 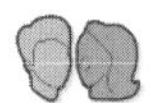

- Divide students into pairs to brainstorm a list of things that make their hearts beat faster. Ask each pair to tell the class at least one of their ideas.
- Give students time to read the questions and think about the experience they would like to relate to their partner. After students have talked in pairs, ask for volunteers to tell their stories to the class.
- As a class, brainstorm answers to the question about clams and their heart rates.

EXPANSION ACTIVITY

- The goal of this activity is to make the idea of heart rate accessible to kinesthetic learners, those who learn best by feeling or doing something.
- Have students check their own heart rates. They can place their hands over their hearts or find a pulse in their wrist. Tell them when to start counting heartbeats. After ten seconds, tell them to stop.
- Multiply the number of heartbeats they counted by six to calculate their heart rate.

REPRODUCIBLE **EXPANSION ACTIVITY**

- This activity aims to expand students' thinking about the human heart beyond the physical realm and into the abstract ideas the heart can represent.
- Teach students idioms that use the word *heart*. Photocopy and distribute BLM 10 "Expressions from the Heart" on page BLM 10 of this Teacher's Edition. Go over the idioms as a class. Then divide students into small groups to discuss the questions.

Sharing Your Experience

2 Making Some Comparisons 

- Refer to the photographs and make sure students understand the comparison between the human eye and a camera.
- Divide students into pairs to match the body parts with the items. Answer questions about unfamiliar vocabulary and draw simple diagrams of the items on the board if needed.
- Join pairs to forms groups of four. Have the groups brainstorm ways in which each body part and item are similar.
- For each item on the list, call on a different group to report on their discussion of the ways the item is similar to the body part.

ANSWER KEY

1. b 2. f 3. e 4. g 5. a 6. c 7. d

Vocabulary Preview

3 Vocabulary in Context

Best Practice

Scaffolding Instruction

This is an example of an activity that provides scaffolded support to students. Throughout the textbook, students are provided multiple opportunities to guess the approximate meaning of new vocabulary that they see in meaningful contexts. This repetition supports students by providing a routine procedure for meeting clear goals. At the same time, examining vocabulary in context is flexible in that it allows students to negotiate meaning in a situation that changes with each new sentence.

- ❑ Go over the list of vocabulary words and definitions. Have students repeat the words after you. Listen for any pronunciation difficulties; for instance, muscles should have only an /s/ sound in the middle. The letter *c* is silent.
- ❑ For each term, ask students to supply the part of speech. For example, they should see that this definition of *hollow* is an adjective.
- ❑ Ask students to read through all of the sentences first, and then go back and find the appropriate vocabulary to fill in the blanks.
- ❑ Ask for volunteers to read each sentence aloud and discuss any additional unfamiliar vocabulary.

ANSWER KEY

1. chambers 2. tick-tock 3. cardiac muscles 4. pumps 5. peel 6. strip 7. varies 8. hollow

Strategy

Listening for Analogies

- Go over the information in the paragraph about analogies and the expressions used to make analogies.
- For each expression, ask students to think of a few additional examples. List the examples on the board to provide more linguistic input. Possibilities include, "My backpack is as heavy as a sack of bricks." "Learning a new language is like climbing a very high mountain." "Getting to know a person is similar to peeling an onion. There's always something new under the next layer."

Before You Listen

1 Considering the Topic

Best Practice

Activating Prior Knowledge

Using a graphic organizer and comparing notes with classmates in this activity help students activate their existing knowledge about the heart. This prepares them to connect that knowledge with the new information they will hear in the conversation. Making connections between prior knowledge and new information is essential for learning a language or any other subject.

- ❑ Ask students to think about the human heart and write what they know about it in the table under the heading, "What I already know about the heart."
- ❑ Divide the class into small groups and have students share their information, writing anything new they learn from classmates in the table under the heading, "What I learned from my classmates."
- ❑ Explain to students that thinking about what they already know about a topic prepares them to learn something new about it. This is because learning involves making new connections in the brain. When people are actively listening to a lecture, by remembering what they already know, making predictions, or asking themselves questions about the topic, they are helping their brains to make new connections.

Listen

2 Listening for the "Gist" or Main Ideas

Best Practice

Making Use of Academic Content

The group study session represented in the listening is an example of real-world academic content. This type of activity allows students to experience situations similar to those they will encounter in academic settings. As students listen to classmates discuss a lecture about the heart, they experience an authentic context in which to interpret the language and concepts presented in this chapter.

- ❑ Ask students if they have ever studied with a group of classmates. Tell them that many university students prepare for exams in this way since it allows them to share information from lectures and readings and to ask each other questions about points that are still unclear. Study groups can also work together to predict which material the professor might ask about on an exam.
- ❑ Direct students' attention to the title of the activity, "Listening for the 'Gist' or Main Ideas." Explain that getting the gist (pronounced /dʒIst/) of something means understanding the main idea or ideas without understanding every detail. This is similar to hearing part of a conversation or reading an article quickly and understanding more or less what it is about, but not catching everything. Assure students that as they listen to the conversation from the study session for the first time, listening for the gist of it is enough. They will listen again later for more detail.

- ❑ Play the audio once all the way through and have students write answers to the questions that follow.
- ❑ Divide students into pairs to compare answers and talk about any information they will need to listen for when they hear the conversation a second time.
- ❑ Play the audio again to give students a chance to listen for more of the details.

ANSWER KEY

1. The students are comparing their notes from Professor Miller's lecture about the heart to make sure they understand everything.
2. He refers to his notes.
3. The size of the person or animal.
4. The piece of cardiac muscle continues to beat all by itself. The students say this happens because nothing tells the heart to beat. The heartbeat starts in the cardiac muscle itself.
5. To pump blood to the rest of the body.

AUDIOSCRIPT

Study Session Conversation: What Makes Us Tick—The Cardiac Muscle

Ali: So what are we studying next, Greta?

Greta: Let's go over the notes from Professor Miller's lecture, Ali.

Ali: You mean the lecture on the heart?

Greta: Uh-huh.

Fred: Great idea. Why don't we go through the notes and make sure we understand everything?

Greta: Sure, Fred.

Ali: OK. Let me just get my notes out. All right. Ready.

Greta: Well, first she said that it was the action of the cardiac muscles that makes an organ as small as the heart so incredibly efficient. And then she talked about how the shape of the heart is similar to a pear. I don't exactly understand that analogy. I mean, which way is the pear supposed to be leaning?

Fred: Well, think of the pictures Professor Miller showed us. In my opinion, it *did* look like a pear, right side up, with the widest part at the bottom, leaning a little to the right.

Greta: Yeah, I get it now. OK, let's talk about the parts. It's got four hollow chambers—two in the top part and two in the bottom part. And what did she say about the walls of the heart?

Fred: She said that they're fairly thick, approximately like a slice of bread, at the bottom. You may not agree with me, but I don't think that's a great analogy. It depends on what kind of bread you have in mind, right? But what she said about the top of the heart makes more sense to me. She said that at the top, they're thinner, about as thin as an orange peel.

Greta: Are you sure about that? I'm fairly certain that it was the other way around.

Ali: No, I'm positive that Fred is right. I have it here in my notes.

Greta: OK. Now what else? Oh, yeah . . . The strips of muscle at the bottom of the heart are like string around a hollow ball. How's that for an analogy?

Fred: That's good.

Greta: You know, I was surprised that the heart is so small. It's only slightly larger than a tightly closed fist. I like how Professor Miller had us each make a fist and look at it so we could see that it was about the same size as a heart.

Ali: Then remember how she told us to open and close our hands? She wanted us to see how the muscles contract and relax over and over again our whole lives.

Fred: Yup. That's the heartbeat. Contraction and relaxation—very regular and even—the beat is just like the tick-tock of a clock.

Greta: But didn't she say that the rate can vary?

Fred: Yeah . . . In general, the rate of the heartbeat varies in relation to the size of the person or animal. An elephant's heart rate is about 25 beats per minute. A small bird's heart rate is about 1,000 beats per minute. The heart of a human infant at birth beats about 130 times a minute. In a small child, it beats about 90 to 100 times a minute. The average adult rate for men is about 75 beats per minute. And the rate for women averages about seven to eight beats faster per minute than the rate for men. Why is that?

Ali: I think she said that's because women are smaller than men, but I don't really understand why that is, do you guys?

Fred: No, not really.

Greta: Let's ask her in class.

Ali: OK. Hmm . . . Anyway, I think it's pretty amazing that this adds up to about 100,000 heartbeats a day for an adult male. That's about 2,600,000,000 heartbeats in a lifetime.

Fred, Greta: Wow!

Ali: Yeah, and another amazing thing is that the heart doesn't have any nerves in it. So, no messages are sent from the brain through the nerves to the cardiac muscles. The brain doesn't tell the cardiac muscles to beat. Nothing does.

Fred: So that means that the heartbeat starts in the cardiac muscle itself?

Greta: That's right. It's different from the other muscles and organs in that way.

Fred: Oh yeah. Remember what Professor Miller said about how a very small piece of cardiac muscle can be kept alive in a dish with special liquid in it? And that the muscle will continue to beat all by itself!

Ali: Uh-huh. Scientists don't really understand how the cardiac muscle does this yet, but I bet that they will in ten or 15 years.

Fred: OK, but how does the heart work with all of the other organs?

Ali: Well, the heart is similar to a pump. Basically, it pumps blood to the rest of the body. Let's see, I've got it here in my notes. The heart pumps approximately five quarts of blood a minute if you are resting and 35 quarts of blood a minute if you are exercising hard. For light activity, the heart pumps 4,500 gallons a day. If you lived until you were 80 years old and just slept all the time, your heart would still pump about 52,560,000 gallons—or 198,961,244 liters—of blood in a lifetime! Can you believe that the heart works that hard?

Fred: Don't look so worried, Ali. I'm pretty sure your heart isn't going to quit yet.

Greta: Right. Remember . . . Professor Miller said that the heart rests a lot, too. In fact, a heartbeat takes eight-tenths of a second, and half of that time the heart rests. So it's both hard-working AND efficient.

Fred: Yeah—I'd say you're going to be around for a good long time!

3 Listening for Analogies 

Best Practice

Organizing Information

This activity uses a graphic organizer to categorize information and accommodate different learning styles. In this case, the chart guides students as they listen for analogies. It provides space for both notes and drawings, so it is effective for both verbal and visual learners. Other types of graphic organizers are used throughout this book.

- Go over the directions and remind students of the three expressions used to make analogies.
- Give students a moment to study the chart and ask any questions they might have about the activity.
- Play the audio of the study session again as students take brief notes on the analogies and expressions they hear.
- Give students time to draw simple pictures to illustrate the analogies.

ANSWER KEY

Item	Analogy	Expression Used
shape of the heart	heart = pear	similar to
walls of the heart	walls of heart = slice of bread at bottom; orange peel at top	like; as… as
strips of muscle at the bottom of the heart	muscles = string around hollow ball	like
size of the heart	heart = fist	the same size as
beat of the heart	beat = tick-tock of clock	just like
action of the heart	heart = pump	similar to

After You Listen

4 Comparing Analogies

Best Practice

Interacting with Others

This collaborative learning activity encourages fluency and confidence. As students share the analogies and expressions they heard in the listening and discuss their opinions with classmates, communication is more important than grammar. Students can practice making contributions to a class as they provide information their classmates might have missed, which builds confidence for future speaking situations.

- In small groups or as a class, have students share the analogies and expressions they heard in the study session conversation. If any students missed information, ask classmates to supply it.
- Explain the purpose of an analogy and ask for students' opinions of the analogies in the listening.
- You may want to play the recording of the study session again so students can hear those analogies they missed.

Talk It Over

5 Setting Contexts for Analogies

- Go over the directions and example. Ask students to hold out a hand and show you what "shaking like a leaf" looks like. Ask if they know or can guess the underlying meaning of this analogy (the man is fearful).
- Discuss the possible situations given in the example. Ask students why a man at a dentist's office might be afraid.

- Divide the class into small groups. Have them discuss the analogies and list four or five situations in which each one might be used.
- Call on some groups to report their ideas to the class.

6 Discussing Analogies

- Keep students in the same small groups and have them discuss the list of analogies on page 68 of the Student Book.
- Have students keep track of the analogies they are not sure about. Explain those analogies in class, or encourage students to find their meanings by asking English speakers outside of class or by doing Internet research.
- If students understand an analogy's meaning, ask them to think of a context in which it might be used and then make a sentence using the analogy.
- Call on each group to report on its discussion. Encourage students to discuss different interpretations of the analogies.
- Ask students for similar analogies from their own language(s) and list some examples on the board.

Reproducible EXPANSION ACTIVITY

- The goal of this activity is to help students remember common analogies by forming associations.
- Photocopy and hand out BLM 11 "Associations Map" on page BLM 11 of this Teacher's Edition.
- Have students write the analogies from Activity 6, "Discussing Analogies," on page 68 of the Student Book in the four larger circles. Encourage them to choose analogies that are interesting, useful looking, or new to them.
- Instruct students to think about each analogy and write anything that comes to mind in the smaller circles. For example, for the analogy "as silent as a grave," a student might write "no noise," "cemetery," "class taking a test," and "library" in the smaller circles.
- Explain that writing down words and the ideas associated with newly learned language helps students make mental connections and remember new material better.
- Have students either share their maps in small groups or tape them to the classroom walls so that everyone can walk around and compare the associations students made with the analogies.

Strategy

Introducing Your Opinion Appropriately

- Give students time to read the introductory paragraph.
- Discuss the difference between facts and opinions. Ask students if they remember some facts they heard in the listening, such as the fact that a small piece of cardiac muscle removed from the heart will continue to beat all by itself. Ask if they remember any opinions, like that expressed by the student who didn't think the slice-of-bread analogy was a very good one.
- Discuss the idea of a *know-it-all*, a person who thinks she or he knows everything. Ask students if they have ever met a person like that, and whether that person was pleasant to be around.
- Go over the expressions to introduce personal opinions. Offer examples such as, "I'm convinced that the students in this class will be very successful." or, "I bet it's going to rain this afternoon."
- Ask students if any of the expressions are new to them. Explain that all of them are used to soften a personal opinion, but there are subtle differences in meaning or tone that English speakers learn over time. The important thing is to know some of these expressions by heart, and to use them to avoid sounding like a know-it-all.

Content Note

- Point out that the "Expressions to Introduce Personal Opinions" are followed by clauses, and that except in the last two expressions on the list, speakers have the option of using *that* as a connector.
  - I imagine we will find out in the next lecture.
  - I imagine *that* we will find out in the next lecture.
- The last two expressions on the list, "In my opinion …" and "Not everyone will agree with me, but …" are also followed by clauses, but *that* is not used as a connector.
  - In my opinion, this English class is an excellent course.

1 Recognizing a Know-It-All 

- ❑ Tell students they will hear a debate between two students, Kenji and Paul.
- ❑ Play the audio of Conversation 1 and ask students to write brief answers to questions 1–4.
- ❑ Ask for volunteers to share their answers with the class.
- ❑ Tell students that they will hear another version of the conversation, and that they should listen for the expressions Paul uses to introduce his opinions.
- ❑ Play the audio of Conversation 2.
- ❑ Ask students which expressions they heard and ask for volunteers to describe the differences between the two conversations.

ANSWER KEY

Conversation 1:

1. yes 2. yes 3. no 4. Paul sounds like a know-it-all because he doesn't use expressions to introduce his personal opinions.

Conversation 2:

I always thought …; I know that not everyone will agree with me …; I'm pretty sure…

AUDIOSCRIPT

Conversation 1

Kenji: I suspect that heart disease is now the number one killer in the United States.

Paul: No, no! It's cancer.

Kenji: Well, I'm almost positive that it's got to be heart disease by now. Didn't Dr. Strong suggest last year that heart disease would soon overtake cancer as the number one ...

Paul: Nope. You're wrong. That couldn't have happened yet. It's still cancer.

Conversation 2

Kenji: I suspect that heart disease is now the number one killer in the United States.

Paul: Oh, I always thought it was cancer.

Kenji: Well, I'm almost positive that it's got to be heart disease by now. Didn't Dr. Strong suggest last year that heart disease would soon overtake cancer as the number one killer?

Paul: Yes, she did, and I know that not everyone will agree with me, but I'm pretty sure Dr. Strong hasn't read the latest statistics on this.

2 Listening for Personal Opinions 

- ❑ Go over the directions and the example. Make sure students understand that they can take notes using their own words, just like when they're listening to a lecture.
- ❑ Play the audio of the study session from Part 2 again.
- ❑ Call on students to read their completed sentences emphasizing the expressions used to introduce opinions.

ANSWER KEY

Answers may vary.

1. Professor Miller is convinced that it is the action of the cardiac muscles that makes an organ as small as the heart so incredibly efficient.
2. In Fred's opinion, the heart looks like a pear.
3. Fred does not agree with the professor's analogy that the walls of the heart are like a slice of bread.
4. Greta is fairly certain that the walls of the heart were thicker on top and thinner on the bottom.
5. Ali is positive that Fred is right. The walls of the heart are thicker on the bottom and thinner on the top.
6. Ali bets that scientists will understand how the heart muscle beats all by itself in ten or fifteen years.
7. Fred is pretty sure that Ali's heart isn't going to quit yet.
8. Fred thinks that Ali will be around for a good long time.

Talk It Over

3 Expressing Personal Opinions 

- ❑ Divide the class into groups of five or more students to discuss the situations.
- ❑ Make sure that students have available the list, "Expressions Used to Introduce Personal Opinions" (on page 68 of the Student Book).
- ❑ Have each group choose one person to be the discussion leader for each situation. The leader is responsible for reading the situation aloud and making sure that everyone in the group has a chance to express their opinion about a situation.

4 Role-Play 

- ❑ Go over the role-play directions with the class and discuss the difference between role-playing and the small group discussions from the last activity. In a role-play, for example, students will express the opinions of their characters and not necessarily their own opinions.
- ❑ Divide students into small groups and set a time limit for choosing a situation, assigning character identities, and practicing the role-play.
- ❑ Call on groups to act out their role-plays for the class; ask the audience to give each group their undivided attention during the role-plays.
- ❑ Have audience members make notes of all the expressions for introducing opinions that they hear.

EXPANSION ACTIVITY

The goal of this activity is for students to practice using expressions to introduce personal opinions.

- Photocopy and distribute BLM 12 "Expressions to Introduce Personal Opinions" on page BLM 12 of this Teacher's Edition. Make one copy for each group of students, depending on class and group size.
- Cut the Black Line Master into strips and fold each strip so that it must be opened to be read.
- Divide the class into small groups and give each group a complete set of folded strips.
- Have students take turns drawing a strip of paper and using it in a sentence expressing a personal opinion.
- The opinions that students express don't necessarily have to be their own. Students may feel less pressure and have more fun if they can say whatever comes to mind, such as, "I'm fairly certain that the earth is flat."

TOEFL® iBT

OPINION QUESTIONS

- Ask a volunteer to read the introductory information aloud as the class follows along. Make sure students understand that the expressions they learned in this chapter are directly applicable to both a test-taking situation and everyday speaking scenarios.
- This is the first time the textbook presents questions similar to those on the speaking section of the TOEFL® iBT. Students may want to know that the TOEFL® iBT has six speaking tasks: The first two are called independent tasks and require students to speak on familiar topics. The remaining four tasks require the use of integrated skills. In these tasks, students are asked to either listen to material and then give a spoken response, or read and listen to material and then give a spoken response. For every task, students are given a short time to prepare and a short time to speak their response into a microphone.

1 Pragmatic Understanding of Opinions: Brief Informal Speeches 

- ❑ Play the audio of the two brief informal speeches and have students answer the multiple choice questions. Allow a 20-second pause after each question.
- ❑ In order to fully exploit the audio, you may want to play each brief informal speech again and pause after each. Ask students which expressions the speakers used to indicate their opinions. Point out that the correct answers were not directly stated by the speakers.

ANSWER KEY

1. b 2. b

AUDIOSCRIPT

Speaker 1

Man: Personally, I don't think that anyone should smoke and I'm positive that smoking causes cancer. Of course, not everyone will agree with me, but I don't think we should make laws about what people can and can't do in restaurants and bars.

Narrator: Question: What is the speaker implying?

Speaker 2

Woman: I should lose some weight. I read in the newspaper that most Americans are eight to 16 pounds overweight, and I'm pretty sure that I'm part of this majority.

Narrator: Question: What does the speaker think?

2 Expressing Opinions 

Best Practice

Cultivating Critical Thinking

This activity asks students to use expressions for giving personal opinions as they answer test questions similar to those in the speaking section of the TOEFL® iBT. This requires students to process the new material presented in the chapter and apply it to a new situation, which helps them to evaluate their understanding of the material and remember it better.

- ❑ With books closed, have students take notes on the opinions expressed in the study session as you play the audio.
- ❑ Explain that students will now practice speaking their answers to questions about the study session.
- ❑ Divide the class into pairs.
- ❑ Have students open their books, but suggest that they only look at each question as it is read by the narrator on the audio. This is similar to actual test conditions.
- ❑ Instruct students to take turns answering the questions. The narrator on the audio will ask a question. Allow 30 seconds for students to answer.
- ❑ Students may have varying degrees of success with this activity the first time they try it, so encourage them to relax and have fun. They should try to speak fluently and continuously for the entire 30 seconds, and they should be sure to express their personal opinion and give reasons for it.
- ❑ Play the audio again with the same pairs reversing the questions they answer.
- ❑ Ask students which of the expressions from the chapter they used.

ANSWER KEY

Students' own opinions will vary.

1. Professor Miller says that the heart resembles a pear, which Fred agrees with. The professor also says that the heart walls are as thick as a slice of bread, but Fred doesn't think that analogy is as good as the first one since there are many kinds of bread.
2. The students agree to refer to Ali's lecture notes to settle the disagreement over whether the heart walls are thicker on the bottom or on the top.
3. In Ali's opinion, scientists will be able to explain how the cardiac muscle beats all by itself.
4. Ali describes the heart's workload over the course of a lifetime, and seems to be concerned about how much work a heart has to do. Fred teases Ali about these apparent worries.

AUDIOSCRIPT

Narrator: Question 1: Fred agrees with Professor Miller in some ways and disagrees in others in regards to what the heart looks like. Explain what each person thinks and then give your own opinion about the appearance of the heart.

Narrator: Question 2: What do the students agree to do to settle a small dispute about their understanding of what was said during the lecture? Do you think this is the best way to handle this or do you have a better suggestion?

Narrator: Question 3: What does Ali think scientists will be able to tell us about the heart in the future? Do you think this is realistic? Why or why not?

Narrator: Question 4: What does Fred tease Ali about? Do you think that this is proper behavior among friends? Why or why not?

EXPANSION ACTIVITY

- The goal of this activity is to give students additional practice with spoken responses.
- Think of familiar topics that students don't need any special knowledge to talk about, such as a favorite book or movie, a personal hero, a dream vacation, or a good place to study.
- Write a number of "test questions" based on the topics and requiring students to give a personal opinion. For example, you might say, "Talk about a favorite book or movie and explain why you like it."
- In a small class, read each question aloud and call on a student to answer it. Bring a timer or look at a watch or clock with a second hand and give the student 15 seconds to think about an answer and 30 seconds to give a spoken response.
- In a large class, give groups of students the questions on strips of paper. Have students take turns drawing strips and answering questions while other group members keep track of the time.

Self-Assessment Log

- ❑ Read the directions aloud and have students check vocabulary they learned in the chapter and are prepared to use.
- ❑ Tell students to find definitions in the chapter for any words they did not check.
- ❑ Have students check the degree to which they learned the strategies practiced in the chapter. Put students in small groups. Ask students to find the information or an activity related to each strategy in the chapter.

Chapter 5

High Tech, Low Tech

This chapter gives students practice taking notes in the context of a class field trip to a space center. In Part 1, students will learn about times when low-tech solutions were the best answer to space-age problems. They will also debate the costs versus the benefits of government space programs and look at vocabulary in context. Part 2 will take students on a simulated space flight and give them practice with diagrams and numbers. In Part 3, students will look at the form and function of the passive voice, and Part 4 presents a very practical technique for taking notes during standardized tests.

Chapter Opener

- ❑ Point out the chapter title, "High Tech, Low Tech," and ask students to brainstorm examples of advanced and old-fashioned technology.
- ❑ Discuss the humor in the quotation. Hoyle indicates that space isn't very far away. But can something that's not very far away still be remote?
- ❑ Direct students' attention to the photo and ask whether they think it illustrates "high tech" or "low tech."
- ❑ Divide students into small groups to answer the Connecting to the Topic questions.

"Space isn't remote at all. It's only an hour's drive away if your car could go straight upwards."

—Fred Hoyle
British astronomer (1915–2001)

Chapter Overview

Lecture: Spaceflight—A Simulation

Learning Strategy: Taking Notes on a Field Trip

Language Function: Shifting Between Active and Passive Voice

Part 1: Building Background Knowledge

Did You Know?

Sharing Your Experience

Vocabulary Preview

Part 2: Taking Notes on a Field Trip

Hints for Taking Notes on a Field Trip

Before You Listen

Listen

After You Listen

Talk It Over

Part 3: Shifting Between Active and Passive Voice

Distinguishing Between Active and Passive Voice

Talk It Over

Part 4: Focus on Testing

Self-Assessment Log

Did You Know?

- ❑ Give students time to read the three vignettes about astronauts who used low-tech solutions for problems in space.
- ❑ Draw a T-chart (a chart with two columns and two headings) on the board. Label one column "Problem" and the other "Solution."
- ❑ Ask students to describe the problem astronauts faced and the solution they found in each case. Write brief notes about the three problems and solutions on the T-chart.

1 What Do You Think? 

Best Practice

Interacting with Others

This activity uses pair discussion to encourage fluency and confidence. As students discuss situations from the "Did You Know?" section, they concentrate on ideas and communication more than on grammar and accuracy. In this way, students practice using English to accomplish an authentic task, which builds confidence for future speaking situations.

- ❑ Divide students into pairs to discuss the three questions.
- ❑ Ask for volunteers to report on their discussions.

Sharing Your Experience

2 Debating the Issue 

Best Practice

Activating Prior Knowledge

The debate in this activity is intended to help students focus on the space program. Thinking about the benefits and drawbacks of government spending for space exploration prepares students to make connections between what they already know about the topic and the new information presented in the chapter. These connections help to increase understanding and retention of the material.

- ❑ Go over the directions as a class. Ask students whether they have participated in debates before.
- ❑ Give students time to read both positions. Explain that it is important for team members to think about how to support their own argument with evidence, and also to predict how the opposing team might support theirs.
- ❑ Make sure students understand that a debate is really an academic exercise. Debaters do not necessarily agree with the position they are supporting. In fact, it is often quite interesting to think from someone else's point of view.
- ❑ Divide the class into two groups and set a time limit for discussion of the positions. Make sure students take notes on their arguments.
- ❑ Subdivide students into groups of four as suggested in the book for simultaneous two-on-two informal debates.

EXPANSION ACTIVITY

- The goal of this activity is to conduct a formal debate using the information generated by the students in Activity 2.
- Divide the class into two groups. Assign one of the groups Position A from Activity 2 and the other Position B.
- Write the format and time limits for the debate on the board and adhere to them strictly. A typical format would look like this:

  Time for groups to plan their arguments (12 min.)

  - Position A: Presentation of argument (5 min.)
  - Position B: Questioning/Cross-examination (2 min.)
  - Position B: Presentation of argument (5 min.)
  - Position A: Questioning/Cross-examination (2 min.)

Time for groups to plan rebuttals (5 min.)

- Position A: Rebuttal (2 min.)
- Position B: Rebuttal (2 min.)
- Position A: Closing arguments (2 min.)
- Position B: Closing arguments (2 min.)

- Explain that in a formal debate, participants take turns presenting or responding to arguments, so there is no interrupting of speakers except by the timekeeper.
- Add that there are judges in a formal debate and a winning and losing team. In a classroom, the instructor acts as judge, declaring a winner and giving feedback on the content of the two teams' arguments.
- After the debate, ask students to describe the debate experience and anything new they learned about the space program.

Content Note

- In the United States, debate is a popular way to learn and practice the use of reasoning and evidence to support arguments. Competitive debate teams are popular at many high schools and universities.

Content Notes

- The "Space Race" between the former Soviet Union and the United States began in October 1957 with the launch of the first Sputnik satellite by the Soviets. Highlights of the two countries' space programs include putting the first human being in space (Soviet Union—Yuri Gagarin, 1961), enacting the first moon walk (USA—Neil Armstrong and Buzz Aldrin, 1969), the Space Shuttle missions (USA), and the International Space Station (joint effort). A new contestant entered the race in the 1990s when China began its space program.
- There is disagreement over whether the enormous cost of space exploration is justified by the advances in technology and scientific knowledge it can generate.

Vocabulary Preview

3 Vocabulary in Context

- ❑ Go over the list of vocabulary words and definitions and have students repeat the words after you. Listen for any pronunciation difficulties they may have; for instance, *acceleration* should have a /k/ sound at the end of the first syllable followed by an /s/ sound at the beginning of the second syllable.
- ❑ For each term, ask students whether they have seen or heard the word before. If they have, ask them in what context. For example, *acceleration* may be a word they've heard in television commercials for cars.
- ❑ Ask students to read through all the sentences first, then go back and fill in the blanks with the appropriate vocabulary. Remind students that not all of the words from the list will be used in the activity.
- ❑ After students complete the activity, ask for volunteers to read each sentence aloud. Discuss any additional unfamiliar vocabulary.

ANSWER KEY

1. Astronauts 2. mission; remote 3. simulate 4. manipulate 5. cargo bay 6. atmosphere; altitude; friction 7. satellite; orbit 8. shuttle 9. solar 10. acceleration

EXPANSION ACTIVITY

- The goal of this activity is to help students learn new vocabulary by using a graphic organizer to think about and categorize terms.
- Photocopy and distribute BLM 13 "Vocabulary Categories" on page BLM 13 of this Teacher's Edition.
- Have students work alone or in pairs and place each term from the vocabulary list in one of the categories. Explain that, to some extent, the placement of the terms is open to interpretation.
- Ask volunteers to say where they placed each word and why they chose a certain category.

FYI

- ❑ Ask students about field trips they have taken in the past and whether or not they were required to take notes during the field trip.
- ❑ Point out that the nature of field trips makes taking notes challenging with so much to see, hear, and chat about.

Strategy

Hints for Taking Notes on Field Trips

Go over "Hints for Taking Notes on Field Trips." Ask students if any of the techniques are new to them and how well they think the techniques would work.

Before You Listen

1 Using the Internet 

Best Practice

Making Use of Academic Content

This pre-listening research activity focuses on real-world academic content. In an academic setting, students often do Internet research to find answers to questions and material for papers and projects. As with any research, it is crucial for students doing research on the Internet to learn ways to locate and evaluate sources. This activity gives students the opportunity to develop valuable research skills in an authentic context.

- ❑ The Internet research on the Lyndon B. Johnson Space Center can be done during class time in a computer lab or as homework.
- ❑ To prepare for the task, conduct a class discussion about finding good sources on the Internet. Ask students which search engines, online databases, or online encyclopedias they regularly use. Ask them for ways to judge whether a website contains reliable information. For example, websites posted by universities or government agencies can often be trusted. Students can also look to see whether a website offers a list of references showing where the information in an article came from.
- ❑ Divide the class into small groups to share and compare the information students found.

2 Discussing the Handout 

Best Practice

Organizing Information

This type of activity uses a graphic organizer to prepare students for the listening activity and to accommodate different learning styles. As students study the diagram in this activity, they encounter vocabulary from the listening as well as a visual representation of the space mission. As students listen, they can verify or correct their earlier ideas about the vocabulary, and follow along with verbal information while looking at the diagram.

- ❑ Go over the directions as a class.
- ❑ Divide the class into pairs to discuss the diagram and the headings.
- ❑ If there are questions about the vocabulary in the headings, assure students that they will understand it better after the listening activity, or that if they do not, you will answer questions about it later. This will allow you to explain the new terms in the context of the space flight simulation.

Listen

3 Taking Notes 

- ❑ Ask students to read over the instructions. Point out that they will listen for main ideas first, including information to confirm or correct their diagrams of the phases of the space mission.
- ❑ Play the audio. Have students refer to the diagram of the stages of the space mission as they listen to the audio and check their guesses about the headings in Activity 2.

- ❑ Play the audio again and have students take notes on the Remote Manipulation Arm shown in the diagram in Activity 3.
- ❑ If any students missed information, play the audio again.
- ❑ After they complete the activity, return students to their pairs from Activity 2 and have them to ask classmates about any of the headings they're still not sure of.

ANSWER KEY-Activity 2

1st circle: EF, 2nd circle: BR, 3rd circle: EO, 4th circle: ET, 5th circle: OCB, 6th circle: RMA, 7th circle: D, 8th circle: L

AUDIOSCRIPT

Field Trip: Space Flight—A Simulation

Guide: Hello. We'd like to welcome Professor Chapman and his aeronautics class to Houston, Texas, and the Lyndon B. Johnson Space Center. Today, without leaving the ground, we are going to experience the excitement of a flight into space.

We are now seated in the space center's amphitheater. The screen in front of you shows the inside of the space shuttle orbiter. The advanced technology used in this presentation will simulate for you what it is like to be a crew member at work on an actual space mission. Our mission today is to capture and repair a $75 million solar observation satellite that has been in orbit since 1980.

OK. Fasten your seatbelts and we will begin our simulated flight on the spaceship *Enterprise*.

All right? Now, imagine we have been inside the orbiter for about two hours making sure everything is ready.

Mission Control: This is Mission Control. It is now T minus 3.8 seconds.

Guide: T stands for takeoff, of course. And we hear the three engines fire.

Mission Control: T minus one second. T minus zero.

Guide: At T minus zero, the two booster rockets fire, and three seconds later we are lifted off the ground by the combined energy of the five engines.

Through the window we see the tower disappear. We feel the effects of acceleration on our bodies as our spaceship speeds up to four times the speed of sound (which is about 1,100 feet per second in the air) and revolves 120 degrees. We are now turned upside down with our heads toward the ground as we climb in the air and go out over the ocean. How do you like the feeling? We won't be right side up until we are in orbit.

Two minutes after takeoff, the fuel in the booster rockets has been used up. They drop away as we continue gaining speed. Six minutes later we have reached 15 times the speed of sound and the graceful spaceship is flying free, heading into orbit around the Earth at a height of 690 miles.

Once we reach full altitude we change our program on the computer. This shuts down the main engines, and the external tank drops away. We can now control the orbiter's movement with small bursts of rocket fire from engines in the nose and tail. Put your hand on the control stick. Move the control stick to the right and we will roll.

Although we don't feel it without gravity, you can see the motion through the window. If you move your wrist on the control forward or backward, we will go up or down. A twist makes us go to the right or left.

Let's have a few of you take turns with this, so you can get the full effect.

Student 1: My turn? OK. Here we go. Lean left!

Student 2: OK, now I'll straighten us up.

Student 3: Anyone for a complete roll?

All Students: Enough! Enough! I'm getting dizzy!

Guide: OK. Let's get ready for the next phase of your mission.

Look through the window. The cargo doors are opening. These doors open when we arrive in orbit and remain open to provide the ship with necessary ventilation throughout our stay in space. As I said before, the purpose of this mission is to repair a $75 million solar observation satellite that has been in orbit since 1980. Since the failure of its control system, the satellite has been moving through space without guidance—moving so fast that it cannot be reached directly by the Remote Manipulation Arm, which we'll call the RMA.

The RMA is a 50-foot mechanical arm attached to the outside of the orbiter. Look at the handout we gave you as you came into the amphitheater. From the drawing, you can see that the mechanical arm is very much like your own arm. The arm is attached to the orbiter at the shoulder, and an elbow and a wrist allow the arm to move and bring satellites into the cargo bay. This maneuver is necessary in order to repair the satellite. There are television cameras at both the elbow and wrist so we can see what's going on. The hand, or what is called the *end effector*, is fitted with three inside wires. A short arm of the satellite is caught by these wires.

If you look out the window, you will see two astronauts in space suits outside. They are going to slow down the satellite manually so we can connect it to the RMA from here inside. Remember, we said that the satellite was moving too quickly to be picked up directly by the RMA.

Student 1: Wow, Look at that!

Student 2: Yeah, they're actually grabbing the satellite with their hands!

Guide: Now it's our turn. The astronauts outside have captured the satellite for us and now we have to get to work. We must manipulate the arm, bending its wrist, elbow, and shoulder joints to lower the damaged satellite into our cargo bay.

Great job! OK, now let's wait while the astronauts repair the satellite in the cargo bay. It should only take a few moments. Just a small part on the outside of it needs to be replaced. Uh-huh, they almost have the old part off. That's it. Now they're putting the new part in place. And tightening it down. There! I think they've got it!

Mission Control: *Enterprise*, this is Mission Control. Congratulations! Your mission has been accomplished. Now prepare for reentry.

Guide: OK, crew, let's get ready for reentry by closing the cargo bay doors. We fire our engines to slow the orbiter so that it begins to fall toward Earth. We enter the atmosphere at an altitude of 400,000 feet. We are now 5,000 miles from our landing site. The friction of air causes us to slow down from our entry speed of 16,000 miles per hour, but it also causes us to heat up. However, we are protected from surface temperatures of 2,750 degrees Fahrenheit by the thermal tiles covering the ship. The heat is so great that our radio communications are cut off for 12 minutes on our descent. Our onboard computers maintain control.

As the atmosphere gets heavier, our craft changes from a spaceship into a glider. The engines shut off as we continue our descent in silence. The ground is coming up at us fast at 10,000 feet per minute, seven times faster than it would in the landing of an airplane. At just 1,500 feet our stomachs feel funny as the pilot pulls up the nose of the spaceship to slow us down. We hear the landing gear open and lock, and very quickly, we touch back down on Mother Earth and come to a stop.

The flight is over. Mission accomplished! Thanks for coming aboard the *Enterprise*.

See you next time on our sister ship *Discovery*.

4 Listening for Measurements and Amounts  

Best Practice

Scaffolding Instruction

Activities 4 and 5 provide scaffolded support to students by preparing them to listen for quantities and statistics through review and practice of numbers. These activities also provide partial notes for students to complete as they listen to the recording of the flight simulation. Scaffolded support assists students as they move through a logical progression of steps toward the goal of independently listening for and taking notes on numbers they hear.

- ❑ For the first part of the activity, divide the class into pairs to practice saying the numbers. Listen for any problems with pronunciation, for example, with the /th/ ending in *one-fourth* and *one-tenth*.

EXPANSION ACTIVITY

- The goal of this activity is to give students additional practice saying numbers in English and an opportunity to ask you questions about them.
- Write a number such as 1,217 on the board and call on a student to say the number.

Repeat with several different numbers, addressing any problems students have as they arise.

- Turn the practice session into a game. Invite the last student who said a number correctly to the board to write a new number and call on a classmate to say it. If the classmate says the number correctly, she or he goes to the board and writes the next number, and so on. If a chosen classmate cannot answer correctly, ask for volunteers to try to say the number.
- Before beginning the second part of the activity, explain that the sentences are partial notes from the field trip and have students read through them. Point out that they are based on the listening passage, but that the wording is not exactly the same as in the audio.
- Play the audio from the field trip again as students listen for numbers to complete the sentences.
- Divide students into pairs or small groups to compare answers and supply information their classmates might have missed.
- Ask whether students have specific questions about any of the numbers or general questions about saying numbers in English.
- Play the audio of the simulation once more and have students complete their sentences or check their answers.

ANSWER KEY

1. 1,100 2. two 3. fifteen 4. 690 5. fifty 6. three 7. 400,000 8. 5,000 9. 2,750 10. 10,000

After You Listen

5 Using Notes to Recall Information 

- ❑ Divide the class into small groups and have students take turns describing the stages of the space mission and the use of the Remote Manipulation Arm, using their notes on the diagrams.
- ❑ Ask for a volunteer from each group to stand up and give their description as a mini-presentation.

Talk It Over

6 Taking Notes on Other Topics 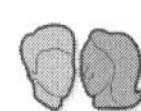

Best Practice

Cultivating Critical Thinking

In this activity, students use the note-taking strategies they practiced earlier in the chapter to prepare for and give a short presentation about a place described by a classmate. This requires students to process the material about note-taking presented in the chapter and apply it to a new situation, which helps them evaluate their understanding of the material and remember it better.

- ❑ Go over the directions so that students understand all parts of the activity.
- ❑ Instruct students to think about and make brief notes on the places they will include in their spoken tour.
- ❑ Have students present their spoken tours to each other. Be sure that the listeners are taking notes so they can later present their partner's town or place.
- ❑ Before students present their reports, give them a few minutes to think about their presentations and perhaps add details to their notes to help them remember important points.

Strategy

Distinguishing Between Active and Passive Voice

- Ask students what they know about the passive voice in English. Ask for an example and, if possible, an explanation of how the passive voice is formed and used.
- Go through each section of the strategy as a class. Ask if students have questions about the passive. (See the "Content Note" for a summary of the use of the passive voice.)

Content Note

- When learning English, a common stumbling block is knowing when to use the passive versus the active voice. Students should be told that the active voice is more common, but there are times when it is desirable to use the passive:

1. The doer of the action is unknown.

   The crime was committed sometime after midnight.

2. The doer of the action is unimportant to the meaning of the sentence.

   Tea is grown in several parts of China.

3. The speaker doesn't want to mention the doer.

   A computer keyboard was ruined when coffee was spilled in the computer lab.

1 Contrasting the Passive and Active Voice 

- ❑ Play the audio and pause after each set of conversations.
- ❑ Have students pay attention to the use of the passive and active voice and answer the questions about the conversations.

Content Note

- On August 29, 2005, Hurricane Katrina hit parts of the United States along the Gulf of Mexico. The states of Louisiana, Mississippi, and Alabama received major damage from wind and the storm surge from the gulf, and the city of New Orleans was flooded when the system of levees protecting it from surrounding waters failed. More than 1300 people died as a result of the hurricane.

  [Source: Associated Press]

ANSWER KEY

Conversations 1 & 2: 1. Conversation 1 contains the passive voice. 2. The passive voice was probably used because the focus was on the damage caused by the hurricane, not on what caused the damage.

Conversations 3 & 4: 1. Conversation 4 contains the passive voice. 2. The passive voice was probably used because the focus is on the insulation foam, not the tile that damaged it. The damaged insulation foam could cause problems, so it is the main subject of concern.

Conversations 5 & 6: 1. Conversation 6 contains the passive voice. 2. The passive voice was probably used because the focus is on the actions, not on who did them. Also, the electric company representative is being careful or polite by not saying who didn't pay the bill.

AUDIOSCRIPT

Conversation 1

Astronaut 1: Wow! Did you see how much damage was caused by Katrina when you drove through town?

Astronaut 2: Yeah, the launch pad was hit, too. Mission Control says that the orbiter liftoff for today has been cancelled until further notice and they'll let us know as soon as it's rescheduled.

Conversation 2

Astronaut 1: I'm really worried about that hurricane. It certainly could cause a serious delay for the launch today.

Astronaut 2: Right. I don't mind the delays so much when we can wait at home, or even on the base. But once we get into our gear and board the shuttle, I really dread any delays.

Astronaut 1: Yeah, me too. I once sat in the shuttle, all suited up, for 8 ½ hours… waiting for a big storm to pass.

Conversation 3

Engineer: Hi, Kim. Can you check out a small problem for me?

Supervisor: Sure. Oh, why is that warning light flashing?

Engineer: I think something strange happened on the lift off.

Supervisor: Look there. Can you see that black spot?

Engineer: Oh, no! Some insulation foam must have broken off and damaged the shuttle!

Conversation 4

Project Supervisor: Hello and welcome to the NASA Space Center.

Reporter: Hello. Murat Boonto from the International Times. Is there going to be a problem bringing the astronauts home safely?

Supervisor: Just a small one. It seems that a small piece of insulation foam was damaged during lift off.

Reporter: What? Was the shuttle damaged, too?

Supervisor: Yes. A protective tile was hit by the foam and we can now see a large black spot on the tile.

Conversation 5

Husband: What happened?

Wife: The lights just went out!

Husband: What do you suppose is the reason?

Wife: (*joking*) Maybe aliens have landed in a spacecraft on our front lawn. But more likely… the electric company probably turned off our electricity because we forgot to pay our bill when we were on vacation.

Conversation 6

Electric company official: Good morning. This is Madison Electric.

Customer:	My name is Ellie Barca and my electricity went out last night.
Electric company official:	Just a minute, Ms. Barca. I'll check your records.
Customer:	Thank you.
Electric company official:	Ah, yes, here they are.
Customer:	What happened?
Electric company official:	Your electricity has been turned off because your bill hasn't been paid.
Customer:	Well... good. We can take care of that. At least it's not because we've been attacked by aliens.

2 Listening for the Passive Voice 

- Play the audio of the flight simulation from Part 2 again as students fill in the blanks in the sentences.
- Divide students into pairs to compare answers or call on students to read each sentence aloud. Make sure the passive is formed correctly, and make sure students notice that the passive can occur with any verb tense.

ANSWER KEY

1. are lifted 2. has been used up 3. be reached 4. is called; is fitted 5. is caught 6. to be picked up 7. has been accomplished 8. are protected 9. are cut off

Talk It Over

FYI

- Review the information in the FYI box with students and ask them to give examples of the passive voice in news reports.

EXPANSION ACTIVITY

- The aim of this activity is to demonstrate the use of the passive voice in news reporting. Students can do the activity as a class or independently at home.
- If the activity is going to be done in class, record a television or radio news broadcast in English that you can play in class. Outside the U.S., look for broadcasts by CNN, the BBC, or Voice of America.
- If students do the activity as homework, suggest television, radio, or Internet sources for news broadcasts in English. On the Internet, National Public Radio (www.npr.org) offers free access to taped portions of its programming, and BBC News offers its weekly radio news program *The World* (www.theworld.org).
- In class or as homework, have students listen to a radio or television news broadcast and identify uses of the passive voice. Tell them to make a note of two or three sentences that use the passive, the context of these sentences, and why the passive was used.
- If the activity is done in class, discuss what students heard; if it is a homework assignment, divide students into small groups to give brief oral reports.

3 Using the Passive Voice to Report the News 

- Divide the class into small groups of three to six students.
- Go over the directions. Instruct students to say, rather than write, the sentences.

- ❑ Call on groups to share stories with the class after they have tried them in small groups.

ANSWER KEY

Answers will vary.

1. The astronauts were given the order to prepare for liftoff.
2. The countdown was begun.
3. The astronauts were asked to check the controls.
4. The controls were checked by the astronauts.
5. All the essential systems were tested.
6. The signal for liftoff was given.
7. The astronauts' cabin was filled with smoke.
8. The fire was quickly put out.
9. None of the pilots was killed.
10. However, two mechanics were injured.
11. Mission Control was shocked by the accident.
12. Afterwards, burned pieces of insulation were found.
13. The public was quickly informed by the media.
14. The next mission was cancelled so that the problem could be fixed.

4 Role-Playing a News Reporter

- ❑ Have students plan their stories in class or as homework.
- ❑ Set a time limit for presentations and specify what type of notes students may use. You may, for example, allow students to write out the passive sentences they plan to use and briefly outline the rest of the presentation, or require that they present from memory so they aren't simply reading aloud.

NOTE-TAKING FOR STANDARDIZED TESTS

- Read the information aloud as students follow along, or give them time to read silently.
- Draw a T-chart (a chart with two columns and two headings) on the board to illustrate the organizational pattern described. Label the left column "Method" and the right column "Operation."
- Have students brainstorm a possible low-tech method of controlling weather damage, such as digging drainage ditches next to fields to prevent flooding.
- Write very brief notes on the T-chart. In the example above, "drainage ditches" in the left column and "prevent flooding" in the right column would be sufficient to jog students' memories when the time came to use the information to answer a test question.

1 Note-Taking Practice 

- ❑ Go over the directions and ask students to imagine the situation: a field trip to a science museum.
- ❑ Play the audio segment. Have students listen to the audio with books closed and take notes in a T-chart, as described above.
- ❑ After the conversation finishes, have students open their books and use their notes to answer the four multiple-choice questions as they hear them in the audio. Allow for a 20-second pause between questions.
- ❑ Discuss whether or not the notes were helpful. Ask students if they need to change their approach to taking notes in any way.

ANSWER KEY

1. c 2. a 3. d 4. b

AUDIOSCRIPT

Guide: OK, everyone. Welcome to the Thompson University Science Museum. Thanks for coming today to see our new exhibit, "Low-Tech Solutions." This exhibit is a slightly humorous look at how clever people have found simple solutions to complicated problems.

Student 1: You mean, like, fixing things with chewing gum and hair pins?

Guide: You're not too far off, as you'll see. Our first exhibit features the mighty, the versatile…aluminum foil. As famous as foil is for replacing pot-covers or cookie sheets, it also fixes cars, satellite dishes, and even computer keyboards. Look at this dirty and rusted-out car muffler, which is the part that keeps cars from running too noisily. Next to it, you see a similar muffler wrapped in three layers of ordinary aluminum foil, kept in place by two "ropes" made of speaker wire from a sound system.

Student 2: Cool. But does it work?

Guide: Listen to this. First I'll play a recording of a car running with a brand new muffler. *[smooth-running noise]* Now I'll press this button, and we can hear the car running with the falling-apart muffler. *[horrible noise]* Finally, let's hear the repaired muffler. *[smooth-running noise]* There. So what do we learn from this?

Student 2: Keep foil in your car.

Guide: Anything else?

Student 3: Yeah. You can save a lot of money if you're smart. A new muffler would have been expensive.

Guide: OK, let's move on. What do you see in this display case?

Student 2: A horn.

Student 1: A clarinet.

Guide: Right. A clarinet. A broken clarinet. Now, this is a finely crafted instrument, made by artistic masters and tested by some very sophisticated machines. So what's wrong with it?

Student 3: You can see from that blow-up photo. One of those hole covers looks thinner or harder or something.

Guide: Right. It looks harder because it has lost a little soft piece that normally goes on the end of the key. That soft cover, called a *pad* makes sure that the tone hole is completely covered when the key is at rest. So, you're a clarinetist just about to go on stage, and one of those pads falls off. What do you do? Rush off to an instrument repair shop?

Student 1: No. You fix it yourself.

Guide: How?

Student 1: Uh, I'm not sure.

Guide: Well here's how the Thompson Orchestra's first clarinetist fixed it. She pulled some chewing gum out of her purse and gave it a few chews. Then she picked up the fallen pad and used the gum to glue it to the end of the key. She got through her performance without any trouble.

Student 3: Pretty clever of her. I had given up chewing gum, but I think I'll start up again.

Guide: Well you'll have to discuss that with your dentist. Now before we move on, let me ask. You're trying to get a DVD out of a DVD player. You know it's in there, but it won't come out because the tray keeps getting stuck. You could take it to a repair shop and pay $40 to have it removed, but what do you really do?

Student 2: I don't know. Shake the player? Pry it out with a butter knife?

Guide: Let's forget about the butter knife method… unless you want a jolt of electricity through your body, but shaking sometimes works. Look here. That's what our next display is about.

Narrator: Question 1: Listen again to part of the exchange.

Guide: OK, everyone. Welcome to the Thompson University Science Museum. Thanks for coming today to see our new exhibit, "Low-Tech Solutions." This exhibit is a slightly humorous look at how clever people have found simple solutions to complicated problems.

Narrator: Which of the following does the tour guide most strongly imply about low-tech solutions?

Narrator: Question 2. According to the tour guide, what item in the exhibit was fixed by using aluminum foil?

Narrator: Question 3. Listen again to part of the exchange.

Guide: Right. It looks harder because it has lost a little soft piece that normally goes on the end of the key. That soft cover, called a *pad* makes sure that the tone hole is completely covered when the key is at rest. So, you're a clarinetist just about to go on stage, and one of those pads falls off. What do you do? Rush off to an instrument repair shop?

Student 1: No. You fix it yourself.

Guide: How?

Student 1: I'm not sure.

Guide: Well here's how the Thompson Orchestra's first clarinetist fixed it. She pulled some chewing gum out of her purse and gave it a few chews. Then she picked up the fallen pad and used the gum to glue it to the end of the key. She got through her performance without any trouble.

Narrator: Why, according to the tour guide, was the solution involving gum especially helpful to the clarinetist?

Narrator: Question 4. Listen again to part of the exchange.

Guide: Well you'll have to discuss that with your dentist. Now before we move on, let me ask. You're trying to get a DVD out of a DVD player. You know it's in there, but it won't come out because the tray keeps getting stuck. You could take it to a repair shop and pay $40 to have it removed, but what do you really do?

Student 2: I don't know. Shake the player? Pry it out with a butter knife?

Guide: Let's forget about the butter knife method… unless you want a jolt of electricity through your body, but shaking sometimes works. Look here. That's what our next display is about.

Narrator: Which of the following is most likely to come next in the tour?

EXPANSION ACTIVITY

- This activity aims to provide students with additional formats for taking notes during standardized tests.
- Photocopy and distribute BLM 14 "Simple Note Formats" on page BLM 14 of this Teacher's Edition.
- Go over the note formats and ask students for example topics for each format. For instance, the "Chain of Events" format could be used to take notes on the space mission simulation from Part 2 of the chapter.

Self-Assessment Log

- ❑ Read the directions aloud and have students check vocabulary they learned in the chapter and are prepared to use.
- ❑ Tell students to find definitions in the chapter for any words they did not check.
- ❑ Have students check the degree to which they learned the strategies practiced in the chapter. Put students in small groups. Ask students to find the information or an activity related to each strategy in the chapter.

Chapter

6

Money Matters

This chapter focuses on banking and investing, paying special attention to World Bank lending to poor countries and whether or not such loans are truly beneficial to those countries. Part 1 will give students background information on development loans as well as useful vocabulary. In Part 2, students will listen for pro and con arguments in a radio interview of a World Bank representative. Part 3 provides the language and practice students need to agree and disagree in appropriate ways, and Part 4 deals with standardized test questions that require students to make inferences.

Chapter Opener

- ❑ As a class, brainstorm things students need money for. Then brainstorm things a country needs money for, such as for building roads or sending representatives to the United Nations.
- ❑ Direct students' attention to the photo. Discuss the sayings in the "Connecting to the Topic" section. List students' answers on the board.
- ❑ Ask a volunteer to read the Cree Indian prophecy aloud. Ask students to describe the attitude toward money it reflects, and whether that attitude is similar to or different from their own.

“Only after the last tree has been cut down,
Only after the last river has been poisoned,
Only after the last fish has been caught,
Only then will you find that money cannot be eaten.”

—Cree Indian prophecy
Native Americans, United States

Chapter Overview

Radio Program: The World Bank Under Fire

Learning Strategy: Understanding and Constructing Pro and Con Arguments

Language Function: Agreeing and Disagreeing

Part 1: Building Background Knowledge

Did You Know?

Sharing Your Experience

Vocabulary Preview

Part 2: Understanding and Constructing Pro and Con Arguments

Expressing Pros and Cons

Before You Listen

Listen

After You Listen

Talk It Over

Part 3: Agreeing and Disagreeing

Agreeing and Disagreeing Confidently, Yet Politely

Talk It Over

Part 4: Focus on Testing

Self-Assessment Log

Did You Know?

- ❑ Give students time to read the information about the World Bank or read the information aloud as students follow along.
- ❑ Ask for volunteers to tell the class about any experience they have or situations they know about involving the World Bank or similar financial institutions.

Content Notes

- The World Bank was founded in the United States in 1944. Its primary goal at the time was to rebuild Europe after World War II, but that goal has been expanded to include reducing poverty worldwide.
- The World Bank is defined as "an independent specialized agency of the United Nations" and has a membership that is nearly identical to the UN. It is not really one single organization, but instead a group of five: the International Bank for Reconstruction and Development (IBRD), the International Development Association (IDA), the International Finance Corporation (IFC), the Multilateral Investment Guarantee Agency (MIGA), and the International Centre for Settlement of Investment Disputes (ICSID).

  [source: www.worldbank.org]

1 What Do You Think? 

- ❑ Divide students into pairs to discuss the pros and cons (arguments for and against) of a new hydroelectric dam. Have them take brief notes on their ideas using a T-chart, a chart with two columns and two headings, with one column labeled "Pros" and the other "Cons."
- ❑ Call on pairs to report on their discussions using the charts to help them remember their ideas.

Sharing Your Experience

2 What Do You Know About Banks? 

Best Practice

Organizing Information

This activity uses a graphic organizer. Graphic organizers can be used when generating ideas for a presentation or paper, when taking notes during a lecture or while reading, or when studying content or vocabulary. By categorizing information and showing relationships between ideas, graphic organizers facilitate understanding and retention of new material. In this activity, students use a sunray graphic organizer to brainstorm ideas about bank services. Other types of graphic organizers are used throughout the book.

- ❑ Go over the directions as a class. You may want to have each group draw a large version of the sunray graphic organizer on paper so that they can write on it easily.
- ❑ Divide the class into small groups and set a time limit for brainstorming ideas about bank services.
- ❑ Draw a very large sunray graphic organizer on the board and ask for a volunteer to come to the board.
- ❑ Ask the groups to take turns reporting their ideas to the volunteer, who will note them on the large sunray graphic organizer. Help the volunteer student by pointing out repetitions of ideas and making suggestions for ways to write brief notes.

3 What Do You Think About Banks? 

Best Practice

Scaffolding Instruction

This activity provides scaffolded support to students. Discussions in pairs and small groups are used consistently throughout the Student Book to help students prepare for topics. This activity also asks students to think about banks as either friends or enemies, which sets the stage for the chapter's learning strategy: listening for pros and cons. This scaffolded support assists students as they progress toward the goal of using English independently in academic settings.

- ❑ Divide the class into small groups and assign one person from each group to be a note-taker and reporter.
- ❑ Ask other group members to read each question aloud and act as discussion leader for that question, making sure every group member expresses an opinion.
- ❑ After the discussion, call on the reporters to stand up and share interesting points made by group members.

Best Practice

Making Use of Academic Content

The following expansion activity uses real-world academic content to increase students' background knowledge of the World Bank. In an academic setting, students often do Internet research to find answers to questions and material for papers and projects. And as with any research, it is crucial that students doing research on the Internet learn to examine sources for bias. By asking students to locate two websites, one with a favorable view of the World Bank and one with a critical view, this activity gives students the opportunity to develop valuable research skills in an authentic context.

EXPANSION ACTIVITY

- The goal of this activity is to give students practice identifying bias in Internet information sources and to provide additional background information on the World Bank.
- Tell students that they will do Internet research to find out more about the World Bank.
- During class or as homework, instruct students to find websites with information about the World Bank. Point out that everything that is written has a point of view, or bias, and that they should find websites or articles reflecting both positive and negative views of the World Bank.
- Photocopy and distribute BLM 15 "Internet Research on the World Bank" on page BLM 15 of this Teacher's Edition.
- Instruct students to provide the requested information: article or website titles or names, URLs, clues about bias, and an interesting piece of information from each site.
- Have students share their information in small groups or as a class.

Vocabulary Preview

4 Crossword Puzzle

- ❑ Make sure that everyone in the class knows how to do a crossword puzzle. Sketch part of a crossword puzzle on the board to show that horizontal sections of the puzzle contain the "Across" words and vertical sections contain the "Down" words. Write a word in the puzzle to show that each small square contains one letter.
- ❑ Tell students to read through the vocabulary words and definitions first, then to try to figure out each puzzle clue without using a dictionary. Point out that the puzzle itself can be helpful since it shows how many letters each word has.
- ❑ After students finish the activity, go over the vocabulary in the context of each clue. Give additional examples and explanations of the terms as needed.

ANSWER KEY

Answers are also on page 215 of the Student Book.

Across: 1. breed 2. borrow 3. irrigation 4. alleviate 5. snails

Down: 1. environmental 2. loan 3. proposals 4. insiders 5. invest 6. fire

Strategy

Expressing Pros and Cons

- Go over the information and the example paragraph. Discuss reasons people consider pros and cons. For example, discussing the pros and cons of something helps people make a reasoned decision, and it helps a student writing a paper demonstrate an understanding of both sides of an issue.
- Ask students what they notice about the expressions in the list. They should indicate that all of the expressions are used to indicate contrast. In this case, the contrast is between the positive aspects (pros) and negative aspects (cons) of an issue.

Before You Listen

1 Matching up Pro and Con Arguments

- Have students work alone or in pairs to match the pros and cons.
- Ask for volunteers to read the resulting sentences aloud to the class, indicating the expression used to change the point of view in each sentence.

ANSWER KEY

1. However, it can also put you into debt…
2. On the other hand, this might leave you with…
3. Instead, it would be much better if they saved…
4. Nonetheless, you will be better off…
5. On the contrary, they could just as easily…

EXPANSION ACTIVITY

- The goal of this activity is to give students practice with the expressions presented in the strategy, "Expressing Pros and Cons."
- Photocopy and distribute as many copies of BLM 16, " Expressions Used to Link Pros and Cons," on page BLM 16 of this Teacher's Edition as you will have small groups of students. Cut out the cards and keep them in sets.
- Divide the class into small groups. Give each group one set of "Expressions …" cards.
- Tell students that they will take turns drawing a card. They should read the card aloud and use the expression in a complete sentence that gives an opinion and states a contrasting point of view. For example, if they draw the expression "on the other hand," they might say, "Studying abroad allows a person to learn about a culture as an insider; on the other hand, the cost can be a real hardship to the student's family."

2 Formulating Challenging Questions

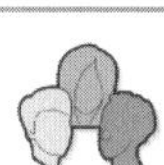

Best Practice

Activating Prior Knowledge

In this chapter, students listen to a radio interview with a representative from the World Bank. In this activity, they think of questions they would like to ask the representative. This encourages students to listen to the interview actively, make comparisons between their own questions and those of the interviewer, and check to see if the content of the interview answers their questions. In short, students make connections between what they already know, what they would like to know, and what they hear in the interview, and these connections help to increase understanding and retention of the material.

- Read the directions aloud. Remind students that they learned the term "under fire" in the vocabulary section. Explain that in battle, this expression means *under attack*. Ask students to explain what it means for the World Bank to be "under fire." They may say that the bank is being criticized for something or questioned about its practices.

- ❑ Divide the class into small groups and have each group generate at least six questions it would like Mr. Cruz to answer. Have students write their questions in the first column of the chart provided. Tell them they will fill out columns two and three later.
- ❑ Call on each group to share their questions with the class and invite everyone to add additional interesting questions they hear from classmates to their own lists. Answers will vary.

Listen

3 Listening for Pros and Cons 

- ❑ Ask students to look at the chart on page 98 of the Student Book before they begin.
- ❑ Have students close their books. Tell students that they will listen to the interview once to get the gist and find out which of their questions are answered. Have them take out their list of questions. Ask students to check off their questions that are addressed in the interview.
- ❑ Play the audio of the interview in its entirety.
- ❑ Have students open their books again to page 98 and look at the chart, "Member Agencies of the World Bank." Tell them that you will play the audio again in three sections, and for each section they will fill out one column of the chart.
- ❑ Play the first part of the interview as students fill out the first column of the chart on the International Bank for Reconstruction and Development (IBRD). If students would like to hear it again, replay the first part of the interview.
- ❑ Repeat the process with the next two segments of the audio for the remaining columns in the chart.
- ❑ Note that there are only two "Cons" for the IDA segment.

ANSWER KEY **Answers may vary.**

Member Agencies of the World Bank		
International Bank for Reconstruction and Development (IBRD)	**International Development Association (IDA)**	**International Finance Corporation (IFC)**
Pros (advantages)	**Pros (advantages)**	**Pros (advantages)**
1. Loans from the IRBD can be restructured to alleviate problems with repayment.	1. The IDA makes loans that are interest free.	1. The IFC can invest in private business and industry.
2. The IBRD lends money for projects that aid economic development.	2. The IDA allows even the poorest countries to begin projects immediately.	2. The government does not have to guarantee the loan, which encourages the growth of private business and industry.
3. The IBRD provides technical assistance along with loans.	3. A major goal is to help people help themselves by sharing knowledge and forming partnerships	3. People in the region spend the money in ways they think are best.
Cons (disadvantages)	**Cons (disadvantages)**	**Cons (disadvantages)**
1. Paying back loans plus interest can be difficult and may force spending cuts in health, education, etc.	1. The IDA is very dependent upon contributions from member nations to support various projects.	1. The IFC is not protected if the business fails.
2. Up to now, the bank could only loan money to buy imported goods, which might discourage the local production of goods.	2. Member nations can dictate what governmental policies are in place before loans are given.	2. The IFC has no control over how a company spends its money.
3. There could be a problem getting local residents to use the technology appropriately.	3.	3. Wealthier nations may have the most influence on which projects are financed.

AUDIOSCRIPT

Radio Program: The World Bank Under Fire

Michelle Barney: Good afternoon. This is Radio K-I-Z-Z, your "total talk" radio station. I am Michelle Barney, financial reporter for Radio KIZZ, and I will be your host for today's program, "The World Bank Under Fire."

I'm sure you are all aware that most of the world's population lives in developing and semi-industrialized countries. These countries do not have enough money to invest in schools, utilities, factories, and highways. One way these countries can get money is by borrowing money from an organization called the World Bank.

In theory, this money should be helping the world's poor. Since the establishment of the World Bank in 1944, most people have assumed that these loans could only do good things for a country. But it turns out that money isn't everything.

For example, many people question the value of a dam built with World Bank money in Ethiopia. That dam was built to provide electricity, but it destroyed the homes and lives of more people than it served with electric power. That dam also destroyed forests and endangered animals and plants. The critics of the World Bank say that this kind of help to developing countries is wasteful, destructive, and unfair. They wonder who is profiting from projects such as this one—the people or large international corporations?

Today we have a spokesperson here with us from the World Bank, Mr. George Cruz. Mr. Cruz has been with the bank for ten years and is part of a team that has been examining the effectiveness of World Bank projects. This World Bank team of insiders is coming to the same conclusions as many critics of the World Bank. They have concluded that many of the projects in the past have been economic failures and serious threats to both the environment and human rights. Mr. Cruz. . .

George Cruz: Well, Ms. Barney, I am very happy to be here today to clarify some things about the World Bank. While much of what you say is true, I think we need to talk about the successes of the World Bank as well as the failures. We also need to talk about the positive changes the World Bank has made in its policies and goals for the 21st century.

But to begin, I'd like to give a brief overview of the World Bank and how it works.

Ms. Barney: Of course. I think that would be very helpful for our listeners.

Mr. Cruz: Now, what we call the World Bank is actually an umbrella term, a general term, for five separate organizations with five slightly different purposes. But the International Bank for Reconstruction and Development is generally what most people think of as the World Bank. In order to borrow money from this branch of the World Bank, a country must be a member. Of course, the money is supposed to be paid back with interest, as with any bank loan.

Ms. Barney: Yes. I guess that's true, but many countries are never able to pay back the loans.

Mr. Cruz: Yes, that has been a serious problem, but we do have a program to restructure the loans, which will alleviate that problem.

Ms. Barney: Yes, restructuring, or reorganizing how the debts are paid back, may help a little, but unless they are forgiven completely so that nothing has to be paid back there are still very serious problems. Isn't it true that in some cases, developing countries have been forced to cut spending on health, education, transportation, and welfare programs in order to reduce their huge debts to the World Bank? I've read that in some countries, the debt to the World Bank is so great that it's now the largest item in the government budgets. Furthermore, these countries have been forced to sell industries and land to foreign corporations in order to pay off debts to the World Bank.

Mr. Cruz: Wait, wait! One thing at a time! First, you're right that developing countries owe a lot of money to the World Bank. However, as of this year, 22 nations have had at least two-thirds of their debts forgiven. They don't have to make any more payments. And, don't forget… there is a danger that if a debt is forgiven completely, that it will ruin that nation's credit rating, because everyone will think that country just doesn't know how to manage money and pay its bills. So we have to be concerned about this, too.

Ms. Barney: I see.

Mr. Cruz: And I hope everyone understands the International Bank for Reconstruction and Development tries to loan money to member countries for projects that will *aid* economic development. In theory, this is good. But up to now, the bank could only loan money to buy imported goods. And to make sure that this rule was followed, the bank paid the sellers directly.

Ms. Barney: Well, this rule is good for the countries and companies that want to sell goods to developing countries, but wouldn't this discourage local production of goods? In the long term, wouldn't this rule do more harm than good to the developing country's economy?

Mr. Cruz: Possibly. That's one of the things we're looking at very seriously. But there are other advantages to getting a loan from this branch of the World Bank. The International Bank for Reconstruction and Development provides technical assistance along with loans. And this is a major part of our new vision for the 21st century.

For example, Cameroon submitted a proposal for a new irrigation system along the Logone River. They hoped that with this new irrigation system, the cash income of the region would be five times greater than before. But the Bank did not approve the project right away because we know that technological advances can sometimes cause environmental problems. Before approving the proposal, the Bank asked environmental consultants to study the project.

The consultants found that the new irrigation system would result in a serious health problem because of snails that live in the area. These snails carry a tropical disease called bilharzia.

Ms. Barney: Excuse me. Was that bilharzia with an *h*?

Mr. Cruz: Yes. Bil-har-zee-uh. Bilharzia. Anyway, the new irrigation system might have spread the snails and the disease they carried to a larger area. So the Bank paid for studies of the river system. Scientists and engineers together determined that if the irrigation system were used only when the snails were not breeding, then the disease would not spread. So, the Bank was able to solve the problem.

Ms. Barney: Yes, I understand what you mean, but wasn't there a problem getting local residents to use the system appropriately? I believe I read that some people were never convinced that the snail disease had really been taken care of, so they would not use the irrigation system at all. And another group of people never believed there was a problem in the first place, so they would not stop using the irrigation system when the snails were breeding.

Mr. Cruz: Yes, that's true. The International Bank for Reconstruction and Development is beginning to see that understanding local needs and culture may be more important than anything else in the success of a project.

Well, let me continue. The second organization under the World Bank umbrella is the International Development Association, or IDA. The IDA has approximately 160 members and makes loans that are interest free. This means that the borrowers do not have to pay any interest and they only pay back the loan amount, or principal. This, of course, is good because it allows even the poorest countries to begin projects immediately. On the other hand, because little or no interest is paid, the IDA is very dependent upon contributions from member nations to support various projects.

The IDA uses the member dues, the yearly membership fees, plus other contributions from member nations, to fund loans to needy countries.

Ms. Barney: So this is how member nations can dictate what governmental policies must be in place before loans will be given, right?

Mr. Cruz: Yes, exactly. The member nations, since they are contributing the money, often wish to have a say in how their money will be handled in a particular country. Some countries may be uncomfortable with the more powerful nations exerting this kind of control over their government policies. However, our major goal for the 21st century is to help people to help themselves, not only by providing money, but also by sharing knowledge and forming partnerships.

So, let's move on to the third organization in the World Bank group: the International Finance Corporation, or IFC. The IFC is different from the International Bank for Reconstruction and Development and the IDA because the IFC can invest in private business and industry, while the other two organizations can only invest in government projects. This is good for the country because the government does not have to guarantee the loan and it encourages the growth of private business and industry. However, the IFC is not protected if the business fails.

Also, the IFC has no control over how a company spends its money. Some people argue that the loan is more effective if people in the region spend the money in ways they think are best, without the IFC telling them what to do. They think that people outside the region do not have a thorough understanding of complex cultural and economic regional issues.

Ms. Barney: Absolutely, but is that ever really possible? I thought that the member nations get voting rights based on the amount of money they contribute to the Bank. Doesn't that mean that the wealthier nations have the most influence on which projects will be financed?

Mr. Cruz: Ideally, of course, the loans are made to countries on the basis of economic need alone.

Robert McNamara, who was secretary of defense when John F. Kennedy was president of the United States, was president of the World Bank for a time. He hoped that the World Bank would be a model of international cooperation free from political

	self-interests. He hoped for a world in which the superpowers would join together to provide financial support for developing nations instead of arguing among themselves. But, we all know that it is difficult to separate economic goals from political interests in today's world.
Ms. Barney:	I couldn't agree more with McNamara's vision. But whether the World Bank can really make this dream a reality is a big question. Well, our time is up and that brings us to the end of this week's program. Our guest today was George Cruz and the topic was "The World Bank Under Fire." Thank you for being with us today, Mr. Cruz.
Mr. Cruz:	My pleasure.
Ms. Barney:	This is Michelle Barney, your host for *World Business Topics*. Please join us next week, same time, same station, K-I-Z-Z, your "total talk" radio.

After You Listen

4 Comparing Pros and Cons 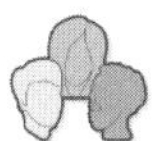

- ❑ Working in the same groups as in Activity 2, instruct students to compare the information they wrote in their charts on page 98.

5 Reviewing Your Questions 

- ❑ Have the groups look again at the list of questions they wrote in the chart in Activity 2 on page 96 and discuss whether their questions were or were not answered satisfactorily. If their question was answered satisfactorily, have students write why in the second column of the chart. If not, have them write why in the third column.

Talk It Over

6 Considering Ways to Invest Your Money 

- ❑ Ask students about their experiences saving and investing money. If students are from different countries, ask them what sorts of investments are most popular in their countries.
- ❑ Go over the directions so that students understand all the steps in the activity.
- ❑ Divide the class into small groups and have students transfer the chart in this activity to large poster paper using markers. Remind them to write large enough that everyone in the room can read their poster.
- ❑ Ask students to add investment ideas to their charts and draw a symbol next to each one.
- ❑ Tape the posters to the classroom walls. Have the groups take turns sharing the investment ideas they thought of.

7 Discussing Pros and Cons of Investments 

Best Practice

Interacting with Others

In this activity, small groups of students must communicate in English to accomplish an authentic task. As students discuss and vote on the investment strategies presented in the previous activity, they concentrate on ideas and communication more than on grammar and accuracy. In this way, they build fluency and confidence for future speaking situations.

- ❑ Working in the same groups as in Activity 6, instruct students to use the chart in this activity to note all the investment ideas generated by the class.
- ❑ Have the groups discuss and note on the chart all the pros and cons they can think of for each idea, and then take a vote on which investment strategy is best overall.
- ❑ Call on students to report on their group's decision and explain the reasons behind it.

Strategy

Agreeing and Disagreeing Confidently, Yet Politely

- Go over the introductory paragraph and ask students to compare the information about agreeing and disagreeing with the norms in their own cultures. Ask, for example, whether professors expect students to react to their statements and whether expressing a personal viewpoint is easy or difficult in their cultures.
- Read through the "Expressions for Expressing Agreement." Explain to students that you'll take turns saying the expressions. You'll say the first expression, "Absolutely," they'll say the second expression, "I'll say!" and so on through the list.
- Ask students whether any of the expressions in the list are new to them.
- Make sure students understand that the expressions are either less formal or more formal, but that all of them are polite. It's easy to agree with someone without worrying about being impolite.
- Read through the "Expressions for Expressing Disagreement." Point out that this list is more complicated and includes informal expressions used only with friends, formal expressions considered rude or aggressive, and polite formal expressions. Make sure students understand these three sections of the list.
- Demonstrate the appropriate sincere, friendly tone to use with the informal expressions by asking students to take turns saying things that are obviously not true; for instance, "I will probably win the lottery today." Respond with one of the informal expressions for expressing disagreement.
- Next, demonstrate how the first list of formal expressions can sound either polite or aggressive. Have students continue making untrue statements. Use formal expressions to respond, but switch between using a firm, yet polite tone of voice and an aggressive, combative tone of voice. Ask students to guess whether you are being aggressive or not.
- Finally, demonstrate polite ways to disagree using the second list of formal expressions and appropriate intonation. Complete the sentences according to what students say. For example, if a student says, "Fish fell from the sky yesterday," you could respond, "I understand what you mean, but I think it's highly unlikely that fish fell from the sky yesterday. Maybe it was just very heavy rain."

Content Notes

- Disagreeing politely requires two "moves" as well as a specific intonation pattern.
- The first move is to agree with the person who just spoke. Agreeing is always polite, so this is a way to show respect for the person's opinion.
  - I understand what you mean,...
- The second move is to use an expression that indicates a change in viewpoint (see Part 2 of the chapter) followed by one's own contrasting opinion.
  - ...but isn't it also true that smokers have rights?
- In terms of intonation, it is important for the person who is disagreeing to indicate that the first move is not the last thing she plans to say. This is often accomplished through rising intonation at the end of the first move. So in the example, the intonation pattern would be something like this:
  - I guess you could say that, but isn't it also true...

- If speakers remember to use these two steps—initial agreement, then an expression to indicate a change in viewpoint followed by a contrasting opinion—in combination with the intonation pattern, they will be able to disagree without hurting anyone's feelings.

1 Listening for Appropriate Uses of Expressions 

- ❑ Play the audio of the conversations all the way through as students write brief answers to the questions in the book.
- ❑ Play the audio again, pausing after each conversation to let students share their ideas about the way agreement or disagreement was expressed.

ANSWER KEY

Answers may vary.

Conversation 1: The student is being rude by using an informal expression expressing disagreement with a professor.

Conversation 2: This student responds appropriately by using a formal, polite expression of disagreement.

Conversation 3: Paul doesn't use an informal expression, so he sounds unfriendly.

Conversation 4: The informal expression Paul uses makes him sound friendly.

Conversation 5: They probably won't reach an agreement easily because the second board member, who disagrees, does not do it politely.

Conversation 6: The conversation is different in that the expression used to show disagreement is formal and polite, so the two board members will feel more like cooperating to reach an agreement.

Conversation 7: Mrs. Franklin is agreeing with the doctor using informal expressions.

Conversation 8: Mrs. Franklin is responding formally in this conversation. This is more appropriate since the doctor is a respected person and seems to be speaking formally in the first place. The formal expressions are also more considerate of the child's feelings.

AUDIOSCRIPT

Listening for Appropriate Uses of Expressions

Conversation 1

Instructor: And furthermore, it is my opinion that if this small country had not received financial aid from friendly countries, the war would have been lost.

Student: You've got to be kidding! Military planning was the key.

Conversation 2

Instructor: And furthermore, it is my opinion that if this small country had not received financial aid from friendly countries, the war would have been lost.

Student: Yes, but isn't it also true that excellent military planning helped?

Conversation 3

Roger: Hey, Paul. Looks like we're having broccoli again! The only time we have anything decent to eat is when my parents visit! Then the food is so good that my parents don't understand why I think the food is overpriced.

Paul: You can say that again, Roger. That's precisely the point. They really do a good job of making parents think we eat that well every day.

Conversation 4

Roger: Hey, Paul. Looks like we're having broccoli again! The only time we have anything decent to eat is when my parents visit! Then the food is so good that my parents don't understand why I think the food is overpriced.

Paul: You can say that again, Roger. They really do a good job of making parents think we eat that well every day.

Conversation 5

First board member: It's obvious that if we don't branch into other areas, eventually the company will fail.

Second board member: I don't believe that! We must cut costs!

Conversation 6

Third board member: It's obvious that if we don't branch into other areas, eventually the company will fail.

Fourth board member: That's more or less true; however, I think that by cutting our costs we can accomplish a great deal.

Conversation 7

Doctor: Mrs. Franklin, your son has a variety of medical problems related to his weight and it's absolutely essential that he get more exercise.

Mrs. Franklin: You can say that again! He's too fat! All he does is watch TV and play video games!!

Conversation 8

Doctor: Mrs. Franklin, your son has a variety of medical problems related to his weight and it's absolutely essential that he get more exercise.

Mrs. Franklin: I couldn't agree with you more, Dr. Lewis. I've been trying to get him to play sports for years.

2 Agreeing and Disagreeing 

- ❑ Go over the directions as a class. Give students time to read the ten sentences and ask you any questions they may have.
- ❑ Model the activity by playing the first part of the audio, pausing at the appropriate place, and agreeing and then disagreeing with the statement after Stop 1. Use expressions from the lists.
- ❑ Divide the class into pairs. Make sure that students have available the lists of expressions for expressing agreement and disagreement.
- ❑ Play the audio, pausing at the points indicated. Have students talk to their partners. They should agree or disagree with each idea using the expressions from the lists on page 101 of the Student Book and give reasons for their opinions.

3 Agreeing and Disagreeing with Items in the News

- ❑ For homework, have each student find an article on a topic they care about, and in which the writer expresses an opinion they can agree or disagree with.
- ❑ Tell students that they will give a brief oral summary of the article, including the author's point of view, and then agree or disagree with that point of view and explain their reasoning.
- ❑ Help students by suggesting places to find articles in English, such as a university or public library, a newsstand with English language newspapers and magazines, or the Internet.
- ❑ Consider giving students written feedback on their summaries. Collect the articles; then give students an idea of how well they expressed the main points and author's opinion, and how well they used language to agree or disagree.

Talk It Over

4 Planning for Economic Prosperity 

Best Practice

Cultivating Critical Thinking

In this activity, students synthesize their knowledge of the world with information about developing countries presented earlier in the chapter. They also apply language strategies for expressing agreement and disagreement as they make proposals for improving economic conditions in a hypothetical country. This complexity and depth of processing promotes retention of the new material and helps prepare students for authentic problem-solving situations.

- ❑ Go over the directions as a class. Call on students to read complete sentences about "The Land of Potential Prosperity" aloud using the list of facts. Point out the map on page 105.
- ❑ Divide the class into small groups and give each group a large sheet of poster paper and markers.
- ❑ Set a time limit for the planning phase of the activity.
- ❑ Remind students that they can practice using expressions for agreeing and disagreeing as they discuss the five actions they will propose for improving economic conditions in the country.
- ❑ Tape the groups' posters to the classroom walls and have groups take turns describing their proposals as they present their posters to the class.

- ❑ Encourage students to react to their classmates' proposals by agreeing or disagreeing with their ideas. They may think they are being polite by saying nothing, but in English-speaking countries, this may be interpreted as a sign that the listeners are uninterested, lacking in individual ideas, or even unintelligent. (Make sure that is not what people think about your students!)
- ❑ Wrap up the activity by having an informal class discussion after the poster presentations. Ask students what they think are the best ways to decrease poverty in the real world.

EXPANSION ACTIVITY

- The aim of this activity is to encourage students to think through one of the actions they proposed for improving economic conditions and represent the steps and outcomes of that action using a flow chart graphic organizer.
- Find out whether students have seen or used flow charts in the past. Draw a sample flow chart on the board consisting of boxes, ovals, and/or diamonds connected by lines showing the steps and effects of an action. (For ideas, enter the words "flow chart graphic organizer" in an Internet search engine and look for examples of flow charts on educational websites.)
- Working in the same small groups as in Activity 4, tell students to choose the action from that activity that would most effectively improve economic conditions in the hypothetical country.
- Have each group design and draw on large poster paper a flow chart that shows their proposed action as a beginning point and the predicted economic improvement as the end point.
- Tape the finished flow chart posters to the classroom walls and proceed as in Activity 4, with each group giving a short presentation of their poster followed by reactions from the audience.

TOEFL® IBT

QUESTIONS ABOUT MAKING INFERENCES

- Review the paragraph with students. Explain that listening for pros and cons allows us to infer, or figure out, whether a speaker has a positive or negative viewpoint about a topic, or possibly what kind of decision a speaker will make in a certain situation.
- The type of standardized test question that asks students to make inferences requires them to listen for details. These details allow the listener to "piece together" information that is not directly stated.

1 Making Inferences: Brief Conversations 

- ❑ Play the audio and have students choose the correct multiple-choice answer(s). Pause for 20 seconds between each conversation.
- ❑ Play the audio again, pausing after each conversation to discuss the details that allowed the inference to be made.

ANSWER KEY

Conversation 1: b (The first part of the woman's statement is a pro; the phrase "on the other hand" signals a con, so "with strings attached," which means with conditions or requirements, must be a con.)

Conversation 2: a & c (The woman says, "Yes, but …," which signals a contrast with the man's statement. Since the man is agreeing with the woman, we can infer that she doesn't want him to agree with her so quickly. We can also infer that she has some instance in mind when it is better to borrow money than to pay cash.)

AUDIOSCRIPT

Conversation 1

Woman: It's nice that banks are beginning to make more loans to people with low incomes. On the other hand, that money comes with a lot of strings attached.

Man: Yeah, I know what you mean.

Question: What is the woman implying?

Conversation 2

Man: You can say that again! I couldn't agree with you more. It's definitely better to pay cash than to pay interest for years and years.

Woman: Yes, but don't forget there are exceptions to that rule.

Question: What is the woman implying?

EXPANSION ACTIVITY

- The goal of this activity is to encourage students to listen closely to the audio portion of a standardized test so that they can understand the details needed to make inferences, and to provide a reference for discussing the details in each conversation.
- After you complete Activity 1, play the audio again as a dictation exercise. Instruct students to write down every word they hear as you play the audio several times, pausing after manageable chunks and repeating portions as necessary.
- Divide students into pairs to compare what they wrote and ask any questions they have about the two conversations.
- Discuss the details in each conversation that enabled the inferences to be made. (Students will have an easier time doing this with a written version of the conversations to refer to.)

2 Making Inferences: Radio Program 

- ❑ Play the audio of the radio program as students take notes on what is implied by the speakers.
- ❑ Remind students that it is helpful to organize their notes in some way. In this case, they might take notes in two columns, jotting down part of the speakers' statements in the left column and the information that can be inferred in the right column.
- ❑ Consider having pairs of students share their notes and make predictions about the inference questions they might hear on a test.
- ❑ Tell students that they will be providing spoken responses to the next inference questions.
- ❑ Play the audio of the radio program segments, pausing after each so partners can take turns listening to and giving 30-second responses.
- ❑ Play the audio a second time so that speakers and listeners can switch roles.
- ❑ Discuss the activity. Ask students how well they predicted the inference questions. Ask whether 30 seconds felt like a long or short time to speak.

ANSWER KEY

Answers will vary.

1. The speaker may be implying that the loans can also have bad results since she uses an expression, "but," to change the point of view after saying that most people assume the loans can only do good things.
2. The speaker may be inferring that Mr. Cruz is qualified to speak on the subject because of his ten years' experience and his involvement with the committee.
3. Mr. Cruz may be inferring that her attitude is negative since he uses an expression of disagreement followed by the idea of the Bank's successes.
4. Mr. Cruz may be inferring that future projects will be more successful thanks to technical assistance from the World Bank, compared with past projects that didn't provide technical assistance.
5. He is implying that local needs and culture were not taken into account enough in past projects but will be extremely important to future projects.
6. Mr. Cruz is implying that McNamara's goals may not be realistic in today's world.

AUDIOSCRIPT

1. **Narrator:** Listen to a part of the radio program again.

Ms. Barney: Since the establishment of the World Bank in 1944, most people have assumed that these loans could only do good things for a country. But it turns out that money isn't everything.

Narrator: What is the speaker implying?

Narrator: Listen to a part of the radio program again.

Ms. Barney: Today we have a spokesperson here with us from the World Bank, Mr. George Cruz. Mr. Cruz has been with the bank for ten years and is part of a team that has been examining the effectiveness of World Bank projects.

Narrator: What is the speaker inferring about Mr. Cruz?

Narrator: Listen to a part of the radio program again.

Mr. Cruz: Well, Ms. Barney, I am very happy to be here today to clarify some things about the World Bank. While much of what you say is true, I think we need to talk about the successes of the World Bank as well as the failures.

Narrator: What is Mr. Cruz implying about Ms. Barney's attitude toward the World Bank?

Narrator: Listen to a part of the radio program again.

Mr. Cruz: The International Bank for Reconstruction and Development provides technical assistance along with loans. And this is a major part of our new vision for the 21st century.

Narrator: What is Mr. Cruz inferring about World Bank projects in the future?

Narrator: Overall, what do you think Mr. Cruz is implying about local needs and culture in relation to both past and future World Bank projects?

Narrator: Listen to a part of the radio program again.

Mr. Cruz: Robert McNamara, who was secretary of defense when John F. Kennedy was president of the United States, was president of the World Bank for a time. He hoped that the World Bank would be a model of international cooperation free from political self-interests. He hoped for a world in which the superpowers would join together to provide financial support for developing nations instead of arguing among themselves. But, we all know that it is difficult to separate economic goals from political interests in today's world.

Narrator: What is Mr. Cruz implying about the ideals of Robert McNamara?

Self-Assessment Log

- ❑ Read the directions aloud and have students check vocabulary they learned in the chapter and are prepared to use.
- ❑ Tell students to find definitions in the chapter for any words they did not check.
- ❑ Have students check the degree to which they learned the strategies practiced in the chapter. Put students in small groups. Ask students to find the information or an activity related to each strategy in the chapter.

Chapter

7

Remarkable Individuals

In this chapter, the Tour de France bicycle race and seven-time winner Lance Armstrong provide material for a discussion of remarkable people. In Part 1, students will build their background knowledge of the race and share their ideas about what makes certain accomplishments remarkable. Part 2 presents expressions used to talk about time and the sequence of events, and students will listen for those expressions in a celebrity profile of Lance Armstrong. In Part 3, students will learn ways to express their likes and dislikes using situation-appropriate expressions, and Part 4 deals with standardized test questions that require students to state a preference.

Chapter Opener

- ❑ Point out the chapter title, "Remarkable Individuals." As a class, brainstorm the kinds of individuals people often consider remarkable and list them on the board. Some examples include artists, political leaders, scientists, and athletes. Ask students if they think everyday people, such as their parents and teachers, can also be remarkable.
- ❑ Direct students' attention to the photo of Lance Armstrong, and divide the class into groups to discuss the "Connecting to the Topic" questions. Call on groups to share their information and ideas with the class.
- ❑ Read the quotation from Lance Armstrong and ask students to restate Armstrong's idea using different words. Guide students beyond the idea of cycling to other pursuits, such as learning a new language.

“ If you worried about falling off the bike, you'd never get on. ”

—Lance Armstrong
U.S. cyclist (1971–)

Chapter Overview

Celebrity Profile: Lance Armstrong, Uphill Racer

Learning Strategy: Listening for Chronological Order

Language Function: Expressing Likes and Dislikes, Pleasure and Displeasure

Part 1: Building Background Knowledge

Did You Know?

Sharing Your Experience

Vocabulary Preview

Part 2: Listening for Chronological Order

Using Words as Clues to Chronological Order

Before You Listen

Listen

After You Listen

Talk It Over

Part 3: Expressing Likes and Dislikes, Pleasure and Displeasure

Choosing Appropriate Expressions of Like and Dislike, Pleasure and Displeasure

Talk It Over

Part 4: Focus on Testing

Self-Assessment Log

Did You Know?

- ❑ Give students time to read the information about the Tour de France or read the information aloud as students follow along.

1 What Do You Think? 

- ❑ Divide students into pairs to discuss the questions.
- ❑ Call on pairs to report their ideas to the class.

Sharing Your Experience

2 What Makes an Accomplishment Remarkable? 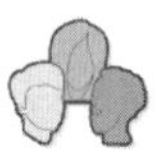

- ❑ As a class, go over the strategy describing the Venn diagram.
- ❑ Divide the class into small groups and go over the directions. Have all group members take notes on their group's discussion.
- ❑ Give each group a large piece of poster paper and markers.
- ❑ Have the groups work together to copy the Venn diagram from the book onto the poster paper, transfer their discussion notes to the diagram in a readable fashion, and illustrate the poster with drawings.
- ❑ Have the groups tape their posters to the walls and walk around the room to look at their classmates' posters.
- ❑ Conduct a class discussion of the posters focusing on common elements among the remarkable accomplishments listed on the posters.

REPRODUCIBLE EXPANSION ACTIVITY

- The goal of this activity is for students to pursue the theme of remarkable individuals through Internet research outside of class and to practice speaking in front of the class.
- As a follow-up to the "gallery walk" in Activity 2, have students choose a famous person mentioned in the posters whom they don't know much about.
- Photocopy and distribute BLM 17 "Researching a Remarkable Person" on page BLM 17 of this Teacher's Edition.
- Instruct students to research their remarkable person using the Internet and fill out the form with information about him or her.
- Call on students to give brief reports about the person they researched.

Vocabulary Preview

3 Sharing Definitions 

- ❑ Point out that the vocabulary words in the list may have more than one meaning, but the meanings here define the words as they are used in the listening.
- ❑ Divide students into pairs to match the words and definitions.
- ❑ Join pairs, forming groups of four, to compare answers and supply missing information.

ANSWER KEY

1. b 2. e 3. l 4. k 5. f 6. h 7. a 8. j 9. d 10. i 11. g 12 c

4 Using Vocabulary 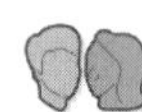

Best Practice

Activating Prior Knowledge

This activity requires students to bring into play their personal experiences and knowledge of the world as they answer questions that include new vocabulary words. In this way, students activate their prior knowledge and make connections between what they already know and the new vocabulary they need to learn, which helps them to understand and remember it.

- ❑ The questions in this activity contain the vocabulary words in context, which helps students make connections and process the new words.
- ❑ Divide students into pairs to take turns asking and answering the questions. Answers will vary.

Strategy

Using Time and Sequence Words as Clues to Chronological Order

- Go over the introductory information about chronological order.
- Ask students if they can think of other instances when simple chronological order is used. For example, when telling a story.
- Point out that *sequence* refers to the order of events—what happens first, next, and so on. Expressions that indicate sequence enable clarity when a speaker doesn't follow simple chronological order.
- Give students a chance to look over the list and ask about any time and sequence words that are new to them or that they are unsure of. Provide examples and explanations as needed.

Content Note

- The expressions listed in the "Time and Sequence Words" table fall into different grammatical categories.

1. The following words can function as prepositions, which are followed by nouns:

after during before until

Example

We went out for ice cream **after** the movie.

2. The following words can function as conjunctions, which connect clauses:

after until before while

Examples

They carried their equipment **while** they were riding.

Until the rain stopped, we did not leave our tent.

Note: Students frequently confuse *during* and *while* due to similar meaning, but *during* only functions as a preposition, and *while* functions primarily as a conjunction.

3. The following expressions are adverbs or adverbials, which function in various sentence positions:

afterward	formerly	recently
at that time	long ago	soon
eventually	now	then
finally	presently	

Examples

She will move to Texas **soon**.

Now, she is living in Idaho.

4. Other expressions in the list have more than one possible grammatical function:

Examples:

Present day scientists do not believe this theory. (used as an adjective)

In the **present day**, fossils of these huge animals can be found all over the world. (used as a noun)

Strategy

Tuning In to the Logic of Chronological Order

- Explain to students that *tune in* means to pay close attention to something in order to better understand it.
- Explain that although time and sequence words are helpful clues, listeners can also use a number of other clues to determine the sequence of events.

- Ask for volunteers to read the bullet points describing ways to tune in to chronological order.
- Reinforce the points by listing them in brief form on the board.

Before You Listen

1 Putting Events in Chronological Order

Best Practice

Scaffolding Instruction

This part of the chapter supports student learning by providing information about understanding chronological order followed by an activity that asks students to determine the chronological order of sentences. The activity is predictable in that the items use a repeated format and procedure, but it is also flexible in that students must negotiate meaning as they move from sentence to sentence within each mini-story and from one mini-story to the next. Instruction, followed by multiple opportunities to participate in an activity that is both predictable and flexible, provides scaffolded support for students as they develop their language skills.

- ❑ Divide the class into small groups and have groups read the sentences in each mini-story aloud and arrange them in sequence.
- ❑ Encourage students to refer to the list of time sequence clues on page 113 of the Student Book or a list that you have written on the board as they answer the questions.

ANSWER KEY

Mini-Story 1: 2, 1, 3

Mini-Story 2: 3, 1, 2

Mini-Story 3: 2, 3, 1

Listen

2 Listening for Time and Sequence Expressions

- ❑ Play the audio once all the way through. Instruct students to listen for the gist and to check any of the time and sequence words they hear from the list on page 113 of the Student Book.

AUDIOSCRIPT

Celebrity Profile: Lance Armstrong, Uphill Racer

Hello. This is Joe Hemmings, and I'm pleased to welcome you to "Celebrity Profile," the show that tells the stories of people in the news who have done remarkable things and lived remarkable lives. I just love the story we're going to tell you today, and I'm certain you will, too.

Lance Armstrong races bicycles. And he's pretty good at it. He's also a father. He's pretty good at that, too. This doesn't sound very special at first, but there is much more to Lance Armstrong's story. Armstrong's win in the 1999 Tour de France bicycle race is one of the most amazing stories in sports history. He was only the second American to win this race, and the win came after he had successfully battled a very deadly form of cancer.

This battle is where our profile begins. When Armstrong found out that he had cancer in October of 1996, his whole world fell apart. He couldn't bear the thought of never racing again, never marrying, and never having children. However, Armstrong says that it was his battle with cancer that transformed his body so he could become the best uphill racer in the world, and transformed his spirit so that he could become a better team member and a husband and father.

By 1996, when he was only 25, Armstrong had already become an international cycling champion. He was riding high on his fame, happy in his role of the wild beer-drinking boy from

Texas. He was young and undisciplined, and the sports writers called him the "Bull from Texas." He had come a long way from his small hometown of Plano, Texas. He was very poor when he left Plano in 1990, but by 1996, he was making over $1 million a year. At that time, though, he still had not won the most famous of all the races: the Tour de France.

In October of 1996, he was told that he had cancer and that he would have to endure treatments of chemotherapy to eliminate 12 tumors in his chest. Eventually, he would have surgery to remove a tumor that had also formed in his brain. Things did not look good. The doctors told him that he had only a 50% chance to live, and they did not even bother to discuss the future of his bicycle-racing career.

When he first began the chemotherapy treatments, he was able to keep up with his teammates on the training rides. Eventually, however, he began to ride more and more slowly. His teammates and friends couldn't stand to see him become depressed by this, so they also rode slowly. He therefore didn't realize just how poor his health had become until one day, a 50-year-old woman on a heavy mountain bike passed him as he was struggling uphill on his superlight racing bike.

Most people thought that Armstrong would never race again, but he says that it was actually the chemotherapy that gave him the body he needed to win the Tour de France. He thinks that, due to the effects of chemotherapy, he was able to lose a lot of heavy muscle that he had built up from swimming as a teenager in Texas. This gave him the opportunity to rebuild his body from scratch, completely from the beginning. This time, he was careful during his training to build the kind of strong and light muscles needed to climb the mountain stages of the Tour de France. And by 1999 he was ready.

However, winning the Tour de France was not the highlight of that year for Armstrong. He and all of his fans were thrilled when his wife Kristin, whom he had married a couple of years before, gave birth to their son Luke in the fall of 1999. And, a couple of years later in 2001, they had twin girls. What a super year *that* was! Armstrong says that facing death helped him learn what was most important in life and that training for his comeback helped him develop the qualities needed for better relationships with friends and family.

But this is not the end of this amazing story. In July of both 2000 and 2001, Armstrong proved that his win in 1999 was not a fluke by winning a second and third time. No one could deny that he was back at the top of his sport. But wait! There's more! Armstrong was asked to be on the 2000 U.S. Olympic team and while he was training, he was hit on a country road by a hit-and-run driver who did not stop to help him. His wife found him two hours later lying in the road with a broken vertebra.

But this remarkable individual could not be stopped. He didn't have time for feeling sorry for himself, and he was back on his bicycle within a few days. He even managed to win a bronze medal at the Olympic Games.

As most of you know, Armstrong did not stop at only three Tour de France wins. I'm delighted to tell you that he went on to win again in 2002, 2003, 2004, and 2005, becoming the only person to ever win this race seven times. And all of the wins in consecutive years! How did he accomplish this remarkable feat? Armstrong has said about himself:

"A slow death is not for me. I don't do anything slowly, not even breathe. I want to die when I'm 100 years old, with an American flag on my back, and the star of Texas on my helmet, after screaming down a mountain on a bicycle at 75 miles per hour. I want to cross one last finish line as my wife and ten children applaud, and then I want to lie down in a field of those famous French sunflowers and gracefully die."

Yes, this would certainly be the perfect ending to a most remarkable life. Since he made this statement, however, Armstrong and his wife, Kristin, have divorced. He began dating singer

Sheryl Crow in 2004. And it was Sheryl Crow who was there cheering at the finish line in Paris when he won in 2004 and for the incredible seventh win in 2005. He retired from professional cycling in 2005, he says, to be able to spend more time sharing parenting responsibilities with his ex-wife and raising money for cancer research.

This is Joe Hemmings. Good night, and please join us next week for another edition of "Celebrity Profiles."

Content Notes

- Lance Armstrong's hometown of Plano is part of the sprawling urban area in northeast Texas known as the Dallas/Fort Worth Metroplex. Plano has a population of approximately 250,000 people.
- In the quotation from the celebrity profile, Armstrong says that he wants to die with the star of Texas on his helmet. The flag of the state of Texas features a single star on a red, white, and blue background, and gives Texas its nickname, the Lone Star State. The star symbolizes the state's struggles for independence.

3 Organizing Information into Chronological Time Periods 

- ❑ Give students time to read through the statements and the four category headings in the chart.
- ❑ Have students fill in the chart based on what they remember from the listening activity. When they listen again, they can verify, add, or change ideas.

ANSWER KEY

Statements	During Armstrong's youth	Before he found out that he had cancer	After he found out that he had cancer	In the future
1. Armstrong was earning over $1 million a year.		✓		
2. He became an international cycling champion.		✓		
3. He was called the "Bull from Texas."		✓		
4. He met Sheryl Crow.			✓	
5. He built up a lot of heavy muscle.	✓			
6. He built strong and light muscles.			✓	
7. He had a son.			✓	
8. He was hit by a car.			✓	
9. He wants to win a race as his wife and ten children applaud.				✓
10. He wants to lie in a field of sunflowers.				✓
11. He was poor.	✓			
12. He won the Tour de France.			✓	

- Play the audio a second time, and instruct students to verify the informaiton in their charts.
- Ask students if any of them are unsure about the chronological order of any of the statements in the chart; if so, call on classmates to volunteer their answers and the reasons for them.

After You Listen

4 Comparing Your Answers 

- Divide students into small groups to compare the information in their charts and discuss the time and sequence clues they used.

Best Practice

Organizing Information

A timeline is a graphic organizer that sets events and the times they occur on a horizontal or vertical line. Events on a timeline can take place in the past, present, and/or future, and longer or shorter time intervals can be represented by more or less space between the events on the line. Using a timeline is an effective way to include a visual element in the chapter's learning strategy of listening for chronological order, and in this way to support different learning styles.

5 Completing a Timeline 

- Ask students to look at the partial timeline of Lance Armstrong's life.
- Point out that some dates, time periods, and events are missing from Armstrong's life.
- Divide the class into pairs and have students complete the timeline using their charts and information they remember from the listening.
- Put pairs together (creating groups of four) to compare timelines and ask about any information they still need.

ANSWER KEY

Answers may vary.

Lance Armstrong's Life

He lived in Plano, Texas.	1980s
He was poor.	in his youth
He left Plano.	1990
He was called the "Bull from Texas."	1991–1996
He had become an international cycling champion.	1996
He found out that he had cancer.	1996
He won the Tour de France.	1999
His son Luke was born.	1999
He won the Tour de France a second time.	2000
He was selected for the U.S. Olympic team.	2000
He was hit by a car.	2000
He won a bronze medal.	2000
He won the Tour de France a third time.	2001
He won the Tour de France a fourth time.	2002
He won the Tour de France a fifth time.	2003
He won the Tour de France a sixth time.	2004
At the finish line in Paris, Sheryl Crow was there cheering.	2004
He won the Tour de France a seventh time.	2005
At the finish line in Paris, Sheryl Crow was there cheering.	2005

EXPANSION ACTIVITY

- The aim of this activity is to provide students additional practice with timelines and sharing personal information.
- Photocopy and distribute BLM 18 "My Life" on page BLM 18 of this Teacher's Edition.
- Give students time to think of their accomplishments and the events that have shaped their lives, and have them plot these events on the timeline.
- Divide the class into pairs or small groups and have students talk about their lives using the timeline as their notes, to help them remember what to say, and as a visual aid to help classmates follow along and see the sequence of events.

Talk It Over

6 Telling a Story

Best Practice

Cultivating Critical Thinking

This story-telling activity gives students a chance to apply the information about time and sequence presented in the chapter to the new task of creating a collaborative story. As students listen to their classmates' contributions and offer their own, they must process language and concepts on a deep level, which promotes retention and allows them to evaluate their understanding of the new material.

- ❑ Read the directions aloud as students follow along in their books.
- ❑ Divide the class into small groups and have students sit in circles to tell their stories.
- ❑ Make sure students have available the list of time and sequence words from page 113 to use while they are creating their sentences.
- ❑ Consider recording the stories for the class to hear. This reinforces the language point and adds an enjoyable listening activity to the chapter. It may be necessary to provide a quiet room and a tape recorder outside of class in order to accomplish this, but it is a worthwhile component of the activity.

Strategy

Choosing Appropriate Expressions of Like and Dislike, Pleasure and Displeasure

- Ask students to think about a typical day, and to estimate how many times in a typical day they mention liking or not liking something. Estimates will differ, of course, but students will most likely agree that they express this type of opinion frequently. They will probably also agree that they would like to know a greater variety of ways to express likes and dislikes in English.
- Go over the introductory information. It is important for students to grasp that using a strong, more emotional expression is more acceptable in informal situations. Using gentler, less emotional expressions reflects the carefulness of speakers in more formal situations.
- Give students time to read through the lists of expressions. Ask them to draw a line separating "I appreciate…" and "I'm delighted…" in the first list, and separating "I dislike…," and, "I don't have time for…" in the second list. Explain that, more or less, these lines separate the gentler, less emotional expressions from the stronger, more emotional ones. Dividing the lists in this way helps simplify matters for students.
- Demonstrate at least one expression from each of the four new sections of the chart using an appropriate tone of voice. For example, use a pleasant, neutral tone to say something like, "I'm pleased you all did your homework." Next, use an excited tone of voice to say something like, "What a terrific group of students I have!"
- Ask for volunteers to offer more examples using expressions from the list. Give feedback on students' tones of voice, levels of emotion, and grammar usage.
- You could also discuss situations in which the expressions might be used. "I hate …" for instance, is quite strong and should be reserved for trusted friends or family members who understand your feelings and not regard you as overly emotional or judgmental.

1 Listening for Consequences of Expressions and Tone 

- ❑ Play the audio of the conversations in its entirety as students write brief answers to the questions in their books.
- ❑ Play the audio again pausing after each conversation to let students share their ideas about the way each speaker expresses like, dislike, pleasure, or displeasure.

ANSWER KEY

Answers may vary.

Conversation 1: The man will probably not get the job because his strong expressions seem very informal and because he indicates a dislike of the very thing the job requires: the ability to work under time pressure.

Conversation 2: The woman will probably get the job because her gentler expressions have an appropriately formal tone and she says she enjoys doing the sort of work that is required.

Conversation 3: Ana expresses the fact that she doesn't enjoy concerts quite strongly. Rafael might not ask her out again because she didn't let him down gently.

Conversation 4: Joyce expresses the fact that she doesn't enjoy experimental theater gently, softening her opinion with her expressions and with an explanation. Rafael might ask Joyce out again because she declined his offer politely.

AUDIOSCRIPT

Conversation 1

Interviewer: I'm happy to say we have quite a few remarkable people working for our company.

Applicant: Now this is my idea of a job!

Interviewer: Ah. . . yes. . . well, we have one Nobel Prize winner in physics and one in chemistry, and they're looking for an assistant to help them organize their notes for a book that must be completed by next month.

Applicant: Oh, no. I can't stand that kind of pressure!

Interviewer: Oh?

Conversation 2

Interviewer: I'm happy to say we have quite a few remarkable people working for our company.

Applicant: That's wonderful! I would love the opportunity to work with them.

Interviewer: Well, we have one Nobel Prize winner in physics and one in chemistry, and they're looking for an assistant to help them organize their notes for a book that must be completed by next month, so you must work hard to keep them on schedule.

Applicant: Actually, I enjoy organizational tasks. I'm sure that I can help them finish on time!

Interviewer: Well, why don't we go and meet them and see what they think?

Conversation 3

Rafael: Hey, want to go to the concert with me on Saturday? There's an amazing cellist who has been playing since she was three years old!

Ana: Oh, no . . . I hate that kind of music.

Rafael: Oh, well, I thought you might like it.

Ana: No, I don't have time for that sort of thing.

Conversation 4

Rafael: Hi! How about going to see that new play at the experimental theater tonight? I really love the director, and they say that the lead actor is sure to win an award for her performance.

Joyce: Thanks, but I don't especially like that type of theater.

Rafael: Oh, sorry, I thought you would.

Joyce:	No, I dislike it because I usually don't understand what's happening.

2 Listening for Expressions of Likes and Dislikes, Pleasure and Displeasure

- ❑ Play the audio of the Lance Armstrong profile as students note all the expressions for likes/pleasure and dislikes/displeasure that they hear.
- ❑ Divide students into pairs to compare charts.

ANSWER KEY

Expressions used for likes/pleasure:

1. I'm pleased to welcome you…
2. I just love the story…
3. He and all of his fans were thrilled when…
4. What a super year…!
5. I'm delighted to tell you…

Expressions used for dislikes/displeasure:

1. He couldn't bear the thought…
2. His teammates and friends couldn't stand…
3. He didn't have time for feeling sorry for himself…

3 Choosing Appropriate Expressions

- ❑ Divide the class into small groups to share answers and discuss their appropriateness.
- ❑ Give students time to read the situations and discuss and write down what they would say in each one. Remind them that the first answer will generally be formal, and the second answer informal.
- ❑ For each situation in the activity, call on a few students to share their statements with the class and explain the language choices they made. Answers will vary.

REPRODUCIBLE — EXPANSION ACTIVITY

- The purpose of this activity is to give students a chance to practice expressing likes and dislikes in the context of party conversation.
- Explain that the interesting people at a party are the ones who have plenty of ideas and opinions to add to a conversation. In this activity, students will role-play people having a conversation at a party.
- Model the use of some of the expressions as they might be used at a party, such as, "I'm happy that our hostess invited me," or, "What a rotten thing the prime minister did last week!"
- Photocopy and distribute as many copies of BLM 19 "The Life of the Party" on page BLM 19 of this Teacher's Edition as you will have groups of 3–4 students. Cut out the expression cards.
- Divide the class into small groups of 3–4 students.
- Explain the rules: Each group will pretend to be people having a conversation at a party. Students are free to bring up any topic they like, from art to zoology, but each person must manage to use all of the expressions on his or her card.
- Choose a group to go first and invite the members to stand or sit at the front of the class. Give each person in the group an expression card and tell them to check off the expressions as they use them in conversation. The conversation is over when every person in the group has used all of the expressions on their card.
- Have the rest of the class listen for expressions they learned in the chapter.

- Repeat the procedure with all the groups, handing out cards only as the groups take the stage so that students aren't distracted by planning their own role-plays while listening to their classmates.
- Take notes during the role-plays and give brief feedback after each one on how well the group used the expressions.

Talk It Over

4 Discussing Goals and Interests 

Best Practice

Interacting with Others

This activity provides high interest subject matter to promote communication in small groups. As students talk about the remarkable accomplishments in the chart, explaining which ones they would or would not enjoy doing, they are more focused on sharing information about themselves, their likes, and their dislikes than they are on vocabulary choices and grammatical rules. In this way, students develop fluency and confidence in their ability to communicate with people using English.

- ❑ Go over the directions and give students time to mark their charts. Be sure that they fill in the blank boxes in the "Other" column.
- ❑ Divide the class into small groups and have students take turns explaining their charts using the expressions on page 118.
- ❑ Ask for volunteers to share and explain what they wrote in the blank boxes.

TOEFL® iBT

QUESTIONS ABOUT EXPRESSING PREFERENCE

- Go over the information about the TOEFL® iBT speaking questions that involve expressing preferences.
- Ask students to create complete sentences using the bullet point phrases and the question in the example about doing laundry.
- Point out that some of the expressions presented in the chapter could also be used to answer this type of question, especially the gentlest expressions on the list, which are neutral in tone. For example, students might say, "I enjoy going to the laundromat because..." or, "I don't care for the on-campus laundry rooms because..."

1 Expressing Preferences 

Best Practice

Making Use of Academic Content

This activity makes use of a number of realistic test questions to give students practice with spoken responses about their preferences. The speaking section of a standardized test is an artificial and high-pressure speaking situation that can challenge even the best speakers of the language. Providing extensive practice with content that mimics actual test content helps prepare students to demonstrate their strengths under stressful test conditions.

- ❑ Divide students into pairs to take turns giving responses to the questions they hear.
- ❑ Play the audio of the questions and have students take turns answering them so that each student answers every question. Remember to allow 20 seconds to prepare and 45 seconds to speak after each one.
- ❑ Conduct a discussion about the questions and the students' responses. Ask, for example, which topics were more difficult and why, and whether students felt comfortable using the language from the chapter in their responses.

AUDIOSCRIPT

Expressing Preferences

Narrator:

Question 1. Lance Armstrong surely prefers biking to any other sport. Other people prefer less strenuous sports. Which type of sport do you prefer? Why?

Question 2. Lance Armstrong would prefer to have many children rather than just one. How about you? Would you prefer to have many children or just one? Why?

Question 3. Some people who are injured stop exercising until they are healed. Others, such as Lance Armstrong, quickly resume their activities, even though it might slow their recovery. Which way of dealing with injuries would you prefer? Why?

Question 4. Whom do you admire more, a person who becomes famous as an academic (a professor, a researcher, etc.) or a person who succeeds in business? Why? You have 20 seconds to prepare your answer and 45 seconds to speak.

Question 5. Some remarkably talented young people become professional athletes instead of going to college. Others finish their college education before turning professional. Which would you prefer for yourself if you had remarkable athletic talent? Why? You have 20 seconds to prepare your answer and 45 seconds to speak.

EXPANSION ACTIVITY

- The goal of this activity is for students to practice stating reasons for preferences without much preparation time.
- Divide the class into two groups. If possible, have students stand or sit facing each other with half of the students on one side of the room and half on the other side.
- Explain that you will read aloud an issue with two possible preferences similar to the topics in the "Focus on Testing" section, and that you will assign one preference to students on one side of the room and the other preference to the other side. Then you will call on students to briefly explain their preferences. (Of course, the preference you assign might not be their true preference, but the goal is to give reasons for a point of view.)
- Keep the pace lively as you read brief, non-controversial issues, such as, "Do you prefer to read a book or see the movie based on that book?"
- Point to one side of the room and say, "Read the book." Then point to the other side and say, "See the movie." (The first side prefers to read the book, and the second prefers to see the movie.)
- Call on students to briefly explain their preferences, alternating between the two sides of the room. Call on at least three students from each side before reading a new topic.
- Students must give different reasons from those of their classmates, and may express either likes or dislikes. For example, they might say, "I prefer to read because I appreciate all the details I get from a book," or, "I prefer to read a book because I dislike paying a lot of money to see a movie."

Self-Assessment Log

- ❑ Read the directions aloud and have students check vocabulary they learned in the chapter and are prepared to use.
- ❑ Tell students to find definitions in the chapter for any words they did not check.
- ❑ Have students check the degree to which they learned the strategies practiced in the chapter. Put students in small groups. Ask students to find the information or an activity related to each strategy in the chapter.

Chapter

8

Creativity

The topic of Chapter 8 is creativity—not just the type of creativity we attribute to artists, but also the creative thinking that inventors and ordinary people need to solve problems. In Part 1, students will learn about three extraordinarily creative people and will have a chance to practice their own "outside the box" thinking. Part 2 presents verbs used to signal important sections of a talk, and students will practice taking notes using those signal words. They will also consider other signals used in communication such as tone of voice, body language, and the sounds, sights, and smells used by animals to communicate. In Part 3, students will learn about expressions used to divulge information, and Part 4 provides practice taking notes during standardized tests using the signal words and other expressions presented in the chapter.

Chapter Opener

- ❑ Ask students to share their ideas about the chapter title, "Creativity." List on the board their interpretations of the word and ideas about creative people.
- ❑ Direct students' attention to the photo and divide them into small groups to discuss the questions in the "Connecting to the Topic" section. Call on groups to share their information and ideas with the class.
- ❑ Read the quotation from Einstein. Ask students to define the intuitive mind versus the rational mind and give examples of each. Ask students which type of thinking Einstein viewed as more valued by society. Ask students which they value more.

"The intuitive mind is a sacred gift and the rational mind is a faithful servant. We have created a society that honors the servant and has forgotten the gift."

—Albert Einstein
Nobel laureate physicist (1879–1955)

Chapter Overview

Lecture: Creativity—As Essential to the Engineer as to the Artist

Learning Strategy: Listening for Signal Words

Language Function: Divulging Information

Part 1: Building Background Knowledge

Did You Know?

Sharing Your Experience

Vocabulary Preview

Part 2: Listening for Signal Words

Listening for Signal Words to Guide Note-Taking

Before You Listen

Listen

After You Listen

Talk It Over

Recognizing Tone of Voice and Body Language Signals

Part 3: Divulging Information

Recognizing When Information is Being Divulged

Talk It Over

Part 4: Focus on Testing

Self-Assessment Log

Did You Know?

- ❑ Give students time to read the information about the three creative people, or read the information aloud as students follow along.

Content Notes

- Grandma Moses, 1860–1961, was a self-taught American painter who lived and died in the state of New York. For many people, her scenes from daily life define the style of art called American primitive.
- Wolfgang Amadeus Mozart, 1756–1791, was born and lived in Salzburg, Austria. Music from his opera *The Magic Flute* was included in the Voyager spacecraft recording meant to represent the music of Earth to extraterrestrials.
- R. Buckminster Fuller, 1895–1983, was born in Massachusetts. He was expelled from Harvard University during his first year there, but went on to write numerous books and receive numerous patents and honorary doctoral degrees.

1 What Do You Think?

- ❑ Divide students into pairs to discuss the questions. Some practical advantages of the geodesic dome might be that it requires no interior support such as columns, and it can be built quickly and inexpensively.
- ❑ Call on pairs to report their ideas to the class.

Sharing Your Experience

2 Creative Solutions to Everyday Problems

- ❑ Divide the class into small groups and go over the directions and the example.
- ❑ Have groups discuss the inventions and take brief notes on their ideas using the chart provided.
- ❑ Go over the list of inventions. Call on members of different groups to report their group's ideas to the class.

ANSWER KEY

Possible answers:

Invention	What it replaced and the problem it solved
paper clip	*Eliminated piles of loose papers that could get lost. Helped people organize their paperwork. Replaced the straight pin.*
lightbulb	*Replaced candles and lanterns. Helped people see at night and reduced accidental fires.*
washing machine	*Eliminated the need to wash clothes by hand and gave people more time to do other things.*
ballpoint pen	*Replaced pens that required nibs and pots of ink. Addressed the need for a more portable writing device.*
refrigerator	*Replaced the icebox or icehouse. Solved the problem of food spoilage.*
rubber band	*Eliminated the need to tie bundles of paper with string, which was more awkward and time-consuming.*
Post-it Note or "sticky" note	*Replaced notes that were attached with tape, staples, paper clips, or rubber bands. Solved one company's problem of what to do with an adhesive that didn't stick very well and made note-writing more convenient.*
Velcro	*Replaced shoelaces, snaps, and buttons. Addressed the need for quick and easy fastening, especially helpful to children and the elderly who might not have*

	nimble fingers or good hand-eye coordination.

EXPANSION ACTIVITY

- The goal of this activity is to encourage students to think about a wide range of inventors and inventions and to share information using spoken communication.
- You will be giving a quiz on little known information and, in this way, creating an information gap between group members and a "quizmaster" who will share the answers with them.
- Tell students that you want to find out how much they know about inventors and inventions.
- Photocopy and distribute BLM 20 "Inventors and Their Inventions" on page BLM 20 of this Teacher's Edition.
- Tell students to make their best guesses as they fill out the chart, matching inventions with inventors. Though students may not have heard of several of the inventors, encourage them to guess.
- Divide the class into small groups to discuss their guesses and the explanations for them.
- Ask each group to choose a quizmaster, a person who is entrusted with the answers, and give each quizmaster a photocopy of BLM 20 "Answer Key" on page BLM 28 of this Teacher's Edition.
- Instruct the quizmasters to go through the inventors one by one and find out if group members know what they invented and/or any details about them.
- If students know about an inventor, the quizmasters should ask them to share what they know with the group.
- When necessary, have the quizmasters supply missing information from the Answer Key.

3 Creative Uses for Common Things

Best Practice

Cultivating Critical Thinking

Students are challenged to think creatively in this activity by reinterpreting their assumptions about what everyday objects, like rubber bands or ballpoint pens, can be used for. In the activity, students use reasoning and communication skills to conceptualize new uses for an everyday object, and in this way improve their thinking and problem-solving skills.

- ❑ Ask students whether they have seen the movie *Castaway* with Tom Hanks. In the movie, Hanks' character survives alone on an island by using objects such as ice skates in creative ways. If students saw the movie, ask what they remember about the character's innovations. If they did not see the movie, ask which objects they would like to have in a similar situation that would help them to obtain food, water, fire, and shelter.
- ❑ Go over the directions.
- ❑ Divide the class into groups of three or four. As a class, assemble a collection of everyday objects available in the classroom and distribute one to each group.
- ❑ Remind students that when they brainstorm, they should try to generate many ideas in a short time.
- ❑ Ask each group to brainstorm at least ten unusual uses for their object.

EXPANSION ACTIVITY

- The goal of this activity is for students to share their creative ideas with the whole class.

- When the groups have completed brainstorming lists in Activity 3, give each group a large piece of poster paper and markers to list their ten creative ideas for using an everyday object.
- When students have completed the posters, ask them to tape the posters to the classroom walls. Gather the class around one poster at a time as each group explains its ideas; if the class is large, have more than one group present at the same time.

4 Creative Analogies 

- ❑ Ask for a volunteer to explain analogies. Students should remember from Chapter 4 that analogies compare new ideas to things that are already familiar.
- ❑ Go over the directions and the example as a class.
- ❑ Tell students that in addition to the language used in this example, they may also use the expressions used to make analogies from Chapter 4: *as… as, (just) like,* and *similar to*.
- ❑ If possible, set the stage for creativity by playing relaxing music as students find their ordinary objects.
- ❑ Divide the class into small groups and have them sit in circles if possible.
- ❑ Ask students to hand their object to the person on their left.
- ❑ Set a time limit for students to write five analogies.
- ❑ Have students share their analogies with group members.
- ❑ Ask for volunteers to share their analogies with the whole class.

Vocabulary Preview

5 Vocabulary in Context

- ❑ Go over the list of vocabulary words and definitions. Have students repeat the words after you and listen for any pronunciation difficulties.
- ❑ For each word, ask students to supply the part of speech. For example, they should see from the suffix that "analytical" is an adjective.
- ❑ Ask students to read through all the sentences first, then go back and find the appropriate vocabulary to fill in the blanks.
- ❑ Ask for volunteers to read each completed sentence aloud.

ANSWER KEY

1. solution, fragmentary 2. circumnavigate 3. inhibited 4. fuse 5. analytical 6. original

Strategy

Listening for Signal Words to Guide Note-Taking

- Go over the paragraph about signal words.
- Ask students to think of some examples of signal words they find useful when listening to English and explain what they mean. For instance, when people hear "on the other hand," they listen for contrast.
- Go over each verb in the list, providing explanations and examples for the verbs students are less familiar with. Point out that this list goes beyond the typical lists of signal words that students have probably seen before because it presents verbs that are commonly used to signal a speaker's next speaking task, such as *explain* or *review*.

EXPANSION ACTIVITY

- This activity aims to solidify students' comprehension of verbs used as signal words and to encourage students to make connections among the verbs.
- Tell students they will categorize all the verbs in the list on page 130 in a way that makes sense to them and create a chart or other graphic organizer with the verbs.
- If students need ideas for graphic organizers, remind them that there are many examples in this book.
- Allow students to use dictionaries and ask questions as they look over the list for possible categories. For example, a student may decide to group synonyms or near-synonyms such as *list* and *outline* or *go over, review* and *summarize*. Another student may categorize the verbs according to a timeline of their appearance in a lecture, or according to the nature of the verb's action, whether it is presenting new information or breaking down a point into components. As students make these decisions about how to categorize the verbs, they are processing the vocabulary as well as being creative.
- Consider suggesting a category called "other" or "miscellaneous" for verbs that don't quite fit into categories so that the task does not cause frustration.
- Divide the class into small groups and have students share the graphic organizers they created and explain the reasoning they used to create them.

Before You Listen

1 Considering the Topic 

Best Practice

Activating Prior Knowledge

As students discuss the answers to the questions in this activity in small groups, they encounter language and concepts they will hear in the lecture. This allows students to consider what they already know about the topic and to ask themselves questions about it, which helps them to focus on and remember the content of the lecture.

- ❑ Explain that this activity will help prepare students to listen to the lecture.
- ❑ Divide the class into small groups and have every student in each group respond to a question before the group moves on to the next question.

Listen

Best Practice

Making Use of Academic Content

This lecture is an example of a real-world model that encourages students to develop listening skills they can use in actual academic settings. As students listen to a professor talk about creativity, they experience an authentic context in which they can interpret the ideas and language from the chapter.

2 Listening for Main Points About Creativity 

- ❑ Play the audio once all the way through. Ask students to close their eyes and imagine the professor, the students, and the lecture hall as they listen for the main ideas.
- ❑ Play only the first half of the audio this time as students listen to fill in the blanks in the sentences, which are similar to sentences in the lecture.
- ❑ Ask for volunteers to read the completed sentences aloud. Briefly discuss each idea, asking students for their interpretations of the sentences.

ANSWER KEY

1. arts; scientists 2. imagining 3. creates
4. creative; repetitive 5. creative ability

- ❑ Now play only the second half of the lecture as students take notes on the blocks to creativity the lecturer describes.

ANSWER KEY

Answers may vary.

1. putting too many limits on solutions to a problem/looking at the problem too narrowly
2. the belief that playfulness and humor in problem solving are for children, not adults
3. the belief that feelings, intuition, and pleasure are bad, whereas logic, reason, and numbers are good
4. the belief that tradition is better than change
5. the belief that scientific thinking and great quantities of money can solve any problem

3 Listening for Signal Words 

- ❑ Play the audio of the lecture again as students listen for and check off the signal words on the list on page 130.

ANSWER KEY

The professor uses the following signal words from the list: analyze; answer; continue; discuss; emphasize; explain; go over; illustrate; list; pick up (where we left off); summarize

Best Practice

Organizing Information

In this activity, students take notes on the lecture using a T-chart, a chart with two columns and two headings. The T-chart allows students to efficiently note signal words and the lecture content that follows those words. In other cases, T-charts can be used to classify information as causes and effects, past and present, or similarities and differences, to name just a few possibilities.

- ❑ Go over the directions and the chart as a class. Practice the activity using the two examples. Start the audio of the lecture and ask students to indicate when they hear the signal words in the examples. Pause the audio at those points and tell students to listen carefully to what comes next.
- ❑ Play the audio of the lecture again all the way through. Have students take notes on the signal words they hear and the content of the lecture just after those signal words.
- ❑ To check listening comprehension, discuss several of the signal expressions and what follows them. Alternatively, put students in small groups to compare charts.
- ❑ Answer any questions students have about the lecture.

ANSWER KEY

Answers may vary.

Signal words	What comes next: what the lecturer does plus what topic/content the lecturer covers
1. *continue*	*goes on with the discussion of the creative process*
2. *pick up where we left off*	*begins with the idea started at the end of the last class: creativity is mysterious*
3. *analyze the creative process*	*examines ideas about creativity, what it is, and how it works in our lives*
4. *Let me emphasize again*	*repeats that everyone is creative and is always creating their own reality*
5. *Let me illustrate this*	*gives example of the "No Smoking" signs*
6. *Now I'll explain*	*shows how art is connected with this process of interpretation and ordering of the world*
7. *I'm going to answer that*	*tells the class that although the mind is creative when we are young, as people get older they fall into repetitive thinking patterns*
8. *Let me list them for you*	*outlines the four main cultural blocks to creativity*
9. *Let's go over each of these ideas*	*lists and explains in depth the four main cultural blocks to creativity*
10. *Let's discuss that further when we have more time.*	*moves on to the conclusion.*
11. *I will summarize*	*briefly restates the main points*

AUDIOSCRIPT

Lecture: Creativity—As Essential to the Engineer as to the Artist

Professor: Today we will continue our discussion of the creative process in general. Then we'll take up the topic of what things might inhibit this creative process in your work. This topic is applicable to any type of work.

Well—to pick up where we left off last time—creativity is mysterious. We all recognize it when we see it, but we don't really understand what it is or how it works. Some people seem to be naturally creative, but we don't know why they are. Is creativity an inborn gift like athletic ability, or is it something that can be acquired, like money or knowledge? Perhaps if we analyze the creative process carefully, we might get some ideas about what it is and how it works in our lives.

The presence of the creative process has always been obvious in the arts. But creativity doesn't play a role only in the arts. Every major scientific discovery began with someone imagining the world differently from the way others saw it. And this is what creativity is all about—imagining the world in a new way. And despite what you may believe about the limits of your own creative imaginations, you do have the ability to imagine the world in an absolutely new way. In fact, everyone does! We're born with it. Cave painters in the Stone Age had it. Musicians in the last century had it. And you have it. And what's more, you use it every day, almost every moment of your life. Your creative imagination is what you use to make sense of your experiences. It is your creative mind that gets meaning from the chaos of your experiences and brings order to your world.

Let me emphasize again that (1) everyone has creative abilities and (2) we are all creating our own realities at every moment. Let me illustrate this by having you look at the large "No Smoking" signs on the walls. Do you recognize the sign at one glance, or do you see it in parts, small sections, letter by letter? When I am being deliberately analytical, I feel I see the world in pieces. What is really going on is that the eye really does "see" things in pieces. It vibrates with great speed, taking brief, narrow pictures of the world. Then the mind combines, or fuses, those individual pictures into a larger picture—a creation. It's this creation that gives us a sense of the whole. So the mind, then, creates an interpretation of what comes in through the senses.

Now I'll explain how art is connected with this process of interpretation and ordering of the world. The artist sees a fragmentary, disordered series of events—pieces of light, color, parts of conversations—and brings them together into a work of art to make the world more understandable. But art is not just an activity for professional artists. The real story is that we do the same things as the artist every day, all the time. In this way, we are all artists and creators in our lives, without effort.

Now you may be wondering at this point why so many people want to be more creative if, as we said, human beings are naturally creative. I'm going to answer that by telling you that although the mind is spontaneously creative when we are very young, as we grow older, the mind tends to become caught in repetitive patterns. Then the mind operates imitatively—not creatively—seeing the world the same way day after day after day. In this state of mind, you are not creating anything new because your mind is not exploring new ways of looking at things.

So the problem seems to be how to remove the barriers to creativity that we build as we grow older. We don't need to add something new to ourselves. We just need to find ways to free the creative ability that is already inside us. To give a practical illustration of what I mean, I'd like to talk about something that I think often inhibits the creative process: our tendency to put too many limits on solutions to a problem. What do I mean by too many limits? Look at your handout. There you see nine dots in three rows. Try to draw no more than four straight connected lines that will touch all nine dots.

Did you solve the problem? You probably had trouble if you were not willing to go outside the limits enclosing the nine dots. Those boundaries are imaginary. Look at this solution.

Students: Wow! I'd never think of that! You've gotta be kidding! It seems so easy now! I got it! Yeah! I got it!

Professor: Great! I'm glad some of you solved the puzzle this way, but there are other solutions, too. Did any of you solve the puzzle in another way? Come on! Don't be shy! No idea is silly as long as it solves the problem. Yes, do you have a solution?

Student 1: Well, you didn't say we had to use only a pen or pencil. So, I cut the dots apart and arranged them in a straight line and then connected them.

Professor: Very original! Anyone else? Any other solutions? Yes, go ahead.

Student 2: How about this: You can tape the handout of the puzzle to a globe and then keep circumnavigating the globe with your pen until you pass through all the dots.

Professor: Wonderful! Very imaginative! Now I have to tell you the solution that my ten-year-old daughter came up with. She solved the problem by using a veeeeery faaaat line! OK. So now you see how your own mind may put limits on the possible solutions to a problem because you're just seeing things in standard, ordinary ways. The fact of the matter is that to be creative, we have to be able to look at things in extraordinary, new ways.

Obviously, when you try to solve a problem creatively, you first have to figure out what the problem is. Don't state the problem too narrowly, too specifically, or you might limit the number of solutions that you will come up with. Let me give you another practical example of solving a problem creatively. Let's say that your problem is to design a playground. If you think the problem is where to put the playground equipment, you are looking at the problem too narrowly. If you think the problem is both designing the playground equipment and then deciding where to place the equipment, you give yourself a much more creative problem with the possibility for a greater variety of solutions. So I can't emphasize this enough: When you state a problem, don't state it too narrowly or you will see it too narrowly and you will limit the possible solutions.

So, you can see now how our creative abilities can be blocked in a variety of ways. But the real deal is that our culture plays a big part in blocking creative potential. Psychologists say that people in many countries seem to have four main cultural blocks to creativity. Let me list them for you. First, we tend to believe that playfulness and humor in problem solving are for children, not adults. Second, we tend to think that feelings, intuition, and pleasure are bad, whereas logic, reason, and numbers are good. Third, most of us think that tradition is better than change. And finally, we believe that scientific thinking and great quantities of money can solve any problem.

Let's go over each of these ideas one at a time. First, despite what you may have heard, humor and creativity are definitely connected. They both open up areas of thought and feeling and connect things or ideas that were never put together before. For example, with a joke—well, wait—let me illustrate. A psychiatrist and a patient are talking and the patient says, "I'm getting really worried about my brother, Doc. He thinks he's a chicken." And the doctor says, "Well, why don't you bring him to me for help?" And the patient answers, "Oh, no. We can't do that." "Why not?" asks the doctor. And the patient answers, "Because we need the eggs."

OK, OK. It's not a great joke, but think about it. You did laugh, so what happened here? You expect that there will be logic to the story and the logic is broken by the surprise punch line, "Because we need the eggs." This is exactly what makes it funny. The punch line about the eggs was not expected. Creativity is also the appearance of the unexpected. And by the way, there's another connection between humor and creativity. To be creative, you must be willing to be laughed at because we often laugh at the unusual. In fact, many of the important ideas in science were laughed at when they were first presented to the public.

OK, so the next item on our list of cultural blocks to creativity is that reason and logic are better than feelings and intuition. Now, although reason and logic are useful, many great ideas come to people while they are dreaming. In fact, one of the most famous works of the composer Richard Wagner came to him in a dream. So be open to your dreams, imagination, and feelings.

The third thing to consider is the relationship of tradition and change. Tradition is valued and worthwhile, but it is often a block to creativity because it represents the ordinary and familiar. The creative process involves things that are new and different. But change is not easy. It takes hard work and great courage. Working for change demands creativity.

And what do you think about the final point—that scientific thinking and lots of money can solve any problem? Yes, in the back, what do you think?

Student 3: Well, I believe that this is true only when scientific thinking is also creative thinking. You know—in the ways you've been telling us about. I also think that the money itself has to be used creatively.

Professor: Yes, very interesting. Let's discuss that further when we have more time.

So, in conclusion, I will summarize what I've said today. Even though the creative process happens unconsciously, the reality is that we can still train ourselves to be more creative people. We can do this by removing the limitations we place on ourselves and by becoming aware of any cultural blocks that may inhibit the creative process.

Well, that's all for today. Thank you, and see you next week.

4 Finding Creative Solutions to a Puzzle 

- ❑ Have students try to solve the dot puzzle on page 131 of the student book individually. Draw the dots on the board and ask for volunteers to come to the board and try their solutions.

ANSWER KEY

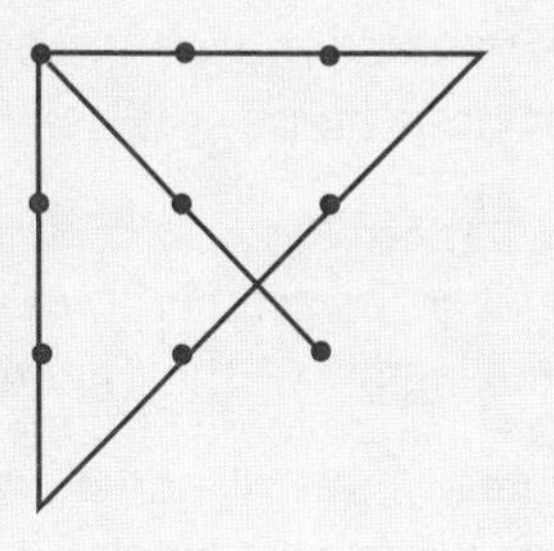

After You Listen

5 Comparing Notes 

- ❑ Divide students into pairs to compare how successful they were with each of the tasks in Activities 2, 3, and 4.

Talk It Over

6 Communicating When You Can't Talk 

- ❑ Go over the directions and bullet points as a class.
- ❑ Divide the class into small groups. Have students use one of the suggested situations or imagine one of their own and brainstorm at least three methods of communication they could use.
- ❑ Give each group a large piece of poster paper and markers and have them list and illustrate their ideas.
- ❑ Call on groups to share their posters with the class and act out their communication techniques.

Strategy

Recognizing Tone of Voice and Body Language Signals

- Give students time to read the information or read it aloud yourself as they follow along in their books.
- Ask students whether body language played an important role in their scenarios in Activity 6.

7 Using Tone of Voice and Body Language Signals

Best Practice

Interacting with Others

In this activity, the whole class uses the dramatic technique of delivering a sentence using a range of emotions. Standing in a circle and experimenting with body language and tone of voice, students experience a classroom dynamic that differs substantially from the norm and takes the focus off of the details of language and places it on the interaction between people in the class. This allows students to integrate the English language with the creative, independent sides of their personalities.

- ❑ Go over the directions.
- ❑ Arrange students in a large circle facing inward.
- ❑ Model the activity by asking students to choose an attitude for you to portray.
- ❑ Have students call out the adjectives, or call them out yourself.
- ❑ Encourage students to use their bodies and voices as each says the suggested sentence or a different one using the selected adjective.
- ❑ Continue until everyone has had a chance to participate. If you exhaust the list of adjectives in the book, encourage students to call out others.

8 Researching the Topic 

- Divide the class into small groups and have each person in the group choose a different animal to research on the Internet.
- Instruct students to take notes on the websites they visit, or print information to read and take notes on later. The goal is for students to learn about animal communication, but to present it using their own words, not sentences copied from another source.
- In class or as homework, tell students to create the outline of a well-organized talk with an introduction, body, and conclusion.
- Ask students to look at their outlines and think about the steps they have to take when giving presentations. For example, they may need to describe an animal's communication system, explain why an animal behaves as it does, and summarize or review the information at the end. With these speaking tasks, students can use signal words to help their listeners follow their ideas.
- Have students prepare and practice their talks in class or as homework.
- On the day students give their presentations, reassemble the groups so members can take turns talking about their animals.
- Alternatively, this research project can culminate with presentations to the whole class. If so, give students individual written feedback on their use of signal words.
- Finish with a group or class discussion of the questions about animal communication versus human communication. Topics to consider include whether or not the same species of animal has different "dialects" in different parts of the world like humans do, or whether animals do anything as creative with their communication systems as humans do when writing a poem or a tongue twister.

Best Practice

Scaffolding Instruction

This part of the chapter supports student learning by providing a logical progression of information and activities that allow students to work toward the goal of understanding a language point. First, students receive information about divulging information followed by commonly used expressions. Next, students listen to brief conversations in which information is divulged, followed by a much longer lecture. Finally, after these receptive activities, students have several chances to create conversations themselves using the expressions presented in this part of the chapter. This series of steps assists students as they progress toward their language acquisition goals.

Strategy

Recognizing When Information Is Being Divulged

- Go over the paragraphs about divulging information. Tell students that divulging information is like letting someone in on a secret. A professor who is divulging information may be revealing something that is not widely known or not easily found in textbooks, so it is important for students to pay close attention.
- Think of some harmless, secret information that you can divulge to the class. Read the first three or four expressions aloud followed by your information. For example, you might say, "Despite what you may believe, there is going to be an end-of-semester class party."
- After you have done this with the first three or four expressions, ask for volunteers to try it with the next expressions on the list and their own secret information.
- Read each informal expression aloud. Tell students that the expressions are generally polite, but would probably not be used in formal situations such as a job interview.

1 Listening for Ways of Divulging Information 

- ❑ Have students read the situations and questions for Conversations 1 and 2.
- ❑ Play the recording of Conversation 1 and ask for volunteers to answer the questions. If some students do not hear the key phrase the first time, play the audio again.
- ❑ Play the recording of Conversation 2 and ask for volunteers to answer the questions. If some students do not hear the key phrase the first time, play the audio again.

ANSWER KEY

Conversation 1

This conversation is formal. The phrases "The fact of the matter is…" and, "Despite what you believe about him…" set a more formal tone.

Conversation 2:

This conversation is informal. The phrases "What's the scoop?" and, "The real story is…" set a more informal tone.

AUDIOSCRIPT

Conversation 1

Albert: Did you hear that Professor Stone was fired from his post as president of the Institute of Behavioral Psychology?

Bonnie: Yeah. I heard that story, too.

Albert: Why do you say it's a story?

Bonnie: Because I've heard what's really going on. The fact of the matter is Professor Stone decided to leave the university in order to pursue a career as a pop singer.

Albert: No kidding—really?

Bonnie: Yup. Despite what you believe about him, he was a great professor, but he's also a fantastic musician and singer.

Conversation 2

Kate: Hey, what gives? That's a really fine motorcycle Jules is riding. I heard he won it in a contest. Is that true?

Doug: I don't know.

Kate: Oh, come on—what's the scoop?

Doug: Well, he's been telling everyone he won it in a contest, but the real story is: he was working nights as a pizza delivery boy and weekends painting houses and didn't want anyone to know.

Kate: I thought he told Susie that working nights and weekends when you should be studying was a bad idea.

Doug: Well, despite what you may have heard, the real story is that he finally found something he wanted badly enough to change his mind about that. We'll have to see if he still thinks it's worth it after mid-term exams.

2 Listening for Information That Is Divulged 

- ❑ Go over the directions as a class.
- ❑ Play the audio of the lecture on creativity from Part 2 again. Have students use the chart to take notes on the expressions for divulging information they hear and exactly what information is divulged.
- ❑ Ask students to look over their notes on the information the professor divulged and share their ideas about how critical the information is to the main points of the lecture.

ANSWER KEY

Phrases the lecturer uses to divulge information	Information divulged
1. And despite what you may believe ...	Your imagination is not limited. You can imagine the world in a completely new way.
2. The real story is ...	All of us, like artists, are creative every day.
3. The fact of the matter is ...	In order to be creative, we have to look at things in new ways.
4. The real deal is ...	Our culture plays a big part in blocking creative potential.
5. Despite what you may have heard ...	Humor and creativity are connected.

Talk It Over

3 Completing Conversations 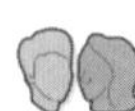

- ❑ Divide the class into pairs and tell students that they are about to be creative with English.
- ❑ Have partners work together to complete as many of the conversations as possible in a set time—perhaps fifteen minutes.
- ❑ Have each pair choose one of their conversations to practice and perform for the class.
- ❑ Consider giving each pair immediate verbal feedback on the expressions from the chapter that they used.

EXPANSION ACTIVITY

- This activity aims to expand on the activities from Part 3, Divulging Information, by asking students to develop mini-lectures on topics of personal interest.
- After completing Part 3, tell students that they will give a two-minute presentation about something they are personally interested in.
- You may want to have students do research or simply develop their mini-lectures based on what they already know.
- Ask students to use two or three of the expressions for divulging information in their talks. To do this, they should think about misconceptions people commonly have about their topic or information that is not commonly known about their topic.
- Give students time to prepare and practice their mini-lectures in class, or assign the preparation as homework.
- Give individual written feedback on students' use of the expressions.

TOEFL® iBT

SIGNAL WORDS AND DIVULGING INFORMATION

- Go over the information about signal words and divulging information.
- Ask students how they could take notes in the listening section of the TOEFL® iBT using signal words and expressions for divulging information. They might suggest using charts with two columns, as they practiced in the chapter, or other ideas.

1 Note-Taking Practice 

- Have students close their books and prepare to take notes.
- Play the audio of the conversation and ask students to take notes using the signal words and other expressions they hear. Do not play the test questions just yet.
- Have students open their books and read the test questions and answer choices. Ask whether they think they could answer the questions using the notes they just took. (On the TOEFL® iBT they will listen to a conversation only once, and may take notes while they listen.)
- Play the audio of the test questions as students answer them. Pause for 20 seconds after each question.
- Discuss the correct answers and whether taking notes using signal words and other expressions helped students choose the correct answers.
- Note that on the TOEFL® iBT students will not have time to pause between the audio passage and the test questions. To offer a more challenging experience similar to that of the TOEFL® iBT, consider playing the audio and questions all the way through.

ANSWER KEY

1. a; d 2. b 3. c 4. a; d 5. c

AUDIOSCRIPT

Student: Excuse me, Professor. I'm not sure that I really followed what you were saying yesterday about specific training in the arts not being an absolute necessity for creativity in the arts to emerge. Would you mind going over that again, please?

Professor: Sure. Let me illustrate my point about creativity this way. Grandma Moses never had an art lesson in her life and yet her paintings are displayed in museums all over the world.

Student: Well, that's true, but she lived a long time. Couldn't she have picked up her skills from a teacher somewhere along the line?

Professor: Apparently not. Furthermore, Grandma Moses is also an example of something else I said during our last class. This was about the equity of creativity. Let me repeat (and I really can't emphasize this enough): creativity is not linked to sex or age or race. It is not linked to any particular type of human being.

Student: Sure. I'm beginning to get what you were talking about. But didn't you also define creativity as being bound by time, place, and culture?

Professor: Well, sort of. What I was describing was that creativity can be stifled by a particular context or or cultural environment that does not appreciate the creative efforts made by an individual in that place and that time.

Student: Oh, I see. Would Van Gogh be a good example of this? You know, he couldn't seem to sell many of his paintings while he was alive, but now they're worth tens of millions of dollars.

Professor: The reality is that he was creative while he was alive. And after he died, his work did not become more creative. Instead, it was the creative imaginations of the viewers of his art that had to catch up to, or rise to, the level of his creative vision. And sadly that took a long time.

Student: Thanks so much for clarifying that. That helped a lot. I just have one more question.

Professor: Yes, of course. Shoot.

Student: Well, this may sound a little naïve, but isn't everything, I mean absolutely everything we do creative on some level? I mean can you give me examples of human activity that isn't creative?

Professor: Good for you! A challenging question! You've stimulated me to think further about that over the next few days and I'll make time for you to lead a discussion on that topic in our next class, OK?

Narrator: Question 1. What was the student confused about? (choose two)

Narrator: Question 2. Why does the professor use Grandma Moses as an illustration?

Narrator: Question 3. Listen to part of the conversation again.

Professor: Furthermore, Grandma Moses is also an example of something else I said during our last class. This was about the equity of creativity. Let me repeat (and I really can't emphasize this enough): Creativity is not linked to sex or age or race.

Narrator: Why does the professor say, "And I can't emphasize this enough"?

Narrator: Question 4. What does the professor imply about Van Gogh's work? (choose two)

Narrator: Question 5. Listen to a part of the conversation again.

Student: Well, this may sound a little naïve, but isn't everything, I mean absolutely everything we do creative on some level? I mean can you give me examples of human activity that isn't creative?

Narrator: Why does the student say, "This may sound a little naïve, but…"?

EXPANSION ACTIVITY

- The goal of this activity is for students to consolidate their knowledge of the chapter material by writing standardized test questions similar to those on the TOEFL® iBT.
- Photocopy and distribute BLM 21 "Writing Test Items" on page BLM 21 of this Teacher's Edition.
- Have each student write three test items similar to those in the Focus on Testing section using part of the audioscript from the lecture on creativity.
- Each test item should include a question that requires listening for signal words or information that is divulged, and four multiple-choice answers. The correct answers should not be marked.
- Tell students to exchange the tests they created and choose the correct answers.
- Have each student return the test to the person who wrote it to have the answers checked.
- Since students are not professional test writers, give them a chance to discuss questions or disagree with answers. It's much less important to get these answers right than it is to think about the type of test question.
- For additional speaking and listening practice, ask for volunteers to read their best questions and answer choices aloud for the class to answer.
- Ask students what they learned about this type of question by writing test items themselves.

Self-Assessment Log

- ❑ Read the directions aloud and have students check vocabulary they learned in the chapter and are prepared to use.
- ❑ Tell students to find definitions in the chapter for any words they did not check.
- ❑ Have students check the degree to which they learned the strategies practiced in the chapter. Put students in small groups. Ask students to find the information or an activity related to each strategy in the chapter.

Chapter

9

Human Behavior

This chapter focuses on human behavior, in particular the tendency to form social groups and associations. In Part 1, students will build their background knowledge about clubs, organizations, and volunteering. In Part 2, they will learn to recognize digressions in a lecture by listening for the signal expressions that help listeners stay on track. Part 3 introduces tag questions, focusing on how they are used by speakers to ask for, confirm, or challenge information. Part 4 demonstrates the way standardized tests utilize expressions that signal the beginning or end of a digression to test the understanding of a speaker's purpose.

Chapter Opener

- ❑ Direct students' attention to the photo and the Alexis de Tocqueville quotation. As a class, brainstorm things people do together that could be considered "forming associations."
- ❑ Divide students into small groups to discuss the photo and the questions in the "Connecting to the Topic" section. Call on groups to share their ideas with the class.

" Americans of all ages, all stations in life, and all types of disposition are forever constantly forming associations. "

—Alexis de Tocqueville
French author and statesman (1805–1859)

Chapter Overview

Lecture: Group Dynamics

Learning Strategy: Recognizing Digressions

Language Function: Using Tag Questions to Ask for Information or Confirmation, or to Challenge

Part 1: Building Background Knowledge

Did You Know?

Sharing Your Experience

Vocabulary Preview

Part 2: Recognizing Digressions

Recognizing Digressions and Returns to the Main Topic

Before You Listen

Listen

After You Listen

Talk It Over

Part 3: Using Tag Questions to Ask for Information, Confirm, or to Challenge

Understanding and Using the Three Types of Tag Questions: Genuine, Rhetorical, and Talk It Over

Part 4: Focus on Testing

Self-Assessment Log

Content Note

- The French writer and historian Alexis de Tocqueville visited the United States in 1831 to observe the democratic system at work. The first volume of his best-known work, *Democracy in America*, was published in 1835, and the second in 1840. Many believe that de Tocqueville's observations about the young country were especially astute, and that as an outsider, he was able to see Americans more clearly than they could see themselves.

Did You Know?

- ❑ Give students time to read the two bullet points about associations.
- ❑ Ask students whether they have heard of any of the organizations mentioned, and whether any of the information is surprising to them.

1 What Do You Think? 

- ❑ Divide the class into pairs and explain that students will take turns speaking for about one minute about each of the two questions.
- ❑ Explain to students that when they are acting as the listener, they should nod, smile, and make polite listening noises, but not add their own comments as if in a conversation.
- ❑ Ask for volunteers to share their thoughts about volunteering with the class.

Content Note

- The high percentage of Americans who volunteer for organizations such as Habitat for Humanity is astounding to many people. These volunteers donate their time for various reasons, including believing in the organization's goals, feeling good about helping others, developing new skills, socializing with new people, and trying out a new career.

EXPANSION ACTIVITY

- The goal of this activity is for students to find out more about the organizations mentioned in the "Did You Know?" section.
- Organize students by having them count off: 1-2-3-4, 1-2-3-4, etc.
- Assign the International Laughter Society to all the ones, the Young American Bowling Alliance to the twos, the Giraffe Project to the threes, and Habitat for Humanity to the fours.
- Tell students to do Internet research on their organization as homework. Explain that each of them will be an expert on that organization for the next class, so they should take notes as they research.
- In the next class, divide the class into groups of four including one expert on each organization.
- Ask students to give their groups an oral summary of what they learned about their organization.

Sharing Your Experience

2 How Sociable Are You? 

Best Practice

Organizing Information

In this activity, students use a chart to break down one day in their lives by hour, activity, and whether they were alone or with other people. This type of graphic organizer provides a way to analyze a complex whole by dividing and classifying its components.

- ❑ Have students think about one day last week and fill out the chart with information about how they spent that day.
- ❑ Divide the class into small groups and have the students use their charts to answer the set of five questions.

- Conduct a class discussion generated by the last two questions focused on relationships and spending time with other people.

Vocabulary Preview

3 Vocabulary in Context

- Go over the directions and the example. Point out that the example sentence includes context clues to the meaning of the term *fields of interest* in the form of examples: *science, art,* and *literature*.
- Students should find plenty of context clues in the sentences and the answer choices. If they want to use dictionaries, ask them to make a best guess about the answers first.
- Go over the sentences and vocabulary and answer any questions about meaning, usage, or pronunciation.

ANSWER KEY

1. a 2. a 3. c 4. a 5. c 6. c

Strategy

Recognizing Digressions and Returns to the Main Topic

- Go over the bullet points about why speakers use digressions.
- Point out that a digression, by definition, moves away from the main topic, and might not be included in the plan or outline of a talk.
- Explain that digressions can make a lecture difficult to follow and are therefore usually clearly signaled.
- Point out that signaling the end of a digression is as important as signaling the beginning in terms of helping listeners follow the lecture.
- Read the lists of expressions aloud, or call on students to read them.
- Discuss any new vocabulary, such as *stray, wander,* or *tangent*.
- Model the use of one of the "Expressions for Announcing Digressions." Think of a topic you can talk to the class about and insert a digression. For example, you could start to talk about the educational requirements for becoming an English instructor, and then use one of the expressions and tell a funny little story about a professor you had.
- Model the use of one of the "Expressions for Announcing a Return to the Main Topic" using the digression you made in the previous section. Repeat the funny little story you told and then use one of the expressions to get back to the subject you were originally talking about.

EXPANSION ACTIVITY

- The goal of this activity is to provide additional exposure to the long lists of expressions involving digressions.
- Before doing the activity, give students time to read over the lists of expressions on page 148 and ask any questions they might have. Tell them they will need to remember as many expressions as possible for this activity.
- Divide the class into pairs and have each pair take out a coin. Make sure that everyone is familiar with the idea of flipping a coin to get "heads" (the side of the coin with a portrait) or "tails" (the other side of the coin). (If the coins your class is using do not have portraits on them, any names for the two sides will be fine.)
- On the board, write "Heads: Announcing Digressions" and "Tails: Returning to the Main Topic."
- Tell students to cover the lists of expressions in their books with a piece of paper.
- Call on a student to flip a coin. If it's heads, he or she must say one of the "Expressions for Announcing Digressions," if tails, one of the "Expressions for Announcing a Return to the Main Topic."
- The second student in each pair should take a look at the list in the book and check their partner's expression. If it was somewhat inaccurate, he or she should say the expression from the book correctly and the first student should repeat it.
- Have the students in each pair reverse roles and do the activity again.
- Tell students that they may use an expression only once. If a student cannot remember any of the expressions, his or her partner may say one from the list for the first student to repeat.
- Students will most likely have a hard time remembering the expressions from these lists, but the point of the activity is for them to remember what they can and refer back to the list to assist their partners.

Before You Listen

1 Considering the Topic 

Best Practice

Activating Prior Knowledge

Whether they are preparing to listen to a lecture or read a chapter in a textbook, students benefit from instructional materials that use questions to activate prior knowledge. As they answer the questions, students recall previously learned information and become aware of gaps in their knowledge, which help them search for the new information they need as they listen or read.

- ❑ Explain that this activity will help students get ready to listen to the lecture.
- ❑ Divide the class into small groups to take turns reading a question aloud. Make sure all group members have a chance to speak.

2 Discussing Digressions 

- ❑ Keeping students in the same small groups, have them discuss these three questions about digressions in informal speaking situations, such as conversations among friends and family.

3 Making an Educated Guess about Digressions 

Best Practice

Making Use of Academic Content

This activity makes use of sentences taken from an academic lecture on human behavior. Presenting realistic content such as this gives students a framework in which to interpret the language and learning strategy presented in the chapter.

- ❑ Go over the directions and the example. Point out that no expressions used to introduce digressions are included here, and students should only fill in the first column at this point.
- ❑ Have students add up the number of items they guessed were digressions and compare their totals.

Listen

4 Listening for Digressions 

- ❑ Play the audio of the lecture once all the way through as students listen for the main ideas.
- ❑ Go over the bullet points and tell students to prepare to take notes on the chart.
- ❑ Play the audio of the lecture again. You might want to pause after each of the statements in the chart to give students a moment to check their guesses and fill out the second and third columns of the chart for the statements that are digressions.

ANSWER KEY

Statement	Main point or digression	Phrase used to introduce the digression	Reason for the digression
1. "This afternoon I'm going to talk about a topic that affects every person in this room—group dynamics."	*main point*		
2. "First, we'll look at patterns of communication in groups, and then we'll look at how groups affect individual performance."	*main point*		
3. "You all went to the discussion session yesterday, didn't you?"	*digression*	*By the way …*	*C; to connect abstract ideas to real experience*
4. "It doesn't seem to matter how large the group is—only a few people talk at once."	*main point*		
5. "I must tell you that all the research I know about has been done in the United States and Canada."	*digression*	*As an aside …*	*PAI; to provide additional information*
6. "The research shows that in groups of eight or more, people talk to the people sitting across the table from them."	*main point*		
7. "If you're planning to be a matchmaker and start a romance between two of your friends, don't seat them next to each other at your next dinner party."	*digression*	*To go somewhat off the topic for a moment …*	*AI; to keep the audience interested*
8. "The theory behind this type of research—research that demonstrates that people do better work in groups—is called social facilitation theory."	*main point*		
9. "In this way, we're like a number of other creatures."	*digression*	*Let me digress a bit …*	*PAI; to provide additional information*
10. "As I mentioned earlier, there is also research that demonstrates the opposite—that individuals perform worse, not better, on tasks when other people are there."	*main point*		
11. "If you don't already know how to do something, you will probably make some mistakes. And if you have an audience, you will continue to make mistakes."	*main point*		
12. "If you can manage it, you should take tests on a stage in front of a large audience."	*digression*	*Let me mention in passing that …*	*R; to relax the audience (digression is humorous)*

How many items did you guess were digressions?

AUDIOSCRIPT

Lecture: Group Dynamics

Professor: This afternoon I'm going to talk about a topic that affects every person in this room—group dynamics. Every person in this room is part of some group, right? For example, you belong to this class. And I'm sure that you belong to other groups too, don't you? Your family, right? A social club perhaps? A soccer, golf, or tennis team? The international student association? What else? Help me out.

Student A: Pi Phi sorority.

Student B: Exam study groups.

Student C: A business students' discussion group.

Student D: Volunteers for a Clean Environment.

Student E: Film Club.

Professor: Good. Thanks. At any one time the average person belongs to five or six different groups. A large part of our sense of identity comes from belonging to these groups. In fact, if I asked you to describe yourself, you might say, for example, "I'm a student, a basketball player, and a member of the film club," wouldn't you? Well, today we're going to look at two interesting aspects of group dynamics, or how groups function. First, we'll look at patterns of communication in groups, and then we'll look at how groups affect individual performance.

In groups, communication seems unsystematic, random, and unplanned, doesn't it? Generally, we don't see any pattern of communication at all. By the way, you all went to the discussion section yesterday, didn't you? Well, what did you notice about the conversations?

Student B: Everyone kept interrupting me.

Professor: Yes! And if you were having a good discussion, people kept interrupting each other and talking at the same time, didn't they? I'll bet students talked pretty much whenever they wanted. Well, let's see what researchers have found concerning communication patterns and group dynamics or how groups function.

The first pattern they have found occurs in groups where there is a lively discussion. It seems like everyone is talking at once, but actually, only a few people are talking. And it doesn't seem to matter how large the group is—only a few people talk at once. Do you know how many? What do you think?

Student C: Three? A few is three, right?

Students: Three? Four? Two?

Professor: Yes, well, the answer is two. Two people do over 50% of the talking in any group.

Now let's look at the second pattern researchers found in group dynamics. When we're in a group, sitting around a table perhaps, who do we talk to? As an aside, I must tell you that all the research I know about has been done in the United States and Canada, so the results I have to share with you may only be valid for these countries. Well, as I started to say, who do people talk to when they're sitting together at a table—people across the table, or people sitting next to them?

Student A: Across the table.

Student B: Next to them.

Professor: Well, the research shows that in groups of eight or more, people talk to the people sitting across the table from them, not to the people next to them. Why do we talk more to the people sitting opposite us? Probably because in our culture we usually make eye contact with the person we're talking to, and it's not as easy to have eye contact with someone who is sitting next to us. It's much easier to maintain eye contact with someone across the table.

To go somewhat off the topic for a moment, if you're planning to be a matchmaker and start a romance between two of your friends, don't seat them next to each other at your next dinner party. On second thought, maybe seating them at a corner of the table would be best, wouldn't it? Then they would be very near each other and would only have to turn slightly in order to look into each other's eyes.

(student laughter)

Well, back to business. Now there's one more point that I'd like to mention regarding conversations in groups (and this might be important to the new romance at your dinner party. Who knows?). The research also shows that, in general, the person in the group who talks the most is regarded as the leader of the group. However, it's true that this person is not usually the most liked in the group, isn't it? D. J. Stang did some research that showed that the person in the group who talked only a moderate amount was liked the most. What use can we make of this information? A new romance would be affected by this aspect of group dynamics, wouldn't it?

But enough of romance and dinner parties. I now want to discuss another important aspect of group dynamics—the effect a group has on an individual's performance. The research tells us that sometimes the effect of the group on someone's performance is positive, and sometimes it's negative. It took quite a while for social psychologists to figure out why this is true.

Some research showed that people did better on a task when they were doing it in a group. It didn't matter what the task was, whether it was slicing tomatoes or racing bicycles; people just performed better when other people were there. It also didn't matter whether the other people in the group were doing the same task or just watching, so competition was not a factor. The first person to notice this phenomenon was Triplett.

Student A: Excuse me, but what was his first name? It wasn't Tom, was it?

Professor: I'm sorry, I don't remember. Please come by my office if you want the complete reference. Anyway, as I was saying, Triplett's research was done quite a long time ago. In 1898, in fact. He watched bicycle racers and noticed that they did much better when they raced against each other than when they raced only against the clock.

This behavior surprised him, so he conducted a simple experiment. He gave a group of children some fishing poles and string. The children were told to wind the string around the fishing poles as fast as possible. Half of the children worked alone. The others worked in pairs. Interestingly, the children who worked in pairs worked faster than those who worked alone.

Well, you're probably not interested in winding string around fishing poles faster, but you *are* interested in doing math problems better, aren't you? F. H. Allport had people work on math problems alone and also in groups of five to six. He found that people did better in the group situation than when they worked alone. The theory behind this type of research—research which demonstrates that people do better when they work in groups—is called social facilitation theory.

Let me digress a bit on this matter of having an audience. In this way, we're like a number of other creatures—ants, for example. Chen did a laboratory experiment with some ants as they were building nests. Chen had some of the ants work alone and some of the ants work with one or two other ants. Guess what! Ants worked harder when they worked with other ants than when they worked alone.

Another famous study was done with cockroaches. Zajonc, Heingartner, and Herman watched cockroaches find their way through a maze while trying to get away from a light. As you may know, cockroaches hate light. They are photophobic, right? The researchers had the cockroaches go through the maze alone and then had them go through the maze with an audience of four other cockroaches. The cockroaches reached the end of the maze faster when they had an audience.

Students: No way! Really? You're kidding, right?

Professor: No, No! Really! This is true.

Well, to continue, as I mentioned earlier, there is also research that demonstrates the opposite—that individuals perform worse, not better, on tasks when other people are there! The theory behind this research, which shows that people do poorly in groups, is called social inhibition theory. R. W. Hubbard did an interesting experiment on this. He had people learn a finger maze. This is a maze that you trace with your finger. The people who had an audience did worse than the people who did the maze alone.

So how can we explain these contradictory results? Zajonc finally came up with a possible reason why people sometimes perform better and sometimes worse in front of an audience. He found that the presence of an audience facilitates or helps you with what you already know how to do. That is, if you *know* what you are doing, having an audience helps you do it better. But if you *don't* already know how to do something, you will probably make some mistakes. And if you have an audience, you will continue to make mistakes. He pointed out that when you are first learning something, you are better off working alone than practicing with other people.

So to recap, the research shows that people generally perform better in groups, *except* if they are performing a new task. In that case they work better alone. And just let me mention in passing that if you can manage it, you should take tests on a stage in front of a large audience with a group of people who are also taking the test. Not very practical though, is it? And I wonder if it's really true for every task we learn. What do you think? Well let's start with that question next time. See you then.

5 Listening for Returns to the Main Topic 

- ❑ Play the audio of the lecture again as students make a check next to each of the expressions they hear.

ANSWER KEY

Expressions That Announce a Return to the Main Topic

____ Anyway...
✓ Anyway, as I was saying...
✓ As I started to say...
____ Back to our main topic ...
✓ (But) Enough of...
____ To come back to what I was saying...
____ To continue with our main point...
____ To get back to the topic at hand...
____ To go on with what I was saying...
____ To return to what I was saying...
✓ Well, back to business...
____ Well, back to work...
✓ Well, to continue (with the main topic)...

6 Listening for Specific Information 

- ❑ Have students read the five questions and answer as many of them as possible from memory.
- ❑ Play the audio of the lecture again as students listen for any information they missed.

ANSWER KEY

1. Differing amounts; two people do over 50 percent of the talking in any group.
2. They talk the most with people sitting across from them.
3. They work better in groups when doing something they already know how to do because having an audience is helpful in that situation. They work better alone when doing something for the first time because having an audience in that situation leads one to make mistakes.
4. They work better with an audience when doing something they already know how to do because having an audience is helpful in that situation. They work better without an audience when doing something for the first time because having an audience in that situation leads one to make mistakes.
5. A person who talks a moderate amount is best-liked. (Answers about why will vary.)

After You Listen

7 Comparing Answers 

Best Practice

Interacting with Others

One of the bases of the communicative approach to language learning is that students acquire language when they are faced with the need to use that language to communicate. In this activity, students must communicate with each other in order to compare answers, compile data, and answer questions. This interaction is a chance for students to improve their English by using it for a concrete purpose.

- ❑ Divide the class into small groups and have students tally their answers from Activities 4 and 5 using the five questions in this activity.

- ❑ Instruct the groups to compare their answers from Activity 6.
- ❑ Tell students to go back and consider how well their answers to the discussion questions in Activity 1 matched the actual content of the lecture.

Talk It Over

8 Reporting on Digressions

- ❑ Assign the activity as homework or make arrangements to attend a lecture or club meeting as a class.
- ❑ Ask students to take notes on the digressions they hear.
- ❑ Divide students into small groups to compare notes and fill out the chart in this activity.
- ❑ Reproduce the chart on the board and call on students to give their groups' answers to the questions.

9 Discussing Group Activities 

- ❑ Go over the directions as a class.
- ❑ Divide the class into small groups to list the principles of group dynamics presented in the lecture. Students may find such a list useful as a reference during their discussions.
- ❑ Ask the groups to choose and list three of the topics from this activity that interest them.
- ❑ Make sure students have the list of "Expressions for Announcing Digressions" and "Expressions for Announcing a Return to the Main Topic" available to use as they discuss their three topics and how the principles of group dynamics apply to them.
- ❑ Ask for volunteers to describe how their group discussions went.

Best Practice

Scaffolding Instruction

This part of the chapter supports student learning by providing a logical progression of information and activities that allow students to work toward the goal of understanding the language point. First, students receive information about the types of tag questions, and then practice the pronunciation of intonation patterns modeled by the instructor. They go on to listen for the structures and intonation patterns in short conversations and a longer lecture. Finally, students use tag questions in role-plays they create. This series of steps supports students as they acquire the new language.

Strategy

Understanding and Using the Three Types of Tag Questions: Genuine, Rhetorical, and Challenging

- Read the introductory material aloud or ask for a volunteer to read it to the class.
- Go over the first type of tag question—the genuine question. Read the example aloud and have students repeat after you. Review both the affirmative and negative forms. Point out that a rising intonation indicates uncertainty; here, the speaker is uncertain about the answer and is asking for information.
- Go over the second type of tag question—the rhetorical tag question. Read the example aloud and have students repeat after you. Point out that a falling intonation indicates certainty; here, the speaker believes they know the answer and just wants confirmation.
- Go over the third type of tag question—the tag question used to challenge. Read the example aloud and have students repeat after you. Model the rising intonation of this type of tag question. Point out that it sounds different from an uncertain rising intonation since the speaker is expressing anger or irritation.
- The challenging tag question—an affirmative tag following an affirmative statement—may be new to students. Explain that the usage of this form is uncommon, and offer a few example situations in which they might hear it. For example, a husband might be angry upon hearing that his wife plans to buy an expensive new car without his knowledge. He might say, "She's buying an expensive new car, is she?" A woman might be upset when she hears that her friend prefers the company of other people. She might say, "She likes her other friends better than me, does she?"
- Review the expressions used as tag questions. Explain that these expressions have a rising intonation with the exception of "Huh," which can function as a rhetorical question with falling intonation as well. Demonstrate the use of "Huh" with both rising and falling intonation.

1 Conveying Intention of Tag Questions with Intonation 

- ❑ Go over the directions and the bullet points. Model and have students repeat the examples.
- ❑ Divide students into pairs to take turns saying the statements and tag questions all three ways.
- ❑ Walk around the classroom and listen to students' intonation, making suggestions and modeling the correct intonation when necessary.

2 Listening for Intonation Patterns 

- ❑ Go over the directions as a class.
- ❑ Ask for a volunteer to read the introduction to each conversation.
- ❑ Play the audio of the conversations, pausing after each to let students answer the questions.

ANSWER KEY

Conversation 1: Steven is asking a genuine question. He wants to know whether Tom will be at the practice.

Conversation 2: Steven is using a rhetorical question. He wants George to know that Tom will be at the practice.

Conversation 3: Steven is using a challenging intonation pattern. He is annoyed by Karl's habitual lateness.

Conversation 4: The boss is asking a genuine question. He doesn't know whether the report will be ready on Wednesday. He may also be making a very indirect request for the report to be finished early.

Conversation 5: *Huh*? *Right*? and *OK*? are used.

AUDIOSCRIPT

Conversation 1

Steven: Our team is having the first practice of the season this Saturday morning at 8:00. You'll be there, Tom, won't you?

Tom: Oh sure! I'll be there early.

Conversation 2

Steven: Our team is having the first practice of the season this Saturday morning at 8:00, George. You'll be there, Tom, won't you?

Tom: Sure will.

Conversation 3

Steven: Soccer practice is at 6:30 this Saturday morning because another team has the field at 8:30.

Tom: Steve, Karl told me he couldn't come to soccer practice until eight.

Steven: What a drag. He's always late. He thinks he's coming at eight, does he? Well, I think he's off the team then. He can't come and go as he pleases and still be on the team.

Conversation 4

Boss: Charlie, I've got an unexpected merchandising meeting this week. The report won't be done by Wednesday, will it?

Charlie: Well, I don't think so, but we'll work on it.

Conversation 5

Josie: Hi, Pete. How are you?

Pete: Fine, how 'bout you?

Josie: Good. You're not cooking tonight, huh?

Pete: You got it. It's Bill's turn, right?

Josie: I think so, but he's going to be late again. I know it.

Pete: In that case, let's start the soup, OK? Otherwise, it'll be nine o'clock before we ever get anything to eat.

Josie: OK, you're right. I'm starving. You cut the carrots and I'll do the potatoes.

3 Listing for the Three Types of Tag Questions

- ❑ Go over the directions and the examples in the chart.
- ❑ Play the audio of the lecture on group dynamics as students listen for the tag questions and classify each one according to its grammatical structure and purpose.
- ❑ Divide students into pairs or small groups to compare answers. If they are unsure about the answers, play the audio again and pause after each tag question to check comprehension.

ANSWER KEY

	Genuine	Rhetorical	Challenging
Affirmative	*It wasn't Tom, was it?*	*Not very practical though, is it?*	
Negative	*... the discussion section yesterday, didn't you?*	*... belong to other groups, too, don't you?*	
		You might say, for example, "I'm a student, a basketball player, and a member of the film club," wouldn't you?	
		... would be best, wouldn't it?	
		... random and unplanned, doesn't it?	
		... talking at the same time, didn't they?	
		... the best liked in the group, isn't it?	
		... this aspect of group dynamics, wouldn't it?	
		... math problems better, aren't you?	
Other	*You're kidding, right?*	*... part of some group, right?*	
		Your family, right?	
		... photophobic, right?	

4 Using Tag Questions to Ask for and Confirm Information 

- ❑ Go over the directions and examples.
- ❑ Divide the class into medium-sized groups and have everyone in the group ask one group member about his or her leisure activities before moving on to the next student.

Talk It Over

5 Using Tag Questions in Role-Plays 

Best Practice

Cultivating Critical Thinking

Students will certainly have fun practicing and performing the role-plays in this activity. They will also synthesize and apply all of the information about tag questions presented in this part of the chapter to a contextualized conversation based on a situation they choose. In this way, students will develop their critical thinking skills as they apply their knowledge of the English language and their own experience to the creation of the role-plays.

- ❑ Go over the direction line and the bullet points so that students understand the steps in the activity.
- ❑ Divide the class into groups of approximately four students.
- ❑ Give the groups time to choose one of the seven suggested situations or to invent their own. They should know who and where they are and what is happening.
- ❑ Have the groups practice their role-plays. Decide whether you want students to write down what they plan to say or simply remember what they can and produce tag questions spontaneously.
- ❑ As each group performs its role-play, have audience members keep a tally of the number and types of tag questions they hear.
- ❑ After each role-play, ask students for a quick summary of that group's total.
- ❑ After all the groups have performed, answer the questions about "Which group ...?" as a class.

REPRODUCIBLE **EXPANSION ACTIVITY**

- The goal of this activity is to give students additional practice with the formation and intonation of tag questions.
- Divide the class into pairs. Give one person in each pair a copy of BLM 22 "Student A" on page BLM 22 of this Teacher's Edition. Give the other person in each pair a copy of BLM 23 "Student B" on page BLM 23 of this Teacher's Edition.
- Explain the procedure. First, all the students should add tag questions to their statements and draw rising or falling intonation lines based on the information given.
- Next, the A students will say all of their statements with tag questions and the B students will respond.
- Then, the B students will say all of their statements with tag questions and the A students will respond.

TOEFL® IBT

DIGRESSIONS IN LECTURES

- Go over the information about standardized test questions involving digressions.
- Check comprehension by asking students: "Are there questions about digressions on standardized tests?" They should indicate that they would not be asked about the content of digressions on standardized tests. However, emphasize that these expressions are important to note because they help listeners understand a speaker's purpose.

1 Transition Phrases: Lecture 

- ❑ Have students close their books and prepare to take notes.
- ❑ Play the audio of the lecture as students listen for the gist and take notes on the main ideas.
- ❑ Have students open their books and answer the questions they hear. Pause for 20 seconds between each question.
- ❑ Play the audio again, pausing after each section to discuss the correct answers.

ANSWER KEY

1. c 2. a 3. c 4. c 5. c

AUDIOSCRIPT

Transition Phrases: Lecture

Professor: Today we're going to look at something very familiar to you all—group work. You know, what teachers tell you to do when the teacher wants to relax. No. Just kidding. Seriously, how many of you have done any group work in a class within, say, the last week? Wow. Almost everyone. Why do your teachers organize group work so much in their classes?

Student 1: Because it's easy.

Professor: Easy for whom? The teacher? The students?

Student 1: Everyone.

Professor: Well, I can speak from the teacher's perspective here. Group work is not especially easy to organize. By the way, we don't do much of it here because there are about 100 of us and this room is like a theater. If I had a better room… Well, never mind. I can assure you that group work, serious group work, requires a lot more planning on the teacher's part than lecturing does. Nothing could be easier than standing up here talking about anything I like. Now, from the student's point of view, is group work easy?

Student 2: Well… yes and no.

Professor: Could you give us some details? Why yes and why no?

Student 2: Well, it's easy because you don't have to do everything yourself. The group is responsible, not just you. But then again, the group can be a pain if they're not very good.

Professor: Beautiful. You've really brought up some important aspects of research on group work. Before we look at these, let me tell you where I stand on group work. I think it's great. All sorts of instructional advantages. But let me get to that later, if we have time. As you said, group work can take pressure off the individual, but it can also cause problems. Let's look at each of these points.

Narrator: Listen again to part of the lecture.

Professor: You know, what teachers tell you to do when the teacher wants to relax.

	No. Just kidding. Seriously, how many of you have done any group work in a class within, say, the last week?
Narrator:	Question 1. What does the professor mean when he says "just kidding"?
	Question 2. Why does the professor say "seriously"?
Narrator:	Listen again to part of the lecture.
Professor:	By the way, we don't do much of it here because there are about 100 of us and this room is like a theater. If I had a better room… Well, never mind.
Narrator:	Question 3. Why does the professor say "by the way"?
	Question 4. What does the professor mean when he says "well, never mind"?
Narrator:	Listen again to part of the lecture.
Professor:	Before we look at these, let me tell you where I stand on group work. I think it's great. All sorts of instructional advantages. But let me get to that later, if we have time.
Narrator:	Question 5. What does the professor indicate by saying "But let me get to that later"?

EXPANSION ACTIVITY

- The goal of this activity is for students to consolidate their knowledge of expressions used to signal digressions and a return to the main topic, and how those expressions might help students answer questions about a speaker's purpose.
- After students have done the listening activity, tell them that they will write a test item for their classmates.
- Have students write a lecture segment on a topic of their choice in which the professor makes a digression and returns to the main topic.
- Next, ask each student to write a question and four multiple-choice answers, similar to those in Part 4 of the chapter, based on their lecture segment.
- If the class is small, call on students to read their lecture segments, questions, and answer choices aloud for the class to answer. In a larger class, divide students into groups to share their test items.
- Consider having students write their answer choices on poster paper or the board to make them more accessible to classmates.

Self-Assessment Log

- ❑ Read the directions aloud and have students check vocabulary they learned in the chapter and are prepared to use.
- ❑ Tell students to find definitions in the chapter for any words they did not check.
- ❑ Have students check the degree to which they learned the strategies practiced in the chapter. Put students in small groups. Ask students to find the information or an activity related to each strategy in the chapter.

Chapter

10

Crime and Punishment

In this chapter, students will consider human beings' responsibility for their own actions in everyday life and in the legal system. In Part 1, students will discuss their own transgressions and temptations and whether crimes are ever justifiable. Part 2 allows students to practice paraphrasing and presents a number of ethical questions. In Part 3, students will learn to express wishes, hopes, and desires, and perform a courtroom drama that explores the issue of temporary insanity. Part 4 introduces standardized test questions that require students to make connections among ideas from a lecture.

Chapter Opener

- ❑ Direct students' attention to the photo and the chapter title, "Crime and Punishment," and ask what experience or knowledge students have of the U.S. and/or their country's legal system.
- ❑ Divide students into small groups to discuss the questions in the "Connecting to the Topic" section. Call on groups to share their ideas with the class.
- ❑ Discuss the quotation from Joan Didion. Ask students to share their own definitions of character. Compare students' definitions with Didion's, and ask whether they agree that character is the source of self-respect.
- ❑ Ask for volunteers to explain the possible connection between the chapter topic and the Didion quotation.

“Character—the willingness to accept responsibility for one's own life—is the source from which self-respect springs.”

—Joan Didion
U.S. novelist (1934–)

Chapter Overview

Lecture: Human Choice—Predetermination or Free Will?

Learning Strategy: Paraphrasing

Language Function: Wishes, Hopes, and Desires

Part 1: Building Background Knowledge

Did You Know?

Sharing Your Experience

Vocabulary Preview

Part 2: Paraphrasing

Paraphrasing What an Instructor Says

Before You Listen

Listen

After You Listen

Talk It Over

Part 3: Wishes, Hopes, and Desires

Understanding and Expressing Wishes, Hopes, and Desires

Talk It Over

Part 4: Focus on Testing

Self-Assessment Log

Did You Know?

- ❑ Give students time to read the three bullet points about crime and punishment.
- ❑ Ask students what they know about Rosa Parks, Dr. Martin Luther King, Jr., and the U.S. civil rights movement.
- ❑ Ask students what they know about the case in Thailand.
- ❑ If appropriate, ask students whether their countries use capital punishment, and whether they think the death penalty is an effective deterrent to crime.

Content Notes

- Rosa Parks was born in Tuskegee, Alabama, in 1913. Before famously refusing to give up her bus seat, she had been secretary of the Montgomery chapter of the National Association for the Advancement of Colored People (NAACP) since 1943. Four days before the incident on the bus, in November of 1955, Parks attended a meeting to discuss the case of Emmett Till, an African-American teenager who had been gruesomely murdered in Mississippi after allegedly flirting with a white woman in a grocery store.
- In her lifetime, Parks received a number of honorary degrees, the Presidential Medal of Freedom, the Congressional Gold Medal of Honor, and many other awards. She eventually moved to Detroit, where she founded a youth development institute. On her death in 2005 at the age of 92, Parks became the first woman to lay in honor in the Capitol Rotunda in Washington, D.C.

Content Note

- The Reverend Martin Luther King, Jr., who was born in 1929, was the key leader of the U.S. civil rights movement in the 1950s and 1960s until he was assassinated in 1968. Inspired by Christian ideals and Gandhi's non-violent protest techniques, Dr. King was a dynamic speaker known for his 1963 "I Have a Dream" speech in Washington D.C. He led numerous marches and was arrested several times. At age thirty-five he became the youngest man to receive the Nobel Peace Prize.

1 What Do You Think? 

- ❑ Divide students into pairs to discuss the questions.
- ❑ Ask for volunteers to share their thoughts with the class.

Sharing Your Experience

2 Wrongs You've Done or Considered Doing 

Best Practice

Activating Prior Knowledge

This activity requires students to recall events from their own lives as they discuss wrongdoing. In this way, students activate their prior knowledge and prepare for the topic of crime and punishment, which helps them to understand and remember new ideas from the chapter.

- ❑ Divide the class into small groups. Have each group choose a leader to read the questions aloud and make sure everyone shares at least one story about wrongs they've done or considered doing.
- ❑ Call on group leaders to share one or two of their group's stories with the class.

Vocabulary Preview

3 Guessing Definitions 

- Go over the directions as a class.
- Model the activity using one of the vocabulary terms. For example, you could point out that *predetermination* has a noun suffix and contains the word *determine*. It also has the prefix *pre*, which means *before*. The meaning of the word should have something to do with determining before, and definition f says "already decided," so that is the best answer choice.
- Divide the class into small groups and have them discuss the vocabulary and match the terms with the definitions.
- When the groups have finished, go over the list of words and call on groups to share the clues that allowed them to guess the correct definitions.
- Answer any questions about the vocabulary, providing explanations and examples of usage as needed.

ANSWER KEY

1. e 2. g 3. h 4. f 5. b 6. a 7. d 8. c

EXPANSION ACTIVITY

- The goal of this activity is for students to share their world knowledge as they develop their understanding of the vocabulary terms *predetermination* and *free will*.
- Divide the class into small groups and ask them to brainstorm a list of ideas based on any degree of belief in predetermination. Ideas include the zodiac, romantic compatibility based on blood type, and destiny.
- Call on students to share their lists of ideas with the class. Write them on the board.
- Conduct a class discussion about predetermination. Ask, for example, whether students believe it's a good idea to marry a person the zodiac describes as incompatible, or whether events in life are determined by free will or are "meant to be."

Strategy

Paraphrasing What an Instructor Says

Go over the information about paraphrasing and ask students for situations in which they might need to paraphrase. For example, they could paraphrase information from the Internet for a report. They might also paraphrase a classmate's words to share group ideas with the class, as in Part 1.

Before You Listen

1 Considering the Topic

Best Practice

Organizing Information

This activity presents a chart for students to use in classifying activities and conditions in their lives as examples of predetermination or free will, central concepts in the chapter. This type of graphic organizer gives students a way to understand the division into two categories visually, which helps accommodate different learning styles.

- ❑ Go over the bullet points to make sure students understand the directions.
- ❑ Have students work alone to fill out the chart and add some ideas of their own.
- ❑ Divide the class into small groups to discuss responses.
- ❑ Call on groups to tell the class about their discussions using the questions in the third bullet point.

2 Practice Paraphrasing

- ❑ Go over the directions and the example paraphrase.
- ❑ Discuss the quotation from Socrates, making sure students understand the meaning and rephrasing the idea several different ways.
- ❑ Ask for volunteers to express the idea in the quotation using their own words, or have everyone in the class write a paraphrase and ask for volunteers to speak or write theirs on the board.
- ❑ Emphasize that there are different ways to say the same thing, and that when paraphrasing, it is important to concentrate on meaning first, just as the class did with the example quotation.
- ❑ Divide students into small groups to compare and discuss their paraphrases. Ask each group to choose one or two of their best paraphrases to share with the class.

ANSWER KEY

Possible answers

1. It's possible that our behavior is automatic—that we have no control over the decisions we make.
2. You might not feel responsible for the things you do if you believe in predetermination.
3. What we do now is interconnected with past actions as well as our future lives.
4. When we must make vitally important decisions our choices become extremely significant.
5. Only people who commit crimes of their own free will are punished.

REPRODUCIBLE

EXPANSION ACTIVITY

- The goal of this activity is for students to critically examine sample paraphrases in order to better judge their own paraphrases.
- Photocopy and distribute BLM 24 and 25 "Paraphrasing" on pages BLM 24 and BLM 25 of this Teacher's Edition.

- Explain that there are two paraphrases for each original statement.
- Ask students to read each original statement and think about the meaning, and then read the two paraphrases and decide which is better.
- Discuss the good and bad points of each paraphrase.

Listen

3 Listening to Paraphrase Parts of a Lecture 

- ❑ Play the audio of the lecture once all the way through as students listen for the main ideas.
- ❑ Ask students to read questions 1–4 so they know which ideas to listen for and paraphrase.
- ❑ Play the audio again, pausing after each section so students can write their paraphrases.

AUDIOSCRIPT

Lecture: Human Choice: Predetermination or Free Will?

Professor: OK, let's get started. Today's lecture about choice is in two parts. The first part of the lecture is about the difference between predetermination and free will. I hope that by the end of class that difference will be clear to you all, because I want to hear your ideas on these two very different views of the world.

The second part of the lecture is about choice in the real world—when life-or-death decisions have to be made.

So, do you believe that our lives are predetermined, or do you believe that we make choices that direct our lives? Basically, if you believe that our lives are predetermined, then you believe that everything we do is decided before we are born. Maybe you think we are programmed to do the things we do. Or perhaps you think a spiritual force makes all our decisions for us. But even if we believe our lives are somehow predetermined, we still appear to be making choices every day. We choose what to have for dinner or what movie to go to. We choose our friends from among the hundreds of people we meet. So the question is: are these really choices, or is the concept of free choice only an illusion?

On the other hand, if you believe that we have free will, then you believe that we do really make all our own decisions. For example, Hindus and Buddhists believe that our choices are made freely and that these choices add up to either a good life or a bad life. This is called *karma*. They also believe in reincarnation. According to this belief, if we don't make enough good decisions during one lifetime, we are reborn to try to do better in the next life.

These two opposing views, predetermination and free will, can have important effects on our lives. How do you think they can affect us? Yes, Craig?

Student 1: Well, if you believe that everything is predetermined. . . then that might make you feel as if you have no control over what happens to you. . . you know. . . no control over your life.

Student 2: And that feeling would certainly affect your behavior. For example, maybe you would feel that if you are not in control, then you don't have to take responsibility for your choices.

Professor: Yes, that's quite possible. Therefore, we should examine these opposing views about choice as a starting point in determining our own attitude toward life. You may recall that Socrates suggested this when he said that the "unexamined life is not worth living."

How many of you have looked at your past actions and said, "I wish I had done that differently" or "If only I had decided to do this instead of what I did"? And certainly we all have worried about the future and thought, "I hope I can do the right thing." Our relationship to the past and to the future seems to be connected with our present choices. That is, all our wishes and hopes for the future are very connected to what we choose now, in the present.

Stop 1

Professor: Now let's talk about choice in the real world. The practical implications of choice increase and intensify when life-or-death decisions have to be made. For example, if you were a judge and your job was to sentence a person to prison or even death for violation of rules or beliefs in your community, you might question the nature of right and wrong before finally reaching a decision. Do any of you recall the character Jean Valjean from *Les Miserables*, who was sentenced to seven years of slavery for stealing a loaf of bread for his starving family? What choice would you have made if you were the judge? I hope you are compassionate and would take time to consider all the possible choices and not decide too quickly.

Students: Wow. That's a tough one. I don't know. I'm really not sure. I need to think about it.

Professor: And what if you were Jean Valjean? Would you have chosen to break the law to feed your family?

Students: Absolutely! Of course! I'd have to! You bet your life I would!

Stop 2

Professor: OK. All right then. But now I want you to think about this. Would you then say that you were not really responsible for the crime? Would you try to get off, be excused, by saying you did it because the society did not provide a job for you and that's why you and your family were so hungry? This is not an easy question, is it?

Now, what about this case? On March 30, 1981, the president of the United States, Ronald Reagan, and three other men were shot on a street in Washington, D.C. John Hinckley Jr., the young man who shot these men, admitted that he felt no remorse about his crime. Three of his four victims recovered; the fourth suffered permanent brain damage.

Fifteen months later, after an eight-week trial that cost $3 million, Hinckley was found "not guilty by reason of insanity." Think about that. Hinckley shot the president of the United States and three other people and was only sent to a mental hospital for counseling and treatment. When the psychiatrists decide that he is well enough, he will be released and sent home. He will not go to prison.

Student 1: Wow! That's incredible!

Student 2: That's terrible!

Student 3: No kidding! I didn't know that!

Professor: Well, it's true. Naturally, many people were very angry that Hinckley received such a small punishment. However, Hinckley's punishment is not my focus here. I want to focus instead on the choice Hinckley made. His actions came from his choice, and his actions injured four people.

Did you know that in the United States, only those criminals who made their choices consciously, willfully, and freely are punished? Yup, that's the law. If it is proven in court that an act, no matter how evil, was caused by influences beyond the control of the person who did it, then that person is not punished for the act.

In other words, in American society, the law says that you are not responsible for choices you make if you are not aware or in control of your actions. This is called legal insanity. How about that!?

Stop 3

Professor: We are faced with other questions—perhaps not as serious—every moment of our lives. Who will I go out with on Saturday night? Shall I go on a diet? Should I go to the movies tonight or should I study for that biology test? Should I make long-range plans for my career? And more important, how should I treat other people?

The poetry, fiction, and theater of every culture reflect the drama involved in making these kinds of choices, but they do not offer simple answers. The only definite rule we are given about making choices is that we have to make them or they will be made for us. Ah, but if only we could make perfect choices, then there would be no problem, right?

In summary, we have touched lightly on the extremely important matter of the nature of human choice and briefly examined the relationship between human choice, crime, and punishment. I hope this lecture has stimulated you to reflect on your own choices—what they are and why you are making them—and to consider how they shape your world view and what your responsibility is for their effects. And remember: whether you think your choices are predetermined or made freely, you cannot get away from making choices, for after all, to choose is to be human.

Stop 4

ANSWER KEY

Possible answers

1. Predetermination is the idea that our lives are mapped out before birth, while free will is the idea that we have control over and make choices about our lives. Believing in either of these ideas affects the way we feel about our lives.
2. Since decisions about crime have major consequences, a judge must consider all aspects of a crime before assigning a punishment.
3. Since Hinckley was found to be legally insane, his crime was considered to be out of his control by the U.S. legal system. Since he could not freely decide his own actions, he was sent to a mental hospital instead of prison.

4. As humans, we make major and minor decisions every day and have no set rules for making those decisions. The professor hopes that he has caused the students to think about their own choices as well as the connection between choosing to commit crimes and being punished.

After You Listen

4 Comparing Notes 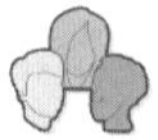

- ❑ Play the audio again as students check their paraphrases and make any necessary changes.
- ❑ Divide students into small groups to share their paraphrases.
- ❑ When the groups are finished sharing their paraphrases, lead a class discussion about the differences they noticed.

Talk It Over

5 Paraphrasing Problems for Group Discussion 

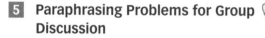

Best Practice

Cultivating Critical Thinking

This activity presents a number of ethical problems for students to discuss and solve in groups. To do this, students must reflect on their personal beliefs as well as the concepts from the chapter and apply both to determine the best course of action in real-world situations. This process allows students to synthesize new ideas with their personal codes of ethics.

- ❑ Go over the information about making unpleasant choices in real-life situations. Ask students if they can think of a few examples, such as not going out with friends in order to study for a difficult class (sacrificing present fun for future success).
- ❑ Go over the four guidelines students will use in their group discussions. You might want to note the guidelines on the board for students to refer to during the activity.
- ❑ Divide the class into small groups to discuss the situations.
- ❑ Call on groups to share with the class the solutions they chose and their reasons for them.

Strategy

Understanding and Expressing Wishes, Hopes, and Desires

- Go over the information about the hopes, wishes, and desires expressed by the lecturer.
- Go over the expressions in the list.
- Review the conditional by asking students for examples of things they wish for and noting them on the board. For instance, students might say, "I wish I could skip the test next week," or, "I wish I were the president of South Korea."
- Demonstrate the similarity in meaning between *wish* and *if only* expressions by transforming the students' own examples. Using the examples above, you could say, "If only I could skip the test next week, I would be so happy," or, "I would make my country a better place if only I were the president."
- Remind students that both *wish* and *if only* expressions indicate pessimism about the possibility of something actually happening.
- Ask for volunteers to share some of their hopes. Write their sentences on the board to reinforce the grammar. For instance, students might say, "I hope to get a good grade in Chemistry," or, "I hope Miguel isn't at home sick today."
- Point out that expressions with *hope* indicate a more optimistic attitude about the possibility of something.

Content Note

- The expressions used to convey wishes, hopes, and desires can be used to talk about the past, present, or future.

Past

- I wish you had called me sooner.
- I hope I didn't keep you waiting long.

Present

- If only I had more money.
- I hope you're having a good time.

Future

- I wish the voters would approve the referendum in the next election.
- I hope scientists develop a vaccine soon.

1 Listening for Wishes, Hopes, and Desires 

- ❑ Play the audio of the conversation as students write the expressions of wishes, hopes, and desires that they hear.
- ❑ Divide students into pairs or small groups to compare notes.

ANSWER KEY

I hope I find one soon.

If only I didn't have to find something inexpensive.

I wish I were making more money.

I certainly hope you're kidding.

AUDIOSCRIPT

Listening for Wishes, Hopes, and Desires

Laura: Have you found a house to rent yet?

James: No, not yet. I hope I find one soon. My family is arriving in a few days, and I want to have a house ready for them when they get here.

Laura: Sounds like you could use some help.

James: Well, maybe a little, but probably all I really need is more money. If only I didn't have to find something inexpensive. I wish I were making more money. Then I would have more choices of houses.

Laura: Well, I may be able to help you out there.

James: You mean you know of a good house for us?

Laura: Not exactly. But I might know of a way for you to make some easy money making some quick deliveries.

James: Uh-oh. This sounds too easy to be legal. But I tell you, I'm getting really desperate at this point. I just might be tempted anyway.

Laura: Well, I certainly hope you're kidding. But you don't have to worry. It's definitely legal. I heard that Pizza Time wants someone to deliver pizzas from 6:00 to 9:00 every night. And the pay's not bad.

James: Oh, is that all? Well, that sounds great! Who do I talk to?

2 Listening to Paraphrase Wishes, Hopes, and Desires

- Instruct students to read the six items before you play the audio again of the lecture on free will or predetermination from Part 2.
- Play the audio again, pausing as necessary so that students may complete the lecturer's sentences and paraphrase them. You may need to play some of the professor's statements more than once.
- Ask for volunteers to share their paraphrases. Discuss the attitude—optimism or pessimism—the lecturer expresses through his choice of expressions.

ANSWER KEY

Answers may vary.

1. **Lecturer:** I hope that by the end of class that difference will be clear to you all. **Possible paraphrase**: The lecturer hopes that by the end of class, the students understand how the two ideas differ.
2. **Lecturer:** I want to hear your ideas on these two very different views of the world. **Possible paraphrase**: The lecturer wants to hear the students' ideas about free will and predetermination.
3. **Lecturer:** I wish I had done that differently. **Possible paraphrase:** The lecturer asks students how many wish they had made a different choice.
4. **Lecturer:** If only I had decided to do this instead of what I did. **Possible paraphrase:** If only I had taken a different course of action.
5. **Lecturer:** I want to focus instead on the choice Hinckley made. **Possible paraphrase:** The lecturer does not want to focus on Hinckley's punishment; he wants to concentrate on Hinckley's decision to shoot.
6. **Lecturer:** I hope this lecture has stimulated you to reflect on your own choices—what they are and why you are making them—and to consider how they shape your worldview and what your responsibility is for their effects. **Possible paraphrase:** In summary, he hopes the lecture will prompt students to examine the choices they make, how those choices affect their personal philosophies, and their responsibility for the consequences of their choices.

3 Expressing Hopes and Wishes

Best Practice

Interacting with Others

In this activity, students complete sentences about their wishes, hopes, and desires and share them in small groups. The content is highly personal, and the activity gives students a chance to reveal facets of themselves not always seen in class. This type of self-expression is more common in English-speaking countries than in many other countries, so the activity provides practice with a speaking skill that may not come easily to some students.

- Tell students that they are going to fulfill the lecturer's wish for them to reflect on their own lives.
- Give students time to think about themselves and complete the partial sentences.
- After they have completed the sentences, have students read them aloud to each other in small groups and explain their wishes, hopes, and desires.
- For this activity, you might not want to ask students to share their ideas with the whole class since they are of such a personal nature.

REPRODUCIBLE

EXPANSION ACTIVITY

- This activity aims to give students practice using the *if only* structure to express hopes and wishes about other people's lives.
- Photocopy and distribute BLM 26 "If Only … A" (page BLM 26 of this Teacher's Edition) for half the students in the class and BLM 27 "If Only … B" (page BLM 27) for the other half.
- Divide the class into pairs. Give one student in each pair a copy of handout A and the other a copy of handout B.
- Go over the example as a class.
- Instruct students to take turns reading their situations aloud to their partners. The partners should respond with an *If only* sentence to express a hope or wish that would be helpful.
- Circulate and monitor students' grammar usage.
- When the pairs are finished, ask for volunteers to perform some of their exchanges for the class.

Talk It Over

4 Expressing Your Hopes and Wishes, Optimism and Pessimism 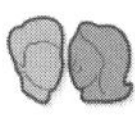

Best Practice

Scaffolding Instruction

This role-play activity provides three opportunities for pairs of students to experiment with the language from the chapter before performing it in front of the class. This practice phase leading to a more challenging task supports learning as students develop the language and communication skills they need to function independently outside of class.

- Go over the directions so that students understand the activity.
- Divide students into pairs to role-play all three situations before choosing one to present to the class.
- Give each pair feedback on their expression of wishes, hopes, and desires.

5 A "Wishes" and "Hopes" Drama 

Best Practice

Making Use of Academic Content

This activity is centered upon real-world issues of the type that students will encounter in academic settings. As small groups prepare to act out a drama, they must consider the trauma experienced by soldiers in combat, a man's failed personal life, murder, and the temporary insanity defense. Dealing with these issues helps prepare students for serious academic discussions.

- Go over the direction line and explain that students will work in groups to plan and present a mini-drama.
- Divide the class into groups of 5–9 students.

- ❑ Have the groups choose a "director" to read the situation aloud and assign or help classmates choose roles.
- ❑ All of the roles must be assigned, so some students may play more than one character.
- ❑ Give students time to plan and practice their dramas. Decide whether you want them to write a script or to simply talk about what they will say and then improvise. Remind students to use the language and ideas from the chapter.
- ❑ Consider videotaping the dramas and watching them as a class. This gives students a chance to listen to and evaluate their own use of English after the pressure of performing the dramas is off. (It's also a lot of fun!)

TOEFL® iBT

IDEA-CONNECTION QUESTIONS

- Go over the information about test questions that require students to make connections between ideas in a lecture.
- Go over the table based on the lecture from this chapter. Explain to students that on the actual test, they will click on the box of their choice using a computer mouse, and that they may change their minds simply by clicking on a different box.

1 Idea-Connection Questions: Lecture 

- Tell students to close their books and prepare to take notes. Mention that taking good notes can be especially helpful with this type of question since it asks about the overall lecture.
- Play the audio of the lecture as students listen and take notes.
- Have students open their books.
- Play the audio of the questions through as students choose the correct answers. Pause for 20 seconds after questions 1, 3, and 4, and for 60 seconds after question 2 to allow students time to choose their answers.
- Go over the students' answers. If necessary, play the audio of the lecture again to clear up any uncertainty or to point out information the students missed the first time.

ANSWER KEY

1. c 2. free choice; no free choice; no free choice; free choice 3. b 4. c

AUDIOSCRIPT

Professor: I think you're all familiar with the age-old debate over free will and predetermination. But recent medical research has added an entirely new dimension to it. In the past, it was mostly a question of whether (1) humans are free to make their own choices or (2) those choices are made for us by some higher power. Now, there's a third choice: My chemicals made me do it.

Neuroscience has identified about 35 chemicals—the neurotransmitters—that help carry messages throughout the brain. Let's use one of them, serotonin, as an example.

One of the first clues pointing to some relation between serotonin and crime came from a large Dutch family whose males were known for particularly violent behavior. Researchers who analyzed the brain chemistry of some family members found a chemical problem. The men had very low levels of MAOA, a chemical that breaks down serotonin. This suggested that too much serotonin could lead to violent behavior.

Later experiments indicated that too *little* serotonin might have the same effect. Violent and impulsive individuals were found to have brain cells that soaked up serotonin very fast. Since this neurotransmitter was known to calm certain people down, researchers reasoned that increasing serotonin levels would solve the problem. Drugs called SSRIs were developed to slow down the re-uptake, or absorbing, of serotonin. They seemed to work. In fact, I think you've all heard of one SSRI, Prozac. It was so effective that it became one of the largest-selling medications of all time.

Anyway, the bottom line is that no one knows exactly how serotonin—or any of its 30-some chemical cousins—really works. It has some relation to criminal violence, but what? Is too much worse than too little? I suspect the answer will involve a lot of factors, a lot of interactions among chemicals, environmental conditions, and even personal experiences. But I'm just guessing.

The one thing we know for sure is that scientific research into brain chemistry is already influencing the criminal courts. If you commit a violent crime because your brain chemicals are out of balance, are you really responsible? Judges have long ruled that a "legally insane" person, a person who cannot distinguish between "right" and "wrong," is not necessarily responsible for his or her crimes. Neuroscience might simply be discovering the chemical reasons for this insanity.

The principle is being tested in the Nevada courts in the case of a young man whom I'll call Jason. Jason was arrested in a hotel lobby, and he quickly admitted that he had, in fact, just committed a murder. A hotel video camera showed him at the scene of the crime. His defense lawyers do not dispute that, unfortunately, he killed someone. However, they have argued that Jason's genetic background is to blame. Jason was raised by a loving and non-violent adoptive father and mother, but investigators found that his biological parents and two brothers lived disturbingly violent lives. All had histories of violently aggressive behavior, mental illness, or both. Jason himself had been diagnosed with serious attention deficit disorder, ADD. The disorder is very often found in people whose brains lack enough serotonin. Further tests of Jason's brain chemistry will reveal more about this troubled young man, but some genetically-based chemical problem is likely. His family's history of criminal behavior goes back more than 100 years.

Jason was 18 years old when he committed murder, so he is legally an adult. But is he legally responsible for the crime? Those who say *no* point out that he has no control over the chemistry of his brain. Under the influence of that chemistry, they say, he could not make a free choice about what he should do. They also point out that he was seeking medical help for his problems, which indicates a desire to get better. Those who *do* hold him responsible say that body chemistry can *affect* decisions but does not *make* them. After all, the definition of legal insanity is very narrow: Not comprehending the difference between "right" and "wrong," and Jason, in seeking help, showed that he *did* understand that difference. Almost everyone has unfortunate influences in life. We have a social obligation, they say, to overcome those limitations, to choose wisely anyway.

Narrator: Question 1. According to the professor, what was one of the first indications of a connection between serotonin levels and violent behavior?

Question 2. In the lecture, the professor mentions some support for the belief that people freely choose whether to commit a crime or not. She also mentions arguments for the opposite—a lack of free choice. Indicate which position each statement supports. Mark an "X" in the proper box for each statement.

Question 3. According to the professor, why is it sometimes helpful to reduce the speed at which serotonin is absorbed by brain cells?

Question 4. Why does the professor start the lecture by mentioning free will and predetermination?

EXPANSION ACTIVITY

- The goal of this activity is for students to make connections between the two lectures from the chapter and express their opinions on mental illness as a legal defense.
- After students finish Part 4, conduct a class discussion about whether legally insane people are responsible for criminal acts they commit. Begin with the specific cases mentioned in the two lectures, those of Hinckley and Jason. Ask students what the two cases have in common. Ask them if they think the two men were responsible for their actions and what, if any, punishments they deserve. Encourage students to give reasons for and explain their personal opinions of mental illness as a legal defense.

Self-Assessment Log

- ❑ Read the directions aloud and have students check vocabulary they learned in the chapter and are prepared to use.
- ❑ Tell students to find definitions in the chapter for any words they did not check.
- ❑ Have students check the degree to which they learned the strategies practiced in the chapter. Put students in small groups. Ask students to find the information or an activity related to each strategy in the chapter.

Name ______________________ Date ______________

Language Learning Survey

Directions: Take this paper and a pen or pencil. Stand up and move around the classroom. Introduce yourself to three different classmates. Ask them these questions about language learning and take brief notes on their answers.

Example A: Hi. My name is Yuki.

B: Hello, Yuki. I'm Elena. Could I ask you a few questions?

A: Sure. No problem.

Questions	Name	Name	Name
How long have you studied English?			
How many languages do you speak?			
What has studying a new language taught you about your native language?			
For you, what is the most challenging part of learning English?			
How has learning English changed you?			

BLM 2

Name ______________________ Date ______________

Learning About Linguists

Directions: Assign one linguist to each group member. Use the Internet to learn basic information about your linguist. Tell the other group members about her or him, as well as your reaction to the linguist's ideas.

To find information, enter your linguist's name in search engines such as Google (www.google.com) or Yahoo (www.yahoo.com), or try online encyclopedias such as Wikipedia (www.wikipedia.org) or Encarta (http://encarta.msn.com).

Benjamin Whorf year born/died: why famous: What do you think?	**Noam Chomsky** year born/died: why famous: What do you think?
Leonard Bloomfield year born/died: why famous: What do you think?	**Deborah Tannen** year born/died: why famous: What do you think?

BLM 3

Name ______________________________ Date ______________

Vocabulary Table

Directions: Complete the table using words from Activity 3 "Vocabulary in Context", on page 28 of the student book, or choose unfamiliar words from the chapter's active and passive vocabulary lists.

Notes: P.O.S. stands for "part of speech", and should identify a word's function, such as noun, verb, or adjective. The context might be part of a sentence containing the word, the name of the lecture where you heard the word, or anything else that helps you remember it.

Word	P.O.S.	Meaning	Context

Name ______________________________ Date ____________________

Making an Outline

Directions: In Part 2 you used an outline to understand the organization of the lecture and take notes, and then to organize your own ideas and take notes to use during a presentation. Outlines can also be used to analyze and take notes on a reading, or to organize your ideas before you write.

The Format of a Formal Outline

Formal outlines use Roman numerals for main ideas. In reading and writing, these main ideas are often the topics of paragraphs or sections. Supporting details and examples are shown using capital letters, numbers, and lowercase letters, with each level representing an increasingly greater degree of detail.

Topic (or Title)

I. ______________________________
  A. ______________________________
  B. ______________________________
    1. ______________________________
    2. ______________________________
      a. ______________________________
      b. ______________________________
  C. ______________________________
II. ______________________________

The Roman Numerals:

1	2	3	4	5	6	7	8	9	10
I	II	III	IV	V	VI	VII	VIII	IX	X

The Content of a Formal Outline:

Depending on your purpose or what your instructor wants, your outline can include:

- ❑ **Complete Sentences:** Full-sentence outlines work well when someone else will read your outline. They can also be helpful when planning a piece of writing, because when you begin the first draft, you have already written several sentences.
- ❑ **Words and Phrases:** If you're making an outline for yourself, you only need to write enough to jog your memory.

BLM 5

Name ______________________________ Date ____________________

Making Excuses

Directions: Although excuses are a part of every culture, your ideas about which excuses to use depend on you as an individual and as a member of your specific culture. Think about yourself and learn about your classmates as you discuss the following questions for each situation below.

1. Is it appropriate to use an excuse in this situation?
2. Does your culture have a typical excuse that people usually use in this situation?
3. What excuse, if any, would *you* use in this situation?

Situations

a. You were supposed to meet your friend at the library to study, but you forgot about it and didn't go.
b. A husband or wife has a great time with friends and gets home much later than expected.
c. A child doesn't do the homework assignment and shows up for class empty-handed.
d. You go to a party and see that all the other guests have brought beautifully wrapped gifts for the hostess. You didn't bring a gift.
e. On your vacation in Paris, you feel lazy and spend most of your time in the hotel room. You don't go to the Eiffel Tower or other popular tourist attractions. When you get back, your family asks about the Eiffel Tower.
f. Two co-workers get angry at each other at a meeting and exchange some heated words. They see each other later as they are leaving work.

 **BLM 6**

Name ______________________ Date ______________

Words on Aging: Partner A

Directions: Below are some quotations about aging by famous people. Your partner has different quotations. Do not show your partner this handout.

Working in pairs, take turns dictating quotations so that both you and your partner have all of them written down. Discuss the meanings of the quotations, as well as your opinions about them. Do you agree with all of the ideas?

The aging process has you firmly in its grasp if you never get the urge to throw a snowball. —Doug Larson
 —Mark Twain
Growing old is mandatory; growing up is optional. —Chili Davis
 —Nikita Ivanovich Panin
Old age isn't so bad when you consider the alternative. —Maurice Chevalier
 —Victor Hugo
Men do not quit playing because they grow old; they grow old because they quit playing. —Oliver Wendell Holmes
 —Agatha Christie

BLM 7

Name ______________________________ Date ____________________

Words on Aging: Partner B

Directions: You have some quotations about aging by famous people. Your partner has different quotations. Do not show your partner this handout.

Working in pairs, take turns dictating quotations so that both you and your partner have all of them written down. Discuss the meanings of the quotations, as well as your opinions about them. Do you agree with all of the ideas?

—Doug Larson
Age is an issue of mind over matter. If you don't mind, it doesn't matter. —Mark Twain
—Chili Davis
In youth the days are short and the years are long; in old age the years are short and the days long. —Nikita Ivanovich Panin
—Maurice Chevalier
Forty is the old age of youth; fifty the youth of old age. —Victor Hugo
—Oliver Wendell Holmes
An archeologist is the best husband any woman can have: the older she gets, the more interested he is in her. —Agatha Christie

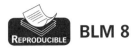

Name ______________________ Date ______________

Venn Diagram

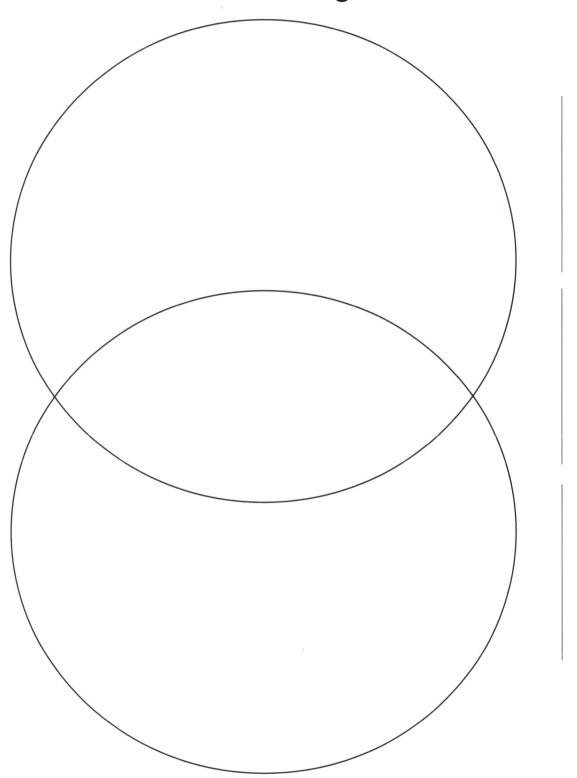

Name ______________________ Date ______________

Cloze Passage

Directions: Fill in the blanks as you listen to the short conversation.

Man: Sorry ______________ at band practice on Thursday. I had a family emergency.

Woman: Really? I'm so sorry. If you ______________, what happened?

Man: No, no, it's OK. I just had to help ______________ grandfather into a nursing home.

Woman: Are you upset ______________?

Man: No. I'm OK.

Woman: When old people can't ______________, a nursing home is the best place to go, right?

Man: Sorry?

Woman: If he can't take care of himself ______________, he'd better go to an institution.

Man: ______________. That's a little cold. This is my grandfather. I love the guy. I've loved spending time at his house. I'm not happy about ______________.

Woman: But why not? You can't take care of him.

Man: Well, not ______________. I have classes, band practice, homework, ______________ study sessions.

Woman: Right. And for your grandfather's care, it's ______________.

Man: Why are you being so hard-hearted about this? It wasn't an easy decision.

Woman: But it's ______________. He'll fit in better there, and he'll have a lot of friends.

Man: Yeah. But to be honest, he ______________ as most of those people. I wonder if he'll really make any friends.

Woman: Still, ______________ if he stayed at home.

Man: OK, OK. We could probably piece something together if we really worked on it. Maybe my parents could juggle ______________. My sister has ______________, but maybe she could drop in on him ______________.

Woman: So you don't really believe this nursing home is the best place for him, do you?

Man: Well, ______________, not really.

Name ______________________________ Date ____________________

Expressions from the Heart

Directions: Take a look at these idioms and expressions that use the word *heart*. Discuss the questions in small groups.

- ***to learn/know something by heart***

  When you learn something by heart, you memorize it. After that, you know it by heart. For example, you might learn a favorite poem by heart so that you can recite it from memory.

- ***to have a heart-to-heart talk with someone***

  You have a heart-to-heart talk with someone when you want to discuss something that is personal and perhaps difficult to say. For example, you might have a heart-to-heart talk with your friend about something he or she did that hurt your feelings.

- ***to have a broken heart/to break someone's heart***

  This expression describes the terrible way we feel when a romantic relationship doesn't work out. You might have a broken heart when someone ends a relationship with you, for example, or you might break someone's heart when you end a relationship with him or her.

- ***to wear your heart on your sleeve***

  People who wear their hearts on their sleeves seldom hide their emotions. They let people see what they are feeling.

- ***to have a change of heart***

  When you have a change of heart, you change your mind about something. For example, you might decide to attend a certain university, but then you have a change of heart and decide to attend a different one.

Discussion Questions:

1. Why would you want to learn something by heart? Think of situations when it is helpful to know something by heart.
2. Describe a heart-to-heart talk you had with someone.
3. Talk about a movie or story in which someone's heart is broken. How does the person's broken heart affect the plot?
4. Do you know anyone who wears their heart on their sleeve? In your culture, is showing emotions a positive or negative trait?
5. Describe a time you had a change of heart about something.

REPRODUCIBLE **BLM 11**

Name ______________________________ Date ____________________

Associations Map

Directions: Choose four analogies from Activity 6, "Discussing Analogies," on page 68 of the Student Book, and write them in the four larger circles. Then think about each analogy and write anything that comes to mind in the smaller circles.

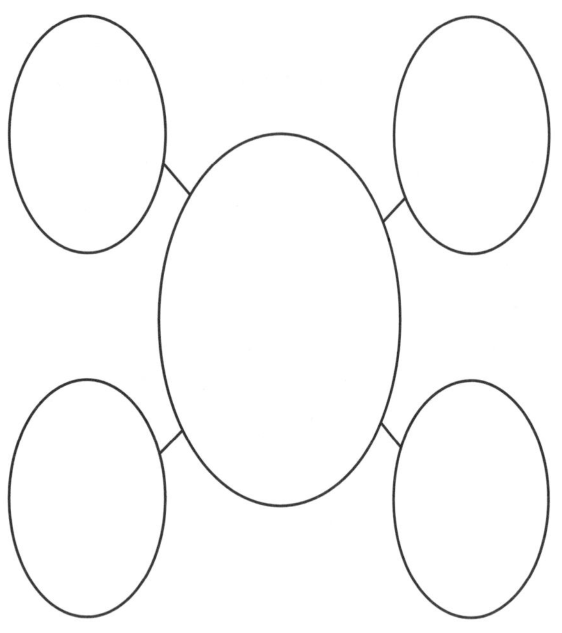

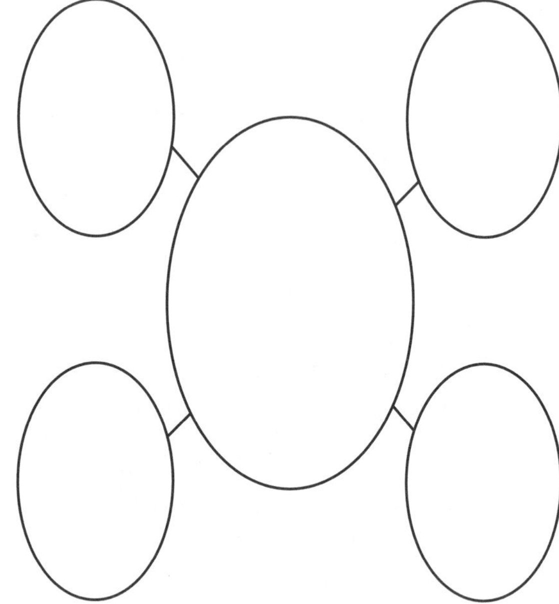

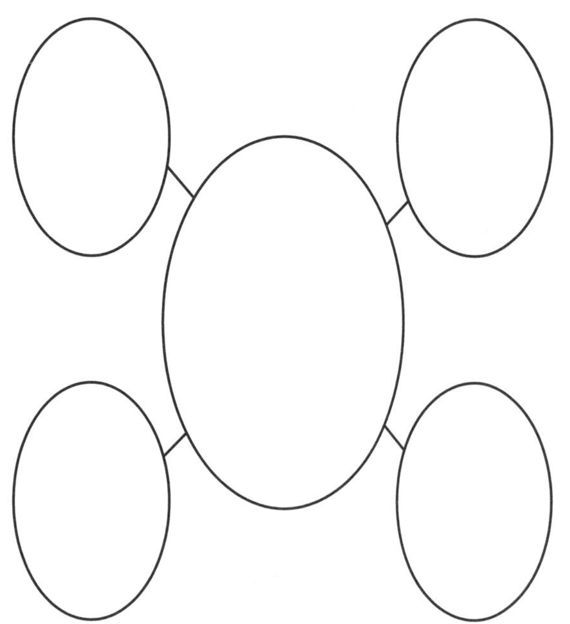

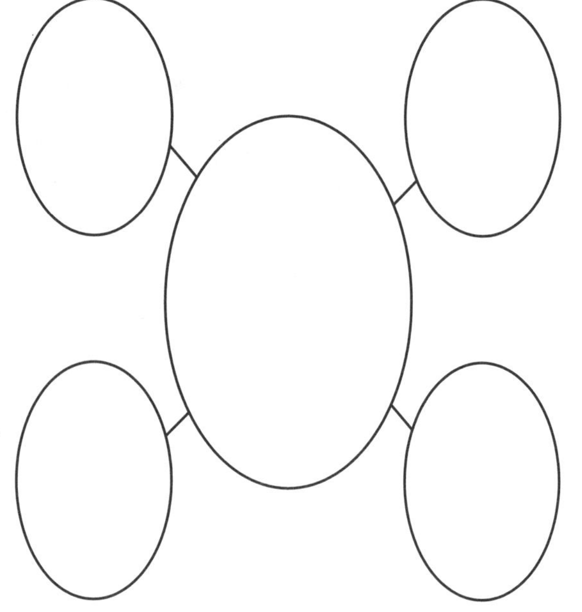

BLM 12

Name ______________________ Date ______________

Expressions to Introduce Personal Opinions

I'm convinced …

I'm (almost) positive …

I'm fairly certain …

I'm pretty sure …

I (strongly) believe …

I bet …

I imagine …

I suspect …

I think I'd say …

In my opinion …

Not everyone will agree with me, but …

Name ______________________ Date ______________

Vocabulary Categories

Directions: Write each term from the vocabulary list under one of the headings in the table below. Be prepared to explain your choices.

Nouns	Verbs	Adjectives
acceleration	manipulate	remote
altitude	shuttle	solar
astronaut	simulate	
atmosphere		
cargo bay		
friction		
mission		
orbit		
orbiter		
satellite		
shuttle		

spacecraft or part of a spacecraft	natural phenomenon
human activity	**person**

Name ______________________ Date ______________

Simple Note Formats

Directions: You learned in the chapter that guessing the possible relationship between ideas you will hear in a lecture can help you take notes. In addition to the two-column note format you practiced in the chapter, try the following:

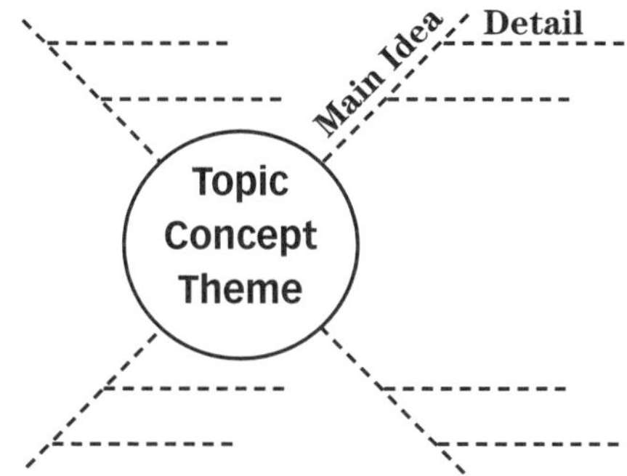

A "Spider Map" shows how supporting ideas relate to a central idea. For example, you might write the result in the center and the causes on each of the spider's "legs."

Chain of Events

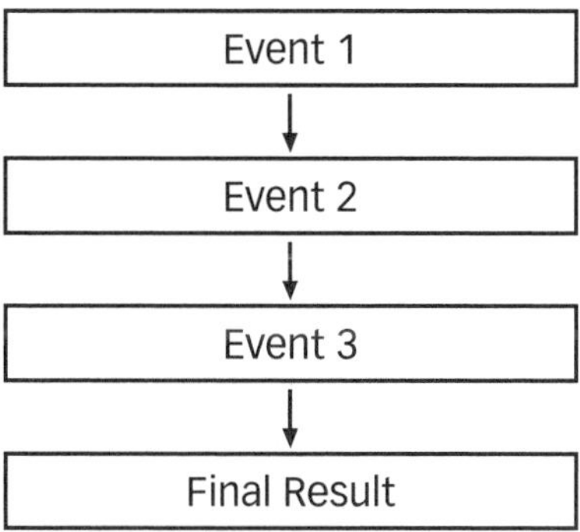

A Chain of Events diagram shows the steps in a process starting with the first and ending with the final result. For instance, a seed sprouts into a seedling, uses sunlight and water to grow, and becomes a tree.

Cycle

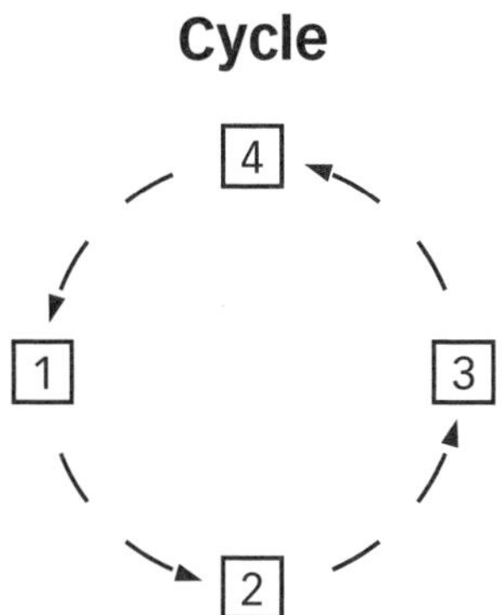

Use a Cycle format to show a repeating set of events such as the rain, evaporation, rain cycle.

Name ______________________________ Date ______________

Internet Research on the World Bank

Directions: Search for information on the Internet about the World Bank. Locate at least one article or website with a positive view of the World Bank, and one with a negative or critical viewpoint. Complete the chart.

	Article or Website #1: Positive Viewpoint	**Article or Website #2: Negative Viewpoint**
Title of article or name of website:		
URL: (Web address)		
Clues about the article's or website's viewpoint:		
One interesting piece of information from the article or website:		

BLM 16

Name ______________________ Date ______________

Expressions Used to Link Pros and Cons

Directions: Make as many copies of this sheet as you have groups of students. Cut out the cards and keep them in sets.

although	**but**
however	**instead**
nonetheless	**on the contrary**
on the other hand	**although**
however	**but**
nonetheless	**on the contrary**

BLM 17

Name ______________________ Date ______________

Researching a Remarkable Person

Directions: On the Internet, search for information about a famous person mentioned in the poster activity. Complete the form and be ready to give a short oral report about the person you researched.

1. Name of person: ______________________

2. Dates and places the person lived: ______________________

____

____

3. Most famous accomplishment: ______________________

____

____

4. Other accomplishments: ______________________

____

____

____

____

5. Your opinion/reaction: ______________________

____

____

____

____

____

____

Name ______________________________ Date ________________

My Life

Directions: Think about your own accomplishments and the events that have shaped your life. Plot the accomplishments and events on the left side of the timeline and the dates on the right side.

My Life

Name ______________________ Date ______________

The Life of the Party

Directions: Cut out the expressions cards. Give one to each student in a group of 3–4 just before they role-play conversations at a party. Tell students to check off their expressions as they use them.

❑ I enjoy … ❑ I can't tolerate … ❑ I love … ❑ I detest … ❑ … irks me	❑ I dislike … ❑ I'm happy … ❑ I can't stand … ❑ That's great! ❑ … bugs me
❑ I don't really like … ❑ I'm thrilled … ❑ I hate … ❑ What a terrific …! ❑ I don't care for …	❑ I'm delighted … ❑ I can't take … ❑ This is my idea of … ❑ I don't have time for … ❑ That's super!

BLM 20

Name ______________________ Date ______________

Inventors and Their Inventions

Directions: Match the inventors with their inventions. Then write the year in which you think the invention was invented.

INVENTOR	INVENTION	YEAR
Alexander Watson-Watt		
Mary Anderson		
Galileo Galilei		
Tokuji Hayakawa		
Bartolomeo Cristofori		
George Crum		
Ruth Wakefield		
Jonas Salk		
Johann Vaaler		
Tim Berners-Lee		

the mechanical pencil
the World Wide Web
the chocolate chip cookie
the thermometer
the potato chip
the windshield wiper
the piano
the polio vaccine
the paper clip
radar

Name ______________________ Date ______________

Writing Test Items

Directions: The script below is part of the lecture on creativity. Read the script and imagine it is part of the listening section of the TOEFL iBT. Write three test items similar to the ones in Activity 1, Part 4 Focus on Testing. Each of the items should have a question that requires listening for signal words or information that is divulged and four answer choices. Do not mark the correct answers.

Let me emphasize again that (1) everyone has creative abilities and (2) we are all creating our own realities at every moment. Let me illustrate this by having you look at the large "No Smoking" signs on the walls. Do you recognize the sign at one glance, or do you see it in parts, small sections, letter by letter? When I am being deliberately analytical, I feel I see the world in pieces. What is really going on is that the eye really does "see" things in pieces. It vibrates with great speed, taking brief, narrow pictures of the world. Then the mind combines, or fuses, those individual pictures into a larger picture—a creation. It's this creation that gives us a sense of the whole. So the mind, then, creates an interpretation of what comes in through the senses.

Now I'll explain how art is connected with this process of interpretation and ordering of the world. The artist sees a fragmentary, disordered series of events—pieces of light, color, parts of conversations—and brings them together into a work of art to make the world more understandable. But art is not just an activity for professional artists. The real story is that we do the same things as the artist every day, all the time. In this way, we are all artists and creators in our lives, without effort.

Now you may be wondering at this point why so many people want to be more creative if, as we said, human beings are naturally creative. I'm going to answer that by telling you that although the mind is spontaneously creative when we are very young, as we grow older, the mind tends to become caught in repetitive patterns. Then the mind operates imitatively—not creatively—seeing the world the same way day after day after day. In this state of mind, you are not creating anything new because your mind is not exploring new ways of looking at things.

BLM 22

Name ______________________ Date ______________

Student A

Directions:

- ❑ Do not show your partner this worksheet.
- ❑ Write tag questions for each statement and draw lines to indicate rising or falling intonation.
- ❑ Say all your statements with tag questions to your partner using the appropriate intonation pattern and structure (affirmative or negative). Your partner will respond after each one.
- ❑ Listen to your partner's statements with tag questions and respond.

1. You studied last night, ______________________?

(You want to confirm that your partner studied.)

2. You enjoy going to school, ______________________?

(This is a rhetorical question. You think your partner enjoys going to school.)

3. This class is awesome, ______________________?

(This is a rhetorical question. You like the class.)

4. You didn't look at the next chapter in the textbook yet, ______________________?

(You want to check to see if this is true.)

5. You're never at a loss for words, ______________________?

(This is a rhetorical question. You admire your partner's speaking ability.)

REPRODUCIBLE **BLM 23**

Name ______________________________ Date ____________________

Student B

Directions:

- ❑ Do not show your partner this worksheet.
- ❑ Write tag questions for each statement and draw lines to indicate rising or falling intonation.
- ❑ Listen to each of your partner's statements with tag questions and respond.
- ❑ Say each of your statements with tag questions to your partner using the intonation pattern and structure (affirmative or negative). Your partner will respond after each one.

1. This is great weather we're having, ______________________?

(This is a rhetorical question. You think the weather is great.)

2. You don't have a little money I could borrow, ______________________?

(You want to check to see if this is true.)

3. We don't have any homework for tomorrow, ______________________?

(This is a rhetorical question. You don't think there is homework for tomorrow.)

4. You've traveled a lot, ______________________?

(You want to check to see if this is true.)

5. The class party will be at your place, ______________________?

(You want to check to see if this is true.)

Name ______________________ Date ______________

Paraphrasing (continued on page BLM 25)

Directions: Read each original statement and think about its meaning. Then, read the two paraphrases that follow and decide which one is better and why.

1. Original

Just as in other degenerative diseases, heart disease is normally present long before we notice any drastic symptoms.

Paraphrases

- **a.** With heart disease, as with other diseases that worsen over time, major symptoms may not occur during the early stages.
- **b.** A long time before we notice major symptoms, heart disease is usually present, just as it is in other degenerative diseases.

2. Original

A child learns language in a natural way and is not conscious of the process. An adult learning a new language relies more on rules and a conscious, disciplined approach to language learning.

Paraphrases

- **a.** Unlike children, adults learn language after studying the rules of a conscious, disciplined approach to language acquisition.
- **b.** Children automatically acquire language without being aware of it. As adults, we deliberately and methodically use rules to learn a new language.

3. Original

Working to improve their economies, developing nations sometimes seek financial assistance from outside sources such as the World Bank.

Paraphrases

- **a.** Developing nations require economic assistance in the form of outside loans, sometimes from the World Bank, as they work to improve their economies.
- **b.** Developing countries may apply for a loan from the World Bank for the purpose of economic development.

Name ______________________ Date ______________

Paraphrasing (continued from page BLM 24)

4. Original

Working as part of a small group may require us to compromise our own ideas to fit with the ideas the group agrees are important.

Paraphrases

a. Members working in small groups sometimes adjust their ideas to conform with those considered important to the whole group.

b. A small group working together inevitably experiences dissension because different members have different goals for the group.

5. Original

Older people who are unable to care for themselves require differing levels of assistance ranging from help in their own homes to living in a facility with round-the-clock nursing services.

Paraphrases

a. Care for elderly people needing assistance can be provided in their own homes or by nursing homes, depending on what they require.

b. A facility with nursing services provides the level of assistance that older people require to be able to care for themselves.

Name ______________________ Date ______________

"If only ...": A

Directions: With a partner, take turns reading situations aloud. After you listen to a situation, use "If only ..." to express a hope or wish that would be helpful to your partner.

Example

Student 1: "This paper is due today, and I'm just not happy with it. I think it really needs more information about climate change."

Student 2: "If only you had another day to work on it." or "If only your professor would give you an extension."

Situations A:

- ❑ I'm a little homesick. My whole family is getting together tomorrow for my mother's birthday party, and I'm stuck here.
- ❑ Can you believe it? My roommate ate all my food again.
- ❑ There's a great program on television tonight, but it's on at the same time as my sociology class.
- ❑ My best friend is always asking to borrow my cell phone, but never offers to help me pay the bill.

Name ______________________________ Date ______________

"If only ...": B

Directions: With a partner, take turns reading situations aloud. After you listen to a situation, use "If only ..." to express a hope or wish that would be helpful to your partner.

Example

Student 1: "This paper is due today, and I'm just not happy with it. I think it really needs more information about climate change."

Student 2: "If only you had another day to work on it." or "If only your professor would give you an extension."

Situations B:

- ❑ I'm really thirsty, but I don't see anywhere around here to get a drink.
- ❑ I'm thinking about getting a part-time job, but I'm worried that if I start working, I might not have enough time to study.
- ❑ I got a really low score on the midterm exam, and I'm not sure I'll be able to pass the course.
- ❑ My apartment is so far from the bus stop that I got soaking wet walking to class in the rain.

BLM #20 Answer Key

Chapter 8 Part 1: (Inventors and Inventions)

1. After your classmates fill in their charts, check their answers.
2. When classmates correctly match an inventor with his or her invention, let them tell the group what they know, such as the nationality of the inventor or how the invention was created.
3. Share the information below if classmates don't know it already.

INVENTOR	INVENTION	YEAR
Alexander Watson-Watt — *Scottish physicist; he invented radar to track storms in order to make it safer to fly airplanes.*	radar	1935
Mary Anderson — *American inventor; she invented a wiper that streetcar drivers could operate from inside the car.*	the windshield wiper	1903
Galileo Galilei — *Italian astronomer; his thermometer consisted of water that rose and fell with the temperature inside a glass tube.*	the thermometer	1593
Tokuji Hayakawa — *Japanese businessman; he invented "The Ever-Ready Sharp Pencil" and later became the CEO of Sharp electronics corporation.*	the mechanical pencil	1915
Bartolomeo Cristofori — *Italian instrument maker; his keyboard instrument could be played at any volume from very soft to very loud.*	the piano	around 1700
George Crum — *Native-American/African-American chef; he cut potatoes into very thin slices and fried them until they were very crisp in order to please a fussy customer.*	the potato chip	1853
Ruth Wakefield — *American hotelier; she owned the Toll House Inn and published a cookbook with her cookie recipe.*	the chocolate chip cookie	1930
Jonas Salk — *Russian-American researcher; his vaccine virtually eliminated the crippling disease.*	the polio vaccine	1947–1955
Johann Vaaler — *Norwegian patent office worker; his original clip had triangular or square ends.*	the paper clip	1890
Tim Berners-Lee – *English computer programmer; since changing the world, he has become a research scientist at MIT.*	the World Wide Web	1989

BLM #22 Answer Key

Student A: 1. didn't you; rising intonation 2. don't you; falling intonation 3. isn't it; falling intonation 4. did you; rising intonation 5. are you; falling intonation

BLM #23 Answer Key

Student B: 1. isn't it; falling intonation 2. do you; rising intonation 3. do we; falling intonation 4. haven't you; rising intonation 5. won't it; rising intonation

BLM #24 Answer Key

Chapter 10 Part 2 Paraphrasing

1. a is a good paraphrase; b uses language that is too similar to the original and it changes its meaning of the original.
2. b is a good paraphrase; a changes the meaning of the original.
3. b is a good paraphrase; a changes the meaning of the original.
4. a is a good paraphrase; b makes sense, but changes the meaning of the original.
5. a is a good paraphrase; b uses language that is too similar to the original and changes its meaning.

Name ______________________ Date ______________ Score ____________

Chapter 1 Test

Section I Listening to a Conversation Answer these questions about the conversation. **(3 points each)**

1. The first student needs clarification on ________.
- (A) why interrupting the professor is impolite
- (B) how languages might affect the way we think
- (C) why languages have such different vocabularies

2. The second student suggests that ________.
- (A) it's fine to interrupt a professor if it's done politely
- (B) it's impolite to interrupt a professor
- (C) shy students should wait for brave students to interrupt a professor

3. The second student talks about bread because ________.
- (A) it's an example of languages having different vocabularies
- (B) having seven types of bread is very unusual
- (C) borrowing words for bread is a linguistic universal

4. "Are you following me?" means ________.
- (A) "Are you as confused as I am?"
- (B) "Are you taking notes on this?"
- (C) "Do you understand me?"

5. The professor talks about eating a croissant in the lecture because ________.
- (A) *croissant* is a word that is borrowed from French
- (B) the professor likes to eat *croissant*
- (C) *croissant* is a type of bread

Section II Listening to a Lecture Answer the questions about the lecture. **(3 points each)**

1. The lecture is about ________.
- (A) comparative linguistics
- (B) historical linguistics
- (C) language learning

2. When grouping languages into families, linguists study ________.
- (A) grammar structures
- (B) the sound system of a language
- (C) vocabulary and phonology

3. The professor implies that the Latin-based languages ________.
- (A) have very different words for basic ideas
- (B) have not changed as much as other languages
- (C) came from an older language

4. Since "Hawaiian regularly transforms the /t/ sound to /k/", we know that ________.
- (A) the Hawaiian language doesn't use the /t/ sound
- (B) the Hawaiian language changes the /t/ sound to /k/
- (C) the Hawaiian language doesn't have many letters

5. What can we predict about the Polynesian languages?
- (A) They will be replaced by English.
- (B) They will borrow a new word for "blood."
- (C) They will continue to change over time.

Section III New Words Fill in each blank with a word from the Word List. **(3 points each)**

collage	paradox	fluently	buy (into)	déjà vu
imitation	transform	innate	linguist	association

1. Dogs have a/n ______________ ability to chase rabbits.
2. The fact that light behaves as both a particle and a wave is a/n ______________.
3. What type of ______________ studies language families?
4. Art teachers try to ______________ students into painters and sculptors.
5. If you have the strange feeling that you have taken this test before, you may be experiencing ______________.
6. I can speak Japanese ______________, but my Korean is not nearly as good.
7. Some pet owners train their animals to form a/n ______________ between good behavior and a reward, such as something good to eat.
8. You probably won't agree with this if you don't ______________ the theory that languages affect the way people think.
9. You can learn some things through ______________, for example, when you try to throw a baseball in the same way as your favorite pitcher.
10. It was an interesting ______________, with a variety of materials the artist had found on the beach.

Section IV Using Language Fill in each blank with a word from the box. (There are more words in the box than there are blanks.) **(8 points each)**

repeat	pardon	understand	again
repeating	interrupt	clear	catch

1. Excuse me. Would you mind ______________________ that?

2. I beg your ______________________. What was that again?

3. May I ______________________? I didn't get the last part.

4. Excuse me. Could you ______________________ that, please?

5. I'm sorry. Would you say that ______________________, please?

TOTAL ____/100 pts.

Name ______________________ Date ______________ Score ____________

Chapter 2 Test

Section I Listening to a Conversation Answer the questions about the conversation. **(3 points each)**

1. The first student isn't sure about ________.
- (A) why anyone would want to learn about cultures
- (B) the value of working in small groups
- (C) getting a good grade in the course

2. In the first student's country, students usually ________.
- (A) do a lot of small-group work
- (B) just listen to a lecture
- (C) do not take notes

3. The second student suggests that ________.
- (A) students don't like listening to lectures
- (B) it's OK not to pay attention during small-group work
- (C) instructors want students to learn more by cooperating

4. Which expression asks for confirmation of understanding?
- (A) "I don't know exactly what you mean. Are you saying . . .?"
- (B) "Maybe you're right, but this is a language class."
- (C) "Do you think it's a good way to learn?"

5. Which of the following is an example of classmates cooperating?
- (A) listening to the audio as a class
- (B) taking notes during a lecture
- (C) listening to each other in small groups

Section II Listening to a Lecture Answer the questions about the lecture. **(3 points each)**

1. The lecture is about ________.
- (A) African lions cooperating to get food
- (B) African lions competing for mates
- (C) the African plains teeming with life

2. An example of lion cooperation is ________.
- (A) four lions hunting one zebra
- (B) male lions fighting over a mate
- (C) lions watching another lion hunt small prey

3. The professor implies that ________.
- (A) lions are very intelligent animals
- (B) lions find it difficult to work together
- (C) lions don't cooperate when they don't have to

4. The student says, "I'm not sure I understand." Another way to say this is, ________.
- (A) "Does that answer your question?"
- (B) "I don't know exactly what you mean."
- (C) "I disagree with your idea."

5. What prediction can we make?
   - (A) The next lecture will be about animal cooperation.
   - (B) The next lecture will be about human competition.
   - (C) The next lecture will be about animal competition.

Section III New Words Fill in each blank with a word from the Word List. (There are more words in the Word List than there are blanks.) **(3 points each)**

awkward	Celsius	ecosystem	ferocious	battle
desolate	Fahrenheit	migratory	beachfront	disposition
fast	teem	catastrophe		

The Antarctic ________(1), which includes only a few animal and insect species, is unique on earth. To begin with, Antarctica is extremely cold. On a summer day, the temperature might reach zero degrees ________(2), which is thirty-two degrees ________(3). On the ________(4), near the water's edge, you may see large birds with a very ________(5) way of walking. They're penguins, of course, whose enemies include the ________(6) leopard seal as well as ________(7) birds that live part of the time in South America and sometimes steal the penguin's eggs. Penguins generally have a quiet ________(8), although males sometimes ________(9) for a mate. One of the most interesting things about penguins is that they must ________(10) for long periods because their nesting grounds are far from their food source—the ocean.

Section IV Using Language Complete the conversation with the phrases from the box. **(8 points each)**

Are you saying that	I see what you mean	I'm not sure I understand
because Mike got a new video game	that I don't have to do chores on Saturday	

Mother: Did you clean up your room like I asked you to?

Child: I didn't clean up my room ________(1).

Mother: I'm not sure I'm getting this. ______________ (2) Mike's new video game is more important than your chores?

Child: No, but it's a really important game.

Mother: ______________ (3). Do you mean to say that the video game is a big part of your life, like your family and your home?

Child: ______________ (4). I'll clean up my room right now.

Mother: That's better. You can play video games with Mike on Saturday.

Child: Am I right? Are you saying ______________ (5)?

Mother: That's right. Now hurry up and clean your room.

TOTAL ____ /100 pts.

Name ______________________ Date ______________ Score ____________

Chapter 3 Test

Section I Listening to a Conversation Answer the questions about the conversation. **(3 points each)**

1. The student didn't understand the part of the lecture about ______.

(A) why Americans live in extended families
(B) the increase in household size
(C) Americans not feeling isolated

2. The professor implied that ______.

(A) many Americans don't like their relatives
(B) Americans should live with their extended families
(C) many people make an incorrect assumption about Americans

3. The average number of people in a U.S. household is ______.

(A) 1.9
(B) 2.5
(C) 2.9

4. The straw-man argument used by the professor was ______.

(A) people outside the U.S. frequently live in extended families
(B) Americans feel isolated because of small household size
(C) the size of households in the U.S. has decreased since 1991

5. According to the conversation, Americans prefer to live ______.

(A) where they can easily visit family members
(B) with several relatives
(C) alone

Section II Listening to a Lecture Answer the questions about the lecture. **(3 points each)**

1. The lecture is about ______.

(A) options for care of the elderly
(B) reasons to consider nursing homes
(C) problems with home healthcare

2. The professor implies that ______.

(A) residents must share rooms in assisted living facilities
(B) elderly people are unhappy in nursing homes
(C) home healthcare isn't a good choice for seriously ill people

3. Families who hire nurses to provide home healthcare ______.

(A) are still responsible for medications
(B) have help with certain medical therapies
(C) don't have to worry about meals

4. "By and large, these facilities look like ordinary apartment complexes." In this sentence, the professor means that ______.

(A) assisted living facilities are seldom a good option

(B) assisted living facilities usually resemble apartment complexes
(C) assisted living facilities are as big as apartment complexes

5. What assumption does the professor make?
(A) Learning about elderly care options will confuse the listeners.
(B) The listeners do not have any elderly relatives.
(C) It's better to learn about elderly care options before one needs to make a decision about them.

Section III New Words Match each word on the left with its definition on the right. Write the letter of the correct definition on the line. **(5 points each)**

_______	**1.** assumption	**a.** people living under one roof, often a family living together
_______	**2.** household	**b.** not closely connected
_______	**3.** extended family	**c.** a family group consisting of parent(s), children, and other close relatives living either together or near each other
_______	**4.** statistics	**d.** brothers and sisters
_______	**5.** data	**e.** alone; separated from other people
_______	**6.** siblings	**f.** a collection of numerical data
_______	**7.** disjointed	**g.** information (which could include facts and statistics)
_______	**8.** isolated	**h.** something someone believes, which may or may not be true

Section IV Using Language Look at the statistics. Then circle the correct adverb of time in each sentence. **(6 points each)**

1. Seventy-seven percent of elderly Polish people have visited their children within the past week.

Elderly Polish people (rarely / typically) see their children at least once a week.

2. In Norway, 8 percent of the elderly live within ten minutes of their children.

Elderly Norwegians (by and large / seldom) live near their children.

3. Eighty-six percent of elderly Americans say they would prefer to live in their own homes.

(Hardly ever / For the most part) elderly Americans prefer to live in their own homes.

4. In Denmark, 58 percent of women and 32 percent of men have seen a sibling within the past week.

Danish women (normally / rarely) visit their siblings more than Danish men.

5. Six percent of elderly people in Great Britain have seen a grandchild within the past week.

(Seldom do / Generally speaking) elderly people in Great Britain see their grandchildren.

TOTAL ____/100 pts.

Name ______________________ Date ______________ Score ____________

Chapter 4 Test

Section I Listening to a Conversation Answer the questions about the conversation. **(3 points each)**

1. The woman wants to run fast ______.
- (A) to rest her cardiac muscles
- (B) to lose weight
- (C) to increase her heart rate

2. The man mentions writing a paper because ______.
- (A) he is not having a good time
- (B) he has a homework assignment due
- (C) he wants to go home

3. The man's opinion is that ______.
- (A) they should exercise more often
- (B) the woman wouldn't enjoy the park
- (C) they would both enjoy going for a walk

4. The man says, "… and check out the gelato stand to see if there are any new flavors …" Gelato is ______.
- (A) a newspaper
- (B) a frozen dessert
- (C) a type of bicycle

5. The woman does not think it is healthy to ______.
- (A) walk in the park
- (B) run fast
- (C) eat ice cream

Section II Listening to a Lecture Answer the questions about the lecture. **(3 points each)**

1. The professor's main purpose is to ______.
- (A) present information about heart attacks
- (B) describe two types of heart disease
- (C) outline ways to prevent heart disease

2. CAD stands for ______.
- (A) cardiac arterial disorder
- (B) coronary artery disease
- (C) cardiac arrest disease

3. The professor says, "… you should do everything possible to avoid a heart attack, which can cause part of the heart to die when it's deprived of oxygen." "Deprived of" means ______.
- (A) getting
- (B) carrying
- (C) lacking

4. The professor compares heart failure to ______.
- (A) an inefficient heart

(B) fluid in the lungs
(C) a leaky water pump

5. The professor implies that ________.
(A) he doesn't believe CAD is caused by high levels of fat in the blood
(B) some people don't share his opinions about preventing heart disease through diet
(C) exercising 30 minutes almost every day is too much for some people

Section III New Words Fill in each blank with a word from the Word List. **(5 points each)**

cardiac muscles	peel	tick-tock	chambers
vary	hollow	strip	pump

1. You might get bored with your exercise routine if you never ________________ it.
2. Blood travels through the four ________________ of the human heart.
3. The ________________ of the human heart is actually the sound of the heart valves opening and closing.
4. You need to remove the ________________ before you eat a mango.
5. Some balls, such as basketballs and soccer balls, are ________________ inside, while golf balls and baseballs are not.
6. Weak ________________ can cause the heart to work inefficiently.
7. He wrote his telephone number on a small ________________ of paper.
8. The heart is able to ________________ blood throughout the entire body.

Section IV Using Language Fill in each blank with a word from the box. (There are more words than questions.) **(6 points each)**

clam	lamb	positive	free	like
pretty	ghost	nice	similar	

1. In some ways, the heart is ________________ to a water pump.
2. I am ________________ that this information will not be on the test.

3. Her face turned as white as a ______________________ when she heard the news.

4. The eye is ______________________ the lens of a camera.

5. The girls in their new dresses were as ______________________ as a picture.

TOTAL ____/100 pts.

Name ______________________ Date ______________ Score ____________

Chapter 5 Test

Section I Listening to a Conversation Answer the questions about the conversation. **(3 points each)**

1. The woman is talking about ______.

(A) a television news story
(B) a radio news story
(C) an Internet news story

2. According to the story, there was a problem with ______.

(A) the space station
(B) a spacecraft
(C) the earth's atmosphere

3. According to the woman, ______ was needed in order to achieve orbit.

(A) more fuel
(B) another Brazilian astronaut
(C) greater acceleration

4. The woman says, "The astronauts were told to return to earth ..." which means that ______.

(A) someone told the astronauts to return
(B) the astronauts did not want to return
(C) the astronauts decided to return

5. The man and woman will probably ______.

(A) ask a friend what happened
(B) listen to the rest of the story
(C) wonder if the spacecraft landed safely

Section II Listening to a Lecture Answer the questions about the lecture. **(3 points each)**

1. The tour guide's main purpose is to ______.

(A) discuss problems with the Apollo 13 mission and how they were solved
(B) defend government spending for the space program
(C) describe the way mission control set the shortest possible course for Apollo 13

2. The tour guide asks if it seems strange to start the tour with the Apollo 13 exhibit because ______.

(A) Apollo 13 did not land on the moon
(B) the Apollo 13 astronauts made it back to earth
(C) the Apollo 13 spacecraft is not in the museum

3. The Apollo 13 astronauts had to travel ______ miles with very limited power.

(A) 2,000
(B) 20,000
(C) 200,000

4. A student tells the tour guide, "... the mission of Apollo 13 wasn't accomplished." The student uses the passive voice because ______.

(A) the focus of the sentence is the mission, not the people who didn't accomplish it

(B) it is uncertain who participated in the mission
(C) the mission took place at an indefinite time in the past

5. One difficult aspect of returning the Apollo 13 spacecraft to earth was ________.
(A) there had been an explosion in the lithium hydroxide canisters
(B) mission control was unable to communicate with the astronauts
(C) the spacecraft was very remote at the time of the explosion

Section III New Words Match each word on the left with its definition on the right. Write the letter of the correct definition on the line. **(3 points each)**

______	**1.** orbit	**a.** travel back and forth frequently
______	**2.** simulate	**b.** of or about the sun
______	**3.** friction	**c.** copy the appearance or effect of something
______	**4.** acceleration	**d.** to control
______	**5.** solar	**e.** the circular path one body makes around another body in space
______	**6.** mission	**f.** an object or vehicle that orbits the earth or another body in space
______	**7.** cargo bay	**g.** the process of increasing speed
______	**8.** satellite	**h.** resistance to motion of two surfaces that are touching
______	**9.** manipulate	**i.** a special job or assignment given to a person or group
______	**10.** shuttle	**j.** an area in an airplane or spaceship used to keep special goods or materials

Section IV Using Language Fill in each blank with either the passive or active form of the verb in parentheses. **(8 points each)**

1. The space program ____________________ (fund) by tax revenue.

2. Some people ____________________ (think) that the costs of the space program are too high.

3. Those people believe that money should ____________________ (spend) on necessities such as food and education.

4. The communications satellites that make cell phones work ______________________ (invent) as a result of the space program.

5. A great deal of military technology also ______________________ (come) from the space program.

TOTAL ____/100 pts.

Name ______________________ Date ______________ Score ____________

Chapter 6 Test

Section I Listening to a Conversation Answer the questions about the conversation. **(3 points each)**

1. The friends are talking about ______.
- (A) loaning money to friends
- (B) getting a new roommate
- (C) spending twenty dollars

2. The woman says, "You can say that again!" which means ______.
- (A) "I disagree with you."
- (B) "Please repeat what you said."
- (C) "I agree with you."

3. According to the conversation, ______ borrowed money from the man.
- (A) the woman
- (B) the man's roommate
- (C) nobody

4. The woman says, "You've got to be kidding!" which means ______.
- (A) "That's really funny."
- (B) "I disagree with you."
- (C) "I agree with you."

5. We can infer from the conversation that ______.
- (A) the woman has a job
- (B) the man doesn't like his roommate
- (C) the man will loan the woman money

Section II Listening to a Lecture Answer the questions about the lecture. **(3 points each)**

1. Dr. Young's main purpose is to ______.
- (A) inform listeners about how to get microcredit
- (B) describe the disadvantages of microcredit
- (C) explain what microcredit is

2. The Grameen Bank was founded ______.
- (A) in 1979
- (B) in Bangladesh
- (C) by Dr. Young

3. According to Dr. Young, one of the advantages of microcredit is ______.
- (A) people can repay the money with interest over time
- (B) poor people cannot borrow money from conventional banks
- (C) poor people can improve their standard of living

4. The radio host says, "On the other hand, isn't it difficult for poor people to repay even small loans?" The man is implying that ______.
- (A) he thinks this is a disadvantage of microcredit

(B) he thinks the Grameen Bank takes advantage of poor people
(C) he can't see any "pros" to microcredit

5. Dr. Young says, "I guess you could say that, Mark, but the system seems to be working and alleviating poverty all over the world," which means ________.
(A) she disagrees with the man
(B) she thinks the peer pressure system is too harsh
(C) she agrees with the man

Section III New Words Fill in each blank with a word from the Word List. (There are more words in the list than there are blanks.) **(3 points each)**

alleviate	environmental	irrigation	free
borrow	insiders	loan	under fire
invest	proposal	snail	breed

1. The stated mission of the World Bank is to ____________ poverty in the world.
2. Some countries ____________ money from the World Bank for infrastructure development.
3. A project in Cameroon built ____________ systems for carrying water to fields.
4. Sometimes the World Bank is ____________ due to concerns about damaging the environment.
5. During part of the year, a species of ____________ could carry a tropical disease.
6. There are other types of animals that ____________ in warm water.
7. ____________ are people who work in or work closely with an organization.
8. The government of Thailand made a ____________ to build a dam on a large river.
9. Local people were worried about ____________ problems such as loss of habitat for fish species.
10. Eventually, the World Bank decided to ____________ in the dam because of the country's need for electricity.

Section IV Using Language Circle the correct word in parentheses. **(8 points each)**

1. **Speaker 1:** This pizza is delicious!

   Speaker 2: That's a laugh!

   Speaker 2 (agrees/disagrees) with Speaker 1.

2. **Speaker 1:** I'll never pass this course. It's just too hard.

   Speaker 2: I'm sorry, but I don't agree.

   Speaker 2 is being (formal/informal).

3. **Speaker 1:** This baseball team is the best in the league.

   Speaker 2: You'd better believe it!

   Speaker 2 (agrees/disagrees) with Speaker 1.

4. **Speaker 1:** We should get together for coffee every week.

   Speaker 2: You're right.

   Speaker 2 is being (formal/informal).

5. **Speaker 1:** I just don't have enough time to have a job while I'm in school.

   Speaker 2: Yes, but isn't it also true that you need more money?

   Speaker 2 (agrees/disagrees) with Speaker 1.

TOTAL ____/100 pts.

Name ______________________ Date ______________ Score ____________

Chapter 7 Test

Section I Listening to a Conversation Answer the questions about the conversation. **(3 points each)**

1. The couple is talking about ______.

(A) which movie Julia Roberts is in

(B) which movie to see

(C) which movie is a comedy

2. The woman says, "Ben Stiller bugs me," which means ______.

(A) she dislikes Ben Stiller

(B) she likes Ben Stiller

(C) she thinks Ben Stiller is funny

3. The woman especially likes ______.

(A) comedies

(B) dramas

(C) James Bond movies

4. The woman suggests a movie that ______.

(A) neither of them will like

(B) takes place in Egypt

(C) is a compromise between suspense and drama

5. The man says, "I just can't take another movie starring Julia Roberts," which means ______.

(A) he doesn't think he would enjoy seeing that movie

(B) he would be delighted if Julia Roberts made another movie

(C) he thinks he already saw the Julia Roberts movie

Section II Listening to a Lecture Answer the questions about the lecture. **(3 points each)**

1. The professor wants to ______.

(A) explain what made Wauneka a remarkable person

(B) compare Wauneka's accomplishments with those of other remarkable people

(C) describe how Wauneka tackled the tuberculosis problem among the Navajo people

2. The professor says, "Today, I am pleased to continue our series on remarkable individuals," which means ______.

(A) he enjoys talking about remarkable individuals

(B) he is happy that the lecture is today

(C) he is hoping the students don't mind if he talks about remarkable individuals

3. Wauneka was elected to the Navajo Tribal Council in ______.

(A) 1910

(B) 1951

(C) 1959

4. The professor says that Wauneka "launched a battle against tuberculosis," which means ______.

(A) Wauneka became infected with the disease

(B) Wauneka began to fight the disease
(C) Wauneka found a cure for the disease

5. Wauneka received the award for Outstanding Worker in Public Health ________.
(A) before she had children
(B) before she was elected to the Navajo Tribal Council
(C) before she received the Presidential Medal of Freedom

Section III New Words Fill in each blank with a word from the Word List. (There are more words in the list than there are blanks.) **(3 points each)**

battle	fluke	keep up with	from scratch
be riding high	chemotherapy	highlight	undisciplined
hit-and-run	vertebra	bull	endure

When I was younger, I thought of my father as a kind of superhero; he was as strong as a ____________ (1) and as handsome as a movie star. I could barely ____________ (2) him when he ran. But that was before his ____________ (3) with cancer, which the doctor found just by a ____________ (4). It was after my father was the victim of a ____________ (5) car accident. He was stopped at a red light when another car struck his car and then just kept going, right through the red light! My father wasn't badly hurt, but when the doctor took an X-ray of his back, he saw a dark spot on a ____________ (6) that didn't look good. It turned out to be a tumor, and it had spread to his backbone from his liver. Soon after that, my father had to ____________ (7) several surgeries and ____________ (8) treatments. To make him feel better, I used to bake him chocolate chip cookies ____________ (9), and he always said that those cookies were the ____________ (10) of his time in the hospital. I'm delighted to tell you that my father is still around and cancer-free, and to me, he's still a kind of superhero.

Section IV Using Language Put the events in chronological order. **(8 points each)**

a) When Richard left the restaurant, all of the employees had gone home for the night.
b) He then caught a glimpse of something shiny under the streetlight.
c) He locked the door and started walking toward his car.

1. Which event should be first? ________

2. Which event should be second? ________

3. Which event should be third? ______
   d) By then, the dog had eaten almost all of it.
   e) Jenna grabbed what remained of the chocolate bar.

4. Which event should be first? ______

5. Which event should be second? ______

TOTAL ____/100 pts.

Name ______________________ Date ______________ Score ______________

Chapter 8 Test

Section I Listening to a Conversation Answer the questions about the conversation. **(3 points each)**

1. The friends are talking about _______.
- (A) the cost of air travel
- (B) a friend's problem
- (C) a friend's mother

2. The woman says, "... what's really going on is... " because _______.
- (A) she thinks the man already knows about Ian
- (B) she hasn't seen the man in a long time
- (C) she wants the man to know the truth

3. The woman says, "... maybe I should explain something... " which means that the next thing she says will probably be _______.
- (A) an example of something
- (B) a reason for something
- (C) a repetition of something

4. The woman suggests _______.
- (A) talking to Ian about his problem
- (B) going to class together
- (C) giving Ian money to buy a plane ticket

5. The man plans to make phone calls to _______.
- (A) Ian's friends
- (B) Ian's family
- (C) Ian's travel agent

Section II Listening to a Lecture Answer the questions about the lecture. **(3 points each)**

1. The main topic of the lecture is _______.
- (A) using creative writing exercises to increase vocabulary
- (B) the value of poetry in prison settings
- (C) ways in which people use creative writing exercises

2. According to the lecture, language learners can improve their reading skills by _______.
- (A) writing a dialogue
- (B) making a word map
- (C) releasing emotions

3. The professor says, "I want to describe one more case... ," which means that the next part of the lecture will contain _______.
- (A) an outline of creative writing exercises
- (B) a definition of creative writing
- (C) details about a particular use of creative writing exercises

4. The professor says, "… but in fact, creative writing is also a *process*… ," which means ______.

(A) creative writing is never finished
(B) the lecture will include an example
(C) this is little known information

5. According to the lecture, the prisoners use poetry writing "… as a tool of self-discovery… ," which means ______.

(A) they realize new things about themselves when they write
(B) they use poetry as a way to forget the past
(C) they write poems as a way to pass the time

Section III New Words Write the letter of the correct definition in each blank. **(5 points each)**

______	**1.** fuse	**a.** the first or only one
______	**2.** analytical	**b.** broken into parts
______	**3.** solution	**c.** answer to a problem
______	**4.** inhibit	**d.** block or frustrate
______	**5.** fragmentary	**e.** considering all details in order to understand completely
______	**6.** original	**f.** join together into a single thing

Section IV Using Language Fill in each blank with the best signal word from the box. (There are more words in the box than there are blanks.) **(8 points each)**

answer	describe	list
repeat	illustrate	continue

1. Welcome back, everyone. Today, we'll ______________ our look at modern architecture with an introduction to the architectural designs of Frank Lloyd Wright.

2. First, I want to ______________ Wright's Prairie Style designs by telling you about some of the features his houses from that period had in common.

3. Wright's Prairie Style designs featured ground-hugging lines, expansive windows, and a central fireplace, to ______________ just a few features.

4. I can ______________________ this style by showing you a picture of Taliesin, Wright's own home.

5. Before I go on, I'd like to ______________________ any questions you might have about the Prairie Style.

TOTAL ____/100 pts.

Name ________________ Date ________________ Score ________________

Chapter 9 Test

Section I Listening to a Conversation Answer the questions about the conversation. **(3 points each)**

1. The main point of the conversation is ________.
(A) the woman wants to change volunteer jobs
(B) the man will give the woman a ride to the food pantry
(C) the woman feels unappreciated at the food pantry

2. The man is surprised to see the woman because ________.
(A) she has a class on Tuesday evenings
(B) she has been very busy volunteering
(C) she usually volunteers at this time

3. The man thinks the woman will like working at the food pantry because ________.
(A) she could help homeless animals
(B) she could help people with children
(C) she could sleep late on Tuesdays

4. The man says, "You'd like a ride there, wouldn't you?" because ________.
(A) he knows she'll want a ride
(B) he assumes she would rather ride her bike
(C) he is checking to see if she wants a ride

5. The friends will probably work at the food pantry ________.
(A) from 7:00 to 8:00
(B) from 8:00 to 10:00
(C) from 6:00 to 8:00

Section II Listening to a Lecture Answer the questions about the lecture. **(3 points each)**

1. The lecturer is talking about ________.
(A) ways to improve campus organizations
(B) ways to keep volunteers happy
(C) ways to recruit volunteers

2. The professor says, "… to return to what I was saying …," which means ________.
(A) he wants to repeat the main points
(B) he wants to get back to the main topic
(C) he wants students to take notes

3. The professor says, "… many people volunteer in order to develop their skill sets," which means that ________.
(A) they want to get better grades
(B) they want to improve their social lives
(C) they want to learn to do new things

4. The professor says, "Let me just mention that …," which means ________.
(A) this is somewhat off the topic

Ⓑ the information is unimportant
Ⓒ he wants to get back to the main topic

5. According to the lecture, training and involvement in goal setting ______.
Ⓐ are important to idealistic volunteers
Ⓑ are important to volunteers who want to improve their social lives
Ⓒ are important to volunteers who want to develop their skill sets

Section III New Words Fill in each blank with a word from the Word List. (There are more words in the box than there are blanks.) **(5 points each)**

eye contact	wind	random	identity
pretty much	field of interest	recap	

1. The good news is that my old watch doesn't need batteries. The bad news is that I have to remember to ______________________ it.

2. Margaret Mead's main ______________________ was anthropology, but she also enjoyed music and art.

3. I think that professors should ______________________ their main points at the end of a lecture.

4. The police were suspicious because the suspect did not make ______________________ while they were talking to him.

5. You can ______________________ assume that Ms. Royko's final exam will be difficult. Her exams are almost always tough ones.

6. Salvador Dali seemed to enjoy his ______________________ as the "mad artist."

Section IV Using Language Fill in each blank with a word from the box. (There are more words in the box than there are blanks.) **(8 points each)**

continue	saying	off	say
digress	on	reminds	way

As you can see, Galileo did not have an easy life. By the ______________________ (1), has anyone in the class been to Italy? To go ______________________ (2) the topic for just a moment, when I traveled there, I saw the part of Florence where Galileo lived, and it was fascinating! Well, to come back to what I was ____________________ (3), Galileo's life was not glamorous. He grew much of his own food in a small garden. Oh, that ____________________ (4) me, if anyone wants them, I brought a sack of tomatoes from my garden. Just come up and help yourselves after class. All right, as I started to ____________________ (5), we have to imagine that Galileo needed the financial support of the de Medici family.

TOTAL ____/100 pts.

Name ______________________ Date ______________ Score ____________

Chapter 10 Test

Section I Listening to a Conversation Answer the questions about the conversation. **(3 points each)**

1. The purpose of the conversation is to ______.
- (A) clarify a point made in a lecture
- (B) discuss the definition of legal insanity
- (C) compare free will and predetermination

2. The student says, "I hope you can help me understand something ...," which means ______.
- (A) the student is optimistic about the professor being able to help
- (B) the student is apologizing for not understanding last week's lecture
- (C) the student is pessimistic about being able to understand

3. The professor says that when people are legally insane, ______.
- (A) they are free to commit crimes
- (B) they do not have free will
- (C) they are more likely to steal cars

4. The professor tells the student not to worry about interrupting because ______.
- (A) the professor is not busy
- (B) the professor is supposed to help students at that time
- (C) the student was absent for last week's lecture

5. The professor says that the legal system ______.
- (A) punishes people who choose to commit crimes
- (B) encourages mentally ill people to commit crimes
- (C) is not in control of a criminal's actions

Section II Listening to a Lecture Answer the questions about the lecture. **(3 points each)**

1. The lecturer is talking about ______.
- (A) early ideas about physical characteristics of criminals
- (B) Darwinism in the nineteenth century
- (C) early theories on causes of criminal behavior

2. We can infer from the lecture that phrenologists ______.
- (A) studied unattractive people
- (B) examined people's skulls
- (C) looked at numerous photographs

3. The professor says that Lombroso, "... hoped that scientists might be able to prevent crime ...," which means that ______.
- (A) he believed the police were unable to fight crime effectively
- (B) he was pessimistic about reducing the number of criminals
- (C) he wanted scientists to help society

4. Which of the following facial features was not mentioned in the lecture?
   (A) drooping eyes
   (B) large nose
   (C) sloping forehead

5. The professor says, "If only it were that easy ...," which means that ________.
   (A) catching criminals was less difficult in the nineteenth century
   (B) the professor wishes scientists could prevent crime
   (C) the professor is pessimistic about using facial features to identify criminals

Section III New Words Match each word or phrase on the left with its definition on the right. Write the letter of the correct definition on the line. **(5 points each)**

______ **1.** programmed — **a.** belief that all events in a person's life have already been decided

______ **2.** life-and-death — **b.** philosophy that good and bad things we do determine what will happen to us

______ **3.** violation — **c.** regret or bad feeling for doing something wrong

______ **4.** remorse — **d.** rebirth of spirits or souls into new bodies or forms of life

______ **5.** free will — **e.** very important, as if your life depends on it

______ **6.** reincarnation — **f.** controlled to do a certain thing or behave in a certain way automatically

______ **7.** karma — **g.** a wrongdoing, a serious mistake or something illegal

______ **8.** predetermination — **h.** freedom that humans have to make choices

Section IV Using Language Fill in each blank with a word from the box. (There are more words in the box than there are blanks.) **(6 points each)**

hope	knew	know	need
use	will	wish	

I'm going to a lecture on world religions next week because I'm very curious about different philosophies of life. I ____________ (1) the lecturer talks about Buddhism because I want to ____________ (2) more about karma and reincarnation. I could also ____________ (3) a reminder about John Calvin and his ideas about predetermination and how God has a plan for every aspect of people's lives. If only I ____________ (4) what that plan was, I could stop worrying about all my decisions! Well, maybe not. I think that according to most religions, people still have free ____________ (5), and I'm choosing to go to that lecture to learn more about all of this.

TOTAL ____/100 pts.

Chapter 1 Test Audioscript

Section I Listening to a Conversation

Student 1: I'm glad we decided to go over the lecture notes together. I need clarification on a few points, but I'm too shy to interrupt the professor in class.

Student 2: I know what you mean, but I really don't think the professor minds if you interrupt as long as you do it politely. Why not give it a try next time?

Student 1: You're right. I'll be brave next time! Now, could we talk about what the professor said about languages affecting our way of seeing the world? That didn't make much sense to me. Did you understand it?

Student 2: I think the idea is that since languages have such different vocabularies, speakers of different languages can think in different ways. Are you following me?

Student 1: I'm not sure ...

Student 2: Well, if your language has seven different words for seven different types of bread that people in your culture usually eat, and my language has only two, then maybe people who speak my language think about bread in a more limited way. And if we start importing a new type of bread from your country, we have to borrow your word for it, too, since our language doesn't have one. Got it?

Student 1: I see. That's why the professor talked about eating a *croissant*!

Section II Listening to a Lecture

Good morning! Today we will begin the next topic in the Introduction to Linguistics course: historical linguistics. As you probably know, most languages belong to a language family, which is a group of related languages. The reason these language families exist is that languages change over time. The interesting thing about historical linguistics is that when you try to determine which languages are in the same family, you have to travel back in time searching for the common language that all the languages in the family descended from.

When grouping languages into families, historical linguists use a technique called "comparative reconstruction", which means comparing modern languages to reconstruct an older "ancestor" language. The two most useful parts of languages to compare are vocabulary and phonology, which is the sound system of a language. Let's start with vocabulary. In comparative reconstruction, linguists look for identical or very similar words for the most basic ideas, such as the natural world or family relationships. Latin-based languages, for instance, have very similar words for "moon": *luna* in Spanish, Italian, Portuguese, and Romanian, and *lune* in French. This similarity means that these languages used to have even more in common than they do now, before all the changes occurred that made them separate languages. This common vocabulary is also a glimpse into the cultures and lifestyles of people in the past. For example, if there is an ancient word for "coffee", we can assume people in a past time and place were familiar with that plant.

The second method of grouping languages into families involves analyzing sounds. Phonological analysis looks for systematic changes in sounds over time, or systematic differences between languages. For example, most of the Polynesian languages have the identical word for "face"—*mata*. The Hawaiian language has a very similar word—*maka*, with a /k/ instead of a /t/. This might seem close enough for most of us, but linguists look for something systematic, and in fact, Hawaiian regularly transforms the /t/ sound to /k/. We can see another example in the word for "blood", which is *toto* in most Polynesian languages, and *koko* in Hawaiian. This systematic difference convinces linguists that Hawaiian is part of the Polynesian language family.

To summarize, the goal of historical linguistics is to reconstruct languages of the past. They do this by comparing the vocabulary and phonology of modern languages in order to find elements from their common past.

Chapter 2 Test Audioscript

Section I Listening to a Conversation

Student 1: Hi, Danny. Let me ask you a question. Does it seem like we spend too much time in small groups in this class?

Student 2: To tell you the truth, I never thought about it. Does the small-group work bother you?

Student 1: Well, I'm just not used to it, I guess. In my country, we usually listen to the professor and take notes, but we don't do much small group work. Do you think it's a good way to learn?

Student 2: I think teachers here see it as a way for students to cooperate and learn more by working together.

Student 1: I don't know exactly what you mean. Are you saying that we can learn from other students? But they don't know any more than we do, right?

Student 2: Maybe you're right, but this is a language class. When we do small-group work, everyone has a chance to talk and practice the new language. And I think we can learn things from each other if we listen carefully. For example, I can learn something from you about your culture, or something from another student who uses a lot of vocabulary words.

Student 1: I see what you mean. If we cooperate with our classmates, maybe we can all learn this language!

Section II Listening to a Lecture

Professor: Welcome back to Zoology 102 everyone! Last time, we talked about situations in which animals are likely to compete, for example, when they're establishing their territory or battling for a desirable mate. Today we will turn our attention to a situation in which one particular animal, the African lion, cooperates in order to get food.

The African plains are teeming with life, and you might think that food is easy to obtain for ferocious predators such as lions. But many of the prey animals are quite large—for example, zebras and water buffalo. Therefore, lions, more often the females, sometimes hunt in groups in order to share these sources of food.

Lions are not designed for long chases, so when they hunt together, they start by carefully positioning themselves. One lion gets in front of the prey animal, while another lion attacks from behind and drives the animal forward. Other lions are usually on the sides so that the animal cannot escape in those directions. As soon as one of the lions has a hold on the animal, the others quickly join in, and the prey animal becomes a shared meal.

Now, lions are famous for their somewhat lazy disposition, and it is not always in the best interest of lions to cooperate when hunting. If a lion is hunting a smaller animal, the other lions may simply watch and wait. Since the hunting lion is likely to be successful by herself, the other lions see no reason to waste their energy helping when they will all be able to share in the meal anyway.

Student: Excuse me, I'm not sure I understand. Do you mean that lions are cooperative sometimes, but will take advantage of each other at other times?

Professor: That's a pretty good summary. From a biological perspective, lions want to conserve their energy and avoid being injured, so not hunting makes sense sometimes. But they also need to eat, so a hungry lion will attack a small prey animal when the opportunity arises, or will hunt as part of a group if the reward is large. Does that answer your question?

Students: Yes, it does. Thanks.

Professor: As you can see, lions do cooperate when hunting, but only if the prey is large enough that another lion will probably not be able to kill it alone. Lions cooperate in other areas of life as well. Next time, we'll talk about why male lions join together in groups, and why nursing females often share their milk.

Chapter 3 Test Audioscript

Section I Listening to a Conversation

Student 1: Did you understand everything in the lecture today?

Student 2: I think so. Was there something that was confusing to you?

Student 1: Yeah, I was confused when the professor talked about Americans living in small households, and not in extended families.

Student 2: Right. The statistics on the handout said that since 1991, the size of the average household in the U.S. has decreased to only 2.5 people.

Student 1: OK, and the professor told us that we could assume Americans feel isolated from their families because of this small household size.

Student 2: Well, the professor said that's an assumption many people make, but according to statistics it's not really true. Americans generally don't feel isolated from their families because their families live nearby and they see each other pretty often. I guess Americans just like living in their own houses, but they still want to see their relatives.

Student 1: I see. I'm glad you understood that part!

Section II Listening to a Lecture

When an elderly person becomes ill or simply unable to do many of the things required in daily life, family members might need to make a decision about the elderly person's care. That difficult moment is probably not the best time to start gathering information on the topic of elderly care options, right? So today in the Seminar on Families and Aging we are going to look at several choices families should know about before deciding on the best situation for them.

Caring for an elderly family member at home appeals to many people emotionally. And if the elderly person isn't seriously ill, and if family members are usually at home and available, then it could be a good option. The important thing to remember is that while you can provide a lot of love, you can't provide much in the way of medical attention.

However, living with the family is still an option for some elderly people with health problems. In that situation, families can hire nurses to provide home healthcare. The family is still responsible for assisting the elderly person with daily activities such as eating and bathing, but the nurse can help with medications and certain therapies.

The next level of elderly care is the assisted living facility. By and large, these facilities look like ordinary apartment complexes, with each senior in his or her own private space. But assisted living facilities offer meals in a large dining room, laundry service, organized activities, and help with daily living activities. As long as the elderly person does not require frequent medical attention, this option is a good one for many families.

Finally, when an elderly person needs skilled nursing care around the clock, it may be time to think about a nursing home. Nursing homes provide the kind of medical therapies that can be difficult or impossible for family members to do, and they are able to assist elderly people with all of their daily activities, even if that means lifting them from a bed and lowering them into a bathtub.

As you can see, deciding how to care for an elderly family member depends a lot on the family's specific situation. If the elderly person is in fairly good health and can still do daily activities by themselves or with a little help from family members, then home healthcare may be an option. But if a higher level of care is needed, families can also consider assisted living facilities and nursing homes.

Chapter 4 Test Audioscript

Section I Listening to a Conversation

Man: (*out of breath*) Hey! Can we slow down? I'm pretty sure I'll die if we keep running this fast.

Woman: Okay, okay. But if we don't run fast, we won't get our heart rates up. You want to get enough exercise, don't you?

Man: Of course I do. But in my opinion, exercise is more beneficial if it's fun, and this is about as much fun as staying up all night to write a paper.

Woman: I guess you're right. They say people exercise more *often* if the exercise is something they enjoy.

Man: You know . . . I'm fairly certain that you would enjoy walking in the park with me. We can still get our heart rates up, but we can also have a conversation, and smell the flowers, and check out the gelato stand to see if there are any new flavors . . .

Woman: Alright, I get it. Let's go over to the park and have a nice, long walk. But we're not stopping to buy ice cream! Exercising is supposed to be *good* for your heart!

Section II Listening to a Lecture

Good morning, everyone. I hope you had a good weekend. I'm sure you remember that we started our unit on the heart last week. Today we'll talk about what can go wrong with the heart when people have heart disease.

You might think of heart disease as one single problem. But in fact, there are several types of heart disease that are quite distinct. Today we'll talk about two types of heart disease: coronary artery disease and heart failure.

If you've ever heard about someone having a heart attack, it was probably caused by coronary artery disease, or CAD. In CAD, the coronary arteries, which supply blood to the heart itself, become narrow or even blocked, resulting in chest pain, or even worse, a heart attack. Believe me, you should do everything possible to avoid a heart attack, which can cause part of the heart to die when it's deprived of oxygen. A heart attack can also cause *you* to die, so keep yourself healthy so that your heart keeps pumping blood the way it should.

Another type of heart disease is called heart failure, which does not mean that your heart stops beating altogether. It means that the heart doesn't pump blood efficiently, just like a leaky water pump that only moves some of the water it's supposed to move. A failing heart doesn't supply the body with all of the oxygen it needs, so it may cause people to become tired and short of breath, and in serious cases, fluid builds up in the lungs and other parts of the body. When this occurs it's called congestive heart failure, and it can eventually lead to death.

Alright, no wonder everyone is talking about ways to keep the heart healthy. You've probably heard that you should exercise for at least 30 minutes almost every day, and I'm positive that's an excellent idea for most people. And you've probably heard that you should eat a diet that is low in cholesterol and saturated fat. After all, the narrowing and blockage of the coronary arteries in CAD are caused by those fats in the blood. Well, not everyone will agree with me, but if you have a family history of heart disease and other risk factors such as high cholesterol, changing your diet probably won't help you much. I strongly believe that taking medications to control the level of cholesterol in the blood is much more effective than trying to control that level through diet.

To sum up, heart disease has several forms, and coronary artery disease and heart failure are just two of them. Next time we'll talk more about ways to prevent heart disease.

Chapter 5 Test Audioscript

Section I Listening to a Conversation

Woman: Hi, Mark. I'm listening to a radio news broadcast about the space station. Would you like to join me?

Man: Sure. What's going on with the space station?

Woman: Well, the spacecraft carrying the first Brazilian astronaut in history was supposed to go to the International Space Station today.

Man: That's great!

Woman: Yes, but there were problems during takeoff. The spacecraft wasn't able to accelerate enough to exit the earth's atmosphere and go into orbit.

Man: So what happened?

Woman: The astronauts were told to return to earth and make an emergency landing.

Man: That's pretty scary. Let's listen and find out if they made it back to earth safely.

Section II Listening to a Lecture

Tour Guide: Hello, and welcome to the National Air and Space Museum. We're going to begin our tour this afternoon with the Apollo 13 exhibit. Does that seem strange to any of you?

Student 1: Well, if I remember correctly, the mission of Apollo 13 wasn't accomplished. They never landed on the moon.

Tour Guide: You're right. The Apollo 13 mission was supposed to be NASA's third moon landing, but one of the spacecraft's oxygen tanks was damaged by an explosion and the crew had to return to earth. But the really interesting thing about the Apollo 13 mission is how the problems caused by the explosion were solved by the astronauts and mission control working together.

Apollo 13 was launched on April 11, 1970, as two connected spacecraft: the lunar module that was supposed to land on the moon's surface, and the command module where the astronauts would spend most of their time in space. The crisis began after two days in space with an explosion in one of the command module's oxygen tanks. Of course, oxygen is critical for people, but it was also needed by the fuel cells that provided heat and electrical power to the spacecraft. The Apollo 13 astronauts were 200,000 miles from earth, and they were in big trouble.

Student 2: So what happened next? How did the astronauts survive without oxygen?

Tour Guide: Well, fortunately, there was still a limited amount of oxygen aboard the spacecraft. From the ground, mission control worked quickly to help the astronauts set the shortest course back to earth and shut down everything possible to conserve power. The crew headed for home with very little oxygen or water in a dark spacecraft where the inside temperature had dropped to 38 degrees Fahrenheit, and they had a *long* way to go.

The best-known part of the return trip involved a very low-tech solution to the problem of removing carbon dioxide caused by the astronauts' breathing. With the command module losing power quickly, the astronauts moved to the smaller lunar module for the journey home. But the square canisters of lithium hydroxide that were needed to remove the carbon dioxide buildup could not be attached to the round hoses in the lunar module. With the help of mission control, astronaut Jack Swigert used cardboard from the back of a notebook, plastic bags, and tape to connect the square canisters to the round hoses! Maybe not the most sophisticated technology, but it got the astronauts safely back to earth.

Chapter 6 Test Audioscript

Section I Listening to a Conversation

Man: Hey, Chris. Do you have a minute?

Woman: Sure. What's up?

Man: I want to ask your opinion about something. My roommate doesn't have enough money for rent this month, and wants to borrow the money from me. But I think it's a mistake to loan money to friends.

Woman: You can say that again!

Man: On the other hand, we're supposed to help our friends when they're in trouble, right? So I should help my roommate.

Woman: Absolutely!

Man: But loans to friends can cause problems if they don't get paid back. Now that I think about it, you never paid me back that twenty dollars I loaned you last month!

Woman: (*jovial tone*) You've got to be kidding! I gave you your twenty dollars as soon as I got my paycheck!

Section II Listening to a Lecture

(Male) DJ Mark: Good morning, Rochester! You're listening to Mark in the Morning on WRTT talk radio. With us today is economics professor Dr. Terry Young. Good morning, Dr. Young, and welcome to WRTT.

(Female) Dr. Young: Good morning, Mark. It's nice to be here.

DJ Mark: Now, I understand that you're a leading expert on microcredit. Could you tell us some of the advantages of microcredit over regular credit?

Dr. Young: Sure, Mark. As you know, banks lend people money based on their credit, their ability to repay the money with interest over time. Well, in 1976, a young economics professor in Bangladesh, Dr. Muhammad Yunus, realized that poor people in his country could not borrow money from conventional banks because their ability to repay a traditional loan was almost nil and they lacked the collateral to access credit. He founded the Grameen Bank, which makes very small loans, usually less than 100 US dollars, to poor entrepreneurs, who use the loans for everything from raising animals to weaving baskets to sell. That is microcredit, and with millions of borrowers, most of them women, using small loans to increase their own standard of living, I think it's easy to see how microcredit helps alleviate poverty in the world.

DJ Mark: Absolutely! On the other hand, isn't it difficult for poor people to repay even small loans?

Dr. Young: It can be, so the Grameen Bank's lending practices are quite different from conventional banks. For one thing, Grameen requires borrowers to make small weekly payments, which are easier to handle than larger monthly payments.

DJ Mark: That's interesting, but Dr. Young, don't a lot of borrowers still default on their loans and never pay them back?

Dr. Young: Not as many as you might think, Mark. The Grameen Bank lends money to groups of five borrowers rather than to individuals. If one member of the group doesn't pay back her loan, none of the members can borrow again in the future. With this system, the bank's repayment rate is excellent.

DJ Mark: I understand what you mean, but isn't that kind of peer pressure rather harsh? I mean, with the group members giving you dirty looks every time they see you . . .

Dr. Young: (*laughing slightly*) I guess you could say that, Mark, but the system seems to be working and alleviating poverty all over the world. Since 1976, the Grameen Bank has expanded to more than 1,500 branches with projects underway in South Asia, Africa, and Latin America.

DJ Mark: Very impressive! I guess microcredit is here to stay, and I'm glad to know a little more about it. Thank you for being here, Dr. Young.

Dr. Young: It was my pleasure.

Chapter 7 Test Audioscript

Section I Listening to a Conversation

Woman: I'm bored. Hey! Why don't we go see a movie!

Man: Sure. I'm up for a movie. How about that comedy with Ben Stiller? It's supposed to be good.

Woman: Hmmm . . . Ben Stiller bugs me. I don't know why. And I don't especially like comedies, to tell you the truth.

Man: OK. What kinds of movies do you like?

Woman: Oh, many kinds! I like suspense movies, and I'm thrilled whenever a new James Bond movie comes out! What about you?

Man: Well, I always appreciate a good drama. I love movies that make you think, you know?

Woman: I've got it! You like drama, and I like suspense, so why don't we go see that movie about the historian who uncovers some secret about the Aztec pyramids? Sort of a suspenseful drama!

Man: That's a good idea, but I'm sorry, I just can't take another movie starring Julia Roberts. She's in it, right?

Woman: She is. Well, maybe we can go some other time. That is, if there's a movie playing that we can agree on!

Section II Listening to a Lecture

Today, I am pleased to continue our series on remarkable individuals by talking about a woman whose name might be new to you. In 1963, Annie Dodge Wauneka became the first Native American to win the Presidential Medal of Freedom. We'll get to that a little later.

Annie Dodge Wauneka, born in 1910, was a member of the Navajo tribe, one of the largest Indian tribes in the United States. The Navajo Nation owns vast areas of land, covering parts of three states in the Southwest, but except for limited oil reserves, the land is poor and dry and the average income among the Navajo is low. As a young woman, Wauneka became aware of the health problems Navajo people suffered as a direct result of this poverty, and after raising her nine children, four of whom had disabilities, she resolved to address those problems by working within the tribal government system.

In 1951, Annie Dodge Wauneka became only the second woman elected to the Navajo Tribal Council, the governing body of the Navajo Nation. Later that same year, she became the Chairman of the Tribal Council's Health and Welfare Committee and launched a battle against tuberculosis, a bacterial infection of the lungs that affected the Navajo at a much higher rate than the general U.S. population. She concentrated her efforts on education about household sanitation and pushed for legislation in the U.S. federal government that provided funds for systems to carry potable running water to tribal homes.

But Wauneka's interest in public health issues did not end with tuberculosis. In her Navajo language radio show, Wauneka raised awareness among listeners of the detrimental health effects of alcoholism among Native Americans. She also worked to provide Navajo children regular medical, dental, and eye exams, and to give parents of newborns baby blankets and clothing. The result of Wauneka's efforts could be seen in the 1960s and 1970s with a thirty-five percent drop in the tuberculosis rate among the Navajo and a twenty-five percent decrease in infant mortality.

For her exceptional work, Annie Dodge Wauneka received many awards and honors, including one for Outstanding Worker in Public Health from the State of Arizona in 1959 and several honorary doctoral degrees. But Wauneka's most notable award was the Presidential Medal of Freedom—the most prestigious non-military award given by the U.S. government—which she received in 1963 for her contributions to the Navajo Nation. The award recognizes a lifetime of service and is granted only by the president and only to remarkable individuals such as Annie Dodge Wauneka.

Sources: National Women's Hall of Fame (www.greatwomen.org)
URL: http://www.lapahie.com/Annie_Dodge_Wauneka.cfm
Creator(s): Harrison Lapahie Jr.

Chapter 8 Test Audioscript

Section I Listening to a Conversation

Man: Hi, Linda. Did I just see you talking to Ian?

Woman: That was him.

Man: Huh! I guess you're one of the lucky ones then. I thought he wasn't talking to anyone these days.

Woman: Well, maybe I should explain something. It might seem as if Ian is avoiding you, but what's really going on is that he's worried that he won't be able to finish his PhD. His father is having health problems, and his mother wants Ian at home.

Man: Oh, I'm sorry to hear that. Do you think there's anything we can do?

Woman: In fact, there is something we can do. Ian said that he wishes he could go home for a visit and see for himself how his father is doing. But the reality is that visiting is just too expensive, so maybe we could get all of his friends to chip in for his airfare.

Man: That's not a bad idea, Linda. If Ian can go home for a visit, he can see what's really going on and then make a decision about finishing his program or not.

Woman: Exactly.

Man: Well, I'm done with classes for today; I'll start making some phone calls.

Section II Listening to a Lecture

Before I ask you to write anything, I'd like to begin our Creative Writing course by talking a bit about ways people use creative writing in their lives. I'll be describing three types of people who use creative writing to accomplish very different things.

First, let's discuss the ways creative writing is a useful tool for writers. I know we usually think of creative writing as "products," including poetry and fiction, but in fact, creative writing is also a *process* writers use to exercise their creativity and solve specific writing problems. Let me illustrate. Imagine a writer who uses the same words again and again and needs to expand her vocabulary choices. She looks up a word in the thesaurus and finds several synonyms and antonyms. She then chooses a synonym that interests her, and looks <u>that</u> word up in the thesaurus. While she's doing all of this, she draws a word map showing vocabulary options inside circles connected by lines to related words. By the time she is finished, she has a visual representation of relationships between dozens of words. The next thing our writer does is make a list of the words from the word map that she likes. She starts playing with combinations of words in phrases and in sentences. Before long, she has accomplished her original goal of expanding her vocabulary usage, and she has done it through creative writing exercises. Other exercises help writers to generate ideas, describe things in detail, and develop fictional characters, to list just a few.

Now, let's consider language students. Can creative writing be of any use to them? I can answer that question with one word: absolutely! Let me explain. One challenge that language learners face is reading in the new language. Creative exercises, such as writing a dialogue between characters from a story, forces learners to use their imaginations, approach the story in a new way, and read it with a fresh perspective. Creative writing exercises also challenge language learners to find precisely the right words, structures, and idioms to convey their ideas.

I want to describe one more case in which creative writing can be used as a tool. In a women's prison in Hawaii, inmates have recently published their first collection of poems. The volunteers who have taught the poetry writing course for the past two years say that the prisoners use poetry as therapy to release painful emotions, and as a tool of self-discovery as the writers acknowledge the facts of their lives that led them to prison.

To summarize, creative writing exercises unlock creativity and encourage problem solving. We'll pick up the topic next time with a look at art therapy.

Chapter 9 Test Audioscript

Section I Listening to a Conversation

Woman: Hi, Brandon. How're you doing?

Man: Not bad. Hey, it's six o'clock. You usually volunteer at the animal shelter on Tuesday evenings, don't you? **[rising intonation]**

Woman: Yeah, usually I do. But I'm getting a little tired of the way I'm treated there. I mean, volunteers want to feel like they're appreciated, don't they? **[falling intonation]**

Man: Of course they do! Hey, maybe you should try volunteering with me at the food pantry. They're really short-handed there, and you enjoy working with families, right? **[rising intonation]**

Woman: Definitely! I'll go with you the next time you volunteer.

Man: That sounds great. I'm signed up for Wednesday mornings from 8:00 to 10:00.

Woman: Hmmm . . . I usually sleep late on Wednesday mornings, but I do want to find a new volunteer job.

Man: It's a date, then. You'd like a ride there, wouldn't you? **[rising intonation]** It would be a very long bike ride.

Woman: I would definitely like a ride. Can you pick me up at 7:45?

Section II Listening to a Lecture

Lecturer: I'm delighted to see so many people here today from campus organizations. And we're all here for the same reason, right?

Participant #1: We need volunteers!

Lecturer: Exactly! None of your organizations could run without volunteers, and today I'm going to suggest some effective ways to keep your volunteers working for you after you've recruited them. If you'll let me digress for a moment, though, I want to ask how many of you have done volunteer work. Raise your hands.

Participants: [*mild group laughter as many people raise their hands*]

Lecturer: Wow! OK. Almost everyone here has done some volunteering. Now, think about one of your volunteer jobs and try to remember why you chose to do it. [*pause*] Now, what eventually made you quit that volunteer job?

Participant #2: For me, it was lonely work. There was nobody to talk to.

Participant #3: I guess at my volunteer job the work was just too easy. I got bored because I wasn't learning anything.

Lecturer: Good! Now, to return to what I was saying, you can keep your volunteers from having the same experience if you understand their reasons for volunteering.

Let's first discuss people who volunteer primarily for social reasons. They want to make new friends, or belong to a group, or get involved in the community where they live. You can meet those people's needs in simple ways like making sure that everyone in your organization learns those volunteers' names! You can also invite volunteers to participate in social activities that don't involve work, such as holiday parties. Also, be sure to inform volunteers about everything your organization does in the community.

Second, many people volunteer in order to develop their skill sets. They want to learn something new, so you need to provide a variety of tasks for them to do, and don't forget to utilize their creativity! Maybe your volunteers can think of new and better ways for your organization to function. Let me just mention that in my own organization, the staff is often just too busy to be very creative.

Anyway, most of the volunteers you'll recruit are people who share your goals, who believe in the ideals of your organization. If you want to keep those people coming back, you have to provide excellent training, which will show them how all your activities contribute to your mission. You also have to get them involved in goal setting, which gives volunteers a chance to direct some of their own efforts toward a cause they believe in.

Remember, if you can meet the needs of your volunteers, you can do much less recruiting at this time next year.

Chapter 10 Test Audioscript

Section I Listening to a Conversation

Student: Excuse me. I hope I'm not interrupting. Do you have a minute?

Professor: Of course! Come in and have a seat.

This is my office hour, so you don't have to worry about interrupting.

Student: Good. Thanks. I hope you can help me understand something you said in last week's lecture.

Professor: Sure. That was the lecture about free will, wasn't it? [*falling intonation on the tag question*]

Student: Yes, and I think you said that mental illness was sometimes used as a legal defense, and I guess I still don't understand the reason for that.

Professor: OK. Within the legal system, a crime is something a person chooses to do. For example, if you have a car that I like, and I decide to steal it from you, I exercise my own free will, so I am responsible for the crime.

Student: But isn't a mentally ill person also responsible? I mean, if the jury decides that the person really committed the crime?

Professor: Under the law, a person who is legally insane is not in control of his or her actions and may not even know whether an action is right or wrong. In that case, they are given treatment in a secure mental health facility rather than prison time.

Student: So if a person is found not guilty by reason of insanity, it means they were not acting of their own free will.

Professor: That's right. At the time of the crime, at least, they were not able to choose or control their own behavior.

Section II Listening to a Lecture

Good afternoon everyone. Let's get started. You'll remember that last time we talked about legal responsibility for criminal behavior, and we'll continue today with theories about what causes criminal behavior. But if you'll let me stray from the subject for a moment, it's interesting to look at a few ideas that early anthropologists had about criminals.

One predecessor of today's criminology was called physiognomy, which can be traced back to ancient Greek philosophers who thought that healthy minds went hand in hand with healthy bodies, and therefore people with deformed or unattractive bodies must have some mental problem as well. Within this school of thought was phrenology, the idea that a person's skull reflected characteristics of the brain underneath it. Since certain areas of the brain were thought to correspond to certain traits, phrenologists thought that by carefully feeling the shape of a person's head, they could understand the person's psychological tendencies. In fact, in the nineteenth century, some American prisons classified criminals according to the bumps on their heads, declaring them to be especially destructive or likely to steal, among other things.

Yes, it's pretty funny, and I'll get back to the main topic, but let me just tell you about one more form of early criminology that I think you'll find amusing. In Italy, again in the nineteenth century, a physician named Cesare Lombroso performed an autopsy on a well-known criminal and noticed that the man's skull reminded him of the skulls of animals he had seen. With Darwinism at the forefront of modern science at the time, Lombroso decided that criminals must be a form of under-evolved human. He hoped that scientists might be able to prevent crime if they could understand it better, or at least identify criminals before they had a chance to commit any crimes.

I know, it sounds pretty crazy, but Lombroso assembled a collection of photographs of criminals and identified facial features he thought they had in common, such as sloping foreheads, large ears, and drooping eyes, which Lombroso thought were more animal than human. In theory, then, if police picked up a suspect, all they had to do was look carefully at his face to determine whether he was a criminal. If only it were that easy, right?

As you can probably guess, the only way to identify criminals is by their actions, not by looking at a person's face or feeling their skull. Now, let's get back to the topic at hand.

(sources: http://human-nature.com/nibbs/03/gibson.html
http://www.criminology.fsu.edu/crimtheory/week4.htm)

Chapter 1 Test Answer Key

Section I

Listening to a Conversation

1. b 2. a 3. a 4. c 5. a

Section II

Listening to a Lecture

1. b 2. c 3. c 4. b 5. c

Section III

New Words

1. innate 2. paradox 3. linguist 4. transform
5. déjà vu 6. fluently 7. association 8. buy (into)
9. imitation 10. collage

Section IV

Using Language

1. repeating 2. pardon 3. interrupt 4. repeat 5. again

Chapter 2 Test Answer Key

Section I

Listening to a Conversation

1. b 2. b 3. c 4. a 5. c

Section II

Listening to a Lecture

1. a 2. a 3. c 4. b 5. a

Section III

New Words

1. ecosystem 2. Celsius 3. Fahrenheit 4. beachfront
5. awkward 6. ferocious 7. migratory 8. disposition
9. battle 10. fast

Section IV

Using Language

1. because Mike got a new video game 2. Are you saying that 3. I'm not sure I understand 4. I see what you mean 5. that I don't have to do chores on Saturday

Chapter 3 Test Answer Key

Section I

Listening to a Conversation

1. c 2. c 3. b 4. b 5. a

Section II

Listening to a Lecture

1. a 2. c 3. b 4. b 5. c

Section III

New Words

1. h 2. a 3. c 4. f 5. g 6. d 7. b 8. e

Section IV

Using Language

1. typically 2. seldom 3. For the most part 4. normally
5. Seldom do

Chapter 4 Test Answer Key

Section I

Listening to a Conversation

1. c 2. a 3. c 4. b 5. c

Section II

Listening to a Lecture

1. b 2. b 3. c 4. c 5. b

Section III

New Words

1. vary 2. chambers 3. tick-tock 4. peel 5. hollow
6. cardiac muscles 7. strip 8. pump

Section IV

Using Language

1. similar 2. positive 3. ghost 4. like 5. pretty

Chapter 5 Test Answer Key

Section I

Listening to a Conversation

1. b 2. b 3. c 4. a 5. b

Section II

Listening to a Lecture

1. a 2. a 3. c 4. a 5. c

Section III

New Words

1. e 2. c 3. h 4. g 5. b 6. i 7. j 8. f 9. d 10. a

Section IV

Using Language

1. is funded 2. think 3. be spent 4. were invented 5. comes

Chapter 6 Test Answer Key

Section I

Listening to a Conversation

1. a 2. c 3. a 4. b 5. a

Section II

Listening to a Lecture

1. c 2. b 3. c 4. a 5. a

Section III

New Words

1. alleviate 2. borrow 3. irrigation 4. under fire 5. snail 6. breed 7. insiders 8. proposal 9. environmental 10. invest

Section IV

Using Language

1. disagrees 2. formal 3. agrees 4. informal 5. disagrees

Chapter 7 Test Answer Key

Section I

Listening to a Conversation

1. b 2. a 3. c 4. c 5. a

Section II

Listening to a Lecture

1. a 2. a 3. b 4. b 5. c

Section III

New Words

1. bull 2. keep up with 3. battle 4. fluke 5. hit-and-run 6. vertebra 7. endure 8. chemotherapy 9. from scratch 10. highlight

Section IV

Using Language

1. a 2. c 3. b 4. e 5. d

Chapter 8 Test Answer Key

Section I

Listening to a Conversation

1. b 2. c 3. b 4. c 5. a

Section II

Listening to a Lecture

1. c 2. a 3. c 4. c 5. a

Section III

New Words

1. f 2. e 3. c 4. d 5. b 6. a

Section IV

Using Language

1. continue 2. describe 3. list 4. illustrate 5. answer

Chapter 9 Test Answer Key

Section I

Listening to a Conversation

1. a 2. c 3. b 4. c 5. b

Section II

Listening to a Lecture

1. b 2. b 3. c 4. a 5. a

Section III

New Words

1. wind 2. field of interest 3. recap 4. eye contact 5. pretty much 6. identity

Section IV

Using Language

1. way 2. off 3. saying 4. reminds 5. say

Chapter 10 Test Answer Key

Section I

Listening to a Conversation

1. a 2. a 3. b 4. b 5. a

Section II

Listening to a Lecture

1. a 2. b 3. c 4. b 5. c

Section III

New Words

1. f 2. e 3. g 4. c 5. h 6. d 7. b 8. a

Section IV

Using Language

1. hope 2. know 3. use 4. knew 5. will

Name ______________________ Date ______________ Score ____________

Interactions/Mosaic Listening/Speaking Placement Test

Directions: Read these directions before listening to the recorded test.

There are four sections in this test, each with a different type of listening and questions. There are a total of fifty questions to answer. You will hear the test questions only once; they will not be repeated.

Sections:

1. Ten question items – after you hear each question, choose the best response. (questions 1–10)
2. Ten statement items – after you hear each statement, select the best conclusion. (questions 11–20)
3. Ten short conversations – after each conversation there is one question to answer. (questions 21–30)
4. Four longer selections – after each longer listening selection, there are five questions to answer about the listening. (questions 31–50)

Section 1 Listen to the question and choose the best response. **(2 points each)**

Example: (You hear:) Where's your sister gone?

(You read:)

(A) to Canada
(B) without her friends
(C) because she was late
(D) yesterday

Choice "a" is the best answer.

1. (A) tomorrow
(B) to visit his sister
(C) just this morning
(D) the train

2. (A) Yes, I must go there.
(B) About five hundred dollars
(C) I'll have a good time.
(D) A few days

3. (A) He's been once.
(B) She's been there for three months.
(C) No, she's still there.
(D) She was there as a child.

4. (A) It's not very fair.
(B) It takes an hour.
(C) It's two dollars.
(D) It's not very far from here.

5. (A) Yes, they can.
(B) The bus stops near the theatre.
(C) There is no way we could make it in time.
(D) It's too bad we missed the eight o'clock show.

6. (A) It's a little too casual.
(B) Yes, the pants fit.
(C) They have three different sizes.
(D) It's a bit tight.

7. (A) They prefer going to the movies.
(B) I haven't really thought about it.
(C) I have no references.
(D) It's either black or white.

8. (A) I would be pleased if she finds a job that she enjoys.
(B) My mother hopes she will go on to college.
(C) I took her on a trip last year.
(D) I want my legs to stop hurting.

9. (A) Yes, the doctor told me to start drinking it more often.
(B) Yes, I needed something to eat.
(C) No, I still drink milk every day.
(D) Sorry, I don't have time.

10. (A) I'm sorry I was late.
(B) I couldn't have come earlier.
(C) Would you like me to come back in a while?
(D) Sorry we left so late.

Section 2 Listen to each statement and then choose the best conclusion. **(2 points each)**

11. (A) Peter's lawyer likes his mother.
(B) Peter likes his mother.
(C) Peter is a liar.
(D) Peter's mother is a lawyer.

12. (A) The flight arrived at 2:30.
(B) The flight took off at 2:30.
(C) The flight will arrive in an hour and a half.
(D) The flight arrived at 1:30.

13. (A) Sixty students went on the sailing trip.
(B) No students went on the sailing trip.
(C) Only a few students arrived to go on the sailing trip.
(D) Nobody signed up for the sailing trip.

14. (A) Judy has to plan something for her birthday.
(B) Someone gave Judy flowers on her birthday.
(C) Judy intends to do something special on her birthday.
(D) Judy bought some plants as a gift.

15. (A) Peter is a fair player.
(B) The match was relatively short.
(C) Peter won the match.
(D) Steve hit the ball fast.

16. (A) Mary was losing her eyesight.
(B) John won the argument with Mary.
(C) Mary forgot why she and John were arguing.
(D) Mary and John argued because it was very hot.

17. (A) Gary preferred Robert to Peter.
(B) Gary preferred Peter to Robert.
(C) Robert liked Peter better than Gary.
(D) Peter liked Gary better than Robert.

18. (A) It's time to plant things in the garden.
(B) Soon it will be warm enough to start planting seeds.
(C) You ought to visit the garden at the sea.
(D) You should be considerate of the garden.

19. (A) The dinner was very good in general.
(B) Dinner was at a restaurant.
(C) Everyone thought the dinner was very good.
(D) Dinner was very good every night.

20. (A) John's brother lives near the club.
(B) John's brother owns the club.
(C) John has never invited his brother to the club.
(D) John's brother has never invited John to the club.

Section 3: Listen to each conversation. Answer the question you hear after each conversation. **(2 points each)**

21. (A) It hasn't rained for many years.
(B) It has rained an unusual amount this year.
(C) It hasn't rained much here.
(D) It hasn't rained this year.

22. (A) He thought the restaurant could have been better.
(B) He agreed with the woman.
(C) He thoroughly enjoyed the restaurant.
(D) It was impossible for the restaurant to be nice.

23. (A) The wind hurt the man's house.
(B) The wind hurt the woman's son.
(C) Paint in the woman's basement was ruined.
(D) Flood water damaged artwork in the woman's house.

24. (A) The man's brother is not strong enough to lift things.
(B) The man's brother is not making any effort to find work.
(C) The brother is unlucky.
(D) The woman is surprised the man's brother is still not working.

25. (A) It's not unusual for him to play in hot weather.
(B) At an earlier time in his life, he played tennis in such weather.
(C) Playing tennis in hot weather uses up his energy.
(D) He's concerned about playing in the heat.

26. (A) It's contradictory.
(B) She doesn't agree.
(C) She wants the man to look at the ducks.
(D) She's angry.

27. (A) He's not planning to purchase anything.
(B) He doesn't need to get anything at this store.
(C) He doesn't agree about the prices.
(D) He doesn't like to buy cheap things.

28. (A) The city nearly burned down.
(B) The mayor was rescued from a burning building.
(C) The mayor was hurt and moved.
(D) The mayor was criticized and left his job.

29. (A) He thinks she should buy a large pizza.
(B) He thinks she should ask for extra mushrooms and cheese.
(C) He likes the mushroom and cheese pizza best.
(D) He thinks the pizzas are too big.

30. (A) The judge was very sure about handling the case.
(B) The judge gave the man a severe punishment.
(C) The judge was difficult to understand.
(D) The judge couldn't decide the theif's punishment.

Section 4 Listen to each longer selection and answer the five questions for the selection. Listen to the first selection. Then answer questions 31–35. **(2 points each)**

31. What do you think T-A-L-K is?
(A) a radio station
(B) a TV station
(C) an animal rescue service
(D) a movie studio

32. What animals are missing?
(A) one dog and two cats
(B) two dogs and one cat
(C) two dogs and two cats
(D) one dog and one cat

33. Which of the animals were taken from a backyard?
(A) None of the animals
(B) All of the animals
(C) Oxen the German Shepherd
(D) Winston the wire-haired terrier

34. Who had a seeing-eye dog?
- (A) Mr. Wilson
- (B) Mrs. Lincoln
- (C) Mrs. Thompson
- (D) Oxen

35. What are the listeners supposed to do if they find one of the pets?
- (A) Call the T-A-L-K phone line.
- (B) Call the police station.
- (C) Call the local animal shelter.
- (D) Wait a week to call.

Directions: The following selection is a lecture in two parts. Listen to Part 1 and answer questions 36–40. **(2 points each)**

36. In what situation does this talk probably take place?
- (A) nutrition class
- (B) business or marketing class
- (C) supermarket training
- (D) a one-day seminar

37. According to the speaker, what is true about product placement?
- (A) It's only important in supermarkets.
- (B) The concept is hardly used in the United States.
- (C) Children are not affected by it.
- (D) It's an extremely important selling tool.

38. The speaker said that children often "pester their parents" in a supermarket. What does *pester* mean?
- (A) nagging and begging
- (B) petting or touching
- (C) wanting candy
- (D) grabbing food

39. What's the speaker's focus?
- (A) product placement outside of the United States
- (B) product placement both in and out of the United States
- (C) product placement in the United States
- (D) products you shouldn't buy

40. What specific examples did the speaker use?
- (A) Candy was the only example.
- (B) Candy was one of the examples.
- (C) The examples were taken directly from the textbook.
- (D) The examples would be on the test.

Directions: Listen to Part 2 of the lecture and answer questions 41–45. **(2 points each)**

41. What products did the speaker talk about?
- (A) expensive products
- (B) headache medicine
- (C) tropical shampoo
- (D) shampoo for oily hair

42. What did the speaker say about U.S. stores?
- (A) All U.S. stores follow the same process for placing items on shelves.
- (B) Most U.S. stores place pricey items at eye level.
- (C) Many U.S. stores place inexpensive items at eye level.
- (D) No U.S. stores place items at eye level.

43. What position was stated by the speaker?
- (A) Inexpensive items are better than expensive ones.
- (B) Expensive items are better than inexpensive ones.
- (C) He didn't endorse inexpensive items or expensive ones.
- (D) He doesn't like candy or shampoo.

44. What did the speaker tell the participants?
- (A) They didn't have any homework.
- (B) They had to get ready for a test.
- (C) They had to do some research.
- (D) They had to finish an assignment in class.

45. When does the class probably meet?
- (A) Tuesday and Thursday nights
- (B) Tuesday nights
- (C) Tuesday mornings
- (D) every other week

Directions: The following selection is a lecture. Listen to the lecture and answer questions 46–50. **(2 points each)**

46. What best describes folk wisdom?
- (A) American folklore
- (B) jokes
- (C) sayings that give advice about life
- (D) different means of expressing oneself

47. Which expression of folk wisdom is *not* mentioned?
- (A) myths
- (B) fairy tales
- (C) songs
- (D) poetry

48. What will the speaker probably focus on in the lecture?

(A) humorous sayings
(B) legends
(C) songs of joy and sorrow
(D) famous American Presidents

49. What source of folk wisdom will be used in the talk?

(A) Abraham Lincoln
(B) Mark Twain and Benjamin Franklin
(C) students in this class
(D) All of the above

50. Which is not mentioned about Ben Franklin?

(A) He loved to eat and drink.
(B) People admired his wit.
(C) He took the bitter medicine.
(D) He told others not to overdo things.

Listening/Speaking Placement Test Audioscripts

Narrator: Section 1

Narrator: Number 1. When did Steve get in?

Narrator: Number 2. How much time will you have to spend in Boston?

Narrator: Number 3. Has she ever been there before?

Narrator: Number 4. How much is the subway fare?

Narrator: Number 5. Should we try to get to the eight o'clock movie?

Narrator: Number 6. Do you think that this jacket fits?

Narrator: Number 7. What are your preferences in art?

Narrator: Number 8. What are your hopes for your niece?

Narrator: Number 9. On the way home from the doctor, did you stop for some milk?

Narrator: Number 10. Couldn't you have arrived an hour later?

Narrator: Section 2

Narrator: Number 11. Peter is a lawyer like his mother.

Narrator: Number 12. Mary's flight was due at one, but it was delayed an hour and a half.

Narrator: Number 13. Sixty students signed up for the sailing trip, but most of them failed to show up.

Narrator: Number 14. Judy's got big plans for her birthday.

Narrator: Number 15. Peter was beaten fairly quickly by Steve in the tennis match.

Narrator: Number 16. In the heat of the argument, Mary lost sight of her original disagreement with John.

Narrator: Number 17. Although Gary liked his uncle Robert, he was fonder of his cousin Peter.

Narrator: Number 18. Considering the season, you really should plant the seeds in the garden before the frost.

Narrator: Number 19. On the whole, the dinner was great.

Narrator: Number 20. John's never been invited to the club by his brother.

Narrator: Section 3

Narrator: Number 21.

Man: The weather has been so hot this summer . . .

Woman: And we haven't had rain like this in years.

Narrator: What does the woman mean?

Narrator: Number 22.

Woman: The restaurant wasn't very good in my opinion.

Man: I thought it couldn't have been nicer.

Narrator: What does the man mean?

Narrator: Number 23.

Man: The storm sounded like it would blow the roof off my house.

Woman: Wasn't it terrible? The flood in our basement ruined my son's paintings.

Narrator: What did the storm do?

Narrator: Number 24.

Man: My brother is having a lot of trouble finding a job.

Woman: What a surprise. I haven't seen him lift a finger.

Narrator: What does the woman mean?

Narrator: Number 25.

Woman: Your serve. Whew. It's gotten very hot.

Man: I know, but I'm used to playing tennis in weather like this.

Narrator: What does the man mean?

Narrator: Number 26.

Man: The less I try to whack the ball, the farther it goes.

Woman: Hmm, that's quite a paradox!

Narrator: What does the woman mean?

Narrator: Number 27.

Woman: Richard told me about this store. He said they have the lowest prices in town.

Man: You think? I don't necessarily buy that.

Narrator: What does the man mean?

Narrator: Number 28.

Man: Did you hear that city hall almost burned down?

Woman: Right, and then the Mayor was removed under fire.

Narrator: What does the woman mean?

Narrator: Number 29.

Woman: How's the pizza here?

Man: Good, by and large, especially the mushroom and cheese.

Narrator: What does the man mean?

Narrator: Number 30.

Woman: That young man got 20 years for stealing a bicycle.

Man: Hmm. The judge sure handed down a hard sentence.

Narrator: What does the man mean?

Female Announcer: This is the T-A-L-K "Lost Pet Watch." Tonight we are telling you about three missing pets.

Blacky is a black-and-white kitten, six months old, who ran away from her owner, Mrs. Lincoln. Her house is next to the high school.

Male Announcer: And then, Oxen, a large German Shepherd, is a guide dog for John Wilson who's been blind since birth. Mr. Wilson cannot get around without his dog. Oxen was last seen running through the Green Acres neighborhood. He's wearing a black collar and has a big scar over his left eye.

Also, Winston, a wire-haired terrier, was taken from Mrs. Thompson's back yard. Winston is a prize-winning purebred worth about $3,000.

Female Announcer: If you have any information, please call our studio at 1-800-PET-HELP. The police station no longer handles missing animal reports. The animal shelter's phone is broken and won't be repaired for a week.

Stay tuned for news here at 103.7.

Narrator: Part 1.

Male Professor: This evening I am going to talk about product placement. Product placement is probably one of the most important concepts I will cover this semester. In the United States special care is taken when placing items in different parts of the supermarket. For example, candy is generally placed next to the cashier or check-out counter. This is because customers are often likely to grab a candy bar while waiting in line. Children, who are waiting in line with their parents, often pester their parents to buy candy for them. Another example has to do with the placement of expensive products.

Oh – Let me turn that off……

Narrator: Part 2.

Male Professor: Now where was I… Right —

Well, many stores in the U.S., not all, will place expensive products at eye level. Imported shampoos, for example, are placed at a level where they are clearly visible and people can easily reach for them. Please note that I am not supporting or endorsing cheap items over expensive ones. Before we end this evening, I want to talk about your next assignment.

Though you might not think of it as homework, I expect each of you to go to a large supermarket before next Tuesday to see where the over-the-counter medicine is placed. I look forward to hearing about your findings in a week.

Narrator: The final selection.

Female Professor: Hello, class. Today we're going to be talking about folk wisdom.

Every culture has many sayings that give advice about life. These sayings are part of what is commonly called "folk wisdom." Of course, folk wisdom is also expressed in other ways, such as myths, fairy tales, legends, and songs. Often, however, folk wisdom is shared in the form of short sayings about the best ways to approach life's joys and sorrows.

Today, we'll look at some of the humorous sayings of three famous Americans: Benjamin Franklin, Abraham Lincoln, and Mark Twain. Then I'll ask you to share some examples of folk wisdom from your own communities.

One characteristic of American folk wisdom is its humor. Humor makes the bitter medicine of life easier to swallow.

Ben Franklin was the first of many Americans to be admired for his humorous folk wisdom. Franklin himself loved to have fun. He liked to eat a lot, drink a lot, and be merry, but he always told others to practice moderation.

Interactions Listening/Speaking Placement Test Answer Key

Section 1

1. c 2. d 3. d 4. c 5. c 6. d 7. b 8. a 9. a 10. c

Section 2

11. d 12. a 13. c 14. c 15. b 16. c 17. b 18. a 19. a 20. d

Section 3

21. b 22. c 23. d 24. b 25. a 26. a 27. c 28. d 29. c 30. b

Section 4

31. a 32. b 33. d 34. a 35. a 36. b 37. d 38. a 39. c 40. a 41. a 42. b 43. c 44. c 45. b 46. c 47. d 48. a 49. d 50. c

SCORING FOR INTERACTIONS/MOSAIC LISTENING/SPEAKING PLACEMENT TEST	
Score	**Placement**
0–27	Interactions Access
28–46	Interactions 1
47–65	Interactions 2
66–84	Mosaic 1
85–100	Mosaic 2

This is a rough guide. Teachers should use their judgment in placing students and selecting texts.